Adventure Guide to

Peru

Nicholas Gill

HUNTER

HUNTER PUBLISHING, INC.
130 Campus Drive, Edison, NJ 08818-7816
☎ 732-225-1900 / 800-255-0343 / fax 732-417-1744
www.hunterpublishing.com
E-mail comments@hunterpublishing.com

IN CANADA:
Ulysses Travel Publications
4176 Saint-Denis, Montréal, Québec, Canada H2W 2M5
☎ 514-843-9882 ext. 2232 / fax 514-843-9448

IN THE UNITED KINGDOM:
Windsor Books International
The Boundary, Wheatley Road, Garsington
Oxford, OX44 9EJ England
☎ 01865-361122 / fax 01865-361133

ISBN 1-58843-593-8
978-1-58843-593-4

© 2007 Hunter Publishing, Inc.

This guide focuses on recreational activities. As all such activities
contain elements of risk, the publisher, author, affiliated individuals
and companies disclaim any responsibility for any injury, harm, or illness that may occur to anyone through, or by use of, the information
in this book. Every effort was made to insure the accuracy of information in this book, but the publisher and author do not assume, and
hereby disclaim, any liability for loss or damage caused by errors,
omissions, misleading information or potential travel problems
caused by this guide, even if such errors or omissions result from neg-
ligence, accident or any other cause.

Cover photo: Tim Graham/Alamy
Other photos by the author and courtesy of PromPerú, Peruvian
Vacations, Enjoy Peru, Julius Tours, among others.

Maps © 2007 Hunter Publishing, Inc.
Index by Inge Wiesen

4   3   2   1

Contents

Introduction	1
History	2
Geography/Land	14
Flora & Fauna	17
National Parks, Reserves	37
Government	40
Economy	41
Peru's People	42
Language	45
Religion	45
Food & Drink	46
Festivals & Events	56
Shopping	61
Arts & Culture	64
Recommended Reading	70
Top 20 Adventures In Peru	71
The Star System	74
Travel Information	74
Documentation	74
Health & Safety	75
Toilets	78
Crime	78
Safety Tips	79
Drugs	79
Liquor Laws	80
Communications	80
Information Sources	81
Newspapers & Magazines	83
Internet	84
Mail & Shipping	84
Currency & Banking	84
Electricity	86
Time Zone	86
What to Take	86
Local Customs	90
Photography	90
Getting Here	92
Getting Around	94
Tour Operators	98
Where to Stay	101
Sports	105
Lima	111
History	114
Getting Here	118
Getting Around	122
The Colonial Center	128
Barrio Chino/Chinatown	138
Callao	138
Pueblo Libre	141
San Borja	143
San Isidro	143
Miraflores	149
Monterrico	164
The Costa Verde	165
Barranco	165
Chorrillos	172
Sports	177
Adventures	178
Tours	181
Language Schools	181
Entertainment	182
Day-Trips from Lima	183
The Southern Coast	187
Chincha Alta	187
Where to Stay	188
Day-Trips from Chincha	188
Pisco	190
Getting Here & Around	190
Sightseeing	191
Where to Stay	191
Where to Eat	191
Day-Trips from Pisco	192
Adventures on Water	194
Ica	195
Getting Here	196
Tourist Information	196
Sightseeing	196
Adventures	197
Wine Tasting	198
Festivals	200
Day-Trips from Ica	201
Where to Stay	202
Where to Eat	203
Nazca	203
Getting Here & Around	205
Tourist Information	205
Sightseeing	205
The Nazca Lines	206
Adventures	208
Day-Trips from Nazca	209
Where to Stay	210
Where to Eat	211
Arequipa	211
Getting Here	213
Getting Around	214
Tourist Information	214
Where to Stay	215
Where to Eat	219
Bars/Clubs/Pubs	221
Sights	222
Tours	231
Shopping	232
Language Schools	233
Festivals	233
Day-Trips from Arequipa	233
Adventures	234
Chivay	237
Where to Stay	237
Restaurants	237
Days-Trips from Chivay	238
Yanque	238
Sightseeing	238
Where to Stay	239
Cabanaconde	239

iv ■ **Contents**

Where to Stay & Eat 240
Sightseeing 240
Tacna 242
Tourist Information 244
Getting Here 244
Getting Around 245
Sightseeing 245
Where to Stay 246
Where to Eat 248
Bars & Clubs 248
Shopping 249
Day-Trips from Tacna 249
Tour Companies 250
To/From Chile 250
The Central Highlands 253
Huánuco 253
Getting Here 253
Banks 254
Sightseeing 254
Where to Stay 255
Where to Eat 256
Bars 257
Day-Trips from Huánuco 257
Tours 258
Huancayo 258
Getting Here 260
Tourist Information 261
Sightseeing 261
Where to Stay 263
Where to Eat 264
Bars/Nightlife 265
Shopping 266
Language Lessons 266
Day-Trips from Huancayo 267
Adventures 267
Huancavelica 268
Getting Here 269
Tourist Information 269
Sightseeing 270
Where to Stay 271
Where to Eat 272
Adventures 272
Abancay 273
Getting Here 274
Banks 274
Where to Stay 274
Where to Eat 274
Tour Companies 275
Andahuaylas 275
Getting Here 276
Bank 276
Sights 276
Where to Stay 276
Where to Eat 277
Day-Trips 277
Ayacucho 278
History 280
Getting Here 280
Tourist Information 281

Sightseeing 281
Shopping 284
Where to Stay 284
Where to Eat 286
Bars 287
Festivals 287
Day-Trips from Ayacucho 288
Tour Companies 291
Cuzco & the Sacred Valley 293
Cuzco 296
History 297
Getting Here 299
Getting Around 304
Tourist Information 304
Sights 306
Barrio San Blas 314
Ruins Around Cuzco 316
Language Schools 318
Where to Stay 319
Where to Eat 326
Bars & Clubs 331
Entertainment 332
Shopping 333
Adventures 337
Festivals 343
Urubamba & Yucay 345
Getting Here & Around 345
Sights 346
Where to Stay 347
Where to Eat 351
Bars 352
Tour Agencies 352
Adventures 353
Pisac 354
Getting Here & Away 354
Sights 354
Where to Stay & Eat 357
Ollantaytambo 358
Getting Here & Away 360
Tourist Information 360
Sights 360
Where to Stay 362
Where to Eat 363
Tourist Agencies 364
Adventures 364
Moray & Maras 365
Chinchero 366
Getting Here 366
Sights 367
Aguas Caliente 368
Getting Here & Around 368
Sights 370
Where to Stay 370
Where to Eat 372
Shopping 373
Massages 373
Machu Picchu 373
History 376
The Ruins 378

Where to Stay	381
The Inca Trail	381
The New Regulations	382
The Trail	384
Alternative Trails	387
Lake Titicaca & Puno	391
Puno	391
Getting Here	393
Getting Around	394
Tourist Information	394
Sightseeing	395
Where to Stay	396
Where to Eat	399
Bars	401
Shopping	401
Tour Companies	402
Festivals	402
Day-Trips from Puno	403
Juliaca	406
Getting Here & Away	406
Banks	407
Where to Stay	407
Lake Titicaca	408
Getting Here & Around	408
Adventures on Water	409
Cordillera Blanca	413
Huaraz	414
Climate	414
Getting Here	416
Tourist Information	417
Sightseeing	417
Where to Stay	420
Where to Eat	424
Groceries	425
Bars & Clubs	425
Shopping	426
Language Schools	426
Festivals	426
Tour Companies	427
Day-Trips from Huaraz	428
Parque Huascarán	430
Adventures	432
Carhuaz	435
Getting Here	436
Where to Stay	436
Yungay	436
Getting Here	436
Sights	436
Caraz	437
Getting Here	437
Where to Stay	437
Where to Eat	438
Tour Agencies	438
Northern Highlands	439
Cajamarca	439
History	441
Getting Here	442
Tourist Information	443
Sightseeing	443
Where to Stay	447
Where to Eat	449
Bars & Clubs	451
Shopping	451
Tour Agencies	451
Festivals	452
Day-Trips	452
Adventures	455
Chachapoyas	456
Tourist Information	456
Getting Here	457
Sightseeing	457
Where to Stay	458
Where to Eat	459
Shopping	460
Tour Companies	460
Day-Trips	460
Huancabamba	463
The North Coast	465
Trujillo	465
Pre-History	466
Getting Here	466
Sightseeing	467
Where to Stay	470
Where to Eat	472
Bars & Clubs	473
Tour Agencies & Guides	474
Festivals	474
Day-Trips from Trujillo	475
Huanchaco	479
Getting Here	479
Where to Stay	480
Where to Eat	480
Tour Companies	482
Adventures on Water	482
Chiclayo	483
Getting Here	483
Tourist Information	484
Sightseeing	484
Where to Stay	485
Where to Eat	487
Bars & Clubs	487
Shopping	488
Tourist Agencies	488
Day-Trips from Chiclayo	488
Tumbes	491
History	491
Tourist Information	492
Getting Here	492
Sightseeing	494
Where to Stay	494
Where to Eat	495
Bars & Clubs	496
Tour Agencies	496
Day-Trips from Tumbes	497
Adventures	498
Getting to/from Ecuador	499
Piura	499

Getting Here	500
Tourist Information	501
Sightseeing	501
Where to Stay	502
Where to Eat	504
Bars	505
Tour Agencies	505
Day-Trips from Piura	505
Mancora	506
Getting Here & Around	506
Tourist Information	507
Where to Stay	507
Where to Eat	510
Bars & Clubs	511
Shopping	512
Adventures	512
Day-Trips from Mancora	512
The Amazon	515
Northern Amazon	515
Iquitos	519
History	520
Getting Here	520
Getting Around	522
Tourist Information	522
Sightseeing	524
Where to Stay	528
Where to Eat	529
Bars/Clubs	530
Adventures	531
Day-Trips from Iquitos	533
Ecolodges	534
River Cruises	539
Adventures	540
Casinos	541
Shopping	541
Festivals	541
Yurimaguas	542
Getting Here	542
Where to Stay	542
Day-Trips	542
Tarapoto	543
Getting Here	543
Tourist Information	543
Where to Stay	544
Where to Eat	545
Bars	545
Adventures on Water	545
Pucallpa	546
Getting Here	547
Getting Around	548
Tourist Information	548
Sightseeing	548
Where to Stay	551
Where to Eat	552
Day-Trips from Pucallpa	552
Shamanic Ceremonies	553
Where to Stay	551
Tours	555
Shopping	555
Contamana	556
The Southeastern Jungle/ Madre de Dios	557
Puerto Maldonado	558
Festivals	558
Getting Here	558
Getting Around	559
Tourist Information	560
Sightseeing	562
Where to Stay	562
Where to Eat	563
Shopping	564
Bars & Clubs	564
Tours & Activities	565
Border Crossing Info	566
Jungle Lodges	567
Boca Manu	575
Getting Here	575
Lodges	575
Tour Operators	575

Maps

Regions of Perú	8
Eco-Regions of Peru	15
Lima Overview	112
Lima Center	129
San Isidro	145
Miraflores	152
Barranco	167
South Coast	189
Nasca Lines	204
Arequipa	212
Tacna	243
Central Highlands	252
Huancayo	259
Ayacucho	279
Sacred Valley	292
Cuzco & the Sacred Valley	295
Cuzco Hotels & Attractions	308
Cuzco Dining & Nightlife	309
Ollantaytambo	359
Aguas Calientes	369
Machu Picchu	375
Inca Trail Tekking	385
Lake Titicaca	390
Puno	392
Huaraz Region	415
Huaraz City	419
Northern Highlands	440
Cajamarca	444
North Coast	464
Tumbes	493
Amazon	516-17
Iquitos	521
Puerto Maldonado	561
Southeastern Jungle	574

About the Author

Nicholas Gill has written for newspapers, magazines, and websites on locations and subjects varying from Guinness beer to the bazaars of Marrakech to the temples at Angkor, Cambodia.

He lived in Peru while he was writing this book, in Lima, Cuzco and in the Lima suburb of Chorrillos. He returns to Peru often and intends to continue exploring and trying to understand this fascinating country as long as he lives.

Acknowledgements

I have met many people along the way, without whose help this book would not have been possible.

Special thanks to the many fellow-travelers who have had a great impact on my writing. For example the Brits Jackie and Martin in Arequipa and Colca Canyon, the bikers Martina and Peter, who helped me get to the continent in the first place, Roland, Jerome, Chris, Tobias and everyone else who made the stay in Pantoja and the trip up the Napo so hellish. Danny of Alaska, Quito and North Carolina for our chance encounter in Mancora. And everyone who was stuck with me for days at a time in Amazon lodges and tours of Lake Titicaca, and of course the many 20-hour bus rides.

In Huaraz, Peruvian Andes Adventures and the Morales family for their generosity in taking me on several hikes in the area and José Olaza for his kind hospitality.

In Iquitos, Peter Jensen, Roldan, and everyone at Explorama for going out of their way to help me and make my stay there more than pleasant, Mayuna Lodge for working with my tight schedule, and the Pilpintuwasi Butterfly Farm for their kindness and dedication. In Puerto Maldonado, Nury, Patricia and everyone at Explorer's Inn for not letting me leave. In Cuzco and the Sacred Valley, my friend and a wonderful vet Karen, Jamie at Luna Rumi, Christian at Kapaj N'an in Urubamba, and everyone at the Amauta Spanish school.

In Lima I would like to thank my friends Sylvana, Marissa, Marina, and Pilar for their help in exploring the city's nightlife. Mariem Valdez and the rest of the Valdez family for their warmth and for treating me like a member of their family.

I would also like to thank my brother Ryan and sister-in-law Lindsey for their kind support, as well as my parents for instilling a love of travel in me that will last the rest of my life.

And last but certainly not least, the sweet and beautiful Claudia Tello Justo, who was my best friend and sometimes travel companion, and who made my entire time in Peru more than worthwhile.

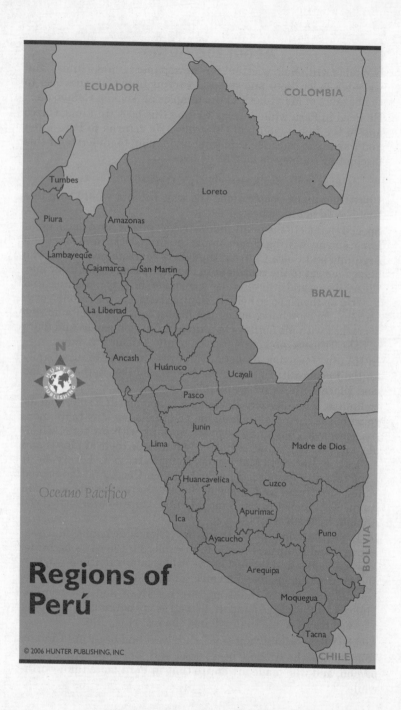

Regions of Perú

© 2006 HUNTER PUBLISHING, INC

Introduction

Kiss the secret stones with Me.
The Torrential Silver Of The Urubamba
Makes The Pollen Fly To Its Yellow Cup.
Pablo Neruda

Peru is one of the most diverse and fascinating countries on the planet. Of the 117 life zones on earth, 84 can be found here. Because of this, Peru's flora and fauna is some of the most unusual on earth. Scientists are only beginning to grasp just how many species exist and how many are still likely to be discovered. Large areas of rainforest and mountains remain unexplored. It was only in the past few decades that research began on the canopy tops, the upper levels of the rainforest, which have opened up a whole new world of plant and wildlife.

IN THIS CHAPTER

- History   2
- Geography   14
- Flora & Fauna   17
- Preservation   32
- Eco-Tourism   32
- Parks & Reserves   37
- Government   40
- Economy   41
- The People   42
- Education   45
- Language   45
- Religion   45
- Food & Drink   46
- Restaurants   55
- Water   56
- Events   56
- Shopping   61
- Arts & Culture   64
- Recommended Reading   70
- Top 20 Adventures   71
- Travel Information   74

As far as history goes, there is more here than anywhere else in the Americas. Most have heard of the Incas and Machu Picchu, but there were many large civilizations here long before the Incas: the Chavín, Chimu, Moche, Wari, Nazca and Paracas. Each group left their mark on the country in some way and their achievements, artifacts, and architecture are more impressive in many ways than that of the Incas.

The adventure possibilities are endless. Each region offers an array of unique activities. On the coast, try surfing, paragliding, fishing, or even sand-boarding. In the Andes, you can hike, climb, raft, bungee jump, fish, or ride horses. In the jungle, there is fishing, wildlife spotting, camping, hiking, and more. There's also wine and Pisco (a grape brandy) tasting, taking part in Andean festivals, dancing the marinera, touring ancient ruins, and sampling the finest cuisine on the continent.

Peru is a country on the rise. Frightened by years of terrorism and economic upheaval, tourists kept clear. Now, with terrorism long gone, the tourist infrastructure is growing. New hotels and restaurants are popping up everywhere, with clever new styles and international flair. New tours are being developed to what were once little-known natural and archeological sights. Roads are being built or improved and flights within the country are increasing. Each year the number of tourists grows. The circuit that was once limited to a few spots such as Lima, Cuzco, Nazca, and Iquitos is expanding to include places such as Huaraz, Mancora, Arequipa, Puerto Maldonado, Chachapoyas, and Cajamarca. It is becoming one of the world's top tourist destinations.

"I will say at the outset that there is only one world, and although we speak of the Old World and the New, this is because the latter was lately discovered by us, and not because there are two." Garcilaso de la Vega

■ History

Pre-History

The Andes are thought to have been inhabited as early as 20,000 years ago, corresponding to the Paleolithic period in Europe. The first peoples were mainly hunters and gatherers.

Civilization took its first big step forward with the domestication of crops such as potatoes and maize and animals such as

llamas, alpacas, and guinea pigs more than 6,000 years ago. Beans, chilies, and cotton were introduced a few thousand years later. Fishing became an important source of food. They used nets, bone hooks, and sometimes reed rafts like the ones in Huanchaco.

Pre-Inca Civilizations

The Incas, the most famous civilization in Pre-Columbian Peru, were actually here for only a few hundred years. It was the people before the Incas that truly shaped the land. The first trace of civilization, thought to be more than 5,000 years old, appears in

Caral stairway

the city of **Caral**, north of Lima. This city has only recently been discovered and is shedding new light on what life during this period may have been like.

About a thousand years before Christ came the **Chavíns**. Their center was near Huaraz, not far from the present-day town of Chavín, although their influence spread throughout the north and along the southern coast. They were the first great civilization to arise. They developed advanced artistic skills and complex religious beliefs. The Chavíns brought great advances in agriculture and architecture as well.

The Chavíns faded around 300 BC and several other cultures arose. In the South the **Paracas**, who were skilled weavers, and later the **Nazca**, known for their mysterious lines that cover the desert, came into power.

Along the north coast, the **Moche** civilization flourished from the third to the eighth centuries. They are responsible for the royal tombs at Sipan, among the most important discoveries in the Americas, and were famous for their realistic ceramics with zoomorphic features. They also created temples in the shape of curtailed pyramids such as the Huacas del Sol and de

Royal tomb at Sipan

la Luna. A serious drought led to a shift in land fertility away from the coast, and the Moche did not survive that.

In the Andes, the **Wari**, or **Huari**, emerged around 600 AD. Their rule covered much of the Andes and parts of the coast. They were fierce military conquerors and imposed their own artistic and religious values on the people they conquered. The resulting resentment eventually led to their demise.

The **Chimu** thrived on the coast from the 12th to 15th centuries as the Wari culture moved back into the mountains. They were architectural geniuses, building the colossal adobe city of Chan Chan. They were also skilled gold and silver jewelers, advanced farmers, and built huge aqueducts that are still used. The Incas conquered the Chimu in the 15th century.

The Beginning of the Incas

The empire, which lasted from the 11th century to the Spanish Conquest in the early 16th century, was one of the greatest planned societies the world has ever known, and the beauty and enchantment of Cuzco reflect that. There is so much history here that it can be difficult to keep straight, particularly when much of it involves myth and legends. The civilization began when the creator and sun god **Viracocha's** offspring **Manco Cápac** (the first ruling Inca) and **Mama Occlo**, arose from the Isle de Sol in Lake Titicaca near Copacabana, Bolivia. They were sent with a golden rod to find the Q'osqo or navel of the world and begin the civilization. He was commanded to find a place where he could push the rod into the ground until it disappeared, and when he found it (Cuzco), that was to become the center of the universe.

The social and political structure was as follows. The Inca himself was surrounded by a religious and secular elite that consisted of a variety of individuals such as defeated chieftains of other cultures and tribes. They were able to make the family, and not the individual, the central unit. Government officials, almost like tax collectors, designated units of 10, 100, 500, 1,000, 10,000, and 40,000 people, with each having its own leader. Each was allotted work for their own group and work that had to be done for the government. Each suyo (or region) of the empire (north, south, east, and west) also had its own ruler or counselor.

Beginning of Cuzco

The capital of the Inca Empire is thought to have been founded around 1100. Previously, Peru had been ruled by a number of cultures; what the Inca did was establish a central government that united them all. They

Cuzco today (N. Gill)

were not the creators of culture that the others were, but they were able to absorb what the others had created and combine them, which was perhaps an even greater accomplishment.

Other cultures occupied the area, such as the Wari, who were there in the 8th and 9th centuries. The first Incas arrived in the 12th century. Other than a few small palaces, the first eight rulers did little to be remembered by. They controlled the area around Cuzco, but expansion was minimal. It wasn't until the Chanka culture arrived in the valley to conquer the Inca, that expansion began. The empire was nearly lost and ruler Viracocha fled. His son Pachacútec took the reigns and in a desperate last battle the Incan army was victorious. The thirst for blood would then begin and the Incan empire would soon become the largest ever seen in the Americas. Over the next quarter-century much of the central Andes came under Inca rule. By the end of the rule of Pachacútec, he had conquered all of Northern Peru and parts of the Ecuadorian Andes.

The Inca Civil War

Tupac Yupanqui

Tupac Yupanqui, much like his father, kept pushing farther north and the empire extended as far as Quito. During the rule of the 11th Inca ruler, Huayna Cápac, the empire would be at its largest, extending south into parts of Bolivia, Chile, and Argentina, and north as far as the Colombian border with Ecuador. During his reign, Europeans discovered the new world. Diseases and epidemics quickly spread from Central America and many died. Huayna Cápac would eventually die of disease as well, but shortly before that he divided the empire into two. Huayna Cápac had two sons, Atahualpa, who was of Quitan descent, and Huáscar, who was of Cusqueñan descent. Each would have his own half of the empire, but neither wanted to share power and a civil war quickly began. Huáscar had the support of the people, but it was Atahualpa who controlled the army. In 1532 he defeated Huáscar's forces near Cuzco and captured him. Atahualpa would then retreat to Cajamarca to rest. Tired and battle-worn, the Incan empire was only beginning to recover. It was at this time that the Spaniards would arrive.

Atahualpa

Conquest

The Spanish first made contact with the Incas during the second voyage of Francisco Pizarro, which reached Tumbes in 1528. After learning of a great empire that flourished there, he went back to Spain to organize a party and funding to conquer it. A few years later, in May of 1532, Pizarro and his men landed in Ecuador, not far from Tumbes, with 179 men, most on horseback. After some small skirmishes with the natives there, they founded the city of Piura in September. They soon learned of the civil war and that the Incan ruler was stationed not far away in Cajamarca. They moved quickly to arrange a meeting. This small group of conquistadors would drastically change the course of Peruvian history.

Pizarro

Cajamarca

Atahualpa meets Pizarro

November 16th, 1532 was the day that would forever change the path of the nation, of the Incas, and of the Spanish. Atahualpa, en route to Cuzco after defeating his brother Huáscar in the north during the Inca civil war, stopped in Cajamarca to rest at the Baños del Inca. The troops were weary and deflated and the power of the Incan Empire as a whole was weakened greatly. The Spaniards arrived on the 15th and were told to wait until the following day. There were

50,000 to 80,000 Inca troops in the area, but still the Spaniards made plans for a surprise attack.

In the afternoon, Atahualpa and an estimated 6,000 armed troops arrived. At a pre-arranged signal, the Spanish troops planned to come into the Plaza on horses and capture the Inca if the opportunity presented itself. Otherwise, they would become friends and wait for a more opportune moment.

The Spanish claim that, when friar Vicente de Valverde presented Atahualpa with a bible, he quickly threw it to the ground. This would be the excuse they needed to attack. Canons were quickly fired and the cavalry trampled the surprised Quechuas. They put up little resistance and by the end of the day thousands were killed. Atahualpa was held prisoner in Cajamarca. He claimed that in exchange for his release he would fill the room he was held in twice over in silver and once in gold. He kept his promise, but he was still not released.

Atahualpa captured

Diego de Almagro soon came from the coast with reinforcements and Atahualpa began to see his fate. He soon sent messages to Quito to arrange for his escape. The Spaniards learned of this and, without a formal trial, executed him on July 26, 1533, in the main Plaza. Before marching to Cuzco to take full control of the empire, the Spanish made the younger brother of Huáscar, Manco, their puppet Inca. They hoped that the people of Cuzco, still loyal to Huáscar, would then hail them as liberators rather than invaders.

Rebellion

After a few years, however, Manco rebelled. An army as large as 100,000 men laid siege to Cuzco, but, in the desperate battle of Sacsayhuaman, the greatly outnumbered Spanish defeated them. Manco retreated to Ollantaytambo, where he was defeated again. He then retreated to Vilcabamba and set up a new Inca state. Manco Inca, after several years in hiding, would be caught and executed, but Vilcabamba would remain. Titu Cusi, who would be crowned Inca, left the stronghold at Vilcabamba in 1567 and was baptized, hoping to have a greater role in the lives of

Manco Capac

Cuzqueños. After he had died, Quispe Titu would be his successor. However, back in Vilcabamba, Tupac Amaru rose to become head of the rebel faction. Another rebellion would

Tupac Amaru II

begin, but Tupac Amaru would be captured and executed just a year later.

More puppet Incas would be installed and Vilcabamba would also survive. Strife among the Incan royalties, the new mixed-blood Incas, and the loyalists in Vilcabamba would divide the great civilization to its end. Tupac Amaru II did manage to lead a strong rebellion attempt in 1780-1781, but it was abruptly defeated.

The Rise of Lima

After conquering the Incas and their capital of Cuzco in the sierra, Pizarro felt the capital of the new Spanish empire in Peru should be along the coast. The Spanish were seafaring people and needed easier access to Panama and Spain. After scouting the coast, they came upon Lima. With the point of Callao serving as the port, the location was perfect. The city quickly became the Vice-Regal, or the Spanish, Capital of South America. With the creation of the Vice-Royalty in 1542, Lima became the capital of a land that included Panama, the majority of South America, and the major trade hub between the colonies and the motherland. The major export was silver bullion from the silver mines in Potosi in what is now Bolivia.

Diego de Almagro

It had its early problems, though, as the thirst for power in those days was great. The two lead conquistadors, Francisco Pizarro and Diego de Almagro, feuded over the land. Almagro took over the city of Cuzco, but the factions later battled and he was killed. His loyal party stormed Pizarro's palace in Lima, assassinated him, and installed Almagro's son, also named Diego, as Governor. Spain sent a new governor the following year and the young Almagro was swiftly executed.

Lima's power faded in the 18th century as Bourbon monarchists emphasized greater control on the colonies. The territories were divided and as a result Lima lost much of its status along with the commercial monopoly it held as other ports opened for trade.

Independence

Peru was the largest stronghold of Spanish power on the continent, with its epicenter in Lima; therefore it was the last to gain independence. Although many remained loyal to Spain at first, most people eventually began to see Peru better off on its own. Venezuelan Simón Bolivar and Argentinean José de San Martín marched to the center of the country from the north and south, after having already liberated Colombia, Venezuela, Ecuador, and Chile. On July 28, 1821, San Martín and his forces marched into Lima without a fight and declared independence to a cheering crowd in the main square. The Spanish armies retreated into the mountains and hung around briefly, but were defeated for good during the Battle of Ayacucho.

Struggles within the New Government

San Martín took a stab at governing the country, as did Bolivar, but both left after a short time. In 1826, Peru elected General José de La Mar as President, and for the first time it had a country of its own. The aforementioned wars took a toll on the initial economy and foreign debt grew as high as five times the annual revenue. Throughout the next century regional war lords regularly attempted – and succeeded – in seizing the power that was left open by the collapse of the Colonial order. The economic troubles seemed to be over in the mid-19th century when Peru began the export of guano and nitrates for fertilizer. Corruption and overspending brought back the economic woes and by 1876 Peru was bankrupt.

War of the Pacific

Due to an alliance with Bolivia, Peru went to war with Chile in 1879. Although the many museums and monuments dedicated to this war would make you think otherwise, Peru lost badly. The 1883 peace treaty gave the nitrate-rich colonies of Tarapacá, Arica, and Tacna to Chile. Tacna did opt to return to Peru on its own in 1929.

New Economy & Immigration

With the loss of guano for revenue, Peru turned to a new economy based on agriculture and mineral exports. There was also foreign investment from countries such as the United States and Great Britain. Peru's population grew steadily in the 19th century due migrant workers, as well as immigration from Europe and Asia.

Modernization

Modernization has become the great goal since independence, although no single leader ever succeeded in achieving it. Lima was the starting point and a few projects kicked it off. First came the Parque de la Exposición, which is still a major recreational area in the city. Second was a new design of the city by Baron Haussmann that was based on 19th-century Paris. Railroads also became a priority and were built throughout much of the country. Many of the projects would push the country even further into debt.

Revolution

The early half of the 20th century saw an expanding middle class and a call for greater government reform. The Alianza Popular Revolucianaria Americana (APRA) was formed and a struggle with those in power ensued for the next three decades. The APRA finally won out, but only after sacrificing the ideals that made it necessary. By the 1960s, radical change was badly desired and, although several reforms were attempted, nothing concrete was ever achieved.

The Years of Terrorism

After a prolonged economic crisis and staggering inflation that reached 7,000% annually in the mid-1980s, a Maoist campaign by the Sendero Luminosa (Shining Path) guerilla group, arose out of the state's failure to meet expectations and a bloody civil war developed. The city of Ayacucho was cut off from the rest of the country for some time. The next 15 years saw the killing of 25,000-30,000 people and an estimated $20 billion of damage was done. Lima was the site of car bombings, dynamite explosions, and kidnappings by the Shining Path Guerilla Group and MRTA during the 1990s. Hundreds of people were killed and millions of dollars in damage left their mark on the city. The leaders of both groups were finally put behind bars in 1992.

Alberto Fujimori

"Right now, things are uncertain."
– former President Alberto Fujimori

The 1990s saw the reign of one of Peru's most memorable presidents, Alberto Fujimori (1990-2001). Although he put an end to the Shining Path and stabilized the economy, the country was filled with other problems. Peru was set on a path of reform, however, for ordinary Peruvians his policies led to great hardship. Poverty levels increased and prices rose. His reign ended when he was accused of sanc-

Alberto Fujimori

tioning a paramilitary death-squad that murdered 25 people. He fled the country. Other charges include illegal phone tapping, diversion of public funds to the intelligence service, bribing of legislators and the transfer of US$15 million (€12.4 million) to his spy chief, Vladimiro Montesinos. He resigned via e-mail, likely the first president ever to do so. It was later found that he was a Japanese citizen and was banned from running for President until 2011. Although still wanted on charges in Peru, Fujimori decided to run for re-election in 2006. In late 2005, the President began making his way back to Peru. He was detained in Chile, however, and at this point his future is uncertain.

Alejandro Toledo

"When we opened the closet to see grandmother's jewels, we found that everything had been stolen."
– President Alejandro Toledo

The US-educated Toledo was South America's first indigenous president. He was widely approved at first, but a poor economy has brought his approval ratings to some of the lowest in Peruvian history. The 2006 elections proved to be quite dramatic, with the country having two very different choices – the leftist former military officer Ollanta Humala and former President Alan Garcia,

Alejandro Toledo

whose time in office was absolutely disastrous. As Venezuelan President Hugo Chavez became more and more involved with Humala, Peruvian voters began to see the election as a choice between Chavez and Garcia. The voters went with Garcia.

■ Geography/Land

With an area of 501,234 square miles, Peru is the third-largest country in South America after Brazil and Argentina. It ranks among the world's 20 largest nations and is larger than Spain, France and Germany put together. Peru occupies the west-central area of South America, on the shores of the Pacific Ocean. It borders Ecuador and Colombia to the north, Chile to the south, Brazil and Bolivia to the east, and the Pacific Ocean to the west. The coast is 3,080 km/1,848 miles long. The country has water rights extending 200 miles from the coast and also has territorial rights to an area of 168 million acres in the Antarctic.

Topography

Llangonaco Lake, near Huaraz (N. Gill)

Peru is divided into three distinct geographic regions: Coast, Andes, and Amazon. The **Coast** amounts to 12% of the country's territory and has 52% of the population. Much of it is made up of desert, the Atacama that stretches south into Chile. Most of the largest cities in the country can be found here, including Lima, Ica, Trujillo, Chiclayo and Piura.

The **Andes**, or the highlands, make up 28% of the land, with 36% of the population. Here you will find the tallest mountains outside of the Himalayas, the largest being Huascarán at 6,768 m/22,199 feet, the world's two deepest canyons, Colca and Cotahuasi, many fertile valleys, and high windswept

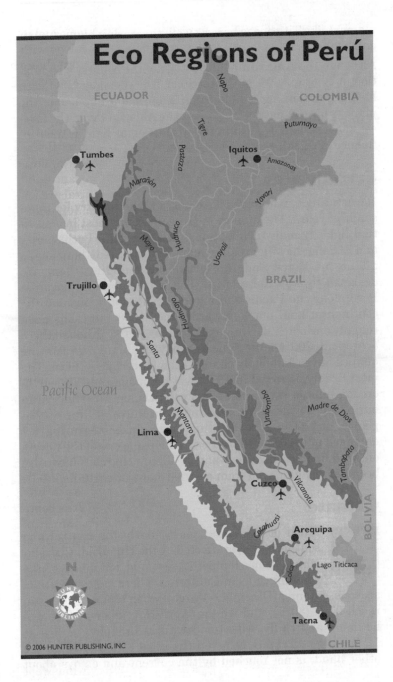

Eco Regions of Perú

ECUADOR
COLOMBIA

Napo

Tigre

Putumayo

Pastaza

● **Tumbes** ✈

Iquitos ✈
Amazonas

Marañón

Yavari

Mayo

Huallaga

Ucayali

BRAZIL

● **Trujillo** ✈

Huancabamba

Santa

Pacific Ocean

Mantaro

Urubamba

Madre de Dios

Lima ●✈

Tambopata

Cuzco ●✈

Vilcanota

Cotahuasi

Arequipa ●✈

Colca

Lago Titicaca

BOLIVIA

N

Tacna ●✈

CHILE

© 2006 HUNTER PUBLISHING, INC

plains. Lake Titicaca is here as well, the world's highest navigable lake.

Although the **Amazon** holds just 5% of the country's population, it contains 60% of the territory. The region is filled with lush vegetation, incredible wildlife and makes up one of the planet's largest natural reserves. The Amazon River, the largest, longest, and deepest in the world, begins here at the confluence of the Marañon and Ucayali rivers.

Earthquakes

Devastating earthquakes have plagued the country for thousands of years. The quakes have been seen almost in a spiritual light by many civilizations. In Lima, both Pachacamac and El Señor de Milagros ceremonies relate to earthquakes as divine messages and the rituals surrounding them are designed to stop the quakes. The Nazca plate sits against Peru along the Pacific shore and is continually pushing the continental land mass upward. Since 1568 there has been roughly one major earthquake every six years, although there are about 200 smaller ones each year. Many devastating quakes have completely changed the landscape in Peru. The most deadly occurred in 1970, when a magnitude 7.8 earthquake-induced rock and snow avalanche on Mt. Huascarán buried the towns of Yungay and Ranrahirca, killing 66,794 people. In 2001, a devastating earthquake measuring 8.1 damaged much of southern Peru, collapsing one of the towers on Arequipa's cathedral. Many of Cuzco's churches have also been heavily damaged from a series of major earthquakes.

Climate

 Much of the **coast**, particularly the central and southern half, is affected by the Humboldt Current, which keeps temperatures mild for much of the year, much as in California. There are two distinct seasons: summer (December-March), when temperatures can reach 27°C (80°F); and winter (April-November), which can be damp and chilly, with temperatures dropping as low as 12°C (53°F). It rarely rains on the coast. The north, on the other hand, is not touched by the current and enjoys about

300 sunny days a year with temperatures reaching as high as 35°C (95°F) in the summer.

In the **highlands** the climate is dry and cold. There are two seasons: dry and rainy. The dry, April-October, has warm sunny days and crisp, cool nights with little rain. The rainy season, December-March, can vary greatly in temperature. The range extends from 20°C (68°F) to 2°C (35°F), although for much of the time it is fairly mild and pleasant.

The **jungle** takes on a tropical feel. Much of the year is humid and sticky. The dry season (April to October) is scorching hot and temperatures often stay above 30°C (86°F). The rainy season (November to March) has frequent heavy rains, which cause the river levels to rise.

El Niño

Whatever I have said about Peru's weather on the coast you can toss out during El Niño years. Abnormal effects on climate across the equatorial Pacific include: sun, temperature, atmospheric pressure, wind, humidity, precipitation, cloud formation, and ocean currents. Cities that sit in the arid desert become prone to flooding. Ica, Piura, Tumbes and many other cities have looked more like Venice at times. Stagnant pools of water bring three times the amount of mosquitoes and malaria. Every three to seven years this occurs.

There is written evidence going back to 1525 regarding the condition, and geological evidence dates back 13,000 years. The Incas would build their cities on hills, keep food stored in the mountains, and their coastal cities were never built near water.

Many farmers and fishermen have learned to adapt, however. Cattle can graze on land that previously had no grass, rice and beans can be planted in the newly irrigated ground, and fishermen can plan for shrimp harvests in the coastal waters that are typically too cold for shrimp.

■ Flora & Fauna

Peru's plant and animal life is second to none. Of the earth's 117 life zones, 84 are found here, which has resulted in a biodiversity far greater than anywhere else on the planet. For example, as many as

1,200 different species have been recorded in an area of 21 sq miles in Madre de Dios. There are 11 eco-regions and three great river basins that include 12,201 lakes and lagoons, with 1,007 rivers. Nearly 13% of the country sits in protected areas, although the number could and should be higher. Plants and animals survive here that are found nowhere else on earth. New species are still being discovered. Many were worshipped and revered as gods for centuries. Animals such as pumas, condors, and serpents are found on pottery, in carvings, in textiles and in the Nazca Lines. The relationship with nature in Peru has long been held at an almost spiritual level.

Plants

In the Amazon, native tribes, who rarely see a doctor, have been using plants as medicine for many generations. Not only are there the hallucinogenic plants such as **Ayahuasca** and **San Pedro**, but there are lesser known plants that will cure everything from snakebites, diarrhea, upset stomach, or fever. Check with your personal shaman, or medicine man, for more information. They can be most easily contacted through the many jungle lodges in Peru.

 Did you know? About 50 major drugs come from rainforest plants, but that is only about 1/7 of the estimated number found here.

Victoria Regia

As expected, the Amazon holds the most diversity in this area. The basin itself is home to the **Victoria Regia**, a huge water lily, and so many fruit-producing plants that they are hard to keep straight. In cloud forests, like the areas around Machu Picchu and parts of the Manu Biosphere Reserve, tropical flowers and plants such as **orchids**, **ferns**, and **bromeliads** all thrive. In the extreme north, near Tumbes, the rare ecosystem is shared only with Ecuador's south and comprises mangrove swamps and aquatic plants. The Andes are home to a variety of trees, shrubs, wildflowers, and herbs. Even the desert that makes up the coast has cactus, palms, and other vegetation. That's just the beginning. In all, Peru has more than 25,000 species of plants (10% of the world total); roughly 5,500 are found only in Peru.

There are more than 3,000 members of the Orchidaceae family found in Peru. Species are found all over the country, with most living in the cloud forest because the 200 inches of rain that falls there each year creates the perfect environment. More than 200 orchid varieties grow in the Machu Picchu Historical Sanctuary.

Trees

Ceiba

The Amazon basin has the most diverse range of trees in the country. The largest and most impressive is without doubt the **ceiba** tree that towers above the forest canopy. The **Brazil nut** tree is quite impressive for its size as well as the delicious nut it produces. There are also interesting species such as the **strangler fig** or the **walking palm**.

In temperate forests, which are the most common in Europe and North America, only a few species of trees are found in every few acres of land. In tropical forests there are 100 to 300.

In the highlands you will encounter **puna**, the shrubs and grasslands that cover the cold plains and mountainsides. Most trees here have small, chunky leaves that help protect against frost. **Mangrove** forests cover the coastal border area with Ecuador.

Strangler fig

Did you know? The ceiba tree once dominated the Amazonian riverbanks but, because of logging, few survive. Their trunks may be as wide as 15 feet across and they can grow more than 160 feet high. Their gigantic crowns are usually covered with epiphytes (smaller plants).

Birds

Toucan

If you count all of the bird species in North America, and then double it, you would have roughly the number found in Peru. There are more than 1,800, the second only to Colombia, which has 1,815 registered species. More than 19% of all the species in the world and 45% of all of the neo-tropical birds are found here.

In the Amazon area there are many different birding areas of interest, such as Manu, Tambopata, and Pacaya-Samiria. Tropical birds such as **toucans**, **parakeets**, **hummingbirds**, and **parrots** are commonplace. **Macaws** are the

Quetzal

quintessential Amazonian birds. There are several species found in the Amazon region; some, such as the military macaw and the red and green macaw are in danger of extinction. Clay-licks, the largest in the world, are filled with flocks of these birds and other parrots that number in the hundreds or sometimes the thousands.

In the cloud forests that make up the eastern slopes of the Andes there is even more diversity than the Amazon basin, with rare species such as **quetzals**, **tanagers**, and even more parrots and macaws. The Andean **cock-of-the-rock** is one of the flashiest birds you will ever see. The bright red males are often found on the pages of tourism brochures.

Hummingbirds, some of the most recognizable birds, are quite numerous and can be found in all parts of the country. There are 116 species, with whimsical names, such as the tyrian metaltail, black-eared fairy, fork-tailed wood nymph, and the white-bearded hermit.

Scarlet macaws

🜋 **Did you know?** Hummingbirds beat their wings in figure eight fashion, at a speed of more than 80 times per second.

Black-eared fairy

Twenty-five percent of all of the **trogon** species live in Peru. These neo-tropical birds are some of the most exciting for bird enthusiasts to encounter. The quetzals, which are the largest, are the most impressive and sought after.

Birds of prey such as **hawks**, **eagles**, **owls**, and majestic **Andean condors** dominate the highlands. The condor, a type of vulture, can have a wingspan as wide as nine feet. It is found at high altitudes in the Andes such as in Colca Canyon, and also on the Paracas Peninsula.

The Islas Ballestas and Islas Palaminos on the coast are home to many migratory and aquatic birds, such as the **Humboldt penguins**, **boobies**, **pelicans**, **gulls**, and **cormorants**. Sightseeing trips to either of the island chains are quite common.

Parakeets in the Northern Amazon (N. Gill)

Even Lima is home to a variety of colorful birds that survive in the parks, beaches, and surrounding desert. Try places like Pachacamac, Parque Kennedy, or Parque El Olivar for a taste of what the rest of the country holds.

 Many species of **parrots** are endangered, but are still being sold on the black market. It is thought that, for every macaw sold, as many as 50 are killed because of poor care or during transport.

Mammals

The mammals of Peru are some of the most fascinating in the world, and also some of the hardest to see. Many tourists come to Amazon lodges for weeks, but see very few. They are there though. Peru has 431 mammal species, most of them nocturnal. With good eyes, some binoculars, and the right guide, you should be able to see some wildlife, though probably not a jaguar.

Capybara

 There are 170 species of **bats** in Peru (40% of all the mammals), while only 40 exist in all of North America.

In the Amazon it all depends on where you are looking. **Capybaras**, the world's largest rodents, **peccaries**, **armadillos**, **tapirs**, and **giant anteaters** can all be found on the ground or riverbanks. In the water, you will find **Amazonian**

manatees, pink river dolphins (they actually are pink), and **giant otters**. In the trees, there are a number of **bats**, such as the fishing bat and vampire bat, sloths, jaguars, ocelots, and more than 20 spe-

Giant anteater (N. Gill)

cies of monkeys. **Sloths** and **monkeys** can best be seen during the dry season, when the waters recede and they come closer to the water to scrounge for food. Night trips into the jungle are among the best ways to see any of the mammals and that is one of the most interesting times to be in the forest.

 Pink river dolphins have been considered sacred to many Amazonian people; therefore they have survived large-scale hunting.

There are six species of cats found here, both spotted and unspotted. They are mostly nocturnal creatures and some of the most difficult to see. If you do see one, consider yourself extremely lucky. Most guides in the jungle have seen just a few in their lives. The largest is the **jaguar**, which can weigh in at 130-260 pounds. Next are the **pumas**, or mountain lions, which are found in much of the Americas and are almost as big as the jaguars. Other smaller cats include **ocelots**, **margays**, **oncillas**, and **jaguarundis**.

As for the **giant otter**, only a few hundred exist here in parks such as Manu, Tambopata, and Pacaya-Samiria. They survive mainly in ox-bow lakes. Viewing the playful creatures is strictly controlled as human interference can limit reproduction. For more information or to see how you can help save these magnificent animals visit The Giant Otter Project through the Frankfurt zoological society at www.giantotters. com.

Elsewhere, in the cloud forests there are many of the same species as in the Amazon, as well as all of the six cat species and the very rare **Andean spectacled bear**, the only bear on the continent. They eat mostly tubers, vegetables, and other

Andean spectacled bear

plant life, although they will occasionally scavenge for dead mammals such as cows or deer. They are known to be extremely shy.

Alpaca in the Cordillera Blanca
(N. Gill)

In the Andes, many of the mammal species have been domesticated, although **pumas** and **vizcachas** (an animal resembling a cross between a rabbit and a squirrel) still run wild. Domesticated animals, such as **cuy**, or guinea pigs, and the **camelids**, **vicuñas**, **llamas**, and **alpacas**, are numerous in the highlands and may have been around for thousands of years.

The camelids survive in highland areas throughout the Andes. Wild herds can still be seen in places like Pampas Galeras and domesticated herds are frequent in small mountain villages. Llamas are the largest and used more as pack animals. Alpacas are slightly smaller than llamas and have longer wool that is often made into everything from gloves, hats, scarves, or sweaters, to blankets and slippers. Vicuñas are the smallest and skinniest. Their fur is short and very fine, but it's their big doe eyes that grab the most attention.

Did you know? Alpaca meat is actually healthier than most meats since it is low in both fat and cholesterol.

Reptiles & Amphibians

Peru has 364 species of reptiles and 315 amphibians. The reptiles are the most difficult to encounter. Other than caimans and iguanas, most will run or hide when they detect a human nearby. They hide in trees, under leaves, and make few sounds. Amphibians are a bit easier. Just a bit. Most are nocturnal and can be seen along forest trails and roadways by shining a flashlight at night, particularly on leaves about six feet from the ground. During the day, search the forest floor, particularly around moist areas near lakes and streams.

Snakes

Of Peru's 364 species of reptiles, 186 are snakes. Of these, few have garnered the notoriety of the **anaconda**. Thanks to Hollywood, myths about these creatures have reached an almost comical level. This member of the boa family is primarily aquatic and lives in rivers, swamps, and ox-bow lakes. They eat other reptiles, birds, and mammals, wrapping around them and squeezing until the animal can no longer breathe.

Anaconda

There are many other interesting species of snakes here, although less well known. Other boas include the **Amazonian tree boa**, the **rainbow boa**, and the **red-tailed boa**.

There are 15 species from the viperid family, the most notorious being the **bushmaster** and **fer-de-lance**. This family makes up most of the country's venomous snakes. The bushmaster is the largest, reaching 7½ to 11 feet and living in mostly lowland, wet forest areas. The fer-de-lance is found in similar locations and reaches a maximum length of six feet.

Most snakes found in Peru are not venomous. Only 32 of the 186 are; those are generally among the hardest to find and are only dangerous to lizards and rodents. So the chance that you will see or be bitten by a poisonous snake is slim.

Turtles

Matamata

There are 16 turtle species in Peru, most found in Amazonian rivers. The **yellow spotted river turtle** is one of the more common, and is often seen near rivers and streams, sunning itself on logs and riverbanks .

The **matamata** is one of the more interesting. The smiling creature looks almost like a rock with a long fleshy nose. It often spends its time on river bottoms waiting until unsuspecting prey swims by.

Several species of sea turtles occur in the Pacific, such as the **olive ridley** and the **leatherback**, but their numbers are far smaller than those of Central America. They mostly live at sea, except when the females come ashore to lay eggs.

The yellowfoot tortoise is the only tortoise found in Peru.

Crocodiles & Caimans

There are five types of crocodiles and caimans found in Peru, most in lakes, rivers, streams, and ponds of the Amazon region. In many restaurants in Iquitos, you can also find them on the menu. They are best seen at night when you can shine a flashlight and see the red reflection in their eyes. Tambopata is perhaps the best place to find them.

The **black caiman** is the largest of the bunch. They can grow up to 21 feet in length and will eat land mammals such as capybaras. The next two aren't particularly dangerous to humans and locals often swim in their vicinity. The **smooth-**

fronted **caiman** dwells in the forests near rivers. It is quite small and only grows to about three feet. The **spectacled caiman** is the most abundant in South America and will grow to eight feet. The

Black caiman (www.enjoyperu.com)

others, like the American crocodile, are found only in Peru's far north near Tumbes.

 Did you know? Many crocodilians survive as long 60 years in the wild.

Frogs & Toads

Yellow-banded poison dart frog

Hundreds of species of frogs can be found in Peru. New species are discovered all of the time as more and more sections of rainforest and cloud forest are surveyed.

Of the **rain frogs**, the largest family of frogs, there are 108 species. They are so named because their heaviest period of breeding occurs just after the rain. Some to look out for are the smoky jungle frog, the Titicaca water frog, and basin white-lipped frog.

As for **tree frogs**, there are 84 species found in Peru. Their bright colors and large eyes set them apart. Watch for the red-skirted tree frog, the giant gladiator frog, the common marsupial frog, and the polka dot tree frog.

🍎 The poison of the poison dart frog is placed on the tips of blowgun darts used by many indigenous Amazonian hunters.

Red and blue poison dart

There are 38 species of **poison dart frogs** such as the Amazon rocket frog and the ruby poison dart frog. They are often brightly colored, which warns predators of their toxicity. They are generally very small, no more than two inches long.

There are also another 40 or so frogs that fit into smaller families, and that's just what has been discovered so far.

Of the **toads**, there are 32 species. Most live in dry areas along the coast and in the highlands.

Did you know? The secretions from the skin of the giant monkey frog are used by the Mayoruna tribe along the border with Brazil to give them magical hunting powers. A powder is made from the secretions and put into open wounds. After vomiting and a high pulse, several days of what is believed to be god-like strength occurs.

Lizards

There 158 species of lizards in Peru; some will be found crawling on the ceiling of your jungle lodge or even on your mosquito net while you sleep.

The **green iguana** spends much of its time in trees near waterways and is sometimes hunted for food. When threatened it often drops from the tree and swims away underwater. It can grow up to six feet long.

Green iguana

The **spiny whorltail** is what you will see crawling all over the stones at Machu Picchu. Also, **common geckos** and **anoles** can be found nearly everywhere.

Other species include **Tschudi's Pacific lizards**, which crawl through sand in the coastal deserts, and the **Amazon thornytail**. Some indigenous people claim a whip from its tail can be fatal.

Insects & Arachnids

Without question, there are more insects on the planet than any other species. Some entomologists believe there are as many as 10 million species. Although they are often overshadowed by mammals and birds, a look at Peru's array of insects is sure to impress even the most conservative bug lover.

There are thought to be 4,300 species of **butterflies** in Peru, possibly more than anywhere else on earth. The neon blue Menelaus' morpho butterfly is one of the most beautiful of all and is commonly seen in tropical forests in Central and South America. Other butterflies common in Peru are the tiger butterfly and the Aurorina's clear

winged satyr. The **Pilpintuwasi Butterfly Farm** near Iquitos is one of the best places to get close-up views of butterflies and their reproduction process.

Ant species are often pointed out on tours of the Amazon. Burchell's army ants capture pray such as insects and small reptiles with their overwhelming numbers and continuing stings. The colonies of such ants that number in the millions move locations every month because it is thought they reduce the numbers of insects so greatly in each area they must look elsewhere. Leaf cutter ants walk in lines of millions carrying green leaves of trees they devoured. Some don't realize that there is a selection process, where certain ants accept leaves worthy of entering the nests, or reject them. The leaves are cleaned and used in gardens inside the nests, where a fungus grows that will feed the larvae and the colony. The Isula ant is well known for its very painful sting. Many jungle guides will get one on a stick for you to see, although they often drop the stick and jump away if it gets too close.

Dragonflies and **damselflies** are found in nearly all of Peru's natural environments. Most are similar to those in North America. The most notable is the helicopter damselfly, which can grow to six inches in length. Of the **beetles**, you won't see John, Paul, George, or Ringo, but you will see montane tiger beetles, green dung beetles, and harlequin long horned beetles.

Other insects you may want to look out for are the **termites**, although you will more likely see their huge nests, **walking sticks**, **praying mantis**, and **orchid bees**, among others.

As for **spiders**, several thousand species are found in Peru. Large, hairy spiders such as tarantulas can be found throughout the Amazon basin and much of the rest of the country, not to mention later in your nightmares. the neo-tropical Colonial spider is known for its web, which can be several yards wide. The webs are communal and may contain as many as 20,000 individuals. It is also safe to say that, of all the species of spiders, very few are dangerous to humans.

 Did you know? Female moths give off a pheromone, or scent, that is carried by the wind. The male will follow the scent, sometimes for miles, until he finds the female.

In the Waters

 Wildlife in Peru is by far not limited to land. Many of the species mentioned above live in rivers, lakes and streams. There are more than 2,000 types of fish found here, which is an astounding 10% of the

Red-bellied piranha

worldwide total. The Amazon waters contain varieties such as the **paiche**, the world's largest freshwater fish, which can weigh as much as 500 pounds and grow as long as nine feet. It is also called the arapaima or piracucu. Here you will also find the tiny **neon tetra**, which has become common in many American fish tanks. The red-bellied piranha, one of several **piranha** species found in the Amazon, has sharp teeth and is attracted to blood, but piranhas are not nearly as dangerous as the movies make them out to be. You can even swim with them if you dare. One fish you do not want to swim with is the tiny **candiru**, known to swim up the urethras of unfortunate women.

The coastal waters are home to many species of fish, including **sea bass**, **tuna**, **mahi-mahi**, **black marlin**, and **king fish**. It isn't just limited to fish, however. There are also **lobsters**, **manta rays**, **squid**, **octopus**, **crabs**, and numerous other creatures. Of the mammals there are **South American sea lions**, **southern fur seals**, **humpbacked whales**,

Southern fur seal

sperm whales, **orcas**, **bottle nosed dolphins**, and **marine otters**.

Surprisingly, there are no great diving sites along the coast. The coral reefs needed to attract colorful, tropical fish and the creatures that feed on them simply aren't there. So the sport has yet to catch on. But, considering that much of the New World's gold was shipped from the port of Callao, and that some ships were attacked by pirates or sank for other reasons, wreck diving could be worth looking into. There are a few places near Mancora that may be able to assist you. Whale-watching also has yet to catch on.

■ Preservation

Although it has fared much better than the Brazilian rainforest, Peru's Amazon region is still in grave danger. More than 750,000 acres of the Peruvian Amazon forest are cut down annually and could disappear completely in the next 50 years. Think about that. Along with the forests, go the diverse, rare, beautiful species that live in them. Some amphibians and reptiles have such small ranges that one company drilling for oil or clearing an area of forest for cow pastures can completely wipe out an entire species.

Birds such as macaws, toucans, and parrots are hunted for their feathers and put up for sale on the black market as pets. Jaguars and other big cats have been hunted out of most regions of the country, with the exception of protected areas. The giant otter, wanted for its fine fur, has already disappeared completely in several other South American nations. Some turtle species, although taken off endangered lists, are anything but safe. In markets, such as the one in Iquitos, hundreds of eggs are stacked in crates for miniscule prices. By the way, some of these turtles only lay one egg at a time. Just look at Lima's beaches. Lima could be the next Río. At one time there were dolphins and seals thriving just off the coast. Now look at it. Sewage from the city of eight million drains not far away and the beach is heavily polluted. The only people that swim there are surfers, who wear a thick wet suit if they are smart. The future looks bleak for many of the world's most incredible creatures unless something is done and done quickly.

■ Eco-Tourism

Eco-tourism is defined as travel to areas of natural and ecological significance to learn about the environment and observe wildlife, usually under the guidance of a naturalist. Sustainment is the key. By visiting these areas you bring money there, learn more about the places, and help preserve them for future generations.

Logging and deforestation are aimed at quick profit rather than sustaining the environment. Over-fishing in the coastal waters and the use of explosives in Amazon Rivers are depleting the fish populations. Corrupt government policies give preference to large corporations rather than to conservation. The introduction of foreign plants and animals often kills native species. Mining, pollution, drugs, cattle grazing... the list goes on and on. A colossal man-made disaster is just waiting to happen. There are protected areas, but government funds are not nearly enough to make the difference they should.

As for bringing gifts to the people and children living in the communities you visit, that can be a double-edged sword. In some places that are heavily visited by tourists, children and sometimes adults put their hands out and beg for candy when they see a tourist. This isn't good when the health of many of these people is already in jeopardy and they often throw the wrappers on the ground anyway. Instead, try giving them a gift they can use. On Lake Titicaca many suffer from sunburn and dry skin. Bring lotion. In other communities in mountains and in the jungle, simple school supplies such as pencils and paper are hard to come by. As far as money goes, it does help, but be reasonable and don't just give it away out of pity. Buy some of their crafts and don't try to bargain down the price too much because it really will amount to only a few cents. Another great gift is a photo. If you have a Polaroid camera or a digital camera with an attached printer, you can give the people a photo of yourself, which they in all likelihood would keep for the rest of their lives.

By visiting the park and supporting the local economy in the correct ways, the benefits can be great. More money into the park itself helps maintain trails, create ecologically friendly viewing platforms, and allows the park to hire more rangers who can help enforce the rules. Allowing local people to earn a living through the park is important; otherwise, they will find their own means of sustaining their income, which may not promote the well-being of the parks. Education and research is a great benefit that ecotourism promotes. For instance, places like the Canopy Walk created by Explorama in Iquitos has led to a far greater understanding of life in the rainforest canopies and the discovery of many new species.

Many will go to extremes to walk around an entrance point into national parks and reserves, sometimes with uncertified guides, to avoid paying a $20 fee. They do not realize how much of a difference that fee makes. Park fees go directly toward maintaining the parkland and protecting the interior of the parks. Some parks may be thousands of acres, but only a few rangers are paid to protect the area and enforce the boundaries. If you stay on the trails you will help prevent further erosion. You have heard the phrase "Leave only footprints." Try not to leave even those.

One of the best things you can do is go with a respected tour operator that follows strict guidelines in operations to have minimal impact on the land, people, and wildlife. A good tour operator will:

- Make contributions to the park visited.
- Provide employment to local residents.
- Use local products, transportation, and locally owned services whenever possible. This includes hiring local guides.
- Keep tour groups small as to not disturb wildlife and habitats.
- Cooperate with researchers.

Many grass roots operations started by young Peruvians and international students are making a difference. Much more action needs to be taken before many of the world's most incredible natural areas are lost forever. One of the best things you can do is give to a non-profit organization such as the ones listed below.

"Produce your own dream. If you want to save Peru, go save Peru. It's quite possible to do anything, but not to put it on the leaders and the parking meters. Don't expect Jimmy Carter or Ronald Reagan or John Lennon or Yoko Ono or Bob Dylan or Jesus Christ to come and do it for you. You have to do it yourself. That's what the great masters and mistresses have been saying ever since time began."
— John Lennon

Non-Profits, NGOs, Volunteering

The **Wildlife Conservation Society** (WCS), www.wcs.org, has several projects ongoing in the country with the vicuña population, with Humboldt penguins, macaw clay licks, and much other wildlife.

The **Civil Association for Conservation of the Peruvian Amazon Environment** (CONAPAC), www.amazon-travel. com/CONAPAC/about.htm, began in Iquitos to help conserve the Amazon forests. It also has a program for visitors to donate to Amazonian schools that desperately need funding.

Inka Porters Project (Porteadores Inka Ñan), www. peruweb.org/porters, is a Cuzco-based organization that works actively with Inca trail operators to help improve working conditions for porters.

Bruce Peru, http://bruceperu.org, is an NGO that helps abandoned children in Peru and offers a large variety of other volunteering opportunities.

Amazon Conservation Association (ACA), www. amazonconservation.org/home, is dedicated to conserving biodiversity through development of new scientific understanding, sustainable resource management and rational land-use policy for the Amazon Basin.

Amazon Medical Project, www.amazonmedical.org, is run by a passionate Wisconsin woman who has dedicated much of her life to bringing modern medical help to people of the area north of Iquitos.

Rainforest Conservation Fund, www.rainforest-conservation.org, is an all-volunteer organization dedicated to preserving the world's rainforests.

Cajamarca Stove Trek, www.socioadventures.com, brings volunteers together for a five-day hike that interacts with the local communities and has the overall goal of building a stove for local families.

Amazon Animal Orphanage, www.amazonanimal-orphanage.org. At the Pilpintuwasi Butterfly farm, this group helps abused, abandoned, and orphaned animals near Iquitos survive.

Peru Verde, www.perverde.org, is an NGO focused on promoting conservation of Peruvian natural resources and ecosystems.

Selva Sur, Conservation Association for the Southern Rainforest of Peru (ACSS), www.inkanatura.com. A very active organization that has purchased more than 10,000 acres of cloud forest and helps the Peruvian rainforest in a variety of areas.

ACT (Action for Conservation through Tourism), act@ gn.apc.org. A charity that helps communities, NGOs, and tour operators develop and market sustainable tourism projects.

Casa de Milagros Orphanage, www.chandlersky.org, is an orphanage in the Sacred Valley.

Association Los Apus, www.localperu.com/contenido/apus. html, helps communities on Lake Titicaca, particularly on the island of Amantani.

Cross Cultural Solutions, www.crossculturalsolutions.org/ Default.aspx?page=peru.home. Volunteering throughout Peru, including in Lima shantytowns.

Mosoq Kausay, www.travatools.com/mosoqkausay, welcomes volunteers of any age interested in permaculture and sustainable agriculture work on conservation and organic farming projects in the Sacred Valley. The program seeks to promote the economy of the local people while allowing them to share the agricultural skills and customs of their ancestors with international volunteers. Activities include learning to plow with oxen and practicing Quechua stonewalling.

Hotels & Tour Operators That Have Begun Their Own Charity/Volunteer Organizations

Incas del Peru (Huancayo), www.incasdelperu.org/discovery.htm.

The Way Inn (Huaraz), www.thewayinn.com/charity.htm.

BuenaVista (Mancora), www.buenavistamancora.com.

Explorama (Iquitos), www.explorama.com

Manu Expeditions (Cuzco), www.manuexpeditions.com.

Pantiacolla Tours (Cuzco), www.pantiacolla.com.

Rainforest Expeditions (Cuzco), www.perunature.com.

Niños Hotel (Cuzco), www.ninoshotel.com.

MirafloresHouse (Lima), www.alberguemirafloreshouse. com.

■ National Parks, Reserves & Sanctuaries

Peru's national parks are run by INRENA, or Instituto Nacional de Recursos Nacionales (www.inrena.gob.pe). Protected areas cover 12.7% of the entire country. There are 10 national parks, as well as several national reserves

Coastline at Paracas National Park (N. Gill)

and sanctuaries. Here are some of the highlights:

■ **Mangalares de Tumbes National Sanctuary** – This is Peru's only swamp forest and it covers 8,320 acres near Tumbes. There is quite a bit of aquatic wildlife that inhabits the mangroves such as snails (33 species), crustaceans (34 species), mollusks (24 species), and fish (105 species), not to mention green iguanas, crab-eating raccoons, and many, many species of birds.

■ **Cerros de Amotape National Park** – Located in the Tumbes and Piura regions, this national park covers 255,600 acres. This is the only area of protected equatorial dry forests in the country. There are four different life zones, which contain many species of plants that are quite rare in Peru, especially orchids, bromeliads, and epiphytes.

Cerros de Amotape National Park

■ **Paracas National Reserve** – Covering 938,000 acres in the Ica region, 609,000 of which are marine environments. The diversity of birds here is great, both of migratory and endemic species. Most of the birds can be found along the coastal area, where you will also encounter two species of sea lions, and the endangered marine otter.

■ **Huascarán National Park** – Established in 1975, this is one of the most visited parks in Peru. Just north of Huaraz, it encompasses almost all of the Cordillera Blanca, cover-

Twin peaks of Huascarán

ing 952,000 acres. There is a wide variety of microclimates, which have given life to 779 species of Andean flora. This is a popular destination for hikers, climbers, and other adventure enthusiasts. The park contains many of the highest mountains in the Americas, including the highest of all, Huascaran, at 22,195 feet.

■ **Machu Picchu Historical Sanctuary & Natural Monument** – This was declared a UNESCO World Cultural and Natural Heritage Site in 1983. It covers 91,250 acres in the Cuzco region, with altitudes ranging from 6,500 to 13,000 feet. A variety of rare flora and fauna inhabit the cloud forests found in this range. Palms, evergreens, cedars, and ferns are among the many plants you will find. As for orchids, this is an incredible place. There are nearly 200 species from 30

genuses. Threatened creatures such as the Andean cock-of-the rock, the spectacled bear, and the pampas cat make their home here.

- **Salinas and Aguada Blanca National Reserve** – This reserve near Arequipa covers over a million acres, with snow-capped mountains, volcanoes, lagoons, meadows and forests. There are several inactive volcanoes such as El Misti (19,089 feet), Chachani (19,680 feet) and Pichu Pichu (17,387 feet). The Salinas lagoons are home to a number of endangered flamingos and other aquatic birds. Around Pampa Cañahuas and Tocra you can see large herds of vicuñas roaming about.

- **Titicaca National Reserve** – This reserve in the Puno region spans 101,000 acres on or around Lake Titicaca. There are more than 60 species of birds that live on the lake, such as Puna ibis, plovers, ducks, herons, and flamingos. Nearly 20 types of frogs are found here as well.

- **Pacaya-Samiria National Reserve** – This is the largest reserve in the country, the second-largest in the entire Amazon, and the fourth-largest on the continent. The 5,824,000 acres in the Loreto region contain a wide variety of flora and fauna, some of it endemic to the reserve. There are 132 mammal species, 330 bird types, 150 reptiles and amphibians, and more than 200 varieties of fish. Several rare and endangered species live in the park, including the black spider monkey, the yellow-chested spider monkey, the woolly monkey, and the giant otter.

- **Manu National Park** – This park is one of the most amazing and diverse natural areas in the entire world. It was named a UNESCO Natural Heritage Site in 1977. The national park covers 479 million acres ranging from 490 to 20,664 feet above sea level. An incredible variety of eco-systems exist within the park. There are 850 species of birds, 200 mammals (100 of which are bats), 120 types of fish, and countless reptiles, amphibians, insects and other creatures. The giant otter, Andean spectacled bear, all of Peru's big cats, armadillos, anteaters, macaws, toucans and many other species live here.

- **Tambopata-Candamo Reserve Zone** – This extends over 769,000 acres and is located in the Madre de Dios area near Puerto Maldonado. The diversity of this park is truly astounding and many world records have been noted here – 1,234 types of butterflies, 592 species of birds, 152 varieties of dragonflies, 135 kinds of ants, 127 species of amphibians, 103 types of mammals, 94 types of fish, 74 different reptiles, 40 termites and 39 varieties of bees. The park is home to the Colpa de Guacamayos, one of the largest natural clay licks in the world, which draws thousands upon thousands of parrots on most days.

■ **Bahuaja-Sonene National Park** – This is in the Madre de Dios and Puno districts, in the provinces of Tambopata and Sandia, respectively. There are 255,710 acres in the park, bordering the country of Bolivia and its Madidi National Park. Like Tambopata-Candamo, which is not far away, there is a diverse population of flora and fauna. Rare species include the giant otter, the harpy eagle, the savannah dog, and the black caiman. The Ese'Eja indigenous population also lives on the land, and is permitted to subsistence hunt.

■ Government

Peru, officially the Republic of Peru, is a constitutional republic. The constitution, written in December 31, 1993, says that citizens may vote after the age of 18 until the age of 70, the exception being members of the military and national police who may not vote. The President is both the chief of state and head of government, and is supported by two Vice-Presidents. The cabinet is appointed by the President, while the Supreme Court is appointed by the National Council of the Judiciary. President Alejandro Toledo has been in office since July 28, 2001. His five-year term ends in 2006. Representatives of Congress, numbering 120, are elected every five years by popular vote. Regional and municipal elections are every four years.

Peru is divided into 24 departments (Amazonas, Ancash, Apurimac, Arequipa, Ayacucho, Cajamarca, Cuzco, Huancavelica, Huánuco, Ica, Junín, La Libertad, Lambayeque, Lima, Loreto, Madre de Dios, Moquegua, Pasco, Piura, Puno, San Martín, Tacna, Tumbes, and Ucayali), plus the Constitutional Province of Callao. Lima is the capital of the country. Also, dozens of indigenous tribes in the Amazon region have been granted their own territories, mostly on national reserves, and they operate independently of the national government.

■ Economy

Like most South American countries, Peru is quite poor. In much of the country people are not part of the market economy and lack electricity and plumbing. The recent openness to trade and investment looks very positive for the future of the economy. Although in recent years Peru's economy as a whole has been improving, 54% live below the poverty line and unemployment for peasant families is widespread.

The hub of all business activity is in Lima. Most national and international companies have their headquarters there and the result is that a significant part of the city resembles most American cities, with chain stores and skyscrapers.

Almost a third of the population works in agriculture (it was twice as high 50 years ago), much of it in subsistence farming. The largest exports are coffee, cotton, sugarcane, rice, potatoes, corn, plantains, grapes, oranges, avocadoes, flowers, coca, poultry, beef, dairy products, and fish. Peruvian exports are expected to increase by 35% in 2006 to roughly $24 billion.

Mining and refining of minerals is significant in many highland areas, such as Cajamarca and Huancavelica. Petroleum extraction and refinement has long been done in jungle and coastal areas although it is likely to be more of a factor soon. Future economic growth will be driven by the Camisea natural gas mega-project, as well as by the export of minerals, textiles, and agricultural products. The project will create a huge pipeline that runs from the Urubamba Valley to the coast, which could have detrimental effects on the environment. A permanent free-trade agreement with the United States is expected to be worked out by 2007, if not before.

For years, visitors were scared away from Peru because of the terrorism that plagued the country. Tour operators in the Amazon would say they were in the Amazon, not Peru, so that visitors would still come. Those days are long gone. Presently, about two million visitors come to Peru annually. This number is increasing each year, as are the revenues and the growth of the tourist infrastructure.

■ Peru's People

 In trying to define Peru's people, it really matters where you are. The population is made up of many ethnic groups that have been mixed with a variety of immigrants. On the coast, in the Andes, or in the Amazon, each region has significantly different ancestral legacies. The coastal area is where you will find the most people with mixed ancestry, or *mestizos*, and what are considered white people. In the Andes you will encounter mainly Ameri-Indians, the legacy of the Incas and their predecessors. The Amazon region is mainly mixed blood, but there are several indigenous tribes that survive. No matter where you go, however, the people are usually friendly, quite proud, and ready to explain to you how great their country is. Families and friendships are usually quite close. When a baby is born, much of the family gets involved in raising it. Whenever there is a birthday, anniversary, graduation, or wedding there will always be a large party.

The population is about 28 million, nearly three-quarters of them living in urban areas. The coast is home to 58% of the population, the highlands 36%, and the jungle roughly 6%.

Their Origins

Pre-Inca

A variety of ethnic groups – the Chavín, the Moche, the Chimu, the Nazca, the Paracas, and the Wari – have survived in Peru since long before the Incas. Many of these groups overlapped and their areas of influence intermingled, which allowed the Incas to dominate them.

Quechuas

The *indigenas* (*indios* is considered an insult) highlanders, or *campesinos* were known in Inca times as Quechuas. They make up around 45% of the population. Peru has the third-highest percentage of Amerindians after Bolivia and Guatemala. Most live in rural areas and survive by subsistence farming, although they also make up the majority of several large cities, such as Cuzco. During the political upheaval of the 80s many fled the highlands to the coast, which is significantly changing the makeup of coastal towns. Most speak Quechua, although many know Spanish as well.

Quechuas

Aymaras

Aymara

These are people derived from another cultural group dominated by the Incas that live on or around Lake Titicaca. Their numbers are significantly smaller than the Quechuas, and most are concentrated on just a few islands. Peru has about 300,000 Aymara-speaking people and there are another two million spread out in Bolivia, Chile, and Argentina.

Mestizos

Mestizos are people of mixed European and Amerindian descent, which defines about 50% of the population and a majority of the coastal population. A little more than 10% are considered white, or of pure European ancestry. The people of Spanish ancestry are sometimes called *Criollos*, although that term now applies mainly to all coastal people and cuisine.

Afro-Peruvians

Brought in during the early years of colonization, black slaves worked on plantations, the railroads and on the Guano islands. Black Peruvians make up 2-3% of the population and most are concentrated in and around the coastal town of Chincha near Ica.

Chinese

Lima's China Town, or Barrio Chino, is the center for all the Chinese on the continent. You will find all sorts of Chinese shops there, not to mention Chinese restaurants. Chinese coolies were recruited to work on railroads and on coastal plantations in the late 1800s. Their influence spread to the cuisine and they created dishes, such as the famous lomo-saltado, which recreated stir-fry for the Peruvian palate. On many street corners you will see Chinese restaurants, or *chifas*. Among the most prosperous Chinese-Peruvians are the Wong brothers, who founded Peru's best supermarket chain. Today's Chinese population is thought to be near one million.

Japanese, Italians, Germans

Many different immigrants have come to Peru in the past century and still make up a small percentage of the population, less than 1%. Tens of thousands of Japanese came in the first quarter of the 20th century to work in coastal sugar plantations. Many stuck around and their influence can be seen most in Lima and in the Nikkei style of cooking, which has had a major influence on modern Peruvian cuisine. Also, La Punta near Callao was settled by Italians and Oxapampa in the central highlands by Germans.

Indigenous People

Ashaninka

There are 42 ethnic groups that still survive in the Amazon, although their population is less than two million. There were once more than 2,000 tribes, with a population of six million. Most of the tribes live in very isolated parts of the jungle and it is just a matter of time before more and more mestizo settlers move into their domains. Some of the best-known are the Amarakaeri, Ashaninka, Shawi, Uitoto, Shipibo, Awajan, Wampis, Tikuna, and Matses.

Cholo is a derogatory term used to define people of the poor highland population. Being a campesino, farmer or person from the country himself, former President Toledo embraced the term, hoping to remove its negative connotations.

■ Education

Most people over the age of 15 can read and write; the literacy rate stands at 87.7% (93.5% for males and 82.1% for females). Schools remain quite bad, and most affluent families in large cities send their children to private or Catholic schools. University education is affordable by just a small percentage of the population, mainly in large coastal cities, which also are home to most colleges and universities. State universities offer a discount based on your economic resources. Some students go to the United States or Europe to study in universities if they can afford it, although that percentage is small.

 Quechua is mainly an oral language and has led to many Quechua speakers being illiterate. In 2005, though, an edition of *Don Quixote* was translated into Quechua.

■ Language

Peru has two official languages: Spanish, used by 73% of the population, and Quechua, the language of the Incas, spoken by 24%. The Aymara language is spoken as well, on Peru's high altiplano along the border with Bolivia. There are also some 50 Amazon languages, including Ashaninka, Aguaruna, and Machiguenga.

English is used by many in the tourist industry and by a significant portion of the youth in large cities such as Lima and Arequipa.

■ Religion

Roman Catholicism is Peru's official religion, practiced by about 90% of all citizens. That doesn't necessarily mean that they all go to church, although many do and many participate in the frequent displays of faith and festivals. With those numbers it may be hard to tell, but the country does enjoy religious freedom. Evangelical churches have been picking up steam in the past few years and about 8-9% follow that faith. Many Andean Catholics also practice animistic religion and worship a number of gods, mountains, the sun, and the moon. This is a legacy of the Incas and other civilizations. Many of the Catholic festivals are paired and intermingled with these indigenous beliefs that relate to the spirits of plants and animals, although Christian ministers have slowly chipped away at these indigenous religions over the past century.

■ Food & Drink

 In an article in January 2004, *The Economist* magazine reported that Peru could "lay claim to one of the world's dozen or so great cuisines." It truly is the last great international cuisine that has yet to be discovered on a worldwide scale. That is changing though. Many upscale restaurants in places like New York and LA, with world-class chefs, are beginning to integrate dishes like ceviche and anticuchos in their menus. On a recent visit to New York, I was able to try *tiradito* at Nobu, if that tells you anything.

There are many reasons that Peruvian food is so dynamic. First is the immense natural diversity that exists within the country. So many different fruits, vegetables, animals, and fish are found here, that the plate easily becomes a canvas for the country's culinary artists. Second is the cultural diversity here and people's willingness to adapt to new flavors. The Incas ruled over an array of cultures themselves, but then came the Spanish, African slaves, the Chinese, Japanese, and Italians. Many dishes are derived from blending ingredients and techniques of these immigrants with whatever local recipe might be prepared. The cuisine is always reinventing itself. It can be spicy, or just spiced up with some picante, or pepper sauce. It can be fried and fatty, fruity and creamy, light or even raw. It truly is one of the most diverse cuisines on the planet.

Lima is being hailed as the gastronomic capital of the continent, and possibly of the Americas. Many internationally trained chefs are coming to Lima to open new restaurants that delight even the most sophisticated diners. Cuzco is next in line. A decade ago international visitors had trouble finding good places to eat. Now they have trouble choosing a restaurant. Some of the best in the country can be found here. Each year a few more open up that completely redefine dining in Cuzco.

Elsewhere, there is Arequipa, which lays claim to its own special cuisine, Iquitos, with its dishes derived from jungle plants and animals, Cajamarca, with cheeses and highland delicacies, Chiclayo, with its sweets, Ica, with wine and Pisco... and on it goes. Each place is home to its own regional recipes and ingredients.

 Did you know? More than 4,000 varieties of potatoes are thought to have originated in Peru, although many of them have since disappeared.

Andean Food

The **potato** is the biggest contribution of the Inca. Entire countries now rely on it for their well being. It is hard to imagine that a few hundred years ago the crop was limited to Peru. When the Spanish arrived, the Inca had already domesticated more than 1,000 varieties. **Papa a la Huancaina** is perhaps the most popular potato-based dish – created in Huancayo, although it is served throughout the country. The creamy sauce is made of cheese, onion, garlic and, most importantly, ají, which gives it a slight zing.

Many Incan recipes have been unchanged for 500 years. **Carapulca** and **pachamanca** are the most notable. Carapulca originally was made with dried meat and potatoes, sometimes with rabbit. It is a hearty stew and is often found in a clay pot at many potlucks and feasts. Pachamanca is usually a part of big Andean feasts. The recipe calls for a hole to be dug in the ground where a fire is set and covered by large stones. A variety of meats wrapped in small leaves and potatoes, corn and beans are thrown in the pit and then covered with dirt. Hours later everyone grabs pieces of the food with their hands. Often a creamy sauce is poured over the food, sometimes right in your hand.

The most famous, or infamous, meats, depending on whom you ask, are **alpaca** and **cuy** (guinea pig). Each is prepared in a variety of ways. Alpaca sometimes is served as a steak or as medallions. Cuy is often served *al horno*, or baked, as well as fried. Picante de cuy is served in a spicy sauce with potatoes. As you might expect, cuy tastes a bit like chicken. It is best eaten by grabbing it on each end, and gnawing on it like an ear of corn. If you are paying less than say, 15 soles for it (this goes for larger cities, not necessarily small highland towns) there is a good chance it is a rat.

Quinoa, a 3,000-year-old grain, used frequently in the Andes has made it onto tables and health food stores in North America for its numerous health benefits. It is low in carbs, high in protein, and contains each of the eight essential amino acids. It can be used in soups, salads, pudding, or risotto and is frequently part of Novo Andina, or New Andean recipes.

Criollo Dishes

When the Spanish arrived, they introduced a variety of cooking techniques and ingredients. During the three centuries of the Vice Royalty they introduced olives, grapes, dairy, beef, chicken, and rice. Recipes such as **ají de gallina** and **papa a la huancaina**, which mix chilies, cheese, and milk for their sauces, are perfect examples of new dishes that became mainstays in Peruvian households.

Other cultures had an influence as well. Two of the most popular dishes in the country – **tacu-tacu** and **anticuchos** – are Afro-Peruvian. Tacu-tacu was once made with leftover seasoned beans and rice, fried together for a nutritious meal. The general recipe today calls for a fried egg on top and plantain on the side. Anticuchos are kebabed beef hearts that are cooked on small charcoal grills in city streets. Novo-Andina recipes often have chicken or fish on the skewer instead. The most typical Chinese-Peruvian fusion dish is lomo saltado. This stir-fries strips of steak, French fries, tomatoes, and onions over white rice.

Causa is a popular appetizer found along the coast. It comprises layers of mashed yellow potatoes with many possible fillings such as avocados and seafood. **Cabrito**, or goat, is used in many northern dishes such as

Antichuchos

seco de cabrito, a kid goat stew. **Papa rellenas** are potato croquettes stuffed with meat, olives, and cheese or other ingredients. The **butifarra** is the most common sandwich and can be found during afternoon tea, for snacks, and in a variety of sizes. A white bun is filled with spiced country ham, onions, and salsa.

 Salsa in Peru is not the tomato-based salsa you find in Mexico; instead, the term applies to all sauces.

Jungle Food

Jungle food can be interesting or just plain bland. I spent two weeks with a mestizo family along the Río Napo and they ate the same thing for nearly every meal: fried plantains or yucca, a fried egg, and a huge pile of white rice. Occasionally there would be soup, a fried fish, or a few very small chunks of beef. That is the most typical.

Juanes are steamed corn meal wrapped in banana leaves much like a tamale and are often filled with chicken, rice, olives, and raisins. **Yuca** is often served fried, or frita, as an alternative to French fries. **Paiche**, the world's largest freshwater fish, is found on most Iquitos menus either as a sandwich, a filet, or in ceviche. **Lagarto** or **caiman** (alligator) is also used in Iquitos in a variety of preparations. There are many other interesting dishes if you look for them, such as **sopa de motelo** (turtle soup), **sajino** (roasted wild boar), or even **tapir**. Keep in mind that some animals are endangered, including many species of turtle. If you go to the Belén market, you will find skewered grubs that are grilled in front of you, among other strange creatures.

Seafood

The Peruvian coast is home to a variety of fish and sea life that have greatly contributed to the cuisine. Meat was actually considered a more refined food until the past century when Japanese immigrants began arriving. It was then that the Nisei cooks recreated the use of pescado and mariscos, fish and seafood. They were the ones who brought ceviche and tiradito up to more modern standards. Some of the names you will encounter are: **lenguado** (sole), **langosta** (lobster), **chorros** (mussels), **conchitas** (scallops), **camarones** (shrimp), **langostinos** (prawns), **cangrejo** (crab), **corvina** (sea bass), **lenguado** (flounder), **pulpo** (octopus), **calamar** (squid), **raya** (manta ray), and **trucha** (trout).

Ceviche

Ceviche is Peru's most famous dish and has been around in some form for centuries. The Incas, for example, ate fish marinated in chincha, a fermented maize beer. Today you can find some variation of it in every part of the country. The dish is fairly simple to make. It uses just five main ingredients: fish, lime, salt, onion and ají. Yucca, sweet potatoes, and corn usually accompany it. It is raw, but not in the way that sushi is. A chemical reaction takes place when the fish is put in the limejuice and it cooks the fish. The juice (leche de tigre) left at the end is thought to cure hangovers and a spoon is usually served so you can slurp it up before you finish. Classic ceviche uses a white fish, usually sea bass. It can be made with shrimp, mixto (with a variety of seafoods), erotico (with conch), or in several other variations. It is made in Ecuador too, but the recipe is quite different; there it is served more as a soup and is much greasier. Ceviche can also be made using duck (pato) or mushrooms (champiñones). It is often eaten in the mornings after a night of drinking (thought to cure hangovers) or for lunch.

Tiradito is the younger cousin of ceviche. It is cooked in lime like ceviche; however, the fish is cut into thinner strips and does not use onions. The most modern variations come from this dish and it can be served in a variety of sauces, usually containing ají, or hot chili peppers.

Street Food

Eating in the street is commonplace here, particularly in the highlands. Food can be found everywhere. Much of it is fried or boiled, so it is generally safe to eat. If you have a weak stomach, however, you may want to hold off. **Humitas** are steamed ground corn with ají and cheese wrapped in a banana leaf (which you don't eat) and can be either sweet or salty. When the Spanish came along, they added fillings such as chicken, cilantro, egg, and chickpeas, calling the recipe **tamales**. Either can be found in a large covered woven bas-

Anticucho seller

ket on street-sides, often near bus stops or terminals. **Empañadas**, kind of like an English pasty, are small pastries filled with meat and potatoes. They are cheap, usually 1 sole or less, and make a great snack to tide you over or to take hiking. **Choclo con queso**, or corn on the cob with cheese, is common in much of the highlands. **Juanes** (see above) are big in Iquitos. **Anticuchos** (see above) are found nearly everywhere.

As for sweets, try **mazamorra morada**. It is a jelly-like dessert made from purple corn and found in most parts of the country. There is one stand set up on Plaza San Blas in Cuzco on most nights. **Picarones**, or pumpkin donuts, are fried right in the street. **Churros** are fried sugary donut sticks that are often filled with cream or manjarblanco, a sweetened milk custard. Also, you will often find simple burger or French fry stands.

Fruits & Vegetables

With so much bio-diversity, you would expect a wide variety of fruits and veggies. In the Andes, you'll find potatoes and chilies; the coast is home to many fruits such as mangoes and limes; coastal plantations grow avocados and asparagus; the Amazon is known for bananas and yucca. This is just the mouth of the Amazon. A quick run through:

Limones, or limes, are often used in a variety of dishes, including ceviche. The Peruvian lime is similar to the key lime. Other fruits include **maracuya** (passionfruit), **bananas**, **pineapples**, **mangoes**, and **papayas**. Fruits found in few other places include **chirimoya** and **lucuma**, which are used in desserts and ice creams. Also the **aguaymanto**, or the Cape gooseberry, which is native to the Andes.

As for vegetables, other than the potato, there are **platanos** (plantains), **yuca** (manioc), **camote** (sweet potato), **choclo** (corn), **aceituna** (olives), **zapallo** (pumpkin), **palta** (advocado), and **alcachofa** (artichoke). Make sure vegetables and fruits are washed in clean water. With almost all tourist restaurants you won't need to ask, but just be wary if buying something street-side, as the water is not often clean.

FOR VEGETARIANS

Vegetarianism isn't wildly popular in Peru, but it does exist. The best vegetarian restaurants are found in cities such as Lima and Cuzco, while many other tourist-driven towns will have one restaurant or two. Try the **Govinda** chain, which has a large menu and is found in most cities. There are also many, many fresh juice stands throughout the country. Chinese restaurants also have a variety of vegetarian dishes.

Drinks

The one soft drink that you will see above all others, even more than Coke or Pepsi, is the neon green **Inka Kola**. This lemongrass-derived cola tastes like a cross between bubble-gum and cream soda. **Herbal teas** are also quite big – Menta (Mint), Herba Luisa (Lemongrass), Puro (Black), Manzanita (Chamomile) and Coca Tea. Although very high-quality coffees are growing on the eastern slopes of the Andes in jungle areas, they haven't really caught on. What is usually served is instant coffee or coffee extract, of which you pour just a bit into a cup of water or milk.

Pisco is a clear, fermented grape brandy that dates back to the 16th century. It was first produced by the Spaniards from Quebranta grapes (a variation of Muscat), in the vineyards of the Ica Valley.

There are four types of Pisco:

Pure – Made from the black Quebranta grapes. It is dry and used in mixed drinks, although it can be drunk straight as well.

Aromatic – from aromatic Muscat, Italia, Muscatel, or Torontel grapes. It is fruitier in taste and aroma than other varieties and served as an aperitif.

Mosto Verde – This variation comes from grape juice that is not entirely fermented to allow some sugar content. It is the most sophisticated and expensive to make.

Acholado – Blended with multiple types of grapes and taken straight or in the famous Pisco sour.

 The origin of Pisco has been a matter of debate between Peruvians and Chileans for years. In 2005, however, the World Intellectual Property Organization recognized Peru as the birthplace of the spirit.

The **Pisco sour** is the national drink. It mixes lime, sugar egg whites, and a dash of bitters. It is often served as a welcome drink at hotels or to lure you into a restaurant. Other variations are the **Maracuya sour** and the **Coca sour**. The **Aguaymanto sour** uses the Cape goosberry as the base.

Other Pisco drinks include the **Chilcano** (Pisco, Sprite and lime), **Pisco martinis**, and **Pisco tonics**. The **Algarobbina** is almost like Peru's version of the white Russian, although sweeter. It uses a sweet syrup made from the fruit of the Algarrobo tree found in the north of the country, along with Pisco and a dash of cinnamon. This drink is second to only the Pisco sour in popularity.

During the days of the California Gold Rush, it was easier to ship Pisco up the coast than to get whisky from the east. Therefore, drinking Pisco became a habit of many miners.

RECIPE FOR PISCO SOUR

Ingredients:
- 1 cup sugar
- 1 cup key lime juice
- 2 egg whites
- 12 ice cubes, crushed
- A few drops Angostura Bitters
- 2 cups Pisco

Preparation:
- Blend Pisco with sugar, lemon juice and Angostura Bitters.
- Add ice and finally the egg white. Blend a few minutes.
- Pour into small glasses and top with afew drops of Angostura Bitters.

Makes 8 servings.

Wine is also quite popular. It is not as renowned as Chilean or Argentine wine, but the Ica region does have several wineries of value. Ica, Tacama and Ocucaje come in red, white and rosé, sweet and dry varieties. Tacama Blanc de Blancs, Gran Tinto Reserva Especial, and Ocucaje's Fond du Cave are recommended.

As for **beer**, there are several varieties. Pilsen is a pilsner, as you might expect. It is brewed in Callao, as well as Trujillo. It is similar to Crystal, found in Lima. Cuzqueña, a lager, is my choice for best beer. Arequipeña is similar to Cuzqueña but from Arequipa. San Juan, from Pucallpa, is the only beer brewed in Peru's Amazon, although construction of a new brewery in Iquitos is underway.

For dark beer there isn't much choice. Cuzqueña has a Malta, which is a very sweet, German-style beer.

The Andes' favorite is **chicha**, a drink made from fermented corn. It was a ceremonial drink for the Incas, and still plays a central role in Andean festivities. There are two varieties.

The first, chichi de jora, is a fermented drink that I personally can't stomach. The second, chicha morada, is made from purple corn and is much better. It isn't alcoholic and tastes a bit like grape juice.

In the jungle there is **masato**, which is chewed up and spit out manioc that is fermented. It is alcoholic, a favorite with people of the jungle, and the taste is not nearly as bad as it sounds.

Aguardiente is sugar cane alcohol, the strong local firewater. It is very strong and is often mixed with jungle roots and plants to make different drinks such as Chuchuhuasi.

■ Restaurants

 Desayuno (breakfast), almuerzo (lunch), and cena (dinner) are the three meals in the Peruvian day. Breakfast is generally light in Peru. It consists of something simple such as bread or a pastry. Most restaurants do not open until 8 am, although hotel restaurants open earlier.

Lunch is the big meal of the day and is taken around mid-day. The idea of having a larger lunch dates to Incan times, because they believed the altitude slowed digestion, so the most filling meal should not be eaten before sleeping.

Many restaurants have menus, or a multi-course meal, for a set price. If you would like to read a menu ask for *la carta*; otherwise they will think you are ordering the special. The special is often the best value and will include an appetizer, main dish, and dessert.

After about 3 pm, most restaurants shut down until dinnertime. Dinner is late, usually no earlier than 9 pm and is very light, consisting of something small such as a sandwich. In isolated towns, most restaurants close by 9 pm.

Breaking Down the Bill & Tipping

There is an 18% restaurant tax added to checks, but this only applies to top end restaurants and hotels. Some will include it in the menu price and will say so. Cheaper restaurants don't add tax.

Tipping is not expected in most of the country, although it is a kind gesture. Most will leave a 10% tip, no matter the restaurant, but only if the service is good. Some higher-end restaurants will add a 10% service charge. If so, you can and should still leave a small tip of 5% or so.

As for tour guides, expect to tip about $5 or more per person per day, depending on the type of tour and the quality of your guide. Taxi drivers are rarely tipped unless they do something extraordinary or helpful.

■ Water

Water from the tap should be treated if you plan on drinking it. Still, the worst that will happen is a case of the runs. You should use bottled water for drinking and teeth brushing. Bottled water is readily available no matter where you are and is generally quite cheap. Make sure the seal is intact before purchase.

National Holidays		
January 1	New Year's Day	Año Nuevo
March-April	Holy Week	Semana Sant
May 1	May Day, Labor Day	Día del Trabajo
June 29	Saint Peter and Saint Paul	San Pedro y San Pablo
July 28-29	Peruvian Independence Day	Fiestas Patrias
August 30	Saint Rose of Lima	Santa Rosa de Lima
October 8	Battle of Angamos	Combate de Angamos
October 20	Lord of the Miracles	El Señor de los Milagros
November 1	All Saints Day	Día de Todos Los Santos
December 8	Day of the Immaculate Conception	Día de la Inmaculada Concepción
December 25	Christmas	Navidad

■ Festivals & Events

There are thought to be more than 3,000 folk festivals in Peru, many of them in the highlands. Most relate to a patron saint or to the Christian calendar. Many were imposed upon the Quechuas by the

Spanish Vice-Royalty to aid in converting them. Others are rooted in Incan beliefs that delve into magic and other gods. Some are exclusively pagan and have remained unchanged for centuries.

January

In Trujillo, the **Marinera Dance Festival** is one of the largest performance arts festivals in the country. The dance is quite complex and involves a man and a woman who each shake a handkerchief in their right hand while moving to difficult footwork. The male wears a wide-brimmed hat and poncho, while the female is dressed in a Moche lace dress. Much of the movable 10-day festival takes place in the Gran Chimú, although parades and festivities occur all over town.

February

The **Virgen de la Candelaria**, which takes place during the first two weeks of the month in Puno, is one of Peru's largest folk festivals and the main reason why the city has earned the nickname of "The Folk Capital of the Americas." The festival is linked to pre-Hispanic agricultural cycles and mining activities in the region. Several hundred musical, dance, and other performance groups come to the city. Villagers come in from the islands and from around the country to drink, dance and wear their best costumes. The dance of the demons, *la diablada*, is one of the most interesting celebrations, with many dressing up in devilish masks and outlandish costumes. The main day is on the 2nd, when the Virgin is led through the city, followed by a colorful procession.

Ica, Peru's wine and Pisco-producing region, holds a harvest festival each February, generally during the second week of the month. The **Festival de la Vendimia** brings together fairs, dances, parades, music, parties, pageants, cock fighting, and the treading of the grapes, all kicked off by the Queen of the Festival.

February/March

As in most Latin American countries, **Carnaval** is widely celebrated. The pre-Lenten festival is particularly big in the Andes. Many festivals have teenagers squirting each other with water or throwing water balloons. The festival takes place the weekend before Ash Wednesday and is biggest in Cajamarca, although festivities occur in most highland cities such as Cuzco and Puno.

March

The town of Lunahuaná, 150 km/90 miles south of Lima, is home to an **Adventure Sports Festival** during the first week of March. The Class IV Cañete River is the center of activities. Events are held in rafting, parasailing, trekking, mountain biking and fishing. Local vineyards also open their doors for tasting.

Semana Santa, or Easter week (March and April), is one of the biggest holidays of the year in most Latin American countries. This is the major religious festival in the Andes and throughout the country. Throughout the Andes the festival is followed by solemn processions, the lighting of candles and masses. The highland city of Ayacucho holds by far the most elaborate festivities.

April

The **Peruvian Paso Horse Festival** takes place at Mamacona Stables at Pachacámac near Lima in mid-April. The horse is derived from a cross breed of the Spanish horse and Arabian stallion and is known for its unique style of walking that almost resembles dancing. The festival revolves around these horses in competitions, parades and costumes.

May

The **Festival of the Crosses** is held throughout the highlands every May 3, particularly in Cuzco, Apurimac, Ayacucho, and Junín. In each community, residents decorate their own crosses and then parade them to neighboring villages. The festival was started to give thanks for a good harvest. Dancing and musical acts are also common.

Qoyllur Rit'I, or the Snow Star Festival, takes place on Ausangate Mountain, high up in the Sacred Valley. The date is movable, but usually in late May or early June. Although it appears to be a Christian festival and images of Christ are prevalent, the pilgrimage attempts to bring man closer to nature and the Apus, the spirits of the mountains. The festival is the largest native Indian pilgrimage in the Americas. More than 10,000 trek up to the snow line. Huge blocks of ice are carried down to the villages as a symbolic irrigation of their land with the holy mountain water.

June

Inti Raymi is the largest festival to take place in Cuzco. Every June 24th, or the day of the Winter Solstice, the Incan Festival of the Sun takes place at Sacsayhuaman near Cuzco. The event is carefully scripted by historians and archeologists to follow the exact ritual that the Inca once did. A ceremony proceeds for much of the day and, at sunset, an actor playing the Inca orders the site to be clear and a party begins in the city that lasts for several days.

July

Independence Day occurs on July 28, but the holiday extends to the 29th as well. Celebrations are held throughout the country and most hotels are booked well in advance.

Cookouts, drinking, music, parades, and fireworks are the norm throughout the country.

October

Procession of Señor de los Milagros in Lima

Señor de los Milagros (Lord of Miracles), the largest procession in all of South America, takes place in Lima's Colonial center from October 18 to 28. The festival originated with a cult of Angolan slaves that began in Colonial times. An image of Christ was painted on the wall of a hut and, despite earthquakes and efforts by the higherups to get rid of it, the image remained and came to be worshipped by the masses. Highly emotional processions are attended by tens of thousands of people, who dress in purple tunics, sing hymns, and pray to the image as it is carried throughout the streets. The two-ton litter is carried from the church of La Nazarenas in a 24-hour procession to the church of La Merced in Barrio Alto.

November

All Saints Day and **Day of the Dead**, November 1-2, are dedicated to remembering those whose lives have passed. Peruvians attend mass and bring flowers to cemeteries. In the highlands, food is shared symbolically with the dead. These traditions were common in Pre-Columbian Peru and continue today, with Christian elements added in.

December

Cuzco's **Santuranticuy Fair** has become one of the largest arts and crafts fairs in the country. Each Christmas Eve artisans lay out blankets with their goods on the Plaza de Armas. The name of the event means "Saints for Sale," which refers to the carved figurines that are placed in Nativity scenes. A variety of other crafts are sold as well. In the evenings, vendors sell ponche, a type of hot rum punch.

■ Shopping

There are innumerable craft markets throughout the country. They can be found almost everywhere, even if just a few Indians lay out a blanket with piles of alpaca gloves, hats, and scarves. Lima is a good place to do whatever shopping you want to do. It will usually be your point of departure so you won't have to carry the goods around during your travels. Things may cost a little bit more, and the selection of hard-to-find items such as retablo boxes (designed to hold altar pieces) is not as good, but the convenience is worth it. Indian markets are found near the traffic circle at Parque Kennedy. For other products, try the **Larcomar Shopping Center**, **Jockey Plaza Mall**, the **Polvos Azules** for black market items, and the independent craftsmen who set up shop in busy squares.

For Alpaca clothing, and by that I mean fine Alpaca, not the poor-quality hats and gloves you can buy for 5 soles in the streets. There are a number of places in Lima, Cuzco and Arequipa. **Alpaca 111** is the best-known and most expensive store and is found in each of those cities, as well as at the airports in Cuzco and Lima.

Some of the less visited cities are where you will come across the best finds, however. **Ayacucho** and its country neighbor of **Quinua** are possibly the best highland craft centers and have a variety of items that can be found only there. **Huancayo** and the surrounding villages are home to a number of different original handicrafts as well. In the north, **Catacaos** near Piura is great for straw and woven items, as well as jewelry and ceramics. In the Amazon, try **Pucallpa**, which is home to a number of famous artists as well as crafts from the indigenous Shipibo tribe.

In general, shops, shopping centers and handicraft markets are open every day (even on holidays) between 9 am and 8 pm. There is no VAT refund for tourists in Peru.

Traditional Crafts

In the way of handicrafts, Peru is one of the world's capitals. There is so much to be found here and within each region the crafts change. Many of the crafts can be highly specific and are found in just one small village in the middle of nowhere. Many of the crafts have been produced unchanged for centuries. Some take root further back, thousands of years. Wherever you go here, in all likelihood there will be unique and affordable crafts to be found. They make wonderful gifts to bring home.

Ceramics are common throughout the country and much knowledge of ancient civilization here comes from designs found on the pottery. Just head to the Larco museum to see what I mean. Everywhere you go, the ceramics are a little different. Pottery is everywhere, particularly in Cuzco, Cajamarca, Huaraz, Trujillo, and Chiclayo. In the jungle, the Shipibo from the Pucallpa area have some of the most unusual designs. Their black and white geometric shapes and lines represent the artist's vision of the world. Other ceramic pieces include devilish masks, figures such as saints, and a variety of crockery and dishes.

The town of Quinua near Ayacucho is home to the **retablo boxes**. The wooden boxes filled with carved figures portray nativity scenes, portraits of daily Andean life, Christian saints, and pre-Colombian gods. Many can be quite gruesome or comical, or just plain cute. The brightly colored boxes come in all sizes from just a few inches to as tall as a person. The Spanish, who learned the practice from the Romans, brought the art to the New World. Also from Quinua are the ceramic churches and chapels. The forms are often cartoonish, with all points sloping inward in vibrant colors. Ceramicists here use a red- and cream-colored clay that is found throughout the area. Ceramic bulls can be purchased here as well. A pair of ceramic bulls is traditionally placed on the tops of houses to protect the families inside. Here, they are called the **Toros de Quinua**, although they can also be found in Cuzco and Puno.

Wooden carving took off during Colonial times, but has been practiced in the country for thousands of years. Some of the best areas to find it are in Huancayo, San Blas in Cuzco, and Ayacucho. Carved church pulpits such as the one in San Blas are highly respected. Everything from highland figures in traditional scenes to animals to kitchen utensils are created in Quinua.

The **mate burilado** is one of the most common craft items found in Peru. The carved dried gourds date back more than 3,500 years and today originate in a small village near Huancayo. With intricate detail and deep tones they portray scenes of everyday life, symbols,  and a variety of designs. They make a great gift and will cost just a few dollars.

Straw hats, baskets, and other **woven items** are popular throughout the north coast and around Lake Titicaca. They are often made from the same native reeds as the Totora rafts. The towns of **Huanchaco** near Trujillo and **Catacaos** near Piura are the best places to find these crafts.

One of the reasons for the Conquest was that Pizarro, on his first voyage, reached Tumbes and realized this was a great civilization with abundant mineral resources – especially gold. The Chavíns were the first to employ gold in their works and nearly every civilization afterwards followed. For the best examples of Pre-Hispanic jewelry, check out Lima's **Gold Museum** or the **Sipan Museum** in Lambayeque. Your most frequent encounters with jewelry in Peru will be cheap, although creative, handmade earrings and necklaces being sold by Bohemian types along beaches or busy squares. If you look a little farther there is a lot more. Easy access to precious metals and stones means that high-quality jewelry is not difficult to find. In many Indian markets there are silver rings, earrings, and necklaces. The quality is good, but don't expect Tiffany's. Moving up, there are many fine jewelers offering Peruvian designs and working with Peruvian resources. **Cuzco's Plaza de Armas** is the best place for this type of jewelry.

Paracas funeral shrouds and Inca and Ayacucho **Wari weavings** are some of the highlights of textile production. The modern tradition is rooted in these traditions and many hundred- and thousand-year-old designs are still commonly used. Cotton and the wool of vicuña, alpaca and llamas are the most common materials. Vertical looms and pedal looms are commonly used for weaving large blankets, but much of it is done by hand. You can witness many highland people with a spool of thread, weaving as they walk. Some of the most common items can be found throughout the highlands such as woven hats, gloves, scarves, and blankets. In Cuzco, Lima, and Arequipa you can find alpaca and vicuña items, sometimes blended with contemporary fabrics made into modern designs such as throw blankets and fine scarves.

Much of the **leatherwork** has been around since Colonial times and includes furniture, belts, and equestrian items such as saddles and harnesses that you can have made to your liking at a fraction of the cost in the US or Europe.

■ Arts & Culture

In addition to handicrafts, some very fine artwork is produced here, as is an abundance of music and dance. Apart from the Latin pop culture, seen in the discos and clubs, art can be found in the streets, churches, the buildings, and especially in the many festivals. Music and dance come naturally to Peruvians of all walks of life. The melting pot of cultures has given way to thousands of different forms and styles, and the number is still growing.

Music

 Peru's musical legacy dates back approximately 10,000 years, as shown by an ancient pututo, a trumpet made from a sea conch, and the zampoña panpipe, a set of 10 or so connected flutes of varying lengths. Other instruments, such as whistling gourds, have been unearthed from Pre-Columbian cultures. Upon Conquest, the confluence of Andean and Western cultures gave birth to more than 1,000 different musical styles.

Afro-Peruvians have always been known as leaders in musical innovation, as well as dance. They invented the cajón, a drum made from a simple wooden box with a hole in it, and created a percussion instrument from the quijada, or the donkey's jawbone. Soulful vocalist **Susana Baca** is the Afro-Peruvian who has garnered the most universal appeal and made a small splash in North America. The Afro-Peruvian musicians called **Peru Negro** are another popular group worth checking out. One of the best records I have found is from David Byrne's Luaka Bop record label, *The Soul of Black Peru*.

Musica criolla blends European and African styles, and occasionally Andean ones as well. This is typical in the coastal cities. A trip to a traditional Peruvian peña (a club dedicated to folkloric music), particularly the ones in Lima and Chincha, is a must for anyone interested in criolla rhythms. **Chicha** is a mix of the huayno (see above) and the Colombian **cumbia**, a type of folk dance music, and is becoming wildly popular across the continent. It sometimes blends the music with rock and other contemporary sounds.

Andean cultures such as the Incas have produced many different varieties of music. The street groups that perform in cities and subways across the US and Europe with flutes, drums, panpipes (and other wind instruments) and guitars, tend to emulate Cuzco's sound, although this is far from all you will hear on a trip to the highlands. Each region of the highlands and altiplano tends to have its own style and different variations of instruments. *El Condor Pasa*, the Andean song that Simon and Garfunkel made into a pop hit, is played often for tourists in many different variations.

The music of the Amazon region takes on a more tropical feel in the way of popular Latin music, although native tribes still use a variety of musical rituals. Drums, chanting, and singing are commonplace. Also of note is the use of a manguaré, or hollow tree trunk called a "semiotic drum" to send messages over distances in the forests.

As for popular music, much of it is either pop songs from across Latin America or American and British pop and classic rock. Salsa is also quite popular. **Reggaeton**, a blend of reggae and Latin dance music, has become the rage in clubs over the last decade. You will no doubt hear the song *Gasolina*, by Puerto Rican Daddy Yankee, on a night out in a disco, although it might possibly be the worst song in the history of the world. Elsewhere, check out the music of Miki Gonzalez, which is considered Andean Chill music and combines electronic music with traditional Andean rhythms and instruments.

The **charango**, a small five- or 10-string, high-pitched guitar, is found mostly in the southern Andes in places such as Cuzco and Puno. Its base was once made with turtle shells, although wood has lately become the norm.

Dance

Like music, dance in Peru is an important element in any community whether on the coast, in the mountains, or the jungle. The best-known Peruvian dance is the **marinera**, originating in Trujillo, where they host an annual competition. The style is quite complex and combines fine footwork, stylish costumes, and a flirtatious attitude. The dance is derived from the zamacueca and the mozamala. The music was composed in honor of the naval hero, Miguel Grau.

The **huayno**, a combination of rural music and traditional folk, is the most beloved dance style in the highland regions. It originated in Pre-Columbian times, but Western influences have brought many variations. It is danced in pairs that turn, hop and tap to the beat of a variety of highland instruments.

Afro-Peruvians have again been in the forefront of dance; just visit any of Chincha's dance halls. The dances are often quite lively – like the **festejo**. The most unusual and perhaps erotic dance is without a doubt the **alcatraz**, which has women dance with tissues attached to their rear ends and men with candles trying to light the tissues as they dance.

Danzante de tijeras

Danzantes de tijeras, or scissor dances, are a test of agility and flexibility. The gymnastic leaps performed in the dance are quite difficult and performed by professionals only in places such as Lima, Arequipa, and Ayacucho. Two sheets of metal are placed together, resembling a pair of scissors, and the resulting sound provides the soundtrack and the name to this dance.

In Colonial times priests believed that the dancers were able to pull off the stunts of the scissor dances because of a pact with the devil. Other feats associated with the dance include sword swallowing, sticking pins in their faces, and eating frogs and snakes.

Literature

The Incas, their predecessors and the jungle tribes never developed a written language. Oral tales were popular, however, the most popular being the Inca creation myth, with its many varieties.

The Inca **Garcilaso de la Vega** (1539-1616), right, son of a Spanish Conquistador and an Incan Princess, is considered one of the country's greatest historians. He wrote down much of what we know about the life and history of the Incas and of the Conquest. When his *Comentarios Reales de los Incas*, or *Royal Commentaries of the Incas*, was published in 1609 in Spain, early in the

Colonial era, the popular idea that the Incas were godless savages changed and a backlash followed.

Mario Vargas Llosa (1936-), who was once a presidential candidate and often considered for the Nobel Prize in Literature, is Peru's premier modern novelist. The Barranco (and London) resident is one of Latin America's most celebrated writers and his works can be found worldwide. Most involve Peruvian politics and society, and are not for light reading. *The Time of the Hero*, his first work, examined life in a Peruvian military academy and caused an uproar upon publication. *The Way to Paradise* deals with a half-Peruvian, half-French woman and years later the life of her grandson, the painter Paul Gauguin.

Trilce, by Peru's legendary poet **Cesar Vallejo** (1892-1938), is one of the country's most admired works of poetry. The avant garde poems are considered among the greatest of Spanish literature.

Ricardo Palma (1833-1919), a Peruvian scholar, author, and once in charge of the national library, wrote and compiled *Tradiciones Peruanas* (1872-1910), or *Peruvian Traditions*. The many volumes of stories combine historical events and fiction about Colonial Peru and are considered some of the most beloved tales in the country.

Painting

Almost all of Peru's paintings postdate the Incas, unless you include the 10,000-year-old petroglyphs in your definition of paintings. Colonialization gave rise to several new styles, such as the Cuzco and Arequipa schools that combined Andean styles with European ones of the time. The Cuzqueña school, for instance, combines Spanish Baroque with indigenous forms and symbols local to that area. Other styles are quite similar, but incorporate more regional themes.

The Amazon is home to a number of world-renowned artists who incorporate native themes into their work. For woodwork there is **Agustín Rivas** of Pucallpa. His style is almost surrealist and has been featured in many international galleries and magazines. **Pablo Amaringo**, once a shaman, also from Pucallpa, is one of the most famous painters who delves into Amazonian spiritual themes. Also, **Francisco Grippa**, of Pevas near Iquitos, is known for his canvases, which are made from local tree barks.

Architecture

Machu Picchu is a given here, but the Incas also had a signature style that can still be seen in many places throughout the country. Their trapezoidal doorways, arches, windows, and niches are the most obvious feature. Large stone walls using colossal polygonal or rectangular stones are also common.

Sacsayhuaman, Cuzco

Each Pre-Columbian civilization had its own style, although much of it was destroyed by the Spanish, by the Incas or just built over. The architecture can still be seen in the many ruins that dot the country. The best examples are Chan Chan, the Huacas del Sol y de la Luna, Túcume, Kuélap, Pachacamac and elsewhere. Also, don't forget the Nazca Lines, which were carved into the desert floor.

Colonial architecture has best survived in churches in cities and towns across the country. The designs are generally a mix of Spanish and Andean themes with intricate stone carvings and elaborate altarpieces.

Other Arts

T'anta wawas are decorated wheat breads that incorporate complex images such as children (wawas), families, homes, crowns of flowers and animals. The breads are produced mainly during festivals, particularly on All Saint's Day. **Fleeting art** is also not unheard of in many highland places. The art is created and lasts for just a short time, sometimes only a few minutes before it is destroyed. For instance you may well see a mosaic of flowers creating a design on a street or square before a marching band comes and walks all over it.

■ Recommended Reading

Literature

Fiction

Vargas Llosa, Mario. *The War at the End of the World*. Penguin, 1997.

Vargas Llosa, Mario. *The Way to Paradise*. Picador, 2004.

Vargas Llosa, Mario. *The Feast of the Goat*. Picador, 2001.

Matthiesson, Peter. *At Play in the Fields of the Lord*. Vintage, 1991.

Poetry

Vallejo, Cesar. *Trilce*. Shearsman Books, 2005.

Neruda, Pablo. *The Heights of Machu Picchu*. Farrar, Straus and Giroux, 1967. The Chilean is considered South America's Walt Whitman. These are some of his poems set in Peru.

History

Hemming, John. *The Conquest of the Incas*. Harvest, 1970.

Frost, Peter. *Exploring Cuzco*. Neuvas Imagenes S.A., 1999.

Burroughs, William. *The Peru Book*, Ohio State University Press, 2007.

Guevara, Che. *The Motorcycle Diaries*. Ocean Press, 2003.

De la Vega, Garcilaso. *Royal Commentaries of the Incas*. University of Texas English, 1987. (English Edition).

Culture & Other Nonfiction

Palma, Ricardo. *Tradiciones Peruanas*. Catedra, 2001. In Spanish.

Higgins, James. *Lima: A Cultural History*. Oxford University Press, 2005.

Landolt, Brenda. *El Ojo Que Cuenta/Eyes That Tell*. IKAM, 2005. Myths, customs and illustrations by indigenous Amazonian people. In English and Spanish.

Matthiesson, Peter. *The Cloud Forest*. Penguin, 1987.

Zarzar Casis, Omar. *Por los Caminos del Peru en Bicicleta*. Editur S.A., 1998. Contains descriptions of 10 of the most beautiful mountain bike tours in different regions of Peru and Bolivia. The detailed tour descriptions are accompanied by a section with technical details on how to get to and from the tours, grades of difficulty, weather conditions, etc.

Smith, Linnea. *La Doctora: The Journal of an American Doctor Practicing Medicine on the Amazon River.* Pfeifer-Hamilton Publishing, 1998. Journal accounts of Linnea Smith, a Wisconsin woman who lives and works as a doctor in the Amazon, near Explorama Lodge.

Wilcox, Joan Parisi. Ayahuasca: *The Visionary & Healing Powers of the Vine of the Soul.* Park Street Press, 2003.

Wildlife Guides

Clements, James E and Noam Shany. *The Birds of Peru: Field Guide to the Birds of Peru.* Lynx Edicions, 2001.

Pearson, David L. and Les Beletsky. *Traveler's Wildlife Guides Peru*. Interlink Books, 2005.

Food

Custer, Tony. *The Art of Peruvian Cuisine*. Quebecor World Peru S.A., 2003.

Marks, Copeland. *The Exotic Kitchens of Peru*. M. Evans and Company, 1999.

Maps

For detailed topographical hiking maps, the best source is the Instituto Geográfico Nacional (IGN). You can visit them at their office in Lima (Av. Aramburu 1190 Surquillo, ☎ 475-3085/475-3075) or online at www.ignperu.gob.pe. Maps are also available at the South American Explorers' Clubhouses in Lima and Cuzco.

■ Top 20 Adventures In Peru

■ **Machu Picchu** – No matter how you get there or just how many tourists are visiting, Machu Picchu, the fortress city of the Incas, is still one of mankind's most incredible creations.

- **Lima's restaurants** – Experience a culinary revolution taking place that is sure to change the way we look at food in all of the Americas. Head to a fine-dining restaurant such as Astrid y Gastón or try some of the country's best seafood dishes at La Rosa Náutica.

- **Kuélap** – The high walls of this mountain-top citadel of the Chachapoyan culture could become the next Machu Picchu, or the next big ancient site in the country.

- **Colca Canyon** – Hike down to the Oasis for a refreshing swim in the world's second-deepest canyon.

- **Andean festivals** – Whether for a religious-oriented festival such as Carnaval or Semana Santa, or a truly ancient affair such as Inti Raymi, the Andean people don't party lightly. The all-out celebrations, combine food, drinking, faith, costumes, dancing, art, and crafts in their all out fiestas.

- **Pisac Sunday Market** – Join the natives who hike with their goods from desolate mountain villages in Pisac's main square and side-streets for Peru's largest Sunday craft market.

- **The Inka Trail and alternative trails** – Hike up and down thousands of stone steps that pass through various ruins en route to Machu Picchu. If the trail is filled up, try one of the pleasant alternatives such as the nature trek past Salkantay or to the isolated ruins at Choquequirao.

- **Climbing in Huaraz** – Join an ice-climbing expedition to one of the world's most beautiful peaks, Alpamayo, or just go for a day-climb in one of the many sites in the Cordillera Blanca.

- **River travel** – Lay for days in an uncomfortable hammock and eat disgusting food in what is one of the most incredible adventures an outsider can attempt in Peru or any country.

- **Jungle lodges** – Search for giant river otters in the day or the black caiman at night on a trip to one of Peru's many Amazon lodges set near some of the world's most diverse eco-systems.

- **Staying on Lake Titicaca** – Stay in a rustic electricity-free cottage on either Amantani or Taquile with a local family. This is one of the best ways to experience peasant life in the country and to open up your eyes to a whole new way of living.

- **White-water rafting** – Whether it is in Tarapoto, Cuzco, or Arequipa, there are a variety of rapids for every skill level.

- **Islas Ballestas** – The poor man's Galapagos are home to sea lions, Humboldt penguins, cormorants, gulls, and a number of other marine birds. Take a boat ride here where you can also see the Candelabra, the Nazca-era design on the nearby shore.

- **Ayahuasca or San Pedro Ceremony** – Participate in a shamanic ceremony by ingesting one of the country's hallucinogenic potions that have been used by locals for centuries.

- **Flying over the Nazca Lines** – To fully appreciate the Nazca Lines, a flight in a tiny aircraft is a must. Circle around each set of these enormous lines that cover many square miles in the desert near Nazca.

- **Mountain biking** – Unheard of not long ago, this sport is taking off in many areas of the country. Try Lima's coastline, in between Cuzco's archeological sites, or in between tiny Amazon villages.

- **Sand boarding** – Head to the sand dunes at the desert oasis of Huacachina for this once-in-a-lifetime sporting experience.

- **Wine and Pisco tasting in Ica** – Head to Ica to get a taste of Peru's largest vineyards. Sample Fond du Cave and a variety of Piscos at the modern facilities of Ocucaje or visit some of the rustic facilities at some of the smaller vineyards and distilleries that still use methods unchanged since Colonial times.

- **Language schools and volunteering** – Whether you want to learn a new skill, a new language, or just want to help people in need, there are many options. For the best of them, try Cuzco, Huancayo, Lima, Cajamarca, and Huaraz.

- **Surfing** – Try your hand at one of the most popular sports on the coast. Visit Lima's crowded beaches or the white-sand beach around Mancora. Or better yet, make the trip to Chicama for the world's longest left-breaking wave.

■ The Star System

If a star ★ appears next to the title of a hotel, restaurant, museum, ruin, or attraction of any kind, that means it is very significant and definitely worth a look. The stars are based on location, scenery, unusual value, or any other factor that makes a place really stand out.

★ If you have the opportunity you should experience this.

★★ This is reason enough to change your plans.

★★★ Don't miss it.

■ Travel Information

Documentation

Visas are not required, except for a few Asian and African countries. North Americans and most Europeans are issued a 90-day tourist card on arrival in Peru or at border crossings. You are given a copy of the tourist card, which you give up upon departure. If your tourist card is lost or stolen, you must apply for a new one at Immigration.

All foreigners should be able to produce their passport or some other recognizable form of identification on demand. Officially, you will need a ticket out of the country to enter and proof of sufficient funds. However, this is rarely asked for.

Be sure to have your passport stamped in and out when you cross any border.

If you want to extend your visa, you can do it in one of two ways. One way is to go to the Immigration office, fill out the required documents and pay the fee (approximately $28). You can do this up to three times (so your total stay will be 180 days if you extend your stay three times). Another option is to cross the border out of Peru and then return; you will be issued a new 90-day tourist card, which in many cases is much easier. Just cross the border, get your passport stamped, come back the next day and a new tourist card is issued.

 When departing the country by air, the departure tax is approximately $28.

Valid foreign drivers licenses are accepted for driving in Peru.

Health & Safety

 The only real health issues I have had while traveling in Peru are mosquito and sand fly bites and sunburn. Nothing worse than I would find back in Ohio. Keep in mind that I have spent several months in the Amazon too, much of it sleeping in hammocks in Third-World conditions. That isn't to say that other diseases and health issues are not of concern; they are and you should take every precaution necessary. However, they are often less of an issue than many would expect.

Diseases

Yellow fever is a virus infection transmitted by the bite of an infected mosquito. The effects vary from mild to life-threatening; some forms even include hepatitis. One in six people infected with the disease experience serious illness; otherwise, they encounter basic flu-like symptoms. The yellow fever virus infects wild monkeys and typically only infects humans who are in close proximity to monkey habitats (i.e., forestry and agricultural workers). Yellow fever infection is very rare in travelers to South America. A vaccination is recommended if traveling to jungle areas. It lasts for 10 years and you will receive a certificate. The vaccination is required if traveling from Peru to Brazil.

Malaria is a risk only in Amazon areas or in the far north near Tumbes. Most will take malaria pills such as Doxycycline or Mefloquine. If you don't take the pills, the chance of getting malaria is still slim. Determine this by finding a county's status through the CDC (☎ 1-888-232-3228 or www.cdc.gov/travel/yellowbk/yfquery.htm) or consult your doctor/travel clinic. Above all, avoiding mosquitoes is the most important part. There are a few things you can do. Stay inside between dusk and dawn, when mosquitoes are most active. Don't wear dark clothing, perfume, cologne, or after-shave, all of which attract mosquitoes. Wear clothes that cover most of your body, stay in screened areas when possible, and use mosquito nets. Use mosquito repellent whenever you go outside, and use repellent with DEET. The affects of malaria include flu-like symptoms such as fevers, headaches, and muscle aches. It may develop as long as a month after getting bitten by a mosquito. Severe cases can lead to nerve damage, seizures, comas, and possibly death.

Dengue is another virus transmitted by mosquitoes and is found in almost all tropical areas. In endemic areas, about one traveler in a thousand will develop dengue. Symptoms develop about five-eight days after being bitten by an infected mosquito and range from very mild infections to severe dengue hemorrhagic fever (DHF).

Diarrhea afflicts about 20-30% of travelers to developing countries. The affliction involves loose and frequent bowel movements, sometimes with cramps, nausea, bloating, fever, and malaise. It comes on strong, usually when you least expect it. Ten percent of cases last more than a week. Let's hope that's not you. To prevent traveler's diarrhea (TD) have all food boiled, peeled, and cooked. Use only bottled water for drinking or teeth brushing and avoid ice in most places. Eat small snacks often, but avoid caffeine and dairy. You must eat though. The nutrients will repair any membrane damage caused by TD.

Chagas is a protozoa that infects more than 16 million Latin Americans, causing around 50,000 deaths annually. The parasite grows in the gastrointestinal tracts of triatomine bugs, known as "kissing bugs," which bite you on the face while you sleep. The bugs are most often found in the ceilings and walls of mud and substandard houses. The feces of the bug are rubbed into any opening on the skin unknowingly. The disease is lifelong.

Most travelers will be affected by some degree of **altitude sickness**, or **sorojchi**. Each person reacts differently to changes in altitude. There is no apparent correlation to level of fitness, body weight, or sex. In areas of high altitude you must increase your breathing rate in order to properly oxygenate the body, as is best seen when walking uphill. Just take a walk around Cuzco and you will definitely notice. Shortness of breath is common and will quickly go away with a brief rest. To acclimatize, the body must adjust to having less oxygen. The process usually takes several days. So, for the first few days at high altitude, drink lots of water to keep hydrated, as much as two liters per day. Steer clear of caffeine, alcohol, and tobacco until you are acclimatized. Get plenty of sleep at night. And take it slow. Drinking coca tea or mate de coca is recommended and thought to help cure the sickness. Sorjchi pills are recommended as well and can be found in most drugstores in Peru. Some people are severely affected by the altitude and the only cure may be to go to a lower altitude. Symptoms include shortness of breath, headaches, nosebleeds, confusion, memory loss, strange dreams, insomnia, nausea, and vomiting. More severe cases lead to swelling of the brain, comas and even death. Some may be at high altitudes for a week before the sickness hits them. Others will know right away and still others will feel no effects.

 For up-to-date travel information check out the US Centers for Disease Control website, www.cdc.gov/travel.

TIPS FOR AVOIDING ILLNESS

■ Drink only bottled, boiled, or treated water.

■ Be careful with raw vegetables and fruits.

■ Avoid eating from street vendors.

■ Rest on the first day of your arrival to the Highlands, and consume light meals to prevent altitude illness (sorojche). Drinking "coca tea" or taking sorojchi pills is recommended.

■ If you travel to the Highlands or to the Jungle, make sure to carry insect repellent and a raincoat.

Electric showers: If you find a strange electric gadget on top of your shower, don't be afraid. The electric shower is actually one of the best ways to guarantee that you get hot water. The trick is to turn on as little water as you can, because the heat is dispersed through the amount of water that comes out. It doesn't increase with the amount of water.

Toilets

Getting to a foreign country and finding out that you no longer know the rules of going to the bathroom or are wondering where the normal amenities are is quite common. Peru has a variety of toilets. The most common problem people encounter is where to put the toilet paper. Usually, you must put it in the wastebasket beside the toilet, most of which have a cover of some sort. This goes for much of Latin America. It isn't so much a problem with the toilets, but with the plumbing. Most upscale hotels have their own system and, unless otherwise stated, you can flush the paper. In poorer areas an outhouse may be used. If that sounds bad, it could be worse. Some roadside stops and country restaurants have just a hole in the ground and, if you are lucky, a place for your feet. Usually there will be a large bucket of water outside with a bowl which you can fill and wash away your mess.

Crime

 Much of the crime in Peru is petty. Pickpockets, camera thefts, grab jobs. In all of my time in Peru I have had one problem, and that was in Chorrillos near Lima. I walked out of a small shop with some basic grocers and a couple of shabby-looking fellows approached me and some Venezuelan friends. They were asking for change but I could see them eyeing my wallet. They quickly grabbed my plastic bag with $8 of groceries and ran away. That was it. If something like that happens, there is no need to get upset. I just walked right back in the store and bought the exact same items from the grocer with an odd look on her face. In rural areas or in large cities armed robberies do occur on occasion. The big coastal cities tend to be worse off than the Andean ones, mainly because of the influx of migrant workers who are living in squalor on the outskirts of most of the cities. Also, on trails that lead just outside of major cities or in between sites, there is need for caution. Armed robberies do happen, but they are rare. If you are the victim of a crime you should immediately contact the tourist police, located in most major cities, or a regular police department, to file a report. If an item is stolen the report will help you file an insurance claim.

Safety Tips

- Carry a copy of identification documents. Keep originals and your valuables in the safety deposit box of your hotel.
- Carry valuables discreetly and never carry large amounts of cash.
- Always keep an eye on your bags and luggage.
- Do not exchange money out in the street.
- Do not walk around late at night through areas with poor lighting or alone.
- Take taxis at night.
- Do not purchase, use, or carry drugs or associate with people who do.

Drugs

For some time Peru was the world's largest coca leaf producer, although in the past few years efforts to stop drug production have decreased the numbers by about 15%. Coca, legal to grow and use in Peru and Bolivia, is often shipped to Colombia where it is processed into cocaine. No matter what the guy in the street tells you in Cuzco or Lima, cocaine and marijuana are illegal. As are ecstasy, opium, heroin, and any other drug that is generally illegal. Penalties are harsh and some will spend years in jail for possession. In places such as Cuzco and Lima, particularly surrounding the nightclubs, undercover cops often offer drugs to clubgoers. If anyone asks you to go to the police station with him or her, make sure it is either on foot or in a marked police car.

Ayahuasca, San Pedro, and other hallucinogens often used in shamanic ceremonies are legal, but they should not be used for recreational purposes.

Liquor Laws

The drinking age is 18 in Peru, although it isn't strictly enforced and anyone over 16 rarely has a problem ordering alcohol in most places. All alcohol is readily available in most grocery stores and carryouts. Bars are open until midnight or later, while most clubs stay open until the next day.

Communications

Telephones

 International and long distance national calls can be made from pay phones. Country and city codes are normally shown in the telephone booths. Public phones take coins as well as cards, which are sold in shops and from street vendors. Make sure you are buying the card corresponding to the telephone company of the phone you want to use. Collect calls cannot be made from pay phones. For telephone information, dial ☎ 103 (Spanish).

■ To make an international call, dial: ☎ 00 + country code + city code + telephone number.

■ To call from one city to the next, dial: ☎ 0 + city code + telephone number.

TELEPHONE CODES	
Department	**Area Code**
Lima	I
Ica	34
Cajamarca	44
Amazonas	44
La Libertad	44
Ancash	44
Arequipa	54

Puno	54
Moquegua	54
Tacna	54
Huánuco	64
Pasco	64
Huancavelica	64
Ayacucho	64
Junín	64
Ucayali	64
Tumbes	74
Piura	74
Lambayeque	74
Apurímac	84
Cuzco	84
Madre de Dios	84
San Martín	94
Loreto	94

Information Sources

 Check out my weekly column at http://southamericatravel.suite101.com for information on traveling in South America.

Tourism Offices

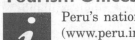 Peru's national tourist organization, **Prom Peru** (www.peru.info/perueng.asp) has offices in Lima, Cuzco, Chachapoyas, Iquitos, Arequipa, Puno, Ayacucho, Huaraz, and Trujillo. Their offices vary on helpfulness and supplies, but nevertheless they are the best source of basic promotional tourist info on sites and activities. If you go to an office they will help you locate an address, as well as give you brochures on different regions, city maps, and lists of services. They often run out of information in English, although I assure you it is available. Their website is

quite extensive and in my opinion better than their offices for most instances.

★★★**South American Explorer's**, Piura 135 (Miraflores), ☎ 51-1-445 3306, fax 51-1-445-3306, www.saexplorers.org. They also have a clubhouse in Cuzco (Choquechaca 188, ☎ 24-5484), as well as in Ithaca, New York, Quito, Ecuador and Buenos Aires, Argentina. SAE is where journalists, film crews, archeologists, international residents, travelers, students and anybody who is anybody goes for information regarding South America. Each clubhouse is a refuge and a resource for travel information, community involvement, home away from home, as well as being an international decompression point. They will hold luggage and accept incoming mail. Wireless Internet access. Library. Book exchange. Bulletin board. Trip reports. Expert advice. Up-to-date travel conditions. Kitchen. They also sell books, information packets, maps, etc. Membership fee required ($50/$80 per couple, including a subscription to their magazine and online access to their travel databases). If you plan on being in Peru for a long time, the membership fee quickly makes up for the price with the many discounts that are offered for language schools, hotels, restaurants, shops – and that's in addition to all of the other useful services they provide. They help organize classes, lectures, and some volunteering activities. Highly, highly recommended.

There are a variety of regional tourist offices that come into play where Prom Peru has yet to appear. These offices are independent of the national scheme and many are quite good. Many cities such as Huancayo, Tumbes, Piura, and Cajamarca have in fact better information than what Prom Peru provides. They are listed in this book when available.

Also try:

www.Andeantravelweb.com. Has a variety of information regarding all travel in Peru, as well as a few places in Ecuador and Bolivia.

www.planeta.com. Site dedicated to ecotourism around the globe with a focus on Latin America.

www.huaraz.com. Excellent site for any information regarding Huaraz and activities in the Cordillera Blanca.

www.peruviantimes.com. Home of the former English newspaper and also sells a guide for foreign residents.

www.vivamancora.com. All the information regarding hotels, restaurants, transportation, and other services related to Peru's northern beaches.

www.cia.gov/cia/publications/factbook/geos/pe.html. The CIA's *World Fact Book* with statistical information of Peru.

www.urbanialima.com. Spanish-language site for what's hot and happening in and around Lima.

www.ruta-inka.com.pe/marcos.asp. The official site for the Inca Trail (Spanish).

www.cocinaperuana.com/english. The best site I have found for Peruvian cooking, recipes, ingredients, and lists of Peruvian restaurants in and outside of Peru.

Clubs & Organizations

www.acap-peru.org. American & Canadian Association of Peru (ACAP).

www.peruvianalpineclub.com. Home of the Peruvian Alpine Club.

www.clubdeperuanos.com. Club Peruano is a website dedicated to Peruvians living abroad.

www.expatperu.com. The number one source for expatriates living in Peru.

Newspapers & Magazines

Peru's major newspaper is *El Comercio* out of Lima, with *La República* following not far behind. There are several bi-lingual tourist journals that are quite good such as *Legado*, *Pachamama*, and *Rumbos*. The *Peruvian Times*, out of Lima, was the country's premier English newspaper, but it is no longer printed. The only English newspaper in Peru at this time is the *Iquitos News*, which is short

on substance and mainly filled with tourist-related information. As far as international newspapers go, they are few and far between. You will almost never find a publication of the same day. The best place to look is on the streets surrounding Parque Kennedy or at Lima's Airport. Anywhere else in the country, you are pretty much out of luck.

Internet

 Internet cafés are all over the country. It is seldom difficult to find a place and the price is always good – less than $1 per hour. Speeds vary depending on where you are and how new the equipment is. Even the smallest towns that only have electricity for limited periods tend to have at least one computer. Because they are so easy to find, I only specify their locations if there is one of exceptional quality or if only one exists in a town.

Mail & Shipping

DHL offices can be found in larger cities and will ship a package home quickly. However, the service is pricey here. Sending items through the post office is much slower and on rare occasions shipments can disappear. Avoid sending items of value by mail.

 Small change: Most places outside the tourist realms of Lima, Cuzco, and Puno often don't carry change for large bills. Try to carry plenty of small bills. Generally, 10 and 20 soles are fine. If you have one for 100 soles, use it in a grocery store or any busy place that is likely to have change.

Currency & Banking

 The Peruvian currency is the nuevo sol (S/.). Circulation is in coins of 5, 10, 20 and 50 céntimos, and 1, 2 and 5 nuevos soles, as well as banknotes for 10, 20, 50, 100 and 200 nuevos soles.Most shops, restaurants and gasoline stations accept US dollars and euros at the daily exchange rate. Most hotels and commercial establishments in cities throughout the country accept major credit cards: Visa, MasterCard, Diners Club and American Express. Travelers' checks are not widely used. BCP banks offer your best chance for exchanging them. Globalnet has standalone ATMs across the country. You can locate them online at www.globalnet.com.pe.

Banking hours in Peru are normally from Mon to Fri, 9 am to 6 pm. In addition, most banks open to the public for a half-day on Sat. In the streets of the main cities there are teller machines installed by the different banks.

Lost Credit Cards

Visa, www.internationalvisa.com, ☎ 01-242-2975.

MasterCard, www.mastercard.com, ☎ 01-311-6000 (24 hrs).

American Express, (in Lima - Lima Tours) ☎ 01-424-5110, fax 330-4482/84/85/86, www.americanexpress.com.

All cards cancelled in Peru can be re-issued from the US. Using DHL, this usually takes about one week. An emergency card takes only one or two days.

Cancellation of Traveler's Checks

American Express: ☎ 001-800-860-2908

To Receive or Send Money

Western Union,

- San Isidro (Main Office), Av. Petit Thours 3595, ☎ 422-0014
- Miraflores: Av. Larco 826, ☎ 241-1220
- Angamos: Av. Petit Thours 5135, ☎ 242-3494
- Central Lima: Jr. Carabaya 693, ☎ 428-7614

There are additional offices around Lima, and also in Arequipa, Cuzco, Chiclayo, Chimbote, Huancayo, Iquitos, Talara, Tarapoto, Trujillo.

Money Exchange

Money should be exchanged in hotels, banks and authorized money exchange offices (service hours 9:30 am to 6 pm). You can often change money in the streets and it is generally safe, but false bank notes are not uncommon. The exchange rate with the US$ varies.

EXCHANGE RATE: I NUEVO SOLE =	
US	US 30¢
Canada	C 34¢
Euro	€0.24
UK	0.17£

Ask about the exchange rate before changing your money. For exchanging other currencies inquire at money exchange offices.

 Prices in Peru are often quoted in dollars rather than soles for large purchase items such as electronics, cars, hotel rooms, and tours. We do the same in the text below.

Electricity

 Electric current is 220 volts, 60 cycles AC. You will not need an adaptor for US appliances. Many large hotels have 110-volt outlets as well.

Time Zone

 Peruvian time is five hours behind Greenwich Mean Time (GMT) and coincides with Eastern Standard Time (EST) in the United States for half of the year. The country does not observe daylight savings time. Peru is on the same time as New York; Santiago de Chile and Caracas are an hour ahead; Río de Janeiro and Buenos Aires are two hours ahead; and Tokyo is 15 hours ahead.

What to Take

 Most people overpack when traveling anywhere. Keep in mind that whatever you need you can buy here – much of it at a much cheaper price. So, instead of buying that nice new jacket for the trip, buy one here. You'll have a souvenir of your visit as well. Things such as t-shirts can be bought for just a couple of dollars. Shoes can be bought in most markets, both dress shoes and sneakers. Most cosmetics are imported from abroad so are more expensive here, but not by much. As for adventure sports, much of the equipment you will need can be rented here, although, if you want a specific quality or model, you may want to bring your own. In Lima you can find just about everything you would find in any major American or European city. Also, there is so much in the way of handicrafts in Peru, that you will probably want to buy a few pieces. So save some room.

Doing laundry is simple here. Just take your pile of clothes to the laundromat, get your receipt and it will be ready for pickup the next day – all nicely folded. Some places in Cuzco and Lima will have it ready within two hours. The price is never more than a few dollars. The *lavanderías* are everywhere too. Most hotels will do your laundry as well, although not as cheaply. So don't try and pack for your entire trip. Plan on doing a wash at least once, and it will make your packing a lot easier.

For the jungle, lightweight pants that can zip off the legs to become shorts are good. That way you can be ready to protect yourself from mosquitoes when needed, or cool yourself off. Binoculars, a zoom lens for your camera, mosquito net if camping, insect repellent, malaria tablets, a wide-brimmed hat, and sun block are essential.

In the Andes the weather can be quite sunny during the day and bitterly cold at night. Daytime temperatures may even require shorts, but at night you'd better be prepared. A warm jacket or sweater is crucial. Keep in mind that wool accessories and clothing are sold everywhere in the highlands, are quite cheap, and make good souvenirs. Leggings and thermal underwear are a good bet also; they don't take up much space and can be worn under your regular clothes.

For the coast, one pair of shorts will likely get you by. Only in the summertime is it warm enough so that you will really need them though. Long pants are the norm and at night it can get a bit chilly, so a light jacket or a sweater is necessary. If going to Tumbes, follow the same rules as you would in the jungle.

If there is one item I recommend for traveling above all others it is without doubt an MP3 player. On it I keep music, of course, but also Spanish lessons, audio books, files. And now, with the iPod Video, I have photos of family and friends, as well as movies. Soon they will be able to read PDF files much like a Palm would, which means that you will be able to carry this guide, which is also available in PDF format, there as well.

The Basics

These clothing items should be the foundation of a 10-day to two-week visit:

- Hiking boots, sandals, and walking shoes or sneakers.
- Four pairs absorbent cotton socks.
- Two pairs lightweight pants or slacks.
- Lightweight shorts (more if spending all of your time at the beach).
- Jeans.
- Three to four t-shirts.
- Two mix-and-match skirt and blouse ensembles (for women)
- Two short-sleeve sport/dress shirts (for men).
- One bathing suit.
- Hooded rain slicker/poncho (heavy-gauge if you'll be in the jungle); or one light to medium jacket (especially if you will be visiting the highlands). If you are going ice climbing or on a serious trekking expedition, a thick or heavy duty material coat such as the ones by North Face are highly recommended.
- Wide-brimmed hat (ones that roll up for packing are good).
- Protective sunglasses.
- Sleepwear (light).
- Flip-flops (for the beach, as slippers, or for showering).
- Prescription medications (including malaria tablets if going to the jungle).
- Personal hygiene products.

- Insect repellent (with DEET).
- Pain reliever.
- Antibiotic ointment.
- Band-aids.
- Sunblock.
- Cosmetics.
- Toilet paper (many bathrooms in rural hotels and other places don't provide toilet paper).
- Hand and body lotion.
- Toothbrush, hairbrush/comb, razor, other daily grooming accessories.

> **Tip:** One item I have found that does wonders in my daily travels is hand sanitizer. A small bottle will go a long way and help you ward off strange germs that appear in rest stop bathrooms, rural living areas, and elsewhere.

Other Items:

- Passport, driver's license, and tourist card.
- Credit card and ATM card (or traveler's checks).
- Concealed money belt.
- Pocket-size high-intensity flashlight.
- Camera (film for traditional cameras; extra battery and memory card for digital ones).
- Pocket-size Spanish dictionary, preferably with phrases if you don't speak the language.
- Small notebook and pens.
- Resealable plastic bags (to keep your camera dry and your cosmetics from leaking).
- Reading material.
- Compass.

> **Tip:** Make copies of all of your important documents such as passports, driver's licenses and credit cards. Keep copies with you and back at home. If anything is lost or stolen this will be a lifesaver.

Local Customs

Dress & Manner

 Kisses on the cheek are customary in coastal cities upon greeting, while in the Andes a light handshake is customary. If ever in doubt a handshake will suffice. Basic greetings usually involve at least a polite hello, how are you? Discussion of subjects such as politics, the economy, and one's marital status or employment are not taboo, but religion often is.

Many come dressed in adventure gear or Jungle Jim outfits, which is fine in most tourist-oriented places. If you plan on fine dining in Lima or Cuzco, or going to clubs in Lima or Arequipa, you may want to bring a dressier outfit or two. In most churches it is generally taboo to wear shorts, flip-flops, tank tops, and anything that is overly revealing.·

As for Peru's Andean population, *indigenas* is the polite term, while *indios* is not. If you are called a gringo, don't take offense. It is a common term and often used. Also, Peruvian society is more male-driven than North America and many European countries. Gringas are safe to travel on their own, but are seen as more sexually open than local women and are often the target of unwanted advances. This is common in all of Latin America. Much of it is harmless, and sexual assaults and rapes are rare. The best thing you can do is ignore any unwanted comments and avoid traveling alone at night.

Photography

 It is absolutely prohibited to take photographs of airports, military bases, places near high-tension towers and police stations. In some churches and museums photography is not permitted. Ask first. Also, be respectful of people. Don't treat them as a part of the scenery. Ask first. Often, they will want a small tip.

Special Considerations

Travelers with Disabilities

 Outside of places like Lima, there are few wheelchair-friendly places in Peru. Many sidewalks are choppy or made of stone, and in Andean cities the streets are often very steep. Very few restaurants, hotels, and public transportation services have adapted to travelers with disabilities. You can contact **Prom Peru** (☎ 1-866-661-PERU, www.peru.info/perueng.asp) for more information regarding this issue. They do have a report available for download at their website. **Apumayo Tours**, www.apumayo.com, and **Inkanatura**, www.inkanatura.com, will help arrange tours for travelers with disabilities.

Traveling with Children

 Lima is the best place for kids, with two zoos, many parks, playgrounds, and kid-oriented activities. If you do the basic tourist trail from Lima to Cuzco and Machu Picchu, the path has been well-trodden by many a child. Elsewhere you will have to be a bit more creative. If your kid isn't afraid of bugs or wildlife, a trip to the Amazon is something they would love to tell all of their friends about. If they don't mind walking a bit, going to ancient ruins such as Machu Picchu or Chan Chan could really be a life-changing experience. Outdoor activities such as horseback riding could be fun as well. For food, they may have issues with many native dishes, but fast food is everywhere, including McDonald's. Chicken and fries restaurants, *pollerias* or *pollo a la brasa*, are everywhere. As hard as it could be at times, bring a child to a country like Peru where people of all walks of life are found, including children of their own age with whom they can interact. This is something that will likely shape their lives in incredible ways.

Gay or Lesbian Travelers

Considering that Peru is overwhelmingly Catholic and quite conservative, homosexuality isn't openly accepted by most people. In coastal cities such as Lima and Arequipa, where the population is more contemporary, sexual orientation is far more open, but in most highland destinatations not as much.

That flag in Cuzco isn't the gay flag, but the symbol of the Tiahuanacu Empire. In places with many tourists, such as Cuzco and Iquitos, homosexuality is much more accepted. Many restaurant, bar, and hotel owners there are homosexuals or openly support them. There are gay nightclubs and bars in Lima, and elsewhere. For most gays and lesbians in Peru, a level of discretion is generally used.

For More Information

Movimiento Homosexual-Lesbiana – ☎ 01-433-6375, mhol@terra.com.pe. This is Peru's best and largest homosexual organization.

www.gayperu.com (Spanish)

www.peruesgay.com (Spanish)

http://gaylimape.tripod.com (English)

Getting Here

By Air

 Peru is linked by direct flights to Houston and Miami, Madrid, and most South American destinations. Many major airlines come here and connecting flights to anywhere in the world are not difficult to find. The main airport is **Jorge Chávez International Airport** (Callao, Lima), which handles most international flights. The airports of Arequipa, Ayacucho, Cajamarca, Cuzco, Chiclayo, Iquitos, Pisco, Pucallpa, Piura, Tumbes, Tacna and Trujillo all have flights to/from Lima. **Taca** and **LAN** fly to Miami and other destinations throughout Latin America. **Continental** flies direct to Houston, Miami, and Newark. **Air Canada**, **American**, **Delta**, and **Air France** also have direct flights to/from the US. For Europe try **KLM**, **Iberia**, and any of the major North American airlines. You may have to go through the US.

 Airport departure tax (TUUA.): domestic flights 12 soles; international flights US$28. Payment must be made in cash before boarding the flight.

Airlines

(Lima offices and telephone numbers)

- **Air Canada** – ☎ 0800-52073, www.aircanada.com.
- **American Airlines** – ☎ 442-8595, inside Hotel Las Americas on Av. Larco (Miraflores), www.aa.com.
- **Continental** – ☎ 221-4340, Belaunde 147 (San Isidro), www.continental.com.
- **Delta** – ☎ 440-4328, Belaunde 147 (San Isidro), www.delta.com.
- **Iberia** – ☎ 411-7800, Camino Real 390 (San Isidro), www.iberia.com.
- **Varig** – ☎ 422-1449, Camino Real 456 (San Isidro), www.varig.com.
- **Avianca** – ☎ 446-9902, Pardo 140 (Miraflores), www.avianca.com.
- **KLM** – ☎ 421-9500, Calderón 185 (San Isidro), www.klm.com.
- **Air France** – ☎ 444-9285, Pardo 601 (Miraflores), www.airfrance.com.
- **Lloyd Aereo Boliviano** – ☎ 241-5510, Pardo 231 (Miraflores), www.lab.com.

On Land

One can enter Peru via the Pan-American Highway through the city of Tacna in the south, or through the city of Tumbes in the north. You can also enter through Loja (Ecuador), which is connected by road to the city of Piura. There are two entry routes from Bolivia: Copacabana - Yunguyo - Puno; and La Paz - Desaguadero - Puno.

By River

The only point of entry by river is along the Amazon, with private river craft services coming from the cities of Leticia (Colombia) and Tabatinga (Brazil) to the port of Iquitos (Peru). Smaller immigration points can be found in Pantoja on the Río Napo bordering Ecuador and near Puerto Maldonado when traveling to/from Boliva or Brazil.

By Lake

Lake Titicaca links Peru to neighboring Bolivia, although direct water routes are difficult to find or expensive.

By Sea

Cruise liners sometimes stop at Callao, Peru's main port. Occasionally, ships call at the ports of Salaverry (Trujillo) and Chimbote (Ancash), in northern Peru; and at San Martín (Ica) and Matarani (Arequipa) in the south.

Cruise Lines Docking in Peru

- **Princess Cruises**, ☎ 800-PRINCESS, www.princess. com.

- **Radisson Seven Seas Cruises**, ☎ 877-505-5370, www. rssc.com.

- **Celebrity Cruises**, ☎ 800-722-5941, www.celebrity-cruises.com.

- **Holland America**, ☎ 206-281-3535, www.holland-america.com.

Getting Around

In most cities you will be able to get around on foot to see any of the sites within the city proper, with the one exception being Lima. In Lima you should treat each suburb as its own city. The center of all tourist activity in almost every Peruvian city is the main plaza, or the Plaza de Armas. Most hotels, restaurants, and tourist-oriented services are generally within a few blocks. Elsewhere, you can take taxis or local transport. To almost every tourist destination outside of a city, there are cheap and frequent organized tours.

Public Transportation

Local and urban buses are often *combis*, a type of minivan with an extra number of seats. They are often crowded and dirty. Most will go for long distances, sometimes as far as several hours away. Ask if they are going to your destination before getting in; and do not take them too late at night.

Taxis

 It is recommended that you take taxis from companies that you call by phone or those authorized by the municipalities (in Lima those are painted yellow and some have a lighted sign on the roof). Taxi meters are not used in Peru, so the price must be negotiated before you get in. Ask at your hotel about the average fare to your destination. Tips are rarely given to taxi drivers. At airports, it is advisable to take only taxis authorized by the management authority. Women should avoid using taxis alone at night. Unmarked taxis that wait for customers outside hotels tend to be safer, but prices are generally two or three times higher.

By Air

 A few inter-regional air trips can be a good option if you are exploring several areas of the country and do not have much time. Most will run just below $100 each way, although Cuzco can be reached for about $150 round-trip. You can get to any airport from Lima.

LAN is the best airline and most consistent, while TANS has had several recent crashes, often is delayed, and does nothing if your flight is canceled other than put you on a flight the next day.

Airlines

(Lima offices and telephone numbers)

- **TACA** – ☎ 213-7000, Espinar 331 (Miraflores), www.grupotaca.com.
- **LAN** – ☎ 213-8300, Pardo 513 (Miraflores), www.lan.com.
- **LC Busre** – ☎ 421-0419, Tulipanes 218 (Lince), www.lcbusre.com.pe.
- **Star Peru** – ☎ 705-9000, Pardo 485 (Miraflores), www.starperu.com.

TANS – ☎ 213-6000, Arequipa 5200 (Miraflores), www.tansperu.com.pe.

Buses

 If you plan on spending more than a few weeks in the country or want to go to some remote areas, taking a long distance bus is likely a must. Bus service varies dramatically here, but prices are generally inexpensive. Comfort is a key issue when reserving a space. Crowded buses on lower quality lines sometimes have three to a seat, various produce in the aisles, and a stink that will frighten away most people. **Ormeño** and **Cruz del Sur** have the best and the most buses to destinations all over the country. They offer several levels of service, which may be *cama* (bed), *semi-cama* (part-bed), as well as regular. With the exception of the highest-level buses, most do not serve a meal but will make a stop at some country restaurant. The food can be anything from delicious to horrid, so if you are having problems eating in established tourist areas, you may want to bring along your own food. Most buses will show movies or play music during much of the trip. At times they will blast loud music so the driver doesn't fall asleep, even if it's 3 am.

Make sure you have a ticket and an assigned seat. Buses are often overbooked or pick up stray passengers, so if you don't have your seat in writing, it is up for grabs. Many people end up standing or sitting in the aisles on crowded buses for hours at a time. Considering that the country is so large, many rides will exceed 20 hours. If time is an issue, ask whether the bus is non-stop. This could shave off quite a bit of time. Fares generally increase around holiday times.

Only a few towns have central terminals (Cuzco, Arequipa, Puno, etc). In other cities you must go to each company's office, which also serves as its terminal. Generally, the offices for all companies are lumped together on one or two streets.

At terminals watch your luggage closely. Many thefts occur here. Before putting your luggage underneath the bus, be sure to get a ticket for it and hold onto that ticket. Also, on the bus, watch your belongings and keep anything valuable with you. I have heard of people climbing underneath seats and stealing bags out from underneath a person's legs. Personally, I have never had a problem with theft on a bus.

Some of the best companies are:

- **Cruz del Sur** – www.cruzdelsur.com.pe.
- **Civa** – www.civa.com.pe.
- **Ormeño** – www.grupo-ormeno.com.
- **Oltursa** – www.oltursa.com.pe.
- **Linea** – www.transporteslinea.com.pe.

Trains

Train travel is limited to just a few routes. Cuzco is the center of all train activity in the country, mainly because you have to go through it to get to Machu Picchu by train (with a stop in Ollantaytambo). From Cuzco you can also travel to Juliaca and Puno by train and vice-versa. Otherwise, there are just a few short routes left of the once great Peruvian railways.

The service from Lima to Huancayo, the highest railway in the world, runs sporadically, mostly on weekends during a few random months each year. You can get from Huancayo to Huancavelica and back by train. This rail line has cars for peasants, which are extremely crowded, as well as first-class cars that resemble basic European trains.

There once was service that went from Arequipa to Puno, but that has stopped running. Daily trains from Tacna to Arica, Chile do still run.

 For more information contact **PeruRail**, www. perurail.com.

Riverboats

Several tour operators in Iquitos take passengers on daily or weeklong cruises on the Amazon, with stops. Some will even travel as far as the mouth of the river at the Atlantic. The other riverboats are where the real adventure is. There once was regular passenger service to places like Iquitos and Yurimaguas but, due to cheap air flights, that has all changed. Most boats now pick up cargo to go with their passengers. What kind of cargo you ask? Cows, pigs, chickens, ducks, corn, rice, bananas, and just about everything else. The food is disgusting and for some reason always cooked by transvestite cooks. I'm serious. The boats are crowded, stop frequently, and are extremely uncomfortable. This is how the local people travel and it is as exotic as anything I have ever experienced. The trips often last for several days. If you are on a very tight budget and want to get to a place like Iquitos, this might be your only choice.

Car Rental

 There isn't really a good reason to rent a car in Peru unless you are working or exploring in a specific area where public transportation is hard to come by. Other than the Pan American Highway, roads tend to be bad, other drivers are often erratic, gas is expensive, taxis are cheap, distances are very great between cities, and inter-regional buses, flights, and trains are inexpensive.

Check each city's section for car rental information. Lima is where you will find the cheapest rates, sometimes as low as $50 a day, although mileage charges often apply. In Cuzco, expect to nearly double that price. A driver's license is needed, as is a credit card. Usually, you must be at least 25 to rent a car.

 You can also hire a taxi for the day or a driver. Negotiate a price because such costs are up for bargaining.

You can rent scooters in many jungle towns and in Cuzco. This is a good way to explore the area for a day and gives you a bit more freedom than public transportation.

Tour Operators

For trips to the jungle, contact any of the hotels or tour operators listed in the *Northern Amazon* or *Southeastern Jungle* chapters; they can usually help arrange your flights, accommodations, and other travel needs. For language schools, trekking, and most adventure and specialized activities handled by local tours look under the section of this guide dealing with the city where you will be traveling for more information.

The next six international companies are popular for arranging exotic yet upscale tours worldwide. In Peru they often combine trips to Lima, Cuzco, and the jungle, as well as sometimes to the Galapagos Islands. They generally include most meals, guides, transportation, and hotels for a flat fee. The companies below those six are based in Peru.

- **Abercrombie & Kent** – www.abercrombiekent.com.
- **Kon-tiki Tours** – www.kontiki.org.
- **Overseas Adventure Travel (OAT)** – www.oattravel. com.
- **GAP Adventures** – www.gap.ca.
- **Peru for Less** – www.peruforless.com, ☎ 877-269-0309. A US-based full-service tour operator with offices in Lima and Cuzco as well, devoted to providing the best-value travel packages to Peru, Ecuador, Bolivia, Argentina, Chile, Uruguay, and Brazil.
- **Southwind Adventures** – www.southwindadventures. com.
- **Inkaterra** – www.inkaterra.com. Runs the Machu Picchu Pueblo Hotel, Reserva Amazonica, Café Inkaterra in Aguas Caliente, its own NGO, and a variety of customized journeys through the Andean Experience, their associated tour group.
- **Inka Natura** – www.inkanatura.com. Arranges upscale tours to many destinations in the country, including some of the leading hotels and sights. Birding tours, Machu Picchu, and Manu are among the most common.
- **Lima Tours** – Office at Larcomar shopping center, ☎ 619-6900, www.limatours.com.pe. This is the best company for city tours, Pachacamac, and anything else in the Lima area. Also books trips on Peru rail for Machu Picchu (which should definitely be booked ahead of time). Arranges gay and lesbian tours as well.
- **Fertur Peru** – Schell 485, ☎ 445-1974, http://ferturperu. tripod.com. Similar to Lima tours.

Culinary

- **Culinary Tour** – www.yanuq.com/magicaltour/magical-tour.htm.

Crafts/Music Lessons

- **Incas del Peru** – www.incasdelperu.com.

Birding

- **Kolibri Expeditions** – ☎ 476-5016, www.kolibriexpeditions.com. Arranges the most complete birding trips all over Peru, including several day-trips from Lima.

Surf Trips

- **Local Tours** – www.localperu.com. This Lima-based company has tours throughout the country, organizes volunteering in the Lake Titicaca area, and surf trips up and down the coast – their specialty.

Gays & Lesbians

- **Above and Beyond Tours** – www.aboveandbeyondtours.com. The official gay and lesbian tour operator for United Airlines has a variety of trips to Peru and South America.

- **Gay Peru** – ☎ 1-447-3366 (Lima), ☎ 0871-871-6168 (United Kingdom), www.gayperu.com/travel. Organized by one of Peru's best gay websites, this company organizes gay and lesbian group tours to many areas of the country.

Where to Stay

The most basic notion is that if rooms do not have private hot-water baths, telephones, or amenities such as a restaurant they cannot legally be called a hotel. This rule is not always enforced, however, and the star rating system is not consistent here. You will find that a three-star in Trujillo is not the same as a three-star in Puno.

Most rates vary by city and by season. During the high season (May-September) in a place such as Cuzco the rates will likely increase by 10-20%. On holidays rates can triple. All rates listed in this book are based on the high season. During this time of the year it is important to book the best hotels at least a month in advance. For the smaller budget options or in out-of-the-way cities, a few weeks or days will usually be enough. Walk-in rates tend to be cheapest, and you can often bargain down the price if there are rooms available.

Hotels

The best hotels are found in large cities, particularly the ones frequented by tourists. Lima and Cuzco have the best options, though cities like Arequipa, Puno, Iquitos, and Trujillo also have a few. International chains such as Holiday Inn, Marriot, and the Best Western are found in a few cities. The best hotels will follow all international standards and will have all of the same amenities as any four- or five-star hotel in North America.

It is also possible to find a hotel on the lower end of the spectrum at say $25 for a double that is perfectly nice but small, charming, and with all of the amenities as a more expensive hotel. If you just want cleanliness, hot water, cable TV, comfort and can do without things such as air-conditioning, heat, and airport transfers, you will likely be perfectly happy with one of these hotels and even happier because you saved a good deal of money.

As for resorts, there are a few and in several styles. Jungle lodges are the most prevalent in the Amazon. The amenities are basic for the most part, and hot water is rare, but they are often quite comfortable. There are many country-style resort hotels in places such as Cuzco and the Sacred Valley. As for beach resorts there a few in and near Mancora; most are small, usually no more than 20 rooms, and the prices are quite reasonable compared to a similar room in, say, the Caribbean.

Many hotels include some sort of breakfast, whether it is a simple bread and tea or a full breakfast buffet.

> ⬿ The most expensive hotels apply an 18% tax, but it is waived for non-Peruvians if they retain a photocopy of their passport.

Hostals, Guesthouses, Hospedajes

Envisioning a hostel, you might think of a place filled with students or people under the age of 22. That isn't so much the case here, although such places do exist. Hostals here generally are cheap hotels, where you may or may not have your own bathroom. Some have dormitory-style beds, but the prices are generally so cheap that getting your own room is just no big deal. Quality will vary dramatically. If you want to meet other travelers, including many solo travelers, these are the types of places you should look for. They often have communal rooms for TV, books, kitchens, laundry, and more, which are great places to pick up travel tips and find travel partners. Hot water can be rare. When it does exist, it is usually more on the warm side, sporadic, or only offered during certain times of the day. Electric showers are found often as well. In some places there are wires hanging down in the shower so be careful and try to adjust before you turn on the water. For electric showers to be actually hot, you sometimes have to turn the power on very low, maybe to just a trickle to concentrate all of the heat in one place. It may not be the best way to shower in the world, but it beats being cold.

Many of the places are family-run or in the home of a local family trying to earn a living. This is good for picking up the language and experiencing how local families live and interact. Most have spent a good deal of time around travelers. They are quite friendly and will want to know a little bit about your home and what you do for a living. Bringing along a few photos of your friends, home, and city is not a bad idea.

Family Homes

In places where you are staying for a period of time, such as attending a language school, staying with a local family is quite common. Such arrangements are often made by the school or by a tour operator and different from guesthouses and hospedajes because you actually live with and become a part of the family, rather than just renting a room from them. You take meals with them, possibly do a chore or two, and may go to community activities and events with them, although you will have your own space. Often, another international visitor will be in the home at the same time.

Camping

 Other than on mountain trails, camping is not as established in Peru as you might expect – possibly because the price of a basic hotel is so cheap. There are really no established campgrounds, although some hotels will allow camping on their property. Camping on beaches is quite common, and for many surfers it is the only way to stay near the best waves.

My Favorite Places to Stay

For details on each of these places, see the section on the area in question.

- **Explorama Lodges** – This is Iquitos' largest lodge operator and their numbers cannot be ignored. They have several lodges in different areas, so you can combine stays at any of them and get the chance to see a number of different habitats, forests, and fauna.

- **Muyuna Lodge** – Muyuna is south of Iquitos, not far from Pacaya Samiria and in close proximity to stunning scenery and wildlife. The price is one of the most reasonable I have found for the quality of the lodge, the guides, and overall accommodations and tours.

- **Explorama Inn** – This Puerto Maldonado legend is the most conservation-minded of any jungle lodge I have ever visited. The amenities are not as luxurious as other lodges, but the real reason you come to the jungle – for wildlife viewing – is the best.

- **Posada del Puruay** – This country estate near Cajamarca takes every opportunity to get you to enjoy the hills and fresh air. Their land is great for horseback riding, hiking, cycling, fishing, and just plain relaxing. The friendly sheepdogs that run around the grounds act as tour guides as well.

- **Casa San Blas** – This new hotel hidden in a small side-street in San Blas in Cuzco is one of the most charming. The rooms are quite affordable and suites with kitchenettes are just a slight bit more.

- **Tambo Viejo** – A restored Victorian style home about 10 blocks from the center of Arequipa is one of the best budget options I have found in the country. There is a long list of amenities, clean rooms, and a vibrant social scene.

- **Hotel Taypikala** – This hotel in Chucuito near Puno is rumored to be owned by an Aymara shaman. The décor here is quite strange and enchanting, which can also be said for the lake and its people.

- **Casa Vieja** – This Chachapoyas inn blends Colonial style with local art. Comfort is quite high and prices are on the budget side.

- **Machu Picchu Pueblo Hotel** – Operated by Inkaterra, this hotel in Aguas Caliente combines the best aspects of staying in the cloud forest with some of the best accommodations in this small tourist town.

- **Hotel Monasterio** – This Cuzco gem is consistently ranked among the world's best hotels. It is set in a monastery that was built over an Incan Palace. The amenities, restaurants, and services are all world-class.

- **Luna Rumi** – This Urubamba retreat is brand new, quiet, and more independent than many of its larger neighbors. The train to Machu Picchu can be caught right outside the front door.

- **Las Arenas de Mancora** – Now associated with the Libertador hotel chain, Las Arenas resembles a quaint, tranquil Caribbean resort with shady palm trees amid white sand and clear blue water, excellent cuisine, a stunning pool, and a number of other amenities.

- **Sonesta Posada El Olivar** – This classic San Isidro hotel is still one of the best options for business travelers and tourists. The suites here are some of the best in Lima.

- **Country Club Hotel Lima** – This high-end venue has long been the center of the social scene for Lima's richest 1%. This national monument is all about classic style and features artwork from the Museo de Osma in Barranco throughout.

- **Rural Farmhouse on Amantani** – A classic tourist spot. A stay with a family on a Titicaca Isle opens you up to a completely different way of living, and allows you to encounter fantastic scenery and some of the brightest stars you will ever see.

Sports

Bullfighting

The **Plaza de Acho Bullring** (Hualgayoc 332 Rimac), ☎ 481-1467, is just over the Río Rimac in downtown Lima. Every October, during Fiestas Patrias, and briefly in March, events are held. Span-ish *toreros* (bullfighters) are most likely to appear. Tickets range from $20 to $100. Bullfights are common throughout the country, although far less sophisticated. In some Andean villages a condor is attached to a bulls back. The event is a symbolic one and relates to the struggle of the Quechuas and the Spanish.

Soccer

Although Peruvians as a nation have not faired well in international play, soccer (*futbol*) is quite popular. The country's last World Cup appearance was in 1982. Universatario (La U) and Alianza Lima, both from the capital are usually the best teams and each match they play against each other tends to be quite rowdy. Teams can be found all across the country, from Iquitos to Cuzco to Trujillo. Inquire at the tourist office in each city for where to buy tickets and schedules. The season runs from late March to November.

Surfing

Cabo Blanco

This has long been one of the country's favorite activities. In fact, many believe the sport was invented in Peru by the fishermen along the north coast who surf the waves back to the shore on their totora reed rafts. Modern surfing with the Maui board hit the country in 1942 and did not look back. There are good spots up and down the coast. Since there are only an estimated 12,000 surfers in the country, the waves are generally crowd-free. The surf season runs during the winter (April to September) on the central coast, while the north coast is best from October to March. Lima is probably the most popular destination for the sheer numbers that surf there, but it is nowhere near as good as other places in the country. Listed below are some of the best locations to catch a wave:

- **Cabo Blanco** – This beach near Mancora produces a short, fast left break that rises to about 12 feet. Ideal in November and December.

- **Mancora's Municipal Beach** – Ideal for its location and easy access, although the waves in this surf town can get quite crowded in the summer.

- **La Herradura** – This Chorrillos beach is one of Lima's classic surf spots. Experienced surfers come for the left-breaking waves that can reach 15 feet in height.

- **Pico Alto** – At Km 43 of the Pan American Highway south of Lima, this spot has the most challenging waves in Peru and should only be attempted by skilled surfers. The waves, which can reach 33 feet in height, draw comparisons to Waimea (Hawaii) and Todos los Santos (Baja California).

■ **Chicama** – Thought to be the world's largest left break that runs from south to west and averages about six feet in height. The site is near Km 614 of the Pan American Highway North.

■ **Punta Rocas** – This spot at Km 45 of the Pan American Highway South is home to international surfing championships in February. The waves here can rise to 16 feet and are known for their consistency.

■ **Isla San Gallán** – One of the Islas Ballestas and home to hundreds of sea lions, this is Peru's best right-breaking wave. You can rent motorboats on El Chaco beach for the 1½-hour ride there.

For More Information

www.wannasurf.com

www.peruazul.com

www.sofiamulanovich.com

www.vivamancora.com

www.localperu.com/localmagazine.html

Golf

Golf is not wildly popular in Peru, but there are a few courses. The best are in Lima, such as the private Lima Golf Club. With reservations, play is available at several San Isidro hotel. Also check out the courses in Trujillo. There is one very rough nine-hole course in Iquitos as well.

Mountaineering/Climbing

The dry season, roughly April to September, is the best time for any high-altitude climbing in Peru. **Huaraz** is without a doubt the center of all activity for any of these sports not just in Peru, but in all of the Americas. Cuzco and Arequipa also have a similar infrastructure that involves equipment rentals, guides, storage, group tours, and acclimitzations, rescue operations, etc. All equipment can be rented in any of these places but, if you are going on a very serious ascent, you probably should bring your own equipment for extra safety. Basic yet challenging climbs are found in places such as **El Misti (Arequipa)** and **Pisco (Huaraz)**, while the likes of Alpamayo and Huascarán are for the experienced only.

Trekking

Peru is one of the world's greatest places for hiking. Just a simple day-trip can get you to unspoiled villages, pristine mountain lakes, and places where no tourist has ever been. The most popular routes are in Cuzco, particularly the **Inca Trail**. The trail is often full and you must reserve months in advance. Keep in mind that there are several other trails that lead to Machu Picchu, all of them cheaper, less crowded, and just as beautiful. Other places for trekking delights include the **Cordillera Blanca** and **Huayhuash**, **Colca Canyon**, **Cajamarca**, and **Huancayo**.

Cycling

Rentals tend to be in poor condition and/or basic. There are a few places that have up-to-date and safe equipment, so be sure to get full details on what you will be renting before your trip. Get it in writing! Otherwise, many bring their own equipment. Keep in mind, though, that domestic flights will charge you a bit extra for bringing along a bike. The sport is best done in **Cuzco** and **Huaraz**, although cycling trips are arranged to all parts of the country including Lima, Arequipa, the Amazon, and throughout the Highlands.

Rafting

White water rafting is quite popular in several areas of the country. Many will go on trips for a week or more exploring the Andes to the Amazon, while camping on riverbanks and cooking their own food. A number of tour operators cater to these kinds of travelers. **Cuzco** provides the greatest diversity in trips. You can take a day-trip on the **Urubamba** or begin the descent from the Eastern highlands to the Amazon basin on the **Apurimac**. Other areas include **Tarapoto**, **Lunahuana**, **Cotahuasi Canyon**, and **Huaraz**. Make sure to check that each guide is certified, all equipment is safe and proper, and rescue operations are in place. Many rivers are quite remote and rafters have died on several occasions. Also, some of the cheaper companies pay no attention to ecological implications of the sport, so be careful and report any unscrupulous companies.

Paragliding

Not a big sport here by any means, but it is done. The **Costa Verde (Lima)** is a good place to look on any given day. The **Gandhi Park**, between San Isidro and Magdalena, is where most enthusiasts launch. **Huaraz** is also a popular spot. In either place, it is likely that you will need your own equipment. Check out www.perufly.com for more information.

Fishing

Most local fishermen use nets for fishing. In the jungle they may use spears. Fishing with a pole is not popular so you should bring your own if you intend to fish. Each of the three regions offers opportunities for the sport. In the Highlands, you can check out mountain streams and rivers in places such as **Urubamba**, **Huancayo**, **Huaraz**, and a number of other places. Trout is the big catch here. On the coast there are a number of places. In Lima you can head to either of the points of the bay, in **Callao** or **Chorrillos** where you will see the most activity. The best fishing is in the warm waters of the north however. Ernest Hemingway once hung out here, fishing off of **Cabo Blanco**. The area boasts the country's best sport fishing with black marlin, tuna, and a number of other high profile fish. In the jungle, fishing for piranha is common on many jungle excursions. For more extreme fishing and specific tours you should contact any of the tour operators or lodges and they will most likely be your best source of information.

Lima

Phone code (01)

With more than eight million people, Lima is one of largest cities in South America. For many, it can be intimidating. The population keeps on mounting and shantytowns spring up in the desert like a armies preparing for war. Public transport can be confusing. Each section is a city of its own, with its own museums, hotels, restaurants, and its own character.

You witness first-hand the continuing socio-economic divisions of Peruvian society, as the country's wealthiest citizens live not far from millions of the poorest. For much of its existence Lima was home to the Colonial

IN THIS CHAPTER

- **History** 114
- **Getting Here** 118
- **Getting Around** 122
- **The Colonial Center** 128
- **Barrio Chino** 138
- **Callao** 138
- **Pueblo Libre** 141
- **San Borja** 143
- **San Isidro** 143
- **Miraflores** 149
- **Montericco** 164
- **The Costa Verde** 165
- **Barranco** 165
- **Chorrillos** 172
- **Sports** 177
- **Adventures** 178
- **Tours** 181
- **Language Schools** 181
- **Entertainment** 182
- **Day-Trips** 183

elite and their Creole (Latin-American-born) descendents, leading many scholars to claim that the real Peru was found in the Andes. but an influx of Andean migrant workers in the last 50 years has brought the so called real Peru into Lima. A new melting pot is emerging here, a new society that is changing the face of modern Peru. It has become one of Latin America's centers of immigration. Since the Conquest, Lima has been the starting point for western society to be imposed upon the continent, but now you will see more than just the Spanish or western influence, but Chinese, Japanese, Italian, German, American, and more.

If you spend some time here, it can become as pleasant as any city on the continent. It is a city of poets, and artists, and interior designers. It is a city of diversity, of oddities, wealth, and

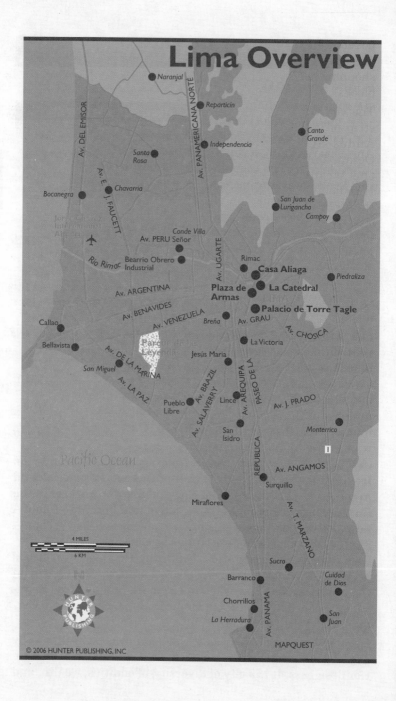

Lima Overview

Naranjal

Reparticin

Canto Grande

Independencia

Av. DEL EMISOR

Av. PANAMERICANA NORTE

Av. E. J. FAUCETT

Santa Rosa

Chavarria

Bocanegra

San Juan de Lurigancho

Campoy

Jorge Chavez International Airport

Conde Villa Señor

Av. PERU

Rio Rimac

Bearrio Obrero Industrial

Av. UGARTE

Rimac

Casa Aliaga

Piedraliza

Av. ARGENTINA

Plaza de Armas

La Catedral

Av. BENAVIDES

Av. VENEZUELA

Breña

Av. GRAU

Palacio de Torre Tagle

Callao

Av. CHOSICA

Bellavista

Av. DE LA MARINA

Parco de la Leyenda

Jesús Maria

La Victoria

San Miguel

Av. LA PAZ

Av. BRAZIL

Av. SALAVERRY

Av. AREQUIPA

PASEO DE LA

Pueblo Libre

Lince

San Isidro

Av. J. PRADO

Monterrico

REPUBLICA

Av. ANGAMOS

Pacific Ocean

Surquillo

Miraflores

Av. T. MARZANO

4 MILES

6 KM

Sucra

Barranco

Cuidad de Dios

Chorrillos

Av. PANAMA

San Juan

La Herradura

MAPQUEST

HUNTER PUBLISHING

© 2006 HUNTER PUBLISHING, INC

poverty. Just when you think you know Lima, it totally surprises you. The city ranges from a cutting-edge, ocean-view shopping center to ancient sites that encompass entire city blocks.

The city lies on a narrow strip of land between the Andes and the Pacific Ocean. Technically, it is in the tropics, but the Humboldt Current cools the air to a more temperate climate. The temperature rarely varies beyond 60-80°F. In summer, from January to April, you will find the beaches packed with Limeños getting as much sun as they can. During much of the rest of the year the capital is covered in a low-hanging grayish fog. The seasons are very gradual, hardly noticeable, and the air is normally humid. There is almost no

Colonial house in Lima's Barranco district (N. Gill)

rain in Lima, but a fine drizzle called garúa does fall from time to time.

It could easily be called the gastronomic capital of South America. Many consider Peruvian food the last great ethnic cuisine that has yet to be discovered. The restaurant scene ranges from *comedors*, where a several-course meal may cost a little more than a dollar, to high-priced luxury restaurants that can rival those of New York or Paris.

It is a major cultural center, with the best museums in the country, fine dining, ancient ruins, and is home to numerous literary figures, artists, and intellectuals. Toss in a booming nightlife, fine dining, numerous adventure sports, and 60 miles of white sand beaches and you have one of the most dynamic cities on the planet.

- **Iglesia San Francisco** – The Colonial church is home to an eerie series of catacombs that are hard to forget.

- **Barranco and Chorrillos** – These seaside suburbs, once resorts for Lima's elite, now are home to an array of interesting architecture, beaches, restaurants, and a thriving arts scene.

- **Pachacamac** – This temple was one of the largest and most revered in all of Pre-Columbian Peru.

- **Dining** – Experience the flavors in one of the dining capitals of the Americas.

- **Nightlife** – Rub shoulders with Lima's beautiful and sophisticated youth in some of the hottest clubs on the continent.

■ History

 There is plenty of evidence of life in pre-Hispanic Lima, with the *huacas* (temples) that can still be seen rising out of the suburbs or Pachacamac to the south. The Incas did not make it here until about 1440 AD, just one century before the Spanish. Lesser-known civilizations such as the Caral-Supe and El Paraiso lived in the region and date back as far as 3000 BC. The Chavín culture, and later the Wari, came in from the sierra and made vague improvements to the area. The Wari constructed most of the seaside shrine of Pachacamac to the south of Lima. The Chancay was the first major local culture to dominate the area, specifically 60 miles north in the Chancay Valley. They left a cultural and commercial influence in their ceramics and textiles.

After conquering the Incas and their capital of Cuzco in the sierra, Francisco Pizarro felt the capital of the new Spanish empire in Peru should be along the coast. After scouting, he determined that the Rimac River Valley was the best spot. The port of Callao provided easy sea access to Panama and then to Spain. The land where the city would sit was inhabited merely by rural farming communities that had been

Francisco Pizarro

absorbed by the Incas, so green areas were plentiful. When the Spanish came, they accepted them as they had done their previous conquerors. There was a native population in the region of about 200,000 at the time who survived on subsistence farming and fishing.

In 1535 the La Ciudad de los Reyes, or the City of Kings, was founded. The city quickly became the Vice-Regal Capital of South America and Lima's Colonial center (now a UNESCO Cultural World Heritage Site) was a sparkling jewel in the Spanish crown. With the creation of the Vice-Royalty in 1542, Lima became the capital of a land that included Panama and the majority of South America. The port of Callao became the major trade hub between the colonies and the motherland. The major export was silver bullion from the mines in Potosi, in what is now Bolivia.

It had its early problems, though, as the thirst for power in those days was great. The two lead conquistadors, Francisco Pizarro and Diego de Almagro, feuded over land and power. Almagro took over the city of Cuzco, but the separate factions soon battled before bewildered Incas and he was killed. His loyal party later stormed Pizarro's palace in Lima, assassinated him, and installed Almagro's son, also named Diego, as Governor. Spain

El Señor de los Milagros procession

sent a new governor the following year and the young Almagro was swiftly executed.

Lima's elite status faded in the 18th century as Bourbon monarchists emphasized greater control on the colonies. The territories were divided and therefore Lima lost much of its power and the commercial monopoly it held as other ports opened for trade.

On October 28, 1746, a large earthquake destroyed much of the city and an estimated 6,000 people died when a resulting tsunami swept into Callao. The practice and procession involving El Señor de los Milagros (Lord of Miracles), the largest religious procession on the continent, began during this catastrophe, although the image was there long before.

 Earthquakes have been a problem for coastal Peru since it was settled. In fact, Pachacamac is thought to have been the Lord of Earthquakes; a primitive cult began and the shrine was built in attempts to suppress his wrath. Oddly enough, it would be Colonial settlers who would begin the tradition of parading the image of El Señor de los Milagros through the streets each October to invoke protection from the tremors.

José de San Martín

Independence came on July 28, 1821, when liberator José de San Martín and his forces marched into Lima without a fight and declared independence to a cheering crowd in Lima's main square. The population grew steadily in the 19th century due to migrant workers and immigration from Europe and Asia.

Lima became the starting point of modernization for the country and a few projects kicked it off. First the Parque de la Exposición was built. Second was a new design of the city by Baron Haussmann that was based on 19th-century Paris. The design used a ring road (still in use), once the old city wall, comprised of Av. Alfonso Ugarte, Paseo Colon, and Av. Grau. Also, a series of avenues were created, radiating from the center and connecting suburbs such as Callao, Miraflores, Barranco, and Chorrillos.

Lima from space

During the 20th century the city's population exploded as migrant workers from the Andes and overseas immigration flooded the city. The population today is 13 times what it was in 1940.

The 1990s saw the city heavily involved with terrorist activity. It became a recruiting ground and also a place of attack. The Shining Path Guerilla Group and Tupac Amaru Revolutionary Movement (MRTA) were responsible for hundreds of killings and millions of dollars in damages. On December 17, 1996, 14 members of the MRTA stormed the home of the Japanese Ambassador to Peru in Lima during a celebration attended by an array of diplomats, dignitaries, and government officials. A hostage crisis ensued and lasted for 126 days. With worldwide media tuned in, the Peruvian special forces successfully raided the embassy by digging a tunnel underneath the house and freeing the 72 hostages still inside. One hostage, two mem-

Lima's Miraflores district

bers of the armed forces, and all 14 of the kidnappers were killed.

With an increase in tourism and bigger businesses moving in, the capital today is one of the most cosmopolitan on the continent.

■ Getting Here

Air

 International flights arrive at **Jorge Chávez Lima Callao International Airport** (☎ 01-517-3100, www.lap.com.pe), on Avenida Elmer Faucett about 10 miles northwest of Lima near Callao. The airport has regular flights to all national destinations, as well as many international destinations. For international flights, check in three hours before departure; for domestic flights, two hours before. Airlines often overbook the flights, so it is very important to get there early.

Getting to & from the Airport

Shuttle buses do not run to the airport, but local buses can be picked up outside the airport for trips to the city; however, none of them go direct to Miraflores or San Isidro and getting your luggage on board will be near impossible. Allow at least 30 minutes to get to the airport from Miraflores.

There are taxis available to and from the airport and prices are fairly reasonable. Leaving the airport, there are several official agencies with stands before you walk outside. They have a list for each part of town and you will get a receipt in the amount for where you are headed and you give that to the cab driver.

For English-speaking airport transfer, contact **Evelyn Ridoutt & Fernando Giorgetti**, Mar de Grau 281, La Perla, Callao, ☎ 420-4100, cellphone ☎ 810-8345. From the airport to Miraflores or San Isidro costs $25. Full-day transfer service is $89. This is a good idea if you want as little hassle as possible.

Airport Services

You can **store luggage** at the airport for $6 a day.

There are **ATMs** and **currency exchange** booths in the airport.

Airport tax on domestic flights is about $4 and on international flights, $28, payable in US dollars or Peruvian soles.

Other services such as phones, rental car agencies, restaurants, duty-free shops, newsstands, and a post office are there as well.

Airline Offices	
TACA	☎ 213-7000, Espinar 331 (Miraflores), www.taca.com
LAN	☎ 213-8300, Pardo 513 (Miraflores), www.lan.com
LC Busre	☎ 421-0419, Tulipanes 218 (Lince), www.lcbusre.com.pe
Star Peru	☎ 705-9000, Pardo 485 (Miraflores), www.starperu.com
TANS	☎ 213-6000, Arequipa 5200 (Miraflores), www.tansperu.com.pe
Air Canada	☎ 0800-52073, www.aircanada.com
American Airlines	☎ 442-8595, inside Hotel Las Americas on Av. Larco (Miraflores) www.aa.com
Continental	☎ 221-4340, Belaunde 147 (San Isidro), www.continental.com
Delta	☎ 440-4328, Belaunde 147 (San Isidro), www.delta.com
Iberia	☎ 411-7800, Camino Real 390 (San Isidro), www.iberia.com
Varig	☎ 422-1449, Camino Real 456 (San Isidro), www.varig.com
Avianca	☎ 446-9902, Pardo 140 (Miraflores), www.avianca.com
KLM	☎ 421-9500, Calderón 185 (San Isidro), www.klm.com
Air France	☎ 444-9285, Pardo 601 (Miraflores), www.airfrance.com
Lloyd Aereo Boliviano	☎ 241-5510, Pardo 231 (Miraflores), www.lab.com.
Wayra Airlines	Pardo 140 (Miraflores), ☎ 243-323, fax 243-3125. This airline just began service in mid-2006. They only had three jets at the time of writing and traveled to only a few cities, including Arequipa and Cuzco. Their expansion plan calls for coverage of most major cities in the country.

Driving

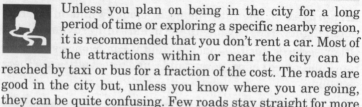

Unless you plan on being in the city for a long period of time or exploring a specific nearby region, it is recommended that you don't rent a car. Most of the attractions within or near the city can be reached by taxi or bus for a fraction of the cost. The roads are good in the city but, unless you know where you are going, they can be quite confusing. Few roads stay straight for more than a few miles, highways are few, and traffic can be quite congested.

All rental agencies have offices at Aeropuerto Internacional Jorge Chávez, while some have offices in the city as well.

CAR RENTAL AGENCIES

- **AVIS** – Av. Javier Prado Este 5235 (Miraflores), ☎ 01-434-1111, ☎ 434-0101.
- **Budget Car Rental** – Av. Canaval and Moreyra 569 (San Isidro), ☎ 442-8703, Mon-Sat, and at the airport, ☎ 575-1637, 24 hours.
- **Hertz Rent-A-Car** – Av. Cantuarias 160, (Miraflores), ☎ 447-2129, Mon-Sat., airport, ☎ 575-1390, 24 hours.
- **National Car Rental** – Av. España 453 (Lima), ☎ 433-3750, Mon-Sat., airport, 24 hours.
- **Euro Car Rent** – Av. Salaverry 1880 (Jesus María), ☎ 265-0278, 24 hours.

Bus

There is no central bus terminal, but most companies have their own terminals in one of two general areas – in the center or on Javier Prado Este in La Victoria or San Borja.

BUS COMPANIES

- **Cruz del Sur** – Jr. Quilca 531, ☎ 424-6158, Esquina de Carlos Zavala and Montevideo, Lima and at Av. Prado Este 1109, La Victoria, ☎ 225-6163, www.cruzdelsur.com.pe. Buses to most major cities.
- **Civa** – Av. 28 de Julio near the Paseo de la República, ☎ 332-5236, www.civa.com.pe. Buses to

all coastal destinations, as well as Cuzco and Ayacucho.

■ **Ormeño** – Paseo de la República 801, La Victoria, ☎ 427-5679, www.grupo-ormeno.com. Has the best buses (Royal Class) to Puno, Cuzco, Arequipa, Ayacucho, Huaraz, Trujillo, Mancora, Tumbes, Piura, Chiclayo, Ica, and Nazca. Also has international buses that go across the continent.

■ **Movil Tours** – ☎ 332-0024, Paseo de la República 749. Buses to Huaraz, Trujillo, Chiclayo, Chachapoyas.

■ **Oltursa** – ☎ 431-2395, Bausate y Mesa 644, www.oltursa.com.pe. Trujillo, Chiclayo and other northern destinations.

■ **Linea** – ☎ 424-0836, Av. Paseo de la República, ☎ 941-959 (La Victoria). Trujillo, Huaraz.

■ **Cial** – ☎ 330-4225, Paseo De La República 646 (La Victoria). To Trujillo, Huaraz, Arequipa, Cuzco.

Lima

BUS TRAVEL TIMES FROM LIMA	
Arequipa	14-16 hours
Nazca	8 hours
Ica	4½ hours
Pisco	3 hours
Cuzco	26-30 hours
Huaraz	8 hours
Tumbes	20 hours
Piura	14 hours
Mancora	20 hours
Trujillo	9-10 hours
Chiclayo	12 hours
Cajamarca	13 hours
Chachapoyas	20 hours
Puno	24 hours
Huancayo	7 hours
Tacna	18 hours

Train

Lima's train station connects to the highest railway in the world, well, sometimes. When in operation, service is generally on just a few weekends a year. It was up and running in 2005 after being shut down for a few years. Call the station for updated information.

Desamparados Train Station – Ancash 201, ☎ 361-2828, ext. 222.

- From Lima to La Oroya and Huancayo: $25/$35 (one way/ round-trip). Leaves Friday from Lima and returns on Sunday. The trip takes 12 hours each way.

■ Getting Around

Taxi

Taxis in Lima are by far the easiest way to get around. They are plentiful and cheap. Taxis can be dangerous for a woman alone at night, however. Your best bet is to call a reputable company and have them meet you rather than get a cab in the street. Unmarked taxis that wait for customers outside hotels tend to be safer, but prices are generally two or three times higher. You should always negotiate a price before you get in the cab. Other than between two main points of interest, you will find that prices vary from cab to cab.

Taxi companies:

- **Taxi Amigo** – ☎ 349-0177
- **Taxi Movil** – ☎ 422-6890
- **Taxi Lima** – ☎ 271-1763
- **Taxi Miraflores** – ☎ 446-3953

Bus

The Lima bus system can be quite confusing. There are a few large American-style buses, but most ride in the small, crowded *collectivo* vans that zip to nearly every corner of the city from every other part. To read the bus destinations, ignore anything written on the sides and concentrate on what is written in front above the windshield. There should be two names, such as Chorrillos-Carabaylo or S.M. Porres-Lima. The names may be either a street or the name of a neighborhood and reference the beginning and ending destination. They will stop everywhere in-between. If a bus is going to a destination at or beyond where you are heading, hop on. Or just shout out the name of your destination to the tout trying to lure you on the bus. For quick reference, here's what to look for:

From **Miraflores** to:

- ■ **Parque de la Expocision** – On Av. Arequipa look for buses with a sign that says Todo Arequipa.

- ■ **Downtown** – Look for Wilson/Tacna.

- ■ **Barranco, Chorrillos** – Heading south or west on Arequipa or Larco take buses that say Chorrillos.

From **Downtown** to:

- ■ **Miraflores** – Any buses that say Chorrillos, Larco, Schell, or Miraflores.

- ■ **Barranco** – Any buses that say Chorrillos.

- ■ From **Chorrillos, Barranco** to:

- ■ **Miraflores** – Chorrillos/Chorrillos.

- ■ **Downtown** – Chorrillos/Chorrillos.

More Information

Post Office

Serpost, Correo Central on the Plaza de Armas, is the best place to send parcels and large packages. They also sell cloth sacks to put them in. Other branches at: Petit Thouars 5201 (Miraflores), ☎ 445-0697; Las Palmeras 205 (San Isidro), ☎ 422-0981; and many others.

Other Shipping Options

DHL/Western Union – There are small braches of each all over town. The main office is at Piérola 808, ☎ 445-3306.

FedEx – Olaya 260 (Surco), ☎ 242-2280.

Banks

Banks and ATMs are plentiful in all parts of town, especially Miraflores, San Isidro, and Barranco. Many banks have a branch on Parque Kennedy and/or Av. Larco in Miraflores. Most of these banks will exchange currency and change travelers' checks. BCP, Banco Continental, BancoWiess, and Interbanc are the most popular. Globalnet has stand-alone ATMs across the country. You can locate them online at www. globalnet.com.pe.

- **Banco de Crédito del Perú** – ☎ 313-2000/311-9898
  Calle Centenario 156 - La Molina
  Jr. Lampa 499 (main office), Lima
  Av. Alfonso Ugarte 1302, Breña
  Av. Larco corner with Shell, Miraflores
  Av. José María Eguren 599, Barranco
  Av. Ricardo Palma 342, San Isidro

- **Banco Wiese Sudameris** – ☎ 211-6000/211-6060
  Dionisio Derteano 102, San Isidro
  Av. Alfonso Ugarte 1292, Breña
  Av. Diagonal 176, Miraflores
  Av. Angamos oeste 291, Miraflores
  Av. Larco 642, Miraflores
  Av. Grau 422, Barranco
  Carabaya 545, Lima
  Jr. Lampa and Jr. Cusco Lima.

- **Citibank** – ☎ 222-2700
  Av. Las Begonias 441, 6th floor, San Isidro
  Av. Camino Real 348, San Isidro

Telephones

Lima's phone code is 01, which need not be dialed when making a local call. If dialing an area outside Lima or calling Lima from another area, you must first dial the phone code and then the number. Pay phones are everywhere, but many accept only telephone cards, which can be purchased from vendors in the street, at mini-markets, gas stations or grocery stores. International calls can be made from booths at Telefonica offices or in many Internet cafés. Rates vary.

Internet

Internet cafés are everywhere. You can rarely walk 10 minutes without seeing one. Most have high-speed connections and range from 1-2 soles per hour.

Dentist

Check with the US or British embassies for an updated list of English-speaking dentists (doctors too).

Hospitals

- **Clínica Angolo-Americana** – Salazar, block 3 (San Isidro), ☎ 221-3656. 24 hours. English-speaking personnel.

- **Maison de Santé** – Adgouin 208-222, (Center) ☎ 428-3000. 24-hours.

- **Clínica San Borja** – Guardia Civil 337 (San Borja), ☎ 475-4000. 24-hours.

- **Instituto de Medicina Tropical** – Brasil 600 (Breña). Treats tropical diseases and can give yellow fever vaccinations and tetanus shots.

Drugstores

There are drugstores on nearly every street in Lima. The most popular chain is **InkaFarma** (☎ 314-2020 for deliveries anywhere in Lima).

Police

- **Main Police Station** – Moore 268 (Magdalena del Mar), ☎ 460-0921, 24 hours.

- **Policia Nacional de Turismo** – Javier Prado Este 2465, fifth floor (San Borja). Next to the Museo de la Nación. 24-hour hotline: ☎ 225-8698. Some staff speak English.

Emergencies

- **Traveler Hotline** – ☎ 574-8000
- **Police** – ☎ 105
- **Fire** – ☎ 116

Maps

Can be bought at SAE or in most bookstores.

Tourist Information

Peru has three offices in Lima:

- The main office in San Isidro, on Jorge Basadre 610, ☎ 511-421-1627, daily 9 am-6 pm, iperu@promperu.gob.pe.
- Aeropuerto Internacional Jorge Chávez, Main Lounge, ☎ 511-574-8000, daily 24 hours.
- On the lower floor of the Larcomar shopping center.

 South American Explorers, Piura 135 (Miraflores), ☎ 445-3306, fax 445-3306, www.saexplorers.org. They will hold luggage and accept incoming mail. Wireless Internet access. Library. Book exchange. Bulletin board. Trip reports. Expert advice. Membership fee required.

Immigration

Migraciones, España 734 (Breña), ☎ 330-4144. You can get a 30-day tourist card extension the same day for $20. First, you must buy the stamped paperwork next door at Banco de la Nación for $7. Bring your passport and the immigration slip you received when entering the country. You may be asked to show an onward ticket or proof of funds, although this is rare. If you go looking like a grungy backpacker, your chance of being hassled will be greater. Also remember, if your trip takes you to any border area, it is almost as easy and usually cheaper to cross the border and get a new visa the next day. Best to go first thing in the morning, as lines get long. Open Mon-Fri, 8 am-1 pm.

Embassies

USA – Encalada Block 17 (Monterrico), ☎ 434-3000, fax 618-2397.

Canada – Libertad 130 (Miraflores), ☎ 444-4015.

Ireland – Alegre 182 (Miraflores), ☎ 273-2903, fax 449-6289.

Great Britain – Larco 1301, floor 23 (Miraflores), ☎ 617-3050, fax 617-3055.

Australia – Belaunde 147, vía Principal 155 Building 3 (San Isidro), ☎ 222-8281.

Switzerland – Salaverry 3240 (San Isidro), ☎ 264-0305.

Japan – San Felipe 356 (Jesus María), ☎ 218-1462, fax 218-1465

Israel – Sánchez 165, floor 6 (Santa Beatriz), ☎ 433-4431.

Italy – Escobedo 298 (Jesus María), ☎ 463-2727.

South Africa – Belaunde 147 (San Isidro), ☎ 440-9996, fax 422-3881

Netherlands – Principal 190, floor 4 (La Victoria).

Argentina – Bermudez 143, floor 2 (Santa Beatriz), ☎ 433-5704.

Bolivia – Castaños 235 (San Isidro), ☎ 422-8231.

Brazil – Pardo 850 (Miraflores), ☎ 421-5650.

Chile – Prado Oeste 790 (San Isidro), ☎ 611-2200.

Colombia – Basadre 1580 (San Isidro), ☎ 442-9648.

Ecuador – Palmeras 356 (San Isidro), ☎ 461-8217.

Venezuela – Arequipa 298 (Lima), ☎ 433-4511.

Gastronomy

Ceviche – Chunks of raw fish marinated in limejuice, onion and hot chili pepper. Served with corn on the cob and sweet potato.

Tiradito – Similar to ceviche, but the fish is cut in strips and served in a sauce. No onions.

Corvina a la Chorrillana – Style of cooking invented in the fishing village of Chorrillos which pairs grilled fish with spicy onions and tomato sauce.

Tacu-tacu – Invented by African slaves. Dish of seasoned beans and rice served with a plantain and a fried egg.

Leche de tigre – A Callao original. A liquid appetizer of limejuice, fish, ají chili pepper. Muy fuerte!

Ají de Gallina – Shredded chicken in a thick sauce of milk, cheese, ají chili pepper and nuts, over white rice.

Causa limeña rellena – Layers of mashed yellow potatoes seasoned with hot chili pepper and lemon, and then stuffed with either tuna, chicken or vegetables. Served cold.

Parihuela – Thick soup of fish and shellfish.

Lomo saltado – The best known of Peru's Chinese fusion dishes. Stir-fried strips of beef sautéed with onion and tomato, mixed in with French fries, with white rice on the side.

Butifarra – Sandwich made of French bread, with country ham, fresh lettuce, and a criollo sauce of onion, lemon and parsley.

Mazamorra morada – Stewed purple maize jelly with fruits.

Suspiro a la limeña – A very rich milk based dessert topped with vanilla cream and meringue. Named because it is soft and sweet like the sigh of a woman from Lima.

■ The Colonial Center

Plaza Mayor

This was the center for Spain's control over the wealth of the new world. The architectural gems, the churches and mansions, are very much worth preserving. The earthquakes of 1746 and 1940 have destroyed many of the buildings, so some now date only to the late 19th and early 20th century. Buildings were torn down to make room for new roads or were left to rot as the center of the city shifted to the suburbs. The 1990s saw a renewed interest in the buildings and a revival of sorts is underway. Most visitors no longer stay in the Center and, unless you have an early flight and want to be 10 minutes closer to the airport, it is recommended you stay elsewhere. There are a few nice hotels here, though, and if your interest is solely to see Colonial architecture and visit museums it can be a pleasant stay. The area can be dangerous at night, so you should always use taxis.

The official center sits between Plaza Mayor and Plaza San Martín, but a much wider area is generally accepted as the Colonial center.

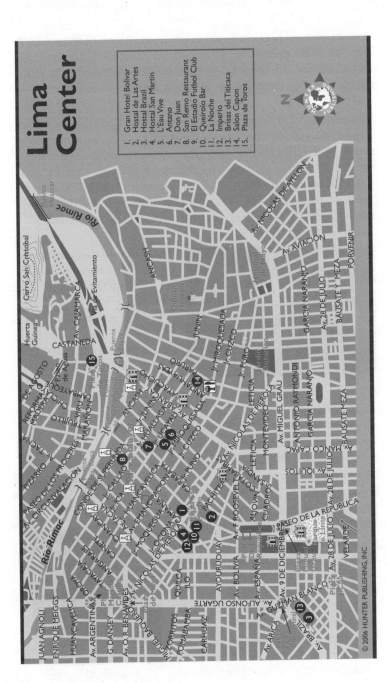

Lima
Center

1. Gran Hotel Bolívar
2. Hostal de Las Artes
3. Hostal Brazil
4. Hostal San Martín
5. L'Eau Vive
6. Antano
7. Don Juan
8. San Remo Restaurant
9. El Estadio Futbol Club
10. Queirolo Bar
11. La Noche
12. Imperio
13. Brisas del Titicaca
14. Salón Capón
15. Plaza de Toros

★★★Colonial Lima only occupied a small part of the modern city. The **Damero de Pizarro** ("Pizarro's Chessboard") extended for 13 blocks by nine blocks. Immigration from Spain and the importation of black slaves quickly expanded the city, however.

The general starting point for tours of the Colonial Center is **Plaza Mayor**, or the **Plaza de Armas**, which is one block south of the Río Rimac and where several other attractions are located. It is the original center of the city that Pizarro first founded, although the earthquake of 1746 destroyed most of the buildings. The central bronze fountain, which dates back to 1651, did survive. The Plaza is a UNESCO World Heritage Site.

Palacio de Gobierno

The **Palacio de Gobierno**, or the Government Palace, on the north side of the square, is the seat of the Peruvian government. The majestic building has priceless works of art and carvings inside. Guided visits are free and are at 8:45 and 9:45 am Mon-Fri and on Sat at 9, 10, and 11 am. You must book 24 hours in advance by calling ☎ 311-3908. No shorts or pants (for women) are allowed. Admission is free. Changing of the guard is Mon-Sat at noon.

Elsewhere in the Plaza, the **Municipalidad de Lima** (City Hall) is on the west side, **La Catedral** is on the east, as is the **Palacio Episcopal** (Archbishop's Palace) and its famed wooden balcony. The Cathedral was completely destroyed in the earthquake, but rebuilt in 1755 on the same design as the original, which was a copy of the Seville cathedral but with three naves.

Palacio Episcopal

Precious oil paintings and carvings surround silver altars. The carved wooden choir stalls are some of the most famous on the continent. The remains of Francisco Pizarro are thought to be in either the glass coffin near the entrance or in the crypt.

Catedral de Lima (Carlos Sala)

Open Mon-Sat 10 am-2:30 pm. Admission 5 soles. The **Museo de Arte Religioso**, or the Museum of Religious Art, inside has free guided tours.

There are a few sites of interests just off the Plaza. The **Philatelic Museum**, located in the central post office, houses a collection of Peruvian stamps and information on the Incan postal system. Open daily 8:15 am-1 pm and 2-6 pm. Admission is free.

Two blocks south of Plaza Mayor is **Iglesia La Merced** (Union and Quesada, ☎ 427-8199). It was built on the site of Lima's first mass in 1534. Notable features on the 18th-century building are the Baroque façade, the altars, and tile work. The silver cross dedicated to Padre Urraca, a 17th-century priest, is frequently prayed to, touched, and alms are left. Open Mon-Sat 8 am-noon.

★★★**Iglesia y Convento de San Francisco** (Plazeula San Francisco, ☎ 426-7377), was also named a UNESCO Cultural World Heritage Site. It is one of the most fascinating attractions in the city and a sure stop on every tour. Built in 1674, the yellow and white

Iglesia de San Francisco (Carlos Sala)

Baroque church withstood the 1746 earthquake. Cloisters are lavishly decorated with Sevillian tiles and carved mudejar, or

Moorish-style, ceilings. The catacombs beneath the church are filled with thousands upon thousands of bones, many of them arranged in intricate patterns. As many as 75,000 bodies were laid to rest here. The tour, which lasts 1½ hours and can be given in English, walks you through the sights mentioned above, a religious art museum, and a 17th-century library with 20,000 books. Open daily 9:45 am-6 pm. Admission 5 soles adults/2.50 soles students.

Palacio Torre Tagle
(Coco Martin)

Palacio Torre Tagle (Ucayali 363), a few blocks east of Plaza Mayor, was built in 1763 and is an excellent example of Colonial architecture. Visitors are no longer allowed inside, so you can only see the carved wooden balconies and the Baroque stone doorway.

Another Colonial remnant, **Casa Aliaga** (Union 224, 447-6624), which can only be viewed vía Lima Tours, is still lived in by the descendents of the original family. Built in 1535, it is the oldest house in Lima. The mansion has a stunning inner patio and a fine array of Colonial-style furniture.

Museo Taurino (Hualgayoc 332, ☎ 482-3360), the bullfighting museum, is just over the Puente de Piedra, a Roman-style bridge that crosses the Río Rimac. Open Mon-Fri 9 am-3 pm and Sat 9 am-2 pm. The **Plaza de Acho Bullring**, once the largest in the world, is next door.

Casa Aliaga interior

Nearby **Plaza Bolivar**, between Av. Abancay and Jr. Ayacucho, is where José de San Martín declared independence. A statue of the liberator now graces its center.

Museo de la Inquisición y del Congreso (Junín 548, ☎ 311-7777), the Museum of the Inquisition, is just across the street from the present House of Congress. The museum is dedicated to the infamous Spanish Inquisition that killed at least 32 people in Lima. The courtroom, or Tribunal Room, has a beautiful, elegant carved wooden ceiling. Many of the other rooms are restored from the Colonial-era house that predates the museum and there are a host of exhibits. The catacombs and prison cells are the most interesting parts of the building. There are somewhat cheesy representations of those accused of heresy in the 18th century being tortured, although the torture tools and settings are realistic. Guided tours are in several languages, but expect to wait for a little while if you don't speak Spanish. Mon-Sun 9 am-5 pm. Admission 5 soles.

The Churrigueresque façade (1720) of **San Agustín** (Ica and Camaná, ☎ 427-7548) is one of the finest examples of that style of architecture. Hours are sporadic.

Façade of San Agustín (www.enjoyperu.com)

Churrigueresque is a term used from the late 18th century to denote the most exuberantly ornamental phase of Spanish architectural decoration, lasting from c. 1675 to c. 1750. The term derives from the Churriguera family, the principal exponents of the style, who worked mostly in Salamanca.

Parts of nearby **Santo Domingo** (Superunda and Camaná, ☎ 427-6793) and its monastery date back as far as 1603. The tombs of San Martín de Porres, a revered saint, and Santa Rosa de Lima, are beneath the sacristy.

★**Las Nazarenas Church** (Huancavelica and Tacna) is one of the most historically interesting places in the city. The church was constructed in the 18th century around a painting of Christ by an Angolan slave. The image is known as *El Señor de Milagros*, or the Lord of Miracles, and each October numerous processions are held in its honor. The image became darkened by all of the candles that were set before it, and had a special meaning for Lima's African population, who felt that Christ was watching over them too. It has become the most adored image in Lima, by all races, classes, and creeds. The image was painted on the house that was used by a black brotherhood in the same location before the church was built. In the earthquake of 1655, the wall holding the image of Christ remained intact and the legend grew from there. The authorities ordered it painted over or removed, but every attempt was thwarted. In the end they gave it official recognition and the church was built.

 Cured of her paralysis by the image of El Señor, a mulatto woman named Josefa Pepa Marmaguillo invented a sweet nougat called a **turron** and gave it out to the poor at Las Nazarenes. Ever since then, each October street vendors sell the Turrons de Dona Pepe.

Plaza San Martín, five blocks southwest of Plaza Mayor, is another impressive main square. As at Plaza Bolivar, a monument of José de Martín is at the center.

★★**Gran Parque Cultural de Lima**, also known as Parque de la Expocision, is a sanctuary of green and shade in a congested part of the city. It some-

Plaza San Martín

times hosts craft and food markets on weekends, children's theater performances, and other special events. There's also a pond with paddleboats, amphitheater, food court, and Japanese garden.

The ★**Museo de Arte** (Paseo Colon 125, ☎ 423-6332) sits on the edge of the park. Several floors are dedicated to more than 7,000 exhibits. There are extensive collections of Pre-Columbian artifacts and pottery, Colonial art, furniture,  modern paintings, and special exhibitions. Open Tues-Sun 10 am-5 pm. Admission 12 soles adults/six soles students.

The nearby **Museo de Arte Italiano** (Paseo de la República 250, ☎ 423-9932) is a small yet wonderful museum that many miss. The Neoclassical building was a gift from Italy in celebration of Peru's independence. There are many statues and paintings, mostly from the early 20th century, crammed into the three high-ceilinged rooms. Open Mon-Fri 9 am-4 pm. Admission 1 sole.

The **Santuario de Santa Rosa** (Tacna block 1, ☎ 425-1279), or the Sanctuary of Santa Rosa, was built on the site of the birth of Lima's first saint. A small garden was built in the 17th century for her prayers and meditations. There is also a small church. Open daily 9 am-1 pm and 3-6 pm. Admission free.

Cerro San Cristóbal, the mountain that dominates downtown Lima, can be reached by a tour that leaves from in front of Santa Domingo. The tour lasts about an hour and leaves every 15 minutes on weekends from 10 am-9 pm. Price is 5 soles. You can go via taxi for about $5 round-trip. A huge illuminated cross that stands there can be seen from across the city and is the objective of a pilgrimage every May 1.

Where to Stay

 Sheraton Lima Hotel and Casino – República 170, ☎ 315-5022, www.sheraton.com.pe. This is the best option in the Center. The hotel has 431 rooms, 85 of which have been recently remodeled. Rooms have all of the amenities you would expect of a five-star hotel. Good location next to Plaza Grau. Free

shuttle service to Miraflores. Dinner shows in Las Palmeras restaurant. Lunch buffet. Bar. 24-hour room service. $$$$

Gran Hotel Bolivar – Union 958, ☎ 619-7777, www.granhotelbolivar.com. A six-level upscale hotel built in 1924 that is probably the best value in the Center. The 272 rooms have wall-to-wall carpeting, mini-fridges, cable TV, hair driers, and every other expected detail. Some have balconies with views of Plaza San Martín. Ernest Hemingway was once a guest. $$$

Gran Hotel Bolivar

Kamana Hotel – Camaná 547, ☎ 426-7204, fax 426-0790, www.kamanahotel.com. Just a few blocks from the main square, this is the best hotel in the very heart of the Center. The 55 rooms have cable TV, safes, private baths, minibars, and phones. Includes continental breakfast. $$

Kamana

Hostal de Las Artes – Chota 1460, ☎ 511-433-0031, artes@terra.com.pe. Dutch/Peruvian owners keep the basic rooms in this 19th century house clean and up-to-date. All rooms have private hot-water baths. Dorm beds are available for less. Solar heating. Book exchange. Gay-friendly. $$

Hostal Brasil – Brasil 497, ☎ 424-1927, www.hostalbrasil.com. Thirty-one rooms of varying sizes. Cozy, but décor is old and outdated. Rooms have private hot-water baths and cable TV. $$

Hostal San Martín – Piérola 882, ☎ 428-5337, fax 423-5744, hsanmartin@oalsnet.com.pe. Near Plaza San Martín. Basic rooms have

HOTEL PRICE CHART	
	under $10
$	$10-$25
$$	$26-$50
$$$	$51-$90
$$$$	$91-$150
$$$$$	Over $150

cable TV, air-conditioning, and private hot-water baths. Includes breakfast. Free airport pick-up. $$

Where to Eat

★**L'Eau Vive** – Ucayali 370, ☎ 427-5612. Dishes from all over the world prepared by a French order of nuns. The nuns sing Ave María each night at 9 pm. Profits go to charity. Open for lunch and dinner. $$$

Antano – Ucayali 332. This pleasant restaurant not far from the previous one serves good traditional Peruvian food. $$

Don Juan – Carabaya 318, ☎ 428-8378. Just steps from the Plaza Mayor is this decades-old restaurant that serves big, hearty portions of Peruvian and International cuisine. Good value. $$

San Remo Restaurant – Pasaje de los Escribaños, ☎ 427-9102. This small upscale café has moderately priced menus. $$

El Estadio Futbol Club – Piérola 926, ☎ 428-8866. Soccer-themed bar and grill on Plaza San Martín with indoor and outdoor tables. $$

DINING PRICE CHART	
$	under $5
$$	$5-$10
$$$	$11-$20
$$$$	$21-$35
$$$$$	over $35

Bars/Clubs

Queirolo Bar – Camaná 900. Crowded and friendly place where the local flavor comes out. Makes its own wine.

La Noche – This jazz bar is the Center's take on the club of the same name in Barranco, which is owned by the same people. Sits next door to Queirolo Bar.

Imperio – Camaná block 9. One of the oldest exclusively gay clubs in Lima.

Peñas

A **peña** is a circle or social group, usually of artists or musicians. Lately, they have started to stage public performances paired with a dinner or buffet.

★**Brisas del Titicaca** – Wakulski 168, ☎ 332-1901, www. brisasdeltiticaca.com. This well-known peña near block 1 of Av. Brasil, is the best in the Center for a dinner and show experience. Buffet of Peruvian food is paired with traditional music and dancing. $$$

■ Barrio Chino/Chinatown

By the late 19th century more than 100,000 Chinese immigrants, called "coolies," had come to Peru to work on the railroads, coastal plantations, or guano islands. Many found themselves in Lima and soon the city was home – and still is – to the largest Chinese population on the continent. Although you can find a **chifa**, or Chinese restaurant, in nearly every city in the country, the best are here. Much as in the rest of the world's Chinatowns, goods from the Orient can be purchased in the many shops near the Central Market. The epicenter is on Calle Capon and Jirón Parura.

Where to Eat

★**Restaurant Oriental Wa Lok** – Jr. Paruro, ☎ 864-878, 427-2656. This restaurant has long been the center of Peru's Chinese dining scene. The restaurant not only perfectly executes Chinese classics, but also has been on the forefront of combining the recipes with Peruvian dishes. $$

Salón Capón – Jr. Paruro 819. The rival to Wa Lok. It is well known for its dim sum, although there are a number of other dishes that it should be known for as well. It has another restaurant at Larcomar. $$

■ Callao

Only a few tourists and yachtsmen venture into Callao, but those that do are well rewarded. This sprawling city not far from the airport extends far into the Pacific on a peninsula, the neighborhood/resort of La Punta. The area can be dangerous and is recommended only during the day, but if you make it there you will find the stunning seaside fort of Real Felipe, a few nice seafood restaurants, a yacht club, the home of Pilsen Callao, and a Colonial port atmosphere that is reminiscent of Old Panama City. The earthquake and subsequent tidal wave destroyed much of the city, although the area around Plaza dos de Mayo has many Colonial buildings with wooden balconies, albeit badly neglected.

Callao has long been considered a part of Lima. It was the principal commercial port for Spain in the entire Pacific during Colonial times. It was once home to the Pacific Steam Navigation Company, which in 1870 was the largest shipping company in the world. It did regular runs from Liverpool to Callao via Panama. The former grounds of the company can still be seen in Callao.

Before railroads arrived, the port was also a transportation hub for people and merchandise going to and from the capital and coastal destinations. With silver bullion from Potosi leaving the port for Spain on a regular basis, it became a major target for pirate activity. In the late 16th century pirate Francis Drake terrorized the port, stealing a cargo-laden ship. Later the Dutch pirates van Spielbergen and L'Hermite attacked the port on several occasions.

To protect against such attacks, **La Fortaleza Real Felipe** was built in 1746. The perimeter is over a mile long and the walls stand an imposing 16 feet high. During the fight for independence, the fort held the rebel fleet at bay for four years, though it was overtaken by siege in 1821. The museum inside has exhibits on Peru's military history, including uniforms, weapons, documents, and other paraphernalia. The most interesting room is dedicated to the women involved. Walking on the top of the walls and towers affords good views of the bay, the coast and the city. Open daily from 9 am-4 pm. Admission 10 soles, which includes a guide.

La Fortaleza Real Felipe

Plaza José Gálvez is the most interesting plaza in Callao. Balconied wooden Colonial buildings still stand, although many are in dire need of repair. A few small ceviche restaurants, souvenir shops, and benches surround it.

The **Museo Naval Julio Elías Murguía** (Av. Monteverde Win 123, ☎ 429-7278, ext. 6794) has models of navy ships and various other military items such as uniforms, weapons, and photographs. Open daily from 9 am-5 pm. Admission 3 soles.

★**La Punta**, the neighborhood at the end of Callao, has some European style to it. Perhaps because it was once home to an Italian colony. There is a nice beach area, a pebble beach, with a promenade, pier, and bandstand.

The **Palomino Islands** just off the coast of Callao are home to a variety of sea life such as sea birds, seals, and maybe a few Humboldt penguins. Tours to the islands can be arranged. See *Adventures on Water* below for more details. Isla San Lorenzo has been made into a high-security prison where the leaders of both Sendero Luminoso (Shining Path) and the MRTA (a revolutionary group) are held.

Where to Eat

★**La Rana Verde** – Parque Gálvez (La Punta), ☎ 429-5279. On the pier beside the Club Universatario de Regattas, this seafood restaurant is one of the best in Lima. Every table has a view of the harbor and the yachts waiting there. The menu is long and even includes chicken and grilled meats. Otherwise, if there is a Limeñan seafood dish that you have wanted to try, they have it and you won't be disappointed. The ceviches and tiraditos are especially good here. Open until 6 pm daily. $$$

■ Pueblo Libre

Pueblo Libre, or freetown, not far from the Colonial Center, is home to several of the city's best museums. During the Colonial period it was used as a rural retreat. It was once known as Santa María Magdalena, but renamed Pueblo Libre, or freetown, when liberators San Martín and Bolivar spent time there. The focal point is **Plaza Bolivar**, with two museums, a few small restaurants and cafés, and a lively square.

The ★**Museo Nacional de Antropologia, Arqueología, y Historia** (Plaza Bolivar) was once the home of viceroy Joaquín de la Pezuela. The museum was founded in 1945 to display the work of archeologist Julio C. Tello (1880-1947) who made many discoveries in the country,

Textile from the Wari culture
(Wilfredo Loayza)

including the Chavín Obelisk, which can be seen there. The

Nasca ceramic
(Wilfredo Loayza)

museum covers civilization in the country from the very beginning to Colonial times. There are a variety of exhibits – stonework, jewelry, pottery, textiles, scale models, burial tombs, mummies, and much more. It isn't as modern or complete as the Larco Museum, but well worth a look. Open Tues-Sat 9 am-5 pm and Sun 9 am-4 pm. Admission 10 soles adults/3 soles students.

The **Museo Nacional de Historia** (Plaza Bolivar, ☎ 463-2009), next door, is less extensive. A collection of early Republican paintings, portraits, manuscripts and other Colonial-era items are on display. The mansion was once home to

San Martín and Bolivar during the 1820s. Open Tues-Sat 9:15 am-5 pm. Admission 10 soles. From here you can take a one-mile path to the museum below (just follow the blue lines).

Mochica ceramic

The ★★★**Museo Arqueológico Rafael Larco Herrera** (Av. Bolivar 1515, ☎ 461-1835, museolarco.perucultural.org. pe) is perhaps the best one in Lima. It is set in an exquisite 18th-century Vice-Royal mansion that was built on top of a seventh-century Pre-Columbian pyramid. The museum and its collections are well maintained and organized. The exhibits trace 3,000 years of Peruvian history, with the largest collection of Pre-Columbian artifacts in the world. Moche dynasty, with some of the most interesting and unique ceramics in the Pre-Columbian world, is the primary focus, although many other civilizations are well represented. There are an estimated 45,000 pieces on display. There is also an impressive gold and silver collection. It is also home of the infamous erotic pottery collection, the *sala erotica*, which shows a variety of Pre-Columbian peoples and sometimes animals engaged in sexual acts. This collection is actually meant to show this one aspect of Pre-Columbian life through their pottery and is taken very seriously. Open daily from 9 am-6 pm. Admission 25 soles

Where to Eat

★**Antigua Taberna Queirolo** – San Martín 1090, ☎ 460-0441, www.antiguatabernaqueirolo.com. This old bodega just around the corner from Plaza Bolivar has an elegant, Colonial style with plenty of woodwork and black and white photographs on the walls. It is good for a quick butifarra (a country ham sandwich with criollo sauce and onions), a snack, glass of wine, or aperitif. It was built in 1880 by two Genoan brothers and has become a landmark of sorts. Wine and Pisco is bottled right next door and can be sampled or purchased. Tours are also given. $$

Olga y Carlos Mamicé – Av. Bolivar 291. This corner restaurant just across the from the two museums at Plaza Bolivar serves a variety of Peruvian dishes and is a good option if looking at millennia-old artifacts has brought out your appetite. $$

■ San Borja

The pleasant middle-class suburb of San Borja offers little in the way of tourist amenities, though it is the home to one major museum.

The ★**Museo de la Nación** – Av. Javier Prado Este 2465, ☎ 476-9933. This vast, sprawling three-level museum just off the highway takes visitors on a tour of Peru's history, all of it, while highlighting the greatest achievements of each culture – from the earliest simple pre-Colombian societies up to the Incas, who lasted until  the Conquest. Ceramics and textiles are well represented, and most of the major ruins are shown in a scale model. The exhibits are chronologically ordered, although many cultures overlap. Explanations for each exhibit are in Spanish and English. Allow at least two hours for your visit. Open Tues-Sun 9 am-6 pm. Admission 6.50 soles adults/3 soles students.

■ San Isidro

San Isidro is Lima's playground for the urban elite and is filled with some of the country's priciest residential complexes, restaurants, boutiques, and businesses. It is consistently ranked as one of the best neighborhoods in all of Peru. San Isidro was developed in the 1920s as a residential area between the Center and Miraflores. The design was based on North American models, with most of the houses having gardens. In recent years it has taken on more of an upper middle class character with all of the living quarters and hotels that surround the park being quite exclusive.

olives were first planted by the Spanish at the founding of the city and El Olivar became the most charming park in all of Lima by the end of the last century.

The land on which the city sits dates back to Pre-Columbian times, as can be see with **Huaca Huallamarca**, also known as Pan de Azucar. The shrine and burial center left by the

Maranga culture dates to between 100 and 500 AD. Recent investigations suggest that the Chavín culture may have been there as well. It isn't as large or impressive as Huaca Pucllana, but if you're in the

Huaca Huallamarca (Mylene d'Auriol)

area it's worth a quick stop. Open Tues-Sun, 9 am-5 pm. Admission 5 soles.

Where to Stay

If price is your concern, avoid San Isidro. There may be a few small, cheap, and convenient hotels on Av. Arequipa, but they are generally not worth the price. If you are looking for luxury, however, this is the place.

★**Swissotel Lima** – Vía Central 150, ☎ 421-4400, www.swissotel.com. Formerly the Oro Verde, this is definitely in the top five of all Lima's hotels. It is sophisticated and classy.

From the moment you walk into the stunning lobby, you know that the rest of the hotel will not disappoint. $$$$$.

★★**Country Club Lima Hotel**, Los Eucaliptos 590,

San Isidro

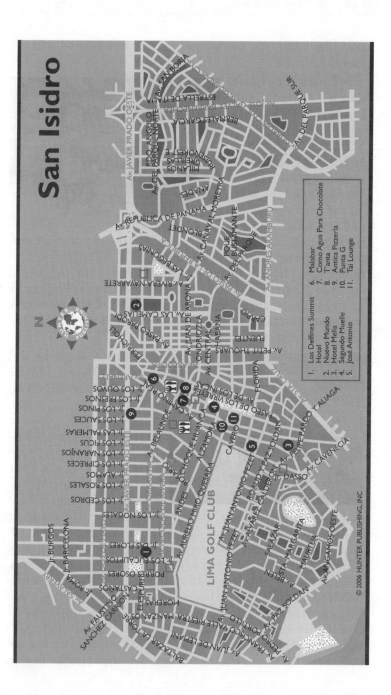

1. Los Delfines Summit Hotel
2. Nuevo Mundo
3. Hotel Melia
4. Segundo Muelle
5. José Antonio
6. Malabar
7. Como Agua Para Chocolate
8. Tanta
9. Antica Pizzeria
10. Punta G
11. Tai Lounge

LIMA GOLF CLUB

© 2006 HUNTER PUBLISHING, INC.

stunning lobby, you know that the rest of the hotel will not disappoint. $$$$$.

★★**Country Club Lima Hotel**, Los Eucaliptos 590, ☎ 1800-745-8883 (in North America) or 611-9000, fax 611-9002, www.hotelcountry.com. Possibly the best hotel in the city. Combines luxury and history.

Built in 1927, the hotel and club quickly became a social center for Lima's elite, visiting dignitaries, bullfighters, and celebrities. Rooms are large and filled with old world antiques; the marble bathrooms have Jacuzzis. It's classic luxury and elegant in the right ways. All of the amenities included. Guests can enjoy the use of the nearby Lima Golf Club and tennis courts. $$$$$

★**Sonesta Posado del Inca El Olivar**, Pancho Fierro 194, ☎ 221-2121, fax 221-2141, www. sonesta.com. Sonesta Peru's flagship hotel, and for good reason. Located beside Olive Grove Park in Lima's financial district, this hotel specializes in business travelers, although any traveler will likely be impressed by the facilities. Some of the features include 24-hour room service, a business center, parking, beauty parlor, fitness center and spa, and indoor/outdoor swimming pools. Rooms are modern, frequently updated and have air conditioning and all the other luxury items you would expect in a five-star hotel. Includes breakfast buffet. Suites are stunning and a good value. Sometimes has weekend deals and packages. The restaurants are worth a visit even if you are not staying in the hotel. Ichi-Ban Sushi Bar might be the best in

Where to Stay ■ 147

Lima and the El Olivar restaurant and bar is headed by one of the best young chefs in Lima. $$$$$

Los Delfines Summit Hotel – Los Eucaliptos 555, San Isidro. ☎ 215-7086, fax 215-7073, www. losdelfineshotel.com.pe. Named after the dolphins Yaku and Wayra that live and train on the grounds. There are 186 rooms, more than 40 of which are suites. The décor is cosmopolitan without being oppressive and maintains a warm, homely feel.

In the Dolphin Bar patrons are treated to a view of the Dolphinarium. The hotel also has one of the most popular casinos in town. $$$$$

Hotel Libertador – Los Eucaliptos 550, ☎ 421-6666, www. libertador.com.pe. One of my favorite luxury hotel chains in Peru, perhaps because it is expanding rapidly in areas that other chains

are ignoring such as Mancora or Tambopata. The Lima location doesn't stand out like some of the other San Isidro hotels, but offers just as much in terms of quality and service. The top-floor restaurant and bar are a nice touch. $$$$

★**NM Lima Hotel** (Nuevo Mundo) – Aliaga 300, ☎ 612-1000, www.nmlimahotel.com. This is a beautiful new 68-room hotel with a hip, trendy flavor. Rooms are stylish without sacrificing comfort. Includes breakfast buffet. Restaurant with 24-hour room service, coffee lounge, and bar. Business center. Highly recommended. $$$$

Hotel Meliá – Salaverry, 2599, ☎ 411-9000, fax 411-9022, melia.lima@solmelia.com. This is officially rated a five-star hotel because it has enough amenities to garner the rating. The pillow menu is an interesting feature. Breakfast and dinner buffets can be had in El Tambo restaurant. $$$

Where to Eat

 Segundo Muelle – Conquistadores 948, ☎ 241-5040, www.segundomuelle.com. On the Malecón with views of the Pacific and the Parque de Amor, this attractive, moderately sized building with a relaxed ambiance is one of San Isidro's best seafood options. To start, try the piqueos (samplers) de causa (layered potatoes) or de tres cebiches (marinated seafood). For the main course try the arroz chaufa con mariscos (seafood fried rice) or the ají de langostinos (like the spicy shredded chicken dish ají de gallina, but with shrimp). Open for lunch only. $$$

José Antonio – Monteagudo 200, ☎ 264-0188. José Antonio is a must if you are looking for straightforward Peruvian fare, artistically prepared using the freshest and best ingredients. The rustic décor has the feeling of a Conquistador's country estate. A few recommended criollo dishes are the apanado (fried breaded steak accompanied with tacu-tacu, fried banana, fried egg, and a raw spicy onion sauce), and the huge Piqueo plate, which has anticuchos (kebabed beef hearts), crispy yucca, corn tamales, chicharrónes (deep fried pork) and other treats. $$$$

Malabar – Camino Real 101, ☎ 440-5200/440-5300. Located on a quiet side street, this restaurant is a definite stop for foodies looking to expand their palate. After graduating from the Culinary Institute of America, Pedro Miguel Schiaffino worked in Italy before starting his own restaurant here. The menu changes frequently and reflects the owner's Cuban-Italian-Peruvian heritage. He is one of the few chefs in Lima to research and use Amazonian ingredients, a trend that I think could explode very soon. The bar is open late and serves Pisco Punch, which uses an 1850 San Francisco recipe. $$$$$

Como Agua Para Chocolate (Like Water for Chocolate) – Pancho Fierro 108, ☎ 224 0174. Named after the excellent movie of the same name. This is one of the best Mexican restaurants in the city. Cantina-like décor and food is authentic. $$$

T'anta – Pancho Fierro 117. Sandwiches, quiche, empañadas, salads, desserts, coffee drinks, cocktails. It has patio and indoor seating and is usually very crowded. $$$

Antica Pizzeria – Dos de Mayo 728, ☎ 222-8437. Part of an upscale chain with locations all over Lima and Peru. Pizzas are good, but the calzones, lasagnas, and pastas are even better. $$$

D'nnos Pizza – Dos de Mayo 790, ☎ 219-0909. For pizza from the biggest and best local chain.

Bars/Clubs

Punto G – Conquistadores 510, ☎ 440-5237. Exclusive club frequented by the rich and cosmopolitan. There isn't even a sign outside, just a pair of white doors. Cocktails are pricey, but all top-shelf.

Tai Lounge – Conquistadores 325, ☎ 422-7351. This Thai restaurant becomes one of the places to see and be seen for beautiful, sophisticated Limeños. Made up of patios and lounge areas where you can show off your new diamond necklaces or $400 pair of pants.

THE TOP 10 RESTAURANTS OF LIMA
■ Astrid y Gastón (contemporary Peruvian)
■ El Señorio de Sulco (criollo)
■ La Mar (seafood)
■ Sonia (seafood)
■ Las Brujas de Cachiche (criollo)
■ Manos Morenos (criollo)
■ La Canta Rana (seafood)
■ La Rosa Náutica (seafood)
■ José Antonio (criollo)
■ Wa Lok (Chinese)

■ Miraflores

In the middle of the 19th century Miraflores slowly replaced the Center as the major area for shopping, restaurants, nightlife, and entertainment. Many wealthy European immigrants redeveloped the area during that time, a character that can still be felt. It didn't have the resort feel of Barranco or Chorrillos, but rather a quiet community good to raise families and was close to commercial outlets. With the constructions of Av. Arequipa in the 1920s and the Vía Expresa in the 1960s the population has steadily climbed. In the year 2000, it stood at around 200,000. For many visitors to Lima, Miraflores is all they see. There is Parque Kennedy and the Larcomar shopping center, the largest hotels in the country, skyscrapers, and tourist amenities galore. But to find the real Miraflores, stroll a little bit farther. Into the back alleys, the leafy corner cafés, the Republican mansions, and the cliffside parks that line the Pacific.

Ave. Diagonal

Parque Kennedy

★**Parque Kennedy** and the adjoining **Parque Central**, are essentially the hub of Lima's tourist district and the focal point of Miraflores. There is shop after shop, restaurants, cafés, hotels, cinemas, a few museums, bars, and clubs all within minutes of the park. It is the hub of international fast food chains as well. The park itself is pleasant enough with flowers, trees, and artisans selling paintings, jewelry and crafts. On weekends there are usually craft vendors and artists selling handicrafts, paintings, and the like.

Calle de las Pizzas, or Pizza Street, which cuts west from across Av. Diagonal, is a short strip of a dozen or so touristy restaurants and clubs. The food is decent, but somewhat over-priced. At night the strip is crowded with partygoers of all ages who crowd the upstairs clubs and discos.

Calle de las Pizzas

The **Parque de Amor**, Park of Love, which sits on the Malecón and overlooks the Pacific has a giant statue of a couple searching for something in one another's tonsils. Wedding parties can be often seen there taking photos.

Farther down the coast, and the end of Larco Avenue, you will come to **Parque Salazar**. The real attraction here is the Larcomar shopping center that sits on the cliff below. See more details under *Shopping*.

For a remarkable amount of Pre-Columbian history within one city block, there's ★**Huaca Pucllana** (Borgoña and Tarapacá, ☎ 445-8695). The adobe structure was made by the Lima culture, which survived from 200-700 AD throughout the central coast. Pucllana means "a place of festive ceremonies." The pyramid itself was built in the fifth century. Wise priests used to organize economic, political, and religious activities to keep social order stable. It has two distinct areas separated by a large wall made of small mud bricks. The east side has a system of halls and plazas that were likely used for civic discussions and activities. The west side includes the pyramid and is more for ceremonial purposes. Burials found at the temple were in ceramic jars or covered in plain cloth and placed over a reed litter with food and objects of everyday use. The center was abandoned by the Lima culture between the seventh and the eighth centuries, but later used by the Wari culture that arrived

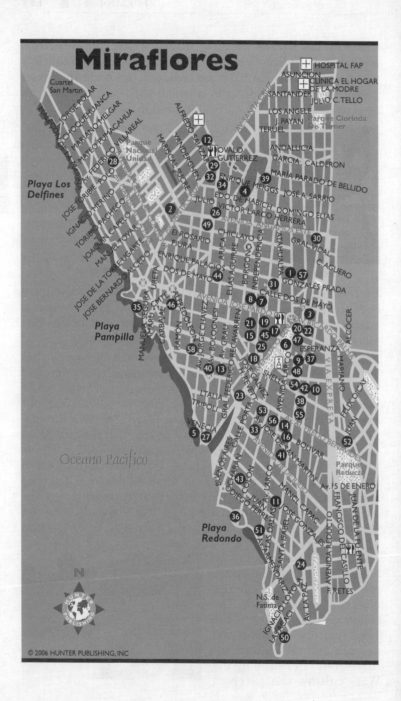

Miraflores

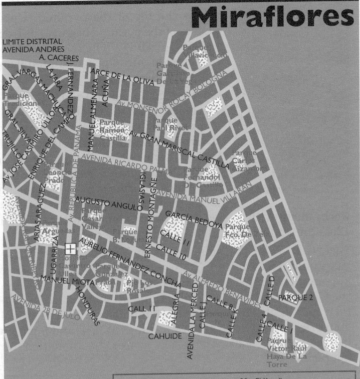

1. SAE
2. Museo Arqueologico Amano
3. House of Ricardo Palma
4. Huaca Pucllana
5. Parque de Amor
6. Parque Kennedy
7. Voluntarios Pub
8. Junius
9. El Tayta
10. Murphy's Irish Pub
11. The Corner
12. Palos de Mogur
13. El Oso Bar
14. Lola Bar
15. O Bar
16. Lava Lounge
17. Café Haiti
18. Café Zeta
19. Café Café
20. La Tiendecita Blanca
21. Scena
22. Tapas
23. Alfresco
24. Dalmacia
25. El Pasaje San Remon
26. Wa Lok
27. Punta Sal
28. La Mar
29. Bohemia café y mas/Etnico
30. El Kapallaq
31. La Gloria
32. Picasso
33. Rafael
34. Cuarto y Mitad
35. El Senorio de Sulco
36. La Rosa Nautica
37. Astrid y Gaston
38. Govinda
39. Huaca Pucllana
40. Brujas de Cachiche
41. Aparthotel San Martin
42. Hostal El Patio
43. Best Western Embajadores
44. Hotel Colonial Inn
45. La Case de los Sanchez
46. Explorer's House
47. IncaHaus
48. Flying Dog
49. Miraflores House
50. Miraflores Park Hotel
51. Marriot
52. Hotel Las Americas
53. Sol de Oro Suites Apart Hotel
54. Sonesta Posada del Inca
55. El Condado Hotel and Suites
56. Holiday Inn
57. Hoteles Mundo
58. Ayllu

Huaca Pucllana

from Ayacucho. They buried their leaders at the top of the pyramid. Upper phases of the pyramid began to be excavated in 1967. There is a small museum on-site. Open Wed-Mon 9 am-5 pm. Admission free.

Another historical site that sits just a few blocks from the Ovalo at the northern end of the park is the **House of Ricardo Palma** (Suarez 189, ☎ 445-5836). It was where the author of the famed *Tradiciones Peruana* lived from 1913 until the time of his death and has memorabilia related to his life and work, along with period furniture. Open Mon-Fri 9:15 am-12:45 pm and 2:30-5 pm. Admission 3 soles.

Tucked away in the side-streets of Miraflores is ★**Museo Arqueológico Amano** (Retiro 160, ☎ 441-2909), open by appointment only. The specialty of the collection is textiles of the Chancay culture, although there are many pieces of pottery and textiles from other Pre-Columbian cultures as well. Tours (in Spanish) are given weekdays at 3, 4, and 5 pm and last about one hour. Admission is free, but donations are appreciated.

Where to Stay

★**Miraflores Park Hotel** – Malecón de La Reserva 1035, ☎ 242-3000, fax 242-3393, www.mira-park.com, www.peruorient-express.com.pe. The most luxurious hotel outside of San Isidro. It earns its five stars officially because of its amenities, with ocean views, a gym, sauna, outdoor pool, and business center. Rooms are elegant, comfortable, clean, and anything you might need they have or will arrange. The restaurants are first-class, as is the Dr. Jekyll and Mr. Hyde Bar. $$$$$

★**Marriot** – Malecón de la Reserva 615, ☎ 217-7000, fax 217-7002, www. marriot.com. Excellent location, just behind Larcomar and every room has sweeping ocean views. Nearly 300 elegant rooms with every amenity imaginable, including hair dry-

ers, coffee makers, cribs, bathrobes, safes, highspeed Internet access (for a fee) and more. A brand new casino (one of the city's most modern) and a small upscale mall are attached. Parking is available. $$$$$

Hotel Las Americas – Benavides 415, ☎ 444-7272. One of Miraflores' best, located at the corner of Larco and Benavides, between Larcomar and Parque Kennedy. Twenty-one floors of rooms with couches, desks, and full bathrooms. Offers corporate discounts for business travelers. Booking online is significantly cheaper. $$$$

Sol de Oro Suites Apart Hotel – Jr. San Martín 305, ☎ 446-9876, fax 447-0967, www.soldeoro.com.pe. This is a five-star apart-hotel right in the center of Miraflores. Room service, laundry, parking, money exchange, business center, a pool, sauna, Jacuzzi, and gym are among the many amenities. The $140-$380 price tag includes breakfast. $$$$$

Sonesta Posada del Inca – www.sonesta.com. Not nearly as nice as the chain's property in San Isidro, but still an excellent value. The 28 rooms have nice little touches such as marble bathrooms and safes. Décor is simple and snug. The Inkafe restaurant is very good. $$$$

El Condado Hotel and Suites – Alcanfores 465-425, ☎ 444-0306, fax 444-1981, www.condado.com.pe. Convenient location near the corners of Larco and Benavides avenues. Rooms are well equipped with cable TV, mini-bars, and safes. Décor is modern and comfortable. Suites available. Gym. Piano bar/restaurant. $$$$

Holiday Inn – Benavides 300, ☎ 610-0700, fax 610-0707, www.holiday-inn.com. Just off Av. Larco. Basic Holiday Inn with no frills and a good value. A bit run-down, but if everything else is full at least you know what you will get. Indoor pool and fitness center. Parking available. $$$

Hoteles Mundo – Petit Thouars 5444, ☎ 241-3160, fax 447-0336, www.hotelesmundo.com. This five-story hotel, not far from the Indian markets is chic, cosmopolitan, and still new. The 46 rooms have air-conditioning, cable TV, desks, anti-allergenic floors, phones, mini-bars, and safes. Décor is homey, clean, and new. Excellent restaurant that serves Peruvian fusion dishes. Excellent value. $$$

Ayllu – José Gálvez 711, ☎ 243-0276, www.ayllu-peru.com. The best hostel in Miraflores and most have yet to hear about it. On a quiet side-street. Everything is sparkling new. There are just five rooms in the hotel, one of them a suite. Each is very cozy, clean, and has cable TV. Most have private baths. free Internet access and breakfast. 24-hour check in. Airport transfers, Spanish lessons. Calls itself a gay hotel that is hetero friendly. Highly recommended. $$

Best Western Embajadores – Juan Fanning 320, ☎ 800-332-7836 (in North America) or ☎ 242-9127, fax 442-9131, www.bestwestern.com. The same quality and reasonable price found throughout Best Western hotels worldwide. An easy choice if you just want something not too expensive, convenient, with medium standards. $$

Hotel Colonial Inn – Espinar 310, ☎ 241-7471, fax 445-7587, www.colonialinn.com. Thirty-four nicely decorated, clean Colonial-style rooms. Restaurant, room service, laundry, private parking, business center, and tours offered in their vintage cruiser. $$$

La Casa de los Sánchez – Diagonal 354, ☎ 444-1177. Convenient location just across from Parque Central. Rooms have all of the basic amenities, although furnishings are a bit worn. Free breakfast and Internet use. $$

Explorer's House, Alfredo León 158, ☎ 241-5002, explorers. house@yahoo.es. Has dorms and double rooms. Breakfast included. Walking distance to Parque Kennedy. Very friendly and welcoming staff who speak some English and are helpful with advice about Lima and Peru. One of the cheapest places in Miraflores. $

IncaHaus – Larco 189, ☎ 242-4350, fax 241-3701, www. incahaus.com. Perhaps the best hostel location in all of Miraflores. The building looks right over Parque Central. Accommodations vary from dorms to private rooms, with private or shared bathrooms. The remodeled house is clean, feels new, and a variety of services are offered. Free Internet access. $$

Flying Dog – Diez Canseco 117, ☎ 445-6745, fax 445-2376, www.flyingdogperu.com. This well known backpacker haunt is just behind IncaHaus. Rooms and rates are comparable to those of Incahaus. Can accommodate longer-term stays as well. $$

Miraflores House – Espinar 611, ☎ 584-2024, www. alberguemirafloreshouse.com. New family-style hostel run by the ever-delightful Francis Pierre Chauvel. He has a wealth of information on traveling in Peru. It's an old, rambling building with lots of personal, eclectic character. There is a long list of services: free Internet, use of kitchen, purified water, karaoke machine, DVDs, two lounge areas and kitchens, plus a book exchange. Dorms and private rooms. Baths are shared or private and have good electric showers. They can arrange long-term stays. Excellent location near Ovalo Gutierrez. $-$$

Lima

Hostal El Patio – Diez Canseco 341-A, ☎ 444-2107, fax 444-1663, www.andix.com/hostalelpatio. Right in the heart of Miraflores. Beautiful vine-covered brick courtyard. Kitchen available for use by guests. All rooms have private bathroom, hot water 24 hours, and a telephone. Continental breakfast included. Suites with kitchenette and cable TV also available. English spoken. Laundry service and money exchange. Airport pick-up is available. free parking. Gay-friendly. Highly recommended. $$

Aparthotel San Martín – San Martín 598, ☎ 242-0500, fax 242-0492, www.sanmartinhotel.com. Excellent location close to the center of Miraflores. Apartments are for two guests (or four with pull-out bed). Spacious suites with living-dining room, double bedroom with closet and bathroom, fully equipped kitchen, cable TV, and telephone. Cafeteria and bar on the top floor. See website for full details of facilities. Prices include continental breakfast. $$$

 Tip: If you need a laundromat (lavandería), try **Lavaqueen** at Larco 1158.

Where to Eat

 ★★**Las Brujas de Cachiche** – Av. Bolognesi 460, ☎ 447-1883, www.brujasdecachiche.com.pe. Named after the mystical neighborhood of Cachiche near Ica, this is an excellent option for classic creole. Try the lomo fino al Pisco con tacu-tacu de Pallares or a tuna fillet with elderberry sauce. Buffet lunches and plates of hors d'oeuvres are also offered. The sprawling mansion setting has a variety of dining rooms and an impressive 1,500-bottle wine cellar. See *Huaringas* below for the attached bar. $$$$

 ★★★**La Rosa Náutica** – Circuito de Playas (at the end of the Costa Verde pier), ☎ 445-0149. The Rosa is a famous restaurant and well loved on the tourist and tour circuit, and for a very good reason: the food is delicious, the view of the Pacific delightful, the service impeccable, and the décor elegant without being stuffy. Dining here is enchanting and shouldn't be missed. $$$$

★★★**Astrid y Gastón** – Cantuarias 175, ☎ 242-5387, www. astridygaston.com. This is the flagship restaurant of Gastón Acurio, one of Lima's and Peru's best chefs. A creative well-trained staff prepares exquisite dishes. Savor plates such as Puerto Montt salmon in a Carmenere wine sauce or slow-roasted baby kid goat with rosemary. The dessert menu is also astounding and worth a trip on its own. The lengthy wine list is available online. This is a definite stop for foodies on a dining tour of Lima. Perhaps Peru's best internationally known modern restaurant. $$$$

Govinda – Schell 634. Vegetarian, cheap menu; open from 12-2 pm, good value. $

Huaca Pucllana – Borgoño Cuadra 8, ☎ 445-4042. Set on the grounds of the Pre-Columbian pyramid of the same name, of which it has stunning views. Dine indoors or in the covered terrace outdoors. Food is a bit overpriced for the quality, but the setting is thought by many to make up for it. Style ranges from Novo-Andina to traditional criollo. $$$

★**El Señorio de Sulco** – Malecón Cisneros 1470, ☎ 441-0389, www.senoriodesulco.com. Opened in 1986 (in Surco) by one of Lima's best-known female chefs, Isabel Alvarez. The restaurant specializes in recovering lost recipes and fusing traditional Peruvian dishes with modern techniques, ranging from simple to exotic. Stewed tongue, suckling pig soaked in Pisco and slathered in a fruity sauce, and squid stuffed with shrimp, scallops, and mushrooms. Soups, seasonal dishes, and buffets are also on the menu. For dessert try Cape gooseberry or coca leaf ice cream. $$$$

El Kapallaq – Petit Thouars 488, ☎ 444-4149. Named after a Moche method of meat preservation, this restaurant's focus is on traditional, yet delicately prepared seafood recipes. Also of interest are the many clay pot stews that are offered. $$$

La Gloria – Atahualpa 201, ☎ 446-6504. One of the best restaurants in town for authentic Mediterranean cuisine. Seafood and pasta are the highlights. The wine list includes a nice selection of Chilean, Argentinean, and Spanish labels. There is also a busy bar area. $$$

Picasso – Santa Cruz 980-982, ☎ 422-1562. The food here is based on both the famous artist's work and his favorite reci-

Lima

pes, which were as strange and appealing as he was. It is Mediterranean for the most part, in style, décor, and taste. $$$

Rafael – San Martín 300, ☎ 242-4149. Chef and owner Rafael Osterling, who once cooked at London's Bibendum and Le Poissonnerie, came to Lima to launch his own restaurant. It is set in a graceful Miraflores mansion in the older part of the neighborhood. The style could be called Peruvian-Mediterranean fusion. The seafood and rice dishes are worth a nibble. The restaurant becomes a bar at night. On Thurs and Fri the tables are pushed back and DJs play electronic music to a dancing crowd. $$$$

Cuarto y Mitad – Av. Espinar 798, ☎ 446 5229. This is one of the places to go for meats and grills. American, Australian, and Argentine beef are all to be found here. There is a decent wine list and the restaurant also operates as a bar. For catering you can inquire at cmurgueitio@hotmail.com. $$$

Bohemia Café y Mas – Santa Cruz 905, ☎ 446-5240, www.bohemiacafé.com. Another restaurant by mogul Gastón Acurio with a frequently changing international menu. There are original takes on comfort foods like Italian spaghetti and cheese and meat fondue or trendy Peruvian dishes like anticuchos de pescado and yuquitos de Huancayo. Also features an array of pizzas, pastas, and sandwiches. There is a bar, Etnico (see below), and a small gallery on the top floor. $$$

Wa Lok – Angamos Oeste 700, ☎ 447-1314. Sprawling and flashy restaurant at Ovalo Gutierrez based on the famed Barrio Chino original. $$$

★**Punta Sal** – Chávez 694, ☎ 242-4524. Also located in San Isidro at Conquistadores 948, ☎ 441-7431. Excellent seafood. Owned by one of Lima's best-known chefs, Adolfo Perret. The ceviche list is long. There are many unique Novo Andina recipes served. The food is very good and, although not the cheapest, is well worth the price. Many tables have ocean views. $$$

La Mar – La Mar 770, ☎ 421-3365. The newest Gastón Acurio creation. This lunch-only seafood restaurant is very crowded, particularly on weekends, with people who want to see and be seen. Dishes range from traditional criollo, Asian fusion, sushi, and pasta. Plates are pleasing to the eye, as well as the palate. The cocktail menu, much of it Pisco-based, is considered by many, better and more creative than the food. $$$$

La Tiendecita Blanca (Café Suisse) – Larco 111, ☎ 445-9797. This café/restaurant has been open for more than half a century. International dishes like pepper steak, potato rosti, veal émince, and cheese fondue are served. The décor features leather furniture, enamel doors and photographs of Lima in the 50s and 60s. A favorite option for Italian, Swiss, and German tourists. $$$

Scena – Francisco de Paula Camino 280, ☎ 445-9688, www.scena.com.pe. This unique restaurant combines art and food at a whole new level. The worldly menu combines Moroccan, Turkish, Arabic, Spanish, Peruvian, French, and Italian flavors with a variety of exotic ingredients. The restaurant also holds shows and exhibits that change frequently and range from a typical gallery-style setting to a circus. $$$$

Tapas – Bonilla 103, ☎ 242-1564. This small, trendy restaurant and bar takes the idea of traditional Spanish tapas and combines them with international flavors and styles, such as Peruvian. There is a lengthy wine list and it stays open fairly late. $$$

Alfresco – Malecón Balta 790, ☎ 242-8960. This lunch-only cevichería has many variations of ceviche and tiradito (a marinated raw seafood dish in a creamy sauce), some of the best and most original in town. Other seafood dishes such as grilled baby octopus and prawn risotto are worth a try too. $$$

Dalmacia – San Fernando 401, ☎ 445-7917. Just a few hundred yards from the Miraflores cliffside, Dalmacia is a quiet, comfortable café that is a great place to savor the day. You can enjoy Mediterranean and Italian dishes, tapas, and Peruvian appetizers. Also a good place for coffee or a glass of wine for lunch or late in the evening. $$

El Pasaje San Remon, or "Pizza Street," has a dozen or so touristy restaurants, bars, and discotecs. Popular, but may sometimes have the feel of a lame college dance club. There are several pizzerias, as well as an English pub, Brazilian restaurant, Cuban restaurant, and others.

Lima

D'nnos Pizza is Lima's dominant pizza chain and has 11 locations scattered throughout the city, including Av. Benevides 1931, and Av. Comandante Espinar 408 in Miraflores. All deliveries can be arranged at the central office number, ☎ 219-0909.

Cafés

★**Café Haiti** – Parque Kennedy (next to McDonald's). A long-time favorite for Peru's artists, writers, and intellectuals. Large, reasonably priced menu with a respectable list of hot drinks. $-$$

Café Zeta – Gálvez and Diagonal. This trendy and popular corner café near Parque Kennedy is good for a relaxing drink or snack. Sidewalk seating. $

Café Café – Olaya 250, ☎ 445-1165, and at Larcomar, ☎ 445-9499. The two locations have large menus dedicated to coffee, tea, snacks, sandwiches, and, above all, desserts. $

Markets

Supermarkets are at **Plaza Vea** (on Av. Arequipa), **Metro** (near Parque Kennedy next to Ripley), and **Wong** (at Ovalo Gutierrez).

There is a great **organic food market** on Saturday near Benevides, across the Vía Expresa, which takes place on a quiet side-street near Parque Reducto. 8 am-3 pm. www.ecologicaperu.com.

Bars & Clubs

Aura – Larcomar Shopping Center, ☎ 242-5516. One of the chic upscale dance clubs in town. Somewhat exclusive. The crowd includes the international jet set, top models, students, and the urban élite. The club occupies two levels, one of which is a large dance floor with a Pacific-view terrace. The décor combines lots of glass, video screens, and a gentle blue lighting to emphasize the "aura" theme. The party starts late and ends early. Wednesdays are for electronic music, while Thursdays through Saturdays feature pop, Latin, and rock music. Drinks are expensive. Admission 40 soles.

Gótica – Larcomar Shopping Center, ☎ 445-6343. Next door and almost identical to Aura, with a slightly (very slightly) less yuppie crowd. One of the better spots in town for electronic music. It has the best resident and guest DJs. Fri nights are for electronic music. The terrace view is stunning here as well. There is a VIP room for the hippest of the hip. Empty before midnight. Admission 35 soles.

★**Huaringas** – Av. Bolognesi 460, ☎ 447-1883, www. brujasdecachiche.com.pe. Excellent lounge/bar area that fills up on weekend nights with young, attractive locals looking to be seen.

El Oso Bar – Recavarren 261. Inside an old run-down house. It doesn't look like much, but people are lined up around the corner to get in. The trendy crowd comes for the trendier music and packed dance floor.

Zuka Lounge – This is the glass-enclosed lounge area at Larcomar Shopping Center. You feel a bit like you are in a fish tank and, as in a fish tank, the people-watching is good. Try a Maracuya sour, a variation of the Pisco sour with passion fruit.

Lola Bar – Bolivar 197, ☎ 241-3000. This narrow bar area can get extremely crowded with Lima's upscale 20- and 30-somethings. The setting is somewhat Victorian, with red walls and couches for lounging. Stylish.

O Bar – Francisco de Paula Camino Cuadra 2. Owned by an expat Frenchman, this small bar is another one that attracts Lima's attractive youth.

Lava Lounge – Bolivar 116, ☎ 241-6606. Chic, exclusive and just opened in 2004. The walls are bright red, and a bit overpowering. Regardless, it's a nice place where the action doesn't get too loud or crazy. The pale-blue unisex toilets are interesting, to say the least.

Voluntarios Pub – Independencia 130, ☎ 445-3939. This two-story pub has one awesomely unique feature: the workers don't get paid. All actually are volunteers and profits go to charity. The place is simple and laid-back with plenty of sofa space. Food and appetizers are served throughout the day and night. Open late Thurs-Sat with DJs spinning a variety of music.

Etnico – Santa Cruz 805, ☎ 446-5240. This is the bar at Bohemia at Ovalo Gutierrez. Think martinis, stylish cocktails, and a beautiful crowd. Couches, cubes, and other interesting seating arrangements make you feel cool even if you are not. The worldly appetizer menu covers five continents.

> **Ovalos** are round intersections or traffic circles with many roads branching off of them. Several have shopping centers or large stores.

El Tayta – This second-level bar on Av. Larco (above Bembos) has a small stage, usually with live music. It gets pretty crowded on the weekends and is a good spot for pitchers of beer with friends.

Murphy's Irish Pub – Schell 627, ☎ 242-1212. Large traditional Irish pub with a loyal crowd of expats and Peruvians. Happy hours 6-9 pm. Live music Thurs-Sat.

The Corner – Larco 1207, ☎ 242-6429. If you just have to catch that game, this is probably the best place in Lima and all of Peru that carries satellite TV with North American and European sports. There is American-style pub food as well. $$

Palos de Mogur – Cavenecia 129, ☎ 221-836, www.palosdemoguer.com. This is a Colombian-based brewpub. If you are sick of Peruvian beer, this is the place to find lagers, stouts, pale ales, and others. They serve a variety of pub foods too.

Peñas

Junius – Independencia 125, ☎ 617-1000, ext 278, www.junius.com.pe. Dinner show combines traditional music and dance with food and drinks. $$$

★La Dama Juana – Larcomar, ☎ 447-3686, www.ladamajuana.com. Another dinner and dance show. It just opened at the end of 2005. The buffet is a bit overpriced, so I suggest eating elsewhere or just ordering the appetizers and drinks. The show is excellent, with dancers from across Peru performing. $$$

■ Monterrico

★★**Museo de Oro del Peru** – Alonso de Molina 1100 (Surco), ☎ 345-1292. Although it isn't as nice as the Museo del Oro in Bogota, Colombia, the entry fee is quite high and an investigation in 2001 claimed that a majority of the artifacts in the museum were fakes. But it's an interesting museum nonetheless. The museum claims the validity issue has been cleared up. Anyway, the collection consists of Inca and pre-Inca gold, jewelry, and ceremonial objects. A few mummies are on hand as well. The Weapons Museum is worth the price of admission on its own. The weapons throughout the ages from cultures all over the world are quite incredible to see. Open daily 11:30 am-7 pm. Admission 30 soles.

■ ★The Costa Verde

The city of Lima actually sits on a cliff, several hundred feet above the Bay of Miraflores. All the way from Chorrillos to Callao there is a major roadway, parking areas, recreation and beach areas at sea level with access

to the water. The name was derived from the vegetation that once grew on the cliffs; although much of it has disappeared, the name has not. During the summer months (January to April), the beaches are packed with sunbathers, outdoor enthusiasts and, at night, partygoers. The water is very dirty, although surfers, boaters, and jet skiers still make use of it. Many resorts have opened up to the north and south of the city, where the water is cleaner. They are frequented mainly by Limeños on the summer weekends. In the north there is Ancon, which is a bit older. In the South look for the resorts of San Bartolo or El Silencio. Also Punta Negra, Santa María, Naplo, Caballeros, and Pucusana.

■ Barranco

The name Barranco means sandy cliff, alluding to where the city sits. Along with Chorrillos, Barranco was a seaside resort for Lima's elite. The Creole bourgeoisie built homes there in the 19th and 20th centuries, as did many affluent German and British immigrants. Although some of the mansions have been neglected, just as many have been restored and Barranco's charm lies in strolling down a tree-lined avenue amidst these grand structures. There are modern houses and apartment complexes along the seaside cliffs, home to some of Lima's most prominent families. It is also where Lima's writers, poets, and artists live and, since the 1980s, has been considered Lima's Bohemian quarter. The last decade has seen a revitalization for Barranco. In turn, an influx of new restaurants, bars, clubs, cafés, and art galleries have made it one of the city's cultural hotspots. Many, including myself, consider it the most beautiful part of Lima.

The ★**Parque Municipal** features a pool with a Romanesque statue and fountain, a small amphitheater, tall trees, and many places to sit. A church, public library, cafés, restaurants, and bars surround it. It is quite peaceful during the day, although at night it becomes filled with people enjoying Barranco's popular nightspots. Small festivals are often held here and on most weekends you can find craft vendors selling their wares.

Puente de Los Suspiros

An attractive promenade called the **Bajada de los Baños** was built leading from the Plaza to the sea; now it is lined with a handful of charming seafood restaurants. Later the famous wooden bridge, the ★★**Puente de Los Suspiros**, the Bridge of Sighs, was built over it. At any given time you are likely to see courting couples walking hand-in-hand across it.

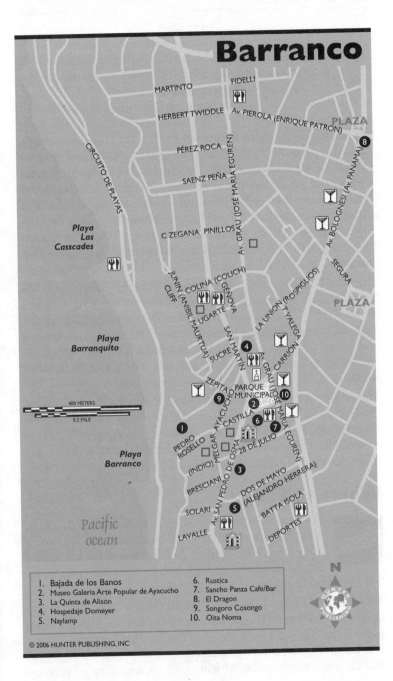

Barranco

MARTINTO FIDELLI

HERBERT TWIDDLE Av. PIEROLA (ENRIQUE PATRON)

PLAZA

PÉREZ ROCA

⑧

SAENZ PEÑA

CIRCUITO DE PLAYAS

Playa
Las
Casscades

C ZEGANA PINILLOS

Av. GRAU (JOSÉ MARIA EGUREN)

Av. BOLOGNESI (Av. PANAMA)

SEGURA

PLAZA

JUNIN (ANIBIL MAURTUA) COLINA (COLICH)
CLIFF GÉNOVA
UGARTE

Playa
Barranquito

SAN MARTIN
SUCRE

LA UNION (ROSPIGLIOS)
T VALEGA
CARRIÓN

④

ZEPITA

GRAU (JOSÉ MARIA EGUREN)

PARQUE
MUNICIPAL

⑨

②

⑩

AYACUCHO

CASTILLA

⑥

⑦

Playa
Barranco

①

PEDRO
ROSELLO

MELGAR

SAN PEDRO DE OSMA

(INDIO)

28 DE JULIO

⑤

BRESCIANI

Av. SAN PEDRO DE OSMA

DOS DE MAYO
(ALEJANDRO HERRERA)

Pacific
ocean

SOLARI

BATTA ISOLA

DEPORTES

LAVALLE

400 METERS
0.2 MILE

③

N

1. Bajada de los Banos
2. Museo Galeria Arte Popular de Ayacucho
3. La Quinta de Alison
4. Hospedaje Domeyer
5. Naylamp

6. Rustica
7. Sancho Panza Cafe/Bar
8. El Dragon
9. Songoro Cosongo
10. Oita Noma

HUNTER PUBLISHING

© 2006 HUNTER PUBLISHING, INC

*"Little bridge hidden by foliage and among yearnings,
little bridge stretched out over the wound of a ravine,
your pieces of timber make thoughts reappear,
the heart clings to your balustrades."*
(Singer and Barranco native Chabuca Grande)

The ★**Museo de Arte Colonial Pedro de Osma** (Pedro de Osma 421, ☎ 467-0141) reflects Barranco's charm and character. It is housed in stunning solid white Colonial mansion that is a work of art in itself. The museum contains a collection of Colonial paintings and furniture, as well as metalwork and sculptures. It sits just off the Parque Municipal. Only 10 visitors are allowed in at any given time. Open Tues-Sun 10 am-1:30 pm and 2:30-6 pm. Admission 10 soles adults/5 soles students.

The small but interesting **Museo de Electricidad** (Pedro de Osma 105), a few doors down, has a few interesting exhibits on electricity. The old electric tram that sits outside is the original tram that used to run between Barranco, Miraflores and Lima. Now it just runs to Chorrillos and back on weekends. Open Tues-Sun 9 am-1 pm and 2-5 pm. Admission 2 soles.

The fairly new **Museo Galeria Arte Popular de Ayacucho** (Pedro de Osma 116) is just across from the Museo de Electridad. If you don't plan on making it to Ayacucho, this is an excellent place to see some of the best crafts that come from Peru's craft capital. Admission free.

Where to Stay

Hostal Gemina – Grau 620, ☎ 477-0712, hostalgemina@yahoo.com. On main street above a busy shopping center. Rooms are a bit dark and dingy, but have private hot-water baths and cable TV. Includes breakfast. $$

The Point Hostel – Malecón Junín 300, ☎ 247-7997, www.thepointhostel.com. Run by two ex-backpackers. Nice location just off the Malecón with views of the Pacific. Internet access, hot water, tourist info, Spanish classes, book exchange, use of the kitchen, surfboards, parking garage, and airport pick-up are among the services. Dorms and doubles. Noisy party atmosphere. $

La Quinta de Alison – 28 de Julio 281, ☎ 247-1515, fax 247-6430. A great location, officially two stars, not far from the center of Barranco. The rooms are small and cozy. Interior rooms are dark, so grab one of the street-side rooms. $$

Barranco Backpacker's Inn – Castilla 260, ☎ 247-1326, www.barrancobackpackers.com. This budget option puts you just steps from Barranco's main Plaza. Rooms have private baths and hot water. Frequented by a younger crowd. Breakfast is included. Can arrange airport pick-up. $$

Hospedaje Domeyer – Domeyer 296, ☎ 247-1413. All rooms carpeted with private bathroom, hot water 24 hours, cable TV and room service. Includes continental breakfast. Laundry service. 15% discount for SAE (South American Explorer's Club) members. $$$

If you need a laundromat, try **Lavandería Neptuno** at Grau 912, ☎ 477-4472.

Where to Eat

★**La Canta Rana** (The Singing Frog) – Genova 101. Excellent neighborhood cevicheria, one of the best in town. Walls are filled to the ceiling with old photos and memorabilia. Nice classic atmosphere. Lunchtime only. Makes excellent chicha morada and Pisco sours. $$$

Restaurant Costa Verde – Circuito de Playas (Playa Barranquita), ☎ 477-5228. Mainly foreigners or locals there to celebrate a special occasion visit this famous seafood destination along the beach. Excellent, yet expensive seafood buffets with gourmet ingredients that are claimed to be in the *Guinness Book of World Records*. The dinner buffet will set you back about $60. $$$$

Al Grano – Montero Rosas 121 (Museo Pedro de Osma), ☎ 252-2828, algrano@speedy.com.pe. Peruvian culinary classics are fused with New Age techniques and styles – such as ravioli stuffed with ají de gallina (a spicy shredded chicken). Hard-to-find gourmet ingredients are used generously here.

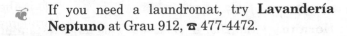

The setting cannot be beat. The restaurant sits inside the Museo Pedro de Osma, a jewel of a Colonial mansion. $$$$

Naylamp – Av. 2 de Mayo 239, ☎ 467-5011, restaurantenaylamp@yahoo.com. This is a courtyard location hidden just off a main street. The restaurant fuses contemporary and traditional Peruvian cooking and seafood. Owner Santiago Solari also produces his own Pisco. The setting is decorated with pre-Inca textiles and ceramics that only add to the charm. $$$$

★Manos Moreños – Pedro de Osma 409, ☎ 467-0421, manosmorenas@terra.com.pe. Set in a Colonial-style mansion with a large patio on a tree-lined street. It serves traditional criollo cooking with specialties like chupe de camarones, piqueos, and arroz con pato a la Chiclayana. Waitresses wear head wraps reminiscent of Afro-Peruvian women that once worked in coastal haciendas. During the evening, Wed to Sun, the restaurant becomes one of the best peñas in town. $$$

El Hornito – Grau 209, ☎ 477-2465. This large restaurant right on Barranco's main square has a great shady patio. The food is Italian, mostly pizzas. It can be crowded on weekend evenings for those looking for pre-clubbing cocktails and snacks. $$

★Bodega Bar Juanitos – Grau 274, ☎ 994-96176. Open for more than 60 years, this narrow, unassuming bodega still packs in the clientele. The look probably hasn't changed a bit, only the faces of the customers. The cured ham sandwiches are a hit, as are all the others. In the day it is filled with poets and writers looking for inspiration, at night with groups of friends sharing pitchers of beer. Although, there isn't a great reason why, it is hard not to fall in love with this place. $

Antica Trattoria – San Martín 201, ☎ 422-7939. Part of the national chain (see the *San Isidro* description above). The bar here is better than most others and is quite popular late in the week and on weekends. Often has live music. $$$

Rustica – Parque de Barranco 105, ☎ 247-9385. The buffet here is pretty crowded on the weekends. It features just about every criollo dish imaginable and the price is modest. It is a good place to start your Peruvian culinary adventures. $$

La Posada del Mirador – Ermita 104, ☎ 477-1120. The food is mediocre, but the restaurant has one of the best views in all of the city. It sits on the end of the Barranco cliffs, above and beyond the Puente de los Suspiros, and has sweeping views to the Pacific and the city. A nice spot for appetizers and a drink. A very romantic place and frequented by couples. $$$

Sancho Panza Café/Bar – Grau 209 A, ☎ 247-9871. Charming and finely decorated wine and tapas bar, with sandwiches, piques (samplers), salads, coffees, and postres (desserts). $$$

Bars/Clubs

★**Mochileros** – Pedro de Osma 135, ☎ 247-1225. This is a great bar set in a 100-year-old mansion, a declared historical sight and a one-time cultural center. It has kept the name, but the bar no longer is a backpacker (mochilero) hotel. There are several different sections. It is packed late at night on Wed through Sat with Lima's 20-somethings and a few backpackers from all over. There is a tree-filled outdoor patio, a smaller intimate lounge inside the Colonial house, and the usually crowded basement area which holds live performances. A variety of events are staged, such as concerts, theater, poetry readings, dance performances, and jazz sessions. Highly recommended.

★★**La Noche** – Bolognesi 307, ☎ 247-2186. This club has been one of the most popular in all of Lima for many years. There are a variety of settings within, each having space for a ton of people. The stage area has the feel of a House of Blues concert hall but without the Disney quality to it. That's a plus, by the way. Monday has jazz nights and is generally packed. Other nights the music delves into rock, indie, and electronic. There are also plays and poetry readings. The work of local artists and photographers is on the walls. There is an unplugged series from May to June. Cover is usually free, but can be as high as 30 soles. Highly recommended.

El Dragón – Nicolás de Piérola 168, ☎ 477-5420. One of Lima's most active clubs that has a variety of music genres played throughout the week. Wednesdays and Thursdays have live jazz or reggae acts, Fridays are for electronic music, and Saturdays vary. After any show, though, the place becomes a packed dance hall. On weekends a line stretches down the street to get in. Highly recommended.

Déjà Vu – Grau 294. Typical discoteca with drink specials, sweaty atmosphere, and open late.

Sargento Pimienta – Bolognesi 755, ☎ 247-3265. A live music hall and dance club, this has been a Barranco institution for decades. The name is the Spanish translation of the Beatles album *Sergeant Pepper*. The most popular beer served are the 2.5-pint bottles and the laid-back younger crowd swills them with ease.

La Estación de Barranco – Pedro de Osma 112, ☎ 247-0344. Located just off Barrancos' municipal park, this bar features a variety of live music throughout the week. Everything from traditional criollo, rock and jazz music to flamenco recitals and stand-up comedy.

Songoro Cosongo – Ayacucho 281, ☎ 247-4730. Not far from the Puente de Suspiros, this bar, named after a book by an Afro-Cuban poet, often features local musicians and poetry on Fridays and Saturdays. The Colonial mansion it occupies was declared a historical site. Also serves criollo food.

There is also a strip of bars and clubs on Carrión between the park and Bolognesi. Most are open all night on the weekends and filled with a young, 18+ crowd looking to party.

Peñas

La Candelaria – Bolognesi 292, ☎ 247-1314, www.lacandelariaperu.com. One of the best-known peñas in Lima and filled mostly with tourists. Dancers are many and thought to be some of the best. Usually a lively crowd that gets involved. Large drink and cocktail menu. A few appetizers are also offered.

Oita Noma – Av. Grau 296 in front of the municipal plaza, ☎ 247-6989, Mon-Sat 8 pm-4 am. This Peña/bar features live music, anything from Latin jazz standards, criollo and traditional rhythms. Hit or miss, depending on the band, the crowd, and the night. Serves food also.

Also try **El Llonja de Barranco** (Salaverry 139, ☎ 247-8011) and **Peña Del Carajo** (Chávez 403, ☎ 247-7977, www.del-carajo.com) for less touristy peñas with live music and shows. It is quite a ways from the center, so the best way to get there is to take a cab.

■ Chorrillos

The once small Indian fishing village of Chorrillos first became a fashionable seaside resort for the elite; now it has been sucked into Lima as a southern suburb. It was given the name (which means "trickles") because small streams of water ran from the cliffs here to the ground below. Some of the city's best seafood restaurants are found here, all of

Playa Herradura and Morro Solar

them visited frequently by mostly Limeños, and are virtually free of international tourists. Also a seafood market with many small shacks surrounded by small tables selling traditional dishes de la mar such as ceviche, tiradito, corvina, and lenguado. The first church was named after St. Peter, the patron saint of fishermen and, each June 29, the saint is paraded through the streets and later on a tour of the harbor. There are no hotels here, other than a few basic ones away from the Malecón, but if you have half a day to spare it can easily be wasted away. **Morro Solar**, the mountain at its end, is topped with lookouts, cell phone towers, a planetarium, several war monuments, and a giant white electric cross that can be seen for as far away as Callao. It is a popular destination for hikers and bikers, although you are advised not to go alone. At sea level, past the Club de Regattas health club and around Morro Solar, you will find **Playa Herradura**. The beach area is lined by a variety of restaurants that get crowded during summer weekends. The waves are said to be some of Lima's best for surfing and body boarding.

Where to Eat

 El Salto del Fraile – Camino a la Herradura ☎ 252-0259. One of the best ocean views in Lima, surrounded on three sides by water. Views overlook Playa Herradura on one side and the Pacific on the other two. It has become famous because everyday at 2 pm a monk (actually a staffer dressed like one) dives into the water. The food is very expensive and, for the most part, mediocre. They have a large menu of seafood, grilled meats, burgers, appetizers, and cocktails so you are sure to find something, though. Ask about lunch specials or buffets. $$$$

★**Sonia** – Lozano 173, ☎ 467-3788. This well-known cevicheria near Parque San Pedro was once a stand at the Chorrillos fish market, and the décor still reflects that. It is said to have invented the cooking styles of "chorrillana" and "a lo macho." The dishes are very reasonably priced and it attracts a wide range of clientele. $$

★**Luchita's** – Zepita 207, ☎ 467-6358. This dazzling building on the corner of Parque San Pedro has been a longtime favorite lunch retreat and has been operating for several decades. It was once run out of a nearby house, the house I lived in actually, and moved up from there. Sit in one of the Colonial dining rooms, the plant-filled courtyard, or the street-side patio. Open generally just for lunch. Ceviche is some of the best in Lima. Also try the criollo dishes like cau cau (tripe stew) and rocoto relleno (stuffed pepper), which are good too. $$

★**Los Pescadores** – The fish market in Chorrillos is where much of Lima's seafood comes from. There are dozens of small stands with outdoor seating that remain open throughout the day and early evening. They are particularly busy on the weekends. Make sure you see a menu or ask for a price before you order, though; several of the stands do their best to swindle upscale customers. $

CEVICHE

Ceviche is Peru's national dish. The fish, generally a firm whitefish, along with other seafood, are soaked in five ingredients: lime juice, onions, salt, onion and ají pepper, minutes before being served. A chemical reaction takes place in those few minutes and the juice actually cooks the fish. Clean, fresh, and simple is thought to be the key to the best ceviche. The leftover juice is called leche de tigre and is believed to cure hangovers. The dish is usually served with a spoon to drink it. Almost always, ceviche is served with a small piece of corn on the cob, sweet potato, and yucca. It is also made in Ecuador, but is slightly different. There it is served almost like a soup and tomatoes are added.

Gay & Lesbian Nightlife

Legendaris – Berlin 363 (Miraflores), www.gayperu.com/legendaris. A newer upscale gay and lesbian dance club. The large ground floor can hold about 250 people. Upstairs has two balconies to watch the action below. Open 11 pm until late. Entry is free on Wed, Thurs and Sun. On Fri and Sat it is 15 soles before midnight, 20 soles after midnight (includes one drink).

Sagitario – Wilson 869, (Downtown), ☎ 424-4383, www.gayperu.com/sagitariodisco. This exclusively gay club is busy every night of the week. It is one of the oldest in the center, although in a bigger and better location. The upstairs balcony overlooks the main dance floor. Entrance is free all night Sun to Thurs and before midnight on Fri and Sat. It is in an unsafe area of town, so take a taxi.

La Sede – 28 de Julio 441 (Miraflores), ☎ 242-2462, www.publasede.com. Both gay- and lesbian-friendly. Can get very crowded on the weekends. Music varies from 80s to Latino pop. Open Wed-Sat.

Kafe Kitsch – Bolognesi 743 (Barranco). One of the best and hippest gay clubs in Lima. Décor, like the name, is kitsch. The fish tank built into the floor is a memorable feature. A good variety of music from 80s pop, Latin top 40, and gay favorites gets the crowded dancing. Open Wed-Sat. No cover.

For more information on gay and lesbian Lima, see www.peruesgay.com (Spanish) or http://gaylimape.tripod.com/ (English).

Shopping

Handcrafts

★**Mercado del Indios**, the Indian Market – Petit Thouars 5245. Handicrafts from all across Peru. Slightly more expensive than elsewhere in the country, but very convenient if you want to buy something you didn't want to carry around or just forgot to pick up. **Artesanias Miraflores** (Av. Ricardo Palma 205) next door is similar.

There are artisans at **Parque Kennedy**, typically on the weekend. Paintings are the norm, but there is usually a good selection of Andean crafts from around Peru. Also, the **Plaza Municipal in Barranco** and **Parque Central** in the center often have craft stands.

For alpaca, there are several options. Most of the stores huddle around the end of Larco avenue, a few blocks from Larcomar. Some of the best are **Alpaca 111** (Larco 671) and **Sol Alpaca** (next door). They also have stores in Larcomar and in Cuzco.

Agua y Tierra – Diez Canseco 298, ☎ 444-6980. This is a great small store on a side-street that sells textiles, jewelry, carvings and other handicrafts, most of which come from Amazonian villages.

Department Stores

Jockey Plaza

Jockey Plaza – (Monterrico). The most upscale mall in town, with expensive international labels such as Kenneth Cole and Cartier.

★★**Larcomar Shopping Center** – www.larcomar.com. Simply stunning. At the end of Av. Larco in Miraflores. An excellent place to find tourist shops, restaurants, souvenirs, chain stores, entertainment, bars, and clubs. Also has bookstores, tour companies, and a DHL/Western Union. The view over the Pacific is quite spectacular.

Larcomar Shopping Center (N. Gill)

Saga Falabella – A huge Macy's-style department store with locations all over Lima and Peru. A new location recently opened in Ripley at Parque Kennedy and Jockey Plaza.

★**Polvos Azules** – Located south of Plaza Grau, across from Parque Central. The authorities overlook this black market. You will find mostly pirated goods such as DVDs, CDs, video games, electronics, clothes, and miles of shoes. It's a good place to buy back your stolen camera.

Camping Equipment

Tatoo Outdoors – At Larcomar. Has backpacks, hiking gear, and other accessories. Expensive.

Bookstores

The area around **Parque Kennedy** has the most bookstores, and is the best place to find books in English. Also try **Zeta** and **Ibero Librerias** in Larcomar shopping center.

Flower Market

At **Puente Santa Rosa**, at **Tacna** and the **Río Rimac**. If sending flowers to anywhere in Peru from anywhere in the world try **Floreria San Borja**, www.floreriasb.com.pe.

■ Sports

Bullfighting

The **Plaza de Acho Bullring** – Hualgayoc 332 (Rimac), ☎ 481-1467 – is just over the Río Rimac from downtown. Every October, during Fiestas

Patrias, and briefly in March, events are held. Spanish toreros (bullfighters) are most likely to appear. Tickets range from $20 to $100.

Horseracing

The **Jockey Club of Peru** – in the Hippodrome de Monterrico, ☎ 435-1035 – has races every Tues and Thurs, beginning at 6 pm, and at 2 pm on weekends.

Soccer

Estadio Nacional – la República between blocks 7 and 9. Hosts the most important soccer matches and other special events.

Golf

Lima Golf Club – (San Isidro). One of the most prestigious courses in Latin America. 18 holes, par 72. Members only, but can be accessed if staying at the Sonesta Posada del Inca El Olivar or the Country Club Lima Hotel, both in San Isidro (see page 144 ff above).

■ Adventures

On Water

Surfing

Although the water that surrounds it is polluted, Lima is a much bigger surfing destination than many expect. At any day of the year, crowds of surfers can be found in select spots up and down Lima's coast. Top spots are by **La Rosa Náutica** in Miraflores, **Playa Waikiki** in Barranco, and **Playa Herradura** in Chorrillos. **Punto Hermosa**, farther south near Pachacamac, is also a favorite destination.

Surf Shops

Tello – Berlin 270 (Miraflores), ☎ 583-1607, telloperu@yahoo.es.

Derrem Surfboards – Aguials 280 near Aramburu and Vía Expresa (San Isidro), ☎ 9913-9094, derrem_surfboards@hotmail.com.

Big Head Surf Shop – Larcomar shopping center, 242-8123, www.bigheadperu.com.

Surf Lessons

Whilar Surfing School – ☎ 252-3247, http://wsurfing.tripod.com. Instructors speak Spanish and English. Many lesson packages available. Equipment rental.

Boating

 Islas Palomino – Arequipa 4960 #202 (Miraflores), ☎ 9949-4867, www.islaspalomino.com. This sea lion observation tour leaves from the port of Callao. Tours visit the mini-archipelago that comprises the Islas Palominos. You will visit the rocky islands of Palomino, San Lorenzo, Cabinzas and El Fronton. You will likely see sea lions, marine birds such as boobies, pelicans, and maybe Humboldt penguins. You can dive in and swim with hundreds of gentle sea lions. It isn't nearly as good as the Islas Ballestas near Pisco, but if you are not going to make it there, this is a good alternative. The tour lasts for four hours and is on a comfortable yacht rather than a large speedboat as in the Ballestas. Departures are daily. Starts at about $30 per person.

Sea lions on Islas Palomino

On Wheels

Biking

 Although the country's best biking destinations are in the Andes, Lima has quite a bit to offer. A few of the major routes:

- **Coastal Road** – The coast road stretches the length of the Costa Verde from Callao to Chorrillos.
- **Pachacamac** – The trip is more than 31 kms/18 miles, much of it through the desert, so bring ample water.
- **Morro Solar** (Chorrillos) – The mountain in Chorrillos has a steady climb over paved and dirt roads.

For a bike tour in Lima or elsewhere in the country, try **Peru Bike Tours** – 28 de Julio 1381, Miraflores, ☎ 241-6367, www. perubike.com. This is the number-one agency offering biking trips around Peru. They are pricey, but they offer the best equipment and arrange tours that suit the riders' needs, skill level, and wants. Up to 15-day all-inclusive tours. Highly recommended.

On Horseback

The area around Lima is filled with natural beauty that few venture out to see. One of the best and only ways to explore it is on a Peruvian Pasofino horse. **Cabalgatas** (☎ 9837-5813, www. cabalgatas.com.pe) offers a variety of tours around Lima and in other parts of the country. Two hours on the beach, mountains, or valleys around Lima are just $45 per person. Will also arrange trips to Pachacamac and the Lurin Valley.

Pasofino horses

In the Air

Paragliding

Along the coast you will often see a paraglider or two floating above Larcomar shopping center and elsewhere on the Costa Verde. The Gandhi Park, between San Isidro and Magdalena, is where most enthusiasts launch. If you would like to go as well but don't have your own equipment, several companies will sell you the experience. **PeruFly** (Jorge Chávez 666, ☎ 444-5004, fax 444-5004, www.perufly.com) offers a variety of in-the-air acrobatic lessons. Hangliding, paragliding, bungee jumping, hot air balloons are offered up and down the coast and throughout he country.

■ Tours

Tour Companies

Lima

Lima Tours – Office at Larcomar shopping center, ☎ 619-6900, www.limatours.com.pe. This is the best company for city tours, Pachacamac, and anything else in the Lima area. Also books trips on Peru rail for Machu Picchu (which should definitely be booked ahead of time). Also arranges gay and lesbian tours.

Local Tours – San Tadeo 261, Surco, ☎ 241-6983, www.localperu.com. Arranges surfing trips, city tours, all sorts of adventure activities, jungle trips, etc.

Inka Natura – Banon 461, (San Isidro) ☎ 444-2022, and at Larcomar shopping center, www.inkanatura.com. Arranges upscale tours to many destinations in the country including some of the leading hotels and sights. Birding tours, Machu Picchu, and Manu are some of the most common.

Fertur Peru – Schell 485, ☎ 445-1974, http://ferturperu.tripod.com.

Equss Peru – ☎ 578-3038, www.equssperu.com. Offers city tours, museums tours, Pachacamac, and nightlife tours.

Kolibri Expeditions – ☎ 476-5016, www.kolibriexpeditions.com. Arranges the most complete birding trips all over Peru, including several day-trips from Lima.

Independent Guides

Mariem Valdez – ☎ 252-1982 (studio), ☎ 9977-9987 (cell), mariemvaldez@hotmail.com. A local artist, longtime traveler, educated in the US who arranges tours and can be a guide around Lima and the country in her spare time. Speaks four languages. Prices vary depending on the number of people.

Also does massages, gives surfing lessons, and rents rooms in Chorrillos. Highly recommended.

■ Language Schools

El Instituto Cultural Peruano NorteAmericano, or ICPNA, offers four weeks of classes (two hours a day Mon-Fri) for about $115, including a book. One of the cheapest places in Lima for lessons. Many different levels offered.

El Sol Spanish School – Solar 469 (Miraflores), ☎ 242-7763, www.elsolidiomasperu.com.

■ Entertainment

Casinos

You can find small gaming halls scattered throughout the city, particularly in Miraflores. Here are some of the best known:

- **Sheraton Lima Hotel and Casino**, Av. Paseo de la República 170 (in the center), ☎ 315-5050, all cards are accepted. Slots are open 24 hours, gaming tables 6 pm-6 am daily.

- **Golden Palace**, Av. República de Panama 3165, San Isidro, ☎ 441-8817, www.casinogoldenpalace.com.pe. Daily 6 pm-6 am. Slots, 24 hours, all card games offered.

- **Casino La Hacienda**, Av. 28 de Julio 511, Miraflores, ☎ 445-3980. All credit cards are accepted. Slots are open 24 hours, gaming tables 6 pm-6 am daily.

Movies

The best in Lima is the **UVB Theaters** at Larcomar Shopping Center in Miraflores. Also try **Cine Planet** – Ovalo Gutierrez (Miraflores), ☎ 452-7000, www.cineplanet.com.pe, **Cinemark** at Jockey Plaza (Monterrico), and **Pacifico**, behind the McDonald's at the oval on Parque Kennedy.

Tip: All theaters in Lima discount their prices on Tuesdays.

Theater

 Teatro Segura – Huancavelica 265 (downtown), ☎ 426-7189. After the Municipal Theater burned down several years ago, the Segura began hosting operas, ballets, and symphonies.

Teatro Britanico – Bellavista 527 (Miraflores), ☎ 447-9760. Usually has performances in English.

Sala Teatral Preludio – Salaverry 2802 (San Isidro), ☎ 261-9777, preludio@telefonica.net.pe. Holds various exhibitions, performances, and cinema.

Centro Cultural PUCP – Camino Real 1075 (San Isidro), ☎ 616-1616, http://cultural.pucp.edu.pe. Hosts a variety of dance troupes, musical acts, plays and a cinema.

■ Day-Trips from Lima

Situated 31 km/18 miles south of Lima on the Pan-Americana (Pan American Highway), the ★★**Pachacamac archeological complex** (☎ 430-0168) is by far the most important Pre-Columbian ruin in the region.

The vast ceremonial center has numerous adobe temples and pyramids dating back as far as 200 AD. The oldest building dates from the Maranga civilization, but it was the Waris who constructed most of the structures here. The Incas made contributions, so there are a variety of cultures represented. The name is derived from the Wari god who was thought to be creator of the world and whose carved wooden statue can be seen in the on-site museum.

When the Incas arrived on the scene about a thousand years after the Waris, rather than destroy the temple and the beliefs associated with it, sensing its power, they allowed it to co-exist with their own religious practices. The Incas added the **Templo del Sol** (Temple of the Sun), which was built of

both stone and adobe, on a rocky hill overlooking the temple and also the **Palacio de Las Mamacuna** (House of the Elect), which was a convent for young maidens to service the deity. The Inca complexes have seen the most excavation. You can climb the stairs to the top of the temple, where there are views of the coast. The Palacio can be entered with a guide for around 5 soles.

These ruins, like most adobe structures, have not withstood the test of time. The Temple still stands, as does the rectangular area beside it where pilgrims would leave their offerings. It was the most important place of pilgrimage in the coastal region, and people would travel from across Peru to make their offerings.

The small museum, visitors' center, café, and craft shops are open during the same hours as the complex. You can ask for a site map at the visitors' center. Most tours will drive from each site to the next. If walking, allow about two hours to see the entire complex. Buy water as the dry desert heat can hit you quickly.

You can get to the complex on a guided tour through any of the agencies listed above. Price depends on the number of people in the group and starts at about $20 per person. The tours last several hours. On the Av. Paseo de la República in Miraflores you can catch a frequent bus that will take an hour or so for less than a $1. Look for any bus that says Pachacamac on the front.

The complex is open daily 9 am-5 pm. Admission 5 soles adult/ 2 soles student.

Tip: If you don't want to pay for a tour and don't want to walk through Pachacamac, there are several other options. You can rent a Peruvian Paso horse to take you around the complex, although this should be arranged in advance by calling the visitors center. Another excellent option is cycling around the site. There are some good tracks and climbs.

★**Caral** – www. caralperu.gob.pe. Believed to be the oldest civilization in the Americas. Dating back to over 3000 BC, this earliest of settlements developed almost simultaneously with the civilizations of Mesopotamia, Egypt, India and China. The site is only recently being excavated and the information learned is disproving much of what was previously believed about early Peruvian societies. The Supe, who lived here, had a social organization with stratified ranks, based on occupa-

Caral overview

The Amphitheater

Supe mother goddess

tion, and an unequal distribution of the socially produced wealth. The site will likely become a first-class national and international tourist destination. There are a variety of pyramids, circular plazas, and other adobe structures on 185 acres.

The Sacred City of Caral, as it is now being called, is located in the Supe Valley, province of Barranca, 182 km/109 miles north of Lima. You can visit the site from 9 am-5 pm. Getting there can only be done on your own at this time. You must drive to Km 184 on the Pan American Highway north and make a right on a small marked road that will lead for 23 km/14 miles to Caral.

The Southern Coast

■ Chincha Alta

Phone code (056)

The Negro/Criollo town of ★**Chincha Alta** (120,000 population) on the road from Lima north of Pisco is an important site for Peru's African culture. Afro-Peruvian rhythms are tops here and can best be heard at the local peñas, particularly the ones in the district of El Carmen. Catacombs that

IN THIS CHAPTER

■ Chincha Alta	187
■ Pisco	190
■ Ica	195
■ Nazca	203
■ Arequipa	211
■ Chivay	237
■ Yanque	238
■ Cabanaconde	239
■ Tacna	242

many slaves once passed through can be visited for $3 per person from **Hacienda San José** in El Carmen (☎ 224-458). The **Festival of Verano Negro** is held at the end of February and that is the best time to visit the peñas. To get here you must take any Lima to Ica/Ica to Lima bus, which will pass through Chincha Alta.

Musica afroperuana

HIGHLIGHTS

■ **Wine and Pisco tasting** – Sample the world's largest Pisco-producing region and some of the finest wine Peru has to offer.

■ **Islas Ballestas** – See seals, frigate birds, and Humboldt penguins in the poor man's Galapagos.

■ **Santa Catalina Monastery** – Walk through the secluded city within a city, one of Peru's most revered Catholic landmarks.

■ **Nazca Lines** – Take a gut-wrenching flight in a five-seater plane for the best view of the Nazca lines.

■ **Adventure** – Trek Colca Canyon, climb El Misti, or raft in Cotahuasi.

Where to Stay

Hostal Sausal – Km 197.5, ☎ 26-2451, sausal@exalmar.com. pe. This resort-style hotel is right on the Pan-Americana (Pan American Highway) and has nice gardens, a great pool, and lots of room for lounging around. $$

★Hacienda San José – About 14 km/8.4 miles from Chincha, ☎ 224-458, hsanjose@terra.com. pe. This isolated historic country estate is surrounded by citrus groves and gardens. Built in 1688, it served as a sugar and honey plantation for nearly 200 years until a notorious rebellion by the slaves took place. A series of catacombs can be seen below the small chapel. Buffet lunches, Afro-Peruvian dance shows, dance classes, and tennis courts make this a great weekend retreat from Lima and at quite a reasonable price. A taxi here should cost 12-15 soles from Chincha. $$$

Day-Trips from Chincha

Wakama (www.wakama-ecoplaya.com) is a great beach resort filled with Limeños. It isn't too far from Lima at 178 km/107 miles (two hours) to the south. The colorful bungalows $$$ are rented for four or eight people and are wildly popular during the summer months

or holidays. Each has private freshwater showers (cold), four-

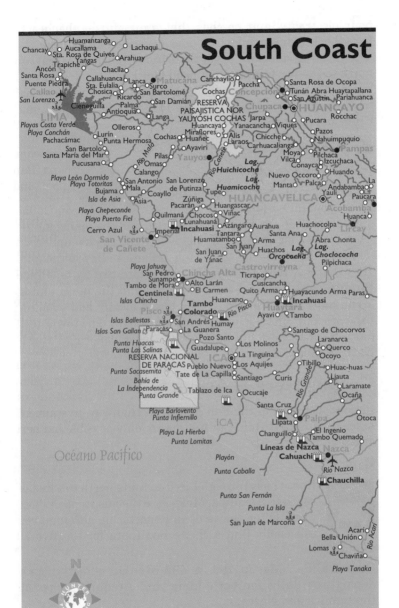

South Coast

Huamantanga
Chancay · Aucallama · Lachaqui
Sta. Rosa de Quives · Arahuay
Ancón · Trapiche · Yangas
Santa Rosa · Chaclla
Puente Piedra · Callahuanca · Lanca · Canchaylio · Paccha · Santa Rosa de Ocopa
San Lorenzo · Sta. Eulalia · Surco · Cochas · Tunán Abra Huaytapallana
Callao · Chosica · San Bartolomé · San Agustín · Pariahuanca
LIMA · Ricardo · San Damián · RESERVA · HUANCAYO
Cieneguilla · Palma · PAISAJISTICA NOR · Rocchac
Antioquia · Langa · YAYOSH COCHAS · Jarpa · Pucara
Playas Costa Verde · Olleros · Huancaya · Yanacancha · Viques · Pazos
Playa Conchán · Miraflores · Alis · Nahuimpuquio
Pachacámac · Cochas · Huañec · Laraos · Carhuacalianga
San Bartolo · Punta Hermosa · Ayaviri · Moya · Pilchaca
Santa María del Mar · Pilas · Vilca · Conayca · Izcuchaca
Pucusana · Omas · Lag. · Nuevo Occoro · Huando
Playa León Dormido · Calango · Huichicocha · Manta · Palca · Andabamba
Playa Totoritas · San Antonio · San Lorenzo · Lag. · Yauli · Paucara
Bujama · Mala · de Putinza · Huamicocha · HUANCAVELICA · Acobamba
Isla de Asia · Coayllo · Tupe · Zúñiga · Huanca
Playa Chepeconde · Pacarán · Huangascar · Huachocolpa
Playa Puerto Fiel · Quilmaná · Chocos · Viñac · Lircay
Cerro Azul · Lunahuaná · Azángaro · Aurahua · Abra Chonta
San Vicente · Imperial · Incahuasi · Tantara · Santa Ana · Lag.
de Cañete · Huamatambo · Arma · Choclocócha
San Juan · San Juan · Huachos · Lag. · Pilpichaca
de Yánac · Orcotocha
Playa Jahuay · Chincha Alta · Ticrapo · Castrovirreyna
San Pedro · Cusicancha
Sunampe · Alto Larán · Quito Arma · Huayacundo Arma Paras
Tambo de Mora · El Carmen · Incahuasi
Centinela · Huancano · Ayavi · Tambo
Islas Chincha · Tambo · Río Pisco
Pisco · Colorado · Santiago de Chocorvos
Islas Ballestas · San Andrés · Humay · Laranarca
Islas San Gallán · Paracas · La Guanera · Querco
Punta Huacas · Pozo Santo · Coyo
Punta Las Salinas · Guadalupe · Los Molinos · Tibillo · Huac-huas
RESERVA NACIONAL · La Tinguiña · Ljauta
DE PARACAS · Pueblo Nuevo · Los Aquijes · Santiago · Curis · Laramate
Punta Sacasemita · Tate de La Capilla · Ocaña
Bahía de · Tablazo de Ica · Ocucaje · Santa Cruz
La Independencia · Río Grande
Punta Grande · Playa Barlovento · Llipata · Palpa · Otoca
Punta Infiernillo · ICA · Changuillo · El Ingenio
Playa La Hierba · Tambo Quemado
Punta Lomitas · Líneas de Nazca · Nazca
Playón · Cahuachi
Punta Caballa · Río Nazca
Chauchilla
Punta San Fernán
Punta La Isla
San Juan de Marcona
Acari
Bella Unión · Río Acari
Lomas · Chaviña
Océano Pacífico · Playa Tanaka

N · HUNTER PUBLISHING

hour electricity, and porches that are right on the beach. Horseback riding, volleyball, and massages are among the activities you can plan. To get there from Chincha you must go north to Puerto Jahuay, then head four km/2.4 miles west. If you do not have your own transportation, you can take a taxi from Chincha (one hour) or ask to be let off of the Lima/Chincha bus at Puerto Jahuay.

■ Pisco

Phone code (034)

Just a short distance west of the Pan American Highway, Pisco (population 60,000) is the largest port between Callao and Matarami. A statue of San Martín and the mansion, the Club Social Pisco, mark the spot where the city's founder set up his headquarters after landing in Paracas Bay in the mid-16th century. Today's Pisco is divided into two parts, **Pisco Pueblo**, with Colonial-style buildings and the main tourist area, and **Pisco Puerto**, consisting of mostly bad-smelling fisheries and the Puerto General San Martín. The town itself has little of interest; but it is a good base for exploring Paracas National Reserve and the Islas Ballestas.

Getting Here & Around

Pisco is just west of the Pan American Highway, five km/3.5 miles from Reparticion. Car rentals are only possible in Lima or Arequipa.

Bus

 Buses pass through Pisco en route north to Lima or south to Arequipa. Make sure the bus stops in Pisco itself. Often they stop in Reparticion, although you can easily find a cheap taxi there for the five-10 minute ride.

Ormeño (San Martín 199, ☎ 532-764) has almost hourly departures daily for both Lima and Arequipa, passing through Ica and Nazca.

Sightseeing

Other than the world-class marine and desert environments nearby, Pisco is only worth a quick look. The **Plaza de Armas** in the center of town is the hub of activity, with most of the hotels, restaurants, and travel agencies being here.

Iglesia de la Compañía

On any given day you can find strolling locals selling tejas here, which are a local sweet made with almonds. The **Iglesia de la Compañía** near the Plaza is the architectural highlight of Pisco, with beautiful hand-carved pulpit and gold-leafed altarpiece.

Where to Stay

The Regidor – Arequipa 201, ☎ 535-220, regidor@mail.cosapidata.com.pe. With TVs, fans, sauna, and a café. This is the only mid-range hotel in Pisco. Most opt to stay in Paracas. $$

Hotel Paracas – On the bay, ☎ 221-1736. In a nice setting near the water and with good, but pricey, food. $$$

El Mirador – Near the dunes at the beginning of town, ☎ 66-5842. Arranges boat trips and can offer full board. $

Where to Eat

There are plenty of small but very good cevicherias and open-sided seafood restaurants near El Chaco, such as **Jhonny Jennifer** ($) and **El Chorito** ($). In Pisco, **El Catamaran** (Comercio 166, $$) has good Italian dishes and **Don Manuel** (Comercio 179, $$) isn't a bad choice either.

Southern Coast

Day-Trips from Pisco

Flamingoes (Heinz Plenge)

On the Paracas peninsula just 15 km/nine miles south of Pisco is the ★**Paracas National Reserve**. It has an almost lunar landscape with miles of drifting sand dunes bordered on one side by high cliffs and rock formations that seem to come right out of the bay. Sandstorms, which lend the park its name, pick up in the late afternoons, the strongest in August. They can last for days. Two **museums** sit side-by-side near the park entrance. The first is unnamed and is free with park admission ($2). It has displays about the park and its animals, birds, the cultures that once lived here, and geological facts. Next door, the small **Archaeological Museum** ($1 extra), has a few artifacts from the Paracas and Ica peoples. If you will be going to the archeological museums in Ica or Lima, though, this one can definitely be skipped.

PARACAS CULTURE

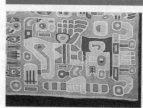

The 9,000-year-old Paracas culture, which peaked from 2000 BC to 500 BC, thrived in the area west of the Andes that is now coastal desert. It is believed that either the dunes kept growing year by year, practically burying the culture beneath the sand, or that heavy flooding pushed the Paracas inland around 200 AD and then the Incas absorbed them. The dry climate today has created the perfect conditions for preserving funerary bundles, as well as huge textiles that are up to seven feet wide with various zoomorphic images such as seabirds and fish. Examples of these textiles, for which the Paracas are best known, are at the archaeological museums in Ica and Lima.

In the bay near the museums, except from January to March, Chilean flamingos can be seen. Andean condors and many other rare species of birds can also be spotted in the park. Bring binoculars. Other sights include a spot on the cliffs

La Catedral

where you can look out for miles at the divide between cliffs and ocean and also see **La Catedral**, a large rock formation that comes right out of the water. Roads are dry, dusty and rough and it is recommended that you go with a tour or by car, rather than trying to walk it. Paracas is often included in Islas Ballestas tours. Contact any travel agency in Pisco.

About 40 km/24 miles inland from the Pan American Highway sits the pleasant valley town of **Lunahuana**. Although small, the town has quite a bit to offer in the way of outdoor activities. Good kayaking can be had upriver on the Río Grande. Rafting (about $25 a trip) is excellent as well, levels being at 4-5 from November to April. The rapids are level 1-2 from May to October. See www.lunahuana.com or call ☎ 946-8309 for more information.

In February the town holds an extreme sports festival. The town is also a good base for a trip to the rarely visited ruins of **Incawasi**, 8 km/4.8 miles west, and **Ungara**, near Cañete.

Several bodegas or wineries sit in the valley, including **Bodega la Reyna de Lunahana** that also produces Pisco and welcomes visitors (☎ 449-6433).

High in the Pisco Valley, 48 km/29 miles from Pisco itself, are the well-preserved Inca ruins of **Tambo Colorado**. Most of the buildings

Tambo Colorado (Lizardo Tavera)

retain their original red-painted walls and adobe bricks. It is a great example of traditional Incan architecture with trapezoidal windows and doorways. You can still make out most of the dwellings and storehouses, all without roofs. To get there, take a taxi from Pisco ($25) or go on a tour with a guide ($10 per person). Alternatively you can get to the site by bus or collectivo (shared taxi) from Pisco ($1.50, three hours).

Adventures on Water

★★Islas Ballestas

The Islas Ballestas are Peru's own version of the Galapagos, albeit much more accessible – one of the world's best places to see rare marine birds such as the Guanay cormorant, Peruvian booby, Peruvian pelican, and the Humboldt penguin. The Paracas Bay is rich in marine plankton, which is nourishment for many fish and their predators. Dolphins and occasionally killer whales can be seen en route to the islands. Surrounded by glowing turquoise waters, the islands themselves are quite scenic with several natural arches and deep caves. The birds number in the tens of thousands and live on the small rocky islands a half-hour by boat from the mainland.

Sea lions can be seen swimming in the rough waters and sleeping and barking on small outcroppings. Hundreds of them gather on one small beach, making an overwhelmingly horrific sound. A truly awesome experience. The females live in harems of 15 or more for each male, each producing one offspring each year. The largest adult male with the largest harem was nicknamed "Mike Tyson" by the locals. Nearby **Isla San Gallán**, a favorite spot for wildlife television shows, where the sea lions number in the thousands, is only accessible for scientific purposes, despite what some may tell you.

Boat tours go to the Islas Ballestas from the dock at El Chaco beach and can be arranged through every hotel and travel agency in Pisco, Paracas, and Ica. They cost roughly $10 for a half-day tour (slightly more from Ica). Agencies pool their clients together, so everyone ends up being on the same boats and all leave together at around 7:30 am, returning at about 11 am. The speedboats seat 30-40 people, four across. A tight fit. Try and get a seat in the front or on the side for the best photos. En route to the islands, boats pass the Nazca-era 50-yard long Candelabra on a hillside facing the Pacific. The tours can be and most often are combined with a half-day trip to Paracas National Reserve. Some hotels in Pisco and Paracas will arrange tours in their own private boats. They are more comfortable and generally more expensive.

For more information, contact the **Zarcillo Connection**, a tour operator at San Francisco 111 (☎ 262-795, www.zarcilloconnection.com). **Paseo Turístico Islas Ballestas** has English-speaking guides (San Francisco 109, ☎ 262-576). Also try **Paracas Isles Tours** (Comercio 128, ☎ 665-872).

 Did You Know? The nitrogen-rich droppings of the birds on the Islas Ballestas are perfect for fertilizer. The shear numbers of birds make it possible to collect the guano commercially and sell it to international markets.

■ Ica

Phone code (034)

Ica (population 200,000), between Pisco and Nazca, is Peru´s wine production capital and plays host to several interesting sites and events. Jerome Luis Cabrera founded the town in 1563, although, because of several large earthquakes, it has moved its center several times. It rarely rains here, except during an El Niño, when the city is prone to flooding. In 1998, the El Niño was particularly bad, leaving Plaza de Armas under three feet of water.

Getting Here

Ica is 70 km/42 miles southeast of Pisco, straddling the Pan American Highway.

Bus

Buses link Ica to Lima, Nazca, Arequipa, and Pisco. Ormeño (at the west end of Salaverry, ☎ 232-622) and Cruz del Sur (west end of town on Municipalidad, ☎ 233-333) offer many connections daily to each location.

Tourist Information

Tourist Offices – Tourist information can be found at a small office at Grau 150, open 8 am-2:30 pm weekdays. Also try the **Touring y Automóvil Club del Peru**, Fermin Tanguis 102, ☎ 219-393, ica@touringperu.com.pe.

Sightseeing

The center of Ica is not much to look at. **Plaza de Armas** is nice for an afternoon stroll, stopping at the occasional souvenir shop (many have local wines), restaurant, or casino. There are two muse-

Catedral de Ica (Anibal Solimano)

ums of interest. The ★**Museo Regional de Ica** is a great one, among the best in the country. It is 1.5 km/.9 mile from Plaza de Armas. You can take bus number 17, although on foot or by cab is also possible. It is perhaps the best place to learn about the Paracas, Nazca, and Ica cultures, which predated the Incas by thousands of years. The modern museum is well laid-out and, although small, incredibly informative. Collections of artifacts include Paracas weavings, mummies, skulls, trophy heads, and quipus (knotted strings used by the Incas for counting). In the rear there is a scale model of the Nazca lines, mirador and all. It is open every day from 9 am-6 pm.

Museo Cabrera at Bolivar 160, although a bit expensive at $5, is sure to make a lasting impression. On display are thousands of carved stones and boulders that seem to depict modern surgical techniques as well as images of day-to-day life. The owner claims the stones are hundreds of years old, although this hasn't been confirmed.

Most of Ica's sights, such as Cachiche, the Bodegas and Wineries, and Huacachina, lie outside the center and can be reached on foot or by cab. The poverty-stricken district of ★**Cachiche**, a place of crumbling adobe house with little or no electricity or plumbing, is a five-minute ride from the Plaza. It is well-known throughout Ica folklore as a place of sorcerers and curaderos (healers), aka white witches. The **Parque a la Bruja** is considered to be a center of high energy, with a dirt pathway dividing the yin and the yang. Many huge date palms have sprouted seven heads and grown in bizarre directions. One of the heads is always cut off, though, seven being an unlucky number. Several animal shapes, such as a bear and an elephant, have mysteriously appeared in the trunks of the palms and can be pointed out if you ask the right person. A golden monument of a ghastly siren marks the spot where practitioners of bad magic were supposedly burned at the stake. A "shaman" has built a small pyramid in the back of a shop at the edge of the park, where he holds shamanic rituals. He also does palm readings, although another "shaman" with pure white hair, who sits in a plastic chair near the monument, looks more authentic.

Adventures

On Foot

Angel Desert Tours (☎ 216-805, www.adticaperu. tk, $12) does a half-day tour to all of Ica's sites. The tour is both on foot and by car, stopping at Plaza de Armas, an old Colonial-style hacienda with Pasofino horses, Huacachina (including sand boarding), Cachiche, and the Tacama and Lazo wineries. Angel, who leads the tours, speaks fluent English and French and knows the area thoroughly.

In the Sand

Sandbroading (Anibal Solimano)

In the high dunes that surround Huacachina, the extreme sport of ★**sandboarding** is a common local activity. But sand boarding is not snowboarding. The speed and mobility of a board in snow doesn't happen in sand, no matter how experienced the rider might be. Turning is slow and difficult. You often stop in your tracks as the entire board gets buried in a pile of cascading sand. It can be frustrating and tiring. There are a few simple things you can do to have a better experience. First of all, make sure the rental office (prices are generally $1 per hour) gives you a stick of wax. Before attempting to slide down the dune, wax the board up as much as possible. Stop and do this often for more speed.

Another tip – start out early because the sun and the sand can get very hot. The hotter the sand, the quicker the wax melts. Also, remember that there are no lifts on these hills. You are walking up! Ask the locals which dune is best. The right slope can make all the difference.

★Wine Tasting

The Ica region is Peru's leading producer of wine, with the area around the city of Ica itself the epicenter. Pisco, a sweet aromatic grape brandy, is also produced here and is said to have originated in the area 400 years ago – although the people of Chile dispute that claim. Like the Napa Valley, this area benefits from the cold Pacific nearby. Local wines are sold at stalls along the Pan American Highway and most of the bodegas (wineries) are close-by and welcome visitors. Much of the wine is still made in traditional presses and aged in clay casks. Degustations (small tastings) are usually free, although a tip or purchase is expected.

One of the biggest names in Peruvian wine, the ★**Tacama Vineyard**, founded in 1885, is also

Pisco (Anibal Solimano)

perhaps the largest, at 445 acres. Professional, well-informed guides offer tours of the Colonial-style hacienda that sits at the foot of the Andes. They lead you through the bottling plant where you can see the many vats and the entire process of creating dozens of vintages such as Grant Tinto, Semi Seco, and Blanco de Blanco that are shipped around the globe. The vineyard uses French advisors who employ the latest Euro-

Barrels of wine at Tacama Vineyard

pean technology. Surprisingly, during part of the year the vineyards are irrigated by the Inca-built Achirama Canal. Three types of Pisco (Puro, Demonio de los Andes, and Pisco de Ica) are also made here, as are several champagnes. Tacama (www.tacama.com) welcomes visitors from 9 am-6 pm every day.

★**Ocucaje** (Pan American Highway Sur Km 335.5, ☎ 056-40-8011, www.ocucaje.com) is another of Peru's more sophisticated, established producers of wine and a long line of Piscos, located about 35 km/21 miles south of Ica. The 16th-century vineyard also makes Fond de Cave, a locally famous and unique blend of Cabernet and Malbec. Winery tours last one hour and cost $3. You can get to the winery via taxi from Ica for $8 each way or as part of a tour. The company also operates the **Ocucaje Sun and Wine Resort** (☎ 40-8001, $$$, more expensive on weekends). They can offer package deals for winery tours, horseback riding, dune buggy rides, and more.

★**Lazo**, on the other hand, is the complete opposite of Tacama and Ocucaje. This bodega (winery) is more typical of Peru, more of an artesian operation, very rustic, but unbelievably interesting. Grapes are still stomped by feet and pressed in an ancient type of wooden press. The wine and Pisco are stored in torpedo-shaped clay vessels and samples for tasting are extracted via a long bamboo stick. The storage area is also part-museum, with many pre-Hispanic artifacts such as jewelry, textiles, oil paintings, chests, statues, and a dusty clutter of just about anything else you could imagine. Don't miss the glass case with mummified human heads.

Right beside Lazo, **El Catador** uses similar techniques. They give short tours, tastings, and explain their own production process. A shop sells their wines, Piscos, and other handicrafts associated with wine-making. Most evenings the restaurants and bar have dancing and music, not to mention a chance to do more sampling. El Catador is a lively spot for the harvest festival.

In the district of La Tinguina, **Bodega Vista Allegra**, founded in 1857 by the Picasso family, blends modern equipment with old-fashioned remnants and has one of the largest wine cellars in Peru. Relaxed tours are given from 9 am to 2 pm.

In the district of Guadalupe, three km/1.8 miles north of Ica, several small bodegas (**Pena**, **Lovera**, and **El Carmel**) aren't much to look at, but are worth visiting for the tastings alone, if you have the time.

Festivals

The ★**Fiesta de la Vendimia**, or harvest festival, is the largest festival in the Ica region. Tourists from Lima fill up the hotels, which more than double their prices. Be sure to reserve well in advance.

The festival is held at Campo Feriado during the first half of March. There is a small entrance fee. Wine and Pisco is free-flowing, and there are horseshows, processions, music, dancing to the Afro-Peruvian festejo, arts, craft fairs, and cockfights. Of particular interest is the Queen of the Festival beauty pageant. The elected queen is the first to tread the grapes in a vat while a crowd of onlookers cheers. Smaller celebrations are also held at many of the bodegas.

Day-Trips from Ica

Huacachina (Anibal Solimano)

Five kilometers/three miles from Ica is the postcard-perfect resort oasis in the desert called ★★**Huacachina**. The emerald-green sulphuric waters are thought to be therapeutic. Many believe they can cure arthritis and rheumatism. Swaying palm trees, pastel buildings, and tall sand dunes in every direction surround the small lake. It is the last of 15 lakes in the Ica area, the others having been dried up through use as local water sources. Water now comes from the highlands. Many charming hotels, guesthouses, cafés, restaurants, shops, and tour operators surround the lake. Activities, such as three-hour dune buggy tours ($15)

Huacachina (Anibal Solimano)

and the local favorite (sand boarding) can be arranged from just about anywhere in town.

 Did You Know? A monument tells the story of the lake being formed by a beautiful princess stripping off to bathe and noticing in a mirror a hunter watching her. Startled, she drops the mirror, which becomes the lake and she became the night sky, coming out every night.

Where to Stay

Las Dunas Sun Resort – Av. La Angostura 400, ☎ 231-013, fax 231-007. A complete desert resort with restaurant, pool, horseback riding, golf course, tennis courts, and its own landing strip for flights to Nazca. $$$

Ocucaje Sun and Wine Resort (see page 200). $$$

Hostal El Carmelo – On the Pan American Highway at the entrance to town, ☎ 232-191. The only mid-range option right in town has a pool, restaurant and even a small winery. $$

Hostal Oasis – Tacna 216, ☎ 234-767. Has hot water, private baths, clean rooms, cable TV, and offers tourist information. $

In **Huacachina** you are mostly limited to budget options such as **Hostal Titanic** (☎ 229-003, $), with a café and pool, or **Casita de Arena** (☎ 215-439), with a small bar and pool. One exception is **Mossone** (☎ 213-630, hmossone@derramajae. org.pe). It has a pleasant patio overlooking the lake, a pool, and rents bicycles and sandboards. Full board with meals is also available. $$$

HOTEL PRICE CHART	
	under $10
$	$10-$25
$$	$26-$50
$$$	$51-$90
$$$$	$91-$150
$$$$$	Over $150

Where to Eat

Restaurant Venezia – Lima 252. Has excellent pizzas, sold by the half or by the slice, and several seafood dishes. $

DINING PRICE CHART	
$	under $5
$$	$5-$10
$$$	$11-$20
$$$$	$21-$35
$$$$$	over $35

El Otro Penoncito – Bolivar 255. The best place in town, with an array of international dishes. $$

La Bruja de Cachiche – Cajamarca 118. "The witch of Cachiche" has many local dishes and offers the chance to sample local wines. $$

There are many cheap Chinese restaurants, or chifas, around Plaza de Armas, with heaping plates of food for a few dollars.

In **Huacachina** there are dozens of small bars and cafés that serve inexpensive meals. The only other option is the restaurant at Mossone. There is no grocery store in Huacachina.

■ Nazca

Phone code (056)

Overshadowed by the majestic Cerro Blanco, the tallest sand dune in the world, sits the small tourist town of Nazca. Being hot, dry, and humidity-free has allowed the world-renowned nearby attraction, the Nazca Lines and numerous cemeteries, mummies and Pre-Incan ruins to remain in good condition for thousands of years.

Did You Know? The Nazca Lines, although undisturbed for thousands of years, were forgotten for some time, until commercial aviation came to the area and the pilots reported seeing strange lines in the desert. By this time, the Pan American Highway, which cuts right through one of the lines, had already been constructed.

Southern Coast

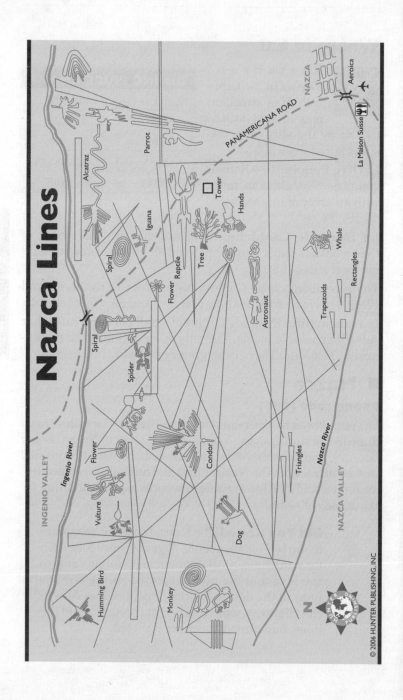

Nazca Lines

© 2006 HUNTER PUBLISHING, INC

Getting Here & Around

Nazca is 444 km/266 miles south of Lima on the Pan American Highway, almost directly between Lima and Arequipa. Car rental is best arranged in Lima or Arequipa.

By Bus

Buses link Nazca with Lima, Arequipa, Ica, and even Cuzco. Departures are frequent, except for Cuzco. **Cruz del Sur** (☎ 522-498), **Ormeño** (☎ 522-058), and **Civa** (☎ 523-019) all depart on Los Incas, within a few blocks west of Plaza Bolognesi.

Tourist Information

Juan Vera of **Nasca Trails** (Bolognesi 550, ☎ 522-858, nascatrails@terra.com.pe) speaks excellent English and can help plan any kind of excursion in the area. Also try **Alegria Tours** (Lima 186, ☎ 523-775, www.alegriatours.com.pe), which has loads of information on walks to nearby sites.

Sightseeing

There is little of interest in Nazca itself. It is just a dry, dusty town made up of hotels, restaurants, tour operators, and tourist shops. Many come for one day to see the lines and then leave that afternoon or in the night. If you do have time to spend here, there are some great side-trips worth discovering.

The **Museo Antonini** (Av. de la Cultura 600, ☎ 523-444) is very modern with good lighting and many artifacts from the pre-Inca ruin at Cahuachi. Photos show the excavation of the site by Professor Orecifi and his crew, who believe the site will reveal the secrets of the lines. Inside, are many examples of jewelry, pottery, and textiles. Outside, in the beautiful courtyard with many rare native plants, there are models of tombs with mummies and a complete recreation of the lines. Open daily 9 am-7 pm. Admission 10 soles.

At the Hotel Nazca Lines, the ★**María Reiche Planetarium** (Bolognesi, ☎ 522-293) is dedicated to the work of the late María Reiche, a German expert who studied the lines for more than 40 years. She believed that the lines hold a vast astronomical calendar for agricultural purposes, although many dispute that claim. The show lasts about 45 minutes, is given in English, and describes many of the constellations in the southern hemisphere and their possible relations to the lines. Afterwards the host will take the group outside to look up at the night sky through their own high-tech telescopes. The show is well worth the time, especially if you know little about astronomy and the stars of the southern hemisphere and want to know more about the lines. Shows are at 7:15 pm and 9:15 pm nightly. Admission $6 or $3 with a student card.

At **Cerro Blanco**, it is possible to sand board. Get there early, at the top no later than 9:30 am to avoid the heat. Ask any tour operator in town for more information.

★★★The Nazca Lines

The Nazca Lines, 22 km/ 13 miles north of Nazca, were made by removing the darker sun-baked stones and piling them on either side of the line, exposing the lighter soil. Why the lines were made is still open to much debate, but scientists have a fairly good idea of  who made them. The Paracas and Nazca peoples are believed to have created the lines between 900 BC to 600 AD. It is also believed that the Huari settlers from Ayacucho made some additions in the seventh century. There are literally hundreds of lines and geometric shapes that stretch for miles, but the animals such as a monkey, dog, spider, whale, and several birds, including a hummingbird with a wingspan of over 100 yards, are the most well-known. There are also images of a tree, hands, and what is thought by some to be an astronaut.

THEORIES BEHIND THE LINES

No one is sure what purpose the lines actually served, but there are plenty of theories. María Reiche, who studied the lines for 40 years, much longer than anyone else, maintained that the lines were an astronomical calendar. In the 1960s Gerald Hawkins supported her claim by computing that the two mounds on the Pampa were aligned with the Pleiades constellation; however, he believed that the occasional alignments with the sun and moon were mere coincidence.

Several scientists such as Von Breuning and Sawyer have claimed that the lines represent running tracks. Author Tony Morrison (*Pathways to the Gods: the Mystery of the Nazca Lines*, Michael Russel, 1978) thinks the lines were ritual walking paths linking huacas, or sites of ceremonial interest.

Isla and Reindel of the Swiss-Liechtenstein foundation mapped the lines for six years using aerial photographs. They believed the lines were offerings involved in the worship of water and fertility, two important elements of coastal culture.

Far stranger theories exist. Due to the fact that the lines are best seen from the air, that there are local legends of flying men, and pottery has been found that seems to show balloonists, American Jim Woodman, believed that the Nazcas flew in hot air balloons.

Most recently, the BBC series *Ancient Voices* supported the claim that the lines are believed to portray the flight of the shaman who consumes psychoactive substances such as San Pedro or Ayahuasca (still practiced today) and enters the world of spirits, making him physically free to fly. In this way the shaman can rid the sick of evil spirits.

In other words, the lines are not meant to be seen from the sky, but from the mind's eye.

Erich von Daniken believes the lines to be extraterrestrial landing sites, and many support his claim.

There are countless other theories, each with their own followers, but no definitive evidence for the true purpose of the Nazca Lines has been discovered as yet.

Adventures

On Foot

 The Nazca Lines can be seen from the mirador (lookout), paid for by Reiche, which stands just beside the Pan American Highway, 22 km/ 13 miles north of Nazca. It is also possible to view from a nearby hill (500 yards from the mirador). From either place it 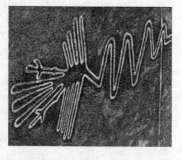 is only possible to see a few of the lines, notably the lizard, the tree, and the hands. The view is difficult to make out. A taxi guide can take you to both places ($4.50 per person).

In the Air

 Several companies in Nazca, as well as in Ica and Pisco, offer flights over the lines. This is the only way to really appreciate how vast an area the lines are spread over and how much work must have been involved in their creation. The planes are small, seating three-five people. They take tight turns and can be turbulent.

 Tip: It is best not to eat just before the flight.

The flights last about 45 minutes from Nazca, offer extraordinary views of the desert, mountains, more than a dozen creatures carved on the ground, and countless other lines. Everyone gets a window seat and the pilots, who are fluent in

English, make loops around every figure to be sure everyone gets the best view. Flights from Nazca average $45 and can be booked just hours in advance. Most leave in the morning from 8 to 10 am or in the afternoon from 3 to 4:30 pm. At other times, conditions are windier and planes are usually not able to take off. Every flight includes a showing of the BBC film on Nazca beforehand and you receive a signed certificate of completion. Every hotel or tourist agency in Nazca can book flights or you can book yourself by phone or online. Contact **Aero Condor** (☎ 522-424, www.aerocondor.com.pe), **Alas Peruanas** (☎ 523-400, www.nazcalinesperu.net), or **Aero Paracas** (☎ 667-231). Aero Condor also arranges flights from Lima ($260) with a stop for lunch in Nazca.

On Wheels

A typical mountain biking itinerary leads from the arid desert around Nazca to an oasis, then on to agricultural land. **Alegria Tours** (Lima 186, ☎ 523-775, www.alegriatoursperu.com) offers a tour with a follow-behind car where you can leave your camera and other belongings. The road is mostly paved and stops at the Paracas ruins and aqueducts.

Day-Trips from Nazca

Huaqeros, or grave robbers, ransacked the cemetery of **Chaucilla**, 30 km/18 miles from Nazca, but many tombs filled with bones, skulls, mummies, and pottery shards dating from 1000 to 1300 AD can still be seen. Tours from Nazca last three hours and cost $5-$10 per person, depending on the number of people. Make sure the tour stops at a potter's or gold mining workshop, where you can see artisans creating works of art from raw materials right before your eyes.

Paradones

Cacsamarca, which has the **Paradones** ruins and aqueducts, are two km/1.2 miles southeast of town. To get there, cross the river to Arica. Although

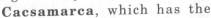

the pre-Incan ruins are not well preserved, the aqueducts are still in working order and provide irrigation for nearby fields. They were built between 300 BC and 700 AD. You can enter the underground aqueducts through the windows, although it is very claustrophobic and wet. Tours from Nazca run about $5, but the walk isn't far and admission just $1.

Six pyramids, each with its own courtyard excavated by Professor Orefici and his team, can be seen at **Cahuachi**, 25 km/ 15 miles west of the Nazca Lines on a dirt road. It is believed to be an important Nazca center and consists of a main temple around a small hill with several adobe platforms. The nearby site of **El Estaqueria** is 200 years old and its function is unclear. It consists of many wooden posts possibly used to dry bodies. There are more than 300 graves here, one containing a mummified dreadlocked and tattooed warrior.

Where to Stay

Hotel Nazca Lines – Bolognesi, ☎ 522-293. Contains the María Reiche Planetarium, as well as a gorgeous pool and courtyard, tennis court, a fine restaurant, and rooms with private patios. They can also arrange package tours for several days with a flight over the lines. $$$

Casa Andina Nasca Hotel – Bolognesi 367, ☎ 52-3563, fax 52-1067, www.casa-andina.com. Casa Andina is the first real chain hotel to come to Nazca and their 60 rooms are some of

the most comfortable and modern in the city. A nice pool and sun terrace add a resort-like ambiance. They offer tours to the natural refuge of San Fernando, where you will see guanacos, Andean condors, and a colony of Humboldt penguins. $$$

Maisson Suisse – ☎ 522-831. This hotel near the airport has 40 rooms with Jacuzzis, a pool, and a pricey restaurant, bar, and gift shop. They also have free camping on the grounds for those flying with Aero Ica. $$$

Hotel de la Borda – On the Pan American Highway at Km 447, ☎ 522-750. In an old hacienda near the airport with modern amenities. $$

Las Casuarinas – Sucre, ☎ 522-803, www.cauarinasnasca. com. A new, quiet hotel just outside of town that has two pools, a restaurant, and a nearby eco lodge. $

Posada Guadelupe – San Martín 225, ☎ 522-245. A basic option with cold-water showers.

Where to Eat

La Kañada – Lima 160. Has a helpful English-speaking owner who hands out free maps of Nazca, displays local artwork, and has good Pisco sours, local wines, and Peruvian dishes. $$

La Taberna – Lima 321. Local and international dishes served in an interesting graffiti-covered ambiance. $

El Portón – Lima at Ignacio Moresky. Has decent Italian dishes, sometimes with live music and dancing. $$

All of the upscale hotels, such as Maisson Suisse and Nazca Lines, have the best restaurants with international menus ($$$) prepared by trained chefs.

■ Arequipa

Phone code (054)

Arequipa (population one million, elevation 7,653 feet) is called "Ciudad Blanca," the White City, because it is constructed almost exclusively of sillar, a white volcanic stone. This is Peru's second-largest city and a close rival to Cuzco in

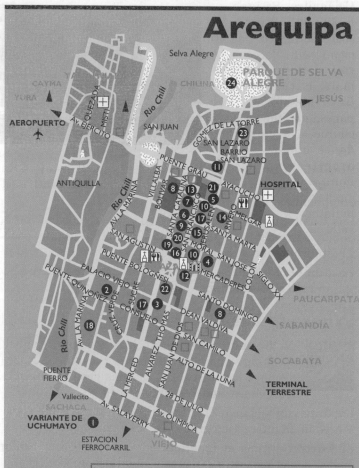

Arequipa

Selva Alegre

PARQUE DE SELVA ALEGRE

CAYMA

YURA

JESÚS

AEROPUERTO

Av. EJERCITO

Río Chili

CHILINA

SAN JUAN

GOMEZ DE LA TORRE

San Lázaro

BARRIO SAN LAZARO

ANTIQUILLA

Río Chili

PUENTE GRAU

AYACUCHO

HOSPITAL

Av. LA MARINA

VILLALBA

BOLIVAR

SANTA CATALINA

SAN FRANCISCO

MERCADERES

SAN AGUSTIN

PUENTE BOLOGNESI

SANTA MARTA

MELGAR

PALACIO VIEJO

PUENTE QUIÑONES

Av. LA MARINA

CRUZ VERDE

SUCRE

CONSUELO

MORAL

SAN JOSE

SANTO DOMINGO

DEAN VALDIVA

PAUCARPATA

SABANDÍA

SOCABAYA

SAN CAMILO

ALVAREZ THOMAS

SAN JUAN ALTO DE LA LUNA

TERMINAL TERRESTRE

Río Chili

PUENTE FIERRO

Vallecito

SACHACA

28 DE JULIO

Av. SALAVERRY

Av. OLIMPICA

VARIANTE DE UCHUMAYO

ESTACION FERROCARRIL

© 2006 HUNTER PUBLISHING, INC

N

HUNTER PUBLISHING

1. Museo de Arte Contemporario
2. Museo de Arqueologia de la Universidad Catolica de Santa Maria
3. Museo Arqueological de la Universidad de San Agustin is at Alvarez Thomas and Palacio Viejo
4. Patio del Ekeko
5. Casona Forum
6. Le Café Art Montreal
7. Déjàvu, Sabor Cubano, Ras El Hanout, Mandala, Zingaro
8. La Trattoria del Monasterio
9. Café Restaurant Rafael
10. Zig Zag Restaurant
11. Casa Andina Arequipa Hotel
12. Sonesta Posada del Inca, Cioccolata
13. La Casa de Klaus, La Leña, Kibosh, La Reyna
14. Café Casa Verde, Ary Quepay
15. El Turko
16. Istanbul at San Francisco
17. Pizzeria Los Lenos
18. Cevicheria El Tiburon
19. Govinda
20. Los Balcones de Moraly Santa Catalina
21. Colonial House Inn
22. Hostal Arequipa Center
23. La Casa de mi Abuela
24. Arequipa Libertador Hotel Plaza Bolivar

Colonial charm. It looks and feels like a Spanish or Italian city. There is a year-round sunny climate, lots of tree-lined streets and parks, magnificent churches, an abundance of Colonial architecture in fountains, arches, cathedrals, and

El Misti (N. Gill)

buildings. It is surrounded by several colossal mountains and volcanoes, such as El Misti (19,133 feet), El Ampato (20,664 feet), El Chachani (19,899 feet) and Sabancaya (22,960 feet). Recently the historic center was named a UNESCO World Heritage Site. Lima and Cuzco usually get the nod as Peru's most important cities; but Arequipa has played an important role as the birthplace of rebellion and migration. Although the area has been plagued with high unemployment and civic strife in recent years, there is no doubt that, without Arequipa, Peru would be a very different country.

 Climate: The weather is relatively mild and sunny with average temperatures of 9-24°C/48-75°F 265 days a year.

Getting Here

Air

 Aeropuerto Alfredo Rodriguez Ballón – Av. Avaicion, Zamacola, ☎ 44-3464. This airport, nine km/5.4 miles northwest of town, has flights to Lima, Cuzco, and Juliaca. The airport can be reached by taxi to/from the center.

Airlines

LAN Peru – Portal de San Agustín 118, ☎ 20-1100, www.lan. com.

Tans Peru – Portal del San Agustín 143-A, ☎ 20-5231, www.tansperu.pe.

Buses

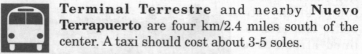

Terminal Terrestre and nearby **Nuevo Terrapuerto** are four km/2.4 miles south of the center. A taxi should cost about 3-5 soles.

Cruz del Sur – ☎ 42-7375, www.cruzdelsur.com. pe. This line makes many daily trips to Lima (13-16 hours) and one to Cuzco (8 pm, 10-12 hours), Puno (8:15 am, five hours), and Tacna (7 am, five hours). All Lima-bound buses stop in Nazca, Ica, and Pisco.

Ormeño – ☎ 42-41870, www.grupo-ormeno.com. Same as Cruz del Sur, but with international buses to Santiago (two days) and Buenos Aires (three days).

Civa – ☎ 42-6563, www.civa.com.pe. Cheaper buses to Lima.

La Reyna – ☎ 43-0612. Has the most buses to Chivay (three hours) that continue on to Cabanaconda (four hours). Several services daily.

Getting Around

Taxi drivers often try to tell you that your preferred hotel is full, particularly smaller guesthouses, and will then try to take you to a place where they receive a commission. Do not believe them. Go to the hotel and check for yourself.

Car Rental

AVIS main office (Palacio Viejo 214 Cercado, ☎ 282-519, fax 212-123) and a counter at the airport (☎ 443-576, avis-aqp@terra.com.pe).

Tourist Information

i

Tourist Offices – **iPeru** has three offices in Arequipa: on the Plaza (Portal de la Municipalidad 110, iperuarequipa@promperu.gob.pe, open every day from 8:30 am-7:30 pm), at Aeropuerto Alfredo Rodriguez Ballón (☎ 44-4564, iperuarequipaapto@iperu.gob. pe, 6:30 am-8:45 pm), and a small booth at the main bus terminal.

Tourist Police, Jerusalén 315, ☎ 239-888.

Hospitals – **Hospital Regional Honorio Delgado Espinoza**, Av. Daniel Alcides Carrión, ☎ 054-23-1818, 24 hours. **Hospital Goyeneche**, Av. Goyeneche (no #), Cercado, ☎ 054 23 1313, 24 hours.

Post Office – **Serpost**, Moral 118, ☎ 21-5247, Mon-Sat 8 am-8 pm, Sun 9 am-1 pm.

Where to Stay

 ★ **A r e q u i p a Libertador Hotel Plaza Bolivar** – Selva Alegre, ☎ 215-110, fax 241-933, arequipa@libertador.com.pe. This 1940 Colonial-style hotel in Selva Allegre is one of the best options for those wanting to be close to the center, while still enjoying the peace and quiet of the natu-

ral surroundings that make Arequipa such a spectacular city. This elegant hotel has 88 rooms, Los Robles restaurant, 24-hour room service, bar, pool, terrace, gardens, spa, gym, and recreation area for children. Rooms have marble bathrooms, air-conditioning, mini-bar, safe, and cable TV. $$$$

Sonesta Posada del Inca – Portal de Flores 116, ☎ 21-5530, fax 23-4374, www.sonesta.com/peru_ arequipa. In the corner of the plaza next to the Cathedral. The upscale hotel, part of the international chain, has an outdoor pool, currency exchange, flight/bus/rental assistance, laundry service, luggage storage, and parking. Each of the 58 rooms includes air-conditioning, heat, mini-bar, in-room phone, cable TV, and a safe. $$$

El Cabildo Hotel – M. Ugarte 411, ☎ 204-060, fax 283-184, cabildohotel@star.com.pe. Located on a quiet residential street in Selva Allegre. There are 45 spotless, stylish rooms and suites with cable TV, mini-bar, security safe and heater. Also, two good restaurants, a piano bar, parking, and Wi-Fi. Attractive hotel all around. $$$

Hostal El Sauce – M Ugarteche 309 in Selva Allegre, ☎ 287-455, fax 281-925, hosteria_elsauce@terra.com.pe. About 10 blocks from the main square, El Sauce has 21 rooms with private bath, mini-bar, phones, and cable TV. Parking and laundry services. Garden breakfast included in price. $$$

Casa Andina Arequipa Hotel – Jerusalén 603, ☎ 20-2070, fax 28-7420, www.casa-andina.com. In the center, six blocks from the Plaza. Features include a restaurant, wireless Internet, 94 rooms (suites with Jacuzzis), telephones, safes, currency exchange, parking. Part of a larger chain with boutique hotels all over Peru that feature brightly colored modern and spacious rooms and breakfast buffets (included in price). $$$

La Maison d'Elise – Av. Bolognesi 104 in Yanahuara, ☎ 256-185, fax 273-935, www.aqplink.com/hotel/maison. A quick cab ride or 20-minute walk from the center. Restaurant, bar/lounge, gorgeous swimming pool (shown at right), colorful buildings and rooms, lots of character. $$$

Los Balcónes de Moral y Santa Catalina – Moral 217, ☎ 201-291, reservas@losbalconeshotel. Set in an old, spacious Colonial house one block from the Plaza. There are 16 rooms with hot/cold private baths, cable TV, phones, and desk. All rooms are on the second level and have a private balcony with views of Chachani Mountain and the cathedral. Includes breakfast. Good value. $$

Colonial House Inn – Puente Grau 114, ☎ 223-533, Colonialhouseinn@hotmail.com. Two-century-old Colonial-style house 10 minutes walk from the Plaza, perfect for those on a budget who don't want to sacrifice character in their hotel. Rooms are large and have private baths with hot water. Also a patio, small breakfast nook, book exchange and laundry. $

The Point – Av. Lima 515 Vallecito, www.thepointhostel. com. This new hostel is owned by the same people who run The Point in Barranco, a legendary backpacker haunt with lots of ties to local nightlife. Large garden and a sunny roof terrace with volcano views. TV room with cable TV and DVDs, free Internet, free breakfast, 24-hour hot water, luggage storage, book exchange, Spanish classes, and a fully equipped kitchen and bar. Not the place for peace and quiet but, if you have come to party, check it out. $

Hostal Arequipa Center – Alvarez Thomas 305-A, ☎ 496-169, is just three blocks south of the Plaza and has nicely decorated rooms with cable TV, hot water, and private bathrooms. Some with Jacuzzis. $$

El Balcón Hostal – 202 Garcia Calderón, ☎ 286-998, balcon@lared.net.pe. This hotel sits on a quiet residential street just a few blocks from the Plaza. Rooms are worn but clean and good value. Includes private baths, TV, phones. There is also an on-site lounge, bar, and restaurant. $$

★**Tambo Viejo** – Av. Malecón Socabaya 107, ☎ 28-8195, fax 28-4747, www.tamboviejo.com. Not far from the bus station, it's well worth the short cab ride or 15-minute walk to Plaza de Armas. The charming Colonial house has taste-ful rooms with hot water and cable TV, book exchange, great views of the city and the volcanoes from their three terraces, a garden, laundry service, café, bar, and Internet. They also offer dorm beds. The helpful staff that speaks good English can arrange trips throughout the region, city and campesina (countryside) tours, as well as book plane and bus tickets. An incredible value. $-$$

La Reyna – Zella 209, ☎ 286-578. Cheap and cozy with a nice rooftop view and small cafeteria. Popular with backpackers. Private rooms or dorms. Most with shared baths. Hot water. Rooms on the lower level near the street can be noisy. They rent some equipment, store luggage, and can arrange Spanish classes and trips to Colca, El Misti, and just about anywhere else in the region. Small café with banana pancakes. $

La Casa de Mi Abuela (My Grandmother's House) – Jerusalén 606, ☎ 241-206, fax 242-761, www.lacasademiabuela. com. Book ahead; this family-run, 50-room hotel is very popular and always receives rave reviews. There is a bar, garden, pool, laundry, and travel agency. Rooms include cable TV, mini-bar, and balconies or terraces. Quite a bit cheaper without a private bath. $

LOCAL GASTRONOMY

- **El Chupe de Camarones** – Shrimp stew with milk, eggs, and oregano.
- **Escribano** – Potato salad with rocoto (Andean pepper), vinegar, olive oil, tomato, and parsley.
- **El Sango** – A sweet made with a wheat base, raisins, honey, milk, and butter.
- **Adobo Arequipeño** – Pork marinated and cooked in vinegar, onions, and chilis.
- **Rocoto Relleno** – Spicy Andean pepper stuffed with meat.

■ **Ocopa Arequipeña** – Potatoes, eggs, olives in a spicy yellow chili sauce. Served cold. One of Arequipa's signature dishes.

■ **Queso Frito** – Fried cheese.

■ **Queso Helado** – Cheese-flavored ice cream (much better than it sounds).

Where to Eat

 Arequipa's dining scene is one of the best in Peru. It lacks the high-priced touristy restaurants of Lima and Cuzco, but has many international (particularly on San Francisco) and local eateries scattered throughout the city. The regional dishes are quite varied and make use of cuy (guinea pig), alpaca, and freshwater shrimp as well as many Andean vegetables.

★**La Trattoria del Monasterio** – Santa Catalina 309, ☎ 204-062, latrattoriadelmonasterio@yahoo.com, is set inside the Convent of Santa Catalina and is one of the White City's most innovative restaurants. Internationally acclaimed Peruvian chef Gastón Acurio, who also owns the famed Lima restaurant Astrid y Gastón, combines Italian cuisine and elegance with that of Arequipeñan flavors. Make reservations. Highly recommended. $$$$

★**Zig Zag Restaurant** – Zela 212, ☎ 206-620, www. zigzagrestaurant.com. Set in a Colonial house with an iron staircase designed by Gustave Eiffel, it is stylish and chic, with food to match. The owners have an ostrich farm and are very enthusiastic about serving the animal in their restaurant and providing information on its health benefits. They also serve massive stone-grilled steaks, alpaca, lamb, and fondues. $$$

They have a crêperie of the same name at Santa Catalina 208 with over 100 varieties of crêpes that are made with high-quality local and foreign ingredients such as crawfish, quinoa, trout, and Roquefort cheese. They also serve a wide variety of sweet crêpes, milkshakes, and other desserts. A good spot for an early evening drink or a nightcap. $$-$$$

Southern Coast

El Turko – at San Francisco 216 and **El Turko II** at San Francisco 315 are cheap, quick, and very good places for kebabs, falafels, or doner kebabs. $

Also try **Istanbul** at San Francisco 31-A, run by the owners of El Turko. $$

Sabor Cubano – San Francisco 205, ☎ 405-297. This is a snazzy little bongo-beating joint that has excellent Cuban sandwiches, piqueos (samplers), coffee, and perhaps the best mojitos (a Cuban rum drink with mint) in all of Peru. $

Ras El Hanout – San Francisco 227, for good Moroccan and Mediterranean in a stylish and exotic setting. $$$

★**Ary Quepay** – Jerusalén 502, ☎ 204-583, www.aryquepay. com. Run by the Verapinto Ramirez family who tend to all facets of restaurant operation. A romantic, rustic atmosphere with plants, patios, watercolor paintings, and candlelight. The long list of dishes includes variations on fish, cuy (guinea pig), alpaca, chicken, beef, shrimp, duck, ostrich, lamb, as well as traditional Arequipeñan recipes. Some vegetarian options as well. English-language menu available. $$

Pizzeria Los Leños – Jerusalén 407, ☎ 289-179. Good wood-fired pizzas in a cozy atmosphere, sometimes with live music.

Café Restaurant Rafael – San Francisco 129. A small stylish place with light meals and drinks. Try the mouthwatering anticuchos (kebabed meat or fish, and sometimes potatoes), chicha (a fermented maize drink), and an array of fine cocktails. $-$$

Zingaro – San Francisco 309, ☎ 217-662. Decent Mediterranean and Peruvian dishes in a pleasant Colonial atmosphere.

Cevicheria El Tiburon – Consuelo 311, ☎ 330-207. A local place just around the corner from several more touristy cevicherias. Virtually no tourists come here. They have excellent ceviche and seafood and it is much cheaper than the other places too. $

For vegetarian try **Govinda**, Santa Catalina 120, ☎ 285-540. Each day of the week it features a different Peruvian or international menu. They deliver too. Run by Hare Krishna.

Mandala – Jerusalén 207. Vegetarian takes on Peruvian, Chinese, and Italian cuisines. $-$$

There are many restaurants overlooking the Plaza, where employees stand on the street and try to entice you inside with discounts and free drinks. Many have traditional regional dishes and a large selection, but it can be hit-or-miss depending on how the chef might be feeling that day. I have found few to be very good. One exception is the **Restaurant Inkafé** at the Sonesta Posada del Inka, which prepares Arequipeñan dishes fused with international cuisine. $$

Café Casa Verde – Jerusalén 406. Donates profits to needy children. Coffee, cappuccino, juices, German breads and cakes. $

Cioccolata – Mercaderes 120, ☎ 247-180. This is the place to go for sweets of any kind. Ice cream, pastries, cakes, pies, as well as food and cocktails, although a bit expensive. Very stylish and could just as easily be in Rome without seeming unusual. $$

Also don't miss the ★**San Camilo Market** for local foods such as ceviche (including ceviche erotico which is considered an aphrodisiac), queso helado (cheese-flavored ice cream...delicious), and regional fruit drinks. The market also has just about everything else that Arequipeñans use, such as textiles, cosmetics, cleaning supplies, toys, and a multitude of other junk.

Also keep an eye out for products from **La Iberica**, an Arequipeñan candy company. Chocolates, toffees, marzipan, and more.

Bars/Clubs/Pubs

 Casona Forum – San Francisco 317. Combines a pizzeria, grill with Swiss cuisine, pub and pool hall, karaoke bar, and discoteca, sometimes with live music, under one roof. Very lively, Thurs-Sat.

Le Café Art Montreal – Ugarte 210. A Canadian-run jazz and blues joint with good food, drinks, and live music Wed-Sat.

Déjà Vu – San Francisco 319. A lively mixed crowd of locals and travelers. The rooftop terrace has great views.

La Casa de Klaus – Zela 207. Run by its German owner and features German and local specialties, as well as imported beers. Klaus raises his own cuy, so it is guaranteed fresh here.

La Leña – Zela 202. A pub that stays open late and draws a stylish, young crowd.

Kibosh – Zela 205, ☎ 626-218. Beer, wood-fired pizzas. Often crowded, with dancing and loud popular music. Open Wed through Sat.

Sights

Any tour of Arequipa should begin with the ★**Plaza de Armas**, as charming as any main square in all of South America. It is slightly smaller than the one in Cuzco, but the architecture surrounding the square, the large central fountain, and the array of palm trees and other trees give it a truly enchanted feel. At night you can often find comedians, clowns, or musicians performing near the fountain to the delight of the crowds. The cathedral is at one end, while the other three corners are marked by three nearly uniform Colonial buildings with second-floor balconies overlooking the Plaza. Many restaurants, tour operators, and souvenir shops can be found here.

Catedral (Heinz Plenge)

The ★**Catedral de la Ciudad de Arequipa**, on the Plaza, was founded in 1612, but due to fires, earthquakes, volcanic eruptions, and construction mishaps, little of what was originally built remains today. One tower collapsed as recently as 2001 during a serious earthquake that damaged much of southern Peru. It was quickly rebuilt by 2003. While most cathedrals in Peru are very solemn, this one has an uplifting, bright atmosphere. There are three vaulted ceilings with a total of 12 supporting columns, each with a statue of an apostle at its base. The intricate wooden pulpit (note the winged devil) was constructed in Lille, France in 1879. The wide tube organ was made in Hamburg, Germany. Open Mon-Sat 7 am-11:30 pm, Sun 7 am-1 pm.

In the street behind the cathedral is a narrow, pedestrian-only street made of cobblestones, with several good shops, restaurants, cafés, and bars where you will find good happy hour specials. Also keep an eye out for the shoelace man, who walks around inside a ball of thousands and thousands of dangling shoelaces and tries to hawk them to the crowds. A hilarious fellow with a good heart and quite the sales pitch.

The **Complejo and Iglesia de la Compañía** (intersection of General Moran and Alvarez Thomas) is a 17th-century Jesuit church, one of the best examples of the mestizo style, and one of the most striking churches in Arequipa. Open daily 10 am-1 pm and 3:30-7 pm. Upscale shops line the cloisters behind the church, selling fine alpaca and jewelry. The **Capilla Real** (Royal Chapel) to its left has a dazzling polychrome cupola. Open Sun-Fri 9 am-noon and 3-6 pm and Sat 11 am-noon and 3-6 pm. Admission 2 soles.

Iglesia de la Compañía
(Wilfredo Loayza)

Also check out the **Iglesia and Complejo de San Francisco** (Zela block 1). There is a good artisan market adjoining the cathedral with lots of lower-end textiles and handicrafts. Open Mon-Sat 7-9 am and 5-8 pm; Sun 7 am-12 pm and 5-8 pm. Convent hours: Mon-Sat 9 am-12:30 pm and 3-5 pm.

Convento Museo La Recoleta (Recoleta 117, ☎ 270-966, convento-la-recoleta@terra.com.pe) is just across the river. It's a Franciscan convent/museum built in 1648, although it was completely reconstructed after the earthquake of 1687. There are two Pre-Columbian exhibitions, two Amazonian, one religious, one pinacoteca (painting gallery), and a library with more than 20,000 volumes. Also contains souvenirs collected on missionary travels in the jungle, mummies, and paintings (including portraits of the 12 Incan emperors).

Open Mon-Sat 9 am-12 pm and 3-5 pm. Admission 5 soles adults/3 soles students.

The **Museo Histórico Municipal de Arequipa** (Municipal Historical Museum Parque San Francisco 407) has lots of memorabilia from the war with Chile, Peruvian naval artifacts, manuscripts, portraits, sculpture, photos, flags, pottery and dolls. Open from Mon-Fri 9 am-5:30 pm. Admission 2 soles.

★★**Museo Santuarios Andinos** (La Merced 110, www.ucsm.edu.pe/santury) is one of the best museums in the country thanks to one very special lady named Juanita, a mummy that was discovered in 1995. Tours are given in several languages including English (be sure to tip guides). Also inside are many capaccochas, or Inca offerings to the Apus (Sacred Mountains) found with Juanita, as well as other artifacts such as gold, jewelry, textiles, and clothing. Juanita is only on display in her icy casing from May-December; the rest of the year she is being analyzed for further scientific data. Open Mon-Sat 9 am-6 pm and Sun 9 am-3 pm. Admission 15 soles; discount with a student card.

JUANITA, LA DAMA DE AMPATO

La Dama de Ampato
(Alejandro Balaguer)

Discovered in 1995 by American anthropologist Dr. Johan Reinhard and local climbing legend Carlos Miguel Zarate (who still helps run Zarate Expeditions in Arequipa), Juanita, has become one of the most famous vestiges of Incan society. The exceptionally preserved 12- to 14-year-old girl, often called "La Dama de Ampato," was found after approximately 500 years packed in ice at a time when an eruption on nearby Mount Sabancaya volcano caused the ice to melt on the Ambato volcano. Quite a bit has been learned about how and why Juanita came to be there. Research has determined that she was chosen as an offering to the volcano and the mountain gods.

Before the sacrifice, it is likely that she traveled to Cuzco with important people of the region and there met with the Inca himself. She was chosen from many children who were thought to be the most perfect in the empire. This was done every four to seven years. Gifts and food were bestowed upon her and 100 white llamas sacrificed in her honor in Cuzco's Plaza de Armas. The Inca then transmitted his divinity to the young girl and, from that point on, she had no choice but to accept her fate. She became clothed in the best garb the Inca Empire could offer, topped by a feathered headset. After the long hike to Ampato, a great celebration, and many rituals, Juanita was put to sleep. Soon after, a sharp blow to her right eyebrow would kill her.

Today, her small body is encased in an icy glass freezer and remains in much the same position as it was found on the Ampato volcano. DNA studies are ongoing to see what else can be learned from the girl, such as her genealogy, state of health, type of diet, viruses and illnesses she may have had and much more. This eternally young girl became a highly important figure to the Incas when she was chosen for this momentous task and has become so once again today for us. Juanita has become a cherished link between ancient and modern Peru.

One of the most fascinating Catholic sites in the entire country, the ★★★**Convento de Santa Catalina** (Santa Catalina 301, www.santa-catalina.org.pe, ☎ 229-798) is where about 450 nuns of the Dominican order lived in total seclusion for four centuries. It was only in 1970 that the convent opened its doors to tourism. Several earthquakes, the

Convento de Santa Catalina

Santa Catalina (Heinz Plenge)

first in 1582, have destroyed many of the oldest sections of the convent. There were times, due to a lack of funds, where the nuns themselves did the repairs. Today, the convent is in excellent condition and an architectural jewel in a city known for its architecture. For its location in a city, this is as peaceful a place as there is. Austere blue, orange, and red walls, all made of sillar (a white volcanic stone), are paired with an abundance of flowers and cobblestone streets. The convent is a town of its own, complete with its own architecture and style. You can visit many of the rooms, now restored, where the nuns slept, cooked, and did their day-to-day living. There are three cloisters, six streets – all named after Spanish cities such as Malaga and Toledo – a cemetery, 80 houses, a square, a church, and an art gallery with hundreds of paintings and portraits of the Arequipa and Cuzco schools, as well as period furniture. The complex covers more than 20,000 square yards in the center of Arequipa. There is also a café with cakes, pastries, and tea made by the nuns. These days only 30 or so nuns remain, aged 18 to 90. They live in a closed-off corner of the northern part of the convent. A small, seldom-read note from the present nuns posted in the convent reads:

"After more than 400 years we are still here because our contemplative vocation is love. This is our great secret of being: to be in love, neither with an ideal nor a project, but with Jesus Christ."

The convent is open every day from 9 am to 4 pm. Admission is 25 soles. Guided tours, which last for about 90 minutes, are given in English, Spanish, and German. A $3 or 10 sole tip is expected.

SOR ANA DE LOS ANGELES

Blessed Sor Ana de Los Angeles has become one of the most famous nuns to ever live at the Santa Catalina convent. Thought to have been born on July 26th, 1620, Sor Ana was delivered to the monastery at the age of three by her parents. When she was 10 or 11 years old her parents removed her from the convent intending to betroth her within a few years. But one day she had a vision of Santa Catalina of Siena and decided to return to the monastery on her own. Although her parents offered her riches to return home, she stayed. That, her mother never accepted. Her brother Francisco, a priest, paid her dowry.

During her long life at the convent she was one of the most popular nuns, even though she could not read or write. This upset some of the others and Sor Ana was thought to have been poisoned on several occasions. Sor Ana often predicted diseases, recoveries, as well as deaths. It is believed that she performed a total of 68 predictions, all of which came true. When she became older she turned blind and was often ill, but never complained.

When she died in 1686, a painter whose body had swelled and was quite ill came to paint her portrait (which still hangs in her room, shown above). As soon as he finished he was healed. Sor Ana's body never needed to be embalmed because it is said to have given off a lovely smell. When she was exhumed 10 months later it was in the same condition. Sor Ana was beatified by Pope John Paul II. The nuns in the monastery have petitioned for her to be made a saint, but the process continues. A small festival is held in her honor on January 10th each year.

The **Iglesia and Convento de Santo Domingo** (Santo Domingo and Rivero) is quite stunning, its white sillar walls contrasting with the brick arches. The white and gold altarpiece is well worth a look too. Open Mon-Sat 7 am-12 pm and 3-7:30 pm, Sun 5:45 am-1 pm and 6:30-7:45 pm.

Architecture of Arequipa

Casa Ricketts

The main feature is the light and shadow contrasts cut into the stone, which is sillar, a white volcanic rock composed of feldspar, oligoclase, glass, quartz, biotite, and ferric oxide. Most of it has come from eruptions of Mount Chachani since Colonial times. The stone, light and easily carved, was used in the construction of almost every building in Arequipa. The stone carvers of the south didn't try to imitate the three-dimensional Baroque style of Cuzco and Lima, but followed a more decorative and ornamental approach. Their's is a plain carving technique that is natural to the Andean people. Emphasis in the carvings is on the flora and fauna of the region. Along with many of the cathedrals, the Colonial

Casa Moral

houses in Arequipa, many of them now banks, share the same style of carving. For example see:

- **Casa Ricketts** – San Francisco 108. Built in 1738. Now the Banco Continental. Mon-Fri 9-1 and 3:45-6; Sun 9-1.
- **Casa del Moral** – Moral 318. Fine example of skilled mestizo carving. Note the gargoyle on the façade. Mon-Fri 9 am-5 pm, Sun 9 am-1 pm.

- **Casa Goyeneche** – La Merced 201. Colonial style from the Cusqueña School. Built for Don Juan de Goyeneche y Aguerreverre in 1782. Now the headquarters of the Banco Central de Reserva in Arequipa. Mon-Sat 9 am-12 pm and 4-6 pm.

Casa Goyaneche

- **Casa Tristán del Pozo** – San Francisco 108. Baroque mestizo dwelling constructed in 1738 for the General Domingo Tristán del Pozo. Now owned by Banco Continental. Mon-Fri 9 am-1 pm and 3:45-6 pm, Sat 9 am-1 pm.

Other Arequipa Museums

The **Museo de Arte de Virreinal de Santa Teresa** (Melgar 303, ☎ 242-531, www.museocarmelitas.com) was just opened in 2005 in the Santa Teresa monastery and is quickly becoming one of the most sought-after places on the tourist circuit. The collection of art and artifacts is outstanding and includes a varied list of paintings, sculptures, and furniture. The exhibition rooms are set within the monastery and are similar to those at Santa Catalina but are without the crowds. Open daily from 9 am-4:30 pm. Admission 10 soles.

The **Museo Arqueológico de la Universidad de San Agustín** is at Alvarez Thomas and Palacio Viejo. A collection of textiles and a few mummies from the Nasca, Inca, Huari, and Tiahuanaco cultures. Open Mon-Fri 8:15 am-4:15 pm.

The **Museo de Arqueología de la Universidad Católica de Santa María** (Cruz Verde 303) has an exhibition of textiles and ceramics from cultures around Arequipa and throughout Peru. Open Mon-Fri 9 am-12 pm, 2-5 pm.

The **Museo de Arte Contemporario** (Tacna and Arica 201), opened in 2003 next to the old rail station. Nice layout with very good contemporary works from mostly little-known Peruvian artists. A pleasant, well-groomed garden surrounds the small building. Open Tues-Fri 10 am-5 pm; Sat-Sun 10 am-2 pm. Admission 3 soles.

Southern Coast

The **San Camillo Market** has just about any item you can imagine, from natural medicines, produce, grains, clothes, CDs and DVDs to cosmetics, all sorts of local culinary specialties and excellent ceviches (see above).

Barrio de San Lazaro is just north of the center as the streets begin to head uphill. It is the oldest district in the city with quiet streets, charming houses, restaurants, hotels, and the Capilla de San Lazaro.

North of the center and San Lazaro, **Selva Alegre**, "the garden of the city," is a relaxing, shady park with lots of trees, benches, a small zoo, and a pond. It has scenic views over the city and of the volcanoes. This where the spectacular Hotel Libertador can be found.

Yanahuara is a residential neighborhood just over the Río Chili. Cross Puente Grau and make a right up Av. Bolognesi to reach the mirador, which is on the same plaza as the church, a 1750 mestizo (mixed Spanish and indigenous style) sillar construction that is quite spectacular. Nice views and photo ops of El Misti.

The most traditional district of Arequipa, **Sabandia**, is about 8 km/4.8 miles. There you can find the Molino de Sabandia, the area's first stone mill that was built in 1621 and is now restored. Taxi is $1.50 each way.

The **Mansion del Fundador**, the mansion of the founder of Arequipa, is a 15-minute cab ride or can be seen as part of the a campesina, or countryside, tour. Made of sillar, this is one of the most traditional and important mansions of the region. Manuel de Carbajal, the city's founder, ordered that the house be built for his son. Remodeled in 1785 by Don Juan Crisostomo de Goyeneche. The house is now a museum, with original furniture, paintings, and a café/bar. Admission is $2.50.

Tours

There are a number of travel agencies in Arequipa, but many are very poorly run. Be sure to check a few before booking anything. It may be wise to pay a little bit extra to get the best equipment and value, particularly if going on a long trek in Colca or a climbing expedition.

Almost every travel agency in the city has a guided city tour that takes you to many of Arequipa's sites such as Santa Catalina and lots of churches and Colonial houses. Prices usually run $20-$25 per person and last all day. Minimum is two people.

Also available is the campesina, or countryside, tour. This brings you to many of the places around Arequipa that you couldn't possibly see on foot, but it can be somewhat disappointing. Prices are the same as for the city tour.

Naturaleza – Santa Catalina 211, ☎ 695-793, www.axb.it/naturelza. They offer tours throughout Peru. They have professional guides with licenses. Good equipment (rentals available). Slightly more expensive than others, but worth the price. Mountain biking from the volcanoes. Trekking in Colca. They work with the local communities and recycle. A very ecological company that provides an authentic experience.

Zarate Expeditions – Santa Catalina 204, ☎ 202-461, www.zarateadventures.com. Founded by Carlos Migual Zarate, who led the expedition with Johan Reinhard that found the mummy Juanita, this company is the best for mountaineering, climbing, and other technical expeditions.

Inca Tours – Jerusalén 410, ☎ 221-650, www.incatoursperu.com. They offer an eight-day llama trek (around $240) that includes Calloma, the Petrogylphs, Inca burial sites, hiking in the valley of the volcanoes, and the chance to interact with lots of llamas.

Gold Tour – Jerusalén 206-B, ☎ 286-359, fax 238-270, goldtourperu@terra.com.pe. Tours to Colca, Volcano Valley, mountaineering expeditions, Machu Picchu, jungle trips, and Nazca.

Shopping

 Leather, antiques, and the finest alpaca items in the country can all be found in Arequipa. There are several good shops for alpaca sweaters, blankets, scarves, and ponchos or just about anything else. Try these:

Alpaca Azul, Santa Catalina 225, near the convent.

Incalpaca, Claustros de la Compañía (which has many fine jewelry shops), Courtyard Two, Store #18.

Alpaca 111, Calle Zela 212.

For nature-conscious gifts, try **Alpaca Cotton Ecological Clothing** at Santa Catalina 300-B, 24-2088. Large selection of upmarket alpaca sweaters and other clothes, jewelry, crafts and rugs.

Saga Falabella – On Av. Ejército in Yanahuara, a 10-minute walk from the center. This huge Lima-based department store with food court and movie theater sells just about everything, including some basic camping equipment.

Patio del Ekeko – Mercaderes 141. They have several upscale shops selling jewelry, textiles, liquor, books, and other highbrow souvenirs. Also an **Illaria Jewelry Store** and **Museo de Arte Textil** (Textile Museum), which shows the evolution of Pre-Columbian Peru in textiles.

Mercado de Artesenia, next to Iglesia San Francisco on Zela, has a variety of handicrafts.

Typical tourist **souvenirs** can be found in almost every shop on the Plaza and on Calle Santa Catalina. There are several **bookstores** with English-language books just off the Plaza on San Francisco.

Av. 28 de Julio has an abundance of **wine and liquor stores** selling local and regional wines and Piscos, often in huge jugs.

Av. Consuelo hosts an amazing number of **bakeries** with finely decorated cakes. You may not need an entire cake, but a walk down this street is sure to be interesting.

Language Schools

Casa de Avila Spanish Institute – Av. San Martín 116 Vallecito, ☎ 213-177. Week-long classes begin every Monday and last until Friday; four hours daily (two hours bookwork and two hours conversation). Beginning, intermediate, and advanced levels are offered in small or private groups. Complete courses take four weeks.

Festivals

Fiesta Jubilares de Arequipa (August 10-20). Arequipeñans are a proud people and are always anxious to stake the claim that they are indeed the center of refined culture in Peru. Hotels are booked well in advance during this 10-day event. Restaurants are crowded. Activities run throughout the festival, including a race up El Misti from the Plaza de Armas. It's a religious, civic, artistic, and cultural celebration. Beauty pageants. Bullfights. A handicraft exhibition also takes place at Fundo El Fierro. Fire-

Virgin of Chapi Procession

works show on August 14. **Día de Arequipa**, the day of the city's founding, is on August 15. The **Virgin of Chapi Procession**, held on May 1st, used to see masses of people making a pilgrimage to her sanctuary (40 km from Arequipa), most of them on foot. However, the sanctuary suffered severe damage in the 2001 earthquake, so the image of the Virgin was moved to the church of Yanahuara, where the celebration now takes place. In the evening fireworks are set off.

Day-Trips from Arequipa

Petroglyphs of Toro Muerto, the UNESCO World Heritage Site, is in the province of Castilla, 164 km/98 miles northwest of Arequipa (2½ to three hours) near the village of Corire. The

area is a volcanic desert set in the midst of a green valley. In just two square miles more than 2,000 images of animals, plants and humans, including scenes from daily life and geometric shapes have been found. There are more petroglyphs here than are found in any other area of similar size in the world. A museum, run by Peru's National Cultural Institute, also keeps watch over the area that was plundered for decades. The museum is the best source of information on the carvings and it also displays examples of ancient technologies and daily life from the people of the area. It takes about two very hot and dry hours to see the site. Bring water and sun protection. Buses leave for Corire hourly from Arequipa (beginning at 5 am) and cost $3. Ask the driver to let you out near the trail to the site or take a $5-$10 taxi from Corire.

Just about the only way people visit the **Valle de los Volcanoes** is on a tour or a trek. The valley is near Andagua, in the province of Castilla, 323 km/194 miles northwest of Arequipa. There are 86 small volcanoes here, making it the best place in the country to see volcanic activity.

Adventures

Climbing

★★**El Misti** (5,822 m/19,096 feet) gives climbers the chance to scale an incredibly high mountain in just two days, although it can be a tough two days. In a matter of 24 hours you will climb roughly 8,000

feet and at a very high altitude. A few words of advice: wear sturdy hiking boots, warm clothes, and bring plenty of water. It is far too common for climbers to have to turn around before they reach the summit because they drank all of their water. An ice axe is not needed, but may help with balance. The walk can be done on your own without a guide (although it should never be done solo), or through a tourist agency in Arequipa.

If going without a guide, be sure to get a good map and information in Arequipa or at the South American Explorer's Club. Basically, you take a taxi from Arequipa to the mining road outside the town of La Independencia early in the morning. Walk along the road for about two hours following the "Mouth of the Lizard," a gap between two ridges at the base of the mountain. The trail should become obvious. After three hours or so, you will reach the edge of the vegetation. Two hours more will bring you to a few campsites and the Monte Blanco shelter. From there, it is four to eight hours to the top, depending on your level of fitness.

Volcan Ampato is 173 km/103 miles north of Arequipa, five hours by 4x4, and sits at 6,288 m/20,625 feet above sea level. This is where Juanita was found. This trip is for serious climbers only and will take three or four days. Best arranged in Arequipa through agencies such as Zarate.

On Water

Rafting

Approximately 12 hours by bus is the deepest canyon in the world, at 3,355 feet deep. This is **Cotahuasi Canyon**. Due to its relative isolation, few actually make the visit. The small, white-washed town of Cotahuasi is the jumping-off point for exploration of the canyon. Trekking, climbing, kayaking, and rafting opportunities await the most dedicated sports enthusiasts. The rafting/kayaking season lasts from May to August, with mostly class 3-5

rapids. There are just a few small hospedajes and comedors (small, local restaurants) here in this town of a few thousand. All information regarding trips to Cotahuasi should be sorted out in Arequipa. Several companies (Reyna, Alex, etc.) in Arequipa have one bus daily to Cotahuasi, leaving between 3 and 6 pm. Cost is about $9.

On Foot

★★★Colca Canyon

The Colca Valley is approximately 162 km/97 miles north of Arequipa, about three hours and 45 minutes by bus. The canyon is 11,150 feet deep and 124 miles long.

Look at the Aquada Blanca National Vicuña Reserve out the bus window, about an hour north of Arequipa, where you can usually see herds of vicuñas. The first town is Chivay, the largest in the valley with several

options for accommodations, restaurants, and a small market. Cabanaconde at the other end of the valley is where most of the trekking opportunities await. It is possible to walk from Chivay to Cabanaconde (70 km/48 miles), stopping at small rural towns and inns where traditional customs, religious practices, and native dress of the Collagua and Cabana people

have survived the onslaught of modernity. It is also possible to hike on the opposite side of the canyon to Coporaque and Ichupampa. but most skip this walk and head strait for Cabanaconde, where they can then trek further down into the canyon. There are more than 17,000 acres of terraces that have helped to prevent erosion and hold back irrigation; many have survived since Inca times. The canyon can be seen year-round. January to April is the rainy season. The rest of the year it is very dry and can be quite cold at nights.

■ Chivay

Phone code (054)

Chivay is small and easy to get around. Everything is within walking distance, although small collectivos/tuk-tuks are very cheap and plentiful. There is a central plaza with attractive arches, a church, and fountain with a few basic hotels and restaurants surrounding it.

Where to Stay

 Hostal Colca River – Zarumilla 116, ☎ 531-172. This has basic rooms with private baths near the market. Very cheap, sometimes less than $2 per person. $

La Casa de Anita – 607 on the Plaza, ☎ 521-114. Simple rooms surrounding a small flowered courtyard. $

Hotel Posada Chivay – Av. Salaverry 325, ☎ 531-032, posadachivay@hotmail.com. All rooms have private bath, hot water, and TV. $$

Pozo del Cielo – Calle Huáscar. On the hill overlooking the town. Fifteen rooms with private baths and electricity. Nice views. Includes continental breakfast. $$$

Casa Andina Colca Hotel – Huayna Cápac, ☎ 53-1020/53-1022, fax 53-1098. Four blocks from the main square. Fifty-two rooms with private baths. Restaurant. Parking. Internet access. Also has a planetarium and observatory for exploring the clear night sky of the valley. $$$

Restaurants

 Lobo's Bar Pizzeria, on the main square, has lots of dishes geared to the tourist. Accepts Visa and MasterCard. They also have a tourist agency that can arrange mountain biking, climbing, and trekking in the canyon (www.isuiza.com). $

McElroy's Irish Pub, on the main square, is the only place in Colca to find a Guinness Stout, a traveler's tradition after days and days of hiking. $

El Chactao Cuyeria, across from the market, near the corner of the main square, serves cuy chactado (fried guinea pig), but also has a decent lomo saltado (stir-fried beef over rice and French fries) and the lemongrass (hierba luisa) tea uses real lemongrass. $

There is a small **market** with lots of local dishes, and basic supplies like cheeses, breads and rice. Open from the morning to early evening. There is a small but good selection of textiles and handicrafts as well.

Days-Trips from Chivay

The ★**Thermal Baths at La Calera** are about four km/2.4 miles from town. They are very clean. There are several outdoor heated swimming pools and one indoor pool at this topnotch establishment just a 10-minute cab ride away. The outdoor pools offer incredible views into the valley and, after a long, exhausting hike, the water is mana from heaven. They also have showers, a sauna, café/bar, and a small museum. To get there, take a taxi or collectivo from the main Plaza. Cost is 1 sole per person. Open from 9 am to 8 pm. Admission 10 soles. Less for nationals.

■ Yanque

Phone code (054)

Rolling farmland and brilliant canyon scenery that makes the rest of the valley so interesting surrounds the small town, farther inside the valley from Chivay. It is a sleepy place, and most of the hotels nearby take advantage of that.

Sightseeing

Museo de Yanque – On the main Plaza, open Tues-Sun 7 am-6:30 pm. A small museum with an emphasis on the unique people and culture of the Colca region and how it differs from other Andean areas.

Where to Stay

Tradicion Colca – Jerusalén 300C, ☎ 205-336, www. tradicioncolca. 8m.com. Nineteen clean, basic rooms with private baths and hot water. Cafeteria. Nice grounds. Can arrange trekking to small canyon villages and thermal baths. $

El Mirador de los Collaguas – Lima 513, ☎ 54-44-8383, www. geocities.com/miradorcolca. Log cabin-ish hotel made of resources from the valley such as stone, wood, hay, and adobe. Eleven rooms

Iglesia de Yanque (Wilfredo Loayza)

with balconies overlooking the canyon. Will arrange trekking, mountain biking, rafting, kayaking, and fishing. La Casa Nostra restaurant. Parking for camper vans. $$$

Libertador Colcalodge – Near Yanque, ☎ 202-587 (Arequipa office), www.colca-lodge.com. Overlooking the Colca River, this country lodge is built entirely of mud bricks and stone, with thatched roof. Hot water (solar) with private baths and buffet breakfast included in price. There are no phones or TVs, but think of that as a plus. Restaurant, bar, living room with fireplace. Access to hot springs. They will arrange treks, mountain biking, rafting. $$$-$$$$

■ Cabanaconde

Phone code (054)

Buses leave and arrive at the town's main Plaza running to and from Chivay (two hours, $1) throughout the mornings, as well as in the late afternoon (although less frequent then). Most begin or continue on to Arequipa.

Where to Stay & Eat

Hotel Villa Pastor – On the main Plaza. Look for the flashing neon sign that says "Restaurant" on top of the building. Nice clean rooms, hot water. They have photocopied maps of the canyon and will even take you to the start of a trail for a small tip. Incredible value. In the off-season you can stay here for under $2 a person. $

There are just a few basic comedors or eating places scattered throughout the town. At night on the Plaza women at stalls sell pasta with fried chicken and potatoes. Very hearty and good before or after a long hike when you are just begging for calories.

Sightseeing

★Cruz del Condor

The mirador (lookout) called the Cruz del Condor is one of the best places in Peru to catch a glimpse of the magnificent Andean condor, which can have a wing span as wide as 10½ feet.

Mirador de Cóndores (Heinz Penge)

This is at one of the deepest points in the canyon. Condors can best be seen in the morning around 9 am and in the afternoon from 4-6 pm You can catch a 7 am bus from Chivay and ask to be let off here, or take the return bus from Cabanaconde at 7:30 and do the same. You can walk back to Cabanaconde from the mirador in about three hours, or hope for a waiting taxi or bus for the 20-minute ride. Many companies in Arequipa offer this as their "one-day canyon tour" – leaving from Arequipa in the morning, stopping at the Cruz del Condor, then for lunch in either Chivay or Cabanaconde and returning in the evening. Nearly all of the time is spent driving, however, and little of the actual canyon is seen.

★★★The Canyon

Unblemished Andean villages line both sides of the canyon and are not more than an hour or two apart. All have small hospedajes or pensions and will cook food (don't expect the Ritz for either), so

Cabanaconde (Heinz Plenge)

if you do not want to carry a tent or food you do not have to. The scenery consists of sparse vegetation, cactus, and the two rocky canyon walls that begin in a cool green river. There are

Herding llamas (Domingo Giribaldi)

plenty of different routes to take. Many people simply walk down to the oasis, stay the night, and walk back up the next day. Others take a round-trip, heading deeper into the canyon, crossing the river, climbing back down to the oasis and then up. If going this way it is recommended that you go counterclockwise because that will mean more downhill walking than up. Other options include hiking in various directions to the small, unspoiled pueblos of Tapay, Pinchollo, or Maca, passing ruins and natural sights along the way.

The Oasis

Cabanaconde campesinas (Heinz Plenge)

The oasis at the bottom of the canyon, Sangalle, is the usual destination for most hikers. They hike the two hours downhill from Cabanaconde in the morning, stay the night and leave the next day, avoiding seeing much of the canyon or the picturesque Andean villages. Some stay longer just to relax. Each of the two campgrounds is equipped with swimming pools, small rustic cabins, showers, bathrooms, and a restaurant/bar. They allow camping for a small fee. Can be quite cold at nights.

Tours

Nearly all tours are arranged from Arequipa, but it is very common and recommended to visit Colca on your own, as most tours provide very little extra. The cost for a two-day tour is about $35-$40 per person. Three-day tours are also available. One-day tours mainly consist of driving to the Cruz del Condor and back from Arequipa. Lots of driving time.

■ Tacna

Phone code (052)

Most skip over Tacna (population 230,000) en route from Arequipa to Chile (36 km/22 miles away) or vice-versa, but there are a few points of interest here that are well worth a day to explore. Patriotism runs deep here. Peru's very first calls for liberation came from Tacna resident Francisco Zela in 1811. The city was taken along with Arica by Chile in 1880 after the War of the Pacific, but in a treaty of 1929 its citizens voted to return to Peru. In 1928, then-President José La Mar gave Tacna the nickname of "Ciudad Heroica."

Tacna enjoys a relatively year-round sunny climate with little rain. Average temperature is 10-22°C/50-72°F.

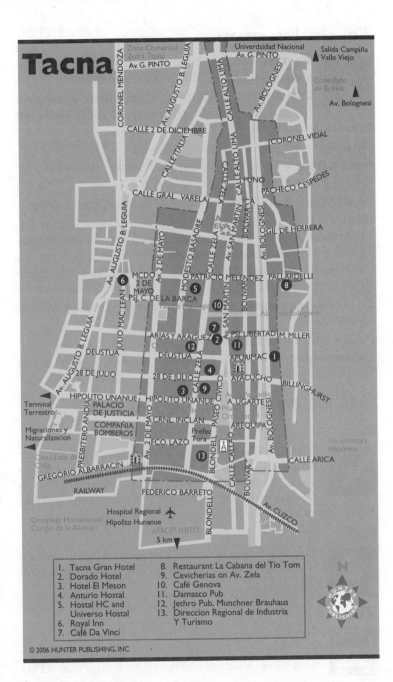

Tacna

Zona Comercial-
Zofra Tacna
Av. G. PINTO
Univerdsidad Nacional
Av. G. PINTO
Salida Campiña
Valle Viejo

Consulado
de Bolivia

Av. Bolognesi

CORONEL MENDOZA
Av. AUGUSTO B. LEGUIA
CALLE ALTO LIMA
Av. BOLOGNESI

CALLE 2 DE DICIEMBRE

CALLE ITALIA

CORONEL VIDAL

CALLE GRAL. VARELA
CALLE ALTO LIMA
PUNO
PACHECO CESPEDES

CALLE ZELA
Av. SAN MARTIN
BOLIVAR
ICA
Av. BOLOGNESI
GIL DE HERRERA

PLAZA
ZELA

Av. AUGUSTO B. LEGUIA
JULIO MAC LEAN

Av. 2 DE MAYO
MODESTO BASADRE
CALLE ZELA

6 MCDO
2 DE
MAYO
PSJ. C. DE LA BARCA
5 PATRICIO MELENDEZ
PALLARDELLI **8**

Teatro Municipal
10
Alameda Bolognesi

DEUSTUA
7
ARIAS Y ARAGUEZ **2** Av. PSJ. LIBERTAD M. MLLER
12 **11**
DEUSTUA
APURIMAC **1**

28 DE JULIO
28 DE JULIO **4** CALLE ZELA AYACUCHO
3 **9** BILLINGHURST

Av. AUGUSTO B. LEGUIA
PRESBITERO ANDIA

Terminal
Terrestro
HIPOLITO UNANUE
PALACIO
DE JUSTICIA
HIPOLITO UNANUE
PASEO CIVICO
A. UGARTE

Migraciones y
Naturalizocion
COMPAÑIA
BOMBEROS
CRNL. INCLAN
AREQUIPA

Consulado de
Chile
FCO. LAZO
Prefec
Tura
13
BLONDELL
CALLE CALLAO
Av. BOLOGNESI

Locomotora
Histórica

GREGORIO ALBARRACIN
CALLE ARICA

RAILWAY
FEDERICO BARRETO
BOLIVAR
Av. CUZCO

Complejo Monumental
Campo de la Alianza
Hospital Regional
Hipolito Hunanue
AEROPUERTO
5 km
BLONDELL

---

1. Tacna Gran Hotel	8. Restaurant La Cabana del Tio Tom
2. Dorado Hotel	9. Cevicherias on Av. Zela
3. Hotel El Meson	10. Café Genova
4. Anturio Hostal	11. Damasco Pub
5. Hostal HC and	12. Jethro Pub, Munchner Brauhaus
Universo Hostal	13. Direccion Regional de Industria
6. Royal Inn	Y Turismo
7. Café Da Vinci	

N

HUNTER
PUBLISHING

© 2006 HUNTER PUBLISHING, INC

Tourist Information

Tourist Office – **Dirección Regional de Industria y Turismo**, Blondell 50, ☎ 722-784.

Consulates – **Chilean Consulate**, Presbitero Andina and Av. Albarracín, ☎ 72-1846. **Bolivian Consulate**, Av. Bolognesi 1751, ☎ 74-5121.

Hospital – **Hipólito Unánue**, Blondell (no #) ☎ 723-431.

Post Office – Av. Bolognesi 301, ☎ 72-4221, open Mon-Sat, 8 am-8 pm.

Pharmacy – **Inkafarma**, Av. San Martín 537, ☎ 74-4096.

Banks – **Banco de la Nación**, Av. San Martín 320, ☎ 74-7474; **Banco Wiese Sudameris**, Av. San Martín 476, ☎ 052-72-7209; **Banco Continental**, Av. San Martín 665, ☎ 72-6551; **BCP**, Av. San Martín 574. All exchange traveler's checks and have ATMs.

Currency Exchange – **Cambios Tacna**, Av. San Martín 612, ☎ 74-3607.

Police – Callao 121, ☎ 71-4141.

Laundromat – **Lavandería Tacna**, Zela 374 A, one of the few lavanderías in Tacna.

Getting Here

Air

Airport Carlos Cirini Santa Rosa, on the Pan American Highway a few kms from town, ☎ 84-4503. Daily flights to Lima. Contact **Aero Continente** (☎ 747-300) for more information. Taxi to town is about $3.

Rail

The rail station is on Calle Gregorio Albarracín 412, ☎ 72-8029. Trains leave for Chile at 9 am and 4 pm ($1).

Bus

There are two stations, one for Chile and Bolivia and the other for national destinations. They are next to each other. Currency exchange and ATMs are in the station. Taxi to the center is about $1. The local departure tax is 1 sole.

- **Cruz del Sur** – www.cruzdelsur.com.pe. Arequipa, Nazca, Lima and Puno.
- **Ormeño** – www.grupo-ormeno.com. Same as Cruz del Sur.
- Buses across the border to Arica are about $1.50.

Getting Around

Most of Tacna's sites are within walking distance from the center. Places like the bus station and duty free zone are a 20-minute walk or a cheap cab ride.

Sightseeing

The **Paseo Civico**, in the center of Tacna, is quite lovely though it's not on the tourist trail. Most of the city's best monuments and attractions can be found on or near it. There are also lots of benches, bright flowers, palms, trees, statues, shops, cafés, hotels, restaurants, and pubs nearby.

Plaza de Armas, featured on the 100 sole note, is home to the Arco Parabolico, the city's proud symbol, which was built in 1959 and looks like a miniature version of the Gateway arch in St. Louis. It is a monument to the heroes of the war of the Pacific. And statues of Admiral Grau and Colonel Bolognesi stand on each side. The arch was designed by German architects and constructed of pinkish quarry stone. It stands 59 feet high and is a nice photo opportunity with the cathedral in the background.

The bronze fountain was created by Alejandro Gustavo Eiffel and thought to be a replica of the one in the Place de la Concorde in Paris.

The **Cathedral** was also designed by Eiffel and his firm. Construction began in 1875 but, due to construc-

Tacna Cathedral

tion difficulties, lack of funds, a change of countries to which Tacna belonged (twice) and a host of other mishaps, the inauguration wasn't until 1954, three quarters of a century later.

The charming, romantic tree-lined, tiled walk, **Alameda Bolognesi**, is also worth a stroll. It was constructed in 1840 for the prefect Manuel de Mendiburu.

Parque de la Locomotora houses the old 1859 No. 3 locomotive that carried supplies and men to Arica during the war with Chile. The park is in the middle of a busy intersection, but a few benches and statues surround it giving it somewhat of a tranquil feel.

There are two houses of historical interest in Tacna that are now museums. **Casa Zela** (Av. Zela 542) is the restored house of Francisco Zela who on June 20, 1811 gave Peru's call for Independence. The house has a courtyard with flowers, paintings of Peruvian generals and military figures, and pottery. It was declared a national monument in 1961. Free admission. Open 8 am-12 pm and 3-7 pm. However you may have to come back several times or wait until someone is around to let you in. **Casa de Jorge Basadre**, on the corner of Inclan and the Paseo Civico, hosts a local art gallery with mostly religious paintings and some photography. There is also a bronze statue and a creepy plaster of the hand and face of the house's former owner. Small and only worth a short look, but pleasant. Friendly, chatty porter. Free admission.

The **Museo Ferroviario** (Railroad Museum) is in an old rail station and one of the most interesting sights in the city. Several large rooms contain dusty remnants. There is a historical document room, mostly from the late 1800s and early 1900s, plus several rooms with old rail apparatus, machines, carts, and several antique engines. Almost all of the tools and equipment are original, making it one-of-a-kind on this continent. Admission 1 sole. Daily from 7 am-5 pm. Ring the bell.

Where to Stay

Tacna Gran Hotel – Av. Bolognesi 300, ☎ 724-193, fax 728-225, reserves@derrama.org.pe. It has a beautiful pool, bar, restaurant, Internet, and lavandería. Rooms are modern, with cable TV and hot water. Suites are available. The nicest hotel in Tacna, and a relatively good value. $$$

Dorado Hotel – Arias Araguez 145, ☎ 713-752, www.doradohotel.com. Elegant hotel right in the center of town. Classic lobby bar, restaurant, and all the amenities you could hope for. $$

Hotel El Meson – Hipólito Unánue 175, ☎ 714-070, fax 721-832, www.mesonhotel.com. Large cozy rooms with cable TV, hot water, minibar, room service. Can arrange rental cars, city tours, and translation services. $$

Anturio Hostal – 28 de Julio 194, ☎ 711-664, www.anturiohostaltacna.com. Good location just off the main strip. Basic, yet clean and cozy. Private bathrooms, hot water, cable TV, restaurant, laundry services. $

Hostal HC (Zela 734, ☎ 74-2042) and **Universo Hostal** (Zela 724, ☎ 71-5441), next door to each other, are clean and have hot water and cable TV.

Royal Inn – Av. Patricia Melendez 574. This is clean, secure, friendly and cheery. Rooms have cold-water showers. $

Lots of cheap hotels can be found near the bus station, but none are very good or clean. $

LOCAL GASTRONOMY

■ **Picante a la Tacneña** – Hot stew made with giblets, dried or salted meat, potatoes, pepper, oil, and oregano.

■ **Picante de guatita** – Hot peppered tripe.

■ **Pastel de choclo** – Fresh corn dish that can be either salty with a pork stew filling or sweet with a raisin filling.

■ **Cuy chactado** – Guinea pig pan-fried underneath a heavy flat stone.

■ **Chicarrones de chanco** – Small pieces of fried pork served with toasted maize.

■ **Tamales** – A dense corn-based lump wrapped in a banana leaf with one of many fillings such as chicken, pork, egg, or olives.

Southern Coast

Where to Eat

Café DaVinci – San Martín 596, ☎ 744-648. Stylish corner building with pastas, pizzas, fish, and many Italian dishes. Try **Leonardo Bar** next door by the same owners for after dinner drinks. Occasional live music. Open from 7 pm to 2 am. $$$

Restaurant La Cabana del Tio Tom – Across from the market. Has typical Tacneña and regional dishes such as cazuela (a rice, vegetable and chicken stew), picante a la Tacneña (a spicy tripe stew), and cojinova frita (fried fish). $

Tradiciones Peruanas Restaurante – Villa Universataria Capanique A, Pocollay, ☎ 848-472. They serve many national dishes and drinks. The menu is reasonably priced, with a glass of wine or Pisco, appetizer, main dish, and dessert for what amounts to just a few dollars. $$

Several good cevicherias are on Av. Zela near the Hotel El Dorado. **Pico Mar** is recommended. Try their chicarron de calamar or ceviche pescado. Both are unbelievable deals that would cost five times as much for any dish with similar ingredients in the United States. They have lunch menus that make it even cheaper. $

Café Genova – San Martín 649, ☎ 74-4809. A popular streetside café open late that serves snacks, desserts, light meals, and coffee drinks. $$

Bars & Clubs

Other than the many casinos that line Av. San Martín, Tacna has little to offer in the way of nightlife. A few restaurants stay open late for cocktails, but other than that there are just a few pubs in a two-block radius that are mostly empty, except on weekends.

- **Damasco Pub**, Pasaje Libertad 54, ☎ 724-473.
- **Jethro Pub**, Arias and Araguez 129.
- **Munchner Brauhaus**, 142 Arias Araguez.

Shopping

Shopping in Tacna usually means the duty-free zone, or **Zona Franca**. Parts of the city have been made into these zones where people from around Peru and Chile come to buy liquor, clothes, electronics, perfumes, jewelry and just about anything else tax-free. Most of the goods are not brand names. The easiest zone to reach is on Av. Colonel Mendoza, but there is also a huge zone of warehouse-type buildings on the Pan American Highway South, Km 1303. See www.zofratacna.com.pe for more information.

 Limits on duty free: You can shop there three times every 12 months, with no more than $1,000 spent per visit. There are also limitations on how much of certain items such as liquor and tobacco you can buy, but, unless you plan on buying cases or truckloads for export, you shouldn't have to worry.

The **Mercado Central** has a mixed array of mostly junk with DVDs, cosmetics, clothing, juice bars, butchers, etc. Nothing of interest other than supplies for daily life. There are a few good craft and antique shops next to the market that are worth a look, however.

Day-Trips from Tacna

- **Monumento a los Heroes del alto de la Alianza** or **the Alto de La Alianza**, is eight km/4.8 miles from the center, near the entrance to the city. About a 15-minute ride from the center by taxi or tour. This was the site of the battle of the same name on May 26, 1880. There is a museum with artifacts and weapons from the battle and the era such as rifles, sabres, uniforms, letters, documents and a scale model of the battle. Daily from 8 am-5 pm.

- **Boca del Río**, about 55 km/33 miles southwest of Tacna, is a small seaside resort with several hotels, hospedajes, and restaurants. Buses from Tacna on a paved road take 30-45 minutes.

- **San Francisco de Miculla Petroglyphs**, just 22 km/13 miles from Tacna, are nearly eight square miles of ancient stone carvings thought to be the earliest art in Peru (9000 BC). Hire a taxi guide in Tacna and negotiate price, or go with one of the tour companies that line Av. Bolognesi.

San Francisco de Miculla (© 2006 UPT)

- **Pocollay** is five km/three miles northwest of the city, a 10-minute drive. The small country town has nice scenery, with orchards, a few bodegas and several traditional restaurants. Many residents of Tacna head here on weekends.

Tour Companies

Several are on Av. Bolognesi, but none are particularly recommended.

To/From Chile

You can go by train, bus, or collectivo. The collectivo cars are big classic American gas hogs, usually a Grand Marquis; for just $3 per person you can make the short, uncomfortable ride fairly quickly that way. They wait outside the international terminals in Arica, Chile and Tacna and leave when full. It's easier to find an immediate ride in the morning. A driver will take you across the border and point you in the right direction for the paperwork. Finding a car with a Peruvian license plate rather than a Chilean one will save you about a $1. This works on both sides.

Border Crossing Information

Crossing between borders here is relatively quick and uncomplicated. Most collectivo drivers will help you through the process anyway. The checkpoint at the border is open from 8 am to 12 am Mon-Fri and 24 hours on the weekend. Remember that Chilean time can vary from one to two hours later than Peruvian time, depending on the time of year. Immigration is closed on public holidays. Chilean visas (not needed for citizens of the US or Canada) must be secured at the Chilean embassy in Tacna. No fruit or vegetables are allowed between borders. If leaving by private vehicle you must purchase four copies of the "relaciones de pasejeros" form available at the kiosk on the border. The drive and process takes one to two hours total, including about 45 minutes of drive time.

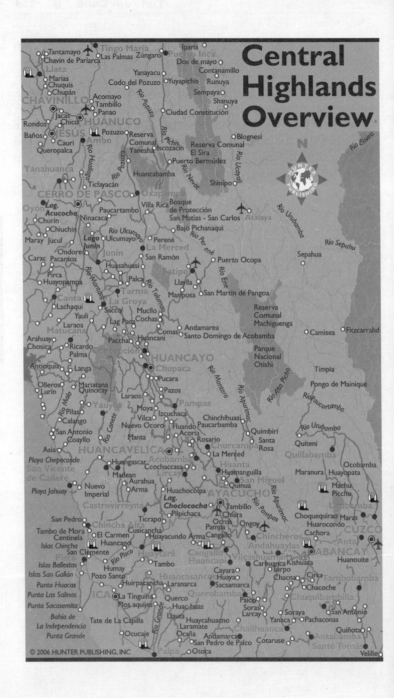

Central Highlands Overview

The Central Highlands

■ Huánuco

Phone code (062)

The local tourist board in Huánuco (population 140,000; elevation 1,895 m/ 6,216 feet) considers its climate to be the best in the world. Although that may be a bit of an overstatement, the brisk mountain air and wealth of sunshine serve

IN THIS CHAPTER	
■ Huánuco	253
■ Huancayo	258
■ Huancavelica	268
■ Abancay	273
■ Andahuaylas	275
■ Ayacucho	278

their purpose. Few tourists make their way here, but if you want to break the trip from Pucallpa to Lima this is the place. There is the temple of Kotosh and a few good restaurants and pubs that can help pass a day with ease.

HIGHLIGHTS

■ **Quinua** – This small village is home to a number of skilled craftsmen and some of the most unusual and elaborate ceramics and carvings in the country.

■ **Hiking in Huancayo** – The pristine beauty of the mountains around Huancayo and the total lack of tourists make this a great alternative to the trails near Cuzco and Huaraz.

■ **Ayacucho** – The Colonial gem is returning as a tourist powerhouse after years of terrorism kept the crowds away.

■ **Semana Santa** – The Easter week festival is the most elaborate in the highly religious city of Ayacucho.

Getting Here

Flights

LC Busre, ☎ 518-113, offers one midday flight to and from Lima three times per week (one hour, $79). **AeroCondor** (2 de Mayo 1253, ☎ 517-090)

also flies to Lima regularly. Both airlines cancel flights frequently due to lack of passengers.

Buses

Transportes Rey (28 de Julio 1215, ☎ 513-623) goes to Pucallpa (nine-12 hours, $8-$10) and Huancayo (eight-10 hours, $5).

ETPOSA (Castillo 800, ☎ 512-903) goes to Pucallpa and Lima. Most Pucallpa-bound buses will stop at Tingo María.

Bahia Continental (Valdizán 718, ☎ 519-999) goes to Lima, Tingo María, and Ayucucho.

You may be able to find collectivo taxis in town to Tingo María, Cerro de Pasco, and La Union. Inquire at **Mya Tours** (Prado 815, ☎ 525-175).

Banks

BCP (2 de Mayo 1005, ☎ 512-213) and **Banco Continental** (2 de Mayo 1137, ☎ 513-348) both have ATMs.

Sightseeing

Huánuco as a town has a few charming tree-lined parks and old Andean cobblestone streets good for a relaxing stroll. The Plaza de Armas and the few blocks surrounding it are where you will find nearly every hotel and the best restaurants.

The **Museo de Ciencias** is at Prado 495, ☎ 518-104. A friendly, chatty older gentleman gives brief tours. They have just about every animal in Peru here – stuffed. Don't forget to check out the case labelled "phenomenon," displaying an eight-legged lamb, ducks drinking tea, and frogs playing musical instruments. Also a small pottery collection, photos, and two mummies. Admission 1 sole. Open Mon-Sat 9 am-noon, 3-6 pm. Sun 10 am-1 pm.

The **Temple of Kotosh**, or the Temple of Manos Cruzada (Temple of Crossed Hands), is a ceremonial site belonging to the Pre-Ina culture of Kotosh, one of Peru's earliest civilized societies. The ruins are in shabby condition, but it looks as if they have done some preservation work lately. The pair of crossed hands made of molded mud is thought to date to between 2000 BC and 100 AD. The actual hands, however, are in the archaeological museum in Lima. Some benches, concrete paths, a scenic bridge over a small stream, a performance area, and a souvenir stand round out the site. Admission 3 soles (1.5 for students). Taxi ride: 5 soles. Open daily 9 am-3 pm.

Where to Stay

Prince Hotel – 28 de Julio 928, ☎ 516-161. On the Plaza. The best of a line of several cheap hotels. Includes cable TV, phone, fans, and private baths with hot water. Suites available with Jacuzzis. $

Grand Hotel Huánuco – Damaso Beraun 775, ☎ 514-222, fax 512-410, www.grandhotelhuanuco.com. Lovely stone building with spotless and timeless Colonial furnishings. Without question the best hotel in Huánuco. All of the amenities are here, such as cable TV, private baths with hot water, telephones, free Internet, 24-hour room service, gym, sauna, and pool. Suites are also available. Excellent restaurant. Price includes breakfast. $$

El Roble – Constitución 629. Small, quiet hospedaje with small-town charm. Friendly, plant-filled balcony. Rooms with or without private baths, hot water.

Gran Hotel Cuzco – Huánuco 616, ☎ 513-578, fax 514-360. Rooms with private baths, supposedly hot water (but it is more like lukewarm). Cable TV. Aged, but a good choice if you want something simple and straightforward. Restaurant. $

Real Hotel – 2 de Mayo 1125, ☎ 511-777, 512-765, realhotel@terra.com.pe. It is the flashy hotel on the Plaza. The second-best hotel after the Grand.

HOTEL PRICE CHART	
	under $10
$	$10-$25
$$	$26-$50
$$$	$51-$90
$$$$	$91-$150
$$$$$	Over $150

Rooms come with cable TV and private baths (lukewarm). Includes access to the pool and sauna. Attached to a good casino with craps, slots, and poker, as well as a restaurant, and discoteca. $$

Where to Eat

 La Sazon de Pedrito – 860 Prado. This is a popular local dive with a cheap menu (5-6 soles) that includes chicha morada (a purple corn drink). Sometimes it is hard to get a table and dishes run out. Try picante de cuy (spicy guinea pig), cabrito a la norteña (a northern-style goat dish), pachamanca (a hearty variety of meats and vegetables cooked in the ground), papas a al huanacaina (potatoes in a cheesy pepper sauce). $

Buena Vida – Abtao 1011. Large, clean and stylish vegetarian restaurant with fruit juices. $

Lookco's – Abtao 1021. Typical fast food burger joint with a variety of styles. Popular with a young crowd. They play live concert DVDs on the TVs. $

El Rodeo – 1019 Abtao. Next to Lookco's, this modest place serves trucha (trout), steaks, and chicharron (fried pork). $

Govinda – Vegetarian restaurant, part of the national chain run by Hare Krishnas. $

La Hacienda – 28 de Julio 1019. Not the same as the bar mentioned below. Small café with wine, sugar cane juice, natural foods. $

DINING PRICE CHART	
$	under $5
$$	$5-$10
$$$	$11-$20
$$$$	$21-$35
$$$$$	over $35

Bars

 Sabor Latina – Adjoined to the Real Hotel. Peña and disco with free admission. One of the few discos in town. Sundays they have pachamanca (a hearty variety of meats and vegetables cooked in the ground).

La Hacienda – 685 Prado. Slick watering hole with attractive wood decor.

Cheers – On the corner of the Plaza. Cheap drinks, chicken and karaoke from a second-floor balcony.

Day-Trips from Huánuco

Road to Tingo María (Renzo Uccelli)

Tingo María is the town 129 km/77 miles north of Huánuco, but there is little in the town itself (and it's known for narco trafficking, so Huánuco is a better base). It sits adjacent to the Parque Nacional de Tingo María, which has a luscious display of green hills, waterfalls, and caves. Cole and Mya Tours (see below) offer full-day trips to Tingo María that visit the park and stop at the waterfall of San Miguel, the Owl cave, sulphuric waters, a mini-zoo, and Tingo María itself. Price about $25 per person, depending on the number of people.

Villa Jennifer – Km 3.5 Catillo Grande, ☎ 969-5059, www.villajennifer.net. This peaceful farm and lodge is near Tingo María and offers bird watching and area tours. Charming, eclectic buildings and rooms. $10 per person including breakfast. Weekend packages available. There is a mini-zoo with caimans and parrots.

San Miguel Falls
(Renzo Uccelli)

Tours

There are just two tour companies in town and both offer roughly the same things – **Cole Travel** (28 de Julio 910, ☎ 991-6465, coletravel@hotmail.com) and **Mya Tours** (Prado 815, ☎ 52-5175, myatourshco@hotmail.com). City tours are four hours and cost just 22 soles. They also run day-tours to Tingo María and can arrange treks on the Yarowilca circuit (three days).

■ Huancayo

Phone code (064)

Huancayo (population 350,000; elevation 3,249 m/10,657 feet), capital and business center of the Junín province, is one of the most under-appreciated highland cities in Peru. Founded in 1572 by Jeronimo de Silva, the city has played host to several major historical events such as the Battle of Junín and the first continental congress. It is easily accessible, at just seven hours from Lima. There are some interesting workshops you can take that go far beyond language lessons, such as carving and music. The available hikes in the area rival those around Cuzco and are far less crowded. It is the home of the national favorite papas a la Huancaina (potatoes in a cheesy pepper sauce). The highest railway in the world can be found here. There are a few good nightlife options. Some interesting restaurants. The best gourd- and wood-carvings in the country. And they say that in the Mantaro Valley there is a party every day of the year.

Cathedral of Huancayo
(Anibal Solimano)

Huancayo

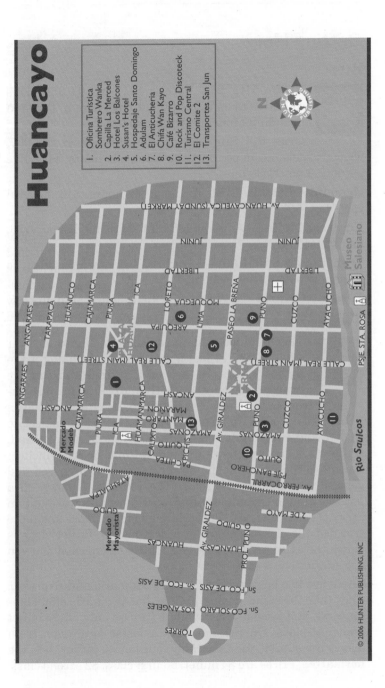

1. Oficina Turistica
2. Sombrero Wanka
   Capilla La Merced
3. Hotel Los Balcones
4. Susan's Hotel
5. Hospedaje Santo Domingo
6. Adulam
7. El Anticucheria
8. Chifa Wan Kayo
9. Café Bizarro
10. Rock and Pop Discoteck
11. Turismo Central
12. El Comite 2
13. Transportes San Jun

Getting Here

Bus

El Comite 2 – Loreto 421, ☎ 804-356. Has collectivo taxis to just about anywhere in the area including Lima and Huancavelica.

Cruz del Sur – Ayacucho 281/287, ☎ 223-367, www.cruzdelsur.com.pe. Buses to Lima (six hours, $10); five per day. 8 am-11:30 pm.

Ormeño – Castilla 1379. To Lima, six hours, $10. Several each day.

Empresa Molina – Angaraes 334. To Ayacucho, 11 hours, $6, four times daily.

Transportes San Juan – Ferocarril 461 and Amazonas. To Tarma, two hours, every hour.

Turismo Central – Ayacucho 274. To Huánuco, six hours, $5.

Train

The highland rail infrastructure climbs to over 4,800 m/15,744 feet above sea level, making it the highest railway in the world. At time of writing the train station only serves Huancavelica. but on occasion the train may go to Cerro de Pasco, La Oroya, and even Lima. This is rare, unfortunately. All times are subject to change and often do. It is a good idea to check a day ahead. Buffet class, contrary to what you may think, does not include a meal in the price. Meals, however, are well prepared and generally cost about 10 soles. The route to Huancavelica passes through 38 tunnels, unspoiled Andean towns, and an array of colorful views. The train tends to get more and more crowded the closer you get to a destination. Buffet class is worth the extra price because it is the least crowded and you are guaranteed a seat.

There are two basic types of trains, Ordinario and Expresso. They take the same amount of time, but Ordinario offers buffet, first, and second class, while Expresso only offers buffet and first class. On Fri and Sun, a faster autovagon train leaves the station and takes only four hours, rather than the normal 6½. Prices are $4 buffet, $3 first class, $2 second class.

The autovagon costs $6. Tickets are sold beginning one day before and the day of the journey from noon to 6 pm.

Huancavelica Station – Augusto Leguia no #, ☎ 752-898, is walking distance from town or a short cab ride ($1). Mon-Sat – Expresso (6:30 am), Ordinario (12:30); Sun – Expresso (2 pm); Fri and Sun – Autovagon (6 pm).

Chilca Station – Ferrocarril 461, ☎ 233-280, is where to go for rail trips other than to Huancavelica. To Lima the trip costs $25/35 (one way/return). Runs infrequently. Leaves Fri from Lima, returns Sun. The trip takes 12 hours each way.

Car Rental

Hertz – Ancash 367 (Plaza Constitución), ☎ 233-705.

Tourist Information

Tourist Office – **Oficina Turistica Sombrero Wanka**. This booth has a big golden hat and is run by Eco Aventura. It has loads of information on the area and offers tours as well. Look for it in Parque Huanamarca.

Tour Company – ★**Incas del Peru**. This is an excellent tour company that has attracted more gringos to little-known Huancayo than anyone else. www.Incasdelperu.org. Lucho Hurtado speaks excellent English and the office is a wealth of information on the region. See more on their tours below.

Banks – BCP, Real 1039. Changes travelers checks and gives cash advances on Visa.

Post Office – Serpost, Huanamarca 350, Mon-Sat 8 am-8 pm, Sun 9 am-1 pm.

Hospital – **Daniel Carrión**, Carrión 1552, ☎ 222-1157. Open 24 hours.

Police – Ferrocarril 580, ☎ 219-851.

Sightseeing

Plaza de la Constitución doesn't have the grandeur of plazas like those of Arequipa or Cuzco, but it does have a certain charm. The Neo-Classical city

Central Highlands

Capilla in Cerrito de La Libertad (Anibal Solimano)

cathedral is there, a craft market is near, and throughout the day it sees quite a bit of human traffic.

The city's most famous church is the **Capilla La Merced** (1839), at Real and Ayacucho, It has been declared a national monument because it was the site where the Peruvian continental congress met for the first time.

Cerrito de La Libertad, 1 km east of the city, is a natural mirador or lookout spot, with a small church, park, amphitheater, small restaurants with regional dishes, and even a zoo. There are wonderful views of the entire city and surroundings.

Two km/1.2 miles from Cerrito de La Libertad you can see the geological formation called **Torre Torre**. The phallic-shaped erosions resemble a smaller version of Utah's Bryce Canyon National Park.

Torre Torre (Anibal Solimano)

The beautiful little gated ★**Parque de la Identidad Wanka** is reminiscent of Parque Guell in Barcelona, Spain. It is one of my favorite small parks in all of Peru. The mix of mosaic, ironwork, gold statues of Andean characters, beautiful plants, flowers and fountains has a very whimsical effect. Impossible not to fall in love with it. Taxi from the center is 3 soles. Admission free.

Museo Salesiano, at Santa Rosa 299, ☎ 247-763, in the Salesian School, is the best museum in Huancayo. The cultural and science center has 7,000 samples of birds, reptiles, and mammals, 750 archeological exhibits, 530 paleontological items, 650 mineral samples, Colonial paintings, and even a stamp collection. Basic, but well organized. Mon-Fri 8 am-12 pm and 2-6 pm. Admission 2 soles.

Where to Stay

 ★**La Casa de La Abuela** (Grandma's House) – Giráldez 691, ☎ 234-383, www.casa_abuela@yahoo.com. This is *the* gringo hotel in Huancayo, but don't let that fool you. It just goes to show how pleasant a place Huancayo can be. The place, run by Grandma herself, is charming and very well kept. Lots of amenities like 24-hour  hot water, travel info, Internet, laundry, kitchen, cable TV, game room, garden, BBQ area and free pickup from the bus station. South American Explorer's Club members and readers of this book receive a 10% discount. $

Hotel Los Balcónes – Puno 282, ☎ 211-041, www.losbalconeshuancayo.com. Near Parque Constitución. Rooms have hot water, cable TV, and phones. Bathrooms are tiled and sparkling clean. Nothing luxurious, but a good deal for the price. Clean, modern restaurant and lounge area. 50 soles for a double. $

Susan's Hotel – Real 851, ☎ 202-251, ☎ 202-722, susans_hotel@hotmail.com. Somewhat modern hotel with sauna and a good seafood restaurant. Room service available. Clean, with new, although shabby, furniture. Price includes hot water, cable TV, and use of the sauna (which can also be used for a small fee if not staying at the hotel). $$

Hotel Turismo – Ancash 729, ☎ 231-072, hotelhyo@correo. dnet.com.pe. Attractive brick hotel in a convenient setting on Plaza Huananmarca. From the inside it looks like a medieval castle with iron chandeliers, Colonial furnishings, and a coat of arms. All the amenities such as private baths, hot water, and cable TV are offered. Price includes breakfast buffet. $$

Hotel Kiya – Giráldez 107, ☎ 214-955, fax 214-957. Rooms have private baths with hot showers. Cable TV is an additional charge. Suites are available. Restaurant with breakfast. $

Hotel Presidente – Real 1138, ☎ 231-736, fax 231-275. Associated with the Hotel Turismo. Modern facilities, private hot-water baths, and price includes breakfast. $$

Hospedaje Santo Domingo – Ica 675. Pleasant two-story building with a flower-filled courtyard and 24-hour hot water.

GASTRONOMY

Papas a la Huancaina – Boiled potatoes in a mildly spicy cheese sauce. Served with a slice of egg and olive.

Pachamanca – Various meats, corns, beans, and potatoes that are cooked in a hole in the ground.

Cuy Colorado – Fried guinea pig in a sauce made of chili, peanuts, and onions.

Caldo de Cabeza – Lambs head soup. Also contains potatoes, onions, and garlic.

Where to Eat

★**Adulam** – Arequipa 952. Several small nooks and a charming patio with ample seating. Lots of plants and clever woodwork. Looks like something out of *Lord of the Rings*. Serves cuy chactado, ceviche, and chicharrónes. Friendly staff. Highly recommended. $$

Antojitos – Puno 588. A longtime popular local hangout with lovely music on most nights after 9 pm. It has a good variety of comfort foods like burgers, pizzas, and anticuchos. Good for drinks. $$

El Anticucheria – Puno 589. Small, but popular dive with a cheap and excellent variety of anticuchos. $

La Cabana and **El Otro Lado** – Giráldez 652, ☎ 22-3303. Opens every day after 5 pm, these two adjoined restaurants have a large menu (that features tourist info on the area as well). Parrilladas, truchas, pizzas, and much more. Cold, try a calientito (a hot, sweet lemon tea). Folklore shows Tues, Fri, and Sat after 9 pm. Happy hour 5-7 pm daily and the bar can get lively at night. $$

Leopardo – Huánuco 716, ☎ 235488. More than two decades in service, it has a wide variety of regional dishes such as mondongo (vegetable and tripe soup), picante de cuy (spicy guinea pig), papas a la Huancaina (potatoes in a cheesy pepper sauce), pachamanca (a hearty variety of meats and vegetables cooked in the ground), and several types of ceviches (marinated raw seafood dishes), tiraditos (marinated raw seafood in a cheesy sauce), and chicharrónes (fried pork). Sometimes has a live show. $$

Chifa Wan Kayo – Puno 550. A basic chifa or Chinese restaurant, but what a clever name (Huancayo in Chinese)! $

Nuevo Horizante – Ica 578. Pleasant but worn vegetarian restaurant with a friendly yellow and green interior. Dirtcheap vegetarian menus (breakfasts too). They also have traditional meat-based Peruvian dishes using tofu and soy. $

Italia Pizzeria – ☎ 233-145 (delivery). Pizza, lasagna, fettuccini, and pizziolas. $

There is a **Casa Sueldo supermarket** at Real 656. On Ica, block 3, there are many good juice stands.

Bars/Nightlife

 La Noche – San Antonio 241, ☎ 223-726. This 18-and-over discoteca (rare in the highlands) is where the local upscale party crowd comes to shake it. A bit out of the center so take a cab.

Café Bizarro – Puno 656. Stylish rock bar that almost seems out of place in Huancayo.

Café Sol y Luna –Puno 584. Small, loud bar.

Central Highlands

Rock and Pop Discoteck – Puno 190. Classic Latin dance house with international music.

Shopping

Feria Dominical (Sunday Craft Market) takes place on numerous blocks of Huancavelica and brings in crafts from the surrounding villages.

There is also a craft market, **Casa del Artesenio**, at Real 481 on Plaza Constitución. Good selection of textiles, jewelry, carved gourds, and woodcarvings.

Language Lessons & Other Courses

Incas del Peru (Giráldez 652, ☎ 223-303, www.incasdelperu.com), offers a wide range of courses for travelers. Spanish language lessons are available in four categories, ranging from Budget to Interactive. They include stays at La Casa de La Abuela and three daily meals. $110-260. Programs start every Monday. Quechua lessons and monthly rates available. Other cultural courses include cooking, weaving, gourd carving, dancing, music, and jewelry making. Prices are $8 per hour and include one-on-one instruction. A minimum of 15 hours is required.

INCAN RECORD KEEPING

The Inca government was very organized and kept detailed records, although they never developed an advanced writing system. Their method of counting, called the quipu, was quite elaborate. The system used knotted cords to keep data. Each knot suggested a unit of 10, 100, 1,000, or 10,000. Each cord was tied to a thicker cord and kept track of items such as crops, soldiers, or gold. Quipucamayocs, or accountants, managed each of the quipus. The cords were different colors or sizes to distinguish what each item was.

Day-Trips from Huancayo

Cochas Chico and **Cochas Grande**, 11 km, is the home of the famous mate burilado, carved gourds that are found across Peru. Collectivos from Giráldez and Amazonas: 1 sole. A few other nearby towns are known for their crafts: **San**

Typical dress in Junín area
(Anibal Solimano)

Agustín de Cajas (hats), **San Pedro** (furniture), and **Hualhuas** (alpaca weavings). All are within 10 km/six miles and can be reached by taxi. Also, in **San Jeronimo**, 25 minutes north, you can find fine crafts made in silver at good prices. Every tour company offers day-trips to the villages ($25-45 per person, depending on the number of people, including lunch and guide). You can follow walking or biking trails to any of these places. Inquire at Incas del Peru for detailed directions.

Wari Wilca Ruins – Seven km/4.2 miles south of Huancayo is the predominant archeological complex in the Mantaro Valley. The site dates to 800 AD and was a place for magical and spiritual rituals. It is believed that the first Wanka couple, the first Waris, rose up from the water there. This is the major stop on the day-long archeological circuit that every tourist office offers ($25-45 per person, depending on the number of people, including lunch and guide).

Adventures

★★Hiking

There are quite a few treks in the area, even rivaling Cuzco in scenic beauty, but the small Andean villages here are far more unspoiled and rarely see a foreign visitor. **Incas del Peru** is the most qualified tour company and offers the widest variety of treks in the region. Other companies, however, may be able to arrange les expensive treks.

Huaytapallana Mountain – This beautiful mountain rarely sees a foreign tourist. Hikes to the top take just a few hours, but can be difficult. Cochas Grande, an emerald lake, and the Huaytapallana glacier are the highlights. Skiing and snowboarding are possible in the high snow-covered zones... but don't expect a lift. One- to three-day treks are offered from Incas del Peru at $30-$105 per person, depending on the number of people and length of the trip. Food and guide are included.

Camino Huanca – Five days. Known to be an authentic Andean experience. Horses and llamas are used to carry packs and equipment. Incredibly scenic and untrodden. $175 per person.

Chancamayo Valley – This five-day trek into the high jungle passes through coffee plantations, waterfalls, cloud forests, and offers the chance to see rare Amazonian wildlife. $175 per person.

■ Huancavelica

Phone code (6495)

Plaza de Armas (Walter Wust)

You will probably be the only tourist in this quiet city of 35,000 at 3,690 m/12,103 feet elevation. Don't let that stop you though. The small town is set amidst high mountains and green hills. There are a few good day-hikes that you can do without a guide. The town was founded not long after the Conquest in 1571, but as early as 1564 the Spanish (with the help of native slaves) began taking mercury from the mines there. The idea to use Huancavelica mercury to extract the silver in Potosi, Bolivia would lead to a significant source of income for the Spanish empire. May to October tends to be warm in the daytime, while the rest of the year tends to be cold and wet. The roads can become quite bad and are sometimes closed during the rainy season.

Getting Here

Bus

Oropesa – O'Donovan 599, ☎ 753-181. Goes to Ica, Pisco, and Lima (12 hours, 25 soles, 5:30 pm).

Exp. Huancavelica – Muñoz 516, ☎ 752-964. Goes to Huancayo (five hours, 10 soles, 5 pm) and to Lima, which is usually a bit faster via this route.

Lobato – Muñoz 489. Has the best buses to Lima (11 hours, 25 soles, 6:30 pm).

Ayacucho – To get to Ayacucho vía Lircay there are infrequent buses. Ask several of the companies on Muñoz if there are any buses leaving for this seven-hours, 221-km/133-mile trip (20 soles).

Train

Huancavelica station – On Av. A.B. Leguia on the south east of the Plaza, ☎ 752-898.

- Mon-Sat – Expresso (6:30 am), Ordinario (12:30 pm)
- Sun – Expresso (6:30 am)
- Fri and Sun – Autovagon (5:30 pm)

Tourist Information

Tourist Office – Dirección de Turismo, Garma 444 (2nd floor), ☎ 752-938. This is a small, but friendly and helpful office that can give directions and maps for local hikes. Mon-Fri 8 am-1 pm, 2-5 pm.

Instituto Nacional de Cultura (INC) – Raimondi 205, on Plaza San Juan de Dios. Has a small museum with pottery and a few mummies. May be able to arrange dance or music lessons if you come on the right day. Tues-Sun 10 am-1 pm and 3-6 pm. Admission free.

Banks – There is a **BCP** at Toledo 384 and it has an ATM. There is also a Multired ATM near the Municipilidad (City Hall).

Sightseeing

The Plaza de Armas is of a quaint Andean style and is calm and pleasant. The city **Cathedral** (1673) is well known for its altarpiece, which is thought to be one of the best Colonial altars in the country. **Mirador Cerro Oropesa**, on the south end of town, was being reconstructed at the time of writing. When finished there will be fountains, statues, benches, and small shops and

Cathedral

restaurants. all with a lovely view of the city and its surroundings.

Street in Huancavelica

At the ★**Sunday Market**, vendors come from as far away as Lircay (80 km) to sell their crafts. The ones from Lircay wear the archetypal dress of the region: austere all-black clothes, though the men also wear bright rainbow-colored pom poms on their belts and women wear colored shawls. Mainly a showcase for textiles, from wool to alpaca, food, and typical market wares. The market crowds much of Torre Tagle on the south end of town.

Huancavelica is known for its many Colonial churches, but they are generally closed to the public. The altars are usually silver here, as opposed to most Colonial churches in the country (gold is standard). Among the best churches are:

- **San Francisco** – 17th-century. This church on Plaza Bolognesi has an astounding 11 altars.

- **Santo Domingo** – 17th-century. Has Italian-made statues of the saint of the same name and the Virgen of Rosario.

- **Santa Ana** – 16th-century. The oldest in Huancavelica, built just after the foundation of the city.

- **San Sebastian** – 17th-century. This church has been restored. The architectural design, with three entrances, is unique in the region.

Santa Ana

Where to Stay

Hotel Presidente – ☎ 752-760. On the Plaza, Huancavelica's nicest hotel and the only non-budget option. Imposing stone building with a Colonial lobby. Rooms have private hot-water baths and cable TV. Much cheaper without bath. Suites are available as well. Also has a good restaurant. $$

La Portada – Toledo 252. Cozy, with hot water and cable TV. $

Hospedaje San José – Huancayo 299, ☎ 752-598. Very basic, but clean and near the train station. Hot water if requested in advance. $

Hotel Camacho – Carabaya 481, ☎ 753-298. Basic, but clean and cared for. Some rooms have private hot-water baths (mornings only) and/or TVs. $

Ascension – Manco Cápac 481, ☎ 753-103. Simple, but rooms have private hot (warm) baths and TVs. $

Savoy – Muñoz 296. Very basic with shared cold-water baths, but clean. $

Where to Eat

Restaurant Diana – 152 Gamarra. Small, pleasant café on a quiet street with more chicken dishes than tables. Breakfast menu available (usually chicken as well). $

Mochicha Sachun – Toledo 303. Simple, hearty Andean fare, chicken, sandwiches. Cheap menus. $

Restaurant Joy – Set lunches and sandwiches. Also has several styles of cuy (guinea pig), such as Colorado and picante. $

Restaurant Fuente de Soda – On the Plaza at the entrance to the theater. An excellent new restaurant that has picante de cuy, trucha (trout), milanesa de pollo and several other regional dishes. Lunch menus are just five soles and include soup, salad, main course, and postre (dessert). Amazing value. $

D'Candela – 432 Muñoz. This peña is also a chifa (Chinese restaurant) with local/regional plates as well. $

There are two marisquerias, or seafood restaurants, beside each other at 434 and 438 Muñoz. Both are similar and will give you your highland ceviche fix.

Adventures

On Foot

Hiking

The hike to the **Mercury Mine** leads to dazzling views of the valley below, passing herds of sheep and llamas, through charming pine forests and mountain streams. The walk should take four to six hours, depending on your physical condition. One way is to walk up to the Mirador on the north end of town. Look at the mountain somewhat above the train station and follow the steps leading up. From there you can take the pack animal trail for 1½ to two hours to the road. The climb goes to about 4,000 m/13,200 feet and can be steep. Follow the road to the

top of the abandoned mining
town of Santa Barbara. You
can go into the mine a little
ways, but be sure to bring a
flashlight. The Mina de la
Muerte, or death mine, was
closed in 1976. From there,
you must hike down into the
valley to the main section of
the town of Santa Barbara,
which includes a scenic stone
church and grassy plaza.
Then follow the road to where
the path splits and you can go
around the mountain to the
more rural eastern end of
Huancavelica or between the
mountains to the forested

Vilca Waterfall

stone path back to Huancavelica. You can also take the stone
path directly to the mines. For the reverse route, just go to the
northeast end of town, climbing the stairs and passing the
bridges between the mountains until you find the path going
up. There are places to rest along the way.

For the next two hikes, get a map from the tourist office. Each
will lead you into small Andean villages that rarely see a tourist and are areas of great natural beauty.

■ **Circuito Potocchi – Sacsamarca** – Six hours
■ **Circuito Santa Barbara** – Five hours

■ Abancay

Phone code (084)

The Apurimac region is little explored. The capital of Abancay
(population 100,000, altitude 2,378 m/7,800 feet) has little to
offer other than a rest in between the trip from Cuzco and
Ayacucho and a base for excursions into the surrounding
countryside. **Santuario Nacional Ampay**, home to Ampay
mountain (5,228 m/17,148 feet) and excellent birding and
camping is 10 km/six miles northwest of town. Also, treks to
Choquequirao, river rafting, biking, and numerous other out-

door adventures can be arranged. The town has become, in recent years, notorious for narco-trafficking. So be cautious.

Getting Here

Bus

There is a brand new terminal at the south end of town (two km from the center). All companies now have their offices there. Taxi to the center $1.

To Andahuaylas (five hours, $4); Cuzco (187 km/112 miles, five hours, $4); Lima via Nazca (18-20 hours, $15-25). For Ayacucho it is best to change buses in Andahuaylas.

Banks

There is a **BCP** with a Visa ATM on the Plaza.

Where to Stay

Gran Hotel – Arenas 196, ☎ 321-144. Some rooms with private hot-water baths, some with TVs. Old and worn, but does the job.

Hostal El Dorado – Arenas 131, ☎ 322-005. Some rooms with private hot-water baths and TVs. Nothing to e-mail home to mom about. $

Hoteles y Turismo Abancay – Barcenas 500, ☎ 321-017, www.apu-rimak.com/hoturs/index.html. Rooms have wood floors and country-style furnishings, cable TV, and private hot-water baths. Suites have Jacuzzis. First-level rooms are slightly more expensive. Nice gardens and a large conference area. Includes continental breakfast. Also a restaurant, bar, and Internet access. $$-$$$

El Encanto de Oro – Arenas 120, ☎ 322-525. Bright, clean, rooms have private baths with hot water, cable TV, and telephones. Also, a location in Andahuaylas. $$

Where to Eat

Restaurant La Delicia – Barcenas 216. Large, mostly vegetarian menu. One of the best places in town offering hundreds of choices. Meat dishes too. $

La Leña – In the small plaza near the market, has parrilladas, chicken, and a nice bar. Rustic, Texas-like saloon atmosphere. $$

Cebicheria Boulevard – At the small park with the statue of an Indian woman in broken chains. Patio tables offer good views of what Abancay has to offer. $

Café Volga – Barceneras 102. Pizzas, omelets, ice cream, tequeños. Small but modern. $

Restauarant Vegetereano – Barceneras 213. Small café with sandwiches, juices, and natural food products. $

Chifa Shanghai – Arenas 198. Popular chifa (Chinese restaurant) with a McDonald's-like atmosphere. Recommended. $

Tour Companies

Apu-rimak Tours and Travel – Sousa and Apurimac, ☎ 321-017, fax 321-017, www.apu-rimak.com. This region is one of the most scenic and under-explored in Peru. This is the only tour company in Abancay. They arrange river rafting in Pachachaca ($35), treks to Choquequirao (two-five days, $200-350), city tours ($33), scenic trips to Cuzco, horseback riding, mountain biking, and climbing Apu Ampay ($110). Can also arrange volunteer work in Apurimac.

THE INCAS & RAP MUSIC

Quechua people always used to pour a little bit of chicha on the floor to thank the Gods before drinking. The practice was later adopted by gangsta rappers in the United States, who would pour some beer on the ground in tribute to their dead comrades, as popularized in many music videos. Also, the name Tupac, used by rappers such as Tupac Shakur, was originally the name of an Inca, Tupac Amaru.

■ Andahuaylas

Phone code (083)

This small town of 25,000 (altitude 3,000 m/9,840 feet) seems little more than a peaceful stop between Cuzco and Ayacucho, but many visit and fall in love with Andahuaylas. The country charm and the beautiful scenery that surrounds the place are enchanting. The town itself has just a few hotels and the restaurants are basic. Plaza de Armas is simple and has a pleasant cathedral that is usually open, as well as a small museum.

Central Highlands

You won't see any other tourists and facilities are few and far between, but if you want to experience a real Andean town that has managed to keep its composure, this is the place.

Getting Here

Air

Aero Condor – Ayacucho 118 (on the Plaza), ☎ 72-1330. Has flights to Lima several times a week ($60-$80, one hour) and sometimes to Ayacucho. The airport is 20 minutes south of town and can be reached by taxi for $3-$4.

Bus

Expresso Los Chankas – Grau 232, ☎ 722-441. To Ayacucho in the evening (10 hours, $7).

Transportes San Jeronimo – Andahuaylas 116, ☎ 721-400. Cuzco (10 hours, $8) and Abancay (five hours, $4).

Expresso Molina – Just over the bridge on Los Sauces. Has buses to Abancay, Ayacucho, and Cuzco. Recommended.

Bank

BCP at Ramón Castilla has a Visa ATM.

Sights

The **Municipal Museum** on the Plaza. Just one small room of pottery, skulls, and a few mummies. Information in Spanish and English. Free. Hours are sporadic.

Where to Stay

El Encanto de Oro – Casafranca 424, ☎ 723-066. Bright, clean rooms have private baths with hot water, cable TV, and telephones. $$

Sol de Oro Hotel – Trelles 164, ☎ 721-152, fax 721-305, soldeorohotel@terra.com.pe. Rooms are homey with private hot-water baths, TVs, and phones. Continental breakfast is included. $$

Imperio Chanka – Clean and new building east of the center. Private hot-water baths and cable TV. Room service. Suites also available. $

There are several small, basic hospedajes on Ramos, all with similar rates and quality. $

Where to Eat

Panificadora – Castilla 599. On a corner of the Plaza. This clean, contemporary bakery has breads, cakes, pastries, coffee, and teas. $

D'Onofrio – Plaza next to the municipal building. Snacks and ice cream. Sparkling clean. $

El Roble – Trelles 264. For local dishes, caldos (soups), etc. $

Chifa El Dragon – Intersection of Ramos and Trelles. It says a lot about the food in Andahuaylas when a Chinese restaurant is the best in town. Also has some criollo dishes. Cheap menus with won ton soup. $

The **Mercado** is at Casafranca and Trelles. Lots of produce, cheeses, and a small craft selection.

Day-Trips from Andahuaylas

★**Puchaca** (www.munipacucha. gob.pe), 17 km/10 miles from Andahuaylas, is a smaller, Andean version of Lake Tahoe. Mountains rise strait out of the cool blue water. Vicuñas graze on the grassy hillsides. There are just a few small restaurants and you can rent small boats and fishing gear. Collectivo taxis ($2) run regularly between the lake and the market at Andahuaylas and leave when full.

Fields above Pachuca

THE LEGEND OF PUCHACA

The area around the lake was once a celestial paradise, so the story goes, inhabited by spiritual and compassionate people. But people from other places discovered the lake and they began to settle there and brought with them corruption, injustice, and ego. One day there was a great celebration. An old ragged man came requesting food and shelter, but every house denied it to him. A modest single woman named "Mama Petecc," let him in and gave him anything he wanted. Thankful, the man advised the woman that a great catastrophe would soon occur in the town and that she should leave with her daughter and not look back. The woman took his advice and left, started to leave, but heard thunder in the sky and turned around. At that point, she was turned to stone. Her statue still stands there today.

About 20 minutes from the town of Pacucha, sit the stone ruins of **Sondor**, a remnant of the Chanka culture that long defended the region from the Incas. The site offers scenic views of the surrounding countryside. From the lake you can hike there in about one hour (ask at the lake for directions), or you can take a taxi from Andahuaylas ($10-$15 round-trip; negotiate).

■ Ayacucho

Phone code (066)

Nearly cut off from the rest of the country during the years of terrorism, Ayacucho (pop. 92,123, 2,760 m/9,053 feet elevation) has now been freed again as a tourist center. There is no more danger in coming here than anywhere else in Peru. The city is home to some of the most elaborate religious festivities. The handicrafts in town and in the nearby town of Quinua are some of the most spectacular in the country. In addition, there are more Colonial churches and architecture than you can count. The vibrant feel of this city of old is slowly returning and it is hard to predict just how this rebirth will affect the Central Highlands.

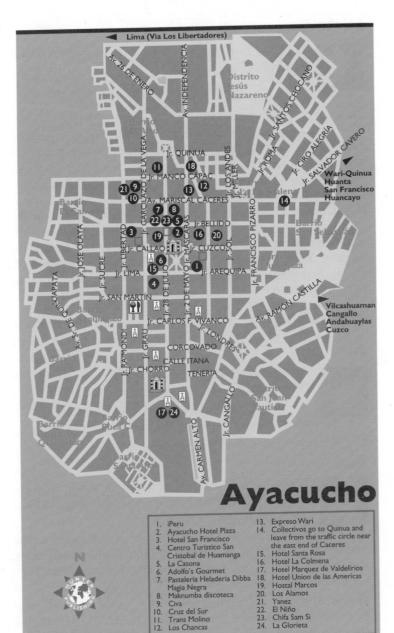

Ayacucho

1. iPeru
2. Ayacucho Hotel Plaza
3. Hotel San Francisco
4. Centro Turistico San Cristobal de Huamanga
5. La Casona
6. Adolfo's Gourmet
7. Pasteleria Heladeria Dibba Magia Negra
8. Maknumba discoteca
9. Civa
10. Cruz del Sur
11. Trans Molino
12. Los Chancas
13. Expreso Wari
14. Collectivos go to Quinua and leave from the traffic circle near the east end of Caceres
15. Hotel Santa Rosa
16. Hotel La Colmena
17. Hotel Marquez de Valdelirios
18. Hotel Union de las Americas
19. Hostal Marcos
20. Los Alamos
21. Yanez
22. El Niño
23. Chifa Sam Si
24. La Glorieta

© 2006 HUNTER PUBLISHING, INC

History

Human remains have been found in the area around Ayacucho, notably at Piquimachay Cave, dating back about 20,000 years. They are the earliest evidence of human activity ever found in South America and date to the Stone Age. From 500-1100 AD, the Wari culture established a solid civilization from this, their capital. The Chankas and the Incas would later overtake the area. The Spaniards founded the modern city in 1539 and called it San Juan de la Frontera de Huamanga, but Simón Bolivar changed the name in 1824 to Ayacucho, or "City of Blood," during the war for Peruvian Independence. In the 1980s and early '90s, the Shining Path Guerillas made the city their own and practically cut it off from the rest of the country. With the days of terrorism long gone, Ayacucho is slowly being restored to its original splendor and bringing back the tourist dollars that have been missing for too long.

Getting Here

Air

Aeropuerto Coronel FAP Alfredo Mendivil Duarte – Ejército 950, ☎ 31-2418.

For flights to Lima (45 minutes), contact TANS, www.tansperu.com.pe, for more information. They usually leave only in the early morning, several times a week.

Bus

There isn't a central terminal in Ayacucho, but most company offices are confined to a few blocks in the north of town.

Civa, Cáceres 1242, ☎ 31-1348, and **Cruz del Sur**, Cáceres 1264, ☎ 31-2813, both go to Lima (575 km/345 miles, nine hours, $10), vía Pisco (six hours) and Ica (six hours) once each day, usually in the evening.

Trans Molino, 9 de Diciembre 458, ☎ 31-2984. Passes Ayacucho en route from Lima to Cuzco (24 hours, $13-$16) in the evening and stops in Andahuaylas (261 km/157 miles, 10 hours). It also goes to Lima five times each day and to Huancavelica (six hours, $7) and Huancayo (10 hours, $7-$8).

Los Chancas, Cáceres 150, ☎ 81-2391, and Expreso Wari. Manco Cápac 451, ☎ 32-6323, both go to Andahuaylas and Cuzco ($14, 24 hours).

Collectivos go to Quinua and leave from the traffic circle near the east end of Cáceres (one hour/2 soles).

Tourist Information

Tourist Office – **iPeru**, Portal Municipal 48, ☎ 066 31 8305, iperuayacucho@promperu.gob.pe. Mon-Sat 8:30 am-7:30 pm, Sun 8:30 am-2:30 pm.

Post Office – Asamblea 295; Mon-Sat 8 am-8 pm.

Hospital – **Hospital Regional de Ayacucho**, Independencia 355, ☎ 31-2180, open 24 hours.

Pharmacy – InkaFarma, 28 de Julio 250.

Tourist Police – Dos de Mayo 100, ☎ 317-846.

Lavandería – **Arco Iris**, Bellido 322, or **Viclar's**, Cáceres 876.

Banks – **BCP**, Portal Union 28, ☎ 81-8305. Has a Visa ATM and will exchange travelers' checks. Also try **Interbanc**, 9 de Diciembre 183, ☎ 81-2480.

Sightseeing

★**Plaza Mayor de Huamanga** is surrounded on four sides by two-story Colonial buildings much like the plazas in Arequipa and Cuzco. Plaza Mayor is much more open, however, and has a less cluttered, more peaceful feel to it. The **City Cathedral** (La Catedral – Mon-Sat 5-7 pm, Sun 9-10 am, 5-7 pm) on the south side of the Plaza, was built in 1612 (although not completed until 1672). It has impressive gold-leafed altarpieces, with Colonial art and paintings. The **Municipalidad**, the **Palacio de Gobierno**, and the **Universidad Nacional de Huamanga** also face onto the square.

If you walk just a few blocks from the Plaza in any direction, you will inevitably run into numerous Colonial churches, mainly Spanish Baroque with hints of Andean influences. In fact, Ayacucho claims to have 33 Colonial churches, one for each year of Christ's life. Many of them, unfortunately, are rarely open to the public. **Templo de Santo Domingo**, 9 de Septiembre block 2, is perhaps the most architecturally creative of the churches, with three Roman arches and two Byzantine-style towers. The façade is oddly composed of reddish colored bricks, but the result is striking. This church plays a large role in the Semana Santa celebrations. **Templo San**

Templo de Santo Domingo
(Carlos Sala)

Cristóbal, at 28 de Julio block 6, is one of the oldest churches on the continent and construction dates back to the founding

Templo San Cristóbal *(N. Gill)*

of the city (it was completed in 1548). Not much remains of San Cristóbal except for one bell tower. **Templo and Convento de San Francisco de Asis**, 28 de Julio block 3, (daily 5:30-6:30 pm) is in the Greco-Roman style and has three naves. The gold-leaf altar is carved in the Churrigueresque style. The temple was built in 1552 and restored in the early 1980s. **Templo de La Merced**, at 2 de Mayo block 2, has the fundamentals of Renaissance design. For die-hard enthusiasts, also try: **Templo de la Compañía de Jesus** (28 de Julio block 1, daily 8 am-noon), **Templo** and **Monasterio de Santa Clara de Asis** (Grau block 3), and the **Templo de Santa Teresa** and **Monasterio de las Carmelitas Descalzas** (28 de Julio block 6).

Ayacucho's often-overlooked Colonial mansions rival the grace and beauty of the churches. On the Plaza itself there are several that you can see in no time at all. For instance, the office of the **Prefecture** (Portal Constitución 15), built in the middle of the 18th century, has a fine courtyard. It is also known as Casa Boza

Street scene in Ayacucho (N. Gill)

and Solis (daily 8 am-6 pm). **Casa Velarde Alvarez**, at Portal Union 47, is one of the oldest mansions in Ayacucho and belonged to the Marquis of Mozobamba. Note the elaborate Andean carvings of snakes, pumas, and alligators. **Casa Vivanco** (28 de Julio 508, daily 8 am-noon, 2-6 pm) holds the **Museo Cáceres**. Inside, you will find a large collection of Cusqueñan-style paintings, as well as Colonial furniture, and military artifacts from the original owner, Miguel Cáceres, a hero of the War of the Pacific with Chile. **Casa Chacon** (Portal Union 28, Tues-Fri, 10:15 am-5:30 pm and Sat 9:45 am-12:15 pm, free admission) holds the **Museo de Arte Popular Joaquín López Antay**. The museum is named after one of the region's most famous carvers of retablo boxes (with images of saints). Much of López Antay's work is on display, as well as

Children of Ayacucho (Heinz Plenge)

textiles, ceramics, and silver work.

The **Barrio Santa Ana** is a landmark of Quechua art and culture. In a quick stroll through this neighborhood you will encounter numerous artesans and their galleries. Head for the **Templo** and **Plazoleta of Santa Ana** and its vicinity to reach the epicenter.

Shopping

 Mercado Artesanal Shosaku Nagase – Plazoleta El Arco. This is an excellent craft market with many vendors bringing in crafts from throughout the Ayacucho countryside such as Quinua. Quality is very high and prices are comparable to anywhere in town.

Where to Stay

 Ayacucho Hotel Plaza – 9 de Diciembre 184, ☎ 812-202, hplaza@ derrama.org.pe. It is the best hotel in Ayacucho and, although far from luxurious, it retains a high and mighty Colonial feel. Some rooms have  balconies. It has 80 mediocre rooms with private hot-water baths, cable TV, and mini-fridges. A good restaurant and bar are also on the premises. Room and laundry service available. Less than a block from the Plaza. $$$

Hotel Santa Rosa – Lima 166, ☎ 31-4614, fax 312-083. One of the best values in Ayacucho. Rooms have cable TV and hot-water baths. Pleasant rooftop terrace and quiet courtyard. Parking. Small restaurant. $$

Hotel San Francisco – Callao 290, ☎ 314-501, fax 314-501, sanfranciscohotel.cjb.net. Well maintained with charming décor and local art. Lovely patio where you can have your free breakfast. Rooms are fairly simple, with cable TV, private hot-water baths, and parquet flooring. $$

Hotel Marquez de Valdelirios – Alameda Bolognesi 720-724, ☎ 818-944. Set in a restored Colonial house near a quiet tree-lined park in Santa Ana. Rooftop terrace with nice city views. Rooms have cable TV and hot water. Breakfast is included. Airport pick-ups availiable. Good value. $$

Hotel Union de las Americas – Manco Cápac 319 (2ᵈ floor), ☎ 319-525. Clean simple, rooms surrounding a cheery, bright covered courtyard. $

Hotel La Colmena – Cuzco 144, ☎ 811-318. Rooms are OK but worn. The location is excellent. Some rooms have private hot-water baths and cable TV. Rooms on the second floor (the ones with private baths) are set amidst business offices and can be noisy during the day. Good restaurant in a flower- and plant-filled courtyard that is often crowded. $

Hostal Marcos – 9 de Diciembre 143, ☎ 316-867. Just a dozen rooms in this bright hotel in an alley just minutes from the Plaza. Rooms are quite clean and have hot-water baths and cable TV. Breakfast is included. Good value and recommended. $$

Los Alamos – Cuzco 215, ☎ 312-782. This two-star has private hot-water baths, cable TV, and room service. Two blocks from the Plaza. Good restaurant in a plant-filled courtyard with ceviche, parrilladas (grilled meats), and pollos a la brasa (roasted chicken). $

Yañez – Cáceres 1210, ☎ 314-918. Very clean and bright, but a little ways from the center. Private hot-water baths and cable TV. Gloomy staff. Breakfast is included. Good value. $

GASTRONOMY

Qapchi – Potatoes, fresh Andean cheese, pepper, milk, oil, and onion.

Mondongo – Corn-based soup with pork, red peppers, and mint.

Puca picante – Potatoes, beef, peanuts, and beet roots served in a hearty tomato-pepper sauce over white rice.

Caldo de cabeza – Literally "head soup." Sheep's head stew with rice, potatoes, and mint.

Adobo ayacuchano -Casserole of marinated beef with chili and spices.

Chaplas – Local round, crusty bread, sometimes served with elderberry.

Central Highlands

Where to Eat

Centro Turístico San Cristóbal de Huamanga – 28 de Julio 178. A Colonial courtyard with a central fountain has several good outdoor cafés with a variety of themes. Sometimes has entertainment.

Café/Bar New York – Burgers, fries, cheesecake. Mostly typical American comfort foods and a few regional items such as calentitos (warm alcoholic herbal tea). $$

Lalos Café – Light snacks, cake, coffee, pizzas, and wine. $$

El Monasterio – Everything Italian. Pizza, pasta, lasagna, calzone, and wine. $$

Brisas del Mar – Probably the best seafood option in Ayacucho. $$

El Niño – 9 de Diciembre 205. Crowded courtyard restaurant just north of the Plaza. Serves mainly pizzas and grills. $$

Pastelería Heladería Dibba – Constitución Portal 7. Clean bakery with ice cream and other desserts. $

Chifa Sam Si – Diciembre 212, attached to Santo Domingo Church. Basic chifa (Chinese restaurant), but exceptionally clean. $

La Glorieta – Bolognesi 204. An excellent option in the quiet suburb of Santa Ana. You can eat regional specialties like puca picante (fried pork with spicy potatoes), pachamanca (a medley of meats and vegetables cooked under the ground), and mondongo (tripe stew) on their shady outdoor patio. $

La Casona – Bellido 463, ☎ 812-733. One of the best restaurants north of the center. Mainly serves regional dishes. Plant-filled stone courtyard with nice views of the moon and stars. Bring your appetite. Portions are far too big. Sometimes full, so call for reservations if you don't want to wait. $$

Adolfo's Gourmet – On the Plaza, 2nd floor, www.adolfosgourmet.com. Has an elegant feel but the menu is surprisingly cheap. The only restaurant overlooking the Plaza. The view is wonderful. Cheap menus, pizza, Andean dishes, jars of cocktails, and a few coffee drinks. $$

Bars

Magia Negra – 9 de Diciembre 293. My favorite bar in town. It has character. For instance, the ceiling consists of dozens of black umbrellas turned upside down. They have good pizzas too.

Maknumba Discoteca – Asamblea and Cáceres. One of the more upscale discotecas in Ayacucho.

Festivals

★★**Semana Santa** (Easter week) is the height of religious celebration for people throughout the Andes. Perhaps the greatest and most famous celebration can be found in Ayacucho. The passion, death and resurrection of Jesus is highly charged and the entire week is set for religious observance. The week kicks off with Jesus riding into Plaza Mayor on a donkey. On Wed, processions carrying the images of the Virgin Mary and Saint John make their way through flower-filled streets and later meet with an image of

Semana Santa
(Domingo Giribaldi)

Christ in the main square. On Holy Friday, beginning at the Monastery of Santa Clara, Christ is paraded through the dark streets on a bed of white roses, followed by a weeping Virgin and many solemn followers holding candles. Prayers and song continue through the night, then a three-hour sermon is delivered on Saturday. Easter Sunday is less somber and one more procession takes place, which is quite spectacular. Semana Santa in Ayacucho is well known throughout Peru. It is advised that you book your hotel at least six months in advance.

Central Highlands

Carnaval (Feb/March) is a three-day festival with lots of drinking of chicha, consumption of Andean dishes, and music.

Day-Trips from Ayacucho

Crafts for sale (Domingo Giribaldi)

★**Quinua** is the home of some of the best crafts in all of Peru. Of particular interests are the retablo boxes – one of more than 40 unique crafts in Ayacucho. The boxes come in many different sizes and generally feature one to three levels of figures depicting often-religious scenes and occasionally daily Andean life. The doors are intricately painted with bright flowers. The retablos once served as portable altars that missionaries used to convert the native people to Catholicism.

Also, the somewhat whimsical ceramic churches, made in nearly every craft shop, are quite impressive.

To get to the center from the road where the buses stop, you must walk up the stone steps, past all of the food vendors and small restaurants (serving many cheap and hearty regional dishes) and you will run into a small stone plaza with a church. There is a

Retablo box

museum (2 soles) on the Plaza, mainly with information and artifacts about the battle of Ayacucho. There isn't a whole lot there so, unless you are a history buff, skip it. There are a few good souvenir shops right such as **Taller de Arte y Escultura El Sol**, **Artesenia Quinuino**, and **Taller Venta Virgen Cocharca**.

Elsewhere, mainly along on San Martín, which leads away from the church, there are several more galleries. Two of the best are **Galeria Sánchez**, which is perhaps the best in town and has one of the largest displays, and **Galeria Ayllu**.

There are three small, basic **hostals** in Quinua, all within a block from the main Plaza. $.

Ceramics for sale in Quinoa (Ayacucho)

To get there you must catch a collectivo van from just north of the traffic circle at the east end of Cáceres. Vans depart frequently and leave when full. They take about an hour to go the 37 km/22 miles from Ayacucho (2 soles). Alternatively, you can take a tour from Ayacucho that will also go to Quinua, as well as to the Wari Ruins and Pampa de Ayacucho.

Santuario Historico de la Pampa de Ayacucho (site of the Battle of Ayacucho) – A 44-m/144-foot obelisk commemorates one of the more famous battles on the continent. This is the site of the Battle of Ayacucho, which emancipated Peru and all of South America from Spanish rule on December 9th, 1824. At the battle, Simón Bolivar declared the name of the city changed from Huamanga to Ayacucho, or "City of Blood." The 44-meter obelisk symbolizes the 44 years from the first revolution of the Inca Tupac Amaru and the battle of Ayacucho. You can walk there from the Plaza in Quinua in about 30 minutes or go with a tour from Ayacucho.

Wari (Carlos Sala)

Wari (Huari) Ruins – This walled center is thought to be one of the first to be constructed in the Andes. It was occupied from approximately 600 to 800 AD and more than 50,000 people are thought to have lived there. Before being conquered by the

Incas, the Wari culture spread throughout the Peruvian Andes from Cuzco to Cajamarca. There are five sites spread over 6,200 acres, with tunnels, stone houses and high walls that are completely surrounded by thick opuntia cacti forests. There is also a small

Wari (Carlos Sala)

visitor center and the **Museo de Sitio Wari** (2 soles). It has photos, scale models, and artifacts from the site. The ruins are open to visitors Tues-Sun 10 am-5 pm. Many of the ruins can be seen from the bus window on the way to Quinua. If you want, you can just ask the driver to stop and let you out. Then hop on the next bus.

Church, Vilcashuaman (Carlos Sala)

Vilcashuaman – This is the spot where the road from Cuzco to the coast and the road that ran through the Andes met, making it the geographical center of the Inca Empire. Vilcashuaman, or Sacred Falcon, was the gathering point of two major highways and became a provincial capital. The earlier grandeur of the city has mostly disappeared thanks to looters and the modern Christian church that sits on the Temple of the Sun. Some of the highlights from historical writings that you can still make out include the Temple of the

Pyramid, Vicashuaman (Carlos Sala)

Moon, three levels of stone terracing, and the five-tiered pyramid of el Ushno. The throne at the top of el Ushno was where the Inca sat and watched over military and religious ceremonies in the plaza below. There are a few basic hospedajes near the site if you prefer to spend more time there. The complex rests 118 km/70 miles from Ayacucho, which is about a three-hour ride. It is best reached by tour from Ayacucho, which generally costs not much more than a round-trip bus ride.

Tour Companies

Eco-Aventura – Portal Independencia 66, ☎ 815-191, warpapicchu@terra.com.pe. City tours, Wari ruins, Quinua, and Vilcashuaman are available, depending on the number of people.

A & R Tours – Portal Union 25, ☎ 311-300, ar_tours@hotmail.com. Offers the same tours as Eco-Aventura.

Pueblo de Huanta, outside of Ayacucho (Carlos Sala)

Sacred Valley

MACHU PICCHU
☐ Hospedaje
Train Station
Aguas Calientes
Intipunku
Wiñay Wayna
Phuyu Pata Marca
Sayacmarca
Runcu Racay
Warmiwañusca
CAMINO INCA
INCA TRAIL
Warmiwañusca
Llulluchapampa
3 Piedras
Wayllabamba
Starada inca

OLLANTAYTAMBO
Km. 88
Q'Orihuayrachina
Patallacta
Train Station

URUBAMBA
☐ Hospedaje
Yucay 28 Km.
19 Km.
Wilcamayu
MONAY
29 Km.
MARAS
Izcuchaca
28 Km.
ANTA
☐ Hospedaje

Río Urubamba 18 Km.
CALCA
Lamay
Coya
PISAQ
CHINCHERO
Laguna
Piuray
Tambomachay 32
Pucapucara
Qenqo
Cusillochayoc
San Sebastián
CUZCO
Train
Station
35 Km.
San Jerónimo

Paucartambo
Huambutio
San Salvador
Tipon
Laguna
Huacarpay
Piquillacta
Urcos A Puno
ANDAHUAYLILLAS
Laguna
de Urcos
Puerto Maldonado
Sicunni, Puno
Arequipa, Bolivia

N

© 2006 HUNTER PUBLISHING, INC.

Cuzco & the Sacred Valley

El Valle Sagrado de los Incas (the Sacred Valley of the Incas) is where it all started. Incan civilization began here when Manco Cápac, as the legend goes, came upon the valley from Lake Titicaca. One of the greatest civilizations the world had ever seen grew from there. The valley is dotted with spectacular Incan and pre-Incan ruins, not to mention the world-renowned site of **Machu Picchu** and several other lost cities. Other noteworthy archaeological sites are the **Pisac** terraces and stone structures that stand high on the mountain overlooking the city, the colossal fortress at **Ollantaytambo**, a once-proud

IN THIS CHAPTER

■ **Cuzco**	**296**
■ **Urubamba & Yucay**	**345**
■ **Pisac**	**354**
■ **Ollantaytambo**	**358**
■ **Moray & Maras**	**365**
■ **Chincero**	**366**
■ **Aguas Caliente**	**368**
■ **Machu Picchu**	**373**
■ **The Inca Trail**	**381**

military facility, and the peaceful town of **Chincero**. Some Incan relics are still in use, such as the salt mines at Maras and the many farming terraces that line the mountainsides.

El Valle Sagrado

The **Río Urubamba** snakes its way through the fertile valley under the usual blue skies, snow-capped mountains, and passing small villages that have changed very little for centuries. The Inca heartland is densely populated. Small pueblos and farms are scattered everywhere, places where roads still don't reach. It is quiet and mystical. Almost like Tuscany before it went Hollywood.

You can make the valley home to a grueling trek or a rafting trip, or just relax at a spa in a sleepy town like Urumbamba. A range of adventure activities are possible here. Each town seems to be a base for some trek or tour. Hiking is one possibility, but you can also go rafting, fishing, kayaking, paragliding, climbing, mountain biking, or horseback riding.

Finally, at the west end, is **Cuzco**, once the Incan capital, and now the tourism capital of the continent. You will find an array of excellent museums, dining, hotels, nightlife, shopping, and historical sites. Almost every tourist that visits Peru comes here. In the high season (May-September) it can be crowded and overbooked. The best time to visit is in April/May or October/November.

Most Cuzco travel agencies offer a one-day tour of the valley, stopping at Chincero, Pisac, and Ollantaytambo, the ruins and markets. Most have English-speaking guides and cost $15-$20 per person.

"The city itself, more than 11,000 feet above sea level, is beautiful – it has a clean terra cotta quality reminiscent of Italian hill towns. But its essence lies less in its architecture than in its setting in the valley, the cold mountain sun reflected from its Inca walls and Spanish steeples, in the mute Indians and haughty llamas, in the relentless bells." – Peter Matthiessen

HIGHLIGHTS

■ **Machu Picchu** – Now practically overrun with tourists most of the year, it is still one of the most enchanting places you will see.

■ **The Inca Trail and Alternative Trails** – Walk the Inca highways to Machu Picchu and other undiscovered ruins, through immaculate mountain passes, and see a way of life that has remained unchanged for centuries.

■ **Cuzco** – Most come for Machu Picchu, but it is this Incan capital and Colonial powerhouse that leaves them more impressed.

■ **Relaxation in the Sacred Valley** – Peru's version of Tuscany, where you can ride horses through the valley or do yoga beside a pure mountain stream.

■ **Shopping at the Pisac Market** – Villagers hike from miles away to bring crafts to the largest and most visited Sunday crafts market in Peru.

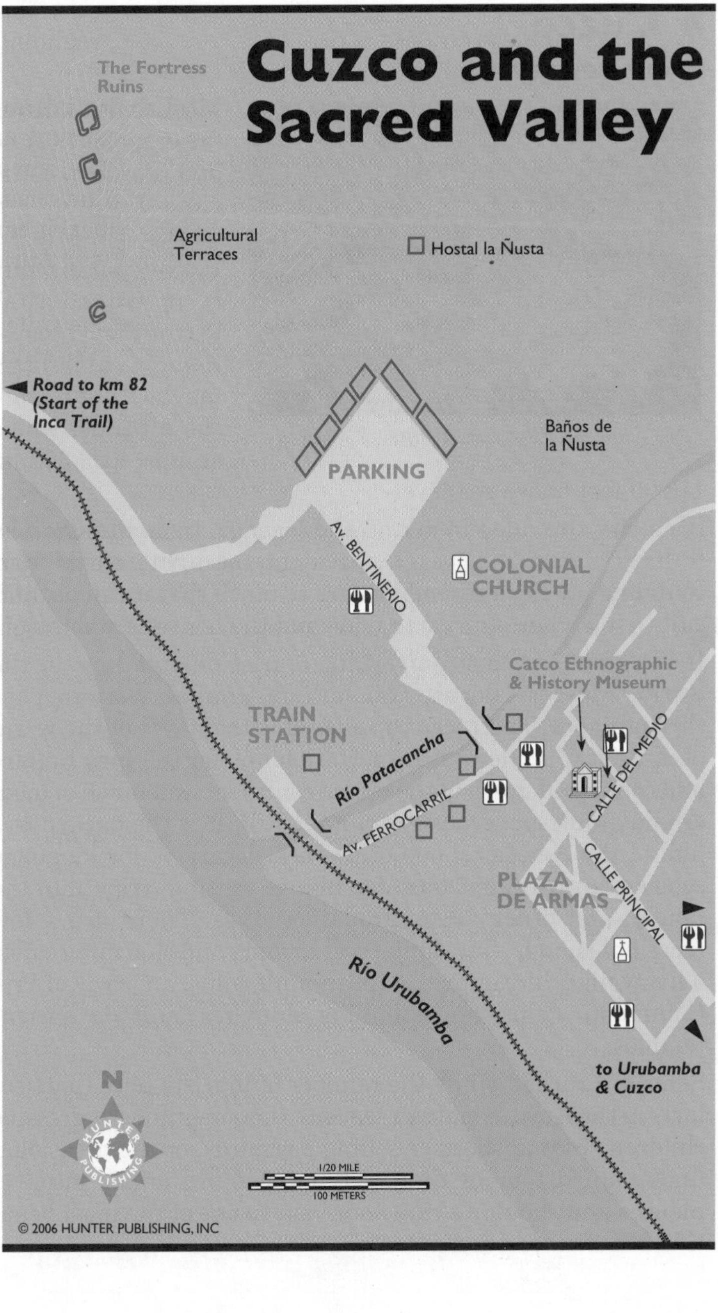

Cuzco and the Sacred Valley

The Fortress Ruins

Agricultural Terraces

☐ Hostal la Ñusta

Road to km 82 (Start of the Inca Trail)

Baños de la Ñusta

PARKING

Av. BENTINERIO

🍴

☩ COLONIAL CHURCH

Catco Ethnographic & History Museum

TRAIN STATION

☐

Río Patacancha

Av. FERROCARRIL

🍴

🍴

🍴

CALLE DEL MEDIO

CALLE PRINCIPAL

PLAZA DE ARMAS

🍴

🍴

Río Urubamba

to Urubamba & Cuzco

N

HUNTER PUBLISHING

1/20 MILE
100 METERS

© 2006 HUNTER PUBLISHING, INC

■ Cuzco

Phone code (084)

Cuzco's Plaza de Armas (N. Gill)

Most come to Cuzco (also spelled Cusco and Q'osqo; population 350,000) en route to Machu Picchu, but to many it is Cuzco that leaves them breathless, although maybe that's from the altitude, which stands, at 3,360 m/ 11,000 feet above sea level.

It's a city shrouded in myths and legends, thought even now to have elements of magic. At night the lights on the surrounding hillsides resemble stars so much that it can be difficult to tell where the earth ends and the heavens start.

It is one of the most important tourist destinations in the world. Most of Peru's two million annual visitors pass through here. The Incas considered it the navel of the world because it was once a transportation hub for the Inca Empire and connected much of the entire continent and much of modern day tourism revolves around it still. It is the backpacker hub of the Americas, one of the best locations for language schools, an excellent base for hiking, rafting, trips into the jungle, and other adventurous activities. There are a few incredible hotels, fine dining restaurants and charming cafés, a lively nightlife, immense Incan-built walls, an array of Pre-Columbian ruins, and stunning churches built on ancient temples.

Some are turned off by the number of tourists here (particularly in the April-Sept high season), the sometimes aggressive children shining shoes or selling postcards, or the occasional undervalued tour or dinner. But these are minor inconveniences and shouldn't ruin your visit to one of the most beautiful cities on earth.

Cuzco temperatures range from 17°C/63°F to -2°C/28°F. The rainy season runs from November to March.

 **The flag:** The rainbow flag often seen in Cuzco is the flag of the Tihuanaco Empire, now the city's own.

History

 The empire, which lasted from the 11th century to Conquest in the early 16th century, was one of the greatest planned societies the world has ever known, and the beauty and enchantment of Cuzco reflect that. There is so much history here that it can be difficult to keep straight, particularly when much of it involves myth and legend.

To know the beginning of Cuzco, you must first know how the Incas began. The civilization began when the creator and sun god Viracocha's offspring Manco Cápac (the first ruling Inca) and Mama Occlo arose from the Isle de Sol in Lake Titicaca near Copacabana, Bolivia. They were sent with a golden rod to find the Q'osqo or navel of the world and to begin the civilization. Manco Cápac was commanded to find a place where he could push the rod into the ground until it disappeared. When he found it, that was to become the center of the universe.

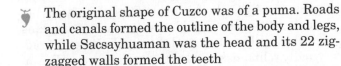 The original shape of Cuzco was of a puma. Roads and canals formed the outline of the body and legs, while Sacsayhuaman was the head and its 22 zigzagged walls formed the teeth

The capital of the Incan Empire is thought to have been founded around 1100 AD. Previously Peru had been ruled by a number of cultures. What the Inca did was establish a central government that united them all and they ran it from here. They were not the scientists and creators of culture that the others were, but they were able to absorb the lifestyle improvements that others had achieved and combine them all, which was perhaps an even greater feat.

Other cultures occupied the area, such as the Wari's who were there in the eighth and ninth century. The first Incas arrived in the 12th century. Other than a few small palaces, the first eight rulers did little that was remembered. They controlled the area around Cuzco, but expansion was minimal. It wasn't until the Chanka culture arrived to take over the Inca, that expansion began. During the rule of Pachacútec, Cuzco developed greatly. Rivers were diverted, buildings such the Qoricancha temple and other palaces were constructed, and the layout of the city was set. A huge central plaza became the center of all social activities.

When the Spanish forces arrived in Cusco in 1533 after capturing Atahualpa, they were hailed because he was seen as a traitor. They believed the Spanish would reinstall Huáscar, but Atahualpa ordered him executed. Soon after, the Spanish began razing the city and took control. In 1536, a rebellion by Manco Inca and his troops nearly took it back. In 1537, a struggle for power from the Spanish side began and Diego de Almagro seized Cuzco from Hernando Pizarro. A year later Pizarro would retake the city and Almagro would be executed. Over the next few decades the Spanish would rebuild much of the city, creating the Plaza de Armas. They tried to instill Catholicism into the hearts and minds of the people, and eventually succeeded, as you can see by the devout religious practice in the city today.

> Integrating Catholicism into Quechua life was not easy. Festivals would involve heavy drinking (which still occurs). And the population only gradually relinquished all of their pagan ways. For instance on Corpus Christi, they would parade the mummies of the Inca rulers through the streets. The mummies were later replaced by 15 religious images.

After the Spanish gained control of the entire country, and with the founding of Lima in 1535, the center of Peru shifted to the coast and the importance of Cuzco dwindled. A 1650 earthquake destroyed many of the Incan buildings, leading to Cuzco's rebuilding in a mostly Baroque style.

The last decade has returned prominence to Cuzco, this time because of tourism. The city is growing now, with new hotels, restaurants, and museums appearing almost weekly and the pace still cannot accommodate the increasing number of tourists. This is really just the beginning. Cuzco is leading the way for tourism to the entire continent and the bubble is unlikely to burst anytime soon.

 The official name of the city has been changed back to the Quechua: Qosq'o. Most street names have been changed to Quechua as well, although both spellings are generally used and accepted.

Getting Here

Air

 Aeropuerto Internacional Velasco Astete (☎ 222-611) is about five km/three miles southeast of the center. Flights to and from Cuzco are often full, especially in the high season. Over-bookings do occur as well, so it is important to get to the airport as early as possible or you will be stuck. Also, the wind sweeping in from the mountains often delays and cancels afternoon flights. In either situation, you will likely be put in line to be on a flight the next day. Some airlines like LAN and TACA will give you free accommodations in such cases, while some, such as TANS, will not.

Airport services include moneychangers, ATMs, an iPeru (tourist information) booth, cafés, gift shops, and car rental desks. Airport departure tax is 12 soles; 35 soles for international flights.

It takes about 20 minutes to get from the airport to the center of town, which can be done by taxi or with a hotel pick-up. Most hotels can arrange pick-up ahead of time. A taxi should costs between 5 and 10 soles, depending on whether you bargain.

Flights

Lima – All of the airlines listed below fly to Lima several times
day (one hour).

Arequipa – LAN.

Puerto Maldonado – The only options are with LAN and TANS
a day. Reserve well in advance during the high season.

La Paz, Bolivia – LAB, Taca.

Airlines

Taca – El Sol 602, ☎ 249-921, www.taca.com.

LAN – El Sol 627 B, ☎ 255-555, www.lan.com.

TANS – ☎ 242-725, San Agustín 315, www.tansperu.com.pe.

Star Peru – El Sol 679 office 1, ☎ 221-896, www.starperu.com.

Aero Condor – Santa Catalina Ancha 315, ☎ 221-136,
aerocondor.com.pe.

LAB – ☎ 222-990, www.lab.com.

> *"From Cuzco the small diesel car to Machu Picchu
> climbs in a series of switchbacks to the high plateaus,
> which surround the city, passing upward through
> groves of eucalyptus trees to the open slopes."*
> – Peter Matthiessen

Rail

To get to Machu Picchu from Cuzco, it is only possible
by rail. During the high season (May-Sept) trips sell ou
reservations should be made more than a day in advan

Estación San Pedro – Cascaparo (no #), ☎ 221-352,
perurail.com. For trains to Aguas Caliente (Machu Picchu Pueblo,
Ollantaytambo.

Estación Wanchac – ☎ 238-722, www.perurail.com. Twenty min
from the center. Open daily 7 am-1 pm and 2-4 pm. Trains to Pur

Estación Poroy – This is the station for the Hiram Bingham tr
You must take a bus or taxi to the suburb about 12 km/7.2 miles aw

Route	Train	Round-Trip	One-Way
Poroy-Machu Picchu-Poroy	Hiram Bingham	$495	Not applicable
Cuzco-Machu Picchu	Vistadome Backpacker	$105 $68	$62 $44
Ollantaytambo-Machu Picchu	Vistadome Backpacker	$71.50 $53	$43 Not applicable
Cuzco-Lake Titicaca	First Class Backpacker	Not applicable Not applicable	$119 $17

Cuzco-Machu Picchu			
Train	**Route**	**Departs**	**Arrives**
Hiram Bingham	Cuzco (Poroy) Machu Picchu	9 am	12:30 pm
	Machu Picchu Cuzco (Poroy)	6 pm	9:25 pm
Vistadome 1	Cuzco Machu Picchu	6 am -	9:40 am
	Machu Picchu Cuzco	3:30 pm	7:20 pm
Vistadome 2	Cuzco Machu Picchu	7 am -	11 am
	Machu Picchu Cuzco	5 pm	9:25 pm
Backpacker	Cuzco Machu Picchu	6:15 am	10:10 am
	Machu Picchu Cuzco	3:55 pm	8:20 pm

Cuzco-Lake Titicaca		
Route	**Departs**	**Arrives**
Cuzco La Raya (20-minute scenic stop) Juliaca Puno (Lake Titicaca)	8 am 4:50 pm	4:35 pm 5:30 pm

The Trains

The Hiram Bingham – This luxury train service runs between Cuzco and Machu Picchu. The train departs from the Poroy Station (20 minutes from the center) at 9 am. The cars (four in all; two of them dining cars, with bar and kitchen) feature elegant interiors, entertainment, meals, wine, bus transfers, guides, entrance to the ruins, and afternoon tea at the Machu Picchu Sanctuary Lodge.

The Vistadome – Glass on all sides allows for the best views of the landscape. It is the quickest route to Machu Picchu. Snacks and refreshments are included. More comfortable than the Backpacker trains.

The Backpacker – This is the cheapest and most uncomfortable train, but it gets the job done.

 Time Savers: It is actually cheaper and quicker by a few hours if you go to Ollantaytambo by road. On the return trip, many passengers get off the train midway at Poroy, where there are buses waiting. This will save an hour and cost about 5 soles.

Bus

Terminal Terrestre

 Peru's bus terminal sits two km/1.2 miles from the center on the way to the airport at Av. Vallejo Santoni, block 2. Below are some of the recommended companies, but there are many, many more at the terminal, lots of them going to the same destinations with departures throughout the day.

Bus Companies

Cruz del Sur – ☎ 22-1909, www.cruzdelsur.com.pe. Has buses to most major cities.

Civa – ☎ 22-9961, www.civa.com.pe. Buses to Lima and Ayacucho.

Ormeño –☎ 22-7501, www.grupo-ormeno.com. Has the best buses (Royal Class) to Puno, Juliaca, Lima, Arequipa, Ayacucho, Huaraz, Trujillo, Mancora, Tumbes, Piura, Chiclayo, Ica, and Nasca. Also to Copacabana and La Paz in Bolivia.

Cial – ☎ 22-1201. To Trujillo, Huaraz, Arequipa, and Lima.

Expreso Molino – ☎ 24-9512. Has the most frequent service to Lima.

Other Destinations by Bus

The Sacred Valley – Urubamba, Chincero, Pisac, Ollantaytambo. There are collectivo cars that leave for each Sacred Valley town. Ask a taxi driver where they are currently departing. Buses leave as follows:

Urubamba (via Chincero) – Av. Grau block 1.

Urubamba (via Pisac) – Calle Puputi block 2.

Ollantaytambo – You must first go to Urubamba and then change buses.

There are also collectivo taxis (10 soles) to **Abancay**. These are quicker than the bus and you can usually find them at the entrance to the bus station.

Puerto Maldonado – This is one of the most exotic road journeys you can take in Peru. Trucks and collectivos leave from Plaza Tupac Amaru and take anywhere from 18 hours to three days, depending on road conditions. Transportation officials consider this the worst road in the country. The trip will be around $20, a little more if you can finagle a seat in the cab with the driver. The scenery is spectacular, although the comfort level is not. A new highway, the Trans Oceanico, is planned to the border with Brazil. Construction is planned to begin in 2006 and will take several years. This will cut the drive time to six hours.

Manu – Make travel arrangements with the lodge where you are staying.

TIME CHART	
To Lima	24-30 hours
To Puno	6 hours
To Juliaca	5 hours
To Arequipa	11 hours
To Ayacucho	22 hours
To Andahuaylas	10 hours
To Abancay	6 hours

Getting Around

Car Rental

AVIS – Aeropuerto Internacional Velasco Astete, Av. El Sol 808, ☎ 620-510, fax ☎ 248-800, avis-cusco@terra.com.pe.

Shuttle

The **Tranvia** is a tourist tram that makes two-hour tours around Cuzco ($2). You can find it on the Plaza de Armas at 10 am and 1 pm each day. Call ☎ 22-4377 for more details.

Taxis

A taxi from just about anywhere in the immediate city to the Plaza should be no more than 5 soles. You should never have trouble finding a taxi in Cuzco, no matter the time of day or night.

BOLETO TURÍSTICO (TOURIST PASS)

This special pass includes Santa Catalina Monastery and Museum, the Contemporary Art Museum, the regional Historic Museum, Museo de Arte Popular, the Cusco Center of Art and Native Folkloric Dances, the Monument to Pachacuteq, and the Qorikancha site museum. Also admits you to the Sacsayhuaman, Pisac, Q'enqo, Pukapukara, Tambomachay, Chinchero, Ollantaytambo, Pikillacta, and Tipon archeological complexes. Each site can only be visited once with the ticket. 70 soles or 35 soles for students. The ticket lasts for 10 days and can be bought at the Oficina Ejecutiva del Comite (☎ 22-6919), in the same building as the iPeru office at Av. El Sol 103. Also one-day tickets that go to limited sites are available for 70 soles/35 soles for students).

Tourist Information

Tourist Office – **iPeru**, Portal Carrizos 250 (Plaza de Armas), ☎ 252-974, iperuava@tsi.com.pe, daily from 8 am-8 pm. Also at the airport in the main lounge, ☎ 23-7364, daily from 6 am-1 pm, iperucus@tsi. com.pe.

South American Explorers – Choquechaca 188 #4, Cusco, ☎ 245-484, www.saexplorers.com. Excellent source of information for hikes in the area. Book exchange, sells guidebooks and maps, and will store luggage. Open Mon-Fri 9:30 am-5 pm and Sat 9:30 am-1 pm.

 Migraciones – Sol 612, ☎ 22-2741. You can renew your tourist card here for an extra 30 days ($27), although, it may be easier just to go to Bolivia if you are heading to Puno anyway, then come back and get a new card. Open Mon-Fri 8 am-noon.

Laundries – **Lavandería Splendid**, Carmen Alto 195, ☎ 237-820, www.splendidlaundry.com. **T'agsana**, Santa Catalina Ancha 345. Also several on Suecia, Procuradoes, and Plateros.

Hospitals – **Hospital Regional**, Av. De la Cultura (no #), ☎ 22-3691. Open 24 hours. **Hospital Antonio**, Plazoleta Belén 1358, ☎ 22-6511. Open 24 hours.

Pharmacy – **Inka Farma**, Sol 174, ☎ 24-2601. Open 24 hours and stocks sorojchi pills.

Post Office – **Serpost**, El Sol 800, ☎ 22-4212. Open Mon-Sat 7:30 am-7:30 pm and Sun 7:30 am-2 pm.

Telephones & Internet – Many places on the Plaza.

Banks – **BCP**, Sol 189. Has ATMs, gives cash advances, and exchanges traveler's checks. **Interbanc**, Sol 380, has ATMs. **Global Net ATMs** is inside Inka Grill and Gato's Market on the Plaza.

Police – **Policia de Turismo** (Tourism Police) – Saphi 510, ☎ 221-961. Open 24 hours.

ALTITUDE SICKNESS

The Peruvain Andes, most notably around Huaraz, are the highest mountains in the world outside of the Himalayas. Many visitors have yet to experience altitudes at this magnitude, and the adjustment doesn't always go easily. Sorojchi, or altitude sickness, affects about half of all tourists who come to Cuzco or Puno. For some, it hits right away and within hours of getting off a plane they are sick in bed with a bucket beside them. This is common. For others, there may be a few days of no ill effects and then the sickness suddenly hits them. To help cure altitude sickness, sorojchi pills are the best option, there is only one kind and you get find them in any drug store in Cuzco. Coca tea is also recommended. I would use it more as a preemptive remedy though. Perhaps have a cup on the first day. You won't fail a drug test for this or get high; the leaves simply increase the oxygen supply in your system. You will also notice a shortness of breath when walking, particularly up the steep streets of San Blas. This is also common and your body takes a few days to adjust. If shortness of breath becomes more serious, most hotels are equipped to supply oxygen treatments.

Sights

Called "Huacaypata," or Warrior's Plaza, during Inca times, Cuzco's ★★**Plaza de Armas** is the heart of the city and perhaps the very center of tourism in all of South America. It

Cuzco's Catedral (Carlos Sala)

was much bigger during Inca times and a small river divided it into two. Today it is home to numerous clubs, restaurants, gift shops, tourist agencies, and churches. There are great views of the Plaza from the pedestrian-only walkway between Plaza del Tricentenario and Huaynapata and also from **Sacsayhuaman**. The **Catedral** and the churches of **El Triunfo** and **Jesus María** are on part of the eastern side of the Plaza, while the church of **La Compañia** is on part the northern side. Colonial arcades fill every space in-between.

The streets heading from the Plaza in every direction also lead to a continuous stream of tourist facilities. To the east is San Blas. To the south is Av El Sol and the train station for Puno. North is Sacsayhuaman. West is Plaza San Francisco and the train station for Machu Picchu.

Iglesia de la Compañía

Procuradores, the narrow pedestrian street heading north, is filled with tourist agencies, cheap restaurants, and gift shops. It has earned the nickname "Gringo Alley." Menu pushers here are aggressive. It is best not to look at or talk to them. Just keep walking.

Hatunrumiyoc (Carlos Sala)

There are two narrow alleys in particular that are prime examples of polygonal Incan stonework. First **Loreto**, which leads south from the Plaza between the churches. The right-hand wall is from Amarucancha, the courtyard of the serpents and the palace of Huayna Cápac, although the church of La Compañía was built over it later. The left-hand wall is from Acllahuasi, the house of the chosen women. It is one of the oldest surviving walls in Cuzco. The Santa Catalina Convent was built over it. Second is the street of ★**Hatunrumiyoc** northeast from the Plaza. It is named after the 12-sided stone embedded in the wall. There are usually a few small children who have learned English hanging around. You can pay them to point out the puma-shape set in a series of stones in a nearby side-street. The stonework here belonged to a palace from Inca Roca, the sixth Inca.

Inca architecture has one unique feature: doors and niches were built in trapezoidal shapes.

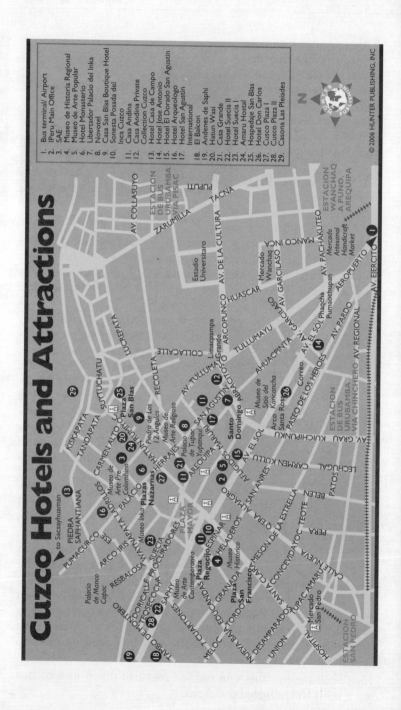

Cuzco Hotels and Attractions

1. Bus terminal/ Airport
2. iPeru Main Office
3. SAE
4. Museo de Historia Regional
5. Museo de Arte Popular
6. Hotel Monasterio
7. Liberador Palacio del Inka
8. Novotel
9. Casa San Blas Boutique Hotel
10. Sonesta Posada del Inca Cuzco
11. Casa Andina
12. Casa Andina Private Collection Cuzco
13. Hotel Casa de Campo
14. Hotel Jose Antonio
15. Hotel El Dorado San Agustin
16. Hotel Arqueologo
17. Hotel San Agustin International
18. El Balcon
19. Andenes de Saphi
20. Hatun Wasi
21. Casa Grande
22. Hotel Suecia II
23. Hotel Suecia I
24. Amaru Hostal
25. Hospedaje San Blas
26. Hotel Don Carlos
27. Cusco Plaza I
28. Cusco Plaza II
29. Casona Las Pleiades

© 2006 HUNTER PUBLISHING, INC

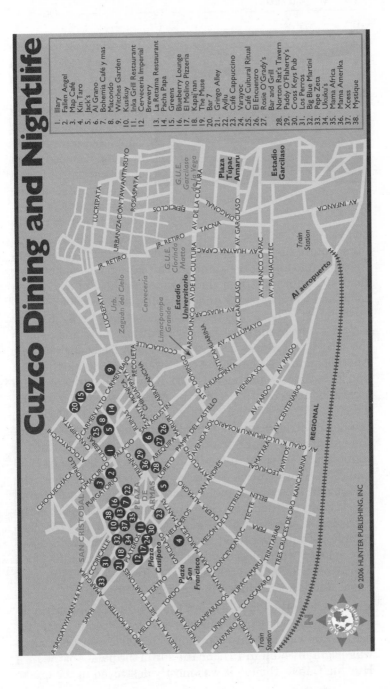

Cuzco Dining and Nightlife

1. Iliary
2. Fallen Angel
3. Map Café
4. Kin Taro
5. Jack's
6. Al Grano
7. Bohemia Café y mas
8. Macondo
9. Witches Garden
10. Kusikuy
11. Inka Grill Restaurant
12. Cerveceria Imperial Brewery
13. La Retama Restaurant
14. Pacha Papa
15. Greens
16. Blueberry Lounge
17. El Molino Pizzeria
18. Kapaj'nan
19. The Muse
20. Bar 7
21. Gringo Alley
22. Ayllu
23. Café Cappuccino
24. Varayoc
25. Café Cultural Ritual
26. El Encuentro
27. Rosie O'Grady's Bar and Grill
28. Norton Rat's Tavern
29. Paddy O'Flaherty's
30. Cross Keys Pub
31. Los Perros
32. Big Blue Martini
33. Pepe Zeta
34. Ukuku's
35. Mama Africa
36. Mama Amerika
37. Xcess
38. Mystique

© 2006 HUNTER PUBLISHING, INC.

The 12-sided stone in Hatunrumiyoc
(Heinz Plenge)

The Renaissance-style ★Catedral de la Ciudad de Cusco (Cuzco City Cathedral) on the Plaza is quite stunning and recently completed a large renovation. Construction of the cathedral began in 1559, just a few years after the Conquest, but took nearly 100 years to complete. The impressive silver altar was made from Potosi silver and weighs almost 900 lbs. The original wood retablo altar sits behind it. The church also holds more than 400 paintings from the Cuzqueña school of art, which combined European and Andean styles. A few are of particular interest. The painting of *The Last Supper* by Marcos Zapata is one of the most famous paintings there and depicts the traditional dinner scene with Andean foods such as cuy. Another painting shows the city after the 1650 earthquake and is the oldest painting in Cuzco. It shows the citizens of the city carrying a crucifix around the Plaza praying for it to stop, which it did. The actual crucifix (*El Señor de los Temblores*, the Lord of Trembles) is adorned in the church to the right of the entranceway to El Triunfo. The church of **El Triunfo** is connected to its right. It was built a few years before in 1556 and is the oldest church in Cuzco. It holds the vault where the remains of Inca historian Garcilaso de la Vega can be found after being returned from Spain not long ago. To the left of the cathedral is the church of **Jesús María**, built in 1733. The complex is built over what was once the Inca Viracocha's palace, mostly with blocks taken from Sacsayhuaman. Open Mon-Wed, Fri, Sat 10-11:30 am and daily 2-5:30 pm, Sun until 5 pm. Admission included in the Boleto Turístico.

Elsewhere on the Plaza is the ★**Iglesia de la Compañía de Jesus**, or La Compañía, which rivals the Catholic cathedral across the way in beauty and opulence. This Jesuit church was originally built in 1571 on the site of the palace of the Inca Huayna Cápac, though it was mostly destroyed in the quake of 1650. It was rebuilt less than 20 years later. The various murals, altars, paintings, and carvings are quite impressive and the façade and nave are wonderful examples of Andean Baroque. Open Mon-Sat 11 am-12 pm and 3-4 pm. Admission free.

Just around the corner is the church and monastery of **Santa Catalina** (Santa Catalina Angosta, ☎ 22-8613). The convent was once on the site of Acllawasi, where the Inca called on the Virgins of the Sun. It is quite fitting that a convent would later take its place. The **Museo de Arte Religioso y Colonial** inside Santa Catalina holds the greatest collection of Cuzqueñan paintings and other artwork in the city. Many of the paintings are by Amerindians You cannot enter the main altar, but can see it behind bars. Admission included in the Boleto Turístico.

One of the city's most important Colonial churches outside of the Plaza, the **Iglesia y Convento La Merced** (Calle Mantas, ☎ 23-1821), was destroyed in the 1650 earthquake and rebuilt in 1654. It houses the remains of the conquistadors Diego de Alamagro (and his son) and Gonzalo Pizarro. The gold monstrance adorned with precious stones is perhaps its most famous feature and on display in the small on-site museum. Open Mon-Sat 8 am-12 pm and 3-4 pm. Admission 5 soles.

The ★★**Convento de Santo Domingo y Qoricancha** or the Temple of the Sun (Av. El Sol and Calle Santo Domingo) is one of the largest tourist draws in Cuzco and one of the few places that nearly everyone visits. The church is symbolic of the Spanish Conquest. The original temple was the most important in the empire and several thousand of the most important priests and their servants were housed there, but the

Convento de Santo Domingo (Jorge Sarmiento)

*Templo Koricancha &
Iglesia de Santo Domingo*

Spanish built Santo Domingo directly on top and enclosed it within. Today the inside cloisters have been removed and five chambers of fine Incan masonry can be seen. Other excavations have led to a variety of stonework, much of it the finest the Incas produced. During Incan times the inside was known as the golden courtyard and the sides were lined with gold panels, life-size gold figures, and gold altars. There was also a huge golden disc that would reflect the light of the sun onto the temple. When the Spanish came, they ripped out all of the gold, melted it down, and divided it up among themselves in strictly controlled portions. Open Mon-Sat 8 am-5 pm, Sun and holidays 2-5 pm. Admission 6 soles or 3 soles for students. English-speaking guides are free, but a small tip is expected ($3-$4).

The **Qorikancha site museum**, underground on Av. El Sol, is small and not outstanding, but worth a quick look. There is a small Pre-Columbian collection and photos from the excavation of Qorikancha. Open Mon-Fri 8 am-5 pm and Sat 9 am-5 pm. Admission included in the Boleto Turístico.

The ★★**Museum of Pre-Columbian Art (MAP)** (Nazarenas Plaza 231, ☎ 242-476) is my favorite Cuzco museum. The artistry of the artifacts is the focus of this modern museum and the result is extraordinary. The aesthetics of each piece are examined, rather than the traditional anthropological background dealt with by most museums. Rooms are dedicated to wood, gold, silver, shell, and bone works from many different Pre-Columbian cultures. There are a few good shops in the court-

yard such as Alpaca 111, H. Stern, as well as some roving ven-

dors and maybe the best restaurant in Cuzco, the MAP café. Open daily 9 am-11 pm. Admission 16 soles or 8 soles for students.

Another excellent museum, the ★**Museo Inka** (Cuesta del Almirante 103, ☎ 237-380) is in what was once the Palacio del Almirante, a Colonial mansion built on top of an Incan palace. The museum traces the development of the Inca from a small regional tribe to one of the greatest civilizations the world had seen. On display are metalwork, jewelry, textiles, ceramics, architectural models, and painted wood Incan drinking cups. You can often find weaving demonstrations (and textile sales) in the courtyard. Open Mon-Fri 8 am-6 pm; Sat and holidays 9 am-6 pm. Admission 5 soles.

Nearby, the **Museo de Arte Religioso** (Hatun Rumiyoc and Herrajes) is inside the **Palacio Arzobispal**, which was erected on the site of another palace built in 1400 for Inca Roca. It includes a variety of religious paintings and Colonial furniture, with the works of indigenous master Diego Quispe Tito. Open Mon-Sat 8:30-11:30 am and 3-5:30 pm. Admission included in the Boleto Turístico.

The **Museo de Arte Contemporario**, the Contemporary Art Museum, has modern art exhibitions that are generally excellent and feature some of the best-known and unknown artists in Peru. Open Mon-Fri 9 am-5 pm. Admission included in the Boleto Turístico.

Colonial furniture and paintings, as well as the evolution of the Cuzqueñan style of painting, can be found at the **Museo de Historia Regional**, the Regional History Museum (inside Casa Garcilaso at Garcilaso and Heladeros). Open daily 8 am-5 pm. Admission included in the Boleto Turístico.

The next museum is near the iPeru office where the tourist tickets are bought, so it is easy for a quick drop in. The **Museo de Arte Popular** is small and won't take more than 20 minutes of your time. It is divided into two rooms, one for contemporary paintings from Peruvian artist and another that is filled with hundreds of dolls, figurines, carvings, and nativity sets with Andean themes. Open Mon-Sat 8 am-6 pm and Sun 8 am-1 pm. Admission included in the Boleto Turístico.

INCA STONEWORK

A privilege of the Incan nobility was to have the walls of their palaces built by highly skilled masons. The artistic legacy of their stonework was the Incas own, not the remnant of some other civilization like much of their other features. The accuracy in which they cut and polished their stones allowed them to fit each piece together without the need of mortar. Most you cannot even fit a piece of paper between, and that goes for today. Powerful earthquakes have torn down much of the city, but have been unable to move these walls. There are two types of walls that were used – course, which had neat rectangular blocks and were preferred, and polygonal, which are shaped every which way to interlock. The latter is thought to be the more amazing today.

 There is a great scene in the movie *Motorcycle Diaries*, where a young kid is giving Che Guevara and his friend a tour of Cuzco. He takes them down Hatunrumiyoc and gives him a speech that you will here almost word-for-word today: "On this side of the street we have the walls that were Inca-built. On the other side is the Spanish-built wall – incapable."

★★Barrio San Blas

The San Blas district of Cuzco is my favorite part of town, filled with narrow winding streets, small cafés and bars, artists' workshops, and some of the most interesting hotels. This neighborhood on the hill is thought of as an artisan district. The reason dates back to the Inca Pachacútec Yupanqui's redesign of the city. The most highly skilled craftsmen from throughout the empire gravitated toward Cuzco, with the duty of sharing all they knew. The ruler asked the municipal architects to leave an area of the city for these artisans; this became San Blas and it led to a technological revolution that helped the Incas establish a far greater society than previously imagined.

Iglesia San Blas

It became a melting pot of artisans, and still is to this day. Many in the galleries have inherited their skills from the generations before them. The crafts take all forms as well: sculpture, pottery, painting, jewelry, textiles, woodcarvings, stonework, religious art and antiques.

Plaza de San Blas

The neighborhood revolves around the **Plaza San Blas**, one of the few parts of the district not on a hill. There you will find a large fountain, several small hotels, many charming cafés and restaurants, and shop after shop of crafts. Several street vendors have made this their permanent home, including a woman who sells Mazamorra Morada, a stewed purple maize jelly with cream, for one sole. The **Iglesia San Blas** stands right on the Plaza. It isn't as flashy or well known as some of the other churches in Cuzco, but the small adobe church has a highly intricate carved wooden pulpit that is thought to be one of the finest in the Americas. Open Mon-Sat 8 am-6 pm, Sun and holidays 2-6 pm. Admission 5 soles.

★★Ruins Around Cuzco

All of the following can be entered with the Boleto Turístico. There aren't entrances to several of the sites, but there are roving inspectors to stamp your tickets. If you take a taxi or bus (take the Pisac bus and get off before Pisac) to the last site, you can easily walk the eight km/4.8 miles along the road and downhill back to Cuzco. At each site there are locals in their finest traditional clothes hoping to get paid for a photo or to sell their crafts.

Sacsayhuaman

The most popular ruin near Cuzco, the Incan fort of ★★**Sacsayhuaman** rarely disappoints. Located on a hill overlooking the city to the north, it is one of the Incas' most impressive architectural feats. The enormous polygonal stone blocks are some of the finest stone masonry you will ever see. Construction began in the 15th century and lasted for almost 100 years, requiring thousands of men to complete it. The limestone blocks, the largest weighing more than 300 tons, were brought from as far as 20 miles away.

It was used as both a fort and for religious and social activities. Much was torn down after the Conquest, to be used for churches and other structures, so only about 20% of the original stonework is left standing. One of the most noteworthy aspects of Sacsayhuaman is the three-tiered zigzag fortifications that served to defend against attackers. Rodadero Hill, opposite the main fortress, once had three large towers, but the Spanish tore them down. There was room in the ramparts for an estimated 5,000-10,000 warriors and their supplies, which should give you an idea of how colossal the site was.

Perhaps the bloodiest battle between the Incas and the Spanish occurred here. Two years after the Spanish took the city, Manco Inca led a rebellion and overtook the fort, using it as a base to carry out raids on the city below. With far greater forces than the Spanish, the Incas nearly recaptured the city as a whole. But in a desperate last battle in 1536 Juan Pizarro and 50 men on horseback stormed the fortress and killed thousands of men. It is said that giant Andean condors feasted on the dead and this is why Cuzco's coat of arms features eight condors.

Fiesta del Inti Raymi (Mylene d'Auriol)

The festival of **Inti Raymi** is held on the clear grassy area and Rodadero Hill. It is possible to walk to Sacsayhuaman from the center of Cuzco by climbing the steps north from San Blas and past the Church of San Cristóbal. The climb to the fort is steep and will take a half-hour or so, depending on how well you have acclimatized. From 8 to 10 pm, it is possible to enter the site to view the stone walls and the valley below by star- and perhaps moonlight.

The site of **Qenko** is four km/2.4 miles from Cuzco, leading away from Sacsayhuaman, about a km away. The name also means zigzag, which relates to the zigzag channels carved into the limestone that were likely used for preparation of chicha (the fermented beverage made from maize by the Inca) or quite possibly blood during ritual sacrifices. The shrine was used for ceremonies and has lightly etched images of a condor, puma, and llama. One of the most interesting features is the hollowed out stone outcropping containing a small alter.

At **Tambo Machay**, water flows from a small, carved channel in the stone wall into a little pool known as the Incas' bath. The shrine is somewhat hidden from the main road so, if you are driving, be on the lookout for the sign. The site is thought to have been related to the Incan water cult.

Puca Pucara is just across the road from Tambo Machay. The name, meaning red fort, reflects the pinkish rock that the post was built with. There isn't much to see, except the wonderful views of the surrounding valley.

Tipón (Carlos Sala)

The agricultural terracing at **Tipón**, 25 km/15 miles from Cuzco, is some of the most impressive that the Incas built. You will also find a temple complex, irrigation canals, and an aqueduct. Many believe the site to be as extraordinary as the ruins at Pisac or Ollantaytambo. It is a bit difficult to get to. The best way is by taxi ($20 round-trip including a wait), which can also stop at Pikillacta. Also, you can catch a combi from Av. Huáscar that goes to Urcos. You must tell the driver to let you off at Tipon, which is a difficult one-hour hike from the road. They are open from 7 am to 5:30 pm.

Pikillacta is actually a pre-Incan site, belonging to the Huari culture. The ceremonial center was built between 700 and 900 AD and comprises mainly two-level adobe buildings that have seen their share of wear. A combi to Urcos will drop you off right at the entrance if you tell the driver.

Language Schools

Amauta Spanish School – Suecia 480, ☎ 262-345, fax 241-422, www.amautaspanishschool.com. Offers on-site accommodations and can arrange home stays with local families, as well as volunteer work. Classes are small and can be helpfully intense. Includes a welcome dinner, various activities throughout each week, and free Internet access. Morning or afternoon classes. Four hours each day. Also has programs in Urubamba and the Manu Biosphere Reserve. Recommended.

Maximo Nivel – Av. El Sol 612, ☎ 25-7200, www.maximonivel.net. Has a variety of classes for different skill levels and can also arrange TEFL certificates for those looking to teach English abroad.

San Blas Spanish School – Tandapata 688, ☎ 24-7898, sbspanishschool@hotmail.com. Offers private and group lessons for reasonable prices.

Mundo Verde Spanish School – Nueva Alta 432-A, ☎ 22-1287, http://mundoverdespanish.com. This Spanish school supports a conservation project in the Peruvian rainforest, developing sustainable resource management in three villages. Volunteers teach English to village children or work on rainforest conservation. In-person interview required. Twenty hours of lessons, $150.

Academia LatinoAmericana de Español – El Sol 580, ☎ 243-364, www.latinoschools.com. Group and private classes. Can arrange volunteer work and home stays. Free dance classes.

Where to Stay

 ★★★**Hotel Monasterio** – Palacios 136 (on Plazoleta Nazarenas), ☎ 241-777, fax 246-983, www.monasterio.orient-express.com. One of the nicest hotels in the entire world, and you will pay the price for it. No joke. It was built in 1565 as the site of the Inca Amaru Qhala's palace, which later became a monastery. The list of special amenities is long. Rooms are luxurious as

Hotel Monasterio (Jorge Sarmiento))

expected and have all the extras, such as oxygen-enriched air to combat altitude sickness. Each room is unique. For $40, a bath butler will bring you a coca sour, a cigar, anti-stress salts, and will run your bath with coca leaves. Its own Baroque chapel has paintings depicting the life of San Antonio Abad. The restaurants are some of the best in Peru, such as Illary (see below). $$$$$

Libertador Palacio del Inka – Plazuela Santa Domingo 259, ☎ 231-961, fax 233-152, www.libertador. com.pe. Just across the street from Qorikancha, the foundations of the building have been here since Incan times. The rooms use quality products and décor is stylish, but nothing is over the top. The restaurant has good Novo Andina cuisine, and there is a

Libertador Palacio del Inka

coffee shop, bar, sauna, gym, business center, and wireless Internet are among the extras. $$$$$

Novotel – San Agustín 239, ☎ 228-282, www.novotelcusco. com.pe. This is one of the newest hotels on the luxury circuit. The décor and design are what I would call Colonial contemporary, with the building a remodeled Colonial and the furnishings contemporary. Rooms are either contemporary or Colonial, depending on your preference. La Cave restaurant is here, plus a coffee shop and bar. $$$$$

Casa San Blas

★**Casa San Blas Boutique Hotel** – Tocuyeros 566, ☎ 251-563, fax 237-900, www. casasanblas.com. Set in a restored Colonial-style house that dates back 250 years, this small boutique hotel set on a steep hill is quite stunning, with quaint décor and original stonework. Rooms have private baths and all of the amenities that a boutique hotel deserves. Also, free Internet access, massage parlor, piano bar, and an excellent restaurant (La Cava de San Blas). Oxygen treatment is available. Suite apartments with kitchens are available for longer stays.

HOTEL PRICE CHART	
	under $10
$	$10-$25
$$	$26-$50
$$$	$51-$90
$$$$	$91-$150
$$$$$	Over $150

Excellent value. Highly recommended. $$$$

Sonesta Posada del Inca Cuzco – Portal Espinar 108, ☎ 227-061, fax 248-484, www.sonesta.com. Not as nice as some of the other hotels in the chain, but the location is excellent and the standard amenities get the job done. The rooms could use a makeover, but are still cozy and a reasonable value. Inkafe restaurant serves creative international dishes and local specialties such as alpaca carpaccio. $$$$

Casa Andina – San Agustín 371, ☎ 252-633, fax 222-908; Santa Catalina Angosta 149, ☎ 233-661, fax 224-461; Portal Espinar 142, ☎ 231-733, fax 231-682; . This up-and-coming bed and breakfast chain has three convenient locations in Cuzco and is a good value overall and include breakfast buffets. All have heated rooms with cable TV, private baths, etc. $$$

Casa Andina Private Collection

Casa Andina Private Collection Cuzco – Plazoleta de Limacpampa Chico 473, ☎ 446-8848, fax 445-4775, www.casa-andina. com. This is one of the chain's flagship locations. As with the other hotels in the private collection, it is quite stunning. The setting is an 18th-century Colonial house with second-level guestrooms, just a few blocks from the center. The price is still reasonable. $$$$

Hotel Casa de Campo – Tandapata 296 B, ☎ 243-069, fax 244-404, www.hotelcasadecampo.com. High up in the San

Hotel Casa de Campo

Blas hill, this sprawling hotel has several levels, all with wonderful views over Cuzco. Breakfast buffet is offered. Will arrange bus and plane tickets, hikes, and a variety of other trips and activities. $$$

Torre Dorada Residencial – Los Cipreses N-5, ☎ 241-698, fax 224-255, www.torredorada.com. This place is big on personal attention, so it might not be a bad choice for older guests. Transportation wherever the guests want to go in Cusco is included in the price of the hotel. Train and airport transfers are include, as is breakfast. $$$

Hotel José Antonio – Av. Pardo 1080, at the corner with Av. El Sol, ☎ 23-9030. This hotel was built in 2003 in a modern style. The 125 rooms have heating, cable TV, mini-bars, hair dryers, and a modem connection. Also a business center, laundry service, restaurant and bar. Includes breakfast buffet. $$$

Hotel El Dorado San Agustín – El Sol 395, ☎ 231-232, fax 24 0993, www.hotelessanagustin.com.pe. Fifty-six rooms with private baths, cable TV, heating, safe, 24-hour room service. Business center, restaurant, bar, laundry service. $$$$

Hotel Arqueologo – Pumacurco 408, ☎ 232-569, fax 235-126, www. hotelarqueologo. com. Another small San Blas hotel. Rooms have heating, private hot-water baths, cable TV, hair dryers, tables, and sofas. The Colonial style

Hotel Arqueologo

is charming here, and rooms vary in size and light. Breakfast buffet is included. The hotel claims that the white Christ (Cristo Blanco) on the hill above covers it with a magical mantle. Within walking distance from Sacsayhuaman. $$$

Hotel San Agustín International – Maruri 390, ☎ 221-169, fax 221-174, www.hotelessanagustin.com.pe. A short walk to the center. The 55 rooms have all of the basic amenities, nothing flashy. $$$$

El Balcón – Tambo de Montero 222, ☎ 236-738, fax 225-352, balcon1@terra.com.pe. Large cozy rooms have private baths, hot water and views over the city. Free coca tea. $$

Andenes de Saphi – Saphi 848, ☎ 227-561, fax 235-588, www.andenesdesaphi.com. Near the base of Sacsayhuaman, the hotel has three flower-filled terraces and a greater appreciation of the natural world than some of the other Cuzco hotels. Rooms are country rustic. Price includes breakfast and airport transfer. $$

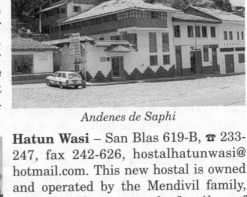

Andenes de Saphi

Hatun Wasi

Hatun Wasi – San Blas 619-B, ☎ 233-247, fax 242-626, hostalhatunwasi@hotmail.com. This new hostal is owned and operated by the Mendivil family, the world-renowned family of Cusqueñan artists. Modern yet simple rooms with private hot-water baths, heaters, cable TV. Includes continental breakfasts. Sun terrace with excellent views of Cusco. The family has several shops in San Blas and wares can be purchased at the hotel as well. $

Casa Grande – Santa Catalina Ancha 353, ☎ 264-156. Big rambling house with a central courtyard, squeaky wooden floors, small museum, parking, TV room, laundry service and an unbelievably warm and inviting staff. Rooms on the top floor are warmer and generally newer. If you are concerned about your budget and can ignore a few minor flaws, this is recommended. Great location.

Hotel Suecia II – Tecsecocha 465, ☎ 23-3282, hsuecia1@
hotmail.com. The rooms are basic, but warm and clean, and
surround a glass-covered courtyard. Shared and private
baths with electric showers. Dorms also available. Good location for the price.

Hotel Suecia I – Suecia 332, ☎ 233-282, hsuecia1@hotmail.
com. Similar to the previous hotel, but one block over.

Amaru Hostal – Cuesta San Blas 541 (San Blas Hill), ☎ 225-
933, www.cusco.net/amaru. Clean and charming with lots of
woodwork (floors, furniture, trim, etc). TV room, restaurant,
luggage storage, book exchange, laundry service. Will arrange
city tours, trips to Machu Picchu and the Sacred Valley.
Rooms with shared and private baths. $$.

★**Hospedaje San Blas** – Plazoleta San Blas 630, ☎ 235 358,
plazadesanblas@yahoo.es. One of my favorite budget options
in Cusco. Sitting right on Plaza San Blas, this pleasant and
quirky little hospedaje is an excellent value. Rooms have
shared bathrooms with electric showers and surround a cov-
ered courtyard. 24-hour reception. TV room with cable TV
and DVDs. Each room is a little different, yet all have a uni-
form charm. The Mandrake café/coffee bar is attached. Excel-
lent value. $

Hotel Don Carlos – El Sol 602, ☎ 226 207, fax 241 375,
dcarloscus@tci.net.pe. One of the better options on Avenida El
Sol. Newly remodeled rooms with cable TV, mini-fridge, and
private baths. Restaurant with 24-hour room service, bar, air-
port transfers, arranges tours. $$$

Cusco Plaza I – Nazarenas 181, ☎ 24 6161, fax 26 3842,
www.cuscoplazahotels.com. On Nazarenas square with the
Monasterio and MAP, this hotel has set up residence in an
18th-century Colonial house. Rooms have private hot-water
baths, cable TV, and heating. Also safes, laundry service, lug-
gage storage, and tourist information. $$$

Cusco Plaza II – Saphi 486, ☎ 263 000, fax 26 2001, www.
cuscoplazahotels.com. Like the previous hotel, it is set in an
18th-century Colonial house with original stone arcs. There
are three patios and a glass-enclosed courtyard. Rooms have
private hot-water baths, cable TV, and heating. Also available

are safes, laundry service, luggage storage, and tourist information. $$$

Casona Las Pleiades – Tandapata 116, ☎ 806 430, www.casonapleiades.com. Bed and breakfast on a quiet side-street in San Blas. Rooms have private hot-water baths. There is a sun terrace, TV lounge, free airport transfer. $$

The Garden House Hotel – Urb. Larapa Grande B-6, ☎ 271-1117, www.cuscohouse.com. A beautiful new hotel about 10 minutes from the center of Cuzco, but close enough so you can easily access the sites.

The Garden House Hotel

It's in a peaceful garden setting, seemingly far-removed from the city. There are just seven double bedrooms with baths, some of them interconnecting family suites. Two sitting rooms with wood fireplaces, a library, dining room, bar, Internet connections, cable TV, and gorgeous views of the city make this one of the best and most convenient escapes to be had in Cuzco. Breakfast is included. $$$

GASTRONOMY

Cuy al horno – Roasted guinea pig.

Tamal – Steamed corn dough, wrapped in a green leaf. Sweet (dulce) or salty (salado).

Chicharrón – Deep-fried pork chunks served with onion and corn.

Kapchi – Bean or potato soup made with milk, eggs, and cheese.

Sopa de quinua – A soup made with the extremely healthy Andean grain.

Saralawa – Soup made with corn, beans, ají pepper, and huacatay.

Where to Eat

Cuzco's dining scene has changed dramatically in the past decade. Before, few restaurants of any stature could be found here. Now, as more and more tourists make their way to Peru, 3- to 5-star restaurants are popping up everywhere with global flare and internationally trained chefs.

★★**Illary** – Plaza Nazarenas (inside Hotel Monasterio), ☎ 243-820. Recently remodeled, chef Michael Rass takes this leading restaurant in the city's leading hotel to new levels. The menu changes often, but ranges from traditional Peruvian to International. A new focus centers on Andean and Cuzqueñan dishes. Gastronomic menus are also available. Reservations are recommended. $$$$$

Fallen Angel – Plaza Nazarenas. Has a kind of LA chic to it that, for some reason, fits in nicely. The glamour aspect consists of images of heaven and hell, lots of drapery and ceiling décor, tables on top of bathtubs, but it isn't overdone. The food is avant-garde, perhaps overly so, but it's still good. Steaks, pastas and salads are the norm, but a few exotic dishes with hard-to-find ingredients will catch your attention. The same owner as Macondo, both of which are gay-friendly. Open late. $$$$

★★**Map Café** – Portal de Panes 115, on the Plaza, ☎ 262-992, www.map-cafe. com. Perhaps the best new restaurant in the city. Inside a glass-enclosed dining room in the courtyard of the Museum of Pre-Columbian Art. The menu is adventur-

ous, without losing its Andean roots. Try dishes like Quinoa fried rice with pickled yacon, Guinea pig confit, or an Oxapampa Camembert sandwich. They also have a long cocktail and wine menu. Highly recommended. $$$$$

DINING PRICE CHART	
$	under $5
$$	$5-$10
$$$	$11-$20
$$$$	$21-$35
$$$$$	over $35

Kin Taro – Heladeros 149, ☎ 226-181. The best place for Japanese in Cuzco. Sushi, tempura, tofu, soups, sake, etc. $$$

Jack's – Choquechaca 509, ☎ 806-960. Has good sandwiches, pastas, and breakfasts. English magazines are available for perusal. Nice bar. Very popular with locals, language students, and tourists alike. Often crowded. $$

Al Grano – Santa Catalina Ancha 398, ☎ 228-032. Asian rice dishes and curries, many vegetarian options as well. Very good and cheap lunch menu. Focus is on Southeast Asian cuisines like Thai, Malaysian, Indonesian, and Indian. Also has a book exchange. $$$

Bohemia Café y Mas – Portal de Carnes 215 (Plaza de Armas), www.bohemiacafe.com. An expansion of the popular Lima restaurant and bar. Large menu with many appetizers, soups, pastas, pizzas, sandwiches, and another 10 main courses. The drink menu is almost as long, with a large number of martinis, many of them Pisco-based. Recommended. $$$$

★**Macondo** – Cuesta San Blas 571, ☎ 229-415. Same owners as Fallen Angel. The name refers to the fictional town in Nobel-prizewinning author Gabriel Garcia Marquez's book *One Hundred Years of Solitude* (a highly rec-
ommended read). Lots of local art adorns the walls, much of it quite edgy. The food is traditional Peruvian, including jungle dishes, and Peruvian fusion. Good cocktail menu with several interesting originals. $$$$

Witches Garden – Carmen Bajo 169, ☎ 974-1569, www.witchesgarden.net. This small, fashionable San Blas restaurant serves Novo Andina and International cuisine. Many interesting chicken dishes as well. The funky soundtrack ranges from Andean, jazz and house to Afro-pop. $$$

★**Kusikuy** – Suecia 339, ☎ 26-2870, www.kusikuycusco.com. The name is Quechua for "happy guinea pig." A trendy setting with straightforward presentations of local specialties using high-quality and fresh ingredients. As you might expect, it's a good place for cuy (guinea pig), which is served on a skewer and standing up (40 soles). Recommended. $$$

★★**Inka Grill Restaurant** – Portal de Panes 115 (on the Plaza de Armas), ☎ 262-992, inkagrill@wayna.rcp.net.pe. This has been one of the best restaurants in Cuzco, and one of the best spots in Peru for Novo Andina cuisine, since its opening. There are several Quinoa dishes, including soup. Alpaca is served as medallions or as a steak. For dessert try the coca-leaf crème brûlée. The décor is dark and castle-like, with huge candles and stone floors and walls. $$$$

Cerveceria Imperial Brewery – Plateros 365. The inside of this microbrewery can be seen from the street in Plateros. What you can't see, however, is the upscale dining room beside it. Oddly, there is only a small bar, so the focus is actually on the food, which is average-tasting, moderately priced international fare. $$$

La Retama Restaurant – Portal de Panes 123, ☎ 226-372. This second-floor restaurant on the Plaza has a truly Andean feel. Everything from the flowers in the vases, the tapestries on the walls, to the food on the table is Cuzqueñan. The nightly folk music shows are a big draw here and highly recommended. $$$

Pacha Papa – This quinta (rustic local restaurant) is just across the street from the San Blas church. Famous for its stir-fried beef, mutton seco, tasty olluquito (small Andean tubers) with meat, and dried alpaca meat. Also try the alpaca anticuchos and alpaca goulash. Order cuy a day in advance. $$$

Greens – Tandapata 700. Just above Plaza San Blas, Greens is a small, trendy place with dark green walls, modern art, candlelit tables, and a small fireplace. The menu is international, with steaks, chicken, and curries. The tropical chicken curry with bananas, peaches and strawberries is interesting. Daily happy hour 6:30-7:30 pm. $$$

★**Blueberry Lounge** – Portal de Carnes 236, on Plaza de Armas. An attractive setting with several cozy lounging areas good for a meal or snack any time of the day. Excellent eggs benedict for breakfast. The lunch and dinner menu are very international, with several Peruvian fusion dishes. Has the same owner as Greens. $$$

El Molino Pizzeria – Plateros 359. Of the many pizza places in town, this is one of the best and most conveniently located. $$$

In front of Gato's market on the plaza, there is a woman that sells **humitas**, or sweet and salty ground corn steamed in a cornhusk, for just half a sole. They are famous among locals and travelers alike and are some of the best in the country. Excellent for a quick snack.

★★**La Cicciolina** – Triunfo 393 (on the northwest corner of El Triunfo and Choquechaka), ☎ 239-510. This second-level restaurant, based on a Melbourne original, combines a tapas bar with Mediterranean, Peruvian and other international flavors to make up one of the most creative and lively menus in Cuzco. Argentine Chef Luis Alberto Scilotto was the former chef at Lima's well-known La Gloria restaurant. The atmosphere is romantic and enchanting, with deep red and yellow walls, contemporary furniture, dim lighting, and the soft glow of candles. Most of the dishes use fresh locally grown ingredients and the pastas are homemade. There is an exquisite wine list as well. A small café and bakery below the restaurant offers take-out service. Reservations are recommended for dinner.

★**The Muse** – Tandapata 684. Cozy café with low ceilings as well as patio seating that looks over Plaza San Blas. Big sandwiches served with sides of pasta salad, excellent juices and coffee drinks. Happy hour from 9:30-10:30 pm, and 12-1 am. Live music on most nights. $$

Bar 7 – Tandapata 690, San Blas, ☎ 431-380, restobar7@hotmail.com. Small San Blas hangout that is good for a drink or meal. The food blends regional foods and ingredients with New Age techniques. Open late. $$$

Cusco Curry House – Nueva Alta 424. Located in Perezosos B&B and perhaps the only English curry house in Peru. Get your fix here. $$

Gringo Alley, or **Procuradores**, has many small tourist-oriented restaurants, with menu hawkers trying to pull you in the door every three steps. Most offer a 10- to 20-sole menu of Peruvian, Mexican, American, or Italian food. They are usually clean, not too bad, offer several courses that will fill you up.

Procuradores (A. Cabrera)

Ayllu – Portal del Carnes 208, ☎ 232-257. This café sits just beside the cathedral. Eye-catching local paintings adorn the walls and the soft sounds of classical music fill the air. The best time to go is for breakfast, but the coffee, pastries, and sandwiches keep diners there throughout the day. $$

Café Cappuccino – Portal Confiturias 141. A pleasant balcony overlooks the Plaza. Good for coffee, tea, a beer, or a light snack such as one of their delicious pastries. Window tables are usually filled. $

Varayoc – Espaderos 142, ☎ 232-404, varayocusco@hotmail. com. Excellent coffees, as well as Swiss dishes like rosti, fondue, pastries, and desserts. $$

Vegetarian

Café Cultural Ritual – Choquechaca 140. Bright and clean vegetarian restaurant and snack bar. Good coffees and juices. $$

El Encuentro – Santa Catalina Ancha 384. One of the best-value vegetarian restaurants in all of Peru. The lunch or dinner menu, at under $2, offers several tasty and nourishing options. A la carte plates are also available. $

Bars & Clubs

Many of the bars and clubs around the Plaza offer free drink coupons (usually for a Cuba libre) to lure you into their club before midnight. It is possible, and often done, to walk from place to place having free drink after free drink. Drink specials, again before midnight, for most of the clubs consist of buy-one-get-one-free or buy-three-at-a-discount. The touts in the street are quite aggressive, but take it in good fun and so will they.

Rosie O'Grady's Bar and Grill – Santa Catalina Ancha 360, www.geocities.com/rosiesincusco. One of Cuzco's legendary gringo haunts. A long wooden bar and a cozy fireplace highlight the pleasant dining area. They serve a variety of pub foods, burgers, and Irish fare. Their TV schedule is posted on a bulletin board outside; the international sports broadcasts probably draw more customers than the food!. $$$

Paddy O'Flaherty's – Triunfo 124. This is a more drinking-oriented pub than Rosie O'Grady's with a focus on sporting events and bar stools rather than dining, although food is served as well. A lively atmosphere of mostly foreigners. Cans of Guinness are available, although pricey. $$

★Norton Rat's Tavern – Loretto 115. This second-level bar on the Plaza is one of Peru's biggest biker hangouts, although you will likely find just about anyone there. Owned by a Clevelander, this dive of a bar with lots of knick-knacks on the walls has good happy hour specials. It's a great place for a beer, or a game of pool or darts.

Cross Keys Pub – Portal Confiturias 233. A good place to catch a European soccer match. Also burgers, curries, and a variety of other English pub foods.

★★Los Perros – Tecseccocha 436, ☎ 226-625. "The Dogs," a chic wine/couch bar owned by an Australian-Peruvian couple, manages to keep a laid-back feel. Wine is sold by the glass or bottle at reasonable prices. Finger foods are also available and delicious, such as the potato skins or cheese plates. Live jazz on Sun or Mon nights. Lots of international magazines for perusal. It gets crowded early, so call ahead to reserve a table. $$$

Big Blue Martini – Tecsecocha 148, ☎ 248-839, bigbluemartini@hotmail.com. Another sofa bar with food and drinks, particularly cocktails, and particularly martinis. Soft blue lighting and an abundance of glass add some extra umph to the hipness.

Pepe Zeta – Teqsecocha 415 (2nd floor), ☎ 223-082. This is a bistro and lounge with a fireplace that attracts a stylish crowd. Music is chilled out, jazz or house, with DJs or live music on the small stage.

★**Ukuku's** – Plateros 316 (2nd floor), ☎ 227-867. This rock club is one of the best places for nightly live music. Not traditional music, but rock, Latino pop, and even Afro-Peruvian. Very cool murals and artwork are hung throughout the place. Tends to draw a more evenly mixed crowd of locals and tourists and stays packed until late.

★**Mama Africa** – Portal Harinas 191 (2nd floor), www.mamaafricaclub.com. One of the best clubs in town, it always draws a large crowd of internationals and locals, plays good music. Has happy hours, and an interesting African theme.

Uptown – Portal Belén 115 (2nd floor). Almost the exact same crowd as Mama Africa, but in a slightly less attractive locale.

Xcess – Suecia 319. This place is often crowded with language students that come to dance to the house, techno, hip-hop, and 80s pop songs.

Mystique – Suecia 320. This bar is next door to Xcess, feeding off of its clientele, and vice versa. It is built on Incan foundations and you can lean against the blocks as you drink a cocktail. Recently went through a light remodeling that put a few needed tables outside the dance floor.

Entertainment

Movies

 Makeshift movie theaters are set up in many clubs on the Plaza de Armas in the afternoons, showing mainly pirated versions of international films, mostly in English. Movies are free, but you must buy a drink or something to eat and prices are very reasonable. Try **Mama Africa**, **Mama Amerika**, **Xcess**, and **Mystique**.

Folkloric Shows

Centre Qosqo de ArteNativo – Has native folkloric dances each night. Open from 7-8 pm. Admission included in the Boleto Turístico.

Teatro Municipal – Meson de la Estrella 149, ☎ 227-321. Holds a variety of performances Thurs-Sun. Has dance and music classes during the summer. Call for details.

Many restaurants such as **La Retama** hold nightly shows.

Shopping

 Cuzco offers the most diverse craft and textile selection anywhere in Peru, not too mention fine jewelry and alpaca clothing. Be sure to bargain, as prices are often inflated. Handicrafts from throughout the Andes can be found here and quality is usually very good.

The main markets are on Av. El Sol. The **Centro Artesenal Cuzco** (El Sol and Tullamayo; open 8 am-10 pm) is the largest and is covered. Prices are a little bit higher than other places, but the selection of mass-produced handicrafts is incomparable. Closer to the Plaza are two more markets, opposite each other. They have better prices and the work is more genuine.

Artesana, San Blas (M. d'Auriol)

The stand on the northeast side of the street next door to one market, run by an older husband and wife team, has the best deals in the city. The selection isn't as big as in the markets, but the quality is just as good.

There are also many small markets and shops on Procuradores, Plateros, and Loreto.

Crafts on sale

The **Barrio San Blas** has been Cuzco's artisan district for centuries and still is. Almost every other doorway has some small workshop and showroom displaying a number of different crafts. Some of the best are ★**Taller Mendival** (on Plaza San Blas, ☎ 23-3247) and **Taller Olave** (also on the Plaza). Each has a variety of Colonial artwork, religious figurines, carvings, frames, ornaments, and jewelry. Taller Mendival is internationally known for the carved, solemn saints with the elongated necks it produces. Otherwise, take a walk up Carmen Alto from the Plaza and also back down to the main square on Hatunrunmiyoc and Cuesta San Blas. You will find hundreds of shops selling every souvenir imaginable.

Books

Every bookstore is on the Plaza and there are several, but English-language books are for the most part very overpriced. My suggestion is to look for a book exchange, of which there are many.

Alpaca

Alpaca 111 – Has locations at Plaza Regocijo 202, Hotel Monasterio, Hotel Libertador, MAP, and the airport. It's the best place for fine alpaca clothing. Recommended.

Alpaca's Best – Confituria 221 (the Plaza). Also in the Hotel Monasterio and Hotel José Antonio.

La Casa de la Llama – Palacio 121.

Other Shops of Interest

Centro de Textiles Tradicionales de Cusco – El Sol 603-A, ☎ 228-117. Non-profit organization that helps preserve Incan textile traditions. Gallery, shop, and small museum.

On-site weaving demonstrations. Expensive, but the quality is very high.

Werner & Ana – Plaza San Francisco 295-A. Boutique of a Dutch-Peruvian couple who blend traditional techniques and materials with high fashion.

Pablo Semanario – Portal de Carnes 244, ☎ 246-093. The famed Urubamba ceramicist has a small shop on the Plaza with his unique style and one-of-a-kind pieces.

Coca Shop – Carmen Alto 115, www.kuychiwasi.org. Products and food made from coca leaves. Also a good source of information on coca.

Mundo Hemp – Qanchipata 596 in San Blas, www.mundohemp.com. Fashionable hemp clothing, housewares, and a small café with hemp cuisine.

Camping/Climbing/Rental Equipment

Tattoo Outdoors and Travel – Plazoleta Las Nazarenas 211, ☎ 26-3099. Has pricey but quality clothing, tents, backpacks, and other gear for sale.

For rentals, you can walk into almost any travel agency or store on the Plaza, Gringo Alley, or Plateros. Prices should just be a few dollars per day per item.

Spas/Massage Services

Yin Yang – Comercio 121, ☎ 258 201, www.yinyang-therapeuticmassage.com. List of massages. Room service available.

Tour Agencies

There are so many tour agencies coming and going in Cuzco that it seems like each day there is a new one opening up. Prices, services, and quality vary greatly and depend heavily on the time of the year and especially the number of people on the tour. You will often find that the people on your tour paid more or less than you. To make sure you get what you paid for, get a written agreement of what your tour includes. This applies to what food you will be eating as well. The prices are always negotiable and you should never take the first offer. Also, it is wise to shop around.

SAS Travel – Portal de Panes 167, Garcilaso 256, ☎ 261-920, fax 237-292, www.sastravelperu.com. A wide range of tours, including treks, rafting, Manu, Puerto Maldonado, Sacred Valley, Cuzco city, horseback riding, four-day tours to Lake Titicaca, and many others. Reliable company with average prices.

United Mice – Plateros 351, ☎ 22-1139, www.unitedmice. com. Well-established company, reliable, with moderate pricing. Mountain biking, rafting, Puno/Cuzco bus trips, Ausangate, Espiritu Pampa, Choquequirao, Salkantay, and the Inca Trail. One percent of profits go to Cuzco street children. English spoken.

Dos Manos – Suecia 480, ☎ 235-620, fax 241-422, www. dosmanosperu.com. Has offices in Arequipa and Puno, and leads tours throughout the country. Every kind of tour possible can be arranged through this company.

Andina Travel – Plazoleta Santa Catalina 219, ☎ 251-892, andinatravel@terra.com.pe. Pricier than some of the other companies but worth it. All sorts of treks available, rafting, mountain biking, customized tours, cultural tours. Specialist in the Lares Valley.

Peruvian Andean Treks – Pardo 705, ☎ 225-701, www. andeantreks.com. American-based company that arranges trips throughout the continent. Expensive, but hires good guides and makes sure everything goes smoothly. Inca trail, llama treks, Vilcabamba, Machu Picchu, and Manu.

Apumayo Expeditions – Garcilaso 265 (office 3), ☎ 246-018, www.apumayo.com. Specialist in rafting. Helped jump-start the clean-up of the Urubamba River. Very eco-friendly company.

Erik Adventures – Plateros 324, ☎ 228-475, www. ericadventures.com. One of the most experienced companies for rafting and kayaking. Offers one- to four-day trips in the Apurimac and Urubamba rivers. Owner is Eric Arenas, a national rafting champion and Olympic rafter. The company also arranges paragliding, bungee jumping, canyoning, horseback riding, climbing, and biking. The emphasis is on the more intense and physically demanding adventures.

Adventure Team Peru – Ruinas 457 # 104, ☎ 241-141, www.adventureteamperu.com. Mountain biking and rafting tours. Also rock climbing, parapenting, and kayaking.

Action Valley – 11 km/6.6 miles out of Cuzco on the road to Poroy, www.actionvalley.com. This adventure park offers a variety of daredevil activities, such as rappelling, bungee jumping (122 m/400 feet), a bungee slingshot, and scaling a climbing wall.

Globos de los Andes – Q'apchik'iijllu 271, ☎ 232-532, www.globosperu.com. This company gives you a bird's-eye view of the Sacred Valley. Prices are high.

Organizacion Internacional de Chamanes y Curanderos del Peru – Choquechaca 490, ☎ 993-3905. Ayuhuasca, Huachuma, Micha, and San Pedro ceremonies available. Courses available as well.

Ayahuasca Wasi – www.ayahuasca-wasi.com. Has weeklong retreats in Tambopata and Pisac, combining Buddhist principles and meditation with a series of Ayahuasca sessions.

For the Cuzco offices of lodges and agencies in Puerto Maldonado and Manu, see the respective sections.

Adventures

On Foot
Walking Tour of Catholic Cuzco

 Cuzco's churches are some of the most spectacular in the New World. Many are as or more spectacular than the famed cathedrals of Europe and combine Andean elements that make them perhaps more interesting as well. Installing Christendom on

Iglesia San Blas

a mass level first began here on the continent. To start this tour, walk or take a taxi to Plazoleta San Blas, where you will find the **Iglesia San Blas**. The church is best known for its mestizo carved wooden pulpit.

Next head up Carmen Alto and make a left down the street of 7 Angelitos and continue down 7 Culebras to the Plazuela Las Nazarenas, home to the MAP museum and the Hotel Monasterio. Here you will find the **Convento Las Nazarenas**, which has an 18th-century fresco inside. Note the mermaid motif on the doorway. From here you will make your way down to the Plaza de Armas, passing the **Museo Inka** along the way.

The **Catedral**, Cuzco's most spectacular Colonial building, is next. The foundation is part of an Incan Palace. The two altars, the silver in front and the carved wood in back are both quite stunning in their own way. There is also a strong collec-

tion of paintings from the Cuzqueñan school. Across the Plaza and just up Mantos in the direction of the stone archway, you will find the **Iglesia y Convento de la Merced** on the left-hand side. This church holds the remains

Iglesia y Convento de la Merced

of Gonzalo Pizarro and the two Almagros, but is best known for its jeweled monstrance on display in the museum.

Turning back to the Plaza and on the right side is the **Iglesia de la Compañía de Jesus**. Rivaling the Catedral in grandeur, the twin towers and fine murals make it perhaps the most photogenic of all. Just around the corner is the **Iglesia y Convento de Santa Catalina**. In addition to the church itself, you can visit the site museum, which has a large collection of religious artifacts and art, perfect for this walk. So, after all of this, you should be ready for the granddaddy of

Convento de Santa Catalina

them all, **Qoricancha**, the Temple of the Sun, or Santo Domingo. Just head south through Loreto, the narrow alley with fine Incan stonework on each side. You will run directly into Qoricancha, perhaps also into little girls in traditional dress holding sheep in hopes of a tip for a photo. After the photo, and giving the girls more and more money until they are satisfied, you will enter the church/temple witnessing the combination of Incan and Spanish religious pride.

Qoricancha

Hiking

For hiking from Cuzco and all of the hikes in the Sacred Valley, you can either take a tour with one of the agencies listed above or go on your own. The one exception is the Inca Trail, where you must go with an agency. See the section on the Inca Trail and alternatives.

The recently rediscovered Incan city of ★★**Choquequirao** is becoming one of the most popular treks in the region. The town, which sits more than two miles above the Apurimac

Choquequirao aquaducts

Gorge, was discovered by Hiram Bingham just before he stumbled upon Machu Picchu, then eventually lost it again. The five-day/four-night trek passes by snow-covered mountain peaks and glaciers, the high jungle, little-known Incan buildings and ruins, raging rivers. There are several locations on the trip where there is a good chance to see the great Andean condor. Prices begin at about $200 for a tour from Cuzco that would include all food, equipment, guides, horses, and bus transportation.

Choquequirao

A five- to seven-day circuit takes you to the top of the area's highest peak, **Ausangate** (6,384 m/20,939 feet). The trip takes you to grasslands filled with herds of alpacas and small rural villages that have changed little since Incan times. The trek starts from the town of Tinqui, which is an eight-hour drive from Cuzco. Tinqui has a small hostel (ausangate@hotmail.com, $) and restaurant. The guides, Francisco Chillihuai and Silverio Crispin, are recommended. Price for a local guide starts at $40 per person, depending on the size of the group. This does not include food or horses. Ausangate is the site of **Q'oyoriti**, the snow star festival held every May or June, which features a midnight trek to the glacier by thousands of Andean peoples. It can also be arranged from Cuzco. Other treks from Tinqui lead to Laguna Sibinacocha (seven-eight days) and Pitumarca (six days).

The way to ★**Vilcabamba** is not necessarily through Cuzco, but you will have to organize the trip from here. The mountain hideout was the last stronghold of the Incas until Manco Inca was killed

Vilcabamba

here in 1544. It is what explorer Hiram Bingham was looking for and thought he had found when he discovered Machu

Picchu. Also known as Espiritu Pampa, the ruins are 70 km/ 42 miles from the lowland town of Quillabamba. It has yet to be excavated on a large scale, so much of it is in pieces and overgrown. To visit here one must hike for about a week round-trip. To start you must go to the village of Huancacalle, reachable by truck (eight hours) from Quillabamba, which is reachable by bus from Cuzco (nine hours, several times a day from the main terminal). In Huancacalle you can rent mules and a guide. The route there is difficult, making many steep climbs and descents before reaching the main site, which sits at about 1,000 m/3,280 feet. You will pass several small, isolated communities and smaller ruins. For more information and maps, contact the SAE clubhouse in Cuzco.

On Wheels

Cycling

 This is a popular one-day trip that passes beautiful Andean lakes and countryside, as well as the sites of Maras and Moray. Moray has four circular terraces set into the earth like an artificial crater, while Maras is one of the most important salt mines of the region. If you don't have much time and really want to go biking, this is an excellent option. Much of it is downhill so you won't need to prepare. You visit unspoiled landscapes, archaeological sites and traditional villages, then return to Cuzco the same day. Prices start at $50 per person.

Motorcycling

Motorcycle tours are on the increase in the area. First it was Harley Davidsons, now it's shifting to motorbikes. The three-day/two-night trip to Pilcapata in Manu National Park is tops. The scenery is among the most stunning in Peru as you make your way down from the high Andes to the jungle, passing some of the world's most diverse flora and wildlife. Prices include a bike (XR 250, 400, or 600), helmet, and gloves. Gasoline and food is up to you. Prices start at around $125.

Scooter Rental

OK, so it isn't a Harley, but if you just want to explore the city on your own, renting a scooter isn't a bad option. You can take it to the nearby ruins, the Pisac market, the suburbs, or just use it to help you get to each museum without your feet falling off from too much walking. You can find a scooter for rent at Tecsecocha 436 (☎ 241-447).

★On Horseback

Although there are a variety of horse treks in the area, including multi-day trips into the Sacred Valley, by far the most popular is the half-day trip that visits the four ruins just outside of Cuzco. The horses ride through the scenic green valley and visit the four Incan ruins of Sacsayhuaman, Q´enko, Puca Pucara, and Tambomachay. The tour lasts about five hours, including a stop for lunch. Many agencies in town offer this tour. Prices start at $40 per person.

On Water

★Rafting

The Sacred Valley is Peru's rafting center and one of the best all-around rafting areas in the world. There are a variety of one-day tours that range in cost from about $20 to $40. For something a little more unusual, and a little more challenging, try the two-day/one-night adventure down the Río Urubamba. The first day goes through a series of Class III rapids, while the second moves up a level to Class IV. The rainy season (December to April) is the best time to do this tour because the river gets faster and the waves and other hydraulics are larger. The tour includes all food, guides, tents, rafting equipment, and transportation to/from the starting/end points. Prices start at about $75. For a three-day trip on the Apurimac that goes through Class III, IV, and V rapids, the prices start at about $200.

Fishing

The Sacred Valley is filled with an abundance of mountain lakes, unpolluted rivers, and streams where a variety of fish thrive. Most trips wind up in the gorgeous Apurimac Valley, using a raft to navigate down the river on Class II rapids. You also drive to various lakes, encountering sleepy rural villages and Pre-Columbian landmarks such as K'eshuachaca, a traditional

Inca bridge. Tours can be several days of camping and cooking your dinner, or just a few hours. Prices vary greatly, so shop around.

Cuzco & Sacred Valley Festivals

Chiaraje (January 20). A war game where community members battle to enhance the fertility of the soil. Takes place in the Canas province.

Semana Santa (Easter week). In remembrance of the death and resurrection of Jesus, each day during Easter week there are processions and the preparation of 12 different non-meat native dishes.

Easter Monday, Señor de los Temblores. Ceremony worshipping the Lord of earthquakes, or Taitacha Temblores. An effigy is paraded around the city while citizens throw nucchu flowers at it. The ceremony is a conjunction of Andean Christian symbols.

Fiesta de las Cruces (May 5). Each community in Cusco and the neighboring areas decorates their crosses and carries them to the other communities. It is thought to show appreciation to the pre-Hispanic gods for an ample harvest.

★★**Qoyllur Rit'i Pilgrimage** (late May or early June), the Snow Star festival. The largest native festival in all of the Americas. Pilgrims climb to the snow-covered Mount Ausangate (6,362 m/20,867 feet) to find the

Qoyllur Rit'i Pilgrimage

snow star that will then be taken back to their villages on blocks of ice to irrigate their land. This is one of the most important manifestations in the Andean religion and is relevant to the indigenous cult of the area mountains and the spirits that live there: the Wamani. The four-hour pilgrimage goes to the Qoyllur Rit'i sanctuary on Sinakhara (4,600 m/

Qoyllur Rit'i Pilgrimage

15,088 feet). The spectacle is said to converge the energy of the divinities, of nature and of man.

★★**Inti Raymi** (June 24). Inca festival that pays tribute to the sun god. Held at the beginning of the winter solstice at Sacsayhuaman, where more than 500 participants re-enact the ritual. The Inca, or at least an actor playing the Inca, is carried in a throne from Koricancha and presides over the festivities until sunset. Tour companies in Cuzco can arrange for tickets to the event, which is the city's largest and most prominent.

Corpus Christi. The Incas once paraded the mummies of dead Inca rulers through the streets, but since Colonial times the ritual has been boringly changed. Sixty days after Easter Sunday 15 images of saints and virgins arrive from throughout Cuzco and greet the body of Christ, which is kept in a gold tabernacle that stands 1.2 m/ 3.9 feet tall.

Inti Raymi

Fiesta del Corpus Christi

Virgen del Carmen (July 15-16). This is the Festival of Mamacha Carmen, the patron saint of mestizos. The attendees of the event scare away any demons by singing (in Quechua) and the effigy is carried in procession. At the end of the procession a mock war is waged against the demons and the faithful emerge victorious.

Virgen de Rosarios (October 10). In Urcos, Combate, and Checaupe. Celebration in homage to the town's patron saint with bullfights, fairs,

Virgen del Carmen

and parades. This is a good place to try pachamancas, which are meals prepared over hot stones in holes in the ground.

Sale of Saints, Santuranticuy (December 24). One of Peru's largest handicraft festivals, held in Cuzco's Plaza de Armas. Painters and artisans create a wide range of Christmas figurines to go with Nativity scenes.

■ Urubamba & Yucay

Serene, beautiful Urubamba is still one of the lesser-known Sacred Valley cities, but that is very likely to change soon. Many young, hip professionals looking to escape the noise and traffic of places like Cuzco and Lima have flocked to the area and are investing in hotels, country lodges, spas, and restaurants that are attracting internationally trained chefs. There are few sites to make the stop worthwhile, if you are not staying here. If you have the money to spend on some of the many outdoor activities offered, need the relaxation of a country spa, or just need a break from the hustle and bustle of the rest of your travels then Urubamba is the place.

Getting Here & Around

Bus

All transportation to and from Urubamba goes to other Sacred Valley cities. There is a small bus terminal about half a mile from town on the main road. From there you can climb aboard a small moto-taxi to wherever it is you want to go. To most Sacred Valley destinations there are buses every 15-30 minutes.

Cuzco – Buses go through either Vía Pisac, which takes two hours or to Chincero, which should take just over an hour. The buses can be extremely crowded.

Ollantaytambo – 30 minutes.

There are also collectivo cars that leave from places up and down the carretera and go to Cuzco, Pisac, and Ollantaytambo.

Train

A vistadome train now departs Urubamba each day at 6:10 am and arrives at 8:20 am, stopping in Ollantaytambo as well. It leaves Aguas Caliente at 4:45 pm and arrives back in Urubamba at 7:15 pm. Price: $43 one-way/$71.50 round-trip. Contact Peru Rail in Cuzco for tickets.

Sights

There are few attractions other than the charm of the valley itself in Urubamba. The **Plaza de Armas** is quaint and quiet, but is scenic, flanked by a church and Colonial buildings filled with restaurants, Internet cafés, small shops, and pisonay trees. The central fountain features a giant ear of maize.

The one place I would recommend to visit above all others is the ★**Pablo Seminario Ceramic Studio** (Berriozabal 111, on the main road, ☎ 201-002, fax 201-177, www.ceramicaseminario. com). Pablo Seminario and Marilú Behar, a famed husband and wife team, are dedicated to sculpting red clay that is found in the valley. They use techniques and designs from Ancient Peruvian cultures and adapt them to their own interesting style. Everything from sculptures, murals, and decorative pottery to dinnerware is made, all of it unique and beautiful. There are

also galleries in Cuzco and the United States where you can purchase the goods. There is a small zoo on the premises with llamas, monkeys, and various birds. Open daily 8 am-7 pm.

The street of **Ramón Castilla** lacks the traditional character of the rest of the town, but this is where you will find banks, pharmacies, and most restaurants.

Yucay is more of an extension of Urubamba than its own town. It is just a few km away and home to several nice lodging options. The Colonial church of **Santiago Apostol** has several oil paintings and alters of interest. You can sometimes find monks selling dairy products, ham, and eggs from their nearby farm. All tourist facilities are found in Urubamba.

Where to Stay

★**Luna Rumi Lodge** – Ccoto-huincho (no #), ☎ 201-797, fax 201-235, www.lunarumi. com. This lodge is quite spectacular and well-run. The train to Machu Picchu will stop (with advance notice) right outside the lodge. Continental break-fast is included. TV room,

with stereo, and library, and big, cozy fireplace. Gorgeous gardens with dozens of varieties of orchids. Patio area. Rooms are sparkling new. They have private steaming hot-water baths with some of the best showerheads I have seen in my life. In the future an on-site spa is planned. Pickups and tours can be arranged. $$$

★**Sol y Luna Lodge** – ☎ 201-620, www.hotelsolyluna.com. Excellent first-class spa with a long list of treatments. The bungalows are just one km/.6 mile from town and are surrounded by extensive gardens that attract a variety of birds (more than 30 species have been sighted). The round rooms are rustic yet modern, emphasizing natural elements. Sauna, gym, yoga, tai chi, and massages. A variety of activities may take place at night, such as cooking demonstrations and pachamanca (a variety of meats and vegetables cooked underground). You can also ride Peruvian Paso horses, or arrange rafting, hiking, biking, or paragliding trips. There is a restaurant and pub on the grounds as well. $$$$

Libertador Tamba del Inka Urubamba – Av. Ferrocarril no #, ☎ 201-126, www.libertador.com. pe. The 76 rooms at this first-class hotel are all in bungalows, the suites having Jacuzzis and private gardens. Rooms are attractive, with plenty of woodwork, and the theme is Andean. All amenities are included, such as mini-fridges, cable TV, phones, and private hot-water baths. The hotel is like a small village confined to 17 acres of land beside the Vilcanota River and surrounded by lush flora and fauna typical of the region. There is a large swimming pool to make those sunny valley days float away in the breeze. $$$$

★**Casa Andina Private Collection Sacred Valley** – 5th Paradero Yanahuara, ☎ 976-5501, fax 445-4775, www.casa-andina.com. This new hotel in Casa Andina's private collection is one of the

finest it has built to date. The rooms and services are top-of-the-line. There are 85 well-equipped rooms in a country-modern style with views of the extensive gardens. The hotel has a gym, and can arrange horseback riding, rafting, trekking, or biking. A new spa is set to open any day now. The banquet room is capable of handling a large convention or business getaway with full folkloric shows and large traditional feasts. The restaurant here is excellent, serving a variety of Novo

Andina creations such as pork tenderloin with aguaymanto and rosemary sauce, trout tartare and quinoa tabbouleh, and elderberry cheesecake. $$$$

K'uychi Rumi – Km. 73.5 Carretera between Urubamba and Ollantaytambo, ☎ 201-169, www.urubamba.com. Think Tuscany. Think villas in the country. Here you can rent two-bedroom fully equipped houses with hot water, kitchen, dining room, and a lounge with a fireplace. There are a total of six houses. They can arrange activities like trekking, tai chi, meditation, rafting, and horseback riding. For activities with other guests, you can head to the feng shui-designed communal house. The name means "rainbow stone" in Quechua, which helps deliver the new age theme. Prices are surprisingly cheap. $$$

Hotel San Antonio Monasterio de la Recoleta – Recoleta (no #), ☎ 201-004, fax 201 666, www.hotelessanagustin.com.pe. Set in what was once a Catholic monastery that was built in the 15th century, this country inn is  one of the best properties this hotel chain has to offer. Rooms surround a central courtyard and are clean and modern, with wood floors and some exposed stone walls. Restaurant, coffee shop, bar, plus 24-hour room service. Suites are not much more expensive. $$$$

San Agustín Urubamba – Ferrocarril (no #), ☎ 201-443, fax 201 025, www.hotelessanagustin.com.pe. This hotel has much of the same charm as the chain's other Urubamba property above, although it is less historic. The 39 rooms are more modern than the other property, but still retain a country Colonial character. On the grounds there is also a spa, pool, Jacuzzi, and sauna. $$$$

Hotel Quinta Patawasi – Pisonayniyoc 220, ☎ 201-386, www.quintapatawasi.com. The brainchild of an old trucker from Oakland and a teacher from Arequipa, this B&B offers personalized attention, including airport pickups, and roundtable dinners. Rooms are basic country style. Multi-day tours of the valley are offered as well. $$$

Willka T'ika Guesthouse – Castilla Postal 70, ☎ 201-508, www.willkatika.com. This is a New Age retreat popular for yoga classes and shamanism rituals. The owner is Carol Cumes, the author of the book *Journey to Machu Picchu: Spiritual Wisdom of the Andes* (Llewellyn, 1998). Employees are local residents. There is a large organic garden with Andean medicinal plants. Rooms face the garden and combine New Age style with country chic. From fire ceremonies, meditation, tai chi, massages, bird and plant life, photography, to archeology, this peaceful hotel can meet your needs. All meals served are vegetarian. $$

Señor de Torrechero – Castilla 114, ☎ 20-1033. Very basic accommodations on one of Urubamba's main streets. Rooms are plain but have bathrooms (cold water).

In Yucay

★**Sonesta Posada del Inca** – Plaza Manco II, Yucay 123, ☎ 201-107, fax 201-345, www.willkatika.com. The deep red and gold hues and Colonial architecture blend in perfectly with the rest of Yucay and the valley. The 84 rooms are rustic, but with all modern amenities, such as TVs and heating. The hotel has an abundance of features – a first-class spa, yoga sessions, a small museum, wedding chapel, and business center. There are extensive grounds and gardens with many places to sit and take in the beauty of the valley. Excellent lunch buffet featuring Novo Andina and International cuisine. Recommended. $$$

La Casona de Yucay Hotel – Plaza Manco II, Yucay 104, ☎ 201-116, fax 201-469, www.lacasona-deyucay.com. Set in a hacienda that dates back two centuries, the hotel is where Simón Bolivar stayed in 1825. La Casona is bright and clean, much of it restored. Stone archways, the fireplace in the lounge, and the large gardens are among the extra touches. It isn't nearly as nice as the Sonesta next door, but it does immerse you in the tranquility that is Yucay. $$$

Where to Eat

★★**El Huacatay** – Arica 620, ☎ 201-790, elhuacatay@yahoo.es. Internationally trained chef Pio opened this restaurant in early 2006 and it has become one of the landmark restaurants in all of the Sacred Valley. It's far more sophisticated than other Urubamba restaurants, which focus mostly on Andean food and pachamanca. The food here is Novo Andino (New Andean) with influences from around the world.

Try the lucuma raviolis or beef filet in a sauce of aguaymanto (an Andean fruit) and quinotto (risotto made with quinua, an Andean grain). There is a contemporary inside dining room and a leafy outdoor patio. Contact the chef if interested in cooking classes.

The Muse Too – Plaza de Armas. The sister location of the San Blas hangout. It is actually bigger then the original with two floors and has a more dominating presence in Urubamba. Still the same great food, drinks, and comfortable couches. Sometimes has live music and trivia games. $$$

Café Cusco – New second-level restaurant and bar that overlooks the Plaza. Attractive minimalist décor and good music. The food is quite good, featuring carpaccio de alpaca, brochettes, anticuchos, sandwiches, and soups. There is an excellent happy hour, with three cocktails for 10 soles. $$$

Alhambra Hacienda Restaurant – On the Carretera, ☎ 201-200, fax 201-100, www.alhambrarestaurant.com. This large hacienda-style restaurant is well equipped to create huge Andean feasts and shows. The food ranges from international and Novo Andina to more traditional regional recipes and cooking techniques such as pachamanca (meats and vegetables cooked under the ground). The kitchen equipment is some of the most modern and sophisticated in the valley. Call or e-mail reservas@alhambrarestaurant.com for reservations. $$$$

La Esquina – On the Plaza, ☎ 201-554. This small restaurant with just a few tables is a good, clean place for snacks, pizza, or a cup of tea. There is also Internet access. $$

Pizzonay – Castilla block 2. Basic Italian comfort menu of pastas, pizzas, soups, and appetizers. Photos of celebrities adorn the walls. $$

Bars

Connection – Castilla 203. Very stylish Internet café, bar, restaurant, with exhibitions by local artists. Good place to catch up with the crowd before they move to Tequila's down the street.

Tequila Club – Castilla 355. Draws a crowd of locals who work in tourism, international volunteers, and tourists. Drinks are cheap and the dance floor isn't overly crowded. It's really the only place in town for a late-night party.

Tour Agencies

Perol Chico – On the highway between Urubamba and Ollantaytambo, Km 77, ☎ 201-694, www.perolchico.com. One of the best horseback riding agencies in the country, Perol Chico has a variety of tours and rides on Peruvian Paso horses, including multi-day trips.

Eco Montana – ☎ 223-216, www.angelfire.com/pe/ecomontana. Run by Omar Zarzar, one of Peru's mountain biking pioneers. Among the best mountain biking tour operators in Peru. The company offers more than 30 tours in Peru, Bolivia, and Chile.

Adventures

On Horseback

Perol Chico (see above) has an Ollanta ride that is one of the most complete horseback tours of the major Sacred Valley sites, although they do offer 12-day rides as well. You take your velvet-gaited Peruvian Paso horse to the fortress at Ollantaytambo, the agricultural terraces of Moray and the saltpans of Salinas. The ride includes three full riding days, with three nights lodging in the Hotel Casa Andina Private Collection in Yanahuara. All meals and soft drinks, round-trip transportation between Cuzco and the riding stable are included in the price of $1,080 per person (two-person minimum). An optional extension to visit Machu Picchu is available.

 The unique walk of the **Peruvian Paso horse** has made it one of the most celebrated horses in the world. The graceful feet almost dance across the earth. The horses are derived from the Spanish breed that was cross-bred with Arabian horses in the coastal deserts of Peru nearly 300 years ago.

On Wheels
Cycling

 This seven-day trip to Huallahualla, Puerto Maldonado, and Lago Sandoval is for moderately experienced cyclists. You first go by bus to Ausangate and Huallahualla. From there the journey begins in the high mountains (4,900 m/11,662 feet) to the low jungle around Puerto Maldonado (300 m/984 feet). In-between you either camp or stay in hostels. The last night you stay at Wasai Lodge in Lago Sandoval, before flying back to

Cuzco. The total length of the trip is 140 km by bike, and 240 km by bus. You need a minimum of five people for this tour to be operable. Offered April to October. Contact **Eco Montana** (see above) for more information.

> 🐛 **Did you know?** The name Quechua is the language that the Incas spoke, but at one time it meant the population as well. The name Inca referred solely to the nobility.

■ Pisac

Mountains above Pisac

Pisac is a small, quiet hamlet in a peaceful valley setting, surrounded by tall mountains and next to a sparkling river. Imposing Incan ruins and stone terraces stand guard on the mountainside behind, overlooking the city. But until recent years it has seen little action. Thanks to increased tourism to Peru, Pisac has become a bustling town on market days where tourists come by the thousands to shop. Hundreds of natives dressed in traditional attire sell and barter their colorful textiles, pottery, and thousands of other items.

Getting Here & Away

Local buses run frequently to Urubamba and Cuzco. Just go to the bridge and wait for one to come. A taxi there will run you about $10.

Sights

★★★ The Pisac Market

Perhaps the most visited market in all of Peru. Traditionally it has been a Sunday event, but tour companies began bringing busloads of tourists on

Tuesdays and Thursdays so there are slightly smaller markets then. But any day of the week there are quite a few vendors set up on the main square.

Pisac Market

The Sunday market begins to get crowded after the 11 am mass (in Quechua) is let out, with a procession led by the town's mayor. The Plaza and its tall pisonay tree is the center of the action, but stalls are set up throughout the Colonial center, crowding every street. The natives come from miles away, from remote mountain villages in their traditional dress, selling alpaca textiles, jewelry, leather, antiques, rugs, ceramics and much more. Bargaining is a must. Prices tend to equal those in Cuzco, but in my opinion the quality is much better. The markets usually wind down by the afternoon.

★ Pisac Ruins

Pisac center

Standing high on a breath-shortening hill above the Colonial town, you will find the other half of Pisac. This are one of the largest ruins in the valley, the terraces rivaling those of Ollantaytambo or Machu Picchu. It is thought that they once were a city, combined with a fort, a ceremonial center, and an agricultural complex.

Pisac Citadel

Much of the ruins consist of stone terracing that is most visible from the valley floor. The terraces on the far side are the most spectacular and lined in a semi-circular pattern.

The **Intihuatana** section is the largest part and the ceremonial center. It holds the **Reloj Solar**, or the hitching post of the sun, which helped the Incas determine the growing season. You can also find the remnants of the palaces of the moon and stars, as well as water channels that led to a ritual bathing site. The views of the valley and mountains from here are quite picturesque, including those of the layout of Colonial Pisac and the mélange of farms.

The **Q'allaqasa**, or military section, is connected to the previous part through a claustrophobic stone tunnel. If you look across the gorge from this site, on the opposing cliffs, you will see hundreds of hollowed-out holes. These were Inca tombs that were raided by huaqeros, or grave robbers. The Q'allaqsa connects by way of a short path to **Kanchiracay**, the agricultural area, where buses and taxis back to Pisac await.

There are two ways of getting to the ruins. One is by taxi or bus, going the back way around the

Pisac ruins (N. Gill)

mountain for roughly 10 km/six miles. This will take you right to one of the main structures. There will still be some walking to do. The other way is by walking from behind the market. You must pass the control booth and show your Boleto Turístico. From there you head up, the way most locals do. You follow the stone stairs and path until you come to what seem to be endless rows of agricultural terraces. You must climb up each of these (look for the small stone stairs that jut out from the walls). To the right a path will form eventually that snakes up the mountain. Much of it goes straight up over stone stairs. The five km/three miles aren't easy and bringing a bottle of water is a must. The climb up should take about an hour and a half. Although the altitude is less than Cuzco, you still need to take it slow and be in relatively good shape.

The ruins are open daily from 7 am-5:30 pm.

Where to Stay & Eat

Hotel Royal Inka Pisac – On the highway to the ruins at Km 1.5, ☎ 203-064, fax 222-284, www.royalinkahotel.com/hpisac.html. This hotel is on the other side of the ruins from the city, but a good location if you are there to get away. Rooms have views of the spectacular ruins and terracing. They are basic

country-style rooms with cable TV, tile floors, heating, private hot-water baths, wooden furniture, and lots of light. There is an indoor swimming pool with panoramic views, Jacuzzi, sauna, beauty and massage salon, and tennis and basketball courts. They also have bicycles to rent if you want to go into town. $$$

Hostal Pisaq – Plaza Constitución, ☎ 20-3062, hotelpisaq@terra.com.pe. The Plaza location makes this ideal if you are just there to shop and need a home base. It is the most attractive of the Plaza hotels, of which there are several. Only some rooms have baths. There is an underground sauna ($10 per group) and a small patio café. $$

Hostal Pisaq

Paz y Luz – www.maxart.com/window/gateway.html. Owned by American tour operator, Dianne Dunn, this bed and breakfast is in a serene setting beside the river. She is trained in Andean energy healing and other spiritual practices. The building is lodge-style with a central fireplace and lots of woodwork. $$

Beho Hospedaje – This medium-sized, quiet guesthouse is just steps from the entrance to the ruins. Rooms are basic, but clean and cozy and surround a pleasant garden. Some rooms have private baths. $

Ulrike's Café – This Plaza restaurant has patio seating and a lively menu that includes cheesecakes and soups. Quite a few vegetarian dishes are offered. Also has a book exchange. $$

Allpa Manka – This second-level restaurant on the corner of the Plaza serves a variety of Andean and Novo Andina dishes. $$$

Horno Colonial – Castilla 572. Local dishes such as trout, chicken, and empañadas. $

There are many Indians selling local foods on the Plaza, particular during market days. Look for the ceviche cart, which has excellent trout ceviche for just a few soles.

Mullo – www.mullu.com.pe. This Plaza art gallery (contemporary designs including jewelry) has a small café with smoothies, coffee, and tea. $$

■ Ollantaytambo

Ollantaytambo, nicknamed Ollanta by locals, has the look and feel of a town that only Disney could have dreamed up, but it is real. Cobblestone streets, plenty of trees, long-forgotten ancient sites, charming boutique hotels and stylish little cafés and restaurants. Pachacútec built the fortress and much of the city, originally called Llacta, in the 15th century. The site of a major train stop, it is has become one of the leading tourist bases in the Sacred Valley, along with Pisac and Urubamba.

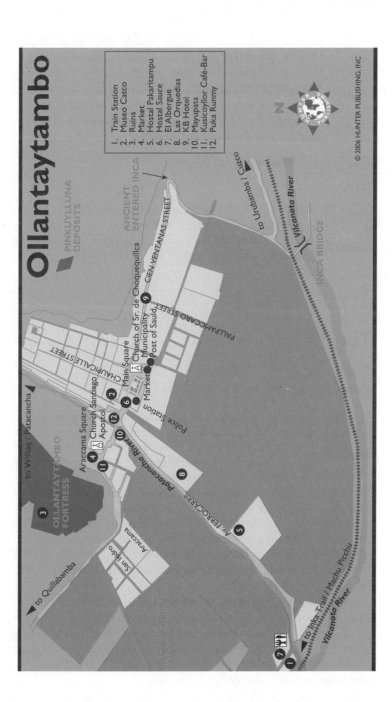

Ollantaytambo

PINKUYLLUNA
DEPOSITS

1. Train Station
2. Museo Catco
3. Ruins
4. Market
5. Hostal Pakaritampu
6. Hostal Sauce
7. El Albergue
8. Las Orquedias
9. KB Hotel
10. Mayupata
11. Kusicoyllor Café-Bar
12. Puka Runmy

ANCIENT
ENTERED INCA

CIEN-VENTANAS STREET

Church of Sr. de Choquequillca
Municipality
Post of Sauld,

PALLPAMCCARO STREET

Main Square
Market

Church Santiago
Apostol

CHAUPIGALLE STREET

Police Station

Aracama Square

OLLANTAYTAMBO
FORTRESS

Patacancha River

AV. FERROCARRIL

Aracama

San Isidro

to Williog / Patacancha

to Quillabamba

to Inka Trail / Machu Picchu

Vilcanota River

to Urubamba / Cuzco

Vilcanota River

INCA BRIDGE

N

© 2006 HUNTER PUBLISHING, INC

If entering Ollantaytambo from Pisac, notice the inclination of the wall on the stone road just before the town. It was an Incan practice to build walls leaning toward the interior of buildings, but this one leans toward the road. Researchers have determined that the road must have been built inside a succession of buildings.

Getting Here & Away

Bus

 Local buses can be found in town near the Plaza. They go to Urubamba, where you can transfer to Cuzco. Colectivo cars will go directly to Cuzco for just a few soles more and are at the Plaza or outside the train station.

Train

See Cuzco.

Tourist Information

www.ollantaytambo.org.

Sights

 The **Plaza Mayor** is small and not nearly as pleasant as most other Andean plazas. It sees quite a bit of tourist traffic, both pedestrians and vehicles, and is not completely enclosed. The few cobblestone streets to the north of the Plaza are much more interesting. Most of the narrow streets are decorated with fine adobe brick and stone walls on both sides. Many were part of canchas – completely walled city blocks (except for one entrance). The canchas in Ollanta are a great example of Incan town planning. The stone city blocks are still intact. Perhaps that is why the pueblo is the only continuously inhabited Inca village.

There is a small **produce market** typical of Andean villages that sits one one side of the main square. It will give you a good idea of the crops grown in the region. You can also buy local dishes here such as anticuchos or corn on the cob. Just make sure everything is cooked. It is generally OK as long as you have a strong stomach.

Below the entrance to the ruins is a **craft market** that sells a variety of goods. I've noticed that there tends to be a greater variety in stone carvings and jewelry here, if that is what you are looking for. They also sell carved and decorated walking sticks, which aren't a bad idea if you are climbing the ruins here and later heading on to Machu Picchu. On Sundays it is a bit livelier, and locals in traditional dress come from miles around. But this is still far smaller than then Pisac market.

The **Museo Catco** (Patacalle, no #, ☎ 204-024), right in the center of town, is worth a quick look if Ollantaytambo has you bored stiff. This small museum has displays of textiles and findings from local ruins, as well

Ollantaytambo fortress

as a variety of tourist and archeological information. Open Tues-Sun 10 am-1 pm and 3-6 pm. Admission 5 soles.

The multi-tiered terraces that line the mountain at the northwest end of town fill almost every view of Ollanta. It is perhaps the most impressive of all the Incan constructions for its size, although not as picturesque as, say, Machu Picchu.

Ollantaytambo ruins

A climb up 200 steps brings you to the top of the **fortress**, but it goes by quickly and is not nearly as difficult as you would think. The fortress was actually only part-fortress. Half was a temple and of equal importance to the Incas. The **temple** area is on top of the terracing and was only half-finished at the time of the Conquest. It was intended to be an astronomical observatory or ceremonial center. The temple construction was started by Pachacutiec using Colla Indians from Lake Titicaca, which explains the similarities of some of the monoliths. It is believed the Colla deserted the work and left many of the stones untouched. Considering that they had to be carried from more than six km/3.6 miles away, who could blame them?

The archaeological complex was once the site of one of the few Spanish defeats in 1536, just after they followed the retreating Manco Inca, who had just lost the battle at Sacsayhuaman. Hernando Pizarro and his force of 70 cavalrymen attempted to climb the terraces and capture the Inca. but arrows, spears, and boulders rained down upon them and the plain below was flooded. The Spanish retreated, but soon returned with a bigger force and Manco Inca had no choice but to flee to Vilcabamba.

In the area between the town and the fortress near the Patacancha River, you will encounter the so-called **Baño de la Ñusta**, or Bath of the Princess. The gray granite waterway and pool were used for ceremonial bathing.

Recently, researchers discovered what appears to be a pyramid, west of the fortress. Some believe it is the real Pacaritambo, the site where four Incan brothers sprung from the earth to start the empire. This is an alternative Incan creation myth.

The site has a 750-m/2,460-foot wall

Baño de la Ñusta

that aligns with the rays of the sun during the winter solstice on June 21. It can best be seen from the opposite side of the river, a one-hour walk west from the Incan bridge. The ruins are open from 7 am to 5:30 pm. You must have a Boleto Turístico to enter.

Where to Stay

Hotel Pakaritampu – Av. Ferrocarril (no #), ☎ 204-020, fax 204-105, www.pakaritampu.com. The best lodging option in Ollantaytambo. The Quechua translation is "house of dawn." It is just a

Hotel Pakaritampu

few years old, but is quickly gaining popularity due to the fireplaces, modern rooms, and their own orchard that supplies fruit. Also home to perhaps the best restaurant in town, which serves a variety of good Peruvian dishes. $$$$

Hostal Sauce – Calle Ventiderio 248, ☎ 204-044, fax 204-048, www.hostalsauce.com.pe.There are just eight rooms here with clean, cozy beds, a rustic décor, and private hot-water baths. There is a lounge area with a wood-burning fireplace, bar, and restaurant and room service. The location just off the Plaza can't be beat. $$$

El Albergue – ☎ 204-014, www.rumbosperu.com/elalbergue. Run by an American woman, this quaint bed and breakfast is right on the railroad tracks. If you miss your train while staying here, you shouldn't be traveling anywhere. The rustic, eclectic house has lots of activity going on. It sits amidst gardens and rivers, and has good views to the mountains and ruins above. Each of the six rooms is a little bit different, but generally all are appealing. Bathrooms are shared. $$

Las Orquedias – Right on the road between the train station and town. ☎ 204-032. Rooms are large but unattractive, with concrete floors, uncomfortable beds, and dingy bathrooms, but if you get stuck here, there may not be many options. $$

KB Hotel – ☎ 204-091, www.kbperu.com. Owned and operated by the KB tour agency (see below), this is one of the better budget choices in town. Rooms vary in size, price, and quality. $

Where to Eat

Mayupata – ☎ 204-009. A favorite spot for tour groups. The menu isn't too big, put the quality of the trout dishes, pastas, burgers, and pizzas is unmatched here. The pleasant river view may put you to sleep after a day of sightseeing. $$

Kusicoyllor Café-Bar – Plaza Arracama (no #), ☎ 204-114. International and Peruvian food, as well as Novo Andina dishes. It has the best wine list and Ollanta and is recommended for a quiet drink or two at night. There are also homemade croissants and ice cream. $$

Puka Rumy – Av. Benitario (no #). A small place with one main dining area and a few outdoor tables. The menu is long, with an array of Peruvian dishes and gringo comfort foods. It is good for appetizers and a drink at night. Friendly atmosphere. $$

Tourist Agencies

KB Tours – ☎ 204-091, www.kbperu.com. Arranges rafting, biking, trekking, and 4x4 excursions from Ollantaytambo.

Adventures

On Foot or Horseback

The area around Ollantaytambo is surrounded by stunning mountain scenery and thick forest, making numerous hikes possible within a short distance from the city. Many can be done on horseback or on foot. Contact any agency in town or the Catco Museum (Patacalle, no #, ☎ 204-024) for more details and pricing.

Pinkuylluna – This two-hour round-trip hike takes you to the little-known ruins at Pinkuylluna. They are thought to be Qollqas, or Incan storehouses.

Pumamarca – One of the most popular options, this four- to six-hour round-trip hike passes through Inca ruins, and the Polylepis forest at Choquechaka.

Ancasqocha – This beautiful mountain lake can be reached on an overnight trip on foot or by horseback.

Yanaqocha – This is a difficult overnight hike. Camping at the mountain lake is expected.

On Water
Rafting

Ollantaytambo is a great spot for accessing some of the best rivers in the Sacred Valley for rafting. The **Chuquicawana** section is one of the most beautiful. The **Urubamba**, south of Cuzco, has river runs

Apurimac Canyon

Class 3 and 4 from May-October, and Class 4 and 5 rapids from December to April. Some rafting or kayaking experience is necessary. Prices start at around $40 per person.

For a trip that is a bit more daring, a trip down **Apurimac Canyon** is a must. It is one of the most profound rafting experiences on the planet, with rapids of Class 3, 4, and 5 plus incredible scenery and sights. The trip lasts three or four nights and experience is necessary for this one. There is a minimum of three people, which you will likely have to gather on your own, as the trip is done only occasionally. Prices start at about $200 per person. Check with KB tours (see above) for more information on either trip.

Birdwatching

The **Q'euna Qocha Polylepis** forest near Ollantaytambo is home to 57 endangered species of birds, including the royal cinclodes, ash-breasted tit-tyrant, and the white-browed tit-spinetail. It can be visited in one day, usually on a tour to Willoq and Patakancha. Contact the Catco Museum (Patacalle, no #, ☎ 204-024) for more information.

■ Moray & Maras

No one is exactly sure what was going on at **Moray** during Inca times. The three agricultural coliseums have irrigation canals and several terraces that served for agro-experimentation. Each level is thought to have a different microclimate and may have been used for the acclimatization and domestication of different crops.

Maras is a striking salt extraction complex. You can access it is via a bridle path. The locals still remove salt from the pans in much the same way as they have for thousands of years. Families pass the pans down from generation

Moray terraces

to generation as they continue this labor-intensive operation. You will likely pass through here on the way to Moray.

Getting to each location is a bit difficult. The easiest way is by taxi or public transport from Chincero to the village of Maras. From there you can walk the nine km/5.4 miles to Moray. You can also hike to Maras from Urubamba, which takes several hours. Ask locals for the best route. And yet another way is via horseback or mountain bike from either Cuzco or Urubamba. Check with just about any tourist agency for more information.

■ ★ Chinchero

There is a calm air that surrounds Chinchero. The small market area, church, and grassy plain that make up much of the town lie amidst a circle of tall mountains, including the snowy peak of Salkantay. It feels secure and a bit mystical. There are no large hotels or fancy restaurants. It has retained its simple Andean character better than other towns on the tourist circuit and is my favorite of the small valley ruins for that reason. At 3,762/12,500 feet, it sits a bit higher than the rest of the valley, so it would be a good idea to acclimate yourself before coming here.

Getting Here

Most buses between Urubamba and Cuzco will stop here, as do most buses on tours of the valley.

Sights

From the parking lot you walk up the hundreds of stone steps until they become too jumbled to climb. At that point, make a left down another stone path, passing a few shops and homes, then walk through the

Chinchero

stone archway. There you will find the main square. The square has several terraces, most of which display Incan masonry skills. One particular wall has 10 trapezoidal niches. If you continue walking to the edge of the plain, there are several hiking trails that branch off in different directions.

Chinchero residents

To the right is the small but attractive 17th-century Colonial adobe church that was constructed on top of an Incan palace of Tupac Yupanqui. It was recently restored and, if you are quiet, you can walk inside. There are a few frescoes worth checking out that adorn the walls and ceiling. The church is open during the same hours as the site. There is a small archeology museum opposite the church that holds some basic Inca relics.

The view here is breathtaking. The Incas considered Chinchero the birthplace of the rainbow. If you are lucky enough, you might just find that pot o' gold.

The site is open 9 am-5 pm. You must show your Boleto Turístico to enter the center.

The **Sunday Market** begins at around 8 am on the main square. It is much less flashy and more traditional than, say, the Pisac market. The selection is much smaller, but prices are better. Here, the villagers and vendors seem to dress in their traditional clothes because that is what they wear. It doesn't feel as if they are doing so to sell you something or to get their picture taken. On any day of the week, there are a handful Indians laying out a blanket full of woven items such

Chinchero fair

as hats, gloves, scarves, and ponchos.

■ Aguas Caliente

Machu Picchu's nearby town, Aguas Caliente (Hot Water) has come a long way. It is slowly taking on the tourist feel of Cuzco, with innumerable hotels, restaurants, and craft shops. It can only be reached by rail. Therefore, much of the town revolves around the rail line, which runs right through the center of it. Many will come just for the day, and the rest come for one night before returning to Cuzco the next morning or afternoon. Prices tend to be higher here than elsewhere and there is little to do other than enjoy the many tourist restaurants and shops. The heat and humidity are a bit more intense here than in Cuzco or elsewhere, as the town and ruins sit in an upper Amazon cloud forest. Many return to Machu Picchu sunburned, so be sure to carry sunscreen.

Most tourist amenities are available, such as Internet cafés, a small medical center and a police station, all within a few minutes of each other. There are no ATMs at this time, but most places accept credit cards and traveler's checks and money can be exchanged at hotels and tour offices.

Getting Here & Around

To get to Machu Picchu from Aguas Caliente you have two options: taking a bus or walking the steep 8-km/4.8-mile road to the top of the ancient citadel.

Buses run from town to the entrance of Machu Picchu every few minutes from 6 am until the evening and

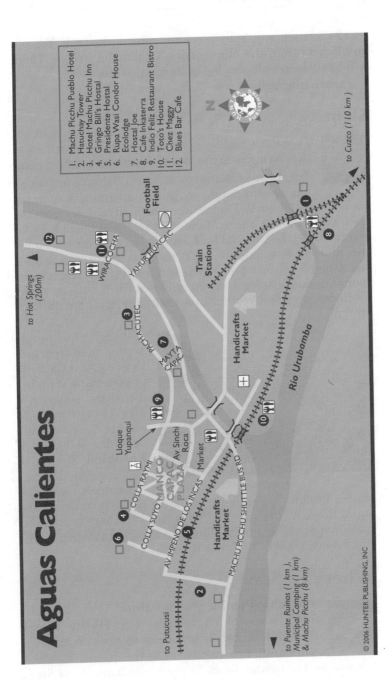

Aguas Calientes

Map Legend:
1. Machu Picchu Pueblo Hotel
2. Hatuchay Tower
3. Hotel Machu Picchu Inn
4. Gringo Bill's Hostal
5. Presidente Hostal
6. Rupa Wasi Condor House
7. Ecolodge
8. Hostal Joe
9. Cafe Inkaterra
10. Indio Feliz Restaurant Bistro
11. Toto's House
12. Chez Maggy
13. Blues Bar Cafe

N

to Hot Springs
(200m)

to Putucusi

to Puente Ruinas (1 km),
Municipal Camping (1 km)
& Machu Picchu (8 km)

to Cuzco (110 km)

Lloque Yupanqui

COLLA RAYMI
COLLA SUYO
AV IMPENO DE LOS INCAS
MANCO CAPAC PLAZA
Av Sinchi Roca
PACHACUTEC
MAYTA CAPAC
WIRACOCHA
YAHUAR HUACAC

Market
Handicrafts Market
Football Field
Train Station
Rio Urubamba
MACHU PICCHU SHUTTLE BUS RD

© 2006 HUNTER PUBLISHING, INC.

cost $4.50 each way. They leave and return when full. You can buy tickets from the office at Río Urubamba Bridge. There will likely be people and buses lined up at the spot.

For **train** information, see Cuzco, page 300.

Sights

 There are really only two attractions worth mentioning in town: the thermal baths and a short hike.

The **Aguas Calientes** of Aguas Caliente are set up like a swimming pool. A hot, steaming swimming pool. The pool is on Av. Pachacútec, about 10 minutes from the town's small Plaza, Plaza Manco Cápac. If you hiked here for several days, the thermal bath will do wonders for your muscles, and will do wonders for that revolting smell coming off of you. Open 5 am-8:30 pm. Admission 5 soles. The streets surrounding and leading to the baths are filled with so many mediocre bars and restaurants that they are hard to keep straight.

Putukusi

Although most people are too tired from getting to Aguas Caliente to even think of hiking anywhere, some actually retain enough energy to climb the sacred mountain of **Putukusi**. The top of the mountain has unparalleled views of Machu Picchu. To get there, you must go to the railroad just out of town. At the sign that says Km 111, there is a trail of stone steps leading up the mountain for about two hours. The climb down is takes half that time.

Where to Stay

★**Machu Picchu Pueblo Hotel** – ☎ 1-800-442-5042, www.inkaterra.com. The Machu Picchu Pueblo Hotel has 85 luxurious rooms with all of the amenities, two restaurants, the Hiram Bingham bar, spa, and a massage room. The grounds comprise 14 acres, with five km/three miles of trails, flora, fauna, and bird-viewing spots. They have a long list of organized hikes and activities available that make the most of being in a cloud forest. Without comparison, the best hotel in Aguas Caliente. $$$$$

Machu Picchu Pueblo Hotel

Hatuchay Tower – Opposite the bus stop, ☎ 21-1200, mapi@ hatuchaytower.com.pe. Rooms here are a bit more modern than most in Aguas Caliente, but don't expect total luxury. Rooms have private hot-water baths and some have balconies overlooking the river. Cable TV and room service are among the amenities. $$$$

Hotel Machu Picchu Inn

Hotel Machu Picchu Inn – Av. Pacachutec, ☎ 21-1011, mapiinn@terra.com.pe. This new hotel right in town has 75 of the most modern rooms. It is one of the best mid-range options and is actually mid-range in value. Still, don't expect so many extras. It is fairly basic. Includes breakfast. $$$

Gringo Bill's Hostal – Raymi 104 (Plaza de Armas), ☎ 211-046, www.gringobills.com. On the main Plaza, 20 m/65 feet from the church. There are a total of 25 rooms, including suites. Each room has a private hot-water bath. Some have balconies. The hotel will accommodate your entire stay in Aguas Caliente from pick-ups, money exchange, arranging guides, lunch, and transportation to Machu Picchu, laundry service, storing your luggage, cooking your meals, planning activities, and more. Low-season prices drop about $10 per room. Recommended. $$$

Presidente Hostal – Los Incas (no #), ☎ 212-034. This charming hostal has 25 rooms right on the rail tracks. Considering the trains don't run at night, you will more likely be put to sleep by the rushing waters of the Río Urubamba, which it faces. Many rooms have great views. $$$

Rupa Wasi Ecolodge

Rupa Wasi Condor House Ecolodge – Huanacaure 110, ☎ 21-1101, rupawasi@hotmail.com. This lodge is just two blocks from the main square, but seems a world away. It is made entirely of cedar wood and has a pleasant garden with orchids and native flora and fauna. Rooms are cozy and country-style, many with panoramic views. There are just five rooms here, all of which have private hot-water baths. One of the most interesting budget options in town. $$

Hostal Joe – Mayta Cápac 103, ☎ 21-1190, trasoc@latinmail.com. If you are looking for cheap and convenient, Joe's is the place. Rooms are basic and worn, but some have private hot-water baths.

Where to Eat

Café Inkaterra – Next to the train station, ☎ 211-122, www.inkaterra.com. This lunch-only restaurant is the most chic and ecologically friendly in Aguas Caliente. It overlooks the Vilcanota River and uses Amazon-style palm thatching for its roof, blending in with the natural setting in a sophisticated way. The food features traditional Andean dishes in contemporary styles such as anticuchos de alapaca (spiced alpaca kebabs). It also serves organic coffee from Quillabamba. $$$

Indio Feliz Restaurant Bistro – ☎ 211-090. This is a French bistro that attracts a largely French clientele and other international travelers. Reservations are needed. French onion soup, chicken in ginger and trout are among the dishes served. Everything is quite good. It is one of the best food finds in town that isn't pizza. $$$

Toto's House – Los Incas, near the tracks, ☎ 21-1020. In a convenient location near the rail line and the river. Has open-air seating overlooking the river and mountains. It is a bit touristy at times, particularly during lunch buffets when live Andean music is performed. Other dishes like trout and pizza are decent. $$

Chez Maggy – Pachacútec 156, ☎ 211-006. This is a branch of the well-known Maggy's in Cuzco and elsewhere in Peru. It is one of the better options for a pizza in Aguas Caliente, and there are many, many pizzerias. They use a clay oven, which makes the dough nice and crisp. They deliver as well. $$

Blues Bar Café – Av. Pachacútec near the hot springs. Of all of the nightlife options here, this is the best. The soundtrack is mostly classic rock and pop hits, which keep the dance floor lively, even with tired trekkers.

Shopping

Aguas Caliente is flourishing in selling crafts, though prices tend to be a bit higher than Cuzco or elsewhere. but it is a town where you often have time to kill. There are vendors set up everywhere, the largest handicraft market is just before the entrance of the train station.

Massages

Call ☎ 974-5617 for massages. They will come to your hotel. $10-$20.

★★★Machu Picchu

I once heard someone who had been traveling around Peru for several months say that they weren't going to visit Machu Picchu. When I asked why, he said that it was too overrun with tourists and there just wasn't the air of mystery surrounding it like some of Peru's lesser-known ruins. Up to a point, he's right. Machu Picchu, particularly during the high season, is overcrowded and has been seen by a ton of people

Machu Picchu (N. Gill)

all over the world. Its image graces the covers of books and posters. but there is a reason why so many people visit the ancient citadel. It is simply stunning, breathtakingly gorgeous. The ancient city is so remote, so high up and surrounded by mountains that are as beautiful as it is. The wind, the sun, the rain, the clouds all seem to converge at this point that remained hidden for so long. It is a dream-like setting if there ever was one. If you are someone who can visit Egypt and not see the Pyramids or the Sphinx, maybe missing Machu Picchu won't be a big deal. Personally, I could not.

It is the one location synonymous with travel to Peru. The site is the most popular on the entire continent and the driving force in tourism to Peru. But it is getting overwhelmed with visitors now. Tourism here increases every year. During the high season, hotels, trains, and tours need to be booked earlier and earlier. From May to Sept, the site is very crowded, with thousands of people visiting it daily. By around noon, most are there at the same time. Restrictions are necessary if Machu Picchu wants to remain for years to come.

Landslides are frequent in the area, and many officials are worried that the site could be a part of one of them if the tourist flow isn't slowed down. UNESCO named the site to its list of endangered world heritage sites and argues that if it sees more than 200-500 visitors each day it will sustain serious damage. That is far below the current numbers. There were plans to run cable cars from Aguas Caliente to the ruins, though after the UNESCO ruling the government placed more stringent rules and the cars were disallowed. Limiting the number of tourists seems on the horizon, even though the powers that be in Lima don't seem to be considering it at this

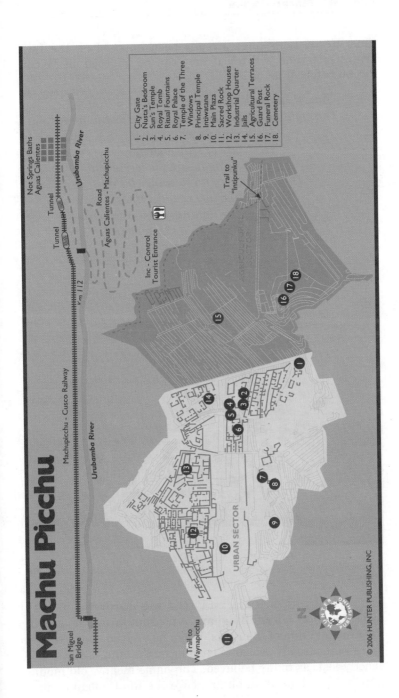

Machu Picchu

1. City Gate
2. Ñusta's Bedroom
3. Sun's Temple
4. Royal Tomb
5. Ritual Fountains
6. Royal Palace
7. Temple of the Three Windows
8. Principal Temple
9. Intiwatana
10. Main Plaza
11. Sacred Rock
12. Workshop Houses
13. Industrial Quarter
14. Jails
15. Agricultural Terraces
16. Guard Post
17. Funeral Rock
18. Cemetery

San Miguel Bridge

Not Springs Baths
Aguas Calientes

Urubamba River

Machupicchu – Cusco Railway

Tunnel

Tunnel

Tunnel

Road
Aguas Calientes – Machupicchu

Km 112

Inc – Control
Tourist Entrance

Trail to "Intipunku"

AGRICULTURAL SECTOR

Trail to Waynapicchu

URBAN SECTOR

N

© 2006 HUNTER PUBLISHING, INC

time. Restrictions have already been imposed on the Inca Trail. Only time will tell if they can be imposed on Machu Picchu before it is too late.

> *And then on the ladder of the earth I climbed*
> *Through the atrocious thicket of the lost jungles*
> *Up to you, Machu Picchu.*
> *High city of scaled stones,*
> *At last a dwelling where the terrestrial*
> *Did not hide in its sleeping clothes.*
> *In you, like two parallel lines,*
> *The cradle of the lightning-bolt and man*
> *Rocked together in a thorny wind.*
> Pablo Neruda

Overview of Machu Picchu (N. Gill)

History

The ancient citadel of Machu Picchu was discovered in 1911 by US explorer Hiram Bingham. A peasant farmer he met in the area told him of the ruins. When he arrived on the scene, there were already peasants farming on the land, so it was not exactly lost, as many believed. The name means "old mountain" in Quechua. It sits high above the Río Urubamba in a remote cloud forest – so well hidden that the Spanish never discovered it. It was a center of worship, an astronomical observatory, and the private country retreat of the Inca Pachacútec. Considering that the Incas kept no writ-

Llamas at Machu Picchu (Jorge Sarmiento)

ten history and the Spanish never found the site, there is not as much known about Machu Picchu as you might have imagined. Much of the information is clearly speculative.

When Bingham found the site, he was looking for and believed he had found the Incan stronghold of Vilcabamba. In 1964 that was determined to be the ruins of Espiritu Pampu, farther into the jungle. Bingham hoped it would lead him to the last of the Incan gold that the Spanish had never melted down. The site was overgrown at the time. Bingham returned again in 1912 and 1915 with a team of archeologists from Yale, clearing much of the vegetation and mapping the site. Later, in 1934, the Peruvian archaeologist Luis E. Valcarcel came and a Peruvian-American expedition visited in 1940-41.

Pachacútec, who initiated the most Incan building projects in the Cuzco area, likely started this one in the mid- to late 1400s. Much of the stonework eventually fell in ruins from the effects of time and nature.

Most believe it was not a significant city in the Incan empire, and many claim that it was likely abandoned even before the Spanish came. It was apparently created, occupied and abandoned in a short span of time, perhaps less than a century.

There were more than 50 burial sites discovered here, with more than 100 skeletons, many of which Bingham believed were female. Therefore, he concluded that Machu Picchu was a site for the Inca's chosen women, the Virgins of the Sun, and that belief held for decades. Later tests of the bones proved the remains to be equally divided between males and females.

The Ruins

The setting, 2,440 m/8,000-feet above sea level, overlooking the Urubamba Valley, shows how much the Incas appreciated the natural world. It is almost cradled by the tall peaks around it, but directly above there was a wide-open sky. With each sunrise there is magic here. The city is bathed in light, piece-by-piece, with the rays of the sun charging through the mist and clouds. Parts of different buildings are aligned to trace the June and December solstice.

The masonry of the stone blocks is extraordinary. Row upon row of terraces, likely used to grow corn and coca leaves, line the steep mountainsides. There are stone aqueducts, and canals, temples, and staircases of the finest masonry.

Generally speaking, the citadel is split into two areas: the agricultural zone, made up of terracing and food storehouses; and the urban zone, featuring the sacred sector, with temples, squares and royal tombs.

Temple of the Sun, Machu Picchu

After entering through the ticket booth, you will walk for about 100 m/328 feet, and most likely, although this may depend on your guide, you will climb a series of steep stairs that breaks off to the left. This will bring you eventually to the **Caretakers Hut**, a restored thatched-roof hut where you will see the classic photographic view of the ruins with the Huayna Picchu Mountain in the background. The earlier you get there the better, because the photos become more and more obscured as the day goes on and the ruins are filled with tourists. The Inca Trail culminates on the path just below the hut. If you follow it back, you will encounter **Intipunku**, or the Sun Gate.

If walking away from the hut, down into the ruins, you will soon come across the **Temple of the Sun** and the **Temple of the Condor**, depending on which combination of paths you take. The Temple of the Sun is the only round building in the complex and was likely the site of astronomical functions. The stonework here is perhaps the finest in the entire complex. The trapezoidal window, which looks out onto the site, has been nicknamed the **Serpent Window**. Nearby, there are a series of connected canals and aqueducts that still work after all of these years.

The Temple of the Condor is thought to be a giant carving of the Andean bird. You have to use your imagination a little bit, but the resemblance doesn't appear to be an accident. The angled rocks at the top are the wings and the smaller, lighter-toned one below is the head. You can crawl through the narrow space behind it and emerge on the other side.

The **Temple of the Three Windows** comes next. It borders one end of the Sacred Plaza. The trapezoidal windows, typical of Incan architecture, look out onto the Plaza below. The **House of the High Priest** is at another side of the Plaza. Connected to it is the more interesting **Sacristy**. The small room offers an intriguing look at the polygonal rocks used in creating the temple. Each of the two rocks at the entrance has 32 angles. The hollowed window-like features on one wall are usually filled with tourists yelling into them to hear an echo.

There will be a staircase behind the Sacristy that climbs to the **Intihua-tana**, or the hitching post of the sun. This is a sundial-like carved rock that served as an astronomical and agricultural calendar. The shape of the rock, when

The Intihuatana (Jordan Klein)

looked at from one angle, almost looks like a scale model of

Huayna Picchu, which sits in the exact same position far beyond.

Huayna Picchu, which means "Young Mountain" in Quechua, is the peak that looms over the ruins. It can be climbed via a steep stone-paved trail. The climb gives bragging rights to those who complete it. I personally climbed it on my first attempt in 23 minutes. The record is 17. My second attempt was much more leisurely and it took about 45 minutes. The average times range from about 45 minutes to an hour and a half. The view at the top is incredible and you can see the entire site, as well as excellent views of the mountains and valleys surrounding you. There are several buildings and terraces that are being restored. The path getting there is steep and at some points very narrow; passing someone coming down can be tricky. If you are afraid of heights this may not be your cup of tea, as there are many points along the walk that will probably send you whimpering. You must sign in at the hut at the beginning of the trail and sign out when you leave. The trail is open from 7am to 1 pm. The last return is at 4 pm.

The **Temple of the Moon** can be reached on the way up or down from Huayna Picchu, although few make the trip. There is a turn-off near the bottom of the mountain that descends lower into the trees before climbing back up again. There is some interesting stonework, consisting of a carved altar, throne, and other caverns and niches that have very little to do with lunar observation. The trip takes about an hour each way.

Admission

The ruins can be seen in a day, although many stick around for a second day to make sure they see every nook and cranny. The site is the most crowded between 10 am and 2 pm. Sundays are particularly full as tourists on a one-day tour that combines the Pisac market and other places in the valley visit Machu Picchu. The complex is open 6:30 am-5:30 pm. The entrance fee is $20; students and nationals pay $10. The Boleto Nocturno, most likely offered during a full moon, gets you into the ruins at night for an extra $10. Guides are available. They are best arranged in Cuzco or Aguas Caliente and run about $10 per person for a two-hour tour.

Where to Stay

★**Machu Picchu Sanctuary Lodge** – ☎ 211-039, fax 211-053, www.monasterio.orient-express.com/web/ocus/ocus_c3a_lodge.jsp. This is an Orient Express hotel, like the Hotel Monasterio in Cuzco.

It is the only hotel within walking distance of the ruins. There are two suites and 29 rooms, about half of which have mountain views. All of the amenities are there, but at this location, who would want to stay in the room? The garden is filled with orchids and hummingbirds. The lunch buffets are open to the public ($$$$$). There is also another restaurant exclusively for guests. $$$$$

WAYS TO SEE MACHU PICCHU

- One-day tour with a same-day return to Cuzco
- Walking the Inca Trail or an alternative trail
- Independently by train

■ ★★★The Inca Trail

The Inca Trail, or the Camino del Inca, was a path through the Andes that led to Machu Picchu. Ruins are lined up along the trail like a connect-the-dots puzzle. It is the highlight of the 127-square-mile national park, the **Machu Picchu Historical Sanctuary**. The zone is filled with great views of mountains, cloud forests, wildlife, and ruins. The park is home to the very rare Andean spectacled bear (which you are unlikely to see), more than 400 species of birds, and a plethora of orchids and other plants. The trail itself is 43 km/27 miles of almost continuous stone stairs.

More than 70,000 people each year take the trip, making it the most popular trail on the continent and one of the most popular in the world. This has led to a series of new regulations aimed at preserving the trail and improving the quality of the trek for everyone on it for years to come. The new regulations were established in 2002 to combat overuse of the trail that had been going on for too long. Since then, prices have gone up and availability has gone down. But many believe it had to be done.

The New Regulations

- An increased entrance fee from $50 to $60. Porters must pay $12 each. For the shorter trail the fee is just $25. Students and children also receive a discount.

- There are only 500 permits issued per day for the trail. This equals about 200 trekkers and 300 guides, porters, cooks, etc. Although this seems like a lot, during the high season they are sold out two or three months in advance. Permits are sold on a first-

The Inca Trail (Alejandro Balaguer)

come, first-served basis. During the rest of the year it is definitely a good idea to reserve a month or two ahead of time.

- A licensed guide must now accompany trekkers. The size of the group must be no more than 16 people and for groups with more than eight, there must be two guides.
- Pets and pack animals such as llamas and horses are not allowed on the trail.
- In 2002 a new law was introduced to set a minimum wage for all porters on the Inca Trail. This followed years of exploitation. The wage is mpw about US$10 per day, but many companies still try and pay less. That is why tipping

is absolutely necessary. The maximum weight that a porter can carry is now 55 lbs (44 lb load + 11 lbs of personal items), and this is checked at a weigh station prior to the start of the trail.

■ The Trail will be closed each February for conservation projects and to give the vegetation a chance to recover. It is also the wettest month of the year. Other treks remain open, however.

■ The UGM (Unidad de Gestion Machu Picchu) now requires companies that arrange treks to meet certain basic requirements, proving that they have professional guides and good camping equipment, radio communications and emergency first aid including oxygen. Licenses are renewed each year.

WEATHER ON THE INCA TRAIL											
	Jan	Feb	Mar	Apr	May	Jun	Jul	Aug	Sep	Oct	Nov	Dec
Max Temp °F	66	66	66	68	68	68	66	68	68	70	70	70
Min Temp °F	45	45	43	41	39	66	32	36	39	43	43	43
Rainy Days	18	13	11	8	3		2	2	7	8	12	16

Tipping

Considering that porters generally come from very poor areas, and make little on the trail for very hard work, a tip is important. The new regulations have set a minimum wage for porters, although many companies still get by paying less. With that said, the less you pay for the trek, the less the porters are going to be paid. If you pay around $250, I can almost assure you your porters are getting the short end of the walking stick. As for tipping, if each person on the trek gives a few dollars to each porter per day, which will amount to perhaps $25-$35 total, it will make a big difference in the lives of these individuals who are going days without seeing their families to carry most of your belongings and equipment. If you are concerned about the treatment of the porters and would like more information, contact the Inka Porter Project (or through the SAE clubhouse in Cuzco).

What to Bring

- Backpack
- Bug Spray
- Flashlight
- Hiking shoes
- Tent (most likely included)
- Canteen (plastic water bottles are not allowed)
- Sunscreen
- Sleeping bag
- Plenty of layers of clothes
- Hat, gloves
- Water purification tablets or drops
- Basic first aid
- High-energy snacks such as candy bars or power bars
- A little cash for things that can be bought on the trail such as snacks, drinks, and for tips

A FEW TIPS WHEN SIGNING UP FOR A TOUR

- Always get in writing what your tour includes such as equipment and even the type of food that will be served.
- Check with several agencies to get an idea of prices, and value. Some may vary greatly and agencies sometimes pool their clients together, even if they have paid different amounts.
- See what the company does to help preserve the trail and what precautions they may take.

The Trail

- **Day 1:** The Inca Trail begins at the town of Qorihuayrachina or, as it's more commonly known, Km 88 of the Ollantaytambo-Aguas Caliente railroad. Prior to that, you will have been picked up at your hotel by bus and

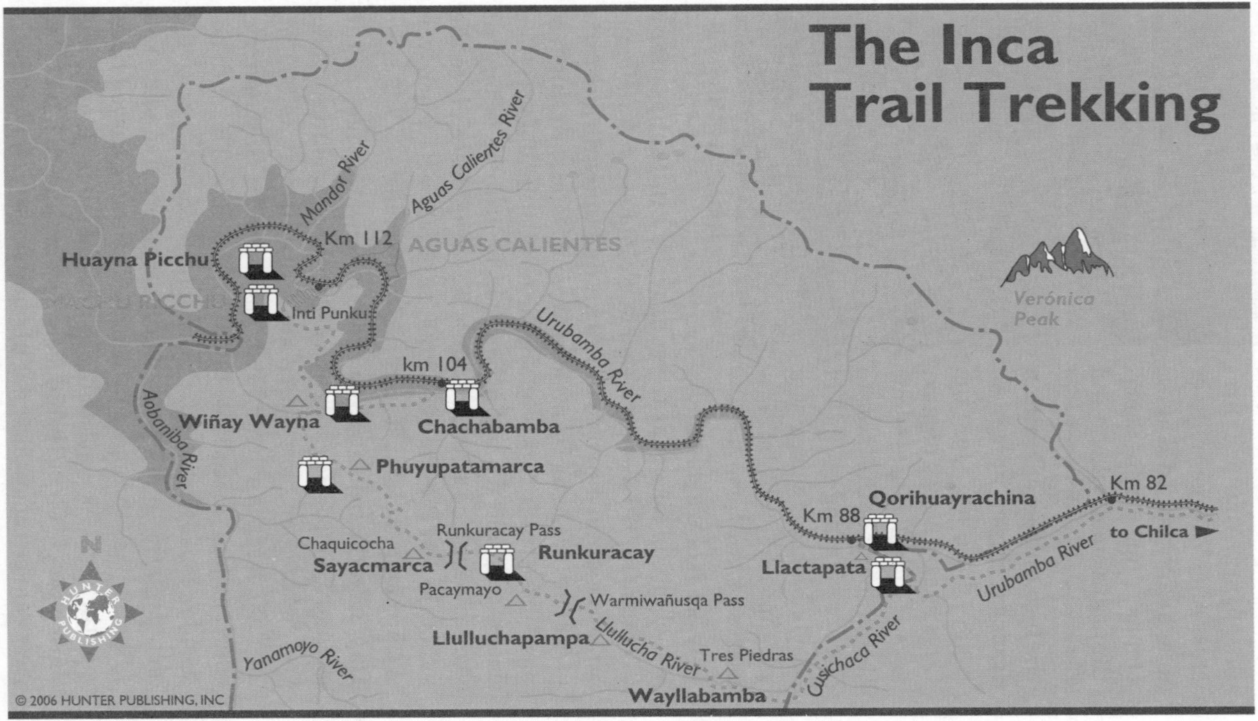

The Inca Trail Trekking

Verónica Peak

Urubamba River

Aguas Calientes River

AGUAS CALIENTES

Urubamba River

Mandor River

Km 112

Huayna Picchu

Inti Punku

Wiñay Wayna

km 104

Chachabamba

Phuyupatamarca

Chaquicocha

Sayacmarca

Pacaymayo

Runkuracay Pass

Runkuracay

Warmiwañusqa Pass

Llulluchapampa

Llullucha River

Tres Piedras

Wayllabamba

Yanamayo River

Aobamba River

Km 88

Qorihuayrachina

Llactapata

Cusichaca River

Km 82

to Chilca

Urubamba River

N

© 2006 HUNTER PUBLISHING, INC

traveled for 3½ hours to this point. You will first cross the Vilcanota River and follow the trail as it climbs up. You pass through a small village and then come to the ruins of the Inca hill fort of **Huillca Raccay**. From here, you walk downhill to the Cusichaca River. The next seven km/4.2 miles follow the left bank of the river to the village of Wayllabamba, where you set up camp. Total distance: 12 km/7.2 miles.

The Inca Trail (Alejandro Balaguer)

- **Day 2:** From Wayllabamba you climb up for about three hours to **Llulluchapampa** (3,680 m/12,070 feet), a meadow. From here you walk another hour and a half to the **Abra de Huarmihuañusca** (4,200 m/13,776 feet), or Dead Woman's Pass, the highest pass of the trail. This is one of the most difficult legs of the entire trek and it's not uncommon for it to be raining or even snowing on tired trekkers. The trail descends to the valley floor at **Pacamayo** (3,600 m/11,808 feet), where you set up camp. Total distance: 11 km/6.6 miles.

- **Day 3:** In the morning you climb for about an hour to the circular ruins of **Runkuracay**. Another 45 minutes takes you to another pass, **Abra de Runkuracay** (4,000 m/13,1200 feet). An hour later you come to **Sayamarca**, which means "inaccesible town" in Quechua. The path descends even lower into the cloud forest. You will notice the orchids, ferns, and mosses becoming more frequent. You will also pass through an Inca-made tunnel, carved right into the rock. As expected, you must climb back up to the third pass (3,700 m/12,136 feet), where you will have clear views of the mountains of Salkantay and Veronica. Soon after, you come to **Phuyupatamarca**, which means "town in the clouds" and is the site of an impressive ruin. To see the ruins, you must climb down a steep set of stairs, passing a series of Ina baths. To leave you must climb down roughly 1,000 steps, which are definitely hard on the knees, so take care. Another few hours of walking brings you to **Wiñay Wayna**, your camping area for the night and also the site of a small hostel, which is always full. Here you can take a shower, grab a bite to eat, use a real toilet, and even sip on a beer. There are some ruins here, mainly agricultural terraces and several stone buildings. Total distance: 16 km/9.6 miles.

■ **Day 4:** From here you wake up bright and early to begin the trail that will lead to Machu Picchu. Many leave by 4:30 am, The sun comes out by 6 am, then starts to clear the mountains by 7 am. The final leg is a nearly vertical climb of 50 stairs to **Intipunku**, the Sun Gate. After that, the ancient citadel of Machu Picchu will lie before you in all of its glory. Total distance: six km/3.6 miles.

Alternative Trails

If the Inca Trail is sold out, do not despair. There are many other hiking options in the area that will lead to Machu Picchu. Many are considered more challenging and more breathtakingly beautiful. The trail fees are lower too (about $25 per day total), so you will likely save money and are unlikely to be slowed down by tour groups of 50, 100, or 200 people.

One popular route is simply a shortened version of the trail. It is often called the **Camino Real de los Incas** or the **Sacred Inca Trail**. It leaves from Km 104 and gives you the experience of walking the real trail without the blisters. From Km 104 there is a four-hour walk uphill to **Wiñay Wayna**. Machu Picchu is just a few hours more. Many stay in Wiñay Wayna, while some head down to Aguas Caliente and return to Machu Picchu the following day. This hike follows the same rules and regulations as the normal trail, so it must be done with a guide.

The most popular alternative Inca trail passes ★★**Salkantay**, the tallest mountain in the Cordillera Vilcabamba at 6,271 m/20,569 feet and the second-highest in the Cuzco area. There are several ways of doing this. I'll explain the most popular. It is more of a nature trek than a way to see ancient ruins. You pass high mountains and sweltering jungle, all in very desolate areas. You can make this trek on your own, without an agency or

Salkantay (Nicholas Gill)

even a guide. Considering that the price is fairly reasonable regardless of which agency you use, most take a guide or hire horses and porters in Mollepata.

On the Salkantay trek (Nicholas Gill)

The trek generally starts in the town of **Mollepata** in the Apurimac Valley to the northwest of Cuzco. It is reachable by an early morning bus. The first night on this trek is cold, as cold a night as I have ever experienced. The camp is beside the snow-covered peak of Salkantay. On a clear night you can see more stars here than almost anywhere. Having a good sleeping bag is essential if you want to sleep. I personally brought a sleeping bag I bought from a Colombian supermarket for about $9. It was frighteningly cold so I ended up putting on every piece of clothing, including gloves and scarves, that I had in my pack. It didn't matter. I could not sleep and was dead-tired the next day, which is the most intense day of hiking on the trek.

Day two is straight up for about half a day. There is usually a great variance in times to complete this part of the trek. Those with greater physical strength and determination may finish hours ahead of the rest of the group. This day alone makes it more difficult than the regular trail; but do not let that stop you. I watched a group of four out-of-shape Germans in their 60s make it. They trudged along slowly and by no means embarrassed themselves.

From this point on, there are a number of variations for the trek. Some take four nights overall, some just three. Others take seven. Some will end in the town of Santa Teresa, a short walk from the train station at the Aobamba hydroelectric plant. It's a one-hour ride from there to Aguas Caliente. Another trek leads to Paucarcancha, Huayllabamba, and then connects with the traditional Inca Trail.

 The Andean condor is the world's largest bird and believed by the Incas to be a messenger between heaven and earth.

Andean condor (*Denis Graham, Rainforest Alliance*)

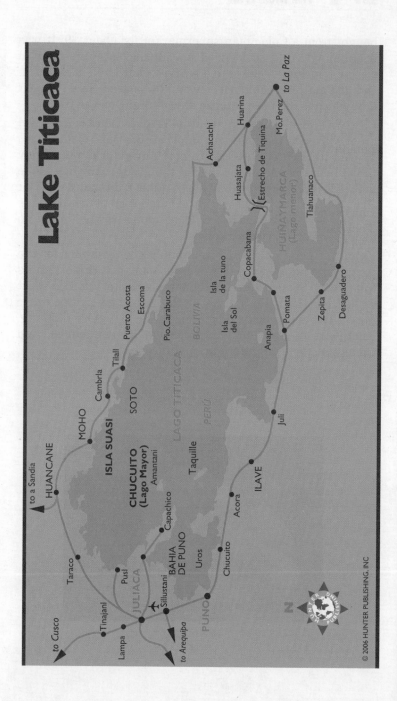

Lake Titicaca

Lake Titicaca & Puno

■ Puno

At 3,827 m/12,553 feet above sea level, and with a population of 100,000, Puno is the base for trips on Lake Titicaca. But the city itself has only a few small attrac-

IN THIS CHAPTER

■ Puno	391
■ Juliaca	406
■ Lake Titicaca	408

tions and the tourist activity is largely confined to one street. There are just a few outlying hotels, a pleasant dock area, and hundreds of blocks of dirty, dusty shanty houses. The Spaniards moved into the area in the early 17th century in search of the Laikakota mines west of Puno. The city was founded in 1668. Puno is thought to be the center of folk art in the country, with more crafts, music, and dance traditions than anywhere else. There are many festivals where the culture and art still thrive as they have for years. Heavy drinking is usually involved as well. There is no doubt about it: Puno can get cold at night. Be sure to dress warmly. Days can be quite hot, though – warm enough for shorts at times. Altitude sickness can also be a problem. Many people actually head to Cuzco to escape the high altitudes.

HIGHLIGHTS

■ **Puno City** – Shop for crafts in the many markets or eat trout in the many restaurants of this tourist hub.

■ **The *Yavari*** – The oldest boat on the lake is docked right outside the Sonesta hotel.

■ **Isla Amantani** – The highlight of many trips to Peru. Interact, eat meals, and stay the night with a local family in this rural retreat.

■ **Islas de Uros** – The floating reed islands are the postcard-perfect image of a unique world.

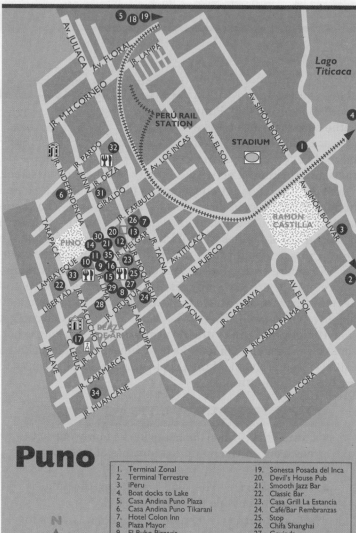

Puno

1. Terminal Zonal
2. Terminal Terrestre
3. iPeru
4. Boat docks to Lake
5. Casa Andina Puno Plaza
6. Casa Andina Puno Tikarani
7. Hotel Colon Inn
8. Plaza Mayor
9. El Buho Pizzeria
10. Inca Bar
11. Apu Salkantay
12. Ukuku's
13. La Choza de Oscar
14. Ekeko's Pub
15. Kamizarakay Rock Pub
16. Positive Vibrations
17. Casa del Corregidor
18. Hotel Libertador Titicaca Lake
19. Sonesta Posada del Inca
20. Devil's House Pub
21. Smooth Jazz Bar
22. Classic Bar
23. Casa Grill La Estancia
24. Café/Bar Rembranzas
25. Stop
26. Chifa Shanghai
27. Govinda
28. Ricos Pan
29. La Casona
30. Le Bistrot
31. Hotel Arequipa
32. Illampu Hostelling
33. Qelqatani Hotel
34. Hotel Balsa Inn
35. Hostal Pukara

Getting Here

Bus

Terminal Terrestre – De Mayo 703, ☎ 36-4733. This is where nearly every bus company has an office and there are frequent departures for places such as Juliaca, Cusco, Arequipa, and Tacna.

Ormeño – ☎ 962-2155. Has service to Lima (20-24 hours, $42, royal class); Cuzco (six hours, $9); and Arequipa (five hours, $7). **Cruz del Sur**, ☎ 35-2451, and **Civa**, ☎ 36-5882, have similar routes, buses, and pricing to those of Ormeño.

Colectur – Tacna 221, ☎ 35-2302. Has buses that go to the border with Bolivia and continue on to Copacabana (three hours, $4) and La Paz (five hours, $7). Almost every tourist agency in Puno offers this same service.

An improved highway has drastically reduced the journey time and made busing to Cuzco easier than the train ride. Some companies (such as **Inka Express** – Avenida Pardo 865 B, ☎ 247-887) offer lunch and a guided tour of the sites along the way.

Local buses go to Juliaca, the border and nearly every small town around the Lake. Most are collectivo minibuses and often wait until full to leave. And I mean full.

Terminal Zonal (Regional Bus Station) – On Av. Simón Bolivar near Carabaya. Colectivos head for the south shore towns of Chimu (10 minutes), Chucuito (30 minutes), Juli (1½ hours) and Yungayo (2½ hours, the Bolivian border), leaving frequently from the early morning to afternoon and costing just a few soles each.

Plane

(See Juliaca).

Train

Peru Rail – La Toree 224, ☎ 051-35-1041, www.perurail.com. This journey has decreased in popularity due to improved roads and faster, easier bus services. Many still opt for the train because of the stunning scenery and greater comfort. Services are offered

Mon, Wed, and Sat, year-round. Backpacker services cannot be reserved in advance. Trains going to or departing from Cuzco leave at 8 am and arrive at 6 pm. They stop in Juliaca and several small towns along the way, including a scenic stop at La Raya, the highest point along the way. The Peru Rail website has a detailed timeline of the journey and what you will see along the way.

To/from Cuzco – $16.66 backpacker; $119 Andean Explorer (includes a three-course lunch).

Getting Around

Tri-taxis, with a seat and two front wheels, are convenient for getting to places nearby and usually cost just 1-3 soles. Regular taxis and motocarros are available as well.

Collectivo buses go to towns along the lake and to the border with Bolivia.

Tourist Information

Tourist Office – **iPeru**, corner of Deusta and Lima, ☎ 364-806.

Laundry – **Lavandería Don Manuel**, Lima block 4, ☎ 352-444. Mon-Sat, 7 am-6 pm.

Banking – **Interbank**, Lima 444; **BCP**, at Lima and Grau, has a Visa ATM and gives cash advances. You can change Bolivian pesos at either bank or from the moneychangers in the street, although rates at the border are similar.

Internet – Access is readily available all over town.

Post Office – SerPost, Moquegua 267 (just east of the Plaza de Armas).

Hospital – Hospital Nacional Manuel Nunez Butron, El Sol 1022, ☎ 369-696. Mon-Fri 7:30 am-1:30 pm.

Police – **Policia de Turismo**, Deustua 538, ☎ 364-806.

Peruvian Immigration – Ayacucho 240, ☎ 357-103. Mon-Fri 8 am-2 pm.

Bolivian Consulate – Arequipa 120, ☎ 351-251, Mon-Fri 8:30 am-2 pm.

Sightseeing

The **Plaza de Armas** sits on the southern end of Jr. Lima and features the **City Cathedral of Puno** (1657), standing proudly on the Plaza's western edge. You can get a glimpse inside from 8 am-noon or 3-

Plaza de Armas

5 pm, although it is far less impressive than most Colonial churches in Peru. It was visited by Pope Paul VI in the mid-60s.

There are a few sites on the Plaza, quite close to the cathedral. The **mansion of Viceroy Count of Lemos**, where he stayed in 1668 as part of an effort to quiet the people and found the

Casa del Corregidor

city, is at Deustua and Conde de Lemos beside the cathedral. Note the Colonial balcony. The **Museo Carlos Dryer**, a municipal museum has a small selection of Incan artifacts, a few mummies, and documents regarding the founding of the city. (Mon-Fri, 7:30 am-3:30 pm, $1). There is also a small craft shop and café at the 17th-century **Casa del Corregidor**, thought to be the oldest house in Puno.

Jr. Lima, which runs for several blocks north of the Plaza, is a pedestrian-only street with many small shops, restaurants, tour agencies, and tourist facilities of all sorts. It is the center of the Puno tourist industry and you will likely find yourself there for one reason or another.

The dock area on Av. Titicaca is lined with craft shops and small places for snacks. Here you can also arrange your own transport on the lake. People will approach you.

★**The** *Yavari* (www.yavari.org) is the most famous boat on the lake and has a long, storied history. James Watt & Co.

The Yavari

built it in Birmingham, England. The 2,766 parts were shipped piece-by-piece to Peru. The *Yavari* and the *Yapura* (its sister ship) were shipped around Cape Horn to the port of Arica, Chile (part of Peru at the time), and then 40 miles inland to Tacna by train. From there man and mule carried it over the Andes to Lake Titicaca, where it was assembled, a daunting task that took six years. It was launched on Christmas Day, 1870. Later, it became a Peruvian Navy ship, a transport vessel, and now a floating museum. Until 1914 the engine was fired by llama dung. In 1987 the Yavari Restoration bought it from the Peruvian Navy. It hasn't been in operation in decades, although it has been restored and the engine still runs. Presently the boat is docked in front of the Sonesta Posada del Inca hotel where you can climb aboard for a free tour (open 8 am-10 pm). In the near future cabins will be available for overnight tours on the lake.

There are two scenic viewpoints on the hills surrounding town. First is **Huajsapata Park**, a few blocks southwest of the Plaza, where there is a white statue of Manco Cápac. The other is from the **Deustua Arch**, built in 1847 by the people of Puno to commemorate the fallen in the Battles of Junín and Ayacucho. To get there, walk north on Independencia to just before Cornejo. It is recommended that you not visit either location alone, as robberies have been known to occur.

Where to Stay

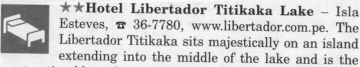

★★**Hotel Libertador Titikaka Lake** – Isla Esteves, ☎ 36-7780, www.libertador.com.pe. The Libertador Titikaka sits majestically on an island extending into the middle of the lake and is the most noticeable and striking hotel in Puno. It has 123 rooms with lake views, private hot-water baths, cable TV, and heating. A good restaurant, small bar, gym, and sauna are on site.

Hotel Libertador Titikaka Lake

The Libertador also has its own dock and arranges day-trips to other parts of the lake. $$$$$

★**Sonesta Posada del Inca** – Sesquicentenario 610, ☎ 36-4111, www.sonesta.com. Excellent views of the lake and with the *Yavari* docked right out front. There is a lovely patio area for drinks and meals among the reeds and blue water. This hotel avoids the hustle and bustle of Puno and is my favorite hotel in Puno for this reason. Rooms are spacious, with private hot-water baths, heating, and cable TV. $$$

Casa Andina Puno Plaza, Grau 270, ☎ 36-7520, fax 36-3712, www.casa-andina.com, and **Casa Andina Puno Tikarani**, Independencia 185, ☎ 36-7803, fax 36-5333. These hotels are two of the best options for comfort and value in Puno's center. All rooms have private hot-water

Casa Andina Puno Plaza

baths, heating, cable TV, and the clean, trendy, and not overly luxuriant décor and amenities that Casa Andina has become known for. $$$

Hotel Colon Inn

Hotel Colon Inn – Tacna 290, ☎ 351-432, www.coloninn.com. Associated with the Best Western, this is a recommended option right in the center. It is in an antique mansion on a corner plot. Rooms aren't overly extravagant, but are cozy and have all the amenities,

Puno – Lake Titicaca

including cable TV and minibars. Restaurant, pizzeria, and a bar are on-site. $$$

Plaza Mayor – Deustra 342, ☎ 363-700, fax 366-089, www.plazamayorhostal.com. Just a block from the Plaza, this tasteful hotel is one of the best in central Puno. Carpeted rooms, private baths, hot water, cable TV, hair dryers, heating, in-room phones, and cable TV. Price includes breakfast buffet. Also offers laundry service, safe, restaurant/bar, fax, and room service. $$$

HOTEL PRICE CHART	
	under $10
$	$10-$25
$$	$26-$50
$$$	$51-$90
$$$$	$91-$150
$$$$$	Over $150

Eco Inn – Chulluni 195, ☎ 36-5525, www.ecoinnpuno.com. This hotel, opened in 2001, is about 10 minutes from the center, near the lake. The 42 rooms have cable TV, wall-to-wall carpeting, and large windows that let in lots of light. Includes a buffet breakfast. Recommended. $$$

Qelqatani Hotel – Tarapacá 355, ☎ 51-366172, www.qelqatani.com. This pleasant mid-range choice is just a few blocks from the Plaza. Rooms are far from lavish, but are clean and have all the amenities. Has a nightly folkloric show in its conference room from 7:30 to 9 pm ($10). A full breakfast buffet is included. $$

Hotel Balsa Inn – Cajamarca 555, ☎ 36-3144, www.hotelbalsainn.com. Your basic official three-star; nothing gaudy. Rooms are carpeted and have heating, cable TV, and phones. A coffee bar and restaurant are on the first floor. Price includes a breakfast buffet. Parking is available. $$

Hostal Pukara – Libertad 328, ☎ 368-448, pukara@terra.com.pe. The hotel is heavily decorated with native art, which you will notice immediately with the huge lobby mural. The 14 rooms all have hot-water baths, cable TV, and heating. Rates include American breakfast served on the rooftop patio. This is an excellent value. $$

Hotel Arequipa – Arequipa 153, ☎ 363-303. Warm, comfortable rooms that have a bit of a hospital feel to them. Some rooms with private baths and TVs. 24-hour hot water is sometimes lukewarm. The small restaurant serves a simple breakfast if you request it in advance. $

Illampu Hostelling – La Torre 137, ☎ 54-353-284. This little hotel hidden in an alley behind El Inti is a good budget option. Rooms have private baths, hot water, and some have TVs. Rooms are basic, but have carpet, clean beds, and new furniture. Bargain price.

El Inti – Torre 137, ☎ 35-1594. Colonial style with basic rooms, hot water and TVs. Nice café/restaurant downstairs. Dirt-cheap.

GASTRONOMY

■ **Pesque** – A dish made up of quinoa, cheese, and eggs.

■ **Chairo** – Stew made from lamb meat.

■ **Salteña** – Small, empanada-like pastry with meat, potatoes, and spices. Delicious.

■ **Quesillos y miel** – A dessert made of curd cheese and honey.

Where to Eat

El Buho Pizzeria –Lima 347. Cozy little restaurant serving a long list of pizzas that are reasonably priced. The menu has a decent pasta list too. The wood-burning stove bakes the pizzas and keeps the place warm. Recommended over the many other pizzerias in Puno. $$

DINING PRICE CHART	
$	under $5
$$	$5-$10
$$$	$11-$20
$$$$	$21-$35
$$$$$	over $35

IncABar – Lima 356, ☎ 368-865. You can tell by the creativity in the sauces that the chef at this stylish place did his training. Dishes with lake fish are the highlight. Also, soups, pastas, and curries are worth a try. Open for breakfast, lunch, and dinner. The café/couch bar is good for some of the pricier cocktails that are hard to find in Puno. $$$

Apu Salkantay – Lima 357, ☎ 363-955. Perhaps my favorite restaurant in Puno. It has character, stylish furniture and décor, creative dishes, and isn't over-priced. Try tartar de trucha, an alpaca sandwich, carpaccio of alpaca, or the Andean cheese selection. $$$

Colonial Door – Lima 345. Simple breakfasts, pizzas, and pancakes. Walls and ceilings are made of reeds. An interesting dining experience. $$

La Caywa – Jr. Arequipa 410. Stylish restaurant with creative dishes. One of the best options in town for trendy, international food. $$

Ukuku's – Libertad 216. Classic gringo restaurant/café with book exchange. Andean dishes and traveler favorites. $

Govinda – Deusta 312. National vegetarian chain run by Hare Krishnas. $

Ricos Pan – Lima 424 & Moquegua 330. The interior of this classy café is surprisingly large and relaxed for its location on Lima. Excellent coffee, cakes, and pastries. $

La Casona – Lima 517. Lace tablecloths with religious artifacts and antiques are the setting for this freshwater fish restaurant. $$

LeBistrot – Arbulu 311. This bar/restaurant/crêperie is in a funky little setting with tapestries on the walls and a reggae beat. Dozens of sweet and savory crêpes, breakfasts, and snacks. $

La Choza de Oscar – Libertad 340. Touristy place with live music on most nights. An array of trout and alpaca dishes. Cheap set menu with a free glass of wine or a Pisco sour. $$

Casa Grill La Estancia – Libertad 137. This is the place in Punotogo for grilled meats. One of the city's more modern restaurants. Lomo, biffe, brochetas, alpaca, and even cuy. They also have many local and regional dishes. $$

Lago de Flores – Lima 357. One of the many modern tourist haunts with pizza on Lima. Alpaca in red wine, peppers, and apple garlic sauce. Pumpkin and tomato soups. Decent wine selection, at least for Puno. $$

Café/Bar Rembranzas – Moquegua 200. Stylish corner café with a long menu of breakfasts, pancakes, and pizzas. $

Stop – Deusta 312. Interesting restaurant/bar with a saloon-like feel and graffiti-covered puzzle-piece walls. Cheap set menus. Burgers, pizzas, alpaca, and trout. $

Chifa Shanghai – Arbulu ☎ 167-171. Locally popular chifa with wanton soup and a main course for 8 soles. $

Restaurant Vegitereana and Medicina Naturales – Libertad 352. Trendy, New-Age café with art on the walls, serving medicinal drinks and organic foods. $

Bars

Devil's House Pub – Jr. Arequipa 401. Corner pub that draws plenty of attention on weekend nights.

Ekeko's Pub – Jr. Lima 355. Street touts lure you inside this cave-like, second-story club with free drinks.

Kamizarakay Rock Pub – Grau 148. Usually has live music and a few travelers inside.

Positive Vibrations – Lima 345 (2nd floor). Typical traveler chill-out bar. A few tables and bar stools, floor seats and pillows, and a wood-burning stove.

Smooth Jazz Bar – Arequipa 454. The name may be a bit overstated. It ain't that smooth, but it's a good place to avoid the typical peña music or traveler dance tracks (aka 80s pop songs).

Classic Bar – 330-A Tarapacá. New discoteca and couch bar that has some style for a Puno bar. The giant framed puzzle on the ceiling is quite impressive.

Shopping

Asociacion Coriwasi – Alfonso Ugarte 150. Large selection of independent vendors selling just about all Puno textiles (including alpaca slippers).

Asociacion de Artesanos La Cholita (Lima 550, 2nd floor) and **Asociacion de Artesanos Tucuy Atipac** (Lima 339, 2nd floor) are good places for typical souvenirs.

Alpaca 111 – Lima 343. This is the best and most expensive place to buy fine alpaca clothing.

Puno – Lake Titicaca

Mercado Central – Has good Puno cheeses; otherwise it is just a typical market with slabs of beef, cheap clothing and cosmetics.

Tour Companies

There are many companies offering the same services and tours for similar prices. The ones listed below are recommended.

Inka Adventures – Ugarte 156, ☎ 51-365-020. Has all of the basic Titicaca tours such as to Sillustani, two-day trips to Amantani and Taquile, and one-day trips to the Uros. Bilingual guides are knowledgeable about the area.

Kollasuyo Tours – Jr. Theodoro Valcarcel 155, ☎ 054-368-642, kollasuyotours@hotmail.com. Arranges trips on Lake Titicaca, to the Sillustani ruins, and train, plane, and bus tickets.

Also try:

Kurni Puno Travel Agency – Jr. Lima 110, ☎ 051-364-565, kurmipunotravel@yahoo.com.

Allways Travel – Tacna 234, ☎ 355-552/367-246, www.titicacaperu.com.

EdgarTours – Lima 328, ☎ 353-444, fax 354-811, edgar-adventures@terra.com.pe.

Zarate Expeditions – Tacna 255 A, ☎ 051-354-180, www.zarateadventures.com. The Puno office for the famed Arequipa-based mountain and adventure guide.

Festivals

 ★**Virgen de la Candelaria** (February 1-14). This two-week festival is one of the main reasons many consider Puno the Folk Capital of the Americas. More than 200 groups of musicians and dancers are brought together to celebrate the Mamacha Candelaria. There are processions, banquets, many performances, and fireworks displays. The festivals date back to Pre-Hispanic times. In the diablada, or dance of the demons, the dancers blow panpipes and wear devilish costumes and masks, while making their offerings to the earth goddess Pachamama.

Day-Trips from Puno

★ Sillustani

This archeological site 34 km/20 miles north of Puno, on a small peninsula on Lake Umayo, is the most notable ruin on the lakeshore. The site is visually pleasing, on top of a hill with barren farmland and the blue of the lake surrounding it. Photos turn

Sillustani (Carlos Sala)

out well from any angle. The funerary towers, or chullpas, were built by the Colla culture, a tribe of Aymara-speaking warriors. The most prominent members of society were laid to rest inside the sealed towers. Personal possessions, food, and other items have been found with the bodies. Similar towers can be seen on several hilltops throughout the region, but the ones at Sillustani are the most striking. Some of the chullpas are more than 12 m/40 feet high and several bear small symbols of creatures such as a snake or alligator. The site can get quite windy on most afternoons, so bring a jacket.

Most visit the ruins on a guided tour from Puno that will also stop at a country house along the way and make other short stops. Tours run about $5-$10 per person and last three hours.

It is possible to take a combination of local buses to the site, but getting back can be difficult.

Chucuito

Chucuito is a small town (population 1,500) just south of Puno (20 minutes) en route to Bolivia. It has excellent views of the lake, one fantastic hotel, a few interesting churches, and a small ruin that is sure to catch your eye or maybe something else. There are some small restaurants, hospedajes, and gift shops that line the main road and around the temple. Regardless of how you feel about the temple, Chucuito does have a rural charm that Puno lacks. Chucuito and all of the rural,

Chucuito (Domingo Giribaldi)

isolated areas along the south shore are known for the Aymara shamans that inhabit them and their mystic ambiance does not go unnoticed if you are attuned to it. To get there you must catch one of the frequent collectivos from Terminal Zonal in Puno (2 soles).

Templo de la Fertilidad – Many guidebooks hype this site simply because they can talk about penises and laugh about it. Personally, I am not overly impressed with the place. It is simply a small stone courtyard containing several dozen stone phalluses. A chain link fence surrounds the area around the temple and gives it an inauthentic feel. The stories behind the site are interesting. Some say local women used to sit on the stones to increase their fertility. Some say the entire site is just an age-old tourist scam. Small craft stands surround the site and children will hound you to pay for a tour. Regardless, the site is far less scenic and photogenic than Chucuito itself.

Where to Stay

★**Hotel Taypikala** – Km 18 (just off the main road in Chucuito), ☎ 356-042, www.taypikala.com. This hotel, meaning vital stone or sacred center, is thought to be surrounded by a strong energy field. It has a New-Age, spiritual feel. Officially rated with three stars, its décor and structure are remarkable. The outside walls look as if they rose straight out of the earth and giant condors sit on the roof. Rooms are comfortable, with heating, private baths, and TVs. On-site restaurant and pub, spa, and massage services. $$$$

Sites between Puno & Cuzco

The Ciudad Rosada, or the pink city, **Lampa** is 23 km/14 miles northwest of Juliaca. Its nickname comes from the pinkish buildings that make up the town. The small church of

La Inmaculada is famous for the hundreds of skeletons of Spaniards that were brought up from the catacombs below to be rearranged in strange patterns. It also has a replica of Michelangelo's *La Pieta* that graces the tomb of a wealthy local citizen. Most come on a tour that stops here en route to Puno from Cuzco or vice versa. You may come from Juliaca via combi; they depart from Av. Huascar near the market and leave when full. The trip takes about 45 minutes (3 soles).

The ruins at **Raqchi** are what remain of the once great Temple of **Viracocha**, one of the most important shrines in the empire. The largest Inca-made roof once was here, supported by 22 stone columns, which can still be seen. The site is undergoing a restoration. It is in the small village of San Pedro. Most Cuzco- or Puno-bound buses pass by Raqchi, though the tour buses make an effort to stop.

Border Crossing Information

Americans and most European citizens do not need a visa to visit Bolivia and are usually granted a 90-day tourist stay without hassle. Canadians, Australians, and New Zealanders are usually issued 30-day stays. If you simply need to get your passport restamped, you can cross the border and come back the next day for a new 90-day stamp. This is much easier than going to an immigration office in Peru. Reports of thefts and light scams by border officials are not uncommon, so keep an eye on your belongings and a good head about you. You should be fine. The border is open from 8 am to 6 pm. Note that Bolivian time is one hour ahead of Peruvian time.

There are two routes to get to Bolivia overland.

Via Yungayo – On this south-shore route you can catch one of the many small, crowded collectivos that depart frequently from Terminal Zonal, on Av. Simón Bolivar near Carabaya. Look for the buses that say Yungayo (2½ hours). From the border there is frequent transportation to the Bolivian resort town of **Copacabana** (10 km/six miles, $1). There aren't Brazilian girls in thong bikinis there, but the town has many quaint hotels and hip restaurants and bars. Half-day tours go to the **Isla del Sol** (by legend, the birthplace of Manco Cápac, the first Inca, and of the sun itself). Alternatively, you can book a Pullman bus from one of the many companies in Puno that continue on to Copacabana and La Paz (most leave at 8 am). The border is generally smooth and well run, although when all the tour buses come through at once, it can be fairly crowded. There are money-changing facilities at the border. For much of the past few years, sporadic strikes have closed the border, so be sure to check ahead.

Via the North Shore – This route is rarely done by tourists and is best taken from Juliaca. You must get a Peruvian exit stamp in Puno, predated by three days. You will have to take many small, crowded, uncomfortable buses and change in several small towns for this to work. You will likely have to stay overnight in very rustic accommodations. Hitchhiking may be necessary. As bad as it sounds, if you have the time and tolerance, you will see some of the most unspoiled towns of the Peruvian altiplano and spectacular scenery that gringos rarely see. Once in Bolivia, however, the journey to any major town such as Copacabana will be as rough as that described above. Good luck.

■ Juliaca

Juliaca is perhaps the most undesirable town in Peru. This is the definition of a third-world shantytown and has very little to offer other than being a base for trips to smaller nearby towns on the Lake, the site of the Puno airport, and a stop on the rail line. It is very impoverished, with people living in tents right on the main streets. The roads are unpaved and unfinished construction projects have left heaps of materials scattered about town. Piles of trash are burned on the roads. Crime is commonplace. Unless you have a good reason for coming here, Don't!

Getting Here & Getting Away

Plane

Aeropuerto Internacional Inca Manco Cápac, Aviacion (no #), ☎ 051-328-974. You can get to and from the airport to the center (two km/1.2 miles) by taxi (4-6 soles). Or, if you are heading to Puno, tourist buses run from here to Puno (an hour, 5 soles) frequently.

Flights are generally sold one-way and range from about $60 to $90.

To Cuzco – (45 minutes), although this flight was not running at the time of writing.

To Lima – (1¾ hour)

To Arequipa – (2 hours 10 minutes)

Airlines

LAN – ☎ 213-8300, www.lan.com.

TANS – ☎ 213-6000, www.tansperu.com.pe.

Bus

The three companies all have similar services and routes. All have terminals on the 12th block of San Martín. Most go to Puno and Cuzco, from where you can make other connections.

Ormeño – ☎ 54-5057, www.grupo-ormeno.com.

Cruz del Sur –☎ 32-2011, www.cruzdelsur.com.pe.

Civa – ☎ 32-6229, www.civa.com.pe.

Train

See Cuzco, Puno, or www.perurail.com.

Banks

Interbank – Nuñez ☎ 227-235

Where to Stay

Suite Don Carlos – Prado 335, ☎ 32-1571, dcarlosjuliaca@terra.com.pe. This is the best option in town, with large new rooms. The newer addition to the hotel has more modern rooms, while the older part is still fine, but a bit worn. Rooms have cable TV, minibars, and hairdryers. $$$

Hotel Royal Inn – San Roman 158, ☎ 32-1561, hotel_royal_inn@latinmail.com. This hotel is centrally located and a good value. Rooms have hot showers and cable TV. The restaurant here is better than most and keeps you from walking outside, a big plus in Juliaca. $$

■ Lake Titicaca

Lake Titicaca

Lake Titicaca pairs some of the world's most stunning scenery with colossal white clouds dancing across a bright blue sky. Snow-capped mountains rise out of the azure blue water in every direction. Sunrise and sunset create colors that you never thought were possible on this earth.

Titicaca, meaning puma, in Aymara, and sacred rock in Quechua, is 194 km/116 miles long at its longest and an average of 65 km/39 miles wide. At 3,810 m/12,497 feet above sea level, it is the highest navigable lake in the world and many legends surround it. The lake is the birthplace of the Tiahuanaco culture and of the first Incas, Manco Cápac and Mama Ocllo, who rose out of the water at the Isla del Sol near Copacabana, Bolivia. The sun, moon, and stars also rose from the lake and made their way to the sky, according to the legend.

There is abundant bird, fish, and plant life on the lake. The totora reeds are what make up the floating islands and are used in the making of the famous reed rafts. There is evidence of reed boats being used on the lake as far back as 4500 years ago. Some believe that the first inhabitants floated on the rafts from Polynesia.

Getting Here & Around

To get to the islands, most go with a Puno tour agency (see below for description). It is possible to go independently, although you really won't save any money, but you have a greater chance of giving money directly to the islanders. The islands of Amantani and Taquile each have their own boats. For Taquile and Amantani, boats leave daily from the dock in Puno at around 7:30 am (25 soles round-trip for Taquile, and a little less for Amantani). There is also a daily boat from Taquile to Amantani (5 soles).

It is possible to get to Bolivia by water as well. Two companies offer this service:

Crillon Tours/Arcobaleno – Lambayeque 175, ☎ 36-4068, www.titicaca.com. Hydrofoil tours are daily; some are overnight, ranging from about $165 to $250, depending on the package.

Transturin – Ayachucho block 1, ☎ 35-2771, leontours@ terra.com.pe. This trip actually goes to Copacabana, Bolivia by bus. From there you hop aboard a catamaran and sail to the Isla del Sol and then to the port of Huatajata before continuing on to La Paz. Overnight stays on the boats are also possible. Prices are similar to those above.

Adventures on Water

The most common way to see the lake is via a tour from Puno. You can simply visit the **Islas de Oros** on a quick half-day trip, but the ★★★two-day trip with a stay on either **Amantani** or **Taquile** is the highlight of a trip to Peru for many, myself included. Most tour companies offer a similar schedule. They pick you up at your hotel early in the morning and head to the docks, where you board a boat (bring sunscreen!). You first visit the Islas Flotantes and are given a brief tour, a chance to ride a reed boat, and time to shop for souvenirs. Next you head to Amantani and meet with your host family. Don't expect anyone to speak English, and there will be no electricity or plumbing. You return to their house for lunch, visit the ruins, have dinner, and at night dress up in traditional clothing and participate in a local dance with live music, local people, and the other members on your tour. On the walk home don't forget to look up into the clear night sky to see some of the most beautiful stars you will ever see. The next day you eat breakfast, say goodbye to your family, climb aboard the boat and head to Taquile. There you will be given a tour around the island, will eat at a local restaurant, and have the chance to visit some of the famed souvenir shops before the ride back to Puno.

★Isla Amantani

Amantani is less developed or touristy than Taquile and is where most tours provide accommodation in the home of a local family. It doesn't have the history of Taquile, but it is much bigger and more traditional. If you show up unannounced you should be able to find accommodation on you own if you ask kindly. There is also a small hospedaje, with basic facilities. Most one-night tours on the lake stay here with local families.

This Quechua-speaking island has double the population of Taquile, at 4,000. The culture here is much more derived from the Aymara Indians. The inhabitants came from Bolivia as early as 500 BC. Presently, there are just eight communities on the island, made up of farms and collections of adobe houses.

There is a small temple atop the pyramid-shaped mountain that dominates the island and is topped by the Incan ruin of Pachamam and Pachatata, dating back more than a thousand years. The climb is well paved and can be tiring at the high altitude, but views of the surrounding lake are absolutely incredible, especially at sunrise or sunset.

★★Isle Taquile

Musicians on Isla Taquile

Taquile is the most visited island on the lake, other than the flotantes or floating islands, and with good reason. The small country houses, farms, stone walls, paths, and views of the water give it a wonderfully rural feel, like Ireland's Ring of Kerry, although the Incan terracing and ruins set it apart. It sits 35 km/21 miles east of Puno (four hours by boat) and has no electricity or roads. The island is just six km/3.6 miles long and has been inhabited for thousands of years. The Quechua-speaking communities here total about 2,000. They rarely leave the island or intermarry with other groups.

Their weaving system is highly intricate, with every knot taking on a special meaning. The men wear tight, floppy-eared hats that they knit themselves, often as they walk around the island. If they are married, they wear a red hat; unmarried is a red and white hat. Different colors also add extra significance. The women are dressed in elaborately decorated, multi-layered skirts. Most of these adornments can be bought in the craft cooperatives on the Plaza, which are highly recommended.

If you want to stay here, there are a few small hospedajes and restaurants on the island. A woman just off the Plaza sells anticuchos de alpaca (kebabed alpaca meat), also available as a sandwich that is excellent and, in fact, better than the food at most of the restaurants on the island, which tend to be overly touristy.

The **Festival of San Diego** (St. James, July 25) is the island's most popular event. A lively feast is combined with music and dancing that may last until the beginning of August.

Isla Suasi

This small island on the north shore near the Bolivian border is difficult to reach if you are not staying at Casa Andina, but it's one of the most isolated and picturesque of all of the lake's islands. There is basic accommodation for those who show up on their own.

Where to Stay

 ★**Casa Andina** – Isla Suasi, ☎ 962-2709, fax 445-4775, www. casa-andina.com. This is the gem of the Casa Andina private collection. Perhaps the best option for those who want the peace and tranquility of the lake,

Casa Andina

resort-like comfort, and a modest price. The hotel is made of local materials, such as stone, adobe, and totora reeds, and is powered by an intricate solar panel system. From Puno, you can reach the hotel in about 2½ hours. Lake views are available from each room, and they feature private baths. The hotel helps arrange activities, such as walking tours of the island, canoeing, and visits with local farmers. A new cultural hut and Andean spa is set to open in 2006. $$$$$

★★★Islas Flotantes de los Uros

On one of the Islas Flotantes

The floating isles are made up of piles of totora reeds, or cattail reeds, that grow on the lake. There are about 40 of the islands and they make up a good part of the Titicaca National Reserve. They aren't exactly floating as they once were; now they are stationary. Many Aymara Indians still inhabit the islands and live by hunting birds and fishing, although tourism brings in a pretty penny as well. Tourism to the islands first began in the 1960s and the islands have since become one of the key tourist attractions in Peru and for the entire continent. Many of the islands have a zoo-like feel with tourists walking around taking photos of people and homes, while buying souvenirs. Some of the more isolated islands are protected, however, and their traditional culture has managed to survive, although the majority of the islanders have converted to Catholicism and a floating church can even be found on one of the islands. After a visit by President Fujimori about a decade ago, solar panels were donated to some of the islands; so don't be surprised if you see several of the reed huts with electricity. The best way to visit the islands is on a tour from Puno. You can also hire a boat on your own from the dock in Puno (price negotiable).

Islas de los Uros

Cordillera Blanca

The Valley of Callejón de Huaylas, 400 km/240 miles northeast of Lima, is the best spot on the continent for climbing and trekking. The valley is 40 km/24 miles wide and runs north-

IN THIS CHAPTER

- **Huaraz**   414
- **Carhuaz**   435
- **Yungay**   436
- **Caraz**   437

south for nearly 200 km/120 miles between the snow-capped mountains of the Cordillera Blanca to the east and the Cordillera Negra to the west. The area is filled with blue skies, green valleys, turquoise lakes, and the highest concentration of glaciers in the world's tropic zone. Although many of the glaciers are receding each year, you can still see a snow-capped peak from nearly every vantage point.

The enthusiasts here are generally a bit more experienced than in Cuzco or other areas. Many come solely to Huaraz and will spend two weeks of their time on a single trek or climb. There are also many day-hikes that are worth the time, passing pre-Colombian ruins, mountain lakes, snow-covered peaks, and small, unspoiled villages. Many who come here need a few days to get acclimatized because of the altitude. Most agencies encourage hikers and climbers to spend a few days in the area, taking short day-trips to adjust. The dry season runs from May-October and is the best time to climb and attempt outdoor activities. The rest of the year sees its share of rain.

The city of Huaraz is the center for most visitors, with enough tourist restaurants, nightclubs, and tourist agencies to satisfy anyone. Other small towns in the area, such as Caraz, Yungay, and Carhuaz, are developing and becoming popular as well, however.

HIGHLIGHTS

- **Chavín** – The most revered ruin of the Chavín culture, one of Peru's largest pre-Inca civilizations.
- **Huaraz** – Rest a few days with some Swiss fondue, and get acclimatized in this mountain town full

of tourist amenities – the adventure sport capital of the continent.

■ **Climbing Huascarán** – Join an ice-climbing expedition to the summit of the world's tallest mountains.

■ **Old Yungay** – Visit this serene sanctuary, site of one of the most devastating natural disasters in recorded history.

■ Huaraz

Phone code (043)

The mountain town of Huaraz (population 100,000), the capital of the department of Ancash, is the base camp for the highest mountains outside of the Himalayas. There are 23 snow-capped mountain peaks that climb above altitudes of 5,000 m/ 16,400 feet, the highest being Huascarán (6,788 m/22,265 feet). The outdoors here screams adventure. You can arrange trekking, climbing, mountain biking, and paragliding, among many other activities. June, July, and August are the peak of the dry season and the best time for adventure activities.

The city itself is unremarkable, with most of the buildings made of concrete and many more in pieces. The town was almost completely destroyed in the 1970 earthquake, which left just one street intact and killed roughly half of the population. It has been rebuilt, but the legacy lingers and much of the Andean character has long since disappeared. The new Huaraz revolves around tourism, and every doorway in the center of town has something to do with it. It is beginning to take on the feel of a ski town or alpine village. The city sits at an elevation of 3,091 m/10,138 feet, so you will need to acclimate yourself for a few days doing day-hikes and enjoying the hotels, restaurants, and nightlife.

Climate

Huaraz has dry and mild weather with an average temperature of 17°C/61°F during the day, and 13°C/ 55°F at night. The rainy season is October through April.

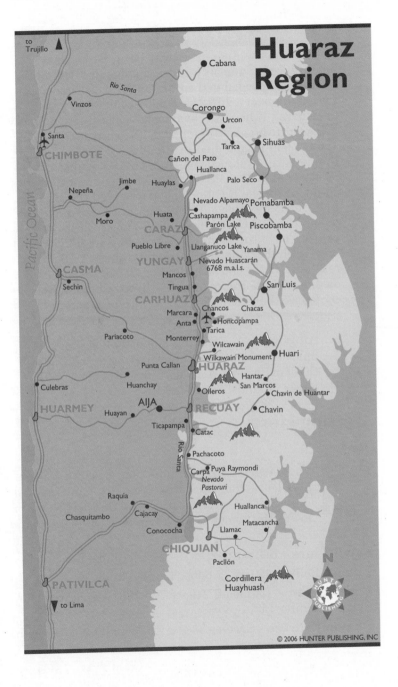

Huaraz Region

to Trujillo

Cabana

Rio Santa

Vinzos

Corongo

Urcon

Santa

Tarica

Sihuas

CHIMBOTE

Cañon del Pato

Huallanca

Palo Seco

Nepeña

Jimbe

Huaylas

Moro

Huata

Nevado Alpamayo

Pomabamba

Cashapampa

Parón Lake

Piscobamba

CARAZ

Pueblo Libre

Llanganuco Lake

Yanama

CASMA

YUNGAY

Nevado Huascarán
6768 m.a.l.s.

Sechin

Mancos

Tingua

San Luis

CARHUAZ

Chancos

Chacas

Marcara

Honcopampa

Pariacoto

Anta

Tarica

Monterrey

Wilcawain

Punta Callan

Wilkawain Monument

Huari

Culebras

Huanchay

HUARAZ

Hantar

Olleros

San Marcos

AIJA

Chavin de Huantar

HUARMEY

Huayan

RECUAY

Chavin

Ticapampa

Catac

Rio Santa

Pachacoto

Carpa

Puya Raymondi

Nevado
Pastoruri

Raquia

Huallanca

Chasquitambo

Cajacay

Matacancha

Conococha

Llamac

CHIQUIAN

N

Pacllón

PATIVILCA

Cordillera
Huayhuash

to Lima

Pacific Ocean

© 2006 HUNTER PUBLISHING, INC

EARTHQUAKES

As with many other places in Peru, earthquakes have played a major role in shaping the region. Here, they have led to the worst natural disasters in Peruvian history. In 1941, 5,000 people were killed in Huaraz when an avalanche caused Laguna Pacacoha to break its damn and flow onto the city. In 1962, 4,000 people died in the town of Ranrahirca thanks to an avalanche on Huascarán. Last but not least, on May 31st, 1970, an earthquake that measured 7.8 on the Richter scale devastated the area. In the end, only about 10% of Huaraz was left standing and 15,000 were killed there. Yungay faired far worse. The entire town was covered by an alluvion, completely burying the entire city and it's 18,000 residents. In the end an estimated 70,000 people had died, all in a matter of minutes. It was the worst recorded earthquake in the Western Hemisphere.

 Alluvion – A cascading mix of water, stone, ice mud and other debris that wipes out nearly everything in its path. A deadly side-effect of an earthquake or landslide.

Getting Here

Bus

 There is no central terminal, but most bus companies leave from the area around Cajamarca and Raimondi or on Fitzcarrald at the north end of town. Most go to Lima, a trip of about eight hours ($8-$12).

Movil Tours – Bolivar 542, ☎ 72-2555. Trujillo, Lima.

Linea – Bolivar 450, ☎ 72-6666. Trujillo, Lima.

Cruz del Sur – Raimondi 242, ☎ 72-8726, www.cruzdelsur.com.pe. Trujillo, Lima.

Chavín Express – Cáceres 338, ☎ 72-4652. Buses to Chavín and other area towns.

Yungay Express – Fitzcarrald 4377, ☎ 72-4377. This goes to Chimbote via the Canyon del Pato. You can transfer in Chimbote to other coastal destinations such as Trujillo. This route is spectacular, but the bus ride is absolute hell.

Minibuses heading north to Carhuaz, Yungay, and Caraz leave from the Centenario just across the river.

Tourist Information

Tourist Offices – **iPeru**, Atusparia #1 (Plaza de Armas), ☎ 72 8812, iperuhuaraz@promperu.gob.pe. **Casa de Guias** – Parque Ginebra 28-G, ☎ 42-1811, www.casadeguias.com.pe. This is one of the most important sources of information in Huaraz if you are planning on trekking or climbing. They can give you extensive background on hikes in the area and safety precautions you should take. The "House of Guides" arranges mountain rescues (by land and helicopter) and registers trekkers before they go out in the wilderness.

Maps – *Cordillera Huayhuash*, from the Alpine Mapping Club, 1:65,000; *Cordillera Blanca and Huayhuash*, from Felipe Diaz, 1:286,000.

Post Office – **Serpost**, Luzuriaga 702, ☎ 42-1030. Mon-Sat 8 am-8 pm.

Banks – **BCP**, Luzuriaga 691, ☎ 72-1692. ATM. **BancoWiese**, Sucre 760, ☎ 72-1500. ATM.

Police – **Comisaria de Huaraz**, Sucre block 2, ☎ 721-330, open 24-hours.

Hospitals – **Victor Ramos Guardia Hospital**, Luzuriaga Block 8, ☎ 421-290. Open 24-hours. **San Pablo Clinic**, Huaylas 172, ☎ 428-811. Open 24-hours.

Laundry – **Lavandería Dennys**, La Mar 561, ☎ 429-232, www.dennysperu.com. 8 am-9 pm.

Sightseeing

The main street, **Calle Luzuriaga**, includes restaurants, tour operators and agencies, banks and the post office. It runs into the **Plaza de Armas**,

Huaraz

which was completely destroyed in the earthquake, but has been partially rebuilt, as has the **Cathedral**.

The **Museo Regional de Ancash** (Luzuriaga 762, ☎ 42-1551) is the one museum here. It isn't huge, nor does it have many exhibits, but there are some fascinating items on display if you are interested in the history of the area. Stone monoliths from the Wari and Recuay cultures are displayed in a small garden. There are also a few mummies and photos of old Huaraz before the earthquake. Open Mon-Sat 9 am-5 pm and Sun 9 am-2 pm. Admission 5 soles.

Jirón José Olaya in the east of town is the last remaining street from old Huaraz. On Sundays, it becomes popular with people selling regional foods, proving that the old Andean character survives.

For the best views of the city and its surroundings, head to the eastern side of the city and the **Mirador Rataquenua**. There are great panoramas here of the northern Cordillera Blanca. The hike there is seven km/4.2 miles and it takes less than an hour. There have been recent reports of thefts and holdups, so do not go alone. To get there, you must turn left on the road past the cemetery, at the end of Luzuriaga, and head uphill. It is also possible to go by car. This is a good first-day hike to help speed up acclimatization.

Wari stonework at Wilcahuain

Huaraz

Av. CONFRATERNIDAD OESTE
Av. CONFRATERNIDAD ESTE
HUAYIAS PALLASCA
Av. CENTENARIO
GUSMAN NAVARRO
CORONGO
MARIANO MELGAR
AUGUSTO B. LEGUIA
Av. CONFRATERNIDAD ESTE
CANDELARIA VILLAR JIRON
GONZALES DE FANNING
JIRON
CARHUAS
BARRONES
DANIEL VILLAIZAN
VICTOR VELEZ
JIRON
SEBASTIÁN DE ALISTE
JIRON MANCO CAPAC
TO EL PINAR
RIO QUILCAY
HUASCARAN
HUALCAN
SAN CRISTOBAL
Av. FITZCARRALD
COMERCIO
JIRÓN 13 DE DICIEMBRE
JIRÓN CARAZ
LAS AMERICAS
AVENIDA RAYMONDI
AVENIDA RAYMONDI
TO PITEC
STADIUM
Av. 27 DE NOVIEMBRE (TARAPACA)
MERCADO
DE LA CRUZ ROMERO
AVENIDA LUZURIAGA
JIRON LACAR
Av. GAMARRA
Iglesia San Francisco
Ministerio de Agricultura
JIRON ITALIA
TO CASMA
LEONIZA ESCANO
JOSE DE SAN MARTIN
JULIAN DE MORALES
ALAMEDA GRAU
Av. CONFRATERNIDAD ESTE
OLAYA
GERRO PUMACAYAN
SOLEDAD
LA ROSA
JOSE SIMON
DE SUCRE
E. PALACIOS
AMADEO FIGUEROA
Av. 27 DE NOVIEMBRE
28 DE JULIO
EULOGIO DEL RIO
ARGUEDAS
AGUSTIN LOLI
DE LA CRUZ ROMERO
GABINO URIBE
Av. GAMARRA
28 DE JULIO
M. VILLANUEVA
RAMON CASTILLA
Iglesia La Soledad
JOSE DE SAN MARTIN
BOLIVAR
D. ANTUNES
C. VALENZUELA
Iglesia Belén
F. SAL Y ROSAS
A. SORIANO
E. OLIVAS
Av. ATUSPARIA
P. COCHACHIN
TO RATAQUENUA
RIO SANTA
TO LIMA
Av. VILLON
Santa Rosa School

1. Linea
2. Yungay Express
3. Jirón Jose Olaya
4. Hotel del Valle
5. The Way Inn
6. Santa Victoria
7. Flor de Canela
8. Bar Strip
9. Craft markets on the plaza:
   The Centro Artesanal Callejon de Huayias and the Feria Artesanal

© 2006 HUNTER PUBLISHING, INC

The **Wari Ruins**, or the **Monumento Arqueológico de Wilcahuain**, are also about seven km from Huaraz. The central stone temple is three levels high, and each level contains seven rooms. It is thought to be a mausoleum that once housed mummy bundles. The complex dates back to 600-900 AD. To get here you can go by taxi (8-10 soles) or hop aboard a combi near the river. Open during daylight hours. Admission 5 soles.

It seems that wherever there are back-breaking, ligament-pulling sports being done in Peru, there is at least one thermal bath in the area? The **hot springs** closest to Huaraz are in the town of Monterrey, six km/3.6 miles north of Huaraz. There are two brownish-colored pools here. They don't look as appealing as you may have expected, but once you get in and feel that hot water, your bones and muscles will thank you. You can get here by cab (5 soles) or by taking the green and white buses in town (1 sole). It is also possible to walk here from the Wari ruins. Open Tues-Sun, 8 am-6 pm. Admission 3 soles.

Where to Stay

Andino Club Hotel – Cochachin 357, ☎ 721-662, www.hotelandino.com. Has the essence of a Swiss chalet. Most of the 41 rooms have terraces with good views of the Cordillera Blanca. The rooms are cozy, with private baths, hot water, cable TV, and are decorated in a modern style with Andean art and décor. Some rooms are equipped with saunas, Jacuzzis and

Andino Club Hotel

fireplaces. The hotel has all business and tourist amenities and will help arrange treks and equipment rentals. It is a favorite of serious climbers and trekkers. $$$$

★**Olaza's** – Arguedas 1274, ☎ 422-529, www.andean-explorer.com/olaza. Rooms are a great value and have hot

water. Only four years old
and well kept. Everything
looks sparkling new. Rooftop terrace has stunning
views of the city and
nearby mountains. Break-
fast, included with the
price, is served there. Also
a cable TV room. The
owner, Tito, can help

Olaza's

arrange tours and is a wealth of information on the area. $$

Churup Albergue – Figueroa 1257, ☎ 4372-2584, www.
churup.com. Charming family-run establishment. A total of
16 rooms, most built in the past year. Almost all of the private
rooms have hot-water baths and new mattresses. Dormitories
are a great value. Other extras include: a book exchange,
Spanish lessons, and laundry service. There are even three
living rooms with fireplaces. $$

La Casa de Zarela – Aruedas 1263, ☎ 348-7883, 421-694,
www.lacasadezarela.com. Has a terrace with BBQ and hammocks, a restaurant with pancakes and burritos and other
backpacker grub, plus its own tearoom. The list goes on and
on. Guest rooms have hot private showers. There is also a
lounge with cable TV and climbing movies to watch. Lots of
climbing information and area info, which many climbers
make use of. $$

San Sebastian – Italia
1124, ☎ 726-960, www.
huaraz.org/sansebas-
tian. This is a beautiful
Colonial-style building
with 20 rooms. The
rooms are uninterest-
ing, but they have writ-
ing desks and hot
showers. The garden
and courtyard make up

San Sebastian

for any shortcomings. The balconied rooms and rooftop ter-
race offer stunning views of the mountains. $$$

Hotel Del Valle – ☎ 432-299, Loreto 780, www.hoteldelvalle. com. The style could be called Grandma's house, with lace curtains and stiff beds. As Grandma would expect, cleanliness is a top priority. Private baths and cable TV are also included. $$$

★**The Way Inn** – Mendoza 821, ☎ 42-8714, www.thewayinn. com. I have never seen a bigger buzz over a backpacker hostel than this. From Colombia to Chile, you will find flyers posted on different bulletin boards by satisfied guests. There is a communal kitchen, communal terrace, communal laundry machine, and communal lounge. Perhaps it is the emphasis on the community that makes this place so well loved? There is also an outdoor bar. Three dorms and four private rooms. Everything is new and clean, with an eclectic mountain spirit to it. Highly recommended. $

The Way Inn Lagoon Bungalow

★★**The Way Inn Lodge** – Located past Llupa on the Pitec-bound road, 15 km/nine miles from Huaraz, www. thewayinn.com. This lodge is so high in the mountains and away from civilization that they had to put in their own septic tank, plumbing, electricity, and water filtration. It is a very desolate spot, but there are great views of the mountains and the natural world. The fine stonework here would have made the Incas proud. Camping is available on grassy terraces and bungalows make up the rest of the accommodations, one of which is partly in a cave. On-site bar, lounge, and restaurant serving an international menu, borderline English pub grub. Much of the food is grown right at the lodge. Breakfast is included. Make arrangements for visiting before showing up. They will help you get there. Can also arrange a variety of hikes and adventure activities. Highly recommended. $-$$$

El Tumi – San Martín 1121, ☎ 421-784, www.hoteleltumi. com. The rooms are older, but clean and well kept, with hot water and cable TV. Cozy. A good restaurant with steaks, pastas, and pizzas. $$

Mi Casa B&B – 27 de Noviembre 773, ☎ 423-375, www. andeanexplorer.com/micasa. The place is family-style, serving local-style food. Owner Alcides is an experienced climber and a professional glaciologist. Rooms are basic and outdated, but have hot-water baths. $$

Edward's Inn – Bolognesi 121, ☎ 722-692, edwardsinn@ terra.com.pe. This is a long-time gringo budget option. Rooms are fairly basic, but are warm and have private baths. The water is solar-powered, so is rarely as hot as you would like. Gear is rented and the owner can provide information on treks and climbs in the area. $$

Santa Victoria – Gamarra 690, ☎ 72-2422, fax 72-4870. This faded green Art Deco building makes you think you are in Los Angeles in the 70s. Rooms, as you can imagine, are outdated, but are spacious and have hot water and cable TV. $$

There are also two good options in nearby Monterrey, both in older Colonial-style buildings that make use of their country locations. These are **Real Hotel Baños Termales Monterrey** (☎ 72-7690, $$$) and **El Patio** (☎ 72-4965, elpatio@terra.com.pe, $$$).

GASTRONOMY

Picante de cuy – Guinea pig served in a spicy sauce with potatoes.

Cuchicanca – Tender pork marinated in vinegar and roasted. Served with boiled potatoes and corn.

Cebiche de pato – Raw slices of duck marinated in orange and lime juice.

Pachamanca – Chicken, beef, and pork and sometimes guinea pig are cooked underground with oca, sweet potatoes, and other vegetables.

Pecan caldo – Broth based on lamb's head, tripe or innards, legs, with mint.

Cordillera Blanca

Where to Eat

★**Crêperie Patrick** – Luzuriaga 422, ☎ 426-037. Cebiche de pato (duck ceviche), alpaca, cuy, huge filled crêpes (sweet and savory), pastas, regional and national dishes, fondues, raclettes, and more. One of the best fine-dining options in town and modestly priced. $$$

Siam de los Andes – Morales and Gamarra. Everything down to the door handles has been imported from the Far East to create an authentic ambiance, although you pay for it. The Thai chef has several excellent curry creations. Also has tom yum soup and good stir-fries. This is probably the best Thai restaurant in the country. $$$$

Bistro de los Andes – Morales 823. Lunch and dinner are a mix of French and Peruvian cuisine. Several good trout and vegetarian dishes. The café/restaurant opens at 5 am for breakfast. Good coffee. $$$

El Salon del Encuentro – Gamarra 790, ☎ 42-6865, and in the Parque del Periodista, ☎ 427-971. Pizzas, pastas, crêpes and good Peruvian dishes too. Friendly service with attention to detail. Also has another restaurant in town at the Parque de Periodisto. $$$

Pachamama – San Martín 687, ☎ 421-834. The glass roof and abundance of plant life gives it a special atmosphere. The food is Peruvian with a French twist. Has a live folk music show on some nights, and dancing as well. There is a giant chessboard on the floor if you want to make a move. $$$

★**Café Andino** – Lucar and Torre 530 (3rd floor), ☎ 421-203, www.cafeandino.com. Good magazine selection and book exchange. Huge fireplace. Couches. Very cozy. One of the best tea selections in Peru. Sells organic Peruvian coffee to take home as well as to enjoy inside. Food and pastries too. Highly recommended. $$

Monte-Rosa/Inka Pub – La Mar 691, ☎ 421-447, www.huaraz.com/monterosa. Great pastas and pizzas. Also has fondue and raclette. Argentine beef. Recommended if you need to replenish your carbs. Sells Victorianox knives and rents/sells mountain gear as well. $$$

California Café – 28 de Julio 562. This place is famous for its all-day North American breakfast and fresh-roasted coffee. Has a free book exchange. $$

Flor de Canela – Luzuriaga 104, ☎ 72-7154. A very lovely restaurant at the corner of Plaza Belén. The dishes are served up by two northern Peruvian women who specialize in northern cuisine. $$$

Chili Heaven – San Martín 687. Chili, burgers, tacos, burritos, and curries. 'Nuff said. $$

El Horno Pizzeria/Café and **El Horno Grill** – In the Parque del Periodista. The same owner runs these two restaurants. One is a pizzeria with a wood-burning oven. The other is a grill that serves a variety of Argentine beef. $$$

Many burger stands set up in the streets near the bar strip. Sex burger is recommended.

Groceries

Comercial Anali – At the eastern end of the central market. Has a variety of foods that you can take on a hike such as sausages, canned goods, cookies, cereals, etc.

Bars & Clubs

 ★**Makondo's** – La Mar 812. This huge cabin-like structure stands out from the rest of the bar strip and usually packs in the late-night crowd. There is a very long winding bar and large dance floor, with a variety of rock and Latin pop hits playing. The top terrace, Los 13 Buhos (The 13 Owls), is a laid-back lounge with good music and a mostly gringo crowd. There is sometimes a cover after a certain time, but usually no more than 10 soles.

El Tambo – La Mar 776. Tied with Makondo as the best dance club in Huaraz, and it is just across the street. There are a few side-tables, but nearly the entire space is dedicated to young locals and foreigners mixing it up on the dance floor. This place is legendary on the Huaraz nightclub scene. Cover ranges from 10 to 20 soles.

Monttrek Pub – Luzuriaga 646. Has a free indoor climbing wall and sells and displays topographical maps of the area, in case you want to talk up your trek over a beer. Serves pizzas,

Cordillera Blanca

pastas, and salads as well. Owned by the Monttrek tour company (www.monttrek.com).

X-Treme – Luzurriaga and Uribe, ☎ 68-2115. Rock and blues music fill the air at this trashy 2nd-floor dive, popular with the backpacker crowd. Increasingly graffiti-filled walls and strong cocktails keep the party flowing.

There are about a dozen bars next to each other around the corner of La Mar and Bolivar. All are fairly small and are crowded late at night on most weekends. There is sometimes live music in some, but little room to dance. Each has a different atmosphere. My advice is to keep popping in until you find one that you like. Moncho Pub/Bar, Anarkia, Waras, and Tupakusi Pub are recommended.

Shopping

Craft Market

There are two craft markets on the Plaza: the **Centro Artesanal Callejón de Huaylas** and the **Feria Artesanal**. Both have similar products, much of it alpaca knit.

Andean Expressions – Arguedas 1246 (beside Olaza's B&B). High quality shirts with Andean designs.

Language Schools

Sierra Verde – Lucar and Torre 538, ☎ 427-954, sierraverde_ls@hotmail.com. Group and individual classes, flexible schedules.

Centro Holistico – Villon 756, ☎ 428-277. Appointments necessary. Massages, physiotherapy, reflex therapy, shiatsu, reiki, marine mud baths and every other spa service you could think of in a mountain town. Very professional and an excellent way to refresh and rehabilitate after a long trek or difficult climb.

Festivals

Carnaval (February). This festival is quite lively here. The most noticeable variation from other places are the games with water, flour, and various other harmless party favors. Generally, you throw water or other things at members of the opposite sex whom you consider attractive.

Semana Santa (April). Easter week in Huaraz is lively, as it is in most Andean villages. The week begins with the entrance of the Señor de Ramos mounted on a burro and each day has a variety of processions. Among the most interesting features are the carpets made from different flowers, such as Flor de Retama, and colored woodchips. They are made in the main streets and show images related to the life, passion, and death of Jesus.

Semana Andinismo (June). This international festival for outdoor sports includes a skiing and snowboarding competition at Pastoruri and Punta Olimpica, a mountain biking competition near Huaraz, as well as rafting, rock climbing, and several other competitions throughout the region.

Tour Companies

★**Peruvian Andes Adventures** – Olaya 532, ☎ 721-864, www.peruvianandes.com. This is one of the best trekking and climbing operators in Huaraz and in all of Peru. It is run by the well-known Morales family. They speak English and are some of the most experienced climbers and trekkers in the area. This are not the cheapest place by any means, but their service is unparalleled and they give the kind of reassurance you want when attempting dangerous treks and climbs. They offer guidance in climbing the highest peaks, such as Huascarán and Alpamayo, as well as popular treks like Santa Cruz, and even day-hikes. Highly recommended.

★**Mountain Bike Adventures** – Torre 530, ☎ 724-259, www.chakinaniperu.com. Owned and run Julio Olaza, who helped pioneer the sport in the region. They rent Trek USA 850 bikes with front suspension, although they don't mind if you bring your own. They offer trips from one day, such as the one in the Cordillera Negra, up to 12 days.

SIEX Sifuentes Expeditions – Huaylas 135, ☎ 426-529, www.sifuentes.biz. This company leads treks to all mountains in the area.

Monttrek – Luzuriaga 646, ☎ 72-1124, www.monttrek.com. This is a good all-around tour operator that can arrange treks, rafting, horseback riding, climbing, and paragliding.

Skyline Adventure School – ☎ 427-097, www.sladventure-school.com. Only operates from May to September. Most of their trips are for serious climbers and trekkers who want to cover some significant ground or scale a high or very technical peak. Some trips may last as much as three weeks. Different trips are offered on different dates so you are more likely to gather a group together. They also offer three-day mountaineering classes and wilderness rescue courses with English instruction.

Discovery Peru – Luzuriaga 834, Huaraz, ☎ 725-689, www.discoveryperu.com. Specialists in climbing in the Cordillera Huayhuash and Cordillera Blanca. Run by a Frenchman named Bruno. Offers climbing courses (beginners, intermediate and advanced) as well as climbs of all major peaks.

Peru Llama Trek – Loli 463, ☎ 997-3405, www.perullamatrek.com.pe. Organizes community- and cultural-based llama treks in the area.

Two for Fly – ☎ 954-6845, twoforfly@gmail.com. Specialists in paragliding.

Aventura Quechua – Sucre 765 #4, ☎ 978-6331, aventuraquechua@hotmail.com. This company runs basic day tours in the area such as to Chavín and some of the more popular treks.

Day-Trips from Huaraz

Chavín de Huantar

For those with less time to spend, there are a variety of day-trips that are well worth your time.

The most visited Pre-Columbian site in the area is without doubt ★**Chavín de Huantar**. The site is less than a km north of the town of Chavín, which is a pleasant small Andean town with many craft shops, country restaurants, a few basic hotels, and an attractive plaza.

It is the best-preserved ruin from the Chavín culture, which thrived from around 1200-300 BC. They were a major force along the Andean range and parts of the coast, with influence spreading from Ecuador to the south. They were not conquerors in the traditional sense, but spread their cultural and artistic influence. The period of expansion is known as the Chavín Horizon or Early Horizon.

The 3,000-year-old Chavín, named a UNESCO World Heritage Site, is built around a depressed square with perfect right angle corners. This is thought to have been a ceremonial gathering place and the center of a feline worshipping cult. An intricately carved archway fronts the main temple, sometimes called the Castillo. There are several tunnels and chambers through the temple, which are now lit. El Lanzón de Chavín, a famous white granite, dagger-like monolithic sculpture that stands 4½ m/15 feet tall, can be found in a passageway behind the main temple. The carving depicts images of the serpent, the bird, and the feline, which were three important deities to the Chavíns. This temple was once dotted with many cabezas clavas, or carved heads that were stuck into the sides of the temple like daggers. There is just one remaining at the rear of the temple. The complex has several other stone constructions, terraces, and stairways. A small museum has a few interesting pieces found at the site.

Getting to Chavín is most often done via a tour from Huaraz that will stop for lunch and at a few scenic stops on the way such as Laguna Querococha (20-30 soles per person). You can come by bus with Chavín Express, which has a daily departure each morning. The trip takes three hours each way. Allow about two hours at the site and for lunch. Open 8 am-4 pm. Admission 10 soles.

★**Llagonacu** are sparkling, glacier-fed turquoise lakes about 50 km/30 miles north of Huaraz, and 28 km/17 miles east of Yungay. On a clear day you'll get incredible views of the beautiful Cordillera Blanca peaks, including Chopicalqui (6,354 m/20,841 feet), Huandoy

Llagonuco lake

Cordillera Blanca

(6,395 m/20,975 feet) and the twin peaks of Huascarán (6,768 m/22,297 feet and 6,655 m/21,828 feet). You can get here from Yungay by bus or taxi ($6 each way). Many tour companies offer this trip as a way to get acclimatized (about $25 per person). To get there and back from Huaraz will take about four hours.

The ★**Pastoruri Glacier**, 57 km/34 miles south of Huaraz, is one of the best day-trips in the area if you want to encounter extreme conditions and locations without great effort. You can literally walk on the glacier and get your feet wet in the snow. It sits at 5,240 m/17,187 feet, so the conditions are fairly rough and snow falls on most afternoons. Horses are there to carry tourists to the glacier from the car if they are very lazy. The trip there by car passes beautiful green valleys at Pachacoto, also the home of the puya raimondii, one of the world's largest flowers. There are some other interesting stops along the way, such as painted caves and underground springs.

THE PUYA RAIMONDII

These huge plants are the largest of the bromeliad family (same family as the pineapple). It is thought to be one of the oldest in the world and only grows in a few isolated places in the Andes. The plant may grow to 12 m/39 feet high and flowers just once in a lifetime, which can be 100 years. It saves all its energy for that one achievement, its life's work.

★★★Parque Nacional Huascarán

A UNESCO Biosphere Reserve and World Heritage Trust Site, the 840,000-acre Parque Nacional Huascarán holds nearly the entire Cordillera Blanca. Besides the highest mountains in the Americas, there are rare flora and fauna, archeological sites that date back millennia, glaciers, lagoons, almost 300 lakes, and more than 40 rivers. Wildlife in the park consists of condors, white tailed deer, guemals, pumas, vicuñas, and foxes. People still

Huascarán

live within the boundaries of the park, most in small mountain villages that have remained untouched by the outside world for centuries.

It was established in 1975 as more and more international visitors began to notice the area's potential for outdoor adventures. The fees are $2 per person per day, and $20 for a multiday pass. You will need to carry a copy of your passport with you. The fee can be paid at any of the stations: Llaganuco, Pastoruri Glacier, or Musho. The fees go toward trail maintenance and to pay park rangers. It is illegal to use off-road vehicles in the park or to hunt.

Equipment Rentals

If you need to rent or buy equipment such as tents, sleeping bags, packs, climbing gear, bikes, or you just need a gas refill for your stove, try either of the following. You can ask them about hiring a guide as well.

Galaxia Mountain Shop – Lescano 603, ☎ 722-792.

MountClimb – Cáceres 421, ☎ 726-060.

Private Guides

If you don't want to take a trek with a tour company, you might consider hiring an independent guide. It is possible to arrange for a single mule driver on up to a full-scale mountaineering expedition with cooks, guides, mules, etc. Each are paid by the day and prices vary, depending on the service and experience. For example, guides run anywhere from $50-$100

per day, mule drivers about $12 per day, and the mules them-
selves average $5 per day. The **Casa de Guias** (see page 417)
is also the headquarters of the mountain guide association of
Peru. It has a list of certified guides and can help determine
what you need for your journey.

Whether you go with an agency, with a private guide, or on
your own, you need to take every precaution. These are very
serious mountains, and the inexperienced should not tackle
them without the help of a professional. Many have died on
the peaks here and many more are seriously injured. Good
maps, safe equipment, and experience in getting out of a dangerous situation are all essential.

ETHICAL TREKKING

■ Use existing campsites.

■ If you carried it in, you can carry it out.

■ Bury "toilets" at least six inches deep and away
from water.

■ Leave plants and stones untouched and unturned.

■ Observe wildlife from a distance.

■ Do not burn wood, paper, or plastic.

Adventures

On Foot
Trekking

 The ★★★**Llaganuco-Santa Cruz** trek is the
most popular in the Cordillera Blanca. It combines
brilliant mountain scenery such as snow-capped
peaks, turquoise lakes and green, flower-filled
meadows. The four- to five-day hike covers roughly 45 km/27
miles with an altitude ranging from 3,000-4,800 m/9,800-
15,700 feet. Due to the popularity of this hike, there are facilities such as campsites and toilets at several spots. The trip
begins at Cashapampa and ends in Vaqueria. Both locations
can be reached by bus within a few hours of Huaraz and the
trail can also be done in reverse as well. The difficulty is moderate. April-October.

The **Olleros to Chavín** walk is a community-based trek using llamas that traces the pilgrimage route to Chavín. The area's peasant farmers actually proposed this idea, hoping to preserve some of their traditions and

Nevado Alpamayo - El Piramide

customs. Art, music, food and medicinal plants of the local people are examined on the four-day walk. The route starts in the small town of Olleros, 30 km/18 miles south of Huaraz. During four days of walking (37 km/22 miles) you will encounter views of Shaqsha (5,703 m/18,705 feet), Cashan (5,686 m/18,650 feet) and Tuctupunta (5,343 m/17,525 feet). You will also visit small, isolated mountain communities such as Shongo and Nunupata, along with the huacas and ruins that are near them. The trek ends at the archeological site of Chavín.

Other good walks in the area include:

Santa Cruz-Yaino – six days, 55 km/33 miles.

Honda-Ulta – eight-nine days, 91 km/55 miles.

Los Cedros-Alpamayo – eight-nine days, 92 kms/55 miles.

Laguna Jahuacocha – five days, 68 km/41 miles.

The **Cordillera Huayhuash** is even more pristine than the other mountain ranges and less explored. Due to problems with terrorism in years past trekkers avoided this area 50 km/30 miles southeast of the Cordillera Blanca. They are returning now, and the 165-km/99-mile circuit is becoming a more and more common trek. The trek usually takes 10 days and goes over five high passes. There are rare birds, turquoise glacier lakes, and panoramic views of these dazzling mountains. There are more than a dozen peaks in the range, the highest being Yerupaja at 6,634 m/21,760 feet. There are also two main circuits that begin and end in Chiquian. One is a large circuit of the range at 20 km/12 miles and another is 40 km/24 miles and heads to Laguna Jahuacocha.

Climbing

Rock Climbing

Rock climbing and climbing overall here is growing in popularity, with new areas being explored all of the time. The best climbs can be found at Huanchac, Monterrey, the Rurec Valley, and the Torre de Paron, aka the Sphinx. You can find full-day rock climbing tours, ranging from easy to moderate difficulty, for about $20 per person, including full gear, guides, and transportation to and from.

Ice Climbing

As exotic as this sport may sound, it is quite common in the area. For scaling many of the snow-capped peaks it is the only option. Ice climbing is highly technical; good guides and equipment are essential. Thus it is one of the more expensive adventure options in the area. Easy access to base camps sets the Huaraz area apart from the world's other major trekking areas. **Pony's Expeditions** and **Peruvian Andes Adventures** (see page 427) have experience organizing climbs to Pisco, Huascarán, Alpamayo, Chopicalqui, Artesonraju, and others. Alpamayo is thought to be one of the most beautiful mountains in the world and is one of the best climbs.

On Wheels

Cycling

There are many cycling options within the confines of the park. Most can be done in a day, but there are a few for serious bikers that offer an experience of a lifetime. A seven-day trip that is frequently completed visits **Querococha, Chavín, Los Conchucos,** and **Llanganuco**. This circuit within the Cordillera Blanca rises and falls, visits the ruins at Chavín de Huántar, climbs the Portachuelo de Llaganuco pass, and descends to the Llaganuco lakes. Stunning views of a handful of tall peaks are quite common on this trip. The journey ends in Yungay.

On Water
River-Rafting/Kayaking

 The best river-rafting in the area takes place on the Santa River, which originates from Lake Conococha and ends in the Pacific. The best section is between Jangas and Caraz.

Fishing

With several hundred pristine mountain lakes in the area, you could imagine that fishing would be a high priority. The sport is allowed in the park from June to August, but you may not fish with nets or explosives. Catches that are below 25 cm/9.75 inches in length must be released.

In the Air
Paragliding/Hangliding

 The flights in this area tend to rely on thermals, which make it possible to fly as far as 80 km/48 miles and reach altitudes of 6,000 m/20,000 feet.

On Skis

 There are no ski resorts here. There is snow, but if you would like to ski it involves a bit of hiking with your equipment on your back. The most accessible location is the Pastoruri Glacier, which is mostly beginner to moderate difficulty. If you want extreme, try some of the slopes on Huascarán, Hualcan, and Copa. You probably won't be able to find ski equipment in Huaraz, so you'll have to bring your own equipment.

■ Carhuaz

This is known by people in Huaraz as an emborracheria, or a place where everyone is drunk. Regardless, the small town of about 7,000 at 2,650 m/8,692 feet is worth going to and making up your own mind. It serves as a good base for treks and is most popularly known as the starting point for trips into the Ulta Valley. The path crosses the Cordillera Blanca at Punta Olimpica (4,950 m/16,236 feet). It will lead to the eastern side of the range and to towns such as Chacas, Huari, and Chavín to the south and Piscobamba and Pomobamba to the north.

Getting Here

 Frequent combis run to Yungay, Carhuaz, and Huaraz (one hour) from the Plaza de Armas.

Where to Stay

 The best hotel is **Hostal El Abuelo** – 9 de Diciembre 257, ☎ 79-4456, hostalelabualo@terra. com.pe. It has cozy, clean rooms with hot-water showers. Breakfast is included. $$

Other than that there are just a few basic hotels that cost roughly 15 soles per person. Don't expect hot water. Restaurants are basic and none are particularly recommended.

■ Yungay

Yungay (2,537 m/8,321 feet, population 10,000) was the site of one of the most tragic natural disasters in all of the Americas. The old city was absolutely swallowed on May 31st, 1970 by a huge avalanche from the western face of Huascarán North, made up of mud, rock, and ice. More than 18,000 were buried – virtually the entire town. The site of the old city has been turned into a sanctuary, Campo Santo. A new city has been rebuilt two km to the south. There isn't much here other than a few very basic hotels and restaurants, but it makes a good base if you are planning on trekking from the lakes at Llaganuco.

Getting Here

 Combis between Caraz and Huaraz pass the Plaza and the old city frequently.

Sights

 ★**Campos Santo**, or Old Yungay, is the sanctuary that has been built over where the old town once sat. Thousands are buried beneath the ground where you walk. You can see some remains of the old town such as the very top of the cathedral and four palm trees that sat on the Plaza de Armas. There is also a smashed and twisted bus that shows just how powerful this alluvion was here. As with other sites in the world where disasters have taken place, tragedy has been replaced by an air of peacefulness. There are many serene, flower-filled gardens. A replica of the façade of the cathedral has been built to honor the dead, and a variety of other monuments were erected. The site offers a perfect view of Huascarán. Open 8 am-6 pm. Admission 2 soles.

■ Caraz

Caraz is one of the few places in the area that has not been heavily damaged by earthquakes. With an elevation of 2,256 m/7,400 feet, a milder climate, and a location near the Cordillera Blanca and the famous Santa Cruz trek, it is becoming a great alternative to staying in Huaraz.

This is an ideal location for preparing an multi-day trek or doing some day-hikes and it has many of the same facilities, though not as many. At the time of writing there was not an ATM, but the BCP bank on the Plaza does cash travelers' checks. It is the starting point to get to Laguna Paron, Cashapampa, the Santa Cruz trek, and trips to Alpamayo. A few km northeast are the ruins of **Tunshukaiko**. The pre-Chavín ruins are thought to be a ceremonial center and possibly a fort of some kind.

Getting Here

 Combis run frequently between Huaraz and Caraz (two hours). Yungay Express (see Huaraz) also runs buses between Huaraz and Chimbote that pass through Caraz.

Where to Stay

 Perla de los Andes – On the Plaza, ☎ 79-2007. Décor is simple, but the rooms have cable TV, and hot-water showers. The location can't be beat. $$

Casa Clara de Asis – On the way out of town toward Huaraz, ☎ 392-172. Country-style, with private hot-water baths. $

Hotel Cordillera Blanca

Hostal Tumshukaico – Melgar 114, ☎ 79-2212, tumshukaico@hotmail.com. Five blocks north of town, but one of the best options for quality and overall value. $

Hotel Cordillera Blanca – www.hotelcordillerablanca.com. A basic two-star with hot-water showers and cable TV. Near the market. $$

Where to Eat

Café de Rat – On the Plaza above Pony's Expeditions. As bad as the name makes this place sound, it is actually one of the best places in town. It attracts mostly travelers with its pizzas, sandwiches, coffees, juices, etc. It also has a warm fireplace and you can sit at the windows and look out onto the Plaza. $$

★**La Capullana** – This is a great country-style restaurant just a km or two outside of town to the north. Ask anyone in town for directions. Sometimes there is live music, dancing and other festivities. They have a large dining area, but the best spot for lunch is on the island in the middle of the small duck pond. You can borrow a canoe and paddle around if you wish. The food is typical of the area and they make a mean cuy. Highly recommended. $$

Tour Agencies

Pony's Expeditions – ☎ 791-642, ☎ 682-848, www.ponyexpeditions.com. A good place to arrange a tour in the area, rent equipment, get guides, mules or buy books, maps, and fuel for cooking stoves.

■ Cajamarca

Phone code (076)

Imagine Wisconsin, but with a charming Colonial capital, an incredible history, and access to stunning ancient sites. This is Cajamarca. The green hills

IN THIS CHAPTER	
■ Cajamarca	439
■ Chachapoyas	456
■ Huancabamba	463

and blue skies that surround the city (population 95,000, 2,750 m/9,020 feet) have made it a country destination for the ages. It is one of the most pleasant Colonial towns in all of Peru and many prefer it to Cuzco. Little remains of the city's Incan foundations, but the Colonial monuments are there and UNESCO has made it a World Heritage Site.

The surrounding area has a wealth of interesting sites, most reachable via day-trips from the city. It is Peru's center for cheese-making, home to a number of regional delicacies, a vibrant carnaval, and a thriving traditional culture. The locals, mostly farmers and artisans, dress in colorful ponchos, straw hats and sandals.

The recently discovered Yanacocha gold mine (www.yanacocha.com.pe), one of the most productive on the continent, has brought a wealth of new investment and prosperity to the area.

HIGHLIGHTS

■ **Baños del Inca** – The almost boiling-hot baths are where the Inca Atahualpa once bathed are now a huge complex for relaxation.

■ **La Collpa and Tres Molina** – Cheese tasting, cows that come when called; what more could you ask for?

■ **Kuélap** – The remote citadel shrouded in mist and mystery may become the next Machu Picchu.

■ **Stove Trek** – Hike an Inca highway and help local families sustain themselves on this five-day trek.

■ **Huancabamba** – Cure what ails you in Peru's center for sorcery.

Northern Highlands Overview

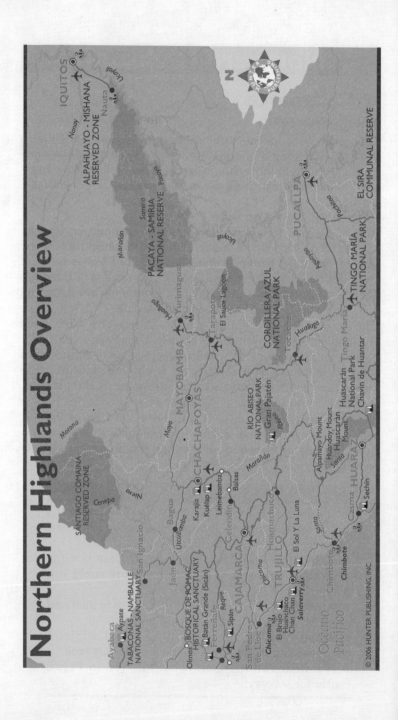

© 2006 HUNTER PUBLISHING, INC.

History

Atahualpa

With a brilliant stroke of luck, good timing and a little force, perhaps the most important incident in Peruvian history and one of the most important in world history occurred in Cajamarca on November 16th, 1532. The moment would forever change the path of the nation, of the Incas, and of the Spanish.

Atahualpa, en route to Cuzco after defeating his brother Huáscar in the north during the Inca civil war, stopped in Cajamarca to rest at the Baños del Inca. The war was a brutal one. The troops were weary and deflated and the power of the Incan Empire as a whole was weakened greatly. At the exact same time, by coincidence, Francisco Pizarro and a few hundred men and horses arrived on the coast. They learned of the Inca's presence here and quickly set up a meeting. This small band of soldiers would drastically change the course of Peruvian history. The Spaniards came to the city on the 15th and found it mostly deserted, as much of the town had accompanied Atahualpa to the thermal baths. The Spaniards were told to stay in the kallankas (halls) surrounding the Plaza and the Atahualpa would meet them the following day. There were 50,000-80,000 troops in the area; nevertheless, the Spaniards made plans for a surprise attack. At a signal, the Spanish troops would come into the Plaza on horses and capture the Inca if the opportunity presented itself. Otherwise, they would become friends and make later arrangements.

Atahualpa and some 6,000 armed troops entered the Plaza in the early evening. The Spanish claim that when friar Vicente de Valverde presented Atahualpa with a bible he quickly threw it to the ground. This would be the excuse they needed to attack. Canons were quickly fired and the cavalry stunned the Indians, who had never seen anything like it before. The Indians barely fought back and by the end of the night more than 7,000 lay slaughtered. Atahualpa was held prisoner in the Cuarto de Rescate, the last Inca building still standing in Cajamarca.

The Spanish success was far beyond their wildest dreams. Atahualpa said that in exchange for his release he would fill the room he was held in twice over in silver and once in gold. Gold and silver made their way to Cajamarca and in 1533 the ransom was complete. Atahualpa was still not released.

 The gold and silver bullion given for the intended release Atahualpa was carefully weighed and measured. There was 26,000 lbs of silver and 13,000 lbs of gold, which today would be valued at around $60 million.

Diego de Almagro brought reinforcements from the coast, which doubled the forces at Cajamarca. Atahualpa sent messages to Quito to arrange for his escape. The Spaniards learned of this and, without a formal trial, executed him on July 26, 1533 in the main Plaza. Before marching to Cuzco to take full control of the empire, the Spanish made the younger brother of Huáscar, Tupac Huallpa, their puppet Inca. The people of Cuzco, still loyal to Huáscar, would then hail the Spanish as liberators rather than invaders. This was the beginning of the end for the great Inca Empire.

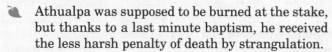 Athualpa was supposed to be burned at the stake, but thanks to a last minute baptism, he received the less harsh penalty of death by strangulation.

Getting Here

Air

 Aeropuerto Armando Revoredo Iglesias – On the highway to Otuzco, Km 3, ☎ 82-2523.

Aero Cóndor (www.aerocondor.com.pe) and **LC Busre** (www.lcbusre.com.pe) have daily flights to Lima. A cab ride there from the center will be no more than 5 soles.

Bus

 There is no central terminal in Cajamarca; but most terminals are clumped together around the third block of Atahualpa, a 3- to 5-sole cab ride or 1.5-km/.

9-mile walk from the center. Most buses head toward the coast to Trujillo (six hours), Chiclayo (six hours), and Lima (12 hours).

Turismo Dias – Sucre 422, ☎ 368-289. Has nice new buses to Chiclayo (15 soles) and Trujillo several times a day. Also to Celendin (five hours); from there you can connect to Chachapoyas.

Linea – Atahualpa 318, ☎ 323-956. Trujillo and Lima.

Ormeño – Evitiamento 750, ☎ 82-4421, www.grupo-ormeno.com.pe. To all coastal destinations.

Cruz del Sur – www.cruzdelsur.com.pe. Same as Ormeño.

Civa – Atahualpa 753, ☎ 82-1460. Morning buses to Lima.

Empresa Atahualpa – Atahualpa 322, ☎ 82-3060. Celendin.

Tourist Information

Regional Tourist Office – In the Complejo de Belén. Mon-Fri 7:30 am-1:30 pm and 3:30-5:30 pm.

Banks – Several on or near the Plaza include **Interbanc**, which has an ATM and Western Union office.

Laundry – **Laundry Dandy**, Puga 545.

Police – Puga no #, ☎ 82-5572. Open 24 hours.

Hospital Regional – Av Urteaga 500, ☎ 82-2414. Open 24 hours.

Post Office – **Serpost**, Puga 778, ☎ 82-4065, open Mon-Sat 8 am-9:15 pm, Sun 8 am-3 pm.

Sightseeing

★**Plaza de Armas** is much smaller than in Inca times, although it sits in more or less the same location. It is the center of all activity here, for locals and tourists alike. Most hotels, restaurants, banks, shops, churches, and tourist agencies are within a couple of blocks. In the center is a fountain that was erected in 1692. On most nights hordes of locals come here to socialize.

The **Catedral**, also known as the Iglesia Matriz Santa Catalina, stands majestically on the west side of the Plaza. The façade is in the Baroque style and made of carved volca-

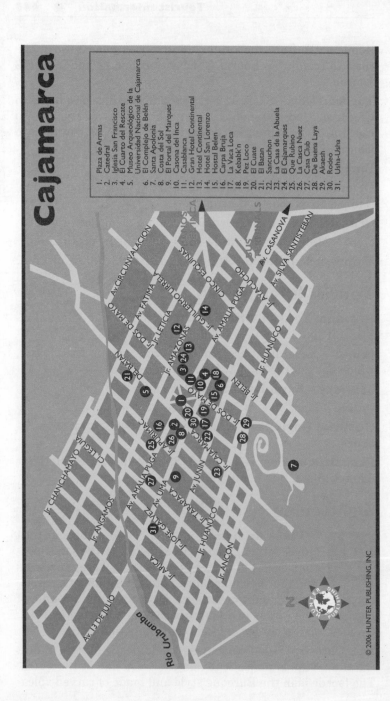

Cajamarca

1. Plaza de Armas
2. Catedral
3. Iglesia San Francisco
4. El Cuarto del Rescate
5. Museo Arqueológico de la Universidad Nacional de Cajamarca
6. El Complejo de Belén
7. Santa Apolonia
8. Costa del Sol
9. El Portal del Marques
10. Casona del Inca
11. Casablanca
12. Gran Hotel Continental
13. Hotel Continental
14. Hotel San Lorenzo
15. Hostal Belen
16. Carpa Bruja
17. La Vaca Loca
18. Kebabk'n
19. Pez Loco
20. El Cuate
21. El Batan
22. Sancuchon
23. La Casa de la Abuela
24. El Cajamarques
25. Que Rubino
26. La Casca Nuez
27. Casa Club
28. De Buena Laya
29. Akaesh
30. Rodeo
31. Usha-Usha

© 2006 HUNTER PUBLISHING, INC

nic stone. Like many other Colonial churches, it lacks a belfry so it could avoid the completion tax imposed by the Spanish crown. Open Mon-Fri 9 am-noon and 4-6 pm.

Iglesia San Francisco, also on the Plaza, is far more impressive. It was originally part of the San Francisco convent. This church is also made from volcanic rock, though the carvings here are more elaborate than on the cathedral. The two towers were completed just a half a century ago, although construction of the rest of the church began in the late 17th century. The **Museo de Arte Colonial** inside has religious paintings and will

Iglesia San Francisco (N. Gill)

also get you a glimpse of the catacombs below the church. **La Sanctuario de la Virgen de Dolores** sits next door. Open Mon-Sat 3-6 pm. Admission 2 soles.

El Cuarto del Rescate

★**El Cuarto del Rescate** (Puga 750) isn't in great condition, but it is worth a look. It really is just a stone room that will take no more than 10 minutes to see, but this is the spot where the Inca Atahualpa was kept prisoner, not the ransom chamber as the name suggests. Atahualpa offered what would amount to two rooms of equal size filled with silver, and another filled with gold in exchange for his release, which never occurred. The room has the trapezoidal niches typical of Incan architecture. It is the only remnant of Incan architecture left in Cajamarca. Open Mon-Sat 9 am-

1 pm and 3-6 pm, Sun 9 am-1 pm. Admission 5 soles (which also includes entrance to Belén and the Museo de Etnografia).

The **Museo Arqueológico de la Universidad Nacional de Cajamarca** (Batán 283, ☎ 821-546), affiliated with the local university, has a nice collection of ceramics, weavings, and other examples of the pre-Inca Cajamarca culture. The museum, where there is a small tourist information booth, also has photographs of the area's principal archaeological sites. Open Mon-Fri 8:30 am-1 pm. Admission 1 sole.

El Complejo de Belén (Belén Block 6) holds a Baroque 18th-century **Bethlemite Chapel** carved out of volcanic rock, two hospitals that are now used by the INC as museums, a stone courtyard, a great bookshop, tourist office, and a terrific coffee shop. The complex was built by the Bethlemite religious order. This is where you will find the **Ethnographical Museum**, which displays local costumes, musical instruments, and various artworks. The carvings on the façade, in the courtyard, and the painted cupola done by highlanders, make the Bethlemite Chapel perhaps the most attractive in Cajamarca. Open Mon-Sat 9 am-1 pm and 3-6 pm, Sun 9 am-1 pm.

Stairs to Mirador at Santa Apolonia
(N. Gill)

The ★**Mirador at Santa Apolonia**, the hill that rises above the south end of the town, affords good views of the city and the green hills that surround it. A small chapel, craft stands, and gardens are here. The pre-Inca altar at the summit is known as the Seat of the Inca. Atahualpa is said to have sat here to review his troops. The altar is believed to have been made during the Chavín period, although, most of the stonework is undeniably Inca. Admission 2 soles. To get there, climb the stairs on Av. Dos de Mayo. There are a few great craft shops on the way up, some with antique furniture or original handicrafts.

Where to Stay

★Costa del Sol – Comercio 773, ☎ 82-2472, www. costadelsolperu. com. This gorgeous brand new modern hotel seems a little out of place in Colonial Cajamarca, but it does bring a type of accommodation that was clearly lacking

Costa del Sol

here. The 72 rooms – including a variety of suites – all have hot-water showers, cable TV, mini-fridges, air-conditioning, and hair dryers. The glass-enclosed dining room looks right out onto the Plaza. There's also a pool, business center, gym, and a casino. $$$

★★Posada del Puruay – Carretera Porcón-Huaygayoc 4.5, ☎ 827-028. This beautiful Colonial mansion sits peacefully in the hills about six km/3.6 miles from the city. Rooms are quite stunning, with lots of woodwork and spotless furniture. Rooms have private hot-water baths, TVs with DVD players (a nice collection of new

Posada del Puruay

films is available to rent), and soft beds. The grounds are equally impressive, with elaborate and well-manicured gardens, access to miles of hiking trails, Paso horses, and trout fishing. The resident sheepdogs are sure to welcome you and may even take you on a short tour. There is an on-site restaurant that is good enough to justify the trip, even if you are not staying at the hotel. Call ahead for reservations. A small bar adjoins the restaurant. $$$$

El Portal del Marqués – Comercio 644, ☎ 828-464, www. portaldelmarques.com. The décor in the rooms is a bit boring and could use some revitalization, but all of the amenities are here. A decent restaurant, business center, casino, and nice garden area make this one of the best budget hotels in the in Cajamarca. $$

Casablanca – Dos de Mayo 446, ☎ 822-141. This hotel right on the Plaza, is next to, and very similar to, Casona del Inca above. Rooms lack views, however. You will find a small chapel in the courtyard out back. $$

Hotel Hacienda San Vicente – On Revolución, one km from the center on Santa Apolonia, ☎ 82-2644, fax 82-1432, hacienda-san-vicente@yahoo.com. The Refugio Ecologico, as they like to call it, has good views of the city from its Santa Apolonia location. Each of the seven rooms is unique, many of them with skylights and some carved right out of stone. The building is quite interesting, with strange combinations of stairs, woodwork, and stone walls that make it feel as if you are in Neverland or Hobbiton. There is also a small. chapel, restaurant, bar, and they have free transport to and from the center. $$

Gran Hotel Continental – Amazonas 781, ☎ 34-1030, fax 36-6640, hotelcontinental@terra.com.pe. Just a block from the center, this business-style hotel has all you could ask for in any hotel, but without the Colonial charm of most of Cajamarca's other lodging options. It also has a good selection of suites – among the best rooms in town. $$$

Hotel Continental – Amazonas 760, ☎ 36-3063, fax 36-3024, hotelcontinental@terra.com.pe. Run by the same owners as the previous hotel and just across the street. It is more or less the same, just a small step down in quality and price. $$

Hotel San Lorenzo – Amazonas 1070, ☎ 822-909, docoforto@yahoo.es. Hot-water showers, cable TV, large rooms and a small café. It's simple and cheap. $

Hostal Belén – Del Comercio 1008, ☎ 830-681. Conveniently located on a corner of the Plaza, this Colonial house has clean, cozy, basic rooms. $

Baños del Inca – At Baños del Inca, ☎ 83-8249. If you plan on spending much of your time at Baños del Inca anyway, these on-site bungalows are a perfect fit. The bungalows come with cable TV, mini-fridges, and have steamy views. $$

★**Laguna Seca** – Manco Cápac 1098, Baños del Inca (six km from the city), ☎ 594-6000, ☎ 82-3149. Reservations in Lima: ☎ 448-5085 (Lima), www.lagunaseca.com.pe/caja_e/cajamarca.htm. This hotel near the Baños del Inca is resort-like and has a quiet country setting. The rooms are equipped with thermal hot-water baths fed by the thermal springs, along with all other amenities if you can find time to leave the large bathtubs. There is an on-site spa, heated pool, and Turkish baths that make good use of the hot water. There are a variety of suites available. They will arrange tours in the area as well, including quick access to horseback riding. $$$$

GASTRONOMY

Caldo verde – A green potato soup spiced with a variety of herbs from the region.

Chicharrón con mote – Fried pieces of pork with steamed corn kernels.

Humitas – Delicious plate prepared with corn that has been milled, when it is creamy; cheese and butter are added, then it is wrapped in corn leaves and boiled.

Cuy con papa – Traditional fried guinea pig served with creamy potatoes.

Cheeses – Tilsit, Edam, Mozzarella, Provolone, Cheddar, Swiss, Dambo, and Mantecoso, among others.

Manjarblanco – Prepared with dairy milk, cinnamon, sugar and potato starch. Also available combined with other flavors such as pineapple and coconut.

Where to Eat

Carpa Bruja – Puga 519, ☎ 34 2844. Hip café with a little bit of LA style. Good for a sandwich, soup, coffee or dessert. 2 for 1 cocktails on most nights. $$

La Vaca Loca – San Martín 320, ☎ 82 8230. Pizzeria with far too cool cow art on the walls. Even cow seat cushions. Calzones and pastas are available too. $$

Kebabk'n – Puga 856. Doner kebabs, falafels, and sandwiches are served at this semi-quick and delicious alternative to fast food. $

Pez Loco – San Martín 333, ☎ 361-806. This trendy restaurant amidst other trendy restaurants serves seafood in the day, and meat at night. $$$

El Cuate – San Martín 345. Probably the best Mexican restaurant outside of Cuzco and Lima. $$$

El Batán – 369 Jr. del Batán, ☎ 826-025. Many consider this Cajamarca's best restaurant. It has an elegant feel but isn't stuffy in the least. The food consists of regional specialties and international dishes, although nothing too exotic or adventurous. There is a pleasant Colonial courtyard, an upstairs art gallery, and live peña music on the weekends. They also have a cheap, three-course lunch menu. $$$

Sancuchon – Junín 1137. At night this sandwich shop becomes a lively bar. $

La Casa de la Abuela – Piedra 671. The name means Grandma's House. It has a uniform country-style décor and cuisine that's a good option for breakfast, lunch, or dinner. And, as always, Grandma's got a sweet tooth. $$

El Cajamarqués – Amazonas 770, ☎ 82-2128. One of Cajamarca's long-standing dining traditions. It's elegant, the food is good and not overly pricey, and the setting is typical Cajamarca Colonial. They also have a charming courtyard filled with exotic birds. $$$

★**Que Rubino** – Puga 589, ☎ 83-0900. This is an excellent and elegant little restaurant and one of my picks for the best in town. Pastas and risottos are paired with grilled meats and seafood (trout and sole). Try the pork chops or filet mignon. The restaurant is bright and clean and so is the food. Ingredients are very fresh and are better quality than most other places here. $$$

La Casca Nuez – Puga 554. Good coffee and desserts lure passersby to this elegant café not far from the Plaza. It has snacks, sandwiches, salads, and at night it's a great spot for a cocktail. $$

Casa Club – Puga 458 A. The Casa Club has a wide variety of dishes, from pizzas and burgers to basic Peruvian. It has a cozy fireplace for those cold days. $$

★**De Buena Laya** – 343 Dos de Mayo. A good variety of regional dishes can be found in this narrow restaurant not far from the main square. Caldo verde is excellent here, as is the cuy and cecina. All is a good value too. $

Bars & Clubs

Akaesh – Dos de Mayo 334, ☎ 368-108, akaeshcafe@hotmail.com. Café/bar with live music and often with drink specials. Open Wed-Sat.

Rodeo – San Martín 354. This is a swanky little place with lots of intimate booths and tables and a small dance floor.

Usha-Usha – Puga 142. The musician/owner sometimes plays live music himself or with others, depending on the light of the moon. It's a typical dive bar with good drinks and is open until the wee hours.

There are a number of small clubs that open their doors late on weekend nights. Ask in town where the current places are, or just listen and you should be able to find them.

Shopping

There are handicraft markets at Belén (Block 7) and on Amazonas.

Colors and Creations – Belén 628. Unique designs in ceramics, textiles, and jewelry.

Also try the several shops on Av. Dos de Mayo on the way to Cerro Santa Apolonia.

Tour Agencies

Socio Adventures – Bambamarca 273, ☎ 83-1118, www.socioadventures.com. Offers a five-day trek to the Cadmalca community near Cajamarca where you will build a cooking stove. Ages 18 and up.

The best way to visit one or more of the archaeological sites beyond Cajamarca is to sign on with one of the tour operators in town. Several of the sites are not accessible by public transportation; going with a guide in a small private colectivo is economical and convenient. Most agencies charge 15 to 20 soles for standard day-trips. Many combine visits (for example, to the Inca Baths, Granja Porcón, La Collpa, and Llacanora; or to Otuzco and Tres Molinos). All of the agencies can be found on the Plaza de Armas and offer similar tours and pricing. On most days the agencies pool their clients together.

Festivals

★★**Carnaval** in Cajamarca is a particularly boisterous affair and it is the most important festival in the region. The festival date is movable, but is generally during the first 15 days of February, with the main festivities taking place from Wednesday to Wednesday. Cajamarca's youth faction makes a habit of soaking each other – and tourists – with water and other liquids (sometimes urine, so watch out!). There are a variety of vibrant festivities throughout the week, with colorful processions, a song contest, a decorated car contest, feasts, parades, dancing, music, and much, much more. Hotels are filled well in advance during this time, so be sure to have reservations.

 Unsha, or the "dance around a tree," is a traditional feast that takes place from Tuesday until Sunday in each of Cajamarca's neighborhoods during Carnaval. This ceremony and feast consists of a dance around a tree decorated with gifts on each of its branches. Dancing couples must try to cut down the tree with an ax. The couple that succeeds in cutting the tree down has to organize next year's feast and get the presents for the branches.

Day-Trips from Cajamarca

The ★★**Baños del Inca** is the huge complex where Atahualpa once bathed, including just before his capture in

Cajamarca. The actual stone bath still stands, although more modern facilities are where you will likely bathe. A tourist ticket is 4 soles, which includes access to your own bath. Bring a towel and swimsuit. Water can get extremely hot. Heated swimming pools are also on-site, as are massage services and a number of other amenities. To get here you can take a combi from Dos de Mayo and Amazonas (2 soles).

Just eight km/4.8 miles northeast of the center, the **Ventanillas de Otuzco** make for a quick and easy side-trip from Cajamarca. Prominent members of the Cajamarca culture, the first to take root in the valley, were buried in the

Ventanillas de Otuzco (Carlos Sala)

windows, or niches, that are carved into the rock. The neat rows of windows make the site look like a prehistoric mansion. Most windows held just one body, but several were large enough for entire families. If you drive another 20 km/12 miles, you will find the **Ventanillas de Combayo**, which are larger and better preserved, although most are satisfied with the ones at Otuzco. To get there you must catch a combi (2 soles) from Del Batán north of the Plaza or take a taxi (10 soles). Organized tours are cheap, leave daily and will stop at a few other nearby sights. Open daily 8 am-5 pm. Admission 3 soles.

Cumbemayo, 20 km/12 miles southwest of the center, is a place of great natural beauty and an ancient marvel. The area is filled with of rolling green hills and is

Ventanillas de Combayo
(Carlos Sala)

Cumbemayo (Mylene d'Auriol)

named for the aqueduct that can be found there. The carved canals are thought to be at least 2,000 years old and may have had a ceremonial purpose. They are carved out of volcanic rock and extends for nine km/5.4 miles. There are also petroglyphs, or cave paintings, with anthromorphic symbols and strange geological formations nearby; both will likely be visited on a tour here.

Granja Porcón, 23 km/14 miles from Cajamarca, is a rural cooperative focusing on agro-tourism such as farming and animal husbandry. About 1,000 residents can be seen working in the fields, planting, milking cows, weaving, and working on a number of other various projects. Both the Peruvian Government and the European Union support the program, and a variety of ecologically friendly methods are being tested, such as a power supply run by hydroelectricity. Public transportation here is limited.

One of the most memorable sights in the area is ★**La Collpa**. It is a cattle ranch that has become a major draw for visitors. There is a small church, gift shop, cheeses for sale, a scenic pond, gardens, and a small zoo at the hacienda. But the highlight of a visit are the cows. Yes, the cows. The handlers beat drums and call out the names of the cows, who come running to their correct stalls for feeding times. They almost dance along as the names are called one by one, "Claudita, Sylvana, Marissa, Marina..." and so on, to the delight of visitors. A tour usually will also stop at **Tres Molinos**, a dairy farm. Here you will get to see the production process for a variety of the local cheeses and manjarblancos (sweet milk spreads).

Adventures

On Foot

The ★**Stove Trek** offered by Socio Adventures (see above) is a five-day trek that allows for plenty of interaction with local communities. The main focus of the trek is the building of a cooking stove for a local family. Cooking stoves in rural communities are a high cause of accidents and death, and this project simply wants to reduce that risk. Visitors are likely to be the first foreigners to visit each local family. Departures are every Mon and Fri from Cajamarca and must be reserved at least five days in advance. Price includes building materials, food, lodging, transport, and a local guide. No prior building skills are needed and the process is not physically demanding.

Treks

Cajamarca is an important crossroads of the nearly 30,000-km/18,000-mile Inca highway system, the Inca trails, known in Quechua as Qhapaq Nan (Great Paths). There are a variety of good hikes around Cajamarca, although the paths are hardly explored. **APREC** (Association for the Rescue of Cajamarca's Ecosystem, at Hotel Laguna Seca, ☎ 89-4600, oper@aprec.org, www.aprec.org) is a nonprofit organization that brings trekkers together with the campesinos living along the trails. APREC guides lead most of the hikes in the area. Some agencies may operate trips as well. Many incorporate area attractions at the beginning or end points, as well as other ruins and natural sights little known outside the realm of the campesinos. Most treks make use of accommodations inside adobe houses, with meals served by local people.

At this time, APREC has four principal routes:

Ingatambo–Granja Porcón. The 16-km/9.6-mile hike takes eight hours, beginning in the sleepy town of Ingatambo, 47 km/28 miles from Cajamarca. The route traces a small stretch of the Cajamarca-Quito highway. The trip ends at Granja Porcón, where you can either return to Cajamarca or stay the night.

Combayo–Cañon Sangal. Starting at Combayo, a two-hour drive from Cajamarca, this hike treads the best-preserved trail near Cajamarca. The little visited Ventanillas de Combayo are the first stop. The 10-km/six-mile hike passes over an area where European cows have not been introduced; therefore, the array of native plants is quite remarkable, as is the bird life.

Cochambul–Baños del Inca. The 20-km/12-mile, two-day hike goes from Cochambul to Laguna San Nicolas, which is a hotspot for pejerrey fishing and where you can see reed rafts being used. Next is Fort Coyer, the site of a battle between the Incas and the Caxamarcans. Chilicat, the next stop, is a town where nearly every resident is involved in the process of making guitars. Finally, you come to the Baños del Inca for a nice soak in the thermal waters.

Cumbemayo-Cajamarca. From Cumbemayo it is possible to walk downhill back to Cajamarca following the Inca road that stretched from Cajamarca to Chan Chan. The trail passes a few small villages and an Inca huaca en route.

■ Chachapoyas

Phone code (041)

The often-overlooked Colonial gem of Chachapoyas (2,334 m/ 7,655 feet, population 25,000) is only beginning to establish itself on the tourist map. With sights like the fortress at Kuélap and the Sarcophagi at Karajia, that is going to quickly change. In five years it will be overrun. The capital of the department of Amazonas is still a little difficult to reach. There is little to do in the town itself, but it is a great base for visits to a number of archeological sights that can be reached on day-trips. The Incas only conquered the Chachapoyan culture a few decades before the Spanish arrived, so Quechua and Incan influence didn't have time to take hold.

 Climate: Average temperature here is between 51-68°F. Wet season is January-April, while the dry season is May-September.

Tourist Information

 Tourist Office – iPeru, Arrieta 588 (on the Plaza), ☎ 47-7292, iperuchachapoyas@promperu. gob.pe.

Hospital – **General Base Chachapoyas**, Triunfo Block 3, ☎ 47-7016. Open 24-hours.

Police – Amazonas 1220, ☎ 47-7017. Open 24-hours.

Post Office – **Serpost**, Arrieta 632, ☎ 47-7019, Mon-Sat 8 am-8 pm.

Laundry – Lavandería Clean, Amazonas 813.

Getting Here

Bus

Movil Tours – Libertad 464, ☎ 478-545, turismo@ moviltours.com. Leaves at 8 pm to Chiclayo, 1 pm to Lima and Trujillo. These are the best buses in and out of Chachapoyas, but none are cama (sleeper). Only normal service.

Transportes Kuélap – Arrieta 412, ☎ 478-128. To Chiclayo leaves at 7 pm, 10½ hours.

Civa – Salamanca 969, ☎ 478-048, iciccia@civa.com.pe. To Chiclayo leaves at 6 pm, 11 hours; to Lima, 12:30 pm, 21 hours, via Trujillo.

Empresa de Transportes Virgen del Carmen – Salamanca 6, ☎ 502-690. To Celendin and Cajamarca. A very rough road and sometimes impassable during the rainy season. Buses only run on Tues and Fri. It may be easier and quicker to go to Cajamarca via Chiclayo.

Sightseeing

There is little to do in Chachapoyas itself; most sights are a few hours outside of town. The **Plaza de Armas** is the hub of all activity and most restaurants, tourist agencies, banks, and hotels are within two blocks of it.

The small town of **Huancas**, a short cab ride from the center, has a mirador overlooking a large canyon and there are a few ceramic workshops.

Where to Stay

★**Casa Vieja** – Chincha Alta 569, ☎ 477-353, www.casavieja-peru.com. My choice for the best accommodation in the city. Rooms have cable TV and private hot-water showers. Clean, modern, and quite comfortable. Much of the restored Colonial house is

Casa Vieja

decorated with handcrafts from the region. Attractive courtyard and dining areas. Continental breakfast is included, as is 15 minutes of Internet use per day. Highly recommended. $$

Puma Urco – Amazonas 833, ☎ 477-871. Just off the Plaza, this small hostal has newly decorated modern rooms with private hot-water baths and cable TV. A cevicheria serves as its restaurant. Can arrange tours and buses. $$

Gran Hotel Vilaya – Ayacucho 755, ☎ 478-154, hotelvilaya@viabcp.com. Most consider this the best hotel in Chachapoyas and it is the most modern. This officially three-star hotel has rooms with hot-water showers, cable TV, and it includes breakfast. The rooms are new, but still a bit bare. $$

Hostal Las Orquedias – Ayacucho 1231, ☎ 778-271, hostallasorquideas@hotmail.com. Although it sits just two blocks from the Plaza, this Colonial-style accommodation feels much farther removed. Perhaps it is that Chachapoyas is so small, or maybe it is the garden in back. Basic country-style rooms have private hot-water baths, cable TV and there is room service available. Includes continental breakfast. $$

Hostal Casona Monsante – Amazonas 746, ☎ 477-702, www.casonamonsante.com. One block from the Plaza, in a historic and well-kept Colonial house with an orchid-filled stone courtyard and attractive woodwork throughout. Rooms are clean and rustically simple, with private hot-water baths and cable TV. $$

Hostal Revash – Grau 517, ☎ 477-391. Creaky wooden floors and hot-water showers give this basic lodging option a bit of character if not much else. The front rooms have balconies with views of the Plaza. $

Hostal El Tejado – Grau 534, ☎ 77-7654. Basic, but clean and friendly. Private hot-water showers and breakfast make it a great value. $

GASTRONOMY

Juanes de yuca – Steamed yucca with chicken wrapped in a banana leaf.

Cecina – Smoked pork or beef.

Enrollado – Tortilla rolled with beef or chicken and other ingredients such as cheese, egg, or raisins.

Chuchuhuasi – Aguardiente drink popular in the eastern lowlands.

Licor de leche or licor de mora – Aguardiente drink made of milk, blackberries, or a number of other ingredients.

Where to Eat

Tradiciones de Chachapoyas – Recreo 540, ☎ 478-643, tradicioneschachas@hotmail.com. A wide variety of typical Chachapoyan food can be found here. Juanes, enrollados, cachangas, cuyes, cecinas, etc. $$

Pizzeria/Bar 505 – Dos de Mayo 505. This place has medio-cre pizzas and Peruvian pub food such as tequeños. But it's one of the best places in town for a drink that isn't a loud disco with terrible music. $

Bar/Pub La Estancia – Amazonas 861. Very similar to the above restaurant, but with more criollo dishes. $

Restaurant Plaza – Grau 534, 2nd floor, ☎ 477-654. Typical Amazonas dishes, heaping plates for ridiculously low prices. The bife apanado (fried steak) is delicious. Atmosphere is white tablecloth all the way and has a nice view of the Plaza. $

Just below the previous restaurant, an anonymous place has essentially the same dishes at a lower cost, but without the atmosphere. Recommended. $

Mas Burger – On the west end of the Plaza. This small, trendy café is generally filled with a younger crowd, who are there for the burgers or chicharrónes. Also has coffee, postres, and ice cream. $

Restaurant Vegetariano El Eden – Grau Block 4. Basic vegetarian fare. Nothing special. $

Café y Mas – Amazonas 836. Small, clean café with good desserts and snacks. $

Shopping

Rusti-K – Amazonas 1105, www.caritas-chachapoyas.org.pe. Small shop with a variety of agricultural and artisan products from area villages.

Tour Companies

Chachapoyas Tours – Grau 534 (2nd floor), ☎ 478-078, www.kuelapperu.com. Tours are a bit pricey, roughly $100 per day, but are more versatile and experienced than most other companies, and they include everything. Will provide logistics for professional teams of writers, photographers, film crews, etc. A variety of tours are offered. They can arrange lodging in lodges such as Choctemal and Levanto outside of Chachapoyas.

Kuélap & Adventure – Ayacucho 771 (2nd floor, office 13), ☎ 777-819, www.kuelapadventure.com.pe.

Turismo Explorer – Ayacucho 920 and Amazonas 869, ☎ 778-060, www.turismoexplorer.com.

Day-Trips from Chachapoyas

★★**Kuélap** (3,100 m/10,168 feet) is Chachapoyas' claim to fame and what will likely make the town an important tourist destination in years to come. The high stone walls and unusual round houses are becoming some of the most posted images for tourism in Peru. Some go so far as to call it the next Machu Picchu, but don't expect that. It is quite different, although just as remote. The citadel is perched on a limestone ridge above the Utcubamba Valley. The 20- to 33-foot wall wraps around the complex, which is 2,200 long by 360 feet wide (at its widest) and vertical cliffs surround much of it. The 15 acres inside the walls are filled with narrow stairways, mysterious geometric designs, and the round houses (rebuilt) that were trademarks of the Chachapoyans.

There are thought to have been as many as 400 of the two-level stone houses, although very little is left of most. The area sits in cloud forest and the flora and bird life are sights in themselves. Fog often blankets the

Chachapoyan house (N. Gill)

mountain and limits the view. During the Conquest, the fortress was intended to be the center of Manco Cápacs rebellion, but the Chachapoyans, still angry with the Incas for conquering them, refused to allow it. Much restoration and excavation work is now being done on the site.

To get here you have several options. The first is a very early bus ride (departing from Grau and Salamanca, 4 am, 3½ hours, 10 soles) that goes directly to the site, passing Tingo, Choctamal, and María. To return, you must hike back to Tingo. which takes a few hours, where there is more frequent transportation. Alternatively, you can hike up to Kuélap from Tingo. The 1,200-m/3,836-foot ascent will take five to six hours. There are several lodging options around Tingo. You can also find full-day excursions on the Plaza de Armas in Chachapoyas for as little as 40 soles per person, depending on the number of people. Open daily 8 am-5 pm. Admission $3.

The mausoleums at **Revash** are a vast complex of tombs near the town of Yerba Buena, about 2½ hours from Chachapoyas. The carved tombs were thought to hold prominent members of the Revash culture that lived in the area about 800 years ago. A tour is necessary to reach the site or you can stay at **El Chillo lodge** ($30 per person, a 30-minute hike from the site) about five km/three miles south of Tingo.

Revash tombs (N. Gill)

The little-known ★★★**Sarcofagos de Karajia** are two hours by car (48 km/29 miles) and 20 minutes on foot from Chachapoyas. This is an incredibly fascinating site that gets very little recognition. It is very strange and mysterious and not that difficult to reach. The 6½-foot-high tombs are elaborately carved out of clay, painted, and some are topped with human skulls. You can see them only from the cliffs below. There is one main section of the tombs, although several others, some unfinished, can be seen on the surrounding cliffs. Many have already been destroyed by huaqueros (grave robbers). This is one of the most interesting sights in all of Peru.

Daily tours from Chachapoyas are not that expensive and are usually combined with a trip to the **Pueblo de los Muertos**, a series of small tombs built into a remote cliffside that resemble the mausoleums at Revash, only much smaller. They are a long hike, with cave paintings and a beautiful waterfall. Admission is 3 soles. The only way to get here is on a tour.

The small town of **Leymebamba** (2,050 m/6,724 feet, population 1,000) is known for its excellent museum. The museum contains many of the 217 mummies that were discovered in a tomb high above the Laguna de los Condores. Most are still in their bundles and in glass cases. Other artifacts such as quipus and ceramics are on display. Open Mon-Sat 9 am-5 pm. Admission 5 soles. The town has simple accommodations. You can hike to the Laguna in about 10 hours from town. Ask for a guide in town or about renting horses. To get to Leymebamba you must take a four-hour bus ride from Chachapoyas (which departs from the Plaza at 3 and 5 am) or go on a tour.

■ Huancabamba

Phone code (073)

Huancabamba (2,000 m/6,560 feet, population 30,000) at 284 km/170 miles from Piura, is one of the more isolated cities in Peru and one of the most difficult to reach. There are few hotels, restaurants, or tourist amenities here, but the mystery and lure of a place such as

Huancabamba

this should not be left out of any guidebook. The area is known for its brujeria, or witchcraft. People from across the country and all walks of life make their way here to find cures for various illnesses, to change their luck, or simply to gain greater insight into their lives. ★★**Shamanic ceremonies** often use hallucinogenic plants such as Ayahuasca or San Pedro. To get here you must come from Piura, Chachapoyas, or north from Ecuador. Slow buses and trucks traverse the highland areas over mostly unpaved, winding roads. The path is difficult and once you arrive it isn't any easier. Most shamans are not in Huancabamba itself, but in the lakes and mountains that surround it, above 4,000 m/13,000 feet and can only be reached by long truck rides or hikes.

There are 14 lakes in the area and the shamans use the mystical healing properties of the water. The largest lake is **Sumbe**, but **La Negra** is thought to have the most power and attracts the best shamans. A typical ceremony will last all night and cost around $50, although if the healer is well known it may cost much more. Ask around in town for more information about where to contact a shaman. The bus station has a list of certified healers. Several very rare species of birds are also found in this area and nowhere else. **Ethipsa** has two daily buses to Piura (☎ 47-3000, eight hours).

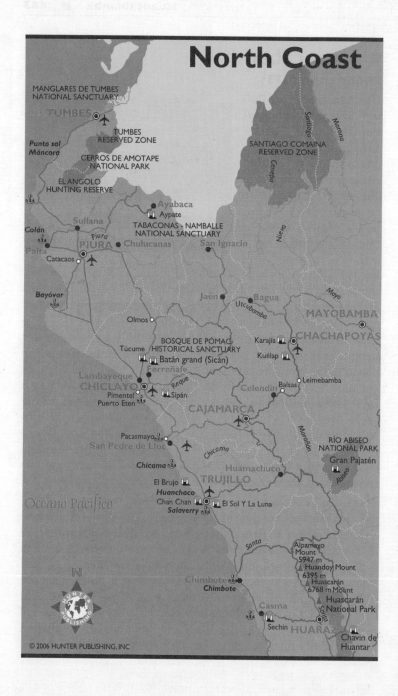

North Coast

MANGLARES DE TUMBES
NATIONAL SANCTUARY

TUMBES

Punta sal
Máncora

TUMBES
RESERVED ZONE

SANTIAGO COMAINA
RESERVED ZONE

CERROS DE AMOTAPE
NATIONAL PARK

EL ANGOLO
HUNTING RESERVE

Ayabaca
Aypate

Sullana

TABACONAS - NAMBALLE
NATIONAL SANCTUARY

Colán

Piura

PIURA   Chulucanas   San Ignacio

Paita

Catacaos

Bayóvar

Jaén   Bagua

MAYOBAMBA

Utcubamba

Olmos   CHACHAPOYAS

Túcume   BOSQUE DE PÓMAC
              HISTORICAL SANCTUARY   Karajía

                    Batán grand (Sicán)   Kuélap

Lambayeque   Ferreñafe

CHICLAYO   Reque   Celendín   Leimebamba

Pimentel   Sípán   Balsas
Puerto Eten

                          CAJAMARCA

Pacasmayo   RÍO ABISEO
San Pedro de Lloc   Chicama   NATIONAL PARK

                                                Gran Pajatén
Chicama

El Brujo   Huamachuco
           Huanchaco   TRUJILLO
Chan Chan   El Sol Y La Luna
        Salaverry

Océano Pacífico

                                        Alpamayo
                                        Mount
                                        5947 m
                                        Huandoy Mount
                                        6395 m
                            Santa   Huascarán
Chimbote   6768 m Mount
        Chimbote   Huascarán
                                         National Park
                        Casma
                                        HUARAZ
                        Sechín   Chavin de
                                        Huantar

© 2006 HUNTER PUBLISHING, INC

The North Coast

The north of Peru sees only a fraction of the visitors who come to the southern half, but that will not be true for long. There are several major Pre-Incan sites that shouldn't be missed. The beaches are the best in the country, particularly the

IN THIS CHAPTER

- **Trujillo** 465
- **Huanchaco** 479
- **Chiclayo** 483
- **Tumbes** 491
- **Piura** 499
- **Mancora** 506

white sand and turquoise waters around Mancora. There are also several natural sites, such as the Mangalares, near Tumbes, as well as the spiritual mysticism to be explored near Hunacabamba.

HIGHLIGHTS

- **Mancora beaches** – The white sand, palm-fringed beaches are comparable to those of the Caribbean and relatively crowd-free.
- **Chan Chan, Túcume, Huaca de La Luna, and Sipan** – These northern archeological sights are the largest and most impressive Pre-Inca ruins on the continent.
- **Huanchaco** – See or ride the traditional reed fishing boats that have been used here for thousands of years.
- **Craft shopping in Catacaos** – Find an endless selection of wooden crafts and ceramics in the handicraft capital of the north.
- **The Mangalares near Tumbes** – An ecosystem unlike the rest of Peru.

■ Trujillo

Phone code (044)

Founded in 1534 by Diego de Almagro, Trujillo (population 650,000) is capital of the department of La Libertad and was named after the Spanish birthplace of Francisco Pizarro. It later became headquarters of the Northern Vice-Royalty, is one of Peru's most important northern cities and has a proud cultural heritage. It is the home of Creole dances such as the marinera norteña, of Peruvian Paso horse breeders, and is famous for its nearby Moche and Chimu sites, as well as the sugar cane and asparagus that are grown in its fields. The city was under several inches of water during the 1998 El Niño.

 Climate: Average annual temperature is 64°F, but during the summers it can get as hot as 82°.

Pre-History around Trujillo

Civilization dates back 12,000 years in La Libertad with the Huaca Prieta, Chavín, Cupisnique, Salinar, and Viru cultures. But there were two that left their mark far more than the others: the Mochica and the Chimu.

The **Mochicas**, third-seventh century AD, were famous for their realistic ceramics with zoomorphic features. They were also known for their temples in the shape of curtailed pyramids, such as the Huacas del Sol and de la Luna.

The **Chimu**, 12th-15th centuries, built the colossal adobe city of Chan Chan. They were skilled gold and silver jewelers, advanced farmers, and built huge aqueducts that are still used. The Incas conquered them in the 15th century.

Getting Here

Air

 Aeropuerto Carlos Martínez de Pinillos – Located on the highway to Huanchaco, 10 km/six miles from Trujillo (☎ 46-4013). Flights go to either Chiclayo or Lima. To get there or away, a taxicab is the best option.

Airlines

Aero Condor – España 106, ☎ 25-5212.

LAN – Pizarro 342, ☎ 221-469, www.lan.com.

Star –Almagro 539, ☎ 47-0137, www.starperu.com.

Bus

Linea – Carrión 140, ☎ 23-5847, www. transporteslinea.com. Chiclayo, Lima, Cajamarca.

Movil Tours – Av. America del Sur 3959, ☎ 28-6538, ostrujillo@moviltours.com. Huaraz, Chiclayo, Lima, and Chachapoyas.

Ormeño – Ejército 233, ☎ 25-9782, www.grupo-ormeno.com. The best buses to the most locations.

Cruz del Sur – Ejército 292, ☎ 20-3780, www.cruzdelsur. com.pe. Many destinations.

Civa – Ejército 285, ☎ 25-1402, www.civa.com.pe. www.civa. com.pe. Many destinations.

Tourist Information

Tourist Offices – **iPeru**, Pizarro 402, ☎ 29-4561, iperutrujillo@promperu.gob.pe. Open Mon-Sat 8 am-7 pm and Sun 8 am-2 pm.

Banks – **BCP**, Gamarra 562. Has a Visa ATM. **Banco Continental**, inside the Casa de la Emancipacion at Pizarro 620, changes travelers' checks.

Post Office – **Serpost**, Independencia 286, ☎ 24-5941. Open Mon-Sat 9 am-8 pm and Sun 9 am-1 pm.

Hospitals – **Clínica Americano-Peruano**, Mansiche 702, ☎ 23-1261. Has English speaking faculty. **Hospital Belén de Trujillo**, Bolivar 350, ☎ 24-5281. Open 24 hours. **Hospital Regional de Trujillo**, Mansiche 795, ☎ 23-1581. Open 24 hours.

Police – **Policia de Turismo**, Independencia 630, ☎ 29-1705. Open daily 8 am-8 pm.

Laundry – **Lavanderías Unidas**, Pizarro 683, ☎ 20-0505.

Sightseeing

Trujillo's **Plaza Mayor** is one of the most majestic in Peru. It is larger than most, and the road sees heavier traffic, but it is well restored and has a gleam to it like a flashy European city. The central

Trujillo's Plaza Mayor (N. Gill)

monument is dedicated to Peru's liberty, which was first declared here. Several Colonial-era mansions surround it.

The **Cathedral** on the northern corner of the Plaza was constructed in the mid-17th century. Inside are paintings from the Cuzqueña and Quitian schools, along with Baroque and Rococo altars. There is a small **Museo Catedralicio** attached with Colonial art and gold and silver objects. Open daily 7 am-12 pm and 4-9 pm.

The Colonial center of the city has been well preserved. 16th-century houses painted in deep yellows, blues, and reds, palaces, and churches stand nearly everywhere you look in the first few blocks around the center. Most are not open on any regular schedule

Iglesia de la Compañía de Jesus

and are usually closed on Sundays. The wrought iron grillwork on many of the Colonial buildings is far more striking than in other Colonial cities.

Colonial houses worth checking out:

Casa de Madalengoitia, or the Emancipation House, is where the Marquis of Torre Tagle in the early 19th century led the separatist movement that resulted in the first proclamation of independence. It houses a collection of 18th-century watercolor paintings.

Casa Ganzoa Chopitea – Independencia 630. This 17th-century house opposite San Francisco church is one of the most finely decorated Colonial mansions in the city. The architects and decorators used a variety of designs throughout. The door is crowned by two lions and is in Rococo style. The windows are Imperial style, the balcony is Neo-Baroque, and the paintings on the wall are Mannerist.

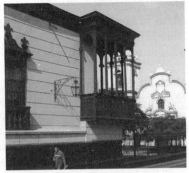

Casa de Mariscal Orbegoso

Casa de Mariscal Orbegoso – Orbegoso 553. This house was constructed in the mid-1700s and retains much of its original Colonial character. It houses a collection of furniture, silver, paintings and mirrors that belonged to former President Mariscal Luis José de Orbegoso y Moncada. It regularly hosts art exhibitions.

Casa Calonge – Pizarro 446. Simón Bolivar stayed in this Neo-Classical house on the Plaza, now the Banco Central de Reserva. The mahogany desk he used is still there on display. There is also a small collection of gold ornaments from the Chimu culture.

Casa Bracamonte – Independencia 441. This Plaza house is rarely open to the public. The façade is quite striking. A white Neo-Classical doorway fronts the yellow building, fine iron grills surrounding the windows, and the woodwork is remarkable.

Casa del Mayorazgo de Facalá – Pizarro 314. The large patio is the most striking part of this 18th-century house, now Banco Wiese. There is a fine stone floor, wooden columns and rails, and a Mudejar corner balcony.

There are several other Colonial churches worth checking out within easy reach of the center. The 17th-century **Iglesia de La**

Colonial buildings in Trujillo (N. Gill)

Merced (Pizarro 550) sits on a small square of its own just north of the Plaza. A Portuguese man named Alonso de las Nieves built it. Some of the highlights include the dome filled with images of the life of Saint Peter Nolasco and the Rococo-style organ, the only one in Trujillo. The striking white and black **Iglesia y Monasterio de El Carmen** (Colon and Bolivar) is home to an important collection of Colonial art. The Carmelite museum inside contains more than 150 paintings from the Quitian School. *The Last Supper*, the most notable painting in the collection, was painted by Otto van Veen, who taught Flemish artist Pedro Pablo Rubens. Admission 3 soles.

Trujillo has no large museums, but there are a couple of smaller, private collections that are quite good. The **Museo de Arqueología, Antropologia, e Historia** (Junín 682, ☎ 249-322, www.unitru.edu.pe/arq/musecount.html) has several pieces from the Huaca de la Luna. Open Mon 9:30 am-2 pm, Tues-Fri 9:15 am-1 pm and 3:30-7 pm, weekends 9:30 am-4 pm. Admission 5 soles. **Museo Cassinelli** (Piérola 601) is actually in the basement of the Mobil gas station. The archeological collection has hundreds of pieces from the Moche, Chimu, and Recuay cultures. There are several rare pieces and also a small erotic collection. Reservations are required to visit. It isn't the Louvre, but it is probably the best museum in a gas station in the world. Admission 6 soles.

Where to Stay

★**Hotel Libertador** – Independencia 485 (Plaza de Armas), ☎ 232-741, fax 235-641, www.libertador.com.pe. This stunning hotel, the only one right on the Plaza, is without question the best in town. It sits in a Colonial mansion and preserves much of the centuries-old character. The service, quality of rooms, and overall ambience are unlike anything else you will find in Trujillo or in all of Northern Peru. **Las Bovedas** restaurant is the best in Trujillo as

Hotel Libertador

well, and features northern dishes such as cabrito, kid goat, and duck. There is a lovely pool and terrace, as well as a sauna and steam bath service. $$$$

Gran Hotel el Golf – Los Cocoteros 500, ☎ 282-515, fax 282-231. This resort hotel's main feature is the swimming pool, which is the center of all activity. Rooms have extras like mini-bars, hair dryers and safes, which you won't find elsewhere in Trujillo. There is a nearby golf course and tennis courts that guests may make use. $$$

Gran Hotel el Golf

Hotel El Gran Marqués – Cienfuegos 145, ☎ 249-582, fax 249-161, www.elgranmarques.com. This hotel is a few km southwest of the center, but has modern amenities and a classier feel than most. The rooms are a bit worn, but they have the feel of a Holiday Inn or similar hotel. All rooms have air-conditioning. Suites are available. There is a restaurant and coffee bar on-site. $$$

Hotel Peregrino – Independencia 978, ☎ 20-3988, elperegrino@viabcp.com. This is a basic mid-range hotel with great value. Rooms have cable TV, hot-water showers, carpeting, writing desks, and mini-bars. The suites are quite a step up and have Jacuzzis. $$

Hotel Peregrino

Hotel Continental – Gamarra 663, ☎ 241-607, fax 249-881, www.hotelcontinentaltrujillo.com. The building and rooms don't appear to have been updated in decades, but have private hot-water baths and cable TV. Includes breakfast. They will arrange airport or bus pick-up with advance notice. $$

Hotel Americano – Pizarro 764, ☎ 241-361. This is a huge hotel right in the middle of the action on Jirón Pizarro. At one time it was one of the best Colonial hotels in Trujillo, but the

lack of upkeep has taken its
toll. The price is still low,
though, and it does have character. Plus the water is hot!
But luxury walked out the
door decades ago. Rooms are
available without bath for
half the price. $

HOTEL PRICE CHART	
	under $10
$	$10-$25
$$	$26-$50
$$$	$51-$90
$$$$	$91-$150
$$$$$	Over $150

Hostal Colonial –
Independencia 618, ☎ 258-
261, fax 223-410, hostalcolonialtruji@latinmail.com. This old
hotel set in a nice Colonial building just a block from the Plaza
is quite a good value. The rooms are so-so, but have hot-water
and cable TV. The restored lobby is quite stunning, though. If
the restoration process continues, expect the price to rise. $

Casa de Clara – Cahuide 495, ☎ 299-997, www.xanga.com/
casadeclara. This is the family home of guides Michael White
and Clara Bravo. The house is in a quiet residential neighborhood fronting a park. It's quite large and there are many communal rooms for TV and socializing. The rooms are basic and
a bit overpriced. $

GASTRONOMY

Cangrejo reventado – Boiled crab.

Pescado a la Trujillana – Steamed fish with egg
and onion sauce.

Cabrito con frijoles – Goat marinated in chicha de
jora and vinagre and served with beans soaked in
onions and garlic.

Pepián de pava – Turkey stew with rice, crushed
corn, coriander and hot chili peppers.

Where to Eat

★Chelsea – Estete 675. Upscale English pub with
some of the best food in town. Lunchtime buffets
daily. Beers on tap. White tablecloth restaurant
during the day with excellent food. It ranges from
criollo to seafood, and international plates. Tequenos con

camarones (spring roll-like snacks stuffed with shrimp) are highly recommended. Sadly, no fish and chips. $$$

DINING PRICE CHART

$	under $5
$$	$5-$10
$$$	$11-$20
$$$$	$21-$35
$$$$$	over $35

Asturias – Pizarro 741. Café with lengthy menu including everything from national plates to burgers and fries. Clean and fast. Good desserts and coffees, juices, cocktails. There's a good chance of seeing another tourist there. $$

Le Valentino – Orbegoso 224, ☎ 29-5339. This is where to come for Italian food with white table cloths. The pastas are good, the pizzas are better. $$$

Café Amaretto – Gamarra 322. This new café right across the street from the San Francisco church, is one of the cleanest in town, with lots of personality. It has the feel and charm of a European café, serving good desserts, snacks, and coffees. It is a great place to come for an evening cocktail as well. $$$

Restaurant De Marco – Pizarro 725. The emphasis is more southern Italian at this small bistro with just a few tables. There is a large menu, especially for such a small place. Much of it is in Italian. $$

Chifa Sam – Pizarro 790. One of the better chifas in town. $

Café/Restaurant – Gamarra 343. This place with the very original name is an imposing white-tablecloth place with a fancy waitstaff. Ironically the food is very, very cheap. There is a good set menu of national dishes. $

Salon de Te R'frescos – Pizarro 777. Café with decent breakfasts, sandwiches, burgers, juices, and desserts. $

Bars & Clubs

Tributo Bar – Alamagro and Pizarro. This is a great bar and live music venue at one corner of the Plaza. It has Beatles posters on the wall and maintains an elegant, Colonial look that fits in nicely in Trujillo. Live jazz on some nights.

North Coast

Nuestra Bar/Pub – Bolognesi 502. Very stylish corner pub just a few blocks from the Plaza. It almost looks like a rat pack hangout where you could sip on a martini and listen to someone play a piano. Windows look out onto the busy street below.

Luna Rota Pub, **Crack Discoteca**, and **Luna Rota Casino** – Av. America Sur 2119, www.lunarota.com. This is an all-in-one complex that attracts a wide variety of locals. Few tourists make the trip here.

Tour Agencies & Guides

Colonial Tours – Located inside Hotel Colonial, it offers reasonably priced tours and has been around longer than most companies.

Michael White and Clara Bravo – See *Casa de Clara* above. These two guides, who also rent rooms in their home-turned-hostel, are the best English-speaking guides in the area. Probably the best Spanish-speaking guides as well.

Festivals

★**National Marinera Festival** (March). Locals hold the national Marinera contest each year at the Gran Chimu Coliseum.

National Surfing Championship (late March). This is an international competition at Malabrigo, home to the world's largest left-hand break.

International Spring Festival (September). Celebration of the arrival of spring. A variety of processions, contests, performances, pageants, and parties are held.

 The Marinera Norteña – This dance, one of Trujillo's most celebrated cultural traditions, is quite complex, as well as beautiful. The most notable aspect is the white handkerchief that is waved in the air with each dancer's right hand to keep pace with each graceful move.

Day-Trips from Trujillo

The Huaca del Sol and Huaca de la Luna temples are located in the district of Moche, five km/three miles to the south of Trujillo, at the foot of Cerro Blanco.

The temples were not originally called Temple of the Sun and Moon, but scientists placed these names upon them for lack of better ones and they have stuck. The **Huaca del Sol** is closed to visitors, but can be seen from a distance. When more funding is available it will open up to tourism as well, but this could be a matter of decades. It is 43 m/141 feet high and, according to legend, 250,000 men using 70 million adobe bricks built it in just three days. The structure served as a ceremonial center and provided housing for the upper classes. It has deteriorated quite a bit since then.

Just 500 yards away, the ★★**Huaca de la Luna** (www.huaca-delaluna.org.pe) is the more impressive of the two and the only one to have been excavated. Much more excavation work remains to be done on the Huaca de la Luna, but it is

Frieze at Huaca de la Luna

open to visitors. Each year the tour changes a little as more information is gathered from the ongoing excavations. There are five overlapping temples, built in different periods during a 600-year span. By unpeeling certain parts of the temple, archeologists were able to find well-preserved decorated walls and huge multi-colored murals with the face of the Moche god named Ai-Apaek. A tomb here contained more than 40 sacrificed warriors. A visitor's center has some information about the site and a variety of vendors sell souvenirs. Open daily from 9 am-4 pm. Admission 10 soles.

To get there you have several options, and the same applies to all of the sites. Combis that say *Campina de Moche* can be picked up from Ovalo Grau at the end of Avenida Moche (every 30 minutes, 1 sole). You can also go with a tour, usually very reasonably priced, or by taxi ($10 round trip with a wait).

Meaning Sun Sun, ★★★**Chan Chan** is the world's largest adobe city. The archeological complex is 4½ km/2.7 miles northwest of the center, a 10-minute ride. The site is huge, larger than you could imagine.

Chan Chan

Much of it is just the remains of adobe walls, but they stretch to the horizon, for miles and miles. It was named a UNESCO Historical and Cultural Heritage Site in 1986.

The complex was built in 1300 AD as the religious and administrative capital of the Chimu Kingdom. An estimated 100,000 people from all walks of life and every social status lived there during its peak. There were nine different sub-cities, called Royal Compounds, within Chan Chan. Each was built by a different ruler, who would later be buried there.

There are three types of buildings on the 7.8-square-mile city that reflect each class: popular, intermediate, and monumental. The monumental is the most impressive and where the Chimu lords and royalty lived. It is represented by a total of nine palaces. Many of the huge city walls are carved with zoomorphic figures, geometrical shapes, and mythical creatures. There is an unseen but vast system of underground aqueducts and channels.

The main section of the site is the **Tschudi Palace**, one of the nine compounds and the most restored. In its heyday, about 1,000 of the most important members of Chimu society lived here. The friezes that adorn the walls are quite interesting and have designs of waves, fish, seabirds, and sea mammals such as otters, which were all important parts of their lifestyle. The friezes that surround the audience rooms in the complex are shaped like nets. The walls here once stood more than 10 m/33 feet high, but are now significantly lower, though some have been built back up.

The site **museum** is quite modern and is free with entry into Chan Chan. It shows a short film that examines what life might have been like at Chan Chan and how it may have looked. This is quite helpful to see before you go inside the complex. Guides await visitors and can be hired for about 20 soles per hour.

To get there, combis from Trujillo leave from the intersection of Pizarro and Av. 28 de Julio, among other places. Most continue on to Huanchaco. People usually come here on a tour that includes the Huaca del Arco Iris and Huanchaco. A taxi should cost 10-13 soles. Open 9 am-4:30 pm. Admission 10 soles (ticket good for 48 hours and includes Huaca Arco Iris and Huaca Esmeralda as well).

★**La Huaca del Arco Iris**, or La Huaca del Dragon, is in the district of La Esperanza, five km/ three miles northeast of Trujillo. Many of the walls are decorated with anthropomorphic figures and rainbows. The highly intricate carvings are well-restored and

Huaca del Arco Iris

quite remarkable. A series of ramps will take you to each of the three levels. The Chimu used the temple as a ceremonial center. Keep an eye out for the biringo, or Peruvian rat dog, which looks like a giant black or gray hairless chihuahua with blotches of yellow hair. It is perhaps the ugliest dog on planet Earth. Tours to Chan Chan usually stop here en route. Open 9 am-4:30 pm. Admission here is included in the ticket for Chan Chan.

La Huaca Esmeralda, is just three km/1.8 miles from the center, in El Cortijo. There are several overlapping terraces at this Chimu site, which dates to around the same time as Chan Chan. A local landowner discovered the site in 1923. El Niños of the past century have greatly eroded it and little restoration work has been done, although you can still make out many of the designs on the friezes. It is between Chan Chan and Trujillo and the same transportation routes apply. Open 9 am-4:30 pm. Admission comes with the entry fee for Chan Chan.

Interior of Huaca de Cao Viejo as it may have originally appeared

Along the coast in the District of Magdalena Huaca de Cao, 34 km/20 miles north of Trujillo, **El Brujo** is one of the oldest and most important coastal ruins. Its construction began more than 5,000 years ago, before ceramics were even invented.

The oldest building is **Huaca Prieta**, built by the Stone Age hunting and gathering culture of the same name. The Mochicas later added **Huaca El Brujo** to the complex. **Huaca de Cao Viejo** is a 27-m-high/88-foot pyramid. It demonstrates the skill of these people in creating murals and sculpted figures, which line the walls. There are several burial sites here from the Lambeyeque culture. The site is about an hour and a half by car from Trujillo. Getting there by bus can be tricky. It is best to go with a guide, but you will need to gather a small group to make it affordable. Open 9 am-4 pm. Admission 20 soles

RECENT FIND

It was announced in mid-2006 that a tattooed female warrior or possibly noble woman was discovered at Huaca El Viejo in Huaca El Brujo near Trujillo. Her tomb had characteristics of both male and female Moche burial rituals, something never uncovered before. The tomb itself was quite elaborate, with many Moche military pieces, sewing needles and thread, a sacrificed woman, gold, and semiprecious stones. Her body was wrapped in fine textiles. Both of her arms and other parts of her body were tattooed with mythological figures and markings that were quite distinct from other Moches. Initial finds believe that she died around 450 AD. Archeologists are still perplexed at who the woman might have been, but all signs point to this being one of the most important finds in years

■ ★Huanchaco

Many travelers prefer to stay at the beach resort of Huanchaco, 12 km/7.2 miles away from Trujillo. You pass Chan Chan on the way here as well, so tours to the ancient sites are readily available. The famous totora reed fishing boats are still used here by some, although at times they seem more like a photo op than anything else. The boats look similar to the ones found in Lake Titicaca, but they are hollow and the fishermen ride on them rather than in them. They are called caballitos, or little horses, and evidence of their existence can be traced back nearly 3,000 years. More than one piece of Mochica pottery at Chan Chan had pictures of the caballitos on them. Watching these boats maneuver in the surf makes a beachfront meal much more entertaining.

The town hugs the beachfront and doesn't extend back more than a few blocks. There is a large **church**, built in 1535-40, that stands on the hill above town and affords good views. The church is thought to be the second-oldest in the country and has been restored. There is an ATM beside the Municipalidad, which is the center of activity in town. Here you will also find the **Artesenias del Norte** that set up stalls, which extend north along the beach. Much of it is jewelry, but there are also a few interesting crafts made from totora reeds, such as miniature caballitos.

Getting Here

Combis from Trujillo leave from the intersection of Pizarro and Av. 28 de Julio, among other places. A taxi here from Trujillo will cost about 8-10 soles.

North Coast

Where to Stay

 Huanchaco International Hotel – On the Huanchaco Hwy, Km 13.5 at Playa Azul, ☎ 461-754, www.huanchacointernational.com. The best resort-like hotel in Huanchaco. Large pool area surrounded by modern bungalows. There are brick floors and older beds, but they have cable TV and private baths. Some suites are available that are more like small condos and can easily sleep four. Popular with vacationing families. $$$

Hotel Bracamonte – Los Olivos 503, ☎ 46-1162, www.camaratru.org.pe/hostalbracamonte/index.htm. This pleasant hotel has 30 rooms with cable TV, telephones, and 24-hour hot-water. The pool area is quite large and lively, surrounded by stonewalls and terraces. The pool hall, book exchange, restaurant, bar, BBQ area, free parking, and laundry service set it apart. $$$

Hunachaco Hostal – Larco 287, ☎ 461-272, www.huanchacohostal.com. This is a charming hotel just a block from the beach on the Plaza. Rooms are basic and lack TVs, but have a beach feel to them. The rooms with shared baths are a steal ($) and allow access to a nice hotel, the pool, and all other amenities for the price of a good ceviche. $$

La Casa Suiza –Los Pinos 451, ☎ 461-285, www.huanchaco.net/casasuiza. This is a long-time backpacker favorite. Owner Heidi passed away in 2005, but the place continues the family tradition with her son Oscar. There are just a handful of rooms, either doubles or dorms. Also, communal rooms for TV, a book exchange, rooftop terrace, and WiFi Internet access. They rent surfboards and wet suits. Attracts a mostly European crowd. $

Los Delfines – Cucardas 129-133, ☎ 461-599. Rooms just a block from the beach with hot-water and cable TV. Good value. $

Where to Eat

 Big Ben – Larco 836, ☎ 461-378, www.bigbenhuanchaco.com. Modern three-story restaurant with ocean-front terraces. One of the pricier restaurants in Huanchaco, with the clientele to prove it. All sorts of seafood dishes, delicately prepared. $$$

Club Colonial – Grau 272, ☎ 461-015. This restaurant occupies a small mansion on the Plaza from the late 18th century. The atmosphere is French Colonial with many antiques, plants, and stained glass doors. The food is a mixture of Peruvian seafood dishes such as ceviche and Franco-Belgian cuisine. Dessert consists of a variety of delicious crêpes. They actually have a small zoo with rare Tumbes caimans and a dozen or so penguins, which is about the last thing you would expect here. $$$

El Kero Restaurant/Pub – La Riviera 115, www.elkero. com. A trendy new restaurant that just popped on the scene. The chef was trained at Le Cordon Blue Peru and likes to get creative with the menu. Try the cangrejo reventado (boiled crab), tiradito (raw fish marinated in lime juice and served in a spicy sauce), pulpo al olivo (octopus marinated in olive oil), or the corvina enrollada (sea bass rolled in a tortilla). They also have steaks, pizzas, and pastas. The pub is open late and draws a youthful crowd. $$$

La Barca – Raimondi 111, ☎ 461-855. Just off the Malecón, this seafood place has all the traditional dishes at reasonable prices. A good choice if you want to watch your budget and still enjoy high-quality food minus the atmosphere. Anticuchos de pescado (kebabed fish), cangrejo reventado (boiled crab), and pescado relleno de mariscos (fish fillet stuffed with seafood) are some of the dishes that stand out. $$

El Mochica – Right on the center of the strip. Nice modern place similar to Big Ben, but slightly cheaper. Terrace with views to the beach and pier. Indoor seating as well when it gets too hot out. $$

Mama Mia – Larco and Independencia. Beachfront dive with a small patio popular for drinks and pizzas. Arranges tours as well to the dunes near town, the ancient sites, and also surfing excursions. $

Otra Cosa – Larco 921, ☎ 461-346, www.otracosa.info. Vegetarian place just off the beach with a variety of sandwiches, pancakes, falafels, and organic Peruvian coffee. All tips go to local charity projects. Can arrange volunteer work and also has tourist information and massage services. $

Tour Companies

Un Lugar Surf School – Bolognesi 473-B, ☎ 957-7170, unlugarsurfschool@hotmail.com. Private or group lessons. Rents boards and wetsuits. Arranges trips to Pacasmayo, Chicama, El Brujo, and Poemape.

Adventures on Water

Reed Boat Rides

If you want to see how the boats float, you can ride on a reed boat and surf back to the beach with a fisherman for just a few dollars (maybe 5 soles). You will probably get a little wet, so wear a swimsuit.

THOR HEYERDAL

Reed boats, Huanchaco

When Norwegian explorer Thor Heyerdal came across the reed boats being used on Easter Island he noticed they were similar to those on Lake Titicaca. He surmised that the people of Polynesia could have come from Peru rather than Southeast Asia. To accomplish this, they would have had to sail on reed rafts like those at Huanchaco and on Lake Titicaca. Heyerdal proved that it was possible. He sailed the Pacific Ocean several times in totora reed boats, on what have become known as the Kon-Tiki expeditions. Those ancient seafarers supposedly were the first to use reed boats, as well as the first to make use of navigation aids such as the ocean currents and constellations.

Surfing

The area's beaches are known for some of the world's longest waves. The very longest is at ★**Chicama**, or Malabrigo, 80 km/48 miles north of Trujillo. If you are not a surfer, there really isn't another reason to come here. The wave is divided into four sections: the point, the cape, the "man" and the "pier." Each section is unique in character. In general, it is a classic left-running Peruvian wave and grows with south- and west-running currents. The ideal size is six feet.

■ Chiclayo

Phone code (074)

Chiclayo (population 500,000), the capital of the department of Lambayeque and Peru's fourth-largest city, is nearly 500 miles north of Lima. It was founded in the 16th century, but it was Lambeyeque 12 km/7.2 miles to the northeast that drew all of the attention until the 19th century. Chiclayo is what you might call "new Lambayeque" and has become one of Peru's fastest growing modern cities. The main Plaza is small and there is very little of interest in the town. but there are so many excellent archeological sites and museums in the area that it is one of the most interesting places in northern Peru.

Getting Here

Air

Aeropuerto Internacional José Abelardo Quiñones Gonzales (Av. Bolognesi, two km/1.2 miles southeast of town, ☎ 23-3192) is served by just two airlines and the flight options are limited. **LAN** (Izaga 770, ☎ 27-4875, www.lan.com) has daily flights to Lima, as does **TANS** (Izaga 763, ☎ 27-1339, www.tansperu.com.pe). A taxi costs about 7 soles to here from the center.

Bus

Ormeño – La Torre 242, ☎ 234-206, www.grupo-ormeno.com. Lima, Mancora, Trujillo, Cajamarca and most other places.

Cruz del Sur – Bolognesi 888, ☎ 427-5679, www.cruzdelsur.com.pe. Same as Ormeño.

Movil Tours – Bolognesi 754, ☎ 27-1940. Chachapoyas (the best buses), Trujillo, Cajamarca, and Lima.

Linea – Bolognesi 638, ☎ 233-497. Lima, Trujillo, and Cajamarca.

Turismo Dias – Cuglievan 190. Has several daily buses to Cajamarca ($5).

There is also a terminal on Av. Bolognesi (#536) a block west of Jr. Balta that has offices for several small bus companies. These travel mostly to highland destinations such as Chachapoyas and Cajamarca.

Transportes Kuélap – To Chachapoyas.

Transportes Mendoza – ☎ 208-785. Has a 1 pm bus to Cajamarca (15 soles). Get your ticket early, because this one can get crowded.

Car Rental

Chiclayo Car Rental can be reached through the Gran Hotel Chiclayo (see below).

Tourist Information

Tourist Police – Pena 830, ☎ 23-5181. Open 24 hours. The office also has tourist information and maps. It is the only tourist information office in town as well.

Hospital – **Hospital Nacional Almanzor Aguinaga Asenjo**, Unanue 180, ☎ 23-7776. Open 24 hours.

Post Office – **Serpost**, Aguirre 140, ☎ 23-7031. Mon-Sat 8 am-8:30 pm, Sun 8 am-2 pm.

Sightseeing

There is very little to see in Chiclayo. The Parque Principal is a nice place to sit and people-watch. It doesn't have the history of the plazas in many other citie, since it was built less than 100 years ago, as was the cathedral that stands on the east side.

The one place that everyone should see is the ★**Witches Market**, which occupies the southwest corner of the Mercado Modelo. It is said to be the largest in Peru. On sale are dried animals, bones, herbs, strange mixtures to cure your ailments or increase your sexual potency. Ask the brujo (witchdoctor for advice).

Where to Stay

Gran Hotel Chiclayo – Villarreal 115, ☎ 234-911, fax 223-961, www.granhotel-chiclayo.com.pe. This hotel has all the amenities you could ask for here. There are a wide variety of suites available, which are the best rooms in the city

Gran Hotel Chiclayo

without question. Gourmet restaurant and a bar/pizzeria, pool, casino, business center, travel agency, and car rental agency. Includes a breakfast buffet, welcome drink, Internet use, and airport transfers. $$$

Costa del Sol – Balta 399, ☎ 227-272, fax 209-342, www.costadelsolperu.com. One of the best new additions to Chiclayo's mid-range hotel scene and it is the best place near the Plaza. There is a rooftop pool, casino, small gym, and a restaurant and bar. Rooms have air-conditioning, mini-fridges, cable TV, hot-water showers, comfy beds, and are either smoking or non-smoking. Suites with Jacuzzis are not much more expensive. Sometimes they have special packages. Includes a welcome drink. $$$

Gloria Plaza Hotel – Grau 397, ☎ 270-744, www.gloriaplazahotel.com.pe. The Gloria Plaza is one of the better options in Chiclayo. The rooms have all the amenities and have a homey character that other hotels lack here. There's a small restaurant and bar and a fountain highlights the pool. $$$

Eras Hotel – De La Vega 851, ☎ 236-333, www.erashotel.com. This is a basic three-star option, which might be one star too many. It just goes to show how little you should trust the ratings system in Peru. The place isn't bad; just don't expect much. The rooms are cozy, clean, have private hot-water showers, and include continental breakfast and airport transfers. $$

Inca Hotel – Gonzales 622, ☎ 235-931, www.incahotel.com. Another high-end budget choice. The Inca lacks character, but is still an excellent value. Each of the 63 rooms has private a hot-water bath, cable TV, air-conditioning, hair dryer, and minibar. There is a large restaurant and bar, plus a small casino. $$

Hotel Central Chiclayo – San José 976, ☎ 231-511, www.hotelcentral-chiclayo.com. A good higher budget option. The hotel is a bit old and worn, but it's cozy and clean. Rooms have cable TV and private hot-water showers. $$

Hostal Royal – San José 787, ℅ 233-421. This Plaza hotel gives the image of a once-grand accommodation that has not been kept up to its former grandeur. The location is good, though, and rooms are equipped with private hot-water baths. $

Piramide – Izaga 726, ☎ 224-036, piramidereal@hotmail.com. Rooms are dingy, but have cable TV and hot-water. $

Latino's – Izaga 600, ☎ 235-437, latinohotelsac@hotmail.com. New, modern hotel on an ugly side-street. Rooms have all the amenities, including a mini-fridge and air-conditioning. $$

GASTRONOMY

Picante de camarones – A spicy shrimp dish.

Tortilla de raya – An omelet with manta ray.

Ceviche a la jhon – Ceviche with octopus, shrimp, conch, and fish.

Mero – Grouper (served in a number of different variations).

Arroz con pato a la Chiclayana – Duck cooked in dark beer and cilantro and served with green rice (green because it absorbs the color of the cilantro).

King Kong – A gorilla-sized sweet with several layers of cookie plus manjar blanco and other creamy fillings such as dulce de leche or dulce de piña.

Where to Eat

Bar/Restaurant Romano – Izaga 706. This attractive Italian restaurant with just a few tables has some of the best Italian food in town. There are about a dozen lasagnas on the menu. The ají de Gallina lasagna is by far the most interesting. $$

La Parra – Izaga 752, ☎ 227-471. Actually two restaurants side-by-side, one a chifa (Chinese), the other a parrilla (grill). The chifa is probably the best in town, and the prices are a bit higher than most. The grill is very good, with a long list of meats. Portions are huge, colossal, and spilling over. Prices are reasonable. $$

Warilke Grill – San José and La Pont. Burgers, chicken, brochettes, anticuchos; everything grilled. Fast food feel with some national plates too. $

Las America's – Aguirre 824. Long-standing old-time diner with mostly criollo dishes. $

Trebol – Beside Las America's on the Plaza, Trebol is clean and modern with a nice selection of desserts and ice creams. $

Grecy Grill – Batán 600. Clean and a bit trendier than most places around, the Grecy has a mass-produced feel, but still manages to be unique. A good variety of national dishes and general snacks like burgers and ice creams. $

Hebron – Balta 605, ☎ 827-709. This sprawling corner location not far from the Plaza specializes in parilladas, or grilled meats, generally Argentine-style. Also, a good selection of sandwiches, salads, and pastas. Playground on-site for kids. $$

Mela – Izaga 602. Quaint little café on a little traveled side street. Excellent cakes and postres. Lunch menus are quiet good and cheap. $

Chiclayo is famous for its sweets, notably the sometimes-giant King Kong snack, which comprises several layers of cookies with manjar blanco and other creamy spreads. There are many small shops on Av. Bolognesi near the bus terminals.

Bars & Clubs

Ozone Discoteca, a few km from the center, is your best chance for weekend nightlife. Take a taxi there as the streets can be dangerous and you won't ever find it otherwise. The modern tent-like structure seems far too trendy for Chiclayo, but the crowd has to come from somewhere.

Shopping

There is a small artisan market near the terminal on Bolognesi.

Tourist Agencies

Moche Tours – 7 de Enero 638, ☎ 224-637, mochetours_chiclayo@hotmail.com. Will arrange tours to all of the museums and archeological sites in the area. It can be expensive if you aren't part of a group.

Sipan Tours – 7 de Enero 77, ☎ 229-053, sipantours@terra.com.pe. Unless you have a group together, this company is quite expensive, although they offer some of the most complete tours around.

Day-Trips from Chiclayo

Lambeyeque

The once-thriving town of Lambayeque, 12 km/7.2 miles northwest of Chiclayo, has been overshadowed in the past century by its faster, more modern neighbor, Chiclayo. It is quiet here now, and retains more of a Colonial air about it than Chiclayo. You can still see Republican-era buildings with wooden balconies and iron grillwork throughout the city. The two museums are the real attraction though. Combis leave from Chiclayo at Pedro Ruiz and Ugarte and de la Vega near Angamos.

The ★★★**Museo Tumbas Reales de Sipan** (tumbasdesipan@hotmail.com) is the best museum in northern Peru and one of the best in the country. It is shaped like a pyramid covered by black glass. The recreated tomb of the Old Lord of Sipan, along with the riches that were found inside, can be seen here. The tomb was only discovered in 1987 and huaqueros, or grave robbers, had only begun to explore the site. That is why there is much to see here. The museum tries to show what the site was like in its heyday, how it was found and excavated, and objects that were found there. The pieces removed from the tomb, often made of gold and turquoise, are some of the most important and impressive in all of the Americas. The pieces depict animals, sea creatures, and the lord of Sipan himself. There are many models and artifacts from the Moche site on display. The entrance is on the third floor. Bags and cameras (not allowed) can be checked on the first floor. Guides can be hired for 10 soles. Open Tues-Sun 9 am-noon and 2:30-4 pm. Admission adult 7.50 soles.

The **Museo Brüning**, just a few blocks away, was closed for remodeling in early 2006. It will never have the artifacts that its neighbor has, but it does have a larger variety of pieces from the Chimu, Vicus, Moche, and Chavín cultures. There is an impressive collection of gold from the Sican, or Lambayeque culture and a smart ceramic display. Open daily 9 am-5 pm. Admission 7 soles.

To me, ★★★**Túcume** is the most fascinating site in northern Peru. At first look it appears to just be a cluster of mountains, but, once you get a little closer, you realize that they are actually pyramids. The sight is peaceful,

there are never crowds, and the bird life here is wonderful, even if you aren't looking for it. The site encompasses approximately 78 square miles. There are nearly 30 pyramids here that date back to 1000 AD, along with walls, and plazas, all comprised of severely deteriorated adobe. Túcume was the capital of the Lambayeque culture and was later inhabited by the Chimus and the Incas. Both the Incas and the Chimus expanded the site. The Incas built a tomb on top of a Chimu structure and several dozen bodies were recently uncovered there. The mirador on Cerro La Raya, or El Purgatorio, has great views of the site and of the surroundings and the climb is highly recommended. The pyramid of **Huaca Larga** is possibly the longest adobe structure in the world at 700 m/2,300 feet long. There is a museum, which will only take a few minutes of your time, but it has good info on the site.

Túcume sits on the Pan American Highway, 41 km/24 miles north of Chiclayo. All buses departing or heading to Chiclayo from the north pass right by it, so you can ask to be left off. If staying in Chiclayo, you can catch a combi to the Brüning Museum in Lambeyeque and then hop on another combi to Túcume. The site is about a km from the Pan-Americana, so it is best to hop aboard a moto-taxi. Open 8 am-4:30 pm. Admission 7 soles.

Considered one of the most important archeological finds of the past century, the **Huaca Rajada at Sipan** (☎ 80-0048) is the place where it all happened. All of the riches found here are now in the museum in Lamabyeque. The Moche burial ground, 35 km/21 miles from Chiclayo, was discovered by Dr. Walter Alva (now the curator of the museum) in 1987. He found it right after the grave robbers did, thanks to a wealth of beautiful pieces suddenly appearing on the black market. Just one of the tombs had been looted at that time and quick police action put an end to further looting. The grave robbers fortunately missed the pyramid of the royal tomb, that of the Lord of Sipan. Buried inside this elaborate tomb was a warrior, a priest, three females, a dog, a llama, a child, and various ceramic and metal pieces. The Lord of Sipan is thought to have been almost god-like to the Moches. Excavations are still ongoing. Some of the tombs have been recreated to look as they did before they were closed hundreds of years before. There is a small site museum. The best way to get here is on a tour from Chiclayo. You can also take a bus from the small terminal at Nicolas de Piérola and Orinete. Open daily 8 am-5 pm. Admission 7 soles.

The town of **Ferreñafe**, 18 km/11 miles northeast of Chiclayo, is home to the modern and impressive ★**Museo Nacional Sican**. Few visit it, however, because of the many other museums in the area. It opened in late 2002 and its focus is on the Lambayeque, or Sican, culture that thrived here from around 750 to 1400 AD. The highlights of the museum are recreations of the incredible 12-m/40-foot tombs that were found at the site. The Lord of Sican (not Sipan) was the most interesting, having been buried upside-down, in the fetal position, with his head detached. There are also pieces here from Batán Grande, a collection of 50 or so pyramids that sit 31 km/18 miles away. There is very little tourist infrastructure in Ferreñafe and it is difficult to reach, but in the next few years I would expect that to change. Open Tues-Sun 9 am-5 pm. Admission 7 soles.

Chiclayo has several pleasant beach areas about 14 km/8.4 miles away. **Pimentel** and **Santa Rosa** are usually crowded on summer weekends. At either place you will see the caballitos, or reed fishing boats. Pimentel is the most popular and there are several good beachfront restaurants (the food is actually much better here than in Chiclayo), a few small hostals (although most people stay in Chiclayo), a rickety old pier, and a row of souvenir stands. A taxi there should run you less than 10 soles.

■ Tumbes

Phone code (072)

Just 30 km/18 miles from the border with Ecuador, Tumbes (population 74,000) is unlike the rest of Peru. The coastal desert has disappeared and become green and lush. This always hot, humid, and sometimes sticky city shares a landscape that is similar to the coast of Ecuador and Colombia with its swampland and mangrove forests. The town itself is nothing special and resembles an Amazonian city more than a coastal one. The real attractions are the national parks that surround it. Although most are difficult to reach, they offer a glimpse into unique environments that the rest of Peru, as diverse as it is, just doesn't have.

History

 Tumbes does have a unique history in that it was the first Peruvian city encountered by Europeans. In 1928 Francisco Pizarro spotted the city as he sailed past from the north. At that time it was an Inca town. Pizarro invited the local chief to dine aboard the ship with him, while two of his men went ashore to explore the city. They returned and told of a great and powerful civilization. That was enough for Pizarro to return to Spain, where he raised the funds to begin his conquest just a few years later. Tumbes has its origins in pre-Inca times, when it was inhabited by a group of natives called the Tumpis. At its peak, the population is estimated to have reached 178,000. During the reign of Pacahacutec, the area was absorbed by the Incan empire. In modern times it was actually a part of Ecuador until the 1940-41 border war, in which Peru came out on top.

FELIPILLO & YACANE

These natives of Tumbes, or Tumbesinos, are thought to have been the first interpreters on the South American continent. They accompanied Pizarro during his conquest of the Incas.

 Climate: The average temperature is 30°C/86°F and frequently rises to over 40°C/104°F. December-March is the rainy season, but that doesn't cool things much at all.

Tourist Information

 Tourist Office – Ministerio de Turismo, Bolognesi 194, 2nd floor (on the Plaza), ☎ 52-3699. There is usually someone there. They are eager to help but don't have much info.

Ecuadorian Consul – Bolivar 123, ☎ 52-5060. Mon-Fri 9 am-1 pm and 4-6 pm.

Post Office – **Serpost**, San Martín 208.

Banks – **BCP**, on Bolivar, has an ATM and will exchange travelers' checks.

Laundry – **Lavandería Flash**, Piura 1002.

Getting Here

Air

 Aeropuerto Pedro Canga Rodriguez, ☎ 52-5102, is a few km north of town. The only airline serving Tumbes at the time of writing was **TANS** (Tumbes Norte 307, ☎ 52-3978, www.tansperu.com.pe), which flies direct to Piura and Lima only.

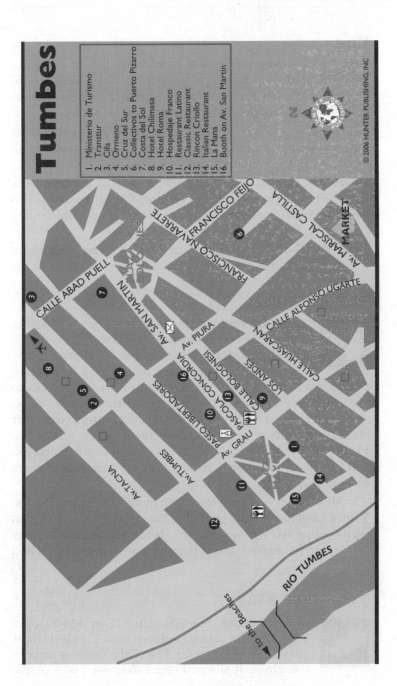

Tumbes

1. Ministerio de Turismo
2. Transtur
3. Cifa
4. Ormeno
5. Cruz del Sur
6. Collectivos to Puerto Pizarro
7. Costa del Sol
8. Hotel Chilimasa
9. Hotel Roma
10. Hospedaje Franco
11. Restaurant Latino
12. Classic Restaurant
13. Rincon Criollo
14. Italian Restaurant
15. La Mana
16. Booth on Av. San Martin

© 2006 HUNTER PUBLISHING, INC.

N

CALLE ABAD PUELL

FRANCISCO FEIJO

FRANCISCO NAVARRETE

Av. SAN MARTIN

Av. PIURA

CALLE ALFONSO UGARTE

Av. MARISCAL CASTILLA

MARKET

CALLE HUASCARAN

PASEO LIBERTADORES

PASCOLA CONCORDIA

CALLE BOLOGNESI

LOS ANDES

Av. TUMBES

Av. GRAU

Av. TACNA

RIO TUMBES

to the Beaches

Bus

Transtur – Piura 448, ☎ 526-860. New air-conditioned mini-vans to the border, Piura, and coastal destinations such as Mancora (20 soles). Departures almost hourly for most destinations.

Cifa – Tumbes 572, ☎ 52-7120. This company has the most buses to Ecuador. Machala (two hours), Cuenca (six hours), and Guayaquil (five hours).

Ormeño – Tumbes 314, ☎ 52-2288, www.grupo-ormeno.com. Has the best service to Lima (18 hours), four times a day. Also stops in Piura (five hours), Chiclayo (eight hours) and Trujillo (10 hours).

Cruz del Sur – Tumbes 319, ☎ 52-4001, www.cruzdelsur. com.pe. Has services similar to those of Ormeño.

Sightseeing

The **Plaza de Armas** is quite modern and lacks the Colonial feel of most plazas in Peru. In its center is a small, colorful pavilion; on the periphery are several restaurants and the public library. Two pedestrian streets, San Martín and Bolivar, run several blocks to the north and are home to many small restaurants, cafés, shops and interesting monuments. There are many craft stands with lots of seashell-based items set up just before Plaza Bolognesi on San Martín. To the east of the Plaza you will find many old wooden houses that are hundreds of years old and falling over, particularly on Calle Grau

The **Malecón** is nice for a stroll and has clear views of the Río Tumbes and its thriving plant life. Floods have destroyed it on many occasions. The new malecón being rebuilt now is likely to be quite impressive and is decorated with mosaic tiles and sculptures.

Where to Stay

Costa del Sol – San Martín 275, ☎ 523-991, fax 525-862, www.costadelsolperu.com. This is the best place in Tumbes, by far. It is really the only modern hotel here. It sits on Plaza Bolognesi, just a couple

of blocks from the main Plaza. There is a refreshing pool (especially important for Tumbes, which might be the hottest, muggiest city ever), a casino, small gym, a restaurant and bar. Rooms have air-conditioning, mini-fridges, cable TV, hot-water showers, comfy beds, and are either smoking or non-smoking. Suites are available too. $$$

Hotel Chilimasa – Airport Road, Manzana 2A, ☎ 52-4555. This hotel is a few km from the center on the way to the air-port and Puerto Pizarro. There are 20 modern rooms, along with a pleasant pool and stone patio. $$

Hotel Roma – Bolognesi 425, ☎ 52-5879, hotelromatumbes@ hotmail.com. This is a classic place for international travelers on a budget. The rooms in the middle of the building have no windows and are less noisy. The rooms on the outside tend to have so many mosquitoes leaking into them that you might as well forget about sleeping. Each room has a fan, cable TV, and private hot-water bath. Everything is basic and worn, but it is right on the Plaza. $

Hospedaje Franco – San Martín 107, ☎ 52-5295. This is a basic hospedaje with cold-water showers and a fan. It sits on a pedestrian-only street near the Plaza. The place is clean and cozy, although it lacks amenities. There are many accommo-dations in this price range between the two plazas, but Franco's is one of the best.

> ### GASTRONOMY
>
> **Conchas negras** – Black conch that thrive in the mangalares (mangroves), found in many seafood dishes such as the local version of ceviche.
> **Tortilla de cangrejo or camarones** – An egg om-elet with crab or shrimp.
> **Chinguirito** – Pipa (the milk of a soft coconut) mixed with aguardiente (alcohol made from sugar cane).

Where to Eat

Restaurant Latino – This place right on the Plaza is a landmark of sorts and attracts plenty of travel-ers and locals alike. The menu is long and has plenty of coastal dishes. The saltado de langostinos (stir-fried prawns, potatoes, and vegetables) is excellent and this is the only place in Peru I have seen it. The mosquitoes tend to be particularly deadly here for some reason, and when the staff notices you continually itching during your meal they are more than happy to bring out a bottle of spray to dab on yourself. Sometimes it has live musica folklorica. $$

Classic Restaurant – Tumbes 185. One of the best restaurants in the city, this place is good for a big plate of ceviche, seafood, and other criollo and norteño (northern) dishes. $$

Rincon Criollo – Bolognesi 253. Criollo dishes, ceviches, and chicharrónes. Sundays are for seafood specials and recommended. It is a small place with just a handful of tables. $

Italian Restaurant – Bolognesi 146. This is a small dive on the Plaza with a popular bar. Pizzas, fettuccines, and lasagnas give you a break from the other places in town, which are generally limited to Peruvian fare or fast food. $

La Mana – Plaza Mayor 142. This second-story restaurant in an aged Colonial building is tucked away in the tree-lined back end of the Plaza. Large open windows look onto the street below. There isn't much selection, but lunch menus are hearty and frighteningly cheap. It is airy, well preserved, and the staff is friendly. $

There is a round booth on Av. San Martín that looks like a gondola cemented in the ground. It has the feel of a small-town diner and is good for a snack like their turkey sandwiches or a cool drink. $

Bars & Clubs

 Hakuna Tropical Disco – The only really worthy disco in town is on the road to the airport a few km away. The Hakuna is an expansive outdoor complex with tiki bars, volleyball, and a sandy floor. Cover varies and you will definitely need a taxi to get there and back, unless you're staying at Hotel Chilimasa nearby.

Tour Agencies

Preference Tours – Grau 427 (on the Plaza next to Hotel Roma), ☎ 524-757, turismomundial@hotmail.com. Tours to the Mangalares, Parque Nacional de Amotape, the Zona Reservada, and city tours. Best if you have a group together.

Day-Trips from Tumbes

Puerto Pizarro

Only 14 km/8.4 miles north of Tumbes lies the fishing village of Puerto Pizarro. It is best known for the manglares, or mangroves, that cover the area. The town is at a point where the Río Tumbes and the Pacific ocean meet, mixing salt and freshwater which is the perfect habitat for the mangroves. An abundance of wildlife are attracted to

Puerto Pizarro (Heinz Plenge)

the mangroves, such as conchas negras, or black conch, which are a delicacy, green iguanas, and a number of sea birds such as pelicans.

An 8,300-acre park, ★★**Los Manglares de Tumbes**, was established here in 1988 to help protect the flora and fauna. It is one part of the larger **Reserva de Biosfera del Noroeste**. The manglares here are actually just one corner of the park. Seeing

Los Manglares (Alejandro Balaguer)

the more isolated and more interesting parts will require a visit to the FPCN office (Tarapacá 4-16, ☎ 52-3412, ptumbes@ mail.cosapidatata.com.pe).

The port itself is a bit chaotic, with tour guides hassling you at every angle. There is one reasonable hotel here ($), although most stay in Tumbes and come here on a day-trip. There are also a few restaurants and souvenir stands. The port is busiest on the weekends when Tumbesinos come to enjoy the beach and seafood restaurants on the Isla de Amor. To get

Peccary, Cerros de Amotape
(Alejandro Balaguer)

here you can take a taxi or hop aboard one of the collectivos that depart from the market area.

The **Parque Nacional Cerros de Amotape** is a rare tropical dry forest, covering 356 square miles. It was created in 1975 to protect its fascinating flora, fauna and rare wildlife such as anteaters, jaguars, deer, peccaries, parrots, and condors. The place to start any trip into the park is at the small village of **Rica Playa**, which has no hotels or restaurants, so bring your own food if you intend to camp. You can catch a combi from the Tumbes market area for the two-hour trip.

Two other, smaller parks adjoin Amotepe, the **Zona Reservada de Tumbes** to the east, where you can spot crocodiles and monkeys, and the **Cota de Caza El Angolo**, where hunting is permitted. The best place to arrange a trip to any of the parks is the FPCN office in Tumbes (see above). They will help set up a visit, including transportation and a guide.

Deer, Cerros de Amotape
(Alejandro Balaguer)

Adventures

On Water

If you go to Puerto Pizarro you will quickly be approached by one of the many certified boatmen to do a ★**mangalares boat tour**. The average tour lasts about two hours, taking you by the mangroves to see the bird life and their stinky poop-covered habitat, and also to look for green iguanas in the trees. There is a stop at the **Isla de Amor** and the point where the fresh water of the river meets the salt water of the Pacific. I actually went there during the week when few other tourists visit. Moments after I stepped on the island I saw a group of men with a gun chasing a dog that had stolen something from them. They were taking aim, but I happened to be in the way, so the dog swam to another island and got away. The Island of Love is actually quite nice though. There are a few small seafood restaurants and sandy patios, a good beach area, and an older gentleman there sells seashells and other souvenirs. If you walk into Puerto Pizarro you will surely be approached by a number of men offering the tour to Isla de Amor. Talk to a few and see what kind of price you can get, because prices vary greatly for the exact same service. There are different lengths as well. If you want, you can spend an entire day visiting various sites at the among the mangroves, such as the Isla de Aves or the Crocodile Sanctuary. Tours generally run from about $8-10 per hour. That's per group, not per person.

Getting to/from Ecuador

The Ecuadorian border town of **Huaquillas** is just 30 km/18 miles from Tumbes. Huaquillas and Aguas Verdes, its Peruvian counterpart, are like one colossal, chaotic outdoor market, with a connecting bridge between them. There are plenty of small hotels and restaurants here, but there is no good reason for stopping. Collectivos run from Tumbes to the border, but the border area is very seedy and it is recommended that you take a direct bus in Tumbes and pass right on through. Buses will go direct from Tumbes to Machala and Guayaquil, the jumping-off point for the Galapagos Islands and a majestic city in its own right. Immigration on each side is open 24 hours a day and fairly quick. North Americans and citizens of most European nations do need a visa to enter Ecuador. Moneychangers are on both sides, particularly around the immigration office. They will often try to shortchange you. Don't forget, Ecuadorian currency is the US dollar.

■ Piura

Phone code (073)

Peru's oldest Colonial city, Piura (population 350,000) was founded in 1532 by Francisco Pizarro, three years before Lima. This occurred just before the Conquistador and his men headed off to Cajamarca to capture Atahualpa and begin the Conquest. The present setting of the city wasn't begun until 1588, however, and went through several major reconstructions due to flooding and earthquakes. It still manages to retain much of its original Spanish character. The city lies 1,035 km/620 miles from Lima and just five hours from the border with Ecuador. It stays warm here for much of the year, particularly during the summer (December-March), when it's steaming hot. The downtown area borders the Río Piura, which has several bridges spanning it. Thanks to major irrigation efforts, significant amounts of rice, cotton, and plantains are grown. During the 1983 El Niño, floods wiped out 90% of the crops and destroyed roads and buildings. Similar damage occurred during the 1992 and 1998 El Niños.

Getting Here

Air

The small **airport** (☎ 34-4505) has just two daily flights to Lima (two hours and 20 minutes) that usually stop in Chiclayo. For more information, contact **LAN** (Grau 140, ☎ 1-213-8200 in Lima, www.lan.com) or **TANS** (Tacna 260, ☎ 30-2067, www.tansperu.com.pe). The airport is just a short two-km/1.2-mile cab ride from the center.

Bus

There is no central terminal in Piura, but most of the companies have stations on Av. Sánchez Cerro, a 10-minute walk from the center.

Transtours – Sánchez Cerro 1113. Has air-conditioned mini-vans to Mancora throughout the day (2½ hours).

Eppo – Sánchez Cerro 1141, ☎ 304-543. Has frequent buses to Mancora (12 soles, three hours).

El Dorado – Sánchez Cerro 1119. Runs slow but frequent, uncomfortable buses to Tumbes (five hours, 20 soles).

Cruz del Sur – Bolognesi and Lima, ☎ 33-7094, www.cruzdelsur.com.pe. This is the best for direct buses to Lima, generally in the afternoon and evening.

Transportes Chiclayo – Sánchez Cerro 1121. Has hourly buses to Chiclayo (10 soles, three hours).

Transportes Loja – Sánchez Cerro 1228. Has direct buses to Tumbes and Machala, Ecuador (seven hours).

Car Rental

Vicus Rent A Car – In the airport, ☎ 999-2051, fax 342-051, www.vicusrentacar.com.pe.

Tourist Information

Tourist Office – On the Plaza on the ground floor of the Consejo Municipal is the local tourism office, which is very helpful and friendly. Also try www.ahorapiura.com.pe, which has links and info to hotels and other tourist services in the area.

Banks – There are several banks on the Plaza, including **BCP** and **Banco Wiesse**.

Post Office – **Serpost**, on the Plaza de Armas.

Sightseeing

The **Plaza de Armas** is filled with monuments and benches, with large, leafy tamarind and ficus trees that help stave off some of the heat. The buildings surrounding it are a mix of modern and Colonial constructions. Much reconstruction was needed here after the 1912 earthquake.

The **Catedral** dates back to 1588 and stands tall at the north end of the Plaza. Much of it has been restored and rebuilt, so only parts are original. Ignacio Merrino, one of

Catedral

Piura's most beloved artists, painted the *San Martín de Porres* mural and several other paintings that adorn the church.

The recently restored **Iglesia de San Francisco**, a couple of blocks to the northeast at Lima and Callao, was where Piura's independence was declared in January of 1821.

Vicus gold statuette
(Anibal Solimano)

There are a few museums in Piura. The best is the **Museo de Oro Vicus** (Huánuco 893, ☎ 30-9267), which isn't far from the bus terminals. The basement has a modern art gallery, while the rest of the floors, reached by a central winding staircase, have Pre-Colombian artifacts. There isn't much here, essentially ceramics, textiles and other archeological finds. The Gold Museum is the only part you must pay for and it has a good collection of gold jewelry and other relics from the Vicus culture, which lived 30 km/18 miles east of the city some 2,000 years ago. Open Tues-Sun 9 am-5 pm. Admission 3 soles.

The other museum, **Casa Grau**, is the birthplace and former home of Admiral Miguel Grau, a hero in the war of the Pacific. The captain of the British-built battleship *Huáscar* was born in this house on July 27, 1834. The ship itself is actually on display in the museum. Open Mon-Fri 8 am-noon and 3-6 pm; weekends 8 am-noon. Admission free, but they accept donations.

Where to Stay

 Los Portales – Libertad 875, ☎ 321-161, fax 323-072, www.hoteleslosportales.com. On the Plaza, this is the best hotel in town. The bright yellow Colonial mansion has wonderful iron grillwork on the windows and is somewhat reminiscent of

Los Portales

the Libertador in Trujillo. All rooms have hot-water showers and TVs; the suites have mini-bars and Jacuzzis. A good restaurant, bar, and pool are on the premises, as is a small casino. Includes a welcome drink and breakfast buffet. $$$

Costa del Sol – Loreto 649, ☎ 302-864, www. costadelsolperu.com. Hidden on a busy side-street a few blocks from the center is Piura's other good hotel. This one is more modern in décor and amenities. There is an attractive outdoor pool, casino, gym, business center, and res-

Costa del Sol

taurant. Rooms are Holiday Inn-like with air-conditioning, mini-fridges, cable TV, hot-water showers, and comfy beds. Suites with Jacuzzis are just a tad more expensive. $$$

Hotel El Sol – S. Cerro 455, ☎ 32-4461, elsol@mail.udep.edu. pe. Basic hotel a few blocks from the center with cable TV, ceiling fans, and private hot-water baths. $

Hotel San Miguel – Apurimac 1007, ☎ 305 122. This is one of the few mid-range facilities around, located in the Plaza las 3 Culturas a few blocks from the main square near the river. Bare bones rooms have cable TV and hot water and there is a cafeteria in the lobby. $$

San Juan Hostal – Sánchez Cerro 1355, ☎ 304-672, fax 201-812, www.ahorapiura.com.pe/hostales/sjuan/sjuan2.htm. Clean, hospital-like feel makes this a sensible stop for the budgeter. Cable TV and private hot-water baths. $

Algarrobo Inn – Los Cocos 389, ☎ 307-450, fax 323-800, http://www.ahorapiura.com.pe/hoteles/algarrobo/index.htm. This is a convenient option if you have an early bus to catch and still want to have cable TV and hot water. Rooms are bare bones, but there are fans to keep the heat at bay and the mosquitoes away. Some rooms have air-conditioning. Internet available in the lobby. A good restaurant has a wide variety of regional dishes, with a cheap menu and breakfast. $

GASTRONOMY

Seco de chabelo – Stew made of beef and plantains.

Seco de cabrito – Stew made with goat meat.

Tamales verdes – Like the regular steamed corn tamale but made with a green tint.

Algarobbina – Cocktail made with egg yolks, sugar, milk, Pisco, syrup from the algarobbo tree, and a pinch of cinnamon. Peru's second cocktail after the Pisco sour.

Chicha de jora – Fermented maize beer that tastes just like vomit and has been a favorite for thousands of years.

Where to Eat

★**Gaditano** – Arequipa 902, ☎ 313-292. This is one of the hottest places in town. It is a corner location with a Colonial feel, smartly decorated with fine artwork and trendy furniture. The food stretches from Peruvian to Spanish, including tapas and a long wine list. The bar stays open somewhat late and serves excellent mixed drinks and wine by the glass. Recommended. $$$

El Taco Taco – Huancavelica 538. Small taco joint near a line of other busy places. Food is fast and cheap. The quesadillas, enchiladas, and burritos are big, filling, and tasty too. $

El Carbon – Huancavelica 552. Simple grill with Argentine beef, sandwiches, and the like.

Los Santitos – Libertad 1014. This picanteria (small local restaurant) has an old-fashioned character that seems typical of Piura. It has adobe walls and a cane roof and wood floors. Their regional plates are some of the best around. $$

Heladeria Venezia – Libertad and Apurimac. Homemade ice cream and very little else, but it is quite popular.

Matteo's Nature Center – On the Plaza, perhaps the only vegetarian restaurant in Piura. $

Capuccino – Libertad 1014. Other than the obvious coffee drinks, this quaint café serves salads, brochettas, sandwiches, cheesecakes, brownies, pecan pie and a variety of other snacks. Just across the way from Venezia. $

Bars

Art Rock Café – Apurimac 343, www.artrockpiura.galeon.com. Set in a small courtyard, this shady bar/café is a good spot to hide from Piura's sweltering heat. It usually has lunch specials with a beer for 10 soles. Ceviche isn't bad here, nor is the chicharrónes. Live music Wed-Sat.

Alex Chopp's – Huancavelica 528. This is a good watering hole that has some pub grub like chicken wings, sandwiches, and even ceviche.

The Bar at Los Portales – Has the most upscale piqeuos (finger foods) and cocktails. It's a fine place for a quiet drink overlooking the Plaza.

Tour Agencies

Servdym Tours – Loreto 654 Dpt. 1, ☎ 996-2600, servdymtours@hotmail.com. Arranges trips into Piura's Andes, Huancabamba, and Mancora.

Day-Trips from Piura

The town of ★**Catacaos**, 18 km/11 miles from Piura, is a definite stop for craft lovers. There is so much in the way of local crafts, much of it found only here, that it is hard not to walk away with bags of goods. There are plenty of woodcarvings, furniture, ceramics, straw weavings, and silver and gold jewelry. It's also a good spot for local cuisine, with many small

Silver filagree, Catacaos
(Anibal Solimano)

North Coast

regional restaurants, called picanterias, scattered around town. It was founded in 1645 and is known for its elaborate Semana Santa celebrations. To get here, you can catch a bus from the Terminal Terrestre El Bosque (Sánchez Cerro block 12 in Piura) or catch one of the frequent collectivo taxis that leave just on the other side of the San Miguel Bridge.

■ Mancora

Phone code (073)

Mancora beach
(Alejandro Balaguer)

★★**Mancora's beaches** are unlike anything you will find on South America's Pacific Coast. They are far beyond the best of those. The municipal beach draws the most crowds, is generally overcrowded, and is very windy. But if you go farther south to beaches such as Las Pocitas, Vichayito, and Los Organos, you will be in a different world. The water is turquoise green, the sand a sparkling white, the skies blue, and palm trees do salsa dances in the wind. It is a peaceful paradise and one of the best beaches in the Americas, including the Caribbean. The sun shines year-round here and the weather rarely strays far from 70-90°F during the day. The town is a bit of a dive, and has become backpacker/party central. The cheapest and worst hotels are here, although there are a few surprises. The bigger resorts, with no more than 20 or 30 rooms, are a bumpy moto ride away.

Getting Here & Around

By Air

The closest **airports** to Máncora are in Tumbes (85 km/51 mils north) and Piura (200 km/120 miles south).

By Bus

Transportes EPPO – Grau Block 4. Has five daily buses to Piura (three hours).

Ormeño – Piura block 5, ☎ 85-8304. Has the best afternoon buses to Lima.

Cruz del Sur – Piura block 5, ☎ 964-0647. Several afternoon and night buses to Lima.

Transtur – Piura block 4. Air-conditioned mini-vans to the border, Piura, and coastal destinations such as Tumbes (20 soles). Departures almost hourly for most destinations.

Colectivos patrol up and down the Pan-American Highway looking for passengers for Tumbes ($2, two hours).

Tourist Information

Anything you ever wanted to know about Mancora can be found at www.vivamancora.com.

Where to Stay

In Town

★★**Buenavista** – ☎ 422-4987, www.buenavista-mancora.com. This is a stunning condo complex that is often rented by the week or month. It is the most luxurious place in Mancora and is hidden just a short walk from the municipal beach.

Buenavista

Each condo is finely decorated, has two levels, two bathrooms, a TV and DVD player, air-conditioning, a kitchen, dining area, and a patio with table and chairs. There is a community room with a bar and a nice pool that is just steps from the beach. The grounds and gardens are well-kept and quite elegant. The owners formerly worked for the United Nations and are active in helping the local community benefit from tourism in Mancora. They may have volunteer opportunities in the near future. There is not another place like this in Mancora. Highly recommended. $$$$

North Coast

Las Olas

Las Olas – www.vivamancora.com/lasolas. This is the best place on the municipal beach, right in the center of all the activity. An excellent spot if you intend on surfing. Each of the 11 rooms has private baths and balconies; great for people-watching. Continental breakfast is included. $$

★**Kimbas Bungalows** – ☎ 25-8373, www.vivamancora.com/kimbas. Kimbas is just five minutes form town near the Cabo Blanco bridge. It is more isolated than most places, although

Pool at Kimbas Bungalows

a few minutes removed from the beach. The hotel grounds are quite attractive and the gardens are dreamily prepared. There is a small pool and community area as well. The bunga-lows are arranged to look like a small village. The rooms are clean, with private baths. $$

Hospedaje Casablanca – A decent, clean guesthouse right in the center of town and very reasonably priced. Rooms have fans and cold-water baths. Some have TVs. There is a book exchange too. $

There are many, many small, cheap hospedajes not far from the beach right in town.

The following hotels on Las Pocitas beaches are listed in order, from nearest to farthest away. Moto-taxis make the bumpy(!) trip between the hotels and the town for 5 soles and they run much of the night.

★**Punta Ballenas** – ☎ 25-8136, www.puntaballenas.com. All rooms have private baths, terraces and TVs and there are several suites as well. The master suite ($180 per night) can sleep four and has a private kitchen and two bathrooms. There is a large pool area surrounded by grass, not far from the beach. From the terrace it is claimed you can often see migrating whales. The bar/restaurant is headed by the owner/chef/joke-master/storyteller Harry Schuler, who likes to get creative with the menu and tries to find the perfect dish or cocktail for your specific mood. $$$

Las Pocitas – ☎ 258-432, www.laspocitasmancora.com. The rooms here are bright and airy, and have private hot-water baths and semi-private porches with hammocks. Each one is a little different, so check a few before making a decision. There is a large beachfront area with many thatched umbrellas for guests. Will arrange massages, surfing lessons, sailing trips, diving, and many other activities. Price includes American breakfast. $$$

Casa de Playa – ☎ 25-8005, www.hotelcasadeplaya.com. This sprawling, bright yellow hotel just seems to keep getting bigger. Each of the 14 rooms has a sea view and a patio with a hanging hammock. The pool area is the largest around and is one of the busiest places to see and be seen. The restaurant sits outdoors and faces the Pacific. $$$

Sunset – ☎ 58-1111, www.hotelsunset.com.pe. The six rooms at this exclusive, quiet hotel have private hot-water baths and large balconies. The beach area here is a bit shady, as there are quite a few palm trees. The Italian restaurant is excellent and worth a trip even if you aren't staying. It is authentic Italian, which means spaghetti and meatballs and pizza are not on the menu. $$$

Los Corales – ☎ 85-8309, www.vivamancora.com/loscorales/index.html. This delightful little complex has just 11 rooms on a nice section of beach. Rooms are bright and cheery and have private hot-water baths, satellite TV, and private patios with hammocks and ocean views. There are brand new suites available as well. There is a charming wood bar and restaurant that serves seafood dishes like ceviche and lobster. The hotel will arrange diving, fishing, and horseback riding. $$

Mancora Beach Bungalows – ☎ 85-8125, ☎ 241-6116 (Lima), www.mancorabeach.com. This large, clean hotel is about four km/2.4 miles from Mancora town. There is a great restaurant that overlooks the pool and the beach. Rooms have high ceilings, fans, private hot-water baths, and patios with hammocks. Some rooms are better than others, so ask to see first. There are two pool areas, one for adults and one for families. Umbrellas and chairs can be used by hotel guests. An overall excellent value. Includes continental breakfast. $$

★★★**Las Arenas** – ☎ 25-8240, www.lasarenasdemancora. com. Now associated with Libertador hotels. This hotel at a bend of Las Poscitas beach is small, a bit more isolated, but stunning. It has the feel of a small Caribbean or South Pacific resort. The restaurant serves an excellent blend of Peruvian and international dishes and will even bring meals out to you poolside, with a piña colada if necessary. Try the tuna sashimi or ceviche de langostinos. Rooms have private hot-water baths, TVs with DVD players, air-conditioning, fans, mini-fridges, and private patios with hammocks. Elegant beach life for a fraction of the cost. Highly recommended. $$$

Where to Eat

The best dining options are in the hotels on Las Pocitas beach. The town is littered with cheap seafood places, chifas, and burger stands. Here are some of the best.

★**The Birdhouse** – This food and shopping complex on the municipal beach draws a steady crowd throughout the day. A deck off the sand plays hosts to a large number of tables that are served by several restaurants (Sirena, Surf and Turf, among others) and Papa Mo's Milkbar, which serves the drinks. The food is mostly seafood although burgers and a variety of other dishes make their way onto the menus. Food is an excellent value and generally very good. $$

★**Sirena** – Piura (no #), ☎ 992-8073. This small boutique has just a few outdoor tables. The inside is mostly for the upscale gift shop that sells accessories and women's items. There is usually a pasta special for fewer than 20 soles that includes a starter, main course, and glass of wine. Entradas are very creative and change frequently. The curry de langosto (lobster curry) is made with coconut and green apples. Excellent choice if it's on the menu. $$$

La Trattoria da Antonio – Piura 352. This small Italian restaurant on the main strip is one of the most elegant in town. Try the penne alla putanesca or one of the many seafood dishes. $$$

Fluid Bar – Piura (no #). This bar filled with a mainly international clientele, has a good selection of Indian curries during the daytime. $$

La Bajadita – Piura (no #). This is more of an evening spot to grab dessert or a snack like manjar blanco pancakes while you listen to laid-back tunes. $

Geko Pizzeria – Piura (no #). This is a basic pizza place with patio seating that you will surely notice as you walk by. There are a variety of international dishes; nothing outstanding, but they cure the munchies. $

Iskay – Piura (no #). Right in the center of the bars, this backpacker hangout is good for a cheap three-course menu or just to kick back and have a drink. $$

Mamiferos – Piura 344. Pizzas, fusion dishes, and good northern seafood plates like mero al horno. Mojitos, margaritas, caipirinhas, and other cocktails make this a great choice for the pre-discoteca scene. Thursday is ladies' night and Saturday there is live music. $$

El Faro Lounge – Piura (no #, beside Interbanc). "The Lighthouse Lounge," crosses a wide variety of genres, serving steaks, national plates, seafood, and crêpes. The catch of the day is usually a good deal. $$

There are many seafood stands that line the municipal beach. You can grab any of the tables on the beach and a waitress will bring out a menu. They are all more or less the same. $

Bars & Clubs

Iguanas – Piura (no #). Corner tiki bar, which is usually crowded with a slightly older (older than 17 that is) crowd of mostly foreigners. Mamiferos and Fluid Bar (see above) are also chilled-out spots.

There are several discotecas right on the main strip, all next to one another. None are particularly good or stand out, so just pop in and see where the crowd is. The weekend here starts on Wed, although there will be a small crowd on any night.

Shopping

The Birdhouse – Several of the best shops in town, including a surf shop that rents boards and wetsuits, can be found here.

For jewelry and handicrafts, many stands and shops dot the Pan American Highway, just north of the cluster of bars. Lots of other stores are sprinkled throughout town as well. Sirena (see above) is the best place for women's swimsuits and other independently designed clothes and accessories.

Adventures

On Water

Mancora is Peru's best-known surfing beach. The waves are best from November-March and the most action is right in front of the municipal beach near all of the hordes of sunbathers. The surf shop at the Birdhouse rents and sells boards and wetsuits. There are many other places in town that do the same.

Day-Trips from Mancora

The **Poza de Barro**, or mud bath, is reachable by a four-hour hike northeast of Mancora or a 30-minute cab ride. The hot, brownish water comes from a natural spring and is thought to have curative properties. Ask in town for directions.

Los Pilares of Quebrada Fernández are about another hour and half on foot from the mud bath. These natural pools are fed by a series of waterfalls. Large boulders which you can jump from or camp on surround them.

Punta Sal

This resort area is 22 km/13 miles north of Mancora. It is far less lively than its neighbor, but the beaches are some of the best around and the majority of the hotels are far more posh.

Playa Punta Sal is a three-km/1.8-mile white sandy beach and

Punta Sal

home to most of the resorts. Other than a few souvenir shops and tourist restaurants, there is very little to do in the town. Much of the activity is confined to the beach.

Getting Here

Minibuses run here and to Mancora frequently. You can also take any bus between Mancora and Tumbes and ask to be left off.

Where to Stay

Punta Sal Club Hotel – Km 1,192 on the Pan American Highway Norte, ☎ 60-8373, 442-5992 (Lima), www.puntasal.com.pe. Includes breakfast, lunch, and dinner. Transportation and water games are extra. Regular rooms, air-conditioned, suites, bungalows. You have your pick and the price varies little. There is a private dining room inside a shipwrecked boat that sits on their property. A lovely restaurant and bar are part of the complex, plus a big pool area, Jacuzzi, playground, tennis courts, volleyball court, game room, and much more. This is an all-out beach resort with very rea-

Punta Sal Club Hotel

North Coast

sonable pricing. They can arrange deep-sea fishing ($400 per day for the boat) and horseback rides. $$$

Caballito de Mar – Km 1187 of the Pan American Highway Norte, ☎ 446-3122 (Lima), www.hotelcaballitodemar.com. The hotel is comprised of 10 bungalows and 23 rooms, all with ocean views, private patios and bathrooms. The rooms right beside the pool area are the most convenient, although the least private. Includes breakfast, lunch, dinner, and a welcome drink. The hotel will arrange activities such as diving, surfing, biking and trips to the Mangalares near Tumbes, hot springs, and surf trips. Prices are far too reasonable for a place like this. $$$ (low season $$).

Hotel Balihai – Km 1196.5 of the Pan American Highway Norte, ☎ 264-1870 (Lima), www.balihaiperu.com. This charming hotel is between Punta Sal and the fishing village of Zorritos. Their rooms are in Indonesian-style cottages with porches and hammocks, modern private bathrooms, and thatched roofs. There is a Peruvian and Indonesian restaurant, a tiki-style bar area, and a gorgeous pool. This hotel can arrange the same tours and activities as Caballito de Mar. $$$

HEMINGWAY'S PICK

Cabo Blanco, 30 km/18 miles south of Mancora, was a favorite of Ernest Hemingway during his trips to Peru in the early 1950s. It is one of the best places for deep-sea sport fishing excursions as well as for surfing. Black marlin and tuna, weighing hundreds of lbs, are the top prizes. There are just a few basic restaurants and hotels. **Hotel Merlin**, ☎ 85-6188, $$, is the best and can arrange fishing excursions. Most surfers camp on the beach during November-March when waves are at their highest.

Punta Sal crab (Heinz Plenge)

The Amazon

■ Northern Amazon

The Amazon is one of Mother Nature's greatest works of art. The river is ever-changing its course. New islands are forming all the time, with new forests and new inhabitants. The river will eventually swallow the islands whole and even newer ones will arise. Sixty-five million years ago (give or take) the Amazon River actually flowed into the Atlantic, but the rise of the Andes cut off the flow of the river, causing it to turn eastward into the Pacific. The Amazon River was "discovered" by a group of Spanish conquistadors led by Francisco de Orellana on Feb. 12, 1542 at the confluence of the Napo River. Yet, we are only beginning to understand how important this area is for the well-being of the planet.

IN THIS CHAPTER

- Northern Amazon   515
- Iquitos   519
- Yurimaguas   542
- Tarapoto   543
- Pucallpa   546

The Amazon rainforest is the largest tropical rainforest on earth. With the Brazilian Amazon being cut down at an ever-increasing rate to make room for cow pastures, Peru's portion of the forest is still relatively wild (although, also disappearing at far too great a rate). Some government officials would like to expand logging operations in the area, so much of the forest could be destroyed in the near future. The Peruvian Amazon is losing roughly 750,000 acres of forest annually to logging, mining, oil drilling and other multinational business ventures. More than 90% of the indigenous populations have disappeared,

Shapra Indian, Ucayali
(Wilfredo Loayza)

along with two-thirds of the languages they spoke. Many tribes are on the verge of extinction and survive only in extreme parts of the forest.

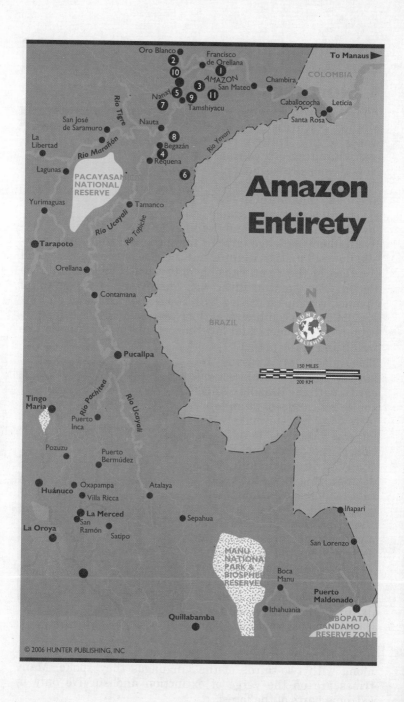

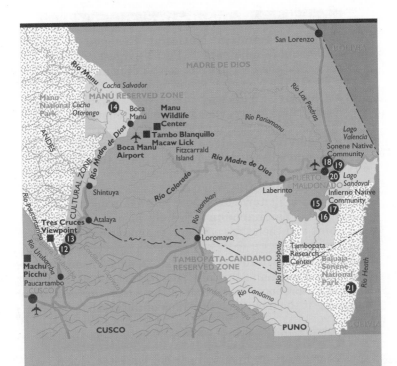

1. Explorama Lodge
2. ExplorNapo
3. Explortambo
4. ACTS
5. Ceiba Tops
6. Muyuna
7. Jacamar
8. Yarapa
9. Tahuayo Lodge
10. Cumaceba Lodge
11. Refugio Altiplano
    Heliconia Jungle Lodge
12. Cock-of-the-Rock Lodge
13. Cloud Forest Lodge
14. Manu Lodge
15. Tambopata Jungle Lodge
16. Explorer's Inn
17. Posada Amazonas
18. Cusco Amazonico Lodge
19. EcoAmazonia Lodge
20. Sandoval Lake Lodge
21. Heath River Wildlife Center

75 MILES

100 KM

HIGHLIGHTS

■ **Pacaya Samiria National Reserve** – The 8,100-square-mile park is Peru's largest single reserve and the best place to see wildlife and isolated tribes in the Northern Amazon region.

■ **Canopy Walkway** – Near Explorama's ExplorNapo Lodge. One of the most renowned wildlife viewing platforms in the world.

■ **Belén floating city** – A wooden shantytown that rises and falls with the river. See one of the most unusual communities in the Americas.

■ **Exotic dining** – Will it be a tapir steak tonight or curried alligator? How about roasted monkey?

■ **Lake Yarinacocha** – Search for pink river dolphins and then take part in a shamanic ceremony.

The Amazon Basin covers more than 2,500,000 square miles and holds more than a fifth of all the freshwater on the planet. The region produces 27% of all of the earth's oxygen, which has given it the nickname the "lung of the earth."

HEALTH RISKS

A certificate of proof will not be requested, but it is wise to get vaccinated against yellow fever – good for 10 years. As for malaria, that is a danger. Most tourists take anti-malarial tablets, either daily or weekly. Ask your doctor which type is preferred for your area of travel, as different types of mosquitoes resist different drugs. Some of the best known are Doxycycline, Mefloquine/Lariam, and Malarone. Most have side-effects such as nausea, vivid dreams, sensitivity to sunburn, and must be taken several weeks before and after your trip. If you go without the medication it doesn't mean you will get malaria. Chances are slim in any case. But it can be fatal, so why risk it? A good mosquito spray is also a must and is best purchased outside of Peru.

Life here is abundant and entirely self-sufficient. There are more than 2,400 species of fish, 50,000 different types of plants, 4,300 types of birds, and 400 mammal species. In Peru, the level of diversity is thought to be among the highest in the world. The Peruvian Amazon covers more than half of the country, although just 5% of the population lives there. Whatever you thought you knew about Peru or the impact of the Incas probably doesn't apply here. The Amazon region walks to the beat of its own drum.

🐦 Many scientists claim that, at the current rate of destruction, the Amazon rainforest could completely disappear in the next 50 years.

■ Iquitos
Phone code (065)

Iquitos, the most isolated large city in Peru (population 400,000), lies more than 1,846 km/1,108 miles NE of Lima, 3,646 km/2,187 miles from the mouth of the Amazon in the Atlantic, and more than 800 km/480 miles downstream from Pucallpa, where you will find the nearest roads leading to the rest of the country. It is the largest city in the world not connected by roads to the outside world. It is a place where adventure awaits at every turn. The food often consists of exotic creatures such as the skewered grubs in the market or the caiman sandwiches in almost every restaurant. The people meander in out of the world's largest jungle on boats and

Iquitos (Julius Tours)

forest paths. You get the sense that international spies are trading secrets in the tropical open-air cafés. It has a New Orleans-like feel with the Río Ucayali (not the Amazon River anymore, as many assume) just off the Malecón, casinos, and flashing lights. Or maybe it just seems that way after weeks in the jungle. Many make this their base for further exploration into the jungle or rivers, but the city itself has several interesting sights as well if you have the time to stay.

History

The official founding of Iquitos was on January 5, 1864, when the Peruvian navy set up a floating port here. But there was some activity in the area beforehand. From 1542, when the conquistadors first arrived near here, to the mid 1800s there was little activity. Only native tribes and the Jesuit and Franciscan missionaries that were trying to convert them inhab-

Native peoples of Iquitos

ited the area. Then came the rubber boom – the first and most important of many booms that would turn Iquitos into the bustling city that it is today. Goodyear's process of vulcanization, invented at this time, created an increased demand for latex, which was found in the rubber trees scattered throughout the jungle. Iquitos suddenly started to flourish in population and wealth. The many rubber barons, such as the famous Fitzcarrald (from the Herzog movie, *Fitzcarraldo*), lived lavishly and imported European materials such as Portuguese azulejos tiles for their opulent houses that still stand today. For a few years the barons even printed their own currency. The boom ended when evenly spaced rubber plantations on the Malay Peninsula were set up. Those trees didn't have to be sought out laboriously in the jungle; the rubber could be extracted in a controlled environment. When that happened, the barons and many others retreated to Europe or elsewhere.

Since the 1960s, however, the tourist, oil, and cocaine booms have brought a resurgence of activity to the city.

Getting Here

Air

Aeropuerto Internacional Francisco Secada Vignetta – Av. Abelardo Quiñones Km 6, ☎ 260-1147. Moto-taxi to/from the airport is about 6-8 soles.

There is a good possibility that by the time this book is out, Spirit Airlines will fly a Miami-Guayaquil-Iquitos route and back, which will save quite a bit of money if you are interested in combining Galapagos and Amazon tours.

Usually there is just one flight a day to or from Pucallpa, Yurimaguas, and Tarapoto, running about $70-$100 each way. Several flights go to and from Lima each day for $60-$110.

Iquitos

1. PromPeru de Armas
2. Inrena's Pacaya Samiria National Reserve Office
3. Iglesia Matriz
4. Casa de Fierro
5. Barrio Belen
6. Belen Market
7. Ari's Burger
8. The Yellow Rose of Texas
9. Bijao Restaurant
10. Estanbul
11. Giornata
12. Fitzcarraldo
13. El Nuevo Meson
14. Antica Pizzeria
15. Sabor A Fiesta
16. Panaderia Huambrillo
17. La Tribu
18. Supermarket
19. NOA
20. Mainuma Lounge
21. El Musmuqui
22. Arandu
23. El Dorado Plaza
24. El Dorado
25. Hobo Hideout
26. Hostal Baltazar
27. Hotel Maranon
28. Doral Inn
29. Rolando's
30. Hotel Victoria Regia
31. Real Hotel Iquitos
32. Hotel Europa

Airline Offices

Star Peru – Prospero 428 (on the Plaza), ☎ 23-6208, reservasiqt@starperu.com.

LAN – Progresso 232, www.lan.com.

Aero Continente – Prospero 232, ☎ 24-3489, www. aerocontinente.com.

TANS – Arica 273, ☎ 22-1549, agiquitos@tans.com.pe.

There are also several other companies at the airport that run small planes and charter services to just about anywhere in the Amazon.

Getting Around

Bus

 There are small collectivo buses in the area that will go to places such as the airport, Bellavista, or Lake Quistococha.

Taxi/Moto-Taxi

This is how most people get around in Iquitos. The three-wheeled carriages, which look almost like Thai tuk-tuks, fill every street in Iquitos and outnumber cars by far; they are sure to put the wind in your hair and the noise in your ears. Very cheap. About a dollar a ride anywhere in town. And they're everywhere. Everywhere.

Car rental?! There is one road out of town that ends after 20 minutes. Where are you going to go?

Tourist Information

i **Tourist Offices** – **PromPeru** has two offices in Iquitos. **Airport**, ☎ 26-0251, Iperuiquitosapto@ promperu.gob.pe. Open daily 8 am-1 pm and 4 pm-8 pm. **Plaza de Armas**, ☎ 23-6144, iperuiquitos@ promperu.gob.pe. Open daily 8:30 am-7:30 pm. **Inrena's Pacaya Samiria National Reserve Office**, Palma 113, Mon-Fri 8 am-4 pm. For maps of the area contact Irene Castro at the **Regional Government Office**, Quiñones Km 1.5. 7 am-12 pm.

Hospitals – **Hospital Regionalde de Loreto**, Av. 28 de Julio (no #), ☎ 252-004. 24-hour attention. **Hospital de Apoyo Iquitos**, Cornejo Portugal 1710, ☎ 264-715. 24-hour attention. **Clínica Ana Stahl**, La Marina 285, ☎ 25-2535.

This private clinic is more expensive than the public hospitals, but well worth the price. 24 hours.

Police – **Comisaria de Moronade Iquitos**, Morona 120, ☎ 23-1123. **Tourism Police**, Lores 834, 24 2081.

Post Office – **Correo**, Av. Arica 402, ☎ 223-812. Mon-Sat 7 am-7:30 pm. **DHL/Western Union**, 212 Prospero.

Embassies – **British Consulate**, in the Regal Bar and Restaurant, Putomayo 182, ☎ 22-2732. **Colombian Consulate**, Araujo 431, ☎ 23-1461. **Brazilian Consulate**, Lores 363, ☎ 231-461. Americans need a visa to cross into Brazil. If you don't already have one you must come here or you will not be allowed in the country. **Peruvian Migraciones**, Cáceres, cuadra 18, ☎ 23-5371. You can extend your tourist card or visa here.

Internet – Iquitos has an Internet café every five meters. Two recommended are: **El Cyber** on the Plaza and **Cocodrilo.net** at Fitzcarrald 215.

Banks – **BCP** is on a corner of the Plaza and has ATMs and exchanges traveler's checks. **BancoWeiss** also has an ATM on the Plaza.

Laundry – **Imperial Launderette**, Putomayo 150, ☎ 23-1768. Mon-Sat 8 am-8 pm.

Recommend Organizations in the Amazon If You Are Looking to Donate:

Amazon Medical Project – (see under Explorama Lodge for more info), www.amazonmedical.org.

Adopt-A-School Program – Provides educational support and school supplies for schools in the rural Amazon. Contact Pam Bucar de Arevalo, PO Box 446, Iquitos, Peru, conapac@explorama.com. Or contact Shawn Stinton at the Detroit Zoological Institute, stinton@detroitzoo.org.

Rainforest Conservation Fund – www.rainforest-conservation.org. All-volunteer organization dedicated to preserving the world's rainforest.

Sightseeing

The **Plaza de Armas** is the hub of all Iquitos activity. The best hotels and restaurants, an array of casinos and flashing lights, and all tourist services are here or a few blocks away. **Iglesia Matriz**, built between 1911 and 1924, has an interesting Swiss clock inside and sits on the south side of the Plaza. The **Casa de Fierro** (see below) is on the east side. The city hall museum, next to

The Amazon

the iPeru office on the north side, has a large collection of plaster and stuffed animals. Admission is free and it's worth a quick look.

★★★**Barrio Belén**, the floating city, is sometimes jokingly called the Venice of the Amazon. Don't expect to sit on a gondola while charming Giuseppe sings *O Sole Mio*. You can, however, pay a local boatman to give you a tour of the area in a motorized canoe. The shanty houses here are built on wooden stilts and on rafts that rise and fall with the water levels. At times in the low water season the water doesn't make it to the city and the houses just sit in the mud and silt. Living conditions are quite poor and you will be amazed at the number of children swimming and playing in the water where their waste is also floating. Just go to the waterfront and a boatman will likely approach you. Prices are about $5 per 30 minutes, per boat, but you can bargain.

The ★**market** that borders Belén is one of the most fascinating in all of Peru. It can be downright filthy at times, but it is worth a look. Other than the typi-

Barrio Belén (iquitos-PERU.com)

cal cuts of meat, food stands, household items, and produce, there are rarities here that set it apart from other markets. On one block, Pasaje Paquito, you can find dozens of stands selling nothing but medicinal plants, potions, cure-all medicines, jungle liquors, jewelry, and charms. Elsewhere you may encounter birds like toucans and macaws, roasted monkeys and grubs, and piles and piles of bananas. Get there early (before 9 am) to see the most action. Eiffel, who built the Eiffel Tower, created the small bandstand that sits in between the market and the barrio as well.

Museo Amazonica (Amazon Museum, 386 Tarapacá, ☎ 23-1072), is small and only has a few exhibits, but the 76 fiberglass statues of Indians in all shapes, sizes, and attires are quite spectacular. There is also some excellent woodcarving, particularly on the ceilings. The photos of old Iquitos are worth a look too. The building itself was put up in 1863. Open Mon-Fri 8 am-1 pm and 3-7 pm. Sat 9 am-1 pm. Admission 5 soles.

Nearby, the **Biblioteca Amazonica** (Amazon Library, Tarapacá 354, ☎ 24-2353) has many volumes on the Amazon and Iquitos, as well as photos, maps,

Floating houses (iquitos-PERU.com)

tribal relics, and an intricately carved wooden ceiling. It maintains a large collection of historical documents on the Amazon Basin. The second-floor windows look out onto the Malecón and the river. There is also Internet access available. Open Mon 3:30-5:45 pm; Tues-Fri 8:30 am-12:15 pm and 3:30-5:45 pm; Sat 9 am-12 pm. Admission free.

The **Camu Camu Gallery** (Trujillo 438, ☎ 253-120), is the Iquitos gallery of Francisco Grippa, who grew up in Northwest Peru and Los Angeles before coming to the Amazon, where he became an internationally renowned painter. One type of canvas he uses is from the chuchuara fig tree. His themes are essentially Amazonian in a European Impressionistic style that has become known as Grippismo. The Iquitos gallery is small, easy to pass up, and sometimes has just a few prints ($20) and originals (up to several thousand dollars). His paintings can also be seen and purchased at the El Dorado Plaza Hotel. His colossal house and studio are downriver in the Amazon town of Pevas (halfway between Iquitos and the border), where you can usually find Grippa himself. This is where to go to if you want the best selection of his work. It is the large modern house on the hill overlooking the river. Ask anyone and they will know where it is.

Malecón Tarapacá is a hub of activity most of the day and night. There are pleasant views over the river and to Belén, as well as restaurants and bars that open up to the sidewalk. On most nights you can catch a crowd of locals enjoying some entertainer or another. There are also a few statues, plenty of benches, and a pink dolphin fountain.

Buildings of the Rubber Boom

Most of the houses from the Rubber Boom are now owned by the military and visitors are not allowed inside to see their full grandeur. But one can hope they will eventually become restaurants and museums. In a short walk from the Plaza de Armas you can see the façades and the azulejos (Portuguese tiles) that line them. A few good examples are:

The Amazon

- **Casa de Barro** – 200-212 Napo. This is the house of Fermin Fitzcarrald, the most eccentric of the rubber barons. It is an adobe house, which is more reminiscent of the Andes, built of materials shipped in from Europe. Fitzcarrald drowned in the river at the age of 36, when his boat sank in a whirlpool as he slept in a cabin.

- **Casa de Fierro** – Perhaps the most eye-catching building on the Plaza de Armas (other than Ari's Burger). Eiffel designed it for the 1889 Paris Exhibition and it reached Iquitos six years later. Many of the iron pieces and metal

  Casa de Fierro at right (N. Gill)

  sheets were carried by hand through the jungle to Iquitos. It now houses a pharmacy, souvenir shop, and restaurant.

- **The Ex Hotel Palace** – At the intersection of Putomayo and Malecón Tarapacá. Art Nouveau building constructed in 1912 in what looks like a Moorish design.

- **Casa Cohen** – 401-437 Prospero, built in 1905, now Los Portales supermarket. Noted for the Portuguese azulejos tiles.

- **Casa Pinasco** – 129-169 Prospero. Built by an Italian family in the early 1900s, but note the English Neo-Classical façade.

- **Casa Morey** – 413-425 Raymondi. Neo-Classical building made almost entirely with European materials.

GASTRONOMY

- **Chonta** – Salad made from noodle-like strips of palm hearts.

- **Ceviche de paiche** – typical Peruvian ceviche that uses the 10-foot-long paiche fish.

- **Juane** – Corn, rice, olives, eggs, and usually chicken wrapped in a bijao leaf and steamed.

- **Inchicapi** – Soup made from chicken, corn, cilantro, and peanuts.

- **Tachaco** – Green bananas and pork that are mashed into balls and fried.

■ **Shambo** – This longtime local favorite popsicle is named after a plant of the same name and appearance. Lots of flavors, mainly of regional fruits.

■ **Jungle animals** – On Iquitos' menus you can find everything from tapir, caiman, and venison to sopa de motelo (turtle soup).

■ **Turtle eggs** – You will find stacks and stacks of these eggs at the market. Each of the turtles lays one egg at a time. Supposedly, their numbers have increased to where they are no longer endangered, but just consider the ecological implications before eating.

■ **Masato** – Drink made from chewed, spit, and fermented manioc root.

■ **Fruits** – Camu camu, cocona, chirimoya, guanabana, and maracuya.

■ **Siete raíces** – mixture of seven roots/barks from the jungle that are soaked in aguardiente (sugar cane alcohol).

■ **Chuchuhuasi** – Bark of the chuchuhuasi tree soaked in aguardiente.

■ **Huarapo** – Fermented sugar cane juice.

■ **Coconachado** – Juice of cocona, sugar, and aguardiente.

Where to Stay

El Dorado Plaza – Napo 258, ☎ 222-555, www.eldoradoplazahotel.com. The El Dorado is the nicest hotel in Iquitos. It calls itself a five-star hotel officially, but it is more like a three-star with a five-star pool and lobby. The pool is gorgeous and makes those hot Amazon days go so much smoother. All the amenities of a good hotel are there – air-conditioning, hot water (often lukewarm), cable TV, mini-bar, phone... plus a good restaurant and bar. They can arrange airport pickups. Touts wait outside the hotel trying to sell tours. You should ignore most street touts, but especially these. $$$$

El Dorado – Napo 362, ☎ 23-1742, fax 22-1985. Not as glamorous as its sister hotel, but with

El Dorado Plaza

more or less the same amenities. Includes breakfast and airport transfer. $$$

Hotel Sol del Oriente – Aberlardo Quiñones Km 2.5 (near the airport), ☎ 260-317, fax 26-0317, www.missloreto.com/hotelsoldeloriente.htm. Perhaps the nicest hotel in Iquitos, but it is near the airport and far removed from town. If you hate the noise of moto-taxis than this is an option, though. Rooms and bathrooms are modern. All of the amenities are included. Gorgeous pool area. $$$

Hobo Hideout – Putomayo 437, ☎ 23-4099. Pleasant and clean backpacker hangout. Dorms only. Kitchen, laundry, and even a small swimming pool. $

Hostal Baltazar – Condamine 265, ☎ 23-2240. This hotel is an excellent value. It is clean, convenient, and cheap. Air-conditioning, cable, private (cold-water) showers. Rooms on the ground floor tend to be slightly more modern. Keep an eye out for the world's friendliest maid, who is known to invite travelers to her home to meet her family and have dinner. $

Hotel Marañon – Nauta 289, ☎ 24-2673, fax 23-1737, hotelmaranon@terra.com.pe. A block from the Plaza. One of the better hotels in the area. Rooms have air-conditioning, hot water, mini-fridge, and cable TV. Also a small pool area, lavandería, Internet, and a restaurant. Continental breakfast included. $$

Doral Inn – Raymondi 220, ☎ 24-3386, fax 24-1970, doralinnhotel_iquitos@hotmail.com. Fairly new accommodation with private baths, hot water, cable TV, and room service. Has a fifth-floor restaurant with a view over the city. Price includes breakfast. $$.

Rolando's – Nauta 307, ☎ 23-1842. Dingy, but cheap and centrally located; comes with private bath. $

Hotel Victoria Regia – Ricardo Palma 252, ☎ 23-1761, ext 43, fax 23-2499, www.victoriaregiahotel.com. Attractive, clean and modern hotel that doesn't overdo it with luxury. Suites available, air-conditioning, cable TV, mini-fridge, phones, hot water and private baths. Also a pool and restaurant with good local dishes like paiche (an enormous freshwater fish), juanes (rice, meat, eggs, olives and spices steamed in a bijao leaf), and inchicapi (chicken and peanut soup). Rates include breakfast and airport pick-up. Also associated with the Heliconia Jungle Lodge (see below). $$$

Hostal El Colibri – Nauta 172, ☎ 24-1737, hostalelcolibri@hotmail.com. Cheap, clean, and pleasant hostel with hot water, private baths, air-conditioning, cable TV. Good location (1½ blocks from the Plaza) and good value. $

Real Hotel Iquitos – On the Malecón one block from the Plaza, ☎ 231-011. Run-down, but good location with views over the Malecón. Rooms have cable TV, air-conditioning, telephones, and mini-bars. $$

Hotel Europa – Prospero 494, ☎ 23-1123, fax 23-5483. Large five-story hotel sits in a noisy, dirty street, and the official three-star rating is a bit high, but includes private baths, hot water, air-conditioning, and cable TV. $$

Where to Eat

★**Ari's Burger** – Prospero 127 at the corner of Napo and Raymondi, ☎ 241-124. Extremely popular any time of day. Resembles a 50s-style open-air American diner with a large menu of burgers, breakfast items, desserts, and the occasional jungle dish. Pretty young waitresses are always friendly and dress in classic malt shoppe shirts, skirts, and hats. $

The Yellow Rose of Texas – Putomayo 180, next to the Iron House and owned by the Texas-born ex-director of tourism for Iquitos. Large menu of many different world comfort foods. Peruvian and jungle foods such as caiman (steaks and sandwiches), but also Louisiana-style Cajun, Tex-Mex, Italian, and British dishes. Also has a free book exchange. Open 24 hours. $

★**La Gran Maloca** – Sargento Lores 170, ☎ 233-126. This is Iquitos' most elegant establishment and set amidst a Rubber Boom-era mansion, with air-conditioning and a beautiful Colonial interior. They serve the best of regional dishes, including the typical steaks and pastas. $$$

Bijao Restaurant – 354 Loreto. Simple place with a small sidewalk patio. Serves light snacks, drinks, and local dishes. $

Estanbul – 386 Raymondi. Has pizzas, pastas, kebabs, falafels, Turkish coffee, and other tastes you probably won't find at many other places in the Amazon. $

Giornata – On the Plaza next to Ari's. It is a good place to go for ice cream (which is good just about anytime in Iquitos). $

The Huasai – Fitzcarrald 102, ☎ 242-222. Good open-air choice with fans and a tropical feel. Cheap lunch menus. $$

★**Fitzcarraldo** – Malecón Maldonado 103 and Napo. A classy open-air restaurant good for just a drink or a decent meal. On the corner, with large open windows and fans.

Dishes such as palm heart soup, smoked pork and banana balls, and caiman in a wine and raisin sauce are particularly good. A few tables sit on the Malecón. $$$

★**Bucanero** – La Marina 124. Owned by the owner of the Yarapa River Lodge. Open only for lunch, but popular. Excellent seafood, including pescado de loreto, paiche, ceviche, tiradito, and plenty of other options. The view over the Río Ucayali is tremendous. One of the best restaurants in Iquitos and very few tourists know about it. $$

El Nuevo Mesón – Malecón Maldonado 153. Serves jungle specialties like boar, tapir, turtle, and caiman. $$

Antica Pizzeria – On Napo between the Plaza and the Malecón. You won't miss this place, with its elaborate façade and decoration that is completely made of what looks like driftwood. It is part of a chain, with restaurants in Lima and elsewhere in Peru. Pizzas are good, calzones are enough for two people. There are a variety of pastas and sauces, as well as lasagnes. $$

Sabor a Fiesta – Nauta 390. This clean corner location a few blocks from the center has a wide variety of choices on their menu, with ceviches, parihuela and good pizzas. $$

Panaderia Huambrillo – Tarapacá 162. A European-style café with coffee and pastries that sits in a quiet location on the Malecón. $

La Tribu – Napo 138. Small bar with a tropical feel. Serves mainly local dishes such as paiche al ajo (an enormous freshwater fish with garlic), lagarto con legumbres (alligator with vegetables), motelo al kion (turtle meat in sauce). This is a good place to try cocktails made with many jungle ingredients such as chuchuhuasi, seven raices, and camu camu that are soaked in aguardiente (sugar cane alcohol). $$

 Supermarket: There is a small nameless corner market on Raymondi 155.

Bars/Clubs

 NOA – Fitzcarrald 298. This is the best discoteca in Iquitos. It is very modern, with two floors, international music, and expensive drinks. Gay-friendly. Usually a $5 cover.

Mainuma Lounge – 254 Fitzcarrald. A new bar and disco next to NOA. Has the atmosphere of an American University pick-up joint.

The Gringo Bar – Putomayo 168, next to the Yellow Rose of Texas. Small bar with sidewalk tables and a slew of expat regulars.

El Musmuqui – 155 Raymondi. Has pitchers of very good mixed drinks like capirinhas and mixtures of jungle liquors.

Arandu – On the Malecón, the popular patio gets filled until late on most nights. Good spot for a beer and to watch the local activity. It is the best of a few bars that make up a small strip.

Copacabana – Trujillo, the 300 block. One of Iquitos' few gay bars.

Adventures

On Water

★★**River Travel** – One journey I took was from Coca, Ecuador to Iquitos, lasting more than two weeks. Five days were spent on a boat, and another 10 or so waiting for it at the border. Both parts of the trip were hell. Unlike the days of old where passenger service was common

Along the Río Napo (N. Gill)

for tourists, the boats are more cargo barges that take on passengers – who end up feeling like cargo themselves. The lower level of the boat is usually filled with an array of animals such as cows, and pigs, chickens, and ducks, all crowded together. Some die on the trip.

The journey is not for the faint of heart. The boat smells terrible and the food is even worse. It's cooked in river water by transvestite cooks (on every single boat), and you are barely able to keep it down. The bathroom (one of them) is usually a metal cabin with holes in it that leak into the river. The sleeping area is overcrowded with as many hammocks as they need to fit. You find your hammock set up in a nice open space, which is gradually surrounded by others. You may find one right above yours with a breastfeeding mother in it. You will see very little wildlife other than an occasional river dolphin or pet/dinner monkey. Occasionally you may be able to get off at a small river town and find some real food, but very rarely. Few tourists take these boats, but, as strange as it sounds, the ones that do often consider it the highlight of their trip – solely because of how surreal it is. The local people have no other choice. This is how they live.

To hop aboard a local boat, all you have to do is go down to Puerto Masusa on La Marina, about 2½ km/1½ miles from the center. There you can look on chalkboards to see which boat goes where and when it is leaving. But the boats almost never leave on time and sometimes leave days late. The only accurate information is from the captain himself. There are four main routes to take, coming to and from Iquitos.

- **To Pucallpa** – Boats leave nearly every other day and take four to six days, depending on the season. $17-$25.

- **To Yurimaguas** – Boats leave about three times a week and take three to four days. You can save a few hours by going to Nauta and taking the boat from there. $25-$30

- **To Ecuador** – This route along the Río Napo is one of the least traveled. Many guidebooks and travel agencies won't even say that it is an option, but I assure you it is. I have made the trip. Look for the boat *Jeisawell* in Iquitos. I hate this boat more than any other boat in the entire world. It is a rotten, dirty, stinking hunk of metal, but it may be the only option. You can catch the boat at Mazan, where via a combined moto carro/ferry ride you can get to/from Iquitos and shave a day off the journey. If heading toward Ecuador, be sure you know when the boat will be arriving in Mazan. If coming from Ecuador, you may have to wait at the border (Pantoja), which has straightforward border proceedings, for as long as two weeks and it is near impossible to get an accurate assessment of when the boat is coming. At the time of writing, a small hotel was being built, although a man named Ruperto will let you stay at his house for $5 a day with three meals. The travel time is four to six days and it costs anywhere from $20-30. Bargain.

- **To Leticia, Colombia/Tabatinga, Brazil** – This downstream route to the tri-border can be reached in three ways. 1. On a **local boat** that will take two days and costs $20. They leave several times a week. 2. Take a **speedboat** (12 hours for $50). Contact Expreso Loreto and Raimondi. They leave at 6 am every other day and include lunch. 3. On a **luxury passenger boat** with one of the tour companies. Once at the border you can literally walk to either of the three checkpoints. Leticia, once a part of Peru, but now Colombia, is the biggest and has the most amenities. From there boats can be picked up to other points in Colombia. There are also flights to the beautiful Colombian cities of

Cartagena and Bogotá. From Tabatinga you can head into the Brazilian Amazon and over to Manaus or still farther to the Atlantic. Remember, Americans need a visa before visiting Brazil.

What you need:

■ A hammock is essential, unless on a boat with cabins, although the cabins are often much worse.

■ Plate/bowl and silverware.

■ Bug spray – Sand flies and mosquitoes usually only come aboard when the boat is stopped, which is often.

■ Extra food – Essential, unless you have a strong stomach.

■ Water (beer and soda can usually be purchased on-board).

DID YOU KNOW?

A guide in the area told me his grandmother used to tell him that wherever he lived he must not be far from a certain type of monkey. He didn't understand why, nor did his grandmother or the rest of their family. It is just something they had always done and the family had stayed safe. When working with a foreign researcher one day, he asked why his family followed this rule and pointed out the monkey. It turned out this species of monkey was highly vulnerable to malaria and only lived in areas where the chance of getting the disease was slim. By following the advice of generations, his family had avoided the disease.

The Amazon

Day-Trips from Iquitos

Puerto Bellavista sits at the northern edge of Iquitos on the Río Mañon. A few small restaurants and bars are at the port and look out onto the river. Many touts working for water taxis and ferries will approach you for a tour down the river. You can get to numerous small mestizo villages such as Pedrecocha or to Yagua and Boras Indian communities with these boats. Private boats and guides are significantly more expensive and faster than the local ferries. The beach, Playa Nanay, is clean and many locals swim in the river there, although the murky water and silt-laden footing scares away most tourists.

Lago Quistococha (Christ's Lake) is seven km/4.2 miles and about a 20-minute taxi ride (10-12 soles) or bus ride (2 soles) from Iquitos. The bus departs from Plaza 28 de Julio. The

1,260 acres of forests, lagoon, and zoo make up the **National Tourist Park**. The lagoon is good for swimming, fishing, floating lazily in a paddleboat, or resting on the artificial beach. You can hike on the pedestrian walk that circles the lake. There is a fish hatchery, one of the few places where you can see the enormous paiche, which can grow up to 10 feet and can be found in many restaurants in Iquitos – although now its numbers are running low. In the zoo you will find many rare animals native to the region. So, if you missed out on a trip to a jungle lodge, you can catch up here. Admission $1.

Unless you are curious about a typical, uninteresting river town, **Pedrecocha** probably won't do much for you. On the edge of town the ★★**Pilpintuwasi Butterfly Farm** is an excellent side-trip that will probably take about a half-day. Austrian Gudrun Sperrer and Peruvian Robler Moreno run this breeding center for more than 43 types of butterflies. You can walk through a large caged area where the butterflies float freely and also an incubation room where you can witness one of nature's most wondrous phenomena. They also have several rare rescued animals here, such as a jaguar, tapir, giant anteater, manatee, and several mon-

Pygmy marmosets at Pilpintuwasi Butterfly Farm

keys. So, if you want to make sure to see some wildlife before or after your jungle trip, this is a good place. At high water, you can catch a boat from Bellavista right to the entrance; otherwise you walk about 20 minutes from the dock at Pedrecocha. Make a left off the boat and follow the signs, or walk up the path to the village and keep left. If you get lost, just ask someone for "las mariposas" (the butterflies) and they will point you in the right direction. Open Tues-Sun 9 am-4 pm. $5 adults, $3 students with card.

Ecolodges

Some people will spend hundreds of dollars but see only minimal wildlife and are disappointed. Chances are you will see some. Just don't expect to see a jaguar or ocelot, as sightings are rare. You must go with the expectation of not just seeing wild-life, but of experiencing one of the most fascinating areas in the world. The Amazon is disappearing. It is no secret. Some believe it will be completely gone in the coming years. Listening to the birds and insects, smelling the

Yagua Indians, near Iquitos (N. Gill)

leaves and flowers, or feeling the strength of the world's largest river system floating beneath you – no price can be set on these experiences. For me personally, this is one part of the world that I could not *not* experience. Most of the lodges are expensive, but they try to make the experience as comfortable as possible in a wild place. All include three full meals a day, usually buffet-style. Most have shared baths and are lit at night by kerosene lamps.

★★**Explorama Lodges** – ☎ 800-707-5275 (in the US), in Peru, ☎ 25-2530, fax 25-2533, www.explorama. com. From the creative mind of Peter Jensen, once the curator of a Wisconsin museum and Pete the Science Guy from the Bozo the Clown show. This first-class company has been around for more than 40 years and is the first, biggest, most popular, and best-organized of all the lodge companies. Some call it the granddaddy of Iquitos jungle lodges. They have a total of five lodges and can arrange just about any itinerary you want. Each lodge is equipped with 24-hour tea, coffee, and water services, and a very attractive dining area and bar. They also have a three-level riverboat that is used on rare occasions. Food is generally buffet-style and excellent. Explorama uses friendly and well-trained, local bilingual guides, many of whom have been with the company for decades. It is a very dignified company that embraces the local community by using their products and promoting several foundations and grass roots organizations that greatly benefit the area. All prices include transportation to and from Iquitos and the lodges and meals. Explorama offers special Internet deals and significant discounts for larger groups. They also offer combined tours to more than one lodge at a time. For example, four days/three nights Explorama and Explornapo is $735 per person or a combined full week at all of the lodges is $899 per person.

■ **Explorama Lodge** – Built in 1864, it is 80 km/48 miles downriver from Iquitos in an area of secondary and some primary growth forests. Clean thatched palm constructions and rooms equipped with mosquito nets and shared bathrooms/showers. Kerosene lamps light the lodge, although some electricity is available to charge camera batteries. Access to the local Yagua Indian community nearby. Macaws and other birds hang around the lodges. When the water is high canoe trips are available right from the lodge. Here you can also encounter Doctor Linnea J. Smith MMD, a Wisconsin doctor, who in 1990 gave up her practice and life at home to dedicate herself to helping those in the Amazon who previously had no access to health care other than that of the shaman. Explorama provides her with meals and transportation, and various individuals and organizations donate all supplies, medicine, and general funding. She runs a six-room clinic near Explorama Lodge that, along with her several local assistants, treats 2,000-2,500 patients a year. For more information, how to make a donation, or how to buy her book, *La Doctora*, visit www.amazonmedical.org. Three days/two nights, $285 per person.

■ **Explornapo Lodge** – Up a small creek (the Sucusari) off of the Río Napo, a major tributary of the Amazon. Explornapo is very similar to Explorama Lodge, but 160 km/96 miles from Iquitos and set in hundreds of thousands of acres of primary forest. The highlight of a trip to this lodge is the nearby ★★★**Canopy Walkway**. The walkway is a third of a mile long, 115 feet high at one point, and the only one in South America and one of just a few worldwide. It was only in the past few decades that scientists began to study the Amazon from high in the tree-top canopies. What they found was an entirely different world, with an abundance of new species that were never thought to have existed. Also **ReNuPeru** medicinal garden, with its own shaman, is found nearby. Five days/four nights, $820 per person.

■ **Explortambos Camp** – A two-hour walk from Explornapo, this campsite is the most rustic of all the Explorama facilities. It can sleep a maximum of 16 people in small,

Canopy walkway at Explornapo (N. Gill)

thatched-roofed structures with mosquito nets. Meals are cooked over an open-hearth fireplace. This is one of the best places to see wildlife such as primates and other mammals because of its low-impact isolation. Stays here are usually combined with stays at Explornapo. Five days/ four nights at Explorama, ExplorNapo, and ExplorTambos, $842 per person.

Explortambos Camp

■ **ACTS Field Station** – The Amazon Conservation of Tropical Study is where many scientists and naturalists go for research. Fortunately, you can join them. The lodge itself is similar to Explorama and Explornapo, and located near the Canopy Walkway. A donation to the reserve and the conservation of the walkway is included in the bill. Reserved mainly for scientific purposes, so contact Explorama for specific details.

■ **Ceiba Tops** – This is the lodge for those who don't want to rough it. It is the only bona fide resort on the Amazon. It actually feels more like a Caribbean island. Rooms have air-conditioning, electricity, mini-fridges, and hot water. There is also a pool complete with waterfall, waterslide, and spa. The dining room and bar/lounge are spectacular. It is just 40 km/24 miles downriver from Iquitos in an area of mostly primary growth forests. The lodge, once called Explorama Inn, is named after a giant ceiba tree that sits on the land and should not be missed. Three days/two nights, $298 per person.

★**Muyuna Amazon Lodge** – Office in Iquitos at Putomayo 163-B, ☎ 242-858, www.muyuna.com. Muyuna prides itself on not paying commissions to street touts, and this is a good thing. They are more budget-minded than some of the similar lodges and tend to

Ceiba Tops

attract a crowd aged between 20 and 40. The lodge sits on the Yanuyacu River about three hours south of Iquitos (120 km/72 miles), near several other lodges. Best to visit in high-water season when more wildlife is near and the lodge is slightly more accessible. Muyuna has local bilingual naturalists, many of whom have worked alongside scientists on various research projects. Their office in Iquitos has a very helpful and friendly staff. They also have dolphin listening equipment. Peruvian-owned. Three days/two nights, $300.

Jacamar Amazon Jungle Lodge – ☎ 866-278-7489 (in the US), www.jacamarlodge.com. Small lodge 155 km/93 miles south of Iquitos on the Tahuayo River. Six thatched-roof bungalows can sleep up to 24 people at a time. Has a dining hall, bar, lounge, and reference library. No electricity, but a small generator is available for charging camera batteries. Can arrange jungle survival and stays with indigenous communities. Three days/two nights, $390 per person. Price breaks for longer stays and larger groups. Off-season discounts as well.

★**Yarapa River Lodge** – Iquitos office at La Marina 124, ☎ 993-1172, 800-771-3100 (in the US), www.yarapariverlodge.com. 177 km/106 miles upstream on the Yarapa River, this lodge is the home of the Cornell University's Esbaran Field Laboratory, where numerous scientists and university students conduct research. With the level of scientific study going on here, you can expect some of the best guides. Full solar powering, composting, and waste management. Four days/three nights, $700. More with private bath.

Tahuayo Lodge – www.perujungle.com. Four hours upstream from Iquitos on the Tahuayo River. Rooms are basic and beds are lined with mosquito nets. Education laboratory and library. Free daily laundry service, which is a huge plus. Recognized as one of the world's 10 best lodges by *Outside Magazine*. Eight days/seven nights, $1,295.

Cumaceba Lodge – Office in Iquitos Putomayo 184, ☎ 23-2229, www.cumaceba.com. This is a good option for those on a budget, but don't expect to see much wildlife at just 30 km/18 miles from Iquitos. Three nights/four days, $200. Also can arrange rustic camping farther into the jungle. Operates **Curaka Adventure Lodge**, as well, 180 km/108 miles upriver near the start of the Amazon. Two nights/three days, $250 per person.

Refugio Altiplano – Raimondi 171, ☎ 224-020, www.refugioaltiplano.org. This lodge fills a specific niche. Its main activities deal in natural medicine, shamanic ceremonies, and spiritual healing. The leader in Ayahuasca hallucinogenic ceremonies. Ceremony house on the grounds. Six days/three ceremonies ($300).

Heliconia Jungle Lodge – www.heliconialodge.com.pe. Located 80 km/48 miles or 1¼ hours downriver from Iquitos. A generator provides electricity for seven hours each day. Twenty-one rooms with private baths and hot water. Three days/two nights, $180. Four days/three nights, $320.

Jungle Lodge Activities

- Piranha fishing
- Stargazing
- Hiking in the jungle
- Camping
- Medicinal plant workshops
- Shamanic ceremonies
- Night walks/canoe trips
- Looking for river dolphins
- Visits to Indian villages
- Visits to Mestizo river towns
- Canopy walks
- Bird watching
- Photography
- Seeing the Victoria Regia

River Cruises

Amazon Tours and Cruises – 336 Requena, ☎ 23-1611, ☎ 305-227-2266 (in the US), 22-2440, fax 23-1265, www.amazontours.net. American-owned and has served parts of the Amazon for 40 years. Operates a handful of luxurious boats with special features like air-conditioning and Jacuzzis. Tours from three days and up. They also have four-day/three-night trips to Leticia/Tabatinga in style ($765 per person

The Amazon

based on double occupancy). Six-night cruises, $1,395. Deals for large groups. They also run tours in the Andes, and to Manaus and Belem, Brazil.

Amazon River Expeditions – Iquitos office is at Ricardo Palma 242, ☎ 421-9195, fax 442-4338, www.amazonriver-expeditions.com. Stops at many places for tours of specific sights such as the confluence of the Ucayali and Marañon rivers – the beginning of the Amazon River. Arranges stays at several lodges. Departs every Sun morning and arrives back in Iquitos on Sat night. Also has trips to the Yanomano rain-forest and the Allpahuayo Mishana National Reserve. Local guides speak English, German, and French. In operation 28 years. Four days/three nights Pacaya Samiria, $485.

Adventures

 Most street guides have very little experience in guiding, are unprofessional, and some have criminal records. Although I have spoken to people who have gotten what they wanted and had a good time, that is not common. Most prices range from $25 to $50 a day, including food and lodging. There are several independent freelance guides in the area who are a much better choice.

Alex Weill Rengifo – ☎ 24-3467, alexweill@mailcity.com.

Randall's Adventure and Jungle Training – ☎ 856-932-9111 in the US, www.jungletraining.com. Led by the only US representative of the Peruvian Air Force School of Jungle Survival, this has been featured on the Travel and Discovery channels. The company can organize any type of jungle training or survival based on clients' desires. Most tours last several weeks and are both physically and mentally demanding. Prices start at $2,500 per person. Military survival school is $1,450 per person.

Amazon Explorer – www.Amazonexplorer.com. This is another hard-core, mentally and physically demanding kind of jungle trip. Programs visit extremely isolated tribes and areas and can be organized to include an emphasis on survival, shamanism, and contact with indigenous tribes. Some trips last two weeks and cost $1,900 per person, although it really depends on the tour.

 Amazon Bike Tours – ☎ 23-1816, biketours2005@yahoo.com, offers half- and full-day mountain biking tours from Iquitos. Designed for riders of various skill levels the tours will take you along jungle trails and through local villages. Prices include bike, helmet, and tour guide, beginning at $25 for a half-day. Group rates are available.

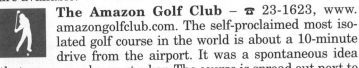 **The Amazon Golf Club** – ☎ 23-1623, www.amazongolfclub.com. The self-proclaimed most isolated golf course in the world is about a 10-minute drive from the airport. It was a spontaneous idea that arose over beers at a bar. The course is spread out next to the Nauta highway, and is 2,340 yards in length. The course is just nine holes. Don't expect top-of-the-line.

Casinos

Royal Inn and Casino – Aguirre 793. The largest in Iquitos, but quite a distance from the center. Also has a hotel. $$$

There are many other casinos in Iquitos, most of them on the Plaza de Armas.

Shopping

Mad Mick's Trading Post, Putomayo 163, dpto. 202, has "everything for the jungle to rent or buy." This is where to go if you are going on a deep trek into the jungle and need serious equipment. But they also have small everyday items like flashlights, mosquito repellent, and boots. They also have a tour office that can help arrange trips to lodges around Iquitos or set up a trip with one of their own guides, who are reasonably economical and far better than strangers in the street.

★**Mercado Artesanal San Juan**, at Quinonez Km 4.5, near the airport. A collection of thatched huts where local artisans are creating the crafts they are selling on-site. Natural medicines, jewelry, textiles, woodcarvings, etc. You can bargain, but prices are relatively cheap and the quality is generally good. Take a moto-taxi there for about 6-8 soles.

The **Centro Artesanal Anaconda**, a thatched-roof market just down from the Malecón, has a good selection of jewelry, ceramics, t-shirts, and small handcarved crafts. Sometimes they hold native dances and music performances.

Raices Cerámica, Loreto 346. This workshop produces all kinds of ceramics, t-shirts and handicrafts, with Amazon themes. Good for chic souvenirs that you won't find anywhere else.

Festivals

Foundation of the Iquitos (January 5) – Civic festival where many find reason to keep the party going after New Year's day.

Fiesta de San Juan (June) – Festival for San Juan Bautista, celebrating water, an important resource for the entire region. Plenty of local dishes find their way to the streets.

■ Yurimaguas

Yurimaguas (population 40,000) is the nearest major port to Iquitos and the one with the most frequent water transportation. It is the biggest port on the Río Huallaga, but still very minor compared with the likes of Iquitos and Pucallpa. The market is quite lively in the mornings before 8 am. You can organize treks in the surrounding jungle through one of the tour agencies on the Plaza.

Getting Here

 The port of **La Boca** is where all the larger boats leave, such as the ones to Iquitos. The port is located some 15 to 20 minutes walk from the center, or a few soles in a moto-taxi. Trips last about three days and leave every other day. You can buy hammocks for the trip at the market for about $5. See the Iquitos section for more information.

To Tarapoto (140 km/84 miles, six hours) try **Expreso Huarmanga**, which has one daily bus at 7 am leaving from its office outside the center. Or try the mini-buses that line up on Tacna and Huallaga. They leave when full, beginning at 4 am.

Where to Stay

 Puerto Patos – San Miguel 720, ☎ 35-2009, www.puertopalmeras.com.pe/pericos. To the north of the city, this quiet place includes continental breakfast in the rate. Rooms overlook the river and are airy, but still hot. They have private baths and hot-water showers. The hotel will help arrange trekking, mountain biking, and general transportation. $$

Hostal Luis Antonio – Jauregui 407, ☎ 35-2065. This is a good budget option where you can add on things like TV and air-conditioning for a slight extra charge. There is also a small pool on the grounds. $

Day-Trips from Yurimaguas

Lagunas, 12 hours upriver from Yurimaguas, is a small village with basic accommodations. Boats between Iquitos and

Yurimaguas stop there, as do more
frequent boats that travel solely
between the two points. You can
arrange canoe trips of several days
with the locals and there is a good
variety of wildlife. Expect to pay
about $15 per person per day.
Lagunas is also a good place to begin
exploration of the Pacaya-Samiria

National Reserve. **Estpel** (☎ 40-1007) is the official guides
association and calling there is a much better option (and
safer) than taking a tour with someone on the street.

■ Tarapoto

Phone code (042)

This city set amid jungle and the eastern lowlands is beginning to attract loads of new tourists seeking relaxation and
adventure. There is little to do in Tarapoto itself (population
100,000, 350 m/1,158 feet elevation) and the restaurants
aren't particularly good outside of those in a few of the nicer
hotels. The Plaza is the hub of activity, but little goes on even
there. The Indian village of Lamas has a small museum, a few
Colonial buildings, and you will be able to purchase crafts. To
get there, take a moto-taxi (20 minutes, 2 soles).

Getting Here

The **airport** (☎ 52-2778) is just a few km from the
center. Flights go to Iquitos and Lima daily, and
smaller companies, with offices at the airport, fly to
various regional destinations. The major airline is
Tans, Plaza Mayor 491, ☎ 52-5339, www.tansperu.com.pe.

Most bus companies head to Chiclayo (15 hours)
and Lima (25-30 hours), although none are very
good or comfortable. **Movil** (Salaverry 858, ☎ 52-
9193) is probably the best company and has the fewest stops. If heading to Yurimaguas, you can catch a collectivo
for the rough, six-hour trip at the market in Shilcayo. You can
also transfer to Chachapoyas via Pedro Ruiz.

Tourist Information

Casa de Turistas – On the Plaza. This is a small
shop with some brochures and useful information.

Where to Stay

Hotel Río Shilcayo – La Flores 224, one km east in Shilcayo, ☎ 522-225. This is a modern facility removed from the hustle and bustle of town. Has a good restaurant, swimming pool, bar, and sauna. Includes breakfast and airport transfers. $$$

Hotel Río Shilcayo

Hotel Nilas – Moyabamba 173, ☎ 527-331, nilas-tpto@terra. com.pe. Has many modern amenities, including a pool, Jacuzzi, gym, Internet access, rooms with cable TV and mini-fridges. $$$

Hostal Luna Azul – Manco Cápac 206, ☎ 52-7604, lunaazulhotel.tripod.com. This hotel has recently gone through a series of improvements and has added air-conditioning to some rooms. Rooms have cable TV and private baths. $$

El Mirador – La Cruz 517, ☎ 522-177. Popular budget option with a rooftop terrace for sharing travel tales. Community feel. Rooms have cold-water showers and fans. Will arrange tours. $

★**Puerto Palmeras** – On the Carretera Km 625, ☎ 511-242-5550 (Lima), fax ☎ 511-444-9663, www.puertopalmeras.com. pe/palmeras.htm. Perhaps the most complete resort in the Peruvian Amazon. It sits on 59 acres of land and includes a beautiful and often crowded pool area. The hotel is built of local materials and the 45 rooms have terraces, TVs, mini-bars, hot showers, and fans. A variety of suites, including some with air-conditioning and Jacuzzis, are available. A nice restaurant and pool bar keep you from having to go into the city. The on-site tourist agency will help arrange activities and tours in the area. They often offer package deals for multi-day stays. Rates include airport transfer. $$$ (They also run the Puerto Patos Lodge at Laguna Azul. $$$)

Where to Eat

La Patarashca – Lamas 261. The best option for Amazonian dishes such as juanes (rice, meat, eggs, olives and spices steamed in a bijao leaf), paiche (a huge freshwater fish), and more. $$

El Camaron – On the Plaza. A variety of national and regional dishes. $$

Bars

Whisky Bar – Morey 157. The best music in town, cheap drinks, and an attractive patio draw gringos and locals alike.

La Alternativa – Grau 401. Dive bar with an extensive menu of Amazonian cocktails.

Stonewasi Taberna – Lamas 222. A good hangout, with the best patio in town.

Adventures on Water

Rafting

Tarapotos rafting is some of the best in the country. Most trips start on the Río Mayo, about 30 km/18 miles from the city. Half- and full-day trips are offered on Class II and III rapids and are quite reasonable at about $20 per person, depending on the size of the group. ★Longer trips lasting up to a week, where you camp on the banks, pass through more difficult Class III and IV level rapids. The best time to go is May-November.

★Pacaya-Samiria Reserve

The largest single natural reserve in the country, this is home to more than 40,000 indigenous peoples of varying ethnicities, as well as brilliant wildlife. An array of rare birds, monkeys, and river animals such as manatees, dolphins, and caimans thrive here. Most visits to the park last at least five days in a dugout canoe, with basic camping, and not venturing far from the river. This is far from luxury but, if done right, a visit here can be one of the best wildlife experiences in the country. January-May sees the most rain and is the time when you will likely see the fewest animals. Much of the park is off-limits to tourists, though many enter illegally. Just a few dozen rangers are in charge of the 8,112-square-mile park; so enforcing

Sloth in Pacaya-Samiria (Julius Tours)

the strict rules is difficult. Hunting is illegal in the park (though fishing is OK), as is visiting with an uncertified guide. If a tourist is caught, there are steep penalties. Permission is needed from INRENA in Lima or Iquitos before visiting the reserve. Entry into the park costs $20 and lasts for as long as you want to stay.

You can reach the park via a lodge from Iquitos or from smaller villages around it, such as Lagunas or Bretaña, with a certified guide. For the most accurate information and advice on how you should visit, go the reserve office in Iquitos.

■ Pucallpa

This is either where the road ends or begins. Literally and metaphorically. Sitting on the Río Ucayali, Pucallpa is Peru's largest river port with road connections inland. The city is

Macaws, Pacaya-Samiria (Julius Tours)

either a dry, dusty, dirty jungle town or a wet, muddy, dirty jungle town, depending on what time of the year you visit. A few roads and streets, particularly around the center, or running to the airport and away from town, are paved. However, most of the town is a mere collection of unconnected cement slabs and dirt that serve as roads and sidewalks. I imagine many more people are injured walking in Pucallpa than by poisonous snakes, insects, or disease. It is growing, though. Business is booming in the industries of lumber, oil, fishing, and, recently, gold mining. The population has grown to over 460,000. The city itself offers very little and the jungle around the city has mostly been cut down. Lake Yarinacocha, just a noisy moto-taxi ride away, is the hub of tourist activity for the area and offers the scenic Amazon environment that most come here for. Average annual temperature: 25°C/77°F (maximum 38°C/100°F and minimum 24°C/75°F). The rainy season runs from November to March.

Getting Here

Aeropuerto Internacional Rengifo is 5.5 km/3.3 miles north of town and is served by just a few airlines that fly to either Lima or Iquitos.

TANS (Arana 615, ☎ 575-421,www.tansperu.com. pe) has one daily flight to and from Lima and Iquitos for $60-$80.

Aero Continente (7 de Junio 561, ☎ 575-643) goes daily to and from Lima for the same price as TANS. A few smaller airlines fly to jungle towns throughout the area, such as Contamana and Tarapoto. Contact **Saosa** (☎ 572-637) for more information.

Quite a few small bus companies are in town. There is no central station, but nearly all of the companies have offices in the first few blocks southwest of the center. They go to Lima (20 hours), Tingo María (eight hours), Hunauco (nine hours), Huancayo (15 hours). Most buses leave in the early morning or in the late afternoon, although times change frequently. Roads are often unpaved and bumpy. All buses cross the Cordillera Azul and can be very cold at night. Dress warmly. Try **Transportes Rey** (Raimondi and 7 de Julio, ☎ 57-5545), **Transmar** (Raimondi 793, ☎ 57-4900), and **Transportes Amazonica** (Tacna 628, ☎ 57-1292).

To Iquitos by Boat

For information on the boats, a good place to start is with the **Capitania** (Castilla 860, ☎ 57-2517). The official in charge can give you a good idea what boats are leaving when. The most accurate information can be found with each boat's individual captain. From January to April (high-water season) most boats dock up near Parque San Martín, while the rest of the year their port is about three km to the northeast. When the river is higher there are more frequent departures, usually daily. The downriver passage to Iquitos takes three-five days and costs

The Amazon

around $20, including meals. See the Iquitos section for more information on river journeys.

Getting Around

 Local buses are small collectivo vans, often crowded. They go to the airport, Yarinacocha, and San Francisco for just a sole or two. It is far easier to take a moto-taxi or traditional taxi, which rarely will cost more than a few dollars to anywhere, in the area. Motorcycles can be rented for about $2 per hour.

Tourist Information

 Tourist Offices – **Dirección Regional de Industria y Turismo**, 111 Dos de Mayo, ☎ 57-1303, ucayali@mincetur.gob.pe. On a dirt road just off the Malecón, this tourist office is perhaps the only reliable source of tourist information in Pucallpa. Staff is helpful and friendly. Hours are sporadic. **Tourist booth** at Yarinacocha, on the waterfront, is flooded with boat captains trying to offer the best deals on a guided tour of the lake.

Laundry – **Lavandería Gasparin**, Portillo 526, ☎ 591-147, Mon-Sat 9 am-1 pm; 4-8 pm. Drop-off or do-it-yourself service. Friendly owner.

Banks – BCP at Raymondi and Tarapacá has an ATM and is the only bank in town where you can exchange travelers' checks.

Western Union – Raymondi 470, ☎ 571-120, in the Laser Viajes y Turismo office that arranges flights, buses, and tours in the area.

Internet cafés – Plentiful, but few are high speed.

Sightseeing

 The brand new futuristic municipal building highlights Pucallpa's **Plaza de Armas** and cathedral that makes you question exactly where you are for a moment. A few good cafés, restaurants, and heladerias (ice cream shops) make it a pleasant place to spend a few hours.

Parque San Martín on the Malecón is nice at sunset. You can watch from one of the many benches as the river vessels carry their cargo. Ice cream and popsicle vendors are every three feet. The steps around the new clock tower are usually crowded with young couples. At the northern end of the park you can find a variety of food stands selling cheap local dishes. Just make sure everything is cooked.

The ★**Parque Natural and Museo Regional** is about five km/three miles from the center. The zoo has an incredible number of animals from the area, including many types of monkeys, birds, jaguars, ocelots, lynx, sloths, and giant river otters. If you can get past the fact that you are in the jungle looking at animals in cages, it is well worth a look. There is also a nice scenic lagoon with quaint bridges that connect you to the museum area. The museum has just a few small buildings with pottery, textiles, and one room with taxidermy. There is a snack bar and a few craft tables on-site. A taxi there should be $1. Open daily 9 am-5 pm. Admission 3 soles.

Art Galleries

UskoAyar – Sánchez Cerro 465. This is the school, gallery, and home owned by the painter and ayahuasca visionary, Pablo Amaringo. Meaning "Spiritual Prince" in Quechua, UskoAyar allows other mostly young artists to display their work here and study. Founded in 1988, Amaringo teaches students to visualize internally what they are going to paint. Amaringo originals can be purchased for several thousand dollars apiece. Photos of the works can be purchased for $20. It is a difficult place to find, so a taxi is the best way to get here. You may have to ask more than one.

One of Pablo Amaringo's children owns a lodge six km/3.6 miles from Pucallpa. There you can arrange for a shaman to conduct an ★★**ayahuasca ceremony**. This is a very secure, serious place for those who are interested. $30 includes the ceremony and a night stay in the lodge.

The Amazon

DID YOU KNOW?

Pablo Amaringo was born in 1943 near the town of Tamanco in a family comprised of farmers, although many ancestors were shamans. When the family lost their farm they moved to Pucallpa, where Pablo was forced to work on the Pucallpa docks. After becoming seriously ill, he began to draw. Not what you think though. With his family living in extreme poverty, he began to make bank notes using Chinese ink. He was soon arrested for counterfeiting, but escaped from jail and fled to Brazil. Two years later he returned to the Peruvian jungle and met with a shaman, who cured him of his illness. He was arrested again for his previous crime and spent several months in jail. For the next decade after his release he began studying the ways of the shamans throughout the Peruvian Amazon. After using ayahuasca on almost a daily basis for years, he became tortured by the spirit world. He abandoned the shamanic practices and turned back to art. His paintings focus on the other worlds he witnessed in his experiences with ayahuasca.

★**Agustín Rivas** – Tarapacá 861, ☎ 57-1834. One of the most important artists of the region. The woodcarvings of Agustín Rivas border on Dali-esque with Amazonian themes. The small gallery located in an upstairs loft has quite a spectacular collection of a few dozen large carvings as well as a few framed documents and paintings. Admission 1 sole. Hours various. Ask at either the bakery or restaurant below to be let in.

WHAT IS AYAHUASCA?

The word refers to a medicinal and magical drink incorporating two or more distinctive plant species capable of producing profound mental, physical and spiritual effects when brewed together and consumed in a ceremonial setting. One of these plants is always the giant woody liana vine called ayahuasca (Banisteriopsis caapi or other species). The other plant or plants combined with ayahuasca generally contain tryptamine alkaloids, most often dimethyltryptamine (DMT). The plants most often used are the leaves of chacruna (Psychotria viridis and other species) and oco yagé, also known as chalipanga, chagraponga, and huambisa (Diplopterys cabrerana).

This drink is widely employed throughout Amazonian Peru, Ecuador, Colombia, Bolivia, western Brazil, and in portions of the Río Orinoco basin. It has probably been used in the western Amazon for millennia and is rapidly expanding in South America and elsewhere through the growth of organized syncretic religious movements such as Santo Daime, União do Vegetal (UDV), and Barquinia, among others.

In traditional rainforest practice, other medicinal or visionary plants are often added to the brew for various purposes, from purely positive healing (blancura) and divination to malevolent black magic (brujeria, magia negra or rojo).

The oldest known object related to the use of ayahuasca is a ceremonial cup, hewn out of stone, with engraved ornamentation, which was found in the Pastaza culture of the Ecuadorean Amazon from 500 BC to 50 AD. It is in the collection of the Ethnological Museum of the Central University (Quito, Ecuador). This indicates that ayahuasca potions were known and used at least 2,500 years ago. Its antiquity in the lower Amazon is likely much greater. – *From www.biopark.org.*

Where to Stay

Hotel Sol de Oriente – San Martín 552, ☎ 575-154, fax 575-510, hsoloriente@qnet.com.pe. Colonial-style furnishings adorn the 45 rooms, with air-conditioning, Jacuzzis, and cable TV. Also a bar, restaurant, Internet access, mini-zoo, beautiful pool area and gardens. It has its flaws, but it is still the nicest hotel in Pucallpa. $$$

Ruiz Hotel – San Martín 475, ☎ 571-280, fax 578-458, hotelruizpucallpa@speedy.com.pe. Attached to a small but decent casino. Rooms with air-conditioning, mini-fridge, cable TV, hot water. Needs an update, but so does the entire town. Laundry, fax, restaurant, room service, and conference room on-site. Suites available. $$$

Hospedaje El Virrey – Jr. Tarapacá 945, ☎ 575-580. Older building, but well-kept. Don't forget to check out the murals of medieval scenes in the lobby. Basic rooms with bath, fan, cable TV, mini-fridge. Better rooms available with air-conditioning and including an American breakfast. $$

Hotel Mercedes – Raimondi 610, ☎ 57-5120, fax 57-1191. Rooms are well-worn and include private baths, hot water, and mini-fridge. Bar, restaurant, and swimming pool are convenient. Suites with lounge areas are available. $$

Hospedaje Komby – Ucayali 360, ☎ 57-1562, fax 59-2074. There is a pool and a good late-night restaurant. Rooms are basic, but include private baths, phone, and cable TV. $

Where to Eat

C'est Si Bon – Independencia 560. Classic ice cream hangout, shiny clean, very attractive decor with local woodcarvings. $$

La Parrillada El Braserito – San Martín 498. The best place for steaks and grilled meats in town. $$

Restaurant Kitty – 1062 Tarapacá. Clean air-conditioned restaurant not far from the waterfront. Dishes like chupe de corvina (sea bass stew), ceviche (raw fish marinated in lime juice), tacu-tacu (seasoned rice and beans), juane (rice, meat, eggs, olives and spices steamed in a bijao leaf), paiche (a freshwater fish from the area). $$

Tika's – 966 Tarapacá, ☎ 577-636 (they deliver). Good burgers, ceviche, sidewalk seating. Nice place for a dinner and a beer with a tropical atmosphere. $

Tropitop – Sucre 401. On a corner of the Plaza. Popular café with breakfast, long list of desserts, sandwiches, and good cremoladas (fruit shakes) made with local fruits. $

Sofia's Restaurant Pizzeria – Next to Tropitop. Has breakfast, pizzas, and sidewalk tables. Quite a few local dishes too. $

El Escorpión – Independencia 430. Good selection of seafood. Economical plates under 10 soles include ceviche (raw fish marinated in lime juice), chicharrón (fried pork), parihuela (seafood soup), and chupe de camarones (soup with prawns).

Piero's – Tarapacá and San Martín, ☎ 577-580 (delivery). Noisy corner spot one block from the Plaza with a long list of good pizzas. $

El Portal Chicken – Independencia 510. Massive restaurant with several floors and sidewalk tables. Roasted chicken and chips. $

You can find lots of cheap local dishes along the waterfront or in the markets. Just be sure to look at it before you buy it. Pucallpa does brew a local pilsner, San Juan, which oddly varies in taste from bottle to bottle.

Day-Trips from Pucallpa

The oxbow lake of ★**Yarinacocha** is seven km/4.2 miles northeast of Pucallpa. (An oxbow lake is formed when a river changes course, leaving an isolated section behind.) Puerto

Callao, Yarinacocha's main port, has loads of bars and restaurants lining the waterfront and is the main tourist drag in the area. If you're looking for peace and quiet, stay somewhere else on the lake. Internet is available at Restaurant Latino, but it is slow and better options exist in town five minutes away. On the lake itself you can see sloths, a variety of bird life, iguanas, and pink and gray river dolphins.

The **Jardin Etno-Botanico Chullachaqui** (Botanical Garden) is about nine km/5.4 miles (30 minutes) from Puerto Callao. It is a stop on many boat tours of Yarinacocha. Admission 2 soles. Open 8 am-4 pm.

Many come to ★**San Francisco** for a quick visit and end up staying for a week. It is just a simple Indian village connected by road and water to the outside world. There is a central craft market where the local Shibipo Indians sell their wares. If looking for a place to stay, just ask in town or a boatman in Puerto Callao and someone will direct you to a small hospedaje or a home stay with a local family. Expect very basic accommodations. There are shamans in the village who often conduct ayahuasca ceremonies for tourists.

The nearby village of **Santa Clara** is only accessible by water and therefore more isolated than San Francisco and more traditional.

★★Shamanic Ceremonies

For the purpose of this book and my own interest, I participated in an ayahuasca ceremony. I went to a small lodge just outside Pucallpa associated with the Usko Ayar school. I had my own room at the lodge and met with a shaman and an assistant in a large plain wooden room built solely for ceremonial purposes. The shaman was an older gentleman in plain clothes. He didn't wear a traditional outfit, but you could sense that he was very serious about what he did.

To begin, I sat down on a mat on one side of the room, while the shaman and his assistant (who was really there to make sure I was OK) sat at different ends. I was given a bucket in case I had to vomit, which is a common reaction to the hallucinogen. The lantern was turned off, and a candle was lit. The shaman poured me a glass of the ayahuasca mixture. It was thick and bitter, a little hard to swallow, but I managed to get it down.

For maybe an hour, maybe longer – it was hard to determine – we sat. In the dark. The only light came from the shaman's hand rolled cigarettes, which he smoked continuously. They asked if I felt anything, which I didn't, so I was given another glass. I didn't eat much that day in preparation, so I didn't vomit. For some time we just waited. Eventually, the shaman began to sing, to chant. I was surprised because I didn't expect it, but it was reassuring. He sang for a long time, took a short break and sang some more. I tried to concentrate on the singing and relax my mind and thoughts, but couldn't.

I was expecting something to happen, but it didn't. They asked me if I felt anything, and I thought I might have. So, after what was probably four hours with the shaman I was walked back to my room. I climbed into my bed and turned off the light. Then boom, it hit me. Swirling colors appeared in the shapes I saw through the dark room. Thoughts of people I knew and loved passed through my mind. Memories that I had forgotten came back to me. Songs ran through my ears. I began to hear the shaman's chants, I could hear myself saying them. The exact words. It was like he was still with me. Still guiding me. To an extent he was. That is the power that they have. This is a general summary of what happened, but I assure you that no words can describe something like this. It isn't that weird night you had at a Pink Floyd concert, but something ancient, something cultural. Each person's experience is unique and may change. For some, it isn't always enlightening. That is why it is important if you take something like the hallucinogen ayahuasca that you not buy it on the street and that you go with a trusted shaman, someone who takes the practice seriously.

> *"Yage (ayahuasca) may be the final fix."*
> *– William Burroughs*

Where to Stay

El Pescador – Basic run-down budget hotel, but it is cheap, on the waterfront, and close to the local nightlife. $

La Maloka – ☎ 596-072. Eco-lodge built on stilts at the end of the Malecón. Rooms and amenities are basic. Good restaurant. $$

Albergue Pandisho – ☎ 57-5041. Located about a half-hour from Puerto Callao by boat. It is a nice relaxing spot that overlooks the lake, has a small restaurant/bar, and even a mini-zoo. The six rooms have bathrooms and electricity is available most of the day. $50 a night for a double.

La Perla – ☎ 961-6004, www.welcome.to/laperla. A 10-minute ride from Puerto Callao. Three doubles and one family bungalow. Shared baths and showers. Solar power. German English-speaking owner offers a variety of tours on the lake. $30 per day per person, including three meals and airport transfers.

Tours

Peke-pekes (wooden launches) can be rented for about $5 an hour and will go to desired locations around the lake. Make sure to let the driver know which stops you want to make before getting on the boat.

A few recommended guides include **Achilles** with his boat *El Patron* and the boats *Henry*, *Antony*, and *Pedro Martin*.

Gilber Reategui Sangama runs **Normita Tours** (www. sacredheritage.com/normita). He offers one-day ($7 per hour), five-day ($35 per day), and 15-day (negotiable) tours on his boat *La Normita*. Multiple-day tours include gasoline, food, water, and tents with mosquito nets and mattresses. Gilber can also arrange visits and ceremonies with a shaman ($10 per person, $17 when only one person is involved) and home stays in the small village of Nueva Luz de Fátima.

Shopping

★★**Maroti Shobo**, at Aquayatia 443 on Yarinacocha's main Plaza, is just up from Puerto Callao. It is a small market of stands and shops that feature the art and crafts of many area tribes. Prices here tend to be the same as in the villages.

Contamana

This small frontier town downriver from Pucallpa is eager to embrace tourism. There are medicinal springs, a gathering site of macaws, waterfalls, and an array of unspoiled natural beauty in the nearby lakes, rivers, and hills. It has a few small hospedajes and restaurants, airstrip, and Internet cafés. **Getting Here:** 15-20 hours by local boat or five hours by speedboat ($20-25) from Pucallpa.

The Southeastern Jungle/ Madre de Dios

IN THIS CHAPTER

- Puerto Maldonado   558
- Boca Manu   575

The Southeastern Jungle gives access to three of the world's best natural reserves: the Manu Reserve, the National Park of Bahuaja-Sonene, and the Tambopata Reserve-Candamo. The combination contains six million acres, making it the largest natural reserve of its kind on the planet. More than 1,250 different species of butterflies, 20,000 types of plants, 1,000 species of birds (13% of the world total), 200 varieties of mammals (7% of the world total), 120 species of reptiles, and 400 types of fish have been identified here. The temperature stays between 31° and 19°C/88° and 66°F, usually on the higher end. But during a weather condition known as a "friaje," where cold air comes in from Patagonia for several days at a time, the temperature can drop as low as 5°C/41°F. Warm clothes become necessary. This also contributes to the natural diversity in the area. Rainy season is November-March, when water levels tend to be higher, but there is a little rain nearly every day.

Access to the area is limited. There are two major points of entry. The frontier town of **Puerto Maldonado** is the base for trips in Tambopata and Bahuaja-Sonene and into Bolivia and Brazil. **Manu** can be accessed by road from Cuzco, or by a small plane to the Boca Manu airstrip. Either way you decide to go, the opportunities for seeing wildlife will not disappoint.

HIGHLIGHTS

- **Manu Reserve** – One of the most diverse areas on the planet. Manu is a once-in-a-lifetime experience.
- **Macaw clay licks** – See hundreds, if not thousands, of macaws and other parrots feeding on the clay cliff sides at the world's largest clay licks.
- **Giant river otters** – Playful and extremely rare; you'll be lucky if you can spot one of these.
- **Puerto Maldonado** – Take a break from wildlife viewing and see how life operates in the Southeastern Jungle's largest city.

■ Puerto Maldonado

Phone code (082)

With a population of 40,000 people, Puerto Maldonado is by far the largest and most important city in the department of Madre de Dios, of which it is the capital. It is 183 m/600 feet above sea level and just 523 km/314 miles from Cuzco, but don't expect to get there by land. Well, at least not in a timely manner. French explorer Faustino Maldonado founded Peru's "Capital of Bio-diversity" on July 10, 1902. Since that time, much like Iquitos, it has been home to a series of booms. First rubber, then logging. Presently the town is experiencing a series of ongoing booms associated with gold, oil, Brazil nuts, coffee, and tourism. All of which are causing a population explosion. The town still doesn't have the colossal feel of hustle and bustle like Iquitos, though. Rather, days drift away like butterflies in this lazy town at the confluence of two rivers, the Madre de Dios and Tambopata. The town itself offers very little for the tourist. There are few decent lodging options, good restaurants are scarce, there are no museums or sights; rather it is a base for trips to nearby lodges and parks. My advice is to avoid Puerto Maldonado altogether, and head directly to the lodges.

Festivals

San Juan (June 24) – Festival celebrated throughout the Amazon, honoring San Juan Bautista (St. John the Baptist) and water, an important element to the region. Local and regional dishes are on display throughout the city as well as arts, crafts, and entertainment.

Getting Here

Air

Aeropuerto Internacional Padre José Aldamiz is located on the Carretera Km 7. **LAN** and **TANS** offer daily flights between Puerto Maldonado and Cuzco, ranging from $45 to $90. In the high season, flights are usually filled several weeks before departure, so reserve well in advance. Flights from Cuzco are also frequently canceled due to wind conditions, so it may be a good idea to arrive in the area a day before your lodge reservation if you want to be safe. The tourism organization, Dir Cetur, has an information booth at the airport with minimal info. Several lodges and hotels in the area have booths there as well. Taxi from the airport is $2 (8 km/4.8 miles), although if you are heading to a jungle lodge a representative will likely be there to pick you up.

Airlines

TANS – Velarde 147, ☎ 571-429, www.tansperu.com.pe.

LAN – Velarde 503, ☎ 213-8200, www.lan.com.

By Truck

There aren't any long distance buses out of town, but transport does reach Cuzco... eventually. Trucks and collectivos leave from Av. Tambopata Cuadra 3 and take anywhere from 18 hours to three days, depending on road conditions. Transportation officials consider this the worst road in the country. A price for the trip will be around $20, a little more if you can finagle a seat in the cab with the driver. The scenery is known to be spectacular, although the comfort level is not. A new highway, the Trans Oceanico, is planned from Cuzco to the border with Brazil. Construction will hopefully begin by the time you read this and will take several years. This will cut the drive time to six hours.

Getting Around

Motocaros, moto-taxis, and regular taxis will take you anywhere in town for just a few soles. Collectivo buses ply the town between the airport, the center, and small villages throughout the area.

Boat

 Madre de Dios Ferry runs across the river to the road that will lead to Iberia and then to Iñapari 250 km/150 miles away on the border with Brazil. You can sometimes find a boat going upriver on the Madre de Dios to Manu, but they are very infrequent. It is much easier to reach Manu via Cuzco.

Motorcycle

As in all Peruvian jungle towns, you can rent a bike (usually something around 100 cc) to take you to some of the hard-to-reach places or just to explore. Look on Prada near the intersection with Velarde for rentals. Price is about 5 soles per hour, but bargain for longer rentals.

Tourist Information

Tourist Offices – **iPeru** in Cuzco (including the airport location) has some information on Madre de Dios. **Minesterio de Industria y Turismo**, Fitzcarrald 252, ☎ 57-1164. This small office has a few brochures on restaurants, hotels, and national park information (all in Spanish), but not much else. They have a booth in the airport that is equally useful. **INRENA**, Cuzco 135, ☎ 57-1604. This National Park office has park info and collects entrance fees, although if going to a lodge you will likely pay the park fees through them.

Banks – **BCP** on the Plaza has a Visa ATM and changes foreign currency and travelers' checks. **Multired** has a standalone ATM on the Plaza next to BCP.

Post Office – **Serpost**, Velarde 675, ☎ 57-1088.

Internet cafés are plentiful, with dozens scattered around town, although nearly all of them are slow.

Laundry – Lavandería (no name), Velarde 898.

Police Station – **Policia Nacional del Peru Madre de Dios**, Alcides Carrión (no #), ☎ 803-504, 24 hours.

Hospitals – **ESSALUD Victor Alfredo Lazo Peralta**, Cáceres Km 3, ☎ 57-1024. **Hospital Santa Rosa**, Cajamarca 171, ☎ 57-1019, 24 hours.

Immigration Office – 26 de Diciembre 356, ☎ 571-069. You can extend your tourist card/visa here for $28. If going to Brazil, get a visa (all Americans need a visa to enter Brazil) in either Lima, as you will not be able to in Puerto Maldonado or at the border.

Bolivian Consulate – Loreto 268, on the Plaza, 2nd floor. If heading to Bolivia it is best to check here beforehand for border formalities.

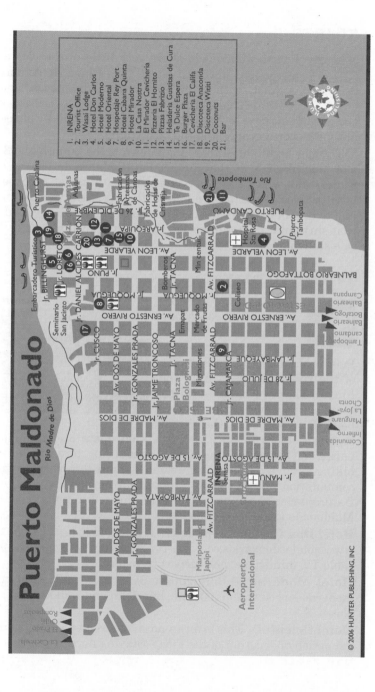

Puerto Maldonado

1. INRENA
2. Tourist Office
3. Wasai Lodge
4. Hotel Don Carlos
5. Hotel Moderno
6. Hotel Oriental
7. Hospedaje Rey Port
8. Hotel Cabana Quinta
9. Hotel Mirador
10. La Casa Nostra
11. El Mirador Cevicheria
12. Pizzeria El Hornito
13. Pizzas Fabrizio
14. Heladeria Gustitas de Cura
15. Te Dulce Espera
16. Burger Plaza
17. Cevicheria El Califa
18. Discoteca Anaconda
19. Discoteca Wititi
20. Coconus
21. Bar

© 2006 HUNTER PUBLISHING, INC

Sightseeing

Puerto Maldonado offers very little in the way of attractions in the city itself. The **Plaza de Armas** is quiet, with a few restaurants, discotecas, and souvenir shops. There is a small park overlooking the waterfront next to Wasai Lodge, which has a mildly pleasant view over the river and the boat traffic.

The major highlight of this jungle town is the 30-m-high/98-foot blue **obelisk** at the intersection of Madre de Dios and Fitzcarrald, which has some interesting statues at its base, but little else. It sits in the middle of the city so the view is limited to the tin roofs of ramshackle houses and the dusty roads that surround them. Admission to use the elevator, 3 soles/1 sole students.

Where to Stay

Wasai Lodge – ☎ 436-8792, www.wasai.com. A jungle lodge that sits right in the city of Puerto Maldonado on the banks of the river just steps from the Plaza. The thatched building complex has the look and feel of being far away from the city. It

organizes tours to the clay licks, Tambopata and Bahuaja parks, and Sandoval Lake, as well as canoeing, bird watching, biking, and ayahuasca ceremonies. Four-day/three-night combination trips to Lago Sandoval, a macaw clay lick in Bahuaja-Sonene National Park, their Tambopata and Maldonado lodges cost $368.

Hotel Don Carlos – Velarde 1271, ☎ 571-029, fax 224-8581, www.hotelesdoncarlos.com. Air-conditioning, swimming pool, cable TV, minifridge, and airport transfers. $$

Hotel Moderno – Billinghurst 359, ☎ 57-1063. Not as moderno as you would imagine, but clean and well kept. Dirt cheap. $

Hotel Oriental – This is a run-down old wood-paneled, budget option on a corner of the Plaza. Staying here is an adventure in itself. $

Hospedaje Rey Port – Velarde 457, ☎ 57-1177. Nothing special, but just a block from the Plaza and rooms have balconies overlooking the noisy street. Basic, but clean and some rooms have showers. $

Hotel Cabana Quinta – Cuzco 535, ☎ 57-1045, fax 57-3336. Down an unpaved, dirty street is one of the nicest hotels in town, even though it barely deserves the three-star rating it has attained. All of the 50 rooms have private baths. Good restaurant with the best breakfast buffet in town. Rooms come with cold-water baths, cable TV, and fans. Superior rooms have hot water and air-conditioning. Has tourist information and can arrange tours. $$

Hotel Mirador – At the corner of Fitzcarrald and the Mirador, this budget place is one of the best in town with cable TV and private baths. Rooms are clean with painted cement floors and the building is new. Basic, but a good value.

BRAZIL NUTS

Madre de Dios is the only region in Peru to grow the often-colossal Brazil nut tree, which is also found in Bolivia and Brazil. Each tree produces about 300 softball-sized fruits a year, each with an average of 15 Brazil nuts. The trees have a certain pollination system that doesn't conform to a plantation set up. So the trees are scattered about the forest and during the first months of the rainy season castañeros, or nut collectors, go from tree to tree collecting them. A 110-lb bag will cost somewhere around $75 in Puerto Maldonado, which is a major export and processing center. You can usually find a woman selling small boxes of the nuts (5 soles), coated in sugar, wherever the buses and boats to the lodges wait.

Where to Eat

La Casa Nostra – Velarde 515, ☎ 57-2647. Relatively simple, but clean and a tourist and guide hangout. Good juice selection, sandwiches, and breakfast. Excellent desserts and decent coffee. Old black and white photos of Madre de Dios remind you where you are. $

Southeastern Jungle

El Mirador Cevicheria – At the eastern end of Fitzcarrald, this simple, but pleasant, cevicheria has a long seafood menu and offers wide views of the jungle and houses below. $

★**Pizzeria El Hornito** – Carrión 271,☎ 572-082 (delivery). Right on the Plaza is one of the best restaurants in town. A long list of thin-crust pizzas (personal and family-size) baked on a wood-burning oven, pastas, and a small wine selection. Only open for dinner. Attached to a small bar (in the rear). $$

Pizzas Fabrizio – Velarde 361. Just a few booths, but pizzas are decent and a little cheaper than El Hornito. $

Heladeria Gustitas de Cura – On the Plaza next to Anaconda. The brightest, cleanest place in town. Sandwiches, ice cream, desserts. They also sell crafts. $

Te Dulce Espera – Velarde 469. Your sweet awaits. Another simple café with snacks, juices, ice cream, and cakes. Friendly staff. $

Burger Plaza – On the Plaza, just a simple burger joint with ice cream. Hours are sporadic. $

Restaurant/Cevicheria El Califa – Piura 266. Decent option for ceviche and a variety of local dishes like hearts of palm and venison. $

Shopping

 Mercado Modelo isn't the fascinating place that is Iquitos' market, but you can find some local specialties such as juane (rice, meat, eggs, olives and spices steamed in a bijao leaf), pan de arroz (bread made from rice), and regional fruits and juices. At night you can find many stands selling roasted chicken and chips for the price of peanuts.

A few craft shops are on the Plaza. The best is **Shabuya** at Arequipa 279.

Bars & Clubs

 Discoteca Anaconda, on the east side of the Plaza, and **Discoteca Wititi**, Velarde 153, are the two main discos in town. They attract the few tourists, international volunteers and a slew of 20-somethings that work in some way in the tourist industry.

Coconuts – On the South side of the Plaza near El Hornito. Draws the same crowd as the two discotecas but is more of a stand-around bar with less dancing.

Bar/Pena 114 – Next to El Mirador on Fitzcarrald it's a wood-paneled local watering hole with a truly tropical feel that never sees a tourist. A good place to get away from it all.

Tours & Activities

City Tours

Peru Tours – Loreto 176, ☎ 573-244, www.perutoursytravel. com. They offer a tour of Puerto Maldonado with guided trips to the few attractions around town, the market, and a few places along the river. Price is 35 soles per person. Discounts available for larger groups.

JungleTours/Freelance Guides

Freelance guides usually hang out at the airport awaiting incoming flights, at tourist hotels, and at La Casa Nostra. The lodges hire the best, so what remains is a mish-mash of whatever is left. Guides charge about $25 per day, not including food and equipment. Negotiate. You can contact the local Guides Association, ☎ 575-606, junglejosi@hotmail.com. Also check at Cabana Quinta and Hotel Wilson for respected guides.

Volunteering/Language Courses/ Meditation Retreats

Tambopata Education Center – ☎ 80-3306 or ☎ 57-3935, www.geocities.com/tambopata_language, in Madre de Dios. They offer English classes to locals and Spanish classes for international students. Volunteer projects include assistant teaching in local schools, working on a reforestation lodge, and helping set up a lodge in the jungle. Volunteers are ages 18-80. They pay $10 per night for accommodation and $27 per night with four hours of Spanish classes daily. Accommodation is in family homes or at a nearby hotel (with pool).

Tambopata Reserve Society (TReeS) – Puerto Maldonado Office, Lambayeque 488, ☎ 57-2788, www.geocities.com/ treesweb. Organization founded by former volunteers and guides from Explorer's Inn. Volunteers work on three separate teams: one for mammals, one for birds, and one for reptiles. Teams spend two weeks at each of five lodges. A variety of projects are available.

Ayahuasca-Wasi – www.Ayahuasca-wasi-com. Traditional Amazonian shamanism is combined with meditation and

Tibetan philosophy for these experimental seven-day seminars. With each seminar there are three ayahuasca ceremonies and also group discussions. They are held at Corto Maltes Lodge (see below) and also at a location in Pisac on certain dates. $850 per person.

Border Crossing Info

To Bolivia – To get to Bolivia there are two options. One is via Brasiléia in Brazil (see below), crossing the river to the Bolivian border town of Cobija, where there is further transportation into Bolivia. The second option is by boat to Puerto Pardo/Puerto Heath. The trip can either be done on a cargo boat (ask at the port; may be hard to find) or by a motorized boat (around $100 in a private boat or $5 for a seat in a peke-peke), which will take half a day. There are immigration officials and basic lodging on each side of the border. From the border, you can continue on into Bolivia down the Madre de Dios River to Riberalta, where connections by road can be made elsewhere in Bolivia. This route sees few travelers and you will wait around for long periods of time to get anywhere.

To Brazil – To get to Brazil you must cross the Madre de Dios River and catch a local bus to Iñapari. From there you can go on foot (one km) to the Brazilian border town of Assis. You must get your Peruvian exit/entry stamp in Iñapari, and money can be changed there as well. A few basic hospedajes sit on each side of the border. If heading to Brazil, you must travel Brasiléia, 115 km/69 miles away, for immigration. All Americans need a visa to enter Brazil. This can be arranged in Lima; you will not be able to do so in Puerto Maldonado or at the border. Also, you *must* have a yellow fever certificate to enter Brazil.

★★★CLAY LICKS

In the first few hours of the light of day, reddish clay cliffs along the Tambopata River become one of the most spectacular canvases of wildlife in the world. Parrots of all sorts begin to arrive in the trees surrounding the lick. They come in pairs or by huge flocks of hundreds. Smaller parrots such as the mealy or orange-cheeked parrot make their way to the cliff side first to begin eating small bits of the clay. The macaws come next. There can be several species of them at a time (or none at all). The precise reason for the attraction to the clay lick is still unknown. Most scientists believe that by ingesting the clay, the parrots are able to obtain some minerals that they lack in their diet and that the clay itself helps to soak up toxins that enter their bodies through unripe fruit and nuts. Collpa Colorado, the largest clay lick in the world, is 120 km/72 miles upstream from Puerto

Macaws at Collpa Colorado (Andes Adventures)

Maldonado (about five hours) and camping trips there can be arranged from most lodges. There are several smaller licks scattered throughout the region, some only minutes from the lodges, and are quite spectacular as well.

Jungle Lodges

Lago Sandoval

This attractive oxbow lake is close to Puerto Maldonado at about two hours up the Río Madre de Dios. The lake has a healthy and thriving population of giant river otters, making it one of the best places to spot this endangered creature. Black caimans, turtles, monkeys, and all sorts of bird life can be seen as well. Stay at Sandoval Lake Lodge or arrange for camping with a guide from Puerto Maldonado. Trails lead to

the lake from some of the other lodges (i.e., Reserva Amazonica).

Sandoval Lake Lodge – ☎ 877-827-8350, www.tropicalnaturetravel.com. One of the best lodge options near Puerto Maldonado. It sits on a bluff overlooking the lake. Rooms have private baths, hot water, electric lighting, and some electricity available in the mornings and evenings. Offers a chance to see giant river otters that live in the lake and the lodge offers an overall focus on wildlife. The lodge also maintains 15 miles of rainforest trails. Three days/two nights, $180-$200 (depending on season).

Lago Valencia

Sixty km/36 miles away from Puerto Maldonado near the border with Bolivia, Lago Valencia is one of the most isolated oxbow lakes, so it has abundant wildlife. Arrange for camping, guides, and transportation from Puerto Maldonado.

Heath River Wildlife Center – Plateros 361, Cuzco, ☎ 251-173, www.tropicalnaturetravel.com/travel/lodges/heath-river-wildlife-center.html. This lodge, opened in 2004, is owned and operated by Ese'eja Indians and Inka Natura. The 10 private bungalows sit on the  Bolivian bank of the Río Heath and have private bathrooms with hot-water showers. The lodge is situated very close to a macaw clay lick and trails lead into Parque Nacional Bahuaja-Sonene. It also has access to the Pampas de Heath, one of the last remaining Amazon savannahs. Four days/three nights, $490-$530, depending on season. Stays are usually combined with a night at Lago Sandoval Lake Lodge.

★★★Tambopata National Reserve

The 769,000-acre park is known for its great diversity of mammals, birds, insects, and plant life. The **Colpa de Guacamayos macaw clay lick**, one of the largest natural licks in the world, is perhaps the highlight of any trip here, but definitely not the only wildlife attraction. Giant river otters are seen in one of the area's oxbow lakes, white and black caimans sit on the banks at night, herds of capybaras are easily spotted anytime of day. Birding here is spectacular. The plant life is stunning. Insects as strange as space creatures will surprise even expert entomologists. In September of 2000, the reserve joined with Bahuaja-Sonene National

Park and Madidi National Park in Bolivia to form a cross-border park system that created the largest area of protected forest on the continent. Guides here tend to be younger and less experienced than in other parts of Peru. Many are students or volunteers from Lima or the US and Europe, but they manage to do a reasonable job. Lodge prices include transfers to/from the airport, three daily meals, guided tours and activities. National Park fees are not included. The entry fee is $10 for the reserve, $30 for the clay lick. The fee must be paid at INRENA in Puerto Maldonado, but, if heading to a lodge, you will likely pay through the lodge. The Puesto de Control El Torre is next to the Explorer's Inn. You must bring a passport to be stamped to get into the reserve. If coming from another park entrance, the fee increases.

★**Libertador Tambopata Lodge** – Inversiones Maldonado S.A. C, Nueva Baja 432, Cuzco, ☎ 245-695, fax 23-8911. In Puerto Maldonado, their office is at the corner of Prada and Velarde, www.tambopatalodge.com. Founded in 1991, this  lodge has been newly remodeled since it became affiliated with Libertador hotels. Rooms are in completely screened-in bungalows with steaming-hot solar-powered water, comfortable beds, mosquito nets, modern private bathrooms, and candle lighting. Solar energy lighting and electricity may soon be available. Food is quite good, with three-course meals for lunch and dinner, and a buffet breakfast. Bungalows have small porches with tables, chairs, and hammocks. It is one of the most comfortable lodges in Peru. There are dining hall and bar areas, a research library with scientific data and reports on studies done at the lodge. Camping trips to the Guacamayos clay lick can also be arranged. Some 25 km/15 miles of hiking trails are set in mainly secondary forests, most of which are on the other side of the river. The lodge is very environmentally conscious (for instance they use fiberglass boats because they last longer and save trees). More than 60 people can be accommodated in a series of small bungalows.

Southeastern Jungle

Three days/two nights, $211 per person, four days/three nights, including clay lick excursions, start at $400. Longer stays can be arranged at a reasonable price.

★★★**Explorer's Inn** – Miraflores office: Alcanfores 459, ☎ 511-447-8888, fax 511-241-8427. Cuzco Office: ☎ 23-5342, Plateros 365. Puerto Maldonado, ☎ 572-078, Fonavi H-15. www.explorersinn.com, www.peruviansafaris.com. The lodge is dedicated to conservation and focused on seeing wildlife more than perhaps any other lodge in Peru. The lodge itself is older, worn, and basic. There are seven fully-screened bunga-

lows (30 rooms) with private baths and mosquito nets. Loads of information is available at the lodge, with a reference library, book exchange, and a small museum. Lectures are frequently given. This is the only lodge

Explorer's Inn (Beto Santillan)

that operates within the actual confines of the Tambopata National Reserve, which is why more wildlife tends to be seen here. They have 37 km/22 miles of trails that you can wander alone or with a guide. Trips to the Guacamayos clay lick and a smaller clay lick nearby can be arranged. In operation since 1975, it is one of the oldest and most established lodges in Peru. Nearly 600 species of birds have been recorded on the property, a number beyond that of any other place on the planet of similar size. They have access to an oxbow lake where a lucky few are able to see a family of giant river otters. Guides are young, well-trained, very friendly and bilingual. Specialized trips and activities can be arranged, including ayahuasca ceremonies. Three days/two nights, $145-$180 per person May-October. Guacamayo clay lick with three nights at the lodge, one night camping, $450. Additional nights, $50. Discounts for large groups and low-season visits.

Posada Amazonas – Miraflores: Aramburu 166, Dept. 4b, ☎ 511-421-8347, fax 421-8183. www.perunature.com. Cuzco: El Triunfo 350, ☎ 23-2772. Puerto Maldonado: Arequipa 401, ☎ 57-1056. Rainforest Expeditions and the Ese'eja Indian community of Infierno, on whose land it sits, own the lodge jointly. Several tribal members are among the guides. It is just one hour upriver from the port and directly adjacent to the border of the National Reserve. The 10 structures that comprise the complex are made of palm fronds,

Posada Amazonas

wood, clay and cane. The 30 rooms have private baths. Programs are similar to those of Explorer's Inn and the Tambopata Lodge. A 35-m/115-foot tower gives guests access to the forest canopy. Three days/two nights, $190.

Picaflor Research Center – ☎ 57-2589, www.picaflor.org. This is 74 km/44 miles upriver from Puerto Maldonado on the Tambopata River. They have 5½ square miles of rainforest as a private conservation area that they maintain with the help of volunteers. They attract a lot of students, backpackers, and long-term travelers. Just six guest rooms with solar power and electricity. Guests usually help with cooking and pumping water. Remote and hands-on. Volunteers pay $150 for 10 nights, and provide three-four hours of work per day. To stay without volunteering for three days/two-nights, the price is $190.

Tambopata Research Center – Miraflores: Aramburu 166, Dep. 4b, ☎ 511-421-8347, fax 421-8183, Cuzco: El Triunfo 350, ☎ 23-2772. Puerto Maldonado: Arequipa 401, ☎ 571-056. www.perunature.com. This lodge is a bit older and has just 13 rooms, but its claim to fame is that it is just 500 m/1,640 feet from the world's largest clay lick. If it is macaws you are after, this is the place. Many Peruvian and international researchers stay here and can be seen at the lodge among the guests. Rooms have mosquito nets and bathrooms are shared. Kerosene lighting. Located five-six hours from Posada Amazonas, so short stays are not always possible and rates are higher than at other places. People usually combine a stay here with one at Posada Amazonas. Note that there are times when the macaws do not appear due to season and weather. Six days/ five nights, $780 (three nights at the Research Center, two at Posada Amazonas).

GIANT RIVER OTTERS

The giant river otter has almost become the symbol of Peru's wild-life. The once highly endangered species has been able to thrive in Madre de Dios because of the strict laws protecting it. They inhabit several of the oxbow lakes (parts of rivers that have been isolated due to a change in the rivers' course) in the area and live in groups of four to eight otters, though as many as 20 have been observed together. They are lively hunters and eat up to nine lbs of fish each day. From June to November, when the young are born, they are more difficult to spot. If you see one or a group of them, at any time of the year, consider yourself lucky.

Cayman Lodge Amazonie – Puerto Maldonado Office, Arequipa 655, ☎ 51-571-970, 51-829-601, www.cayman-lodge-amazonie.com. A French- and Peruvian-owned lodge opened in 2005. It is 2½ hours upstream from Puerto

Cayman Lodge Amazonie

Maldonado on the Tambopata River. Owner Daniel is from a family of guides and is one of the most experienced in the area. The lodge offers one of the longest and most flexible lists of programs, including trips to the clay licks, Lakes Condenado and Lake Sachavacayoc, camping, and shamanic ceremonies, as well as ornithology, botany, and medicinal plant tours for professionals. Three days/two nights, $180. Five-day/four-night shamanic program, $400.

Other Lodges

Corto Maltes – www.cortomaltes-amazonia.com. On the Madre de Dios River, 30 minutes from Puerto Maldonado. Walking distance (five km/three miles) from Lago Sandoval. Rooms have private hot-water baths, electricity, and small porches with hammocks. Can arrange ayahuasca ceremonies, massages, and anti-stress therapies. Four days/three nights, $220.

Reserva Amazonica – www.inkaterra.com. Formerly Cuzco Amazonico, this lodge is on 28,000 acres of a private ecological reserve, 15 km/10 miles downriver from Puerto Maldonado. Bungalows are built in the traditional style of the Ese-Eja, an area native group. Rooms have comfortable beds, mosquito nets, and porches with hammocks. This is the only lodge where you can find a massage room. Three suites are available with private baths and solar-heated water. A new canopy walkway, the only one in Puerto Maldonado, gives guests access to the forest canopy. Eight km/4.8 miles of trails. Specialized programs for children and families. Food quality and comfort is considered some of the best among the lodges. Four days/three nights, $260.

★★★Parque Nacional Manu

This UNESCO World Biosphere Reserve and World Heritage Site covers 7,800 square miles or 5,266,800 acres. For much of the park, however, access is limited to a few Indian tribes, who choose to remain isolated with no outside contact. Only a small number of researchers and a few thousand visitors are given permission to enter the park annually. The multiple-use zone, also known as the Reserved Zone, is where a some lodges and permanent establishments have been allowed. The park is one of the best-known throughout the world for its diverse wildlife. The elevation ranges from 4,300 to 200 m/14,000 to 660 feet above sea level, greatly contributing to its biodiversity. Over 800 species of birds are found here, 200 species of mammals, and many others. Few areas of the world can compare. More than 30 indigenous communities live in Manu, but you are not

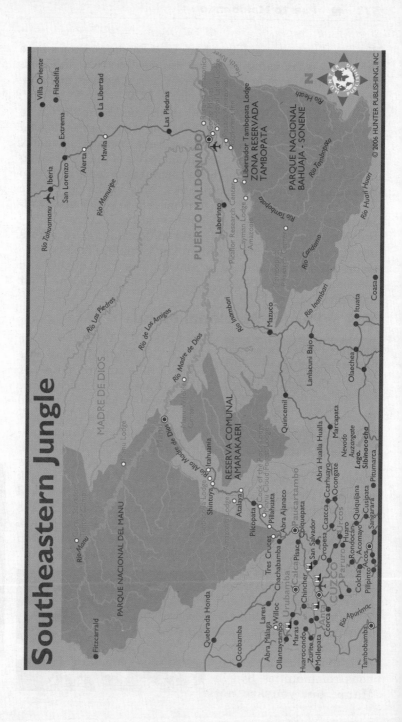

Southeastern Jungle

likely to encounter them. Areas just outside the park, such as
the land held by the Manu Wildlife Center, also offer excellent
wildlife-watching opportunities – sometimes better than Manu
itself. The entrance fee for the Reserved Zone is $45 per person.

Manu National Park Office – Bastidas 310, Cuzco, ☎ 240-
898, pqnmanu@cosapidata.mail.com.pe. They can issue a per-
mit for the Reserved Zone.

■ Boca Manu

Getting Here

Most tour companies use a combination of flying to/from the
Boca Manu airstrip and driving, although some may also
travel by boat downriver to Puerto Maldonado.

Bus

Most lodges in the Manu area are accessible by road
from Cuzco. They will likely arrange private transport, but you may be able to save some money using
local transport. Depending on where you are
headed, travel time can be anywhere between five to 24 hours
and depends heavily on the season. Breakdowns are frequent,
so even though it may save you a few bucks, it is best to
arrange travel in Cuzco through a tour company. Shintuya is
the closest town to the park and will take nearly 24 hours to
reach. There is basic accommodation there.

Lodges

Amazonia Lodge – Cuzco: ☎ 84-23-1370, Matara 334, www.
amazonialodge.com. This well-known birding site was
founded in 1980 on a former tea plantation. A 65-foot-high
viewing platform gives access to the forest canopy. Very
attractive lodge and grounds; rooms are new, clean and comfortable. Shared bathrooms are modern with hot water. Nine-
day birding tour offered on select dates April-November
($1,630). Accommodation only (no transportation), $60 per
person per night.

★★**Manu Cloud Forest Lodge** – See *Manu Nature Tours*,
www.manuperu.com. Just six hours from Cuzco, this lodge in
the cloud forest is near a 400-foot waterfall. The lodge is quite
spectacular and comfortable and the setting is one of the most
scenic in the entire country. There is accommodation for 16-20
people and rooms have private hot-water baths and verandas

overlooking a small creek. Also a sauna. Four days/three nights, $648 (includes round-trip bus from Cuzco). They also offer additional activities such as mountain biking ($45) and whitewater rafting ($98).

Cock of the Rock Lodge – See *Inkanatura*, www. tropicalnaturetravel.com/ travel/lodges/cock_of_the_ rock.html. The lodge sits at 1,600 m/5,248 feet, high in the Manu cloud forest on the eastern slopes of the Andes. A 183-km/110-mile, eight-hour drive from Cuzco. Mosquito-free. You'll have a chance to see the

Cock of the Rock Lodge

cock-of-the-rock, the spectacled bear, the woolly monkey, and other unique wildlife. The 10 private bungalows have private baths and balconies. Three days/two nights, $450.

Manu Wildlife Center – www.manuwildlifecenter.com, www.inkanatura.com, www.manuexpeditions.com. This lodge has 22 bungalows with private baths and hot-water

One of thousands of bird species in Parque Nacional Manu (Peru Verde)

showers. It's a 90-minute dugout canoe ride from the Boca Manu airstrip, near the confluence of the Manu and Alto Madre de Dios River. The area has one of the highest levels of diversity in the area due to the unusually high number of microhabitats, but it is not actually within the formal boundaries of the national park. Manu Expeditions and the Peru Verde Conservation Group own it jointly. There are 39 km/23 miles of trails around the lodge. Near the Blanquillo clay lick. Four days/three nights, $990.

Pantiacolla Lodge – See *Pantiacolla Tours*, www.pantia-colla.com. Set on a bluff overlooking the Alto Madre de Dios with 1,200 m/3,936 feet of mountains behind it. That means few mosquitoes! There are 2,500 acres of land with many miles of trails. Accommodates Spanish students in conjunction with Amauta Spanish School in Cuzco. Also organized to care for visiting children and families. Rooms are fairly reasonable ($55 per person), but rates do not include transportation or tours.

The next two options are the only *permanent* accommodations within the Parque Nacional Manu itself.

★**Manu Lodge** – See *Manu Nature Tours*, www.manuperu.com. The only lodge with services inside the park itself. This basic lodge sits on a small oxbow lake about one km from the Río Manu and has 14 double rooms with shared cold-water baths. There are 20 km/12 miles of trails leading from the lodge.

★**Cocha Salvador Tented Camp** – See *Manu Expeditions*, www.manuexpeditions.com. The safari-style campsite is just 500 m/1,400 feet from the largest oxbow lake in Manu. It has raised supports with walk-in tents, cots, and shared modern bathrooms. The lake is home to a family of giant river otters. Several more primitive campsites are available nearby on sandy beaches (during the dry season).

Tour Operators

Manu Nature Tours – Cuzco: Avenida Pardo 1046, ☎ 252-721, 252-521, fax 234-793, www.manuperu.com. Books tours to Manu Cloud Forest Lodge and Manu Lodge.

Inkanatura – Cuzco: Plateros 361, ☎ 251-173, fax 245-973. Lima: Manuel Bañon 461 (San Isidro), ☎ 440-2022, fax 422-9225, www.inkanatura.com. Books tours to many lodges such as Sandoval Lake Lodge, Cock of the Rock Lodge, and the Manu and Heath Wildlife Centers. Also runs tours to other destinations across Peru. Six-day/five-night trip, staying at a combination of lodges in the Manu area, $1,310.

Pantiacolla Tours – Cuzco: Plateros 360, ☎ 238-323, www.pantiacolla.com. This company has ecological tours to Manu's Reserved Zone, five days ($745), seven days ($815), and nine days ($785). Each tour combines stays in the Reserved Zone with nights in the cloud forest, trips to the clay lick, and the Pantiacolla Lodge and includes all transportation costs from

Cuzco. Also has a program with Manu's Yine Indians. The three-day tour intermingles the tourists and the Yine Indians in activities such as paddling dugout canoes, traditional body-painting, pottery workshops, bow-and-arrow-shooting. The Yine explain their way of life, knowledge of the forest and plants, traditional medicines, and tell stories. $290 with two nights in Yine Lodge and can also be combined with a five- or seven-day tour.

Manu Expeditions – Cuzco: Pardo 895, ☎ 226-671, www.manuexpeditions.com. This is one of the best-known companies for Manu. They run the Manu Wildlife Center and the Cocha Salvador Safari Camp. British owner Barry Walker is a renowned ornithologist. They offer four- ($980), six- ($1,235), and nine-day ($1,585) trips to Manu with a combination of camping and stays at lodges, as well as horseback treks in the Andes and specialized bird-watching tours.

Manu Ecological Adventures – Cuzco: Plateros 356, ☎ 261-640, www.manuadventures.com. Five- to eight-day trips to the Reserved Zone, shaman ceremonies, bird-watching, and specialized trips.

Spectacled Bear in Parque Nacional Manu (Peru Verde)

Index

Abancay, 273-275

Accommodations, 101-105; Abancay, 274; Aguas Caliente, 370-372; Andahuaylas, 276-277; Arequipa, 215-218; Ayacucho, 284-285; Barranco, 168-169; Boca Manu, 575-577; Cabananconde, 240; Cabo Blanco, 514; Cajamarca, 447-449; Caraz, 437-438; Carhuaz, 436; Chachapoyas, 458-459; Chiclayo, 485-486; Chincha Alta, 188; Chivay, 237; Chucuito, 404; Colonial Center, 135-137; Cuzco, 319-325; Huancavelica, 271-272; Huancayo, 263-264; Huanchaco, 480; Huánuco, 255-256; Huaraz, 420-423; Ica, 202; Iquitos, 528-529; Isla Suasi, 411; Juliaca, 407; Machu Picchu, 381; Mancora, 507-510; Miraflores, 154-158; Nazca, 210-211; Ollantaytambo, 362-363; Pisac, 357-358; Pisco, 191; Piura, 502-503; Pucallpa, 552-553, 556; Puerto Maldonado, 566-567, 571-578; Puno, 396-399; Punta Sal, 513-514; San Isidro, 144-148; Tacna, 246-247; Tarapoto, 544-545; Trujillo, 470-472; Tumbes, 494-495; Urubamba and Yucay, 347-351; Yanque, 239; Yurimaguas, 542-543

Adventures, 71-74; Cajamarca, 455-456; Chorrillos, 178-181; Cuzco, 337-343; Huancavelica, 272-273; Huancayo, 267-268; Huanchaco, 482-483; Huaraz, 432-435; Ica, 197-198; Iquitos, 531-532; Islas Ballestas, 195; Lake Titicaca, 409-411; Lima, 178-181; Mancora, 512; Nazca, 208-209; Ollantaytambo, 364-365; Tarapoto, 545-546; Urubamba and Yucay, 353-354

Aguas Caliente, 368-373; getting here and around, 368-370; map, 369; massages, 373; shopping, 373; where to eat, 372-373; where to stay, 370-372

Amazon region, 515-582; health tips, 518-519; Iquitos, 519-541; map, 516-517; Northern Amazon, 515-519; Pucallpa, 547-557; Tarapoto, 542-547

Andahuaylas, 275-278; day trips, 277-278; getting here, 276; sightseeing, 276; where to stay and eat, 276-277

Andes, 14, 16

Archeology, 3-4; Caral, 185-186; Pachacamac, 183-185; Paracas National Reserve, 192

Arequipa, 211-237; adventures, 234-237; architecture, 228-230; day trips, 233-234; festivals, 233; getting around, 214; getting here, 213-214; language schools, 233; map, 212; shopping, 232; sightseeing, 221-230; tour operators, 231; tourist information, 214-215; where to eat, 218-221; where to stay, 215-218

Ayacucho, 278-291; day trips, 288-291; festivals, 287-288; getting here, 280-281; history, 280; map, 279; shopping, 284; sightseeing, 281-284; tour operators, 291; tourist information, 281; where to eat, 286; where to stay, 284-285

Bahuaja-Sonene National Park, 40

Barranco, 166-173; accomodations, 168-169; map, 167; Peñas, 172-173; restaurants, 169-171

Barrio Chino/Chinatown, 138

Bars and clubs: Arequipa, 221-222; Ayacucho, 287; Barranco, 171-172; Cajamarca, 451; Chiclayo, 487-488; Colonial Center, 137; Cuzco, 331-332; Huancayo, 264; Huánuco, 257; Huaraz, 425-426; Iquitos, 530; Mancora, 511-512; Miraflores, 162-164; Piura, 505; Puno, 401; San Isidro, 149; Tacna, 248; Tarapoto, 545; Trujillo, 473-474; Tumbes, 496; Urubamba and Yucay, 352

Biking see Cycling

Bird watching, 20-22; Islas Ballestas, 194; Ollantaytambo, 365; Puerto Maldonado, 571

Boat tours: Chorrillos, 173; Pucallpa, 556-557; Puerta Pizarro, 498-499

Boca Manu, 575-578

Boleto Turístico (tourist pass), 304

Border crossings, 405-406; Bolivia, 570; Brazil, 570; Chile, 250-251; Ecuador, 499

Bullfighting, 105; Lima, 177-178

Buses, 96-97; Cuzco, 302-303; Lima, 120-121, 122-123

Cabanaconde, 239-242; sightseeing, 240-242; tour operators, 242; where to stay and eat, 240

Cabo Blanco, 514

Cajamarca, 439-456; adventures, 455-456; day trips, 452-454; festivals, 452; getting here, 442-443; history, 441-442; map, 444; shopping, 451; sightseeing, 443-447; tour operators, 451-452; tourist information, 443; where to eat, 449-451; where to stay, 447-449

Callao, 138-141

Camping, 103

Camping equipment, 335

Car rental, 98; Arequipa, 214; Cuzco, 304; Lima, 120

Caral archeological site, 185-186

Caraz, 437-438

Carhuaz, 435-436

Casinos: Chorrillos, 182; Iquitos, 541

Central Highlands, 252-291; Huancayo, 258-268; Huánuco, 253-258; map, 252

Ceramics, 62-63

Cerros de Amotape National Park, 37

Chachapoyas, 456-463; day trips, 460-462; getting here, 457; shopping, 460; sightseeing, 457; tour operators, 460; tourist information, 456-457; where to stay and eat, 458-460

Chiclayo, 483-491; day trips, 488-491; getting here, 483-484; shopping, 488; sightseeing, 484-485; tourist information, 484, 488; where to stay and eat, 485-486

Children, traveling with, 91

Chincero, 366-368

Chivay, 237-238

Chorrillos, 173-177; nightlife, 175-176; restaurants, 174; shopping, 176-177

Chucuito, 403-404

Climate, 16-17; Arequipa, 213; Huaraz, 414; Inca Trail, 383; Tumbes, 492

Climbing see Mountaineering

Colonial Center, 128-138; accomodations, 135-137; peñas, 138

Communications, 80-84

Contamana, 559

Cordillera Blanca, 413-438; Caraz, 437-438; Carhuaz, 435-438; Huaraz, 414-435; Yungay, 436-437

Costa Verde, 165

Credit cards, 85

Crocodiles and caimans, 26-27

Cruises, 541

Currency and banking, 84-85, 86, 124, 254, 523

Cuzco, 5-6, 295-345; adventures, 337-343; Barrio San Blas, 314-316; entertainment, 332-333; festivals, 343-345; getting around, 304; getting here, 299-303; history, 297-299; hotel and attractions map, 308-309; language schools, 318-319; map, 295; ruins, 316-318; shopping, 333-335; sightseeing, 306-318; spas, 335; tour operators, 335-337; tourist information, 304-305; where to eat, 326-330; where to stay, 319-325

Cycling, 108; Cuzco, 341; Huaraz, 434; Iquitos, 540; Lima, 179-180; Nazca, 209; Urubamba and Yucay, 353-354

Dance, 66-67

Disabilities, travelers with, 91

Documents, 74-75

Driving, 120

Duty free zone/Zona Franca, 249

Earthquakes, 16; Huaraz, 416; Lima, 116

Eco-tourism, 32-34

Ecolodges, 535-541

Ecuador: getting to/from, 499

El Niño, 17

Electricity, 86
Embassies, 126-127; Iquitos, 523
Festivals and holidays, 56-60;
  Arequipa, 233; Ayacucho, 287-
  288; Cajamarca, 452; Cuzco and
  Sacred Valley, 343-345; Huaraz,
  426-427; Ica, 200-201; Iquitos,
  541-542; Isle Taquile, 411; Puerto
  Maldonado, 562; Puno, 402;
  Trujillo, 474
Fishing, 109; Cabo Blanco, 514;
  Cuzco, 342
Flora and fauna, 17-20; birds, 20-
  22; fish and sea mammals, 30-32;
  insects and arachnids, 29-30;
  mammals, 22-25; plants, 18-19;
  reptiles and amphibians, 25-29;
  trees, 19-20
Flying, 208-209
Folkloric shows, 333
Food and drink, 46-55; see also Restaurants

Gay and lesbian travelers, 91-92,
  100, 175-176
Golf, 107, 178; Iquitos, 540; Lima,
  178
Guided tours, 181-182

Handicrafts, 61-64; Ayacucho, 284;
  ceramics, 62-63; Chorrillos, 176-
  177; Cuzco, 333-334; Huancayo,
  266; Huaraz, 426; jewelry, 63-64;
  leatherwork, 64; mate burilado,
  63; Mercado del Indios, 176;
  retablo boxes, 62-63; weavings,
  64
Health and safety, 75-80, 518-519;
  Lima, 125
Hiking see Walking and hiking
History, 2-14; Ayacucho, 280;
  Cajamarca, 441-442; Cuzco, 297-
  299; Iquitos, 520; Lima, 114-118;
  Machu Picchu, 376-377; Trujillo,
  466; Tumbes, 491-492
Holidays and festivals, 56-60
Horse racing: Lima, 178
Horseback riding, 180; Cuzco, 342;
  Lima, 180; Ollantaytambo, 364
Huancabamba, 463
Huancavelica, 268-273; adventures,
  272-273; getting here, 269-270;
  shopping, 266; sightseeing, 270-
  271; tourist information, 269-270;
  where to stay and eat, 271-272

Huancayo: adventures, 267-268;
  day trips, 267; getting here, 260-
  261; language lessons, 266; map,
  259; sightseeing, 261-263; tourist information, 261; where to
  stay and eat, 263-265
Huanchaco, 479-483; adventures,
  482-483; getting here, 479;
  where to stay and eat, 480-482
Huánuco, 253-258; banks, 254; day
  trips, 257; getting here, 253-254;
  sightseeing, 254-255; tour operators, 258; where to stay and eat,
  255-257
Huaraz, 414-436; adventures, 432-
  435; city map, 420; climate, 414;
  day trips, 428-430; festivals,
  426-427; getting here, 416-417;
  language schools, 426; map, 415;
  shopping, 426; Sightseeing, 417-
  420; tour operators, 427-428;
  tourist information, 417; where
  to eat, 424-425; where to stay,
  420-423
Huascarán National Park, 38

Ica, 195-203; adventures, 197-198;
  day trips, 201-202; festivals,
  200-201; getting here, 196;
  sightseeing, 196-197; tourist information, 196; where to stay
  and eat, 202-203; wine tasting,
  198-200
Immigration, 126
Inca stonework, 314
Inca Trail, 381-389; alternative
  trails, 387-389; map, 385; regulations, 382-383; tipping, 383-
  384; weather, 383; what to
  bring, 384
Inernet cafés: Lima, 125
Information sources: clubs and
  organzations, 83; recommended
  reading, 70-71; tourism offices,
  81-82; Web sites, 82-83
INRENA (Instituto de Recursos
  Nacionales), 37
Internet cafés, 84, 125, 523
Iquitos, 519-541; adventures, 532-
  534, 541-543; day trips, 534-535;
  festivals, 543-544; getting here
  and around, 520-522; history,
  520; map, 521; shopping, 543;
  sightseeing, 524-527; tourist information, 522-524; where to

eat, 529-530; where to stay, 528-529, 535-541
Isla Amantani, 409-410
Isla Suasi, 411
Islas Flotantes de los Uros, 412
Isle Taquile, 410-411
Jewelry, 63-64
Juliaca, 406-407
Jungle lodges, 571-578

Kayaking see Rafting

Lake Titicaca and Puno, 390;
    Juliaca, 406-408; Lake Titicaca,
    408-412; map, 390; Puno, 391-406
Lambeyeque, 488-491
Language, 45
Language schools, Arequipa, 233;
    Chorrillos, 182; Cuzo, 318-319;
    Huancayo, 267; Huaraz, 426;
    Puerto Maldonado, 569-570
Lima, 9-10, 111-186; adventures,
    178-181; Barranco, 166-173; Bar-
    rio Chino/Chinatown, 138-141;
    Callao, 138-141; Chorrillos, 173-
    174; Colonial Center, 128-138;
    Costa Verde, 165; day trips, 183-
    186; entertainment, 182-183; get-
    ting here, 118-122; history, 114-
    118; language schools, 182; map,
    112; Miraflores, 150-164;
    Montericco, 165; Pueblo Libre,
    141-143; San Borja, 143; San
    Isidro, 143-149; sports, 177-178;
    tour operators, 181-182
Literature, 67-69

Machu Picchu Historical Sanctuary
    and Natural Monument, 38-39,
    373-381; admission, 380; history,
    376-377; map, 375; ruins, 378-
    379; where to stay, 381
Mail and shipping, 84, 123
Malaria, 518-519
Mammals, 22-25
Mancora, 506-514; adventures, 512;
    day trips, 512-514; getting here
    and around, 506-507; shopping,
    512; tourist information, 507;
    where to eat, 510-511; where to
    stay, 507-510
Mangalares de Tumbes National
    Sanctuary, 37
Manu National Park, 39

Markets: Chinchero, 367; Iquitos,
    524; Miraflores, 162; Pisac, 354-
    355
Massages: Aguas Caliente, 373;
    Cuzco, 335
Miraflores, 150-164
Money matters, 124; currency, 84-
    85; exchange rates, 85-86; tip-
    ping, 55
Monterico, 165
Moray and Maras, 365-366
Motorcycles: Cuzco, 341; Puerto
    Maldonado, 564
Mountaineering, 107-108;
    Arequipa, 234-235; Huaraz, 434
Movies, 182; Cuzco, 332-333

National parks, 37-40; Huaraz,
    430-432
Nazca, 203-208; adventures, 208-
    209; getting here and around,
    205; Lines, 206-208; map, 204;
    sightseeing, 205-206
North Coast, 464-514; Chiclayo,
    483-491; Huanchaco, 479-483;
    Mancora, 506-514; map, 464;
    Piura, 499-506; Trujillo, 465-
    479; Tumbes, 491-499
Northern Amazon, 515-519
Northern Highlands, 439-463;
    Cajamarca, 439-456;
    Chachapoyas, 456-462;
    Huancabamba, 463; map, 440

Ollantaytambo, 358-365; adven-
    tures, 364-365; getting here and
    away, 360; map, 359; sightsee-
    ing, 360-362; tour operators,
    364; tourist information, 360;
    where to stay and eat, 362-364

Pacaya-Samiria National Reserve,
    39, 548-549
Pachacamac archeological com-
    plex, 183-185
Packing tips, 86-89; Inca Trail, 384
Paracas National Reserve, 37-38
Paragliding, 109; Huaraz, 435;
    Lima, 180-181
Parks and reserves, 37-40
Parque Nacional Huascarán, 430-
    432
Parque Nacional Manu, 578
Peñas: Barranco, 172-173; Colonial
    Center, 138; Miraflores, 164

Petroglyphs, San Francisco de Miculla, 250; Toro Muerto (UNESCO World Heritage Site), 233-234

Pisac, 354-358; getting here and away, 354; market, 354-355; ruins, 355-357; where to stay and eat, 357-358

Pisco: day trips, 192-194; getting here and around, 190-191; sightseeing, 191; where to stay and eat, 191

Piura, 499-506; day trips, 505-506; getting here, 500-501; sightseeing, 501-502; tour operators, 505; tourist information, 501; where to stay and eat, 502-505

Plants, 18-19

Pucallpa, 546-556; day trips, 556; getting here and getting around, 549-550; sightseeing, 551-553; tourist information, 551; where to stay and eat, 554-556

Pueblo Libre, 141-143

Puerta Pizarro, 497-498; adventures, 498-499

Puerto Maldonado: festivals, 562; getting here and getting around, 562-564; guided tours, 569; language schools, 569-570; map, 566; shopping, 568; sightseeing, 566; tourist information, 564; where to stay and eat, 566-568, 571

Puno, 391-406; day trips, 403-406; festivals, 402; getting here and around, 393-394; map, 392; shopping, 401-402; sightseeing, 395-396; tourist information, 394; where to stay, 396-399

Punta Sal, 513-514

Rafting, 108-109; Arequipa, 235-236; Cuzco, 342; Huaraz, 435; Ollantaytambo, 364-365; Tarapoto, 545-546

Reptiles and amphibians, 25-29

Restaurants, 55-56; Abancay, 274-275; Aguas Caliente, 372-373; Andahuaylas, 277; Arequipa, 219-221; Ayacucho, 286; Barranco, 169-171; Barrio Chino/Chinatown, 138; Cabanaconde, 240; Cajamarca, 449-451; Callao, 140-141; Caraz, 438; Chachapoyas, 459-460; Chiclayo, 487; Chivay, 237-238; Chorrillos, 174; Colonial Center, 137; Cuzco, 326-330; Huancavelica, 272; Huancayo, 264-265; Huanchaco, 480-482; Huánuco, 256; Huaraz, 424-425; Ica, 203; Iquitos, 529-530; Mancora, 510-511; Miraflores, 158-162; Nazca, 211; Ollantaytambo, 363-364; Pisac, 357-358; Pisco, 191; Piura, 504-505; Pucallpa, 552-553; Pueblo Libre, 142-143; Puerto Maldonado, 567-568; Puno, 399-401; San Isidro, 148-149; Tacna, 248; Tarapoto, 545; tipping, 55-56; Trujillo, 472-473; Tumbes, 495-496; Urubamba and Yucay, 351-352

Riverboats, 97-98; Iquitos, 531-533; Pucallpa, 547

Rubber Boom buildings, 526-527

Ruins: Cuzco, 316-318; Huaraz, 418, 420; Machu Picchu, 378-380; Pisac, 355-357

Sacred Valley, 294-389; Aguas Caliente, 368-373; Chinchero, 366-368; Cuzco, 296-345; festivals, 343-345; Inca Trail, 381-389; Machu Picchu, 373-381; map, 292; Moray and Maras, 365-366; Ollantaytambo, 358-365; Pisac, 354-358; Urubamba and Yucay, 345-354

Salinas and Aguada Blanca National Reserve, 39

San Borja, 143

San Francisco de Miculla Petroglyphs, 250

San Isidro, 143-149

Sandboarding, 198

Scooters: Cuzco, 341-342

Shamanic ceremonies, 553

Shopping, 61-64; Aguas Caliente, 373; Arequipa, 232; Ayacucho, 284; Cajamarca, 451; Chachapoyas, 460; Chiclayo, 488; Chorrillos, 176-177; Cuzco, 333-335; Huancayo, 266; Huaraz, 426; Mancora, 512; Pucallpa, 555; Puno, 401-402; Tacna, 249

Shuttle: Cuzco, 304

Sillustani, 403

Soccer, 105-106; Lima, 178

Sorojchi (altitude sickness), 305-306
Southeastern Jungle/Madre de Dios, 557-580; Boca Manu, 575-5787; map, 556; Puerto Maldonado, 558-574
Southern Coast, 187-251, 246-247; Arequipa, 211-237; Cabanaconde, 239-242; Chincha Alta, 187-190; Chivay, 237-238; getting around, 245; getting here, 244-245; Ica, 195-203; map, 189; Nazca, 203-211; Pisco, 190-195; sightseeing, 245-246; Tacna, 242-243; tourist information, 244; where to stay and eat, 246-247; Yanque, 238-239
Spas, 335
Sports see also individual sports, 105-109
Star system, 74
Surfing, 106-107; Huanchaco, 483; Lima, 178-179

Tacna, 242-251; day trips, 249-250; getting here and getting around, 244-245; map, 243; shopping, 249; sightseeing, 245-246; tourist information, 244; where to stay and eat, 246-248
Tambopata National Reserve, 573
Tambopata-Candamo Reserve Zone, 39-40
Tarapoto, 543-547
Taxis, 95; Cuzco, 304; Iquitos, 522; Lima, 122
Telephones, 124
Theater, 183
Thermal baths: La Calera, 238
Time zone, 86
Tipping, 55-56; Inca Trail, 383-384
Titicaca National Reserve, 39
Tour operators, 98-100; Abancay, 275; Arequipa, 231; Ayacucho, 291; Boca Manu, 577-578; Cajamarca, 451-452; Caraz, 438; Chachapoyas, 460; Huánuco, 258; Huaraz, 427-428; Lima, 181-182; Piura, 505; Puno, 402; Trujillo, 474; Tumbes, 496; Urubamba and Yucay, 352-353
Tourism offices, 81-82
Trains, 97; Cuzco, 300-302; Huancayo, 260-261; Lima, 122

Transportation, 94-98
Travel information, 74-105; accomodations, 101-105; diseases, 75-77; documents, 74-75; electricity, 86; getting here and getting around, 92-98; internet cafés, 84; Lima, 126; local customs, 90; money matters, 84-86; packing tips, 86-90; safety, 78-80; tour operators, 98-101; tourism offices, 81-82; web sites, 82-83
Trees, 19-20
Trekking, 108; Cajamarca, 455-456; Huaraz, 432-433
Trujillo, 465-479; day trips, 475-479; festivals, 474; getting here, 466-467; history, 466; sightseeing, 467-470; tour operators, 474; tourist information, 467; where to stay and eat, 470-473
Tumbes, 491-499; climate, 492; day trips, 497-498; getting here, 492, 494; history, 491-492; map, 493; sightseeing, 494; tour operators, 496; tourist information, 492; where to stay and eat, 494-496

Urubamba and Yucay, 345-354; adventures, 353-354; getting here and around, 345-346; sightseeing, 346-347; tour operators, 352-353; where to eat, 351-352; where to stay, 347-351

Volunteering, 35-36; Puerto Maldonado, 569-570

Walking and hiking: Arequipa, 236-237; Cuzco, 339-341; Huancavelica, 272-273; Huancayo, 267-268; Ica, 197-198; Iquitos, 540-541; Nazca, 208
Water, drinking, 56
Wildlife, 20-32
Wildlife preservation, 32
Wine: Ica, 198-200

Yanque, 238-239
Yungay, 436-437
Yurimaguas, 542-543